THE PAPERS OF
BENJAMIN FRANKLIN

SPONSORED BY

The American Philosophical Society

and Yale University

BENJAMIN FRANKLIN
Né à Boston, dans la nouvelle Angleterre, le 17 Janv. 1706.

Honneur du nouveau monde et de l'humanité,
Ce Sage aimable et vrai les guide et les éclaire;
Comme un autre Mentor, il cache à l'œil vulgaire,
Sous les traits d'un mortel, une divinité.   Par M. Feutry.

Duplessis Pinxit Parisiis 1778.   Tiré du Cabinet de M. Le Ray de Chaumont &c.   Chevillet Sculpsit.

Benjamin Franklin

THE PAPERS OF
Benjamin Franklin

VOLUME 32   *March 1 through June 30, 1780*

BARBARA B. OBERG, *Editor*

ELLEN R. COHN AND JONATHAN R. DULL, *Senior Associate Editors*

KAREN DUVAL, *Associate Editor*

LESLIE J. LINDENAUER, *Assistant Editor*

CLAUDE A. LOPEZ, *Consulting Editor*

KATE M. OHNO, *Editorial Assistant*

New Haven and London   YALE UNIVERSITY PRESS, 1996

As indicated in the first volume, this edition was made possible through the vision and generosity of Yale University and the American Philosophical Society and by a substantial donation from Henry R. Luce in the name of Life Magazine. *Additional funds were provided by a grant from the Ford Foundation to the National Archives Trust Fund Board. Subsequent support has come from the Andrew W. Mellon Foundation and the Pew Charitable Trusts through Founding Fathers Papers, Inc. Major underwriting of the present volume has been provided by the Florence Gould Foundation. Generous sponsors include the American Philosophical Society, the Earhart Foundation, the French-American Foundation, the Kemper Educational and Charitable Fund, Dorothy W. Bridgwater, Da Capo, Dr. and Mrs. William W. Glenn, Frank B. Jones, Candace and Stuart Karu, Richard N. Rosenfeld, John and Deane Sherman, Mr. and Mrs. Malcolm N. Smith, and George F. Waters. Contributions from the Friends of Franklin, the Friends of the Franklin Papers, Donald A. Petrie, Louise K. Smith, the* Saturday Evening Post *Society, and other individuals also help to sustain the enterprise.* The Papers of Benjamin Franklin *is a beneficiary of the generous and long-standing support of the National Historical Publications and Records Commission under the chairmanship of the Archivist of the United States. The National Endowment for the Humanities, an independent federal agency, has provided significant support for this volume. For the assistance of all these organizations and individuals, as well as for the indispensable aid of archivists, librarians, scholars, and collectors of Franklin manuscripts, the editors are most grateful.*

Publication of this volume was assisted by a grant from the National Historical Publications and Records Commission.

Library of Congress catalog card number: 59–12697
International standard book number: 0–300–06617–1

♾ The paper in this book meets the guidelines for permanence and durability of the Committee on Production Guidelines for Book Longevity of the Council on Library Resources.

Printed in the U.S.A.

Administrative Board

Edmund S. Morgan, Yale University, *Chairman*
Edward C. Carter II, American Philosophical Society
Robert Darnton, American Philosophical Society
David B. Davis, American Philosophical Society
Mary M. Dunn, Schlesinger Library, Radcliffe College
Paul LeClerc, New York Public Library
Robert Middlekauff, University of California, Berkeley
Barbara B. Oberg, Yale University
John G. Ryden, Yale University Press
Gordon S. Wood, American Philosophical Society

Advisory Committee

Thomas Boylston Adams
Thomas R. Adams
I. Bernard Cohen
John C. Dann
Sir Frank C. Francis
Andrew Heiskell

To

EDMUND S. MORGAN

with admiration, gratitude, and affection

Contents

Foreign-language surnames and titles of nobility often run to great length. Our practice with an untitled person is to provide all the Christian names at the first appearance, and then drop them; a chevalier or noble is given the title used at the time, and the full name is provided in the index.

*Denotes a document referred to in annotation.

CONTENTS

xxiv

CONTENTS

xxvi

List of Illustrations

The earliest surviving example of the second passport form issued at Passy. It differs from the first form (xxx, facing page 181) chiefly in the addition of the border, which Franklin removed in subsequent issues. Reproduced by courtesy of Mrs. F. T. Lewis, Fairport, New York. Photograph by James M. Via.

This plate is attributed to the manufactory of Pont-aux-Choux, in Paris, which closed its doors shortly before the opening of Clark & Cie.'s pottery works in Montereau, from which Franklin purchased his set of creamware. No example of Montereau pottery has survived. Both manufactories employed English workers. Photograph reproduced by courtesy of the Musée National de la Céramique à Sèvres.

"Plan of the Siege of Charleston in S. Carolina," drawn by Samuel Lewis. The map was first published in Charles Smith, *The American War, from 1775 to 1783: with Plans* (New York, 1797). The engraving was by Tanner, probably Benjamin (1775–1848), a New York engraver. See R.V. Tooley, *Tooley's Dictionary of Mapmakers* (Tring, Eng., 1979), p. 609.

Contributors to Volume 32

The ownership of each manuscript, or the location of the particular copy used by the editors of each rare contemporary pamphlet or similar printed work, is indicated where the document appears in the text. The sponsors and editors are deeply grateful to the following institutions and individuals for permission to print or otherwise use in the present volume manuscripts and other materials which they own.

INSTITUTIONS

Académie des sciences, Paris
American Philosophical Society
Algemeen Rijksarchief
Archives de la Marine, Paris
Archives du Ministère des affaires
    étrangères, Paris
Bibliothèque du Port, Brest
Boston Public Library
Chicago Historical Society
Columbia University Library
Dibner Library of the History
    of Science and Technology,
    Smithsonian Institution
Harvard University Library

Henry E. Huntington Library
Historical Society of Pennsylvania
Library of Congress
Massachusetts Historical Society
National Archives
New Hampshire Historical Society
New Jersey Historical Society
New-York Historical Society
Public Record Office, London
University College, London
University of Pennsylvania
    Library
Yale University Library

INDIVIDUALS

Albert M. Greenfield,
    Philadelphia, Pennsylvania
Mrs. Martin M. Kendig, Chicago,
    Illinois
Mrs. F. T. Lewis, Fairport,
    New York

Mrs. Henry Sage, Albany,
    New York
Mrs. Richard R. Wood, Wawa,
    Pennsylvania

Statement of Methodology

Arrangement of Materials

The documents are printed in chronological sequence according to their dates when these are given, or according to the date of publication in cases of contemporary printed materials. Records such as diaries, journals, and account books that cover substantial periods of time appear according to the dates of their earliest entries. When no date appears on the document itself, one is editorially supplied and an explanation provided. When no day within a month is given, the document is placed at the end of all specifically dated documents of that month; those dated only by year are placed at the end of that year. If no date is given, we use internal and external evidence to assign one whenever possible, providing our explanation in annotation. Documents which cannot be assigned a date more definite than the entire length of Franklin's stay in France (1777–85) will be published at the end of this period. Those for which we are unable to provide even a tentative date will be published at the conclusion of the series.

When two or more documents have the same date, they are arranged in the following order:

1. Those by a group of which Franklin was a member (*e.g.*, the American Commissioners in Paris)
2. Those by Franklin individually
3. Those to a group of which Franklin was a member
4. Those to Franklin individually
5. "Third-party" and unaddressed miscellaneous writings by others than Franklin.

In the first two categories letters are arranged alphabetically by the name of the addressee; in the last three, by the name of the signatory. An exception to this practice occurs when a letter to Franklin and his answer were written on the same day: in such cases the first letter precedes the reply. The same rules apply to documents lacking precise dates printed together at the end of any month or year.

Form of Presentation

The document and its accompanying editorial apparatus are presented in the following order:

1. *Title*. Essays and formal papers are headed by their titles, except in the case of pamphlets with very long titles, when a short form is substituted. Where previous editors supplied a title to a piece that had none, and this title has become familiar, we use it; otherwise we devise a suitable one.

Letters written by Franklin individually are entitled "To" the person or body addressed, as: To John Adams; To John Adams and Arthur Lee; To the Royal Society.

Letters to Franklin individually are entitled "From" the person or body who wrote them, as: From John Adams; From John Adams and Arthur Lee; From the Committee of Secret Correspondence.

Letters of which Franklin was a joint author or joint recipient are titled with the names of all concerned, as: Franklin and Silas Deane to Arthur Lee; Arthur Lee to Franklin and Silas Deane. "Third-party" letters or those by or to a body of which Franklin was a member are titled with the names of both writers and addressees, as: Arthur Lee to John Adams; The American Commissioners to John Paul Jones.

Documents not fitting into any of these categories are given brief descriptive headings, as: Extract from Franklin's Journal.

If the name in the title has been supplied from external evidence it appears in brackets, with a question mark when we are uncertain. If a letter is unsigned, or signed with initials or an alias, but is from a correspondent whose handwriting we know, the name appears without brackets.

2. *Source Identification*. This gives the nature of the printed or manuscript version of the document, and, in the case of a manuscript or a rare printed work, the ownership and location of the original.

Printed sources of three different classes are distinguished. First, a contemporary pamphlet, which is given its full title, place and date of publication, and the location of the copy the editors have used. Second, an essay or letter appearing originally in a *contemporary* publication, which is introduced by the words

xxxiii

"Printed in," followed by the title, date, and inclusive page numbers, if necessary, of the publication. Third, a document, the manuscript or contemporary printed version of which is now lost, but which was printed at a later date, is identified by the words "Reprinted from," followed by the name of the work from which the editors have reproduced it. The following examples illustrate the distinction:

Printed in *The Pennsylvania Gazette,* October 2, 1729.
Reprinted from William Temple Franklin, ed., *Memoirs of the Life and Writings of Benjamin Franklin* . . . (3 vols., 4 to, London, 1817–18), II, 244.

The Source Identification of a manuscript consists of a term or symbol (all of which are listed in the Short Title List) indicating the character of the manuscript version, followed by the name of the holder of the manuscript, as: ALS: American Philosophical Society. Since manuscripts belonging to individuals have a tendency to migrate, we indicate the year in which each private owner gave permission to publish, as: Morris Duane, Philadelphia, 1957. When two or more manuscript versions survive, the one listed first in the Source Identification is the one from which we print.

3. An editorial *Headnote* precedes some documents in this edition; it appears between the Source Identification and the actual text. Such a headnote is designed to supply the background of the composition of the document, its relation to events or other writings, and any other information which may be useful to the reader and is not obtainable from the document itself.

4. The *Text* of the document follows the Source Identification, or Headnote, if any. When multiple copies of a document are extant, the editors observe the following order of priority in determining which of the available versions to use in printing a text: ALS or ADS, LS or DS, AL or AD, L or D, and copy. An AL (draft) normally takes precedence over a contemporary copy based on the recipient's copy. If we deviate from the order set forth here, we explain our decision in the annotation. In those instances where multiple texts are available, the texts are collated, and significant variations reported in the annotation. In selecting the publication text from among several copies of official French

correspondence (*e.g.*, from Vergennes or Sartine) we use the version which is written in the best French, on the presumption that the French ministers used standard eighteenth-century spelling, grammar, and punctuation.

The form of presentation of the texts of letters is as follows:

The place and date of composition are set at the top, regardless of their location in the original manuscript.

The signature, set in capitals and small capitals, is placed at the right of the last line of the text if there is room; if not, then on the line below.

Addresses, endorsements, and notations are so labeled and printed at the end of the letter. An endorsement is, to the best of our belief, by the recipient, and a notation by someone else. When the writer of the notation has misread the date or the signature of the correspondent, we let the error stand without comment. Line breaks in addresses are marked by slashes. Different notations are separated by slashes; when they are by different individuals, we so indicate.

5. *Footnotes* to the Heading, Source Identification, Headnote, and Text appear on the pages to which they pertain. References to documents not printed or to be printed in later volumes are by date and repository, as: Jan. 17, 1785, APS.

Method of Textual Reproduction

1. *Spelling* of all words, including proper names, is retained. If it is abnormal enough to obscure the meaning we follow the word immediately with the current spelling in brackets.

2. *Capitalization and Punctuation* are retained. There is such variety in the size of initial letters, often in the same manuscript, that it is sometimes unclear whether the writer intended an upper or lower case letter. In such cases we make a decision on the basis of the correspondent's customary usage. We supply a capital letter when an immediately preceding period, colon, question mark, exclamation point, or dash indicates that a new sentence is intended. If a capital letter clearly indicates the beginning of a new thought, but no mark of punctuation precedes it, we insert a period. If neither punctuation nor capital letter indicates a sentence break, we do not supply them unless their absence renders comprehension of the document nearly

impossible. In that case we provide them and so indicate in a footnote.

Dashes were used for a variety of purposes in eighteenth-century personal and public letters. A dash within a sentence, used to indicate a break in thought, is represented as an em dash. A dash that follows a period or serves as a closing mark of punctuation for a sentence is represented as an em dash followed by a space. Occasionally correspondents used long dashes that continue to the end of a line and indicate a significant break in thought. We do not reproduce the dash, but treat it as indicating the start of a new paragraph.

When there is an initial quotation mark or parenthesis, but no closing one, we silently complete the pair.

3. *Contractions and abbreviations* are retained. Abbreviations such as "wd", "honble", "servt", "exclly", are used so frequently in Franklin's correspondence that they are readily comprehensible to the users of these volumes. Abbreviations, particularly of French words, that may be unclear are followed by an expanded version in brackets, as: nre [navire]. Superscript letters are brought down to the line. Where a period or colon is a part of the abbreviation, or indicates that letters were written above the line, we print it at the end of the word, as: 4 th. for 4.th. In those few cases where superscript letters brought down to the line result in a confusing abbreviation ("Made" for "Mad^e"), we follow the abbreviation by an expanded version in brackets, as: Made [Madame].

The ampersand by itself and the "&c." are retained. Letters represented by the "y" are printed, as: "the" and "that". The tailed "p" is spelled out, as: "per", "pre", or "pro". Symbols of weights, measures, and money are converted to modern forms, as: *l.t.* instead of ⅄ for *livres tournois*.

4. *Omissions, mutilations, and illegible words* are treated as follows:

If we are certain of the reading of letters missing in a word because of a torn or taped manuscript or tightly bound copybook, we supply the letters silently.

If we cannot be sure of the word, or of how the author spelled it, but we can make a reasonable guess, we supply the missing letters in brackets.

When the writer has omitted a word absolutely required for clarity, we insert it in italics within brackets.

5. *Interlineations* by the author are silently incorporated into the text. If they are significant enough to require comment a footnote is provided.

Textual Conventions

/	denotes line break in addresses and different hands in notations.
⟨roman⟩	denotes a résumé of a letter or document.
[*italic*]	editorial insertion explaining something about the manuscript, as: [*one line illegible*]; or supplying a word to make the meaning clear, as: [*to*].
[roman]	editorial insertion clarifying the immediately preceding word or abbreviation; supplies letters missing because of a mutilated manuscript.
(?)	indicates a questionable reading.

Abbreviations and Short Titles

AAE	Archives du Ministère des affaires étrangères.
AD	Autograph document.
Adams Correspondence	Lyman H. Butterfield, Richard L. Ryerson, *et al.*, eds., *Adams Family Correspondence* (6 vols. to date, Cambridge, Mass., 1963–).
Adams Papers	Robert J. Taylor, Richard L. Ryerson, *et al.*, eds., *Papers of John Adams* (10 vols. to date, Cambridge, Mass., 1977–).
ADB	*Allgemeine Deutsche Biographie* (56 vols., Berlin, 1967–71).
Adm.	Admiral.
ADS	Autograph document signed.
AL	Autograph letter.
Allen, *Mass. Privateers*	Gardner Weld Allen, ed., *Massachusetts Privateers of the Revolution* ([Cambridge, Mass.], 1927) (Massachusetts Historical Society *Collections*, LXXVII).
Almanach des marchands	*Almanach général des marchands, négocians, armateurs, et fabricans de France et de l'Europe et autres parties du monde* . . . (Paris, 1779).
Almanach royal	*Almanach royal* (91 vols., Paris, 1700–92). Cited by year.
Almanach de Versailles	*Almanach de Versailles* (Versailles, various years). Cited by year.
Alphabetical List of Escaped Prisoners	Alphabetical List of the Americans who having escap'd from the Prisons of England, were furnish'd with Money by the Commissrs. of the U.S. at the

	Court of France, to return to America. A manuscript in the APS, dated 1784, and covering the period January, 1777, to November, 1784.
ALS	Autograph letter signed.
APS	American Philosophical Society.
Archaeol.	Archaeological.
Assn.	Association.
Auphan, "Communications"	P. Auphan, "Les communications entre la France et ses colonies d'Amérique pendant la guerre de l'indépendance Américaine," *Revue Maritime*, new series, no. LXIII and LXIV (1925), 331–48, 497–517.
Autobiog.	Leonard W. Labaree, Ralph L. Ketcham, Helen C. Boatfield, and Helene H. Fineman, eds., *The Autobiography of Benjamin Franklin* (New Haven, 1964).
Bachaumont, *Mémoires secrets*	[Louis Petit de Bachaumont *et al.*], *Mémoires secrets pour servir à l'histoire de la république des lettres en France, depuis MDCCLXII jusqu'à nos jours; ou, Journal d'un observateur* . . . (36 vols. in 12, London, 1784–89). Bachaumont died in 1771. The first six vols. (1762–71) are his; Mathieu-François Pidansat de Mairobert edited them and wrote the next nine (1771–79); the remainder (1779–87) are by Barthélemy-François Mouffle d'Angerville.
Balch, *French in America*	Thomas Balch, *The French in America during the War of Independence of the United States, 1777–1783* (trans. by Thomas Willing Balch *et al.*; 2 vols., Philadelphia, 1891–95).
BF	Benjamin Franklin.

BF's accounts as commissioner	Those described above, XXIII, 20.
BFB	Benjamin Franklin Bache.
Bigelow, *Works*	John Bigelow, ed., *The Works of Benjamin Franklin* (12 vols., New York and London, 1887–88).
Biographie universelle	*Biographie universelle, ancienne et moderne, ou histoire, par ordre alphabétique, de la vie publique et privée de tous les hommes qui se sont fait remarquer* . . . (85 vols., Paris, 1811–62).
Bodinier	From information kindly furnished us by Cdt. Gilbert Bodinier, Section études, Service historique de l'Armée de Terre, Vincennes.
Bodinier, *Dictionnaire*	Gilbert Bodinier, *Dictionnaire des officiers de l'armée royale qui ont combattu aux Etats-Unis pendant la guerre d'Indépendance* (Château de Vincennes, 1982).
Boudriot, *John Paul Jones and the Bonhomme Richard*	Jean Boudriot, *John Paul Jones and the Bonhomme Richard: a Reconstruction of the Ship and an Account of the Battle with H.M.S. Serapis* (trans. by David H. Roberts; Annapolis, 1987).
Bowler, *Logistics*	R. Arthur Bowler, *Logistics and the Failure of the British Army in America, 1775–1783* (Princeton, 1975).
Bradford, *Jones Papers*	James C. Bradford, ed., *The Microfilm Edition of the Papers of John Paul Jones, 1747–1792* (10 reels of microfilm, Alexandria, Va., 1986).
Burke's Peerage	Sir Bernard Burke, *Burke's Genealogical and Heraldic History of the Peerage Baronetage and Knightage with War Gazette and Corrigenda* (98th ed., London, 1940). References in ex-

ceptional cases to other editions are so indicated.

Burnett, *Continental Congress* — Edmund C. Burnett, *The Continental Congress* (New York, 1941).

Burnett, *Letters* — Edmund C. Burnett, ed., *Letters of Members of the Continental Congress* (8 vols., Washington, 1921–36).

Butterfield, *John Adams Diary* — Lyman H. Butterfield *et al.*, eds., *Diary and Autobiography of John Adams* (4 vols., Cambridge, Mass., 1961).

Cash Book — BF's accounts described above, XXVI, 3.

Chron. — *Chronicle.*

Claghorn, *Naval Officers* — Charles E. Claghorn, *Naval Officers of the American Revolution: a Concise Biographical Dictionary* (Metuchen, N.J. and London, 1988).

Clark, *Ben Franklin's Privateers* — William Bell Clark, *Ben Franklin's Privateers: a Naval Epic of the American Revolution* (Baton Rouge, 1956).

Clark, *Wickes* — William Bell Clark, *Lambert Wickes, Sea Raider and Diplomat: the Story of a Naval Captain of the Revolution* (New Haven and London, 1932).

Clowes, *Royal Navy* — William Laird Clowes, *The Royal Navy: a History from the Earliest Times to the Present* (7 vols., Boston and London, 1897–1903).

Cobbett, *Parliamentary History* — William Cobbett and Thomas C. Hansard, eds., *The Parliamentary History of England from the Earliest Period to 1803* (36 vols., London, 1806–20).

Col. — Column.

Coll. — *Collections.*

comp. — compiler.

Croÿ, *Journal* — Emmanuel, prince de Moeurs et de Solre et duc de Croÿ, *Journal inédit du duc de*

	Croÿ, 1718–1784 (4 vols., Paris, 1906–07).
d.	*denier.*
D	Document unsigned.
DAB	*Dictionary of American Biography.*
DBF	*Dictionnaire de biographie française* (18 vols. to date, Paris, 1933–).
Dictionary of Scientific Biography	Charles C. Gillispie, ed., *Dictionary of Scientific Biography* (18 vols., New York, 1970–90).
Deane Papers	*The Deane Papers, 1774–90* (5 vols.; New-York Historical Society *Collections,* XIX–XXIII, New York, 1887–91).
DF	Deborah Franklin.
Dictionnaire de la noblesse	François-Alexandre Aubert de La Chesnaye-Dubois and M. Badier, *Dictionnaire de la noblesse contenant les généalogies, l'histoire & la chronologie des familles nobles de la France . . .* (3rd ed.; 19 vols., Paris, 1863–76).
Dictionnaire historique	*Dictionnaire historique, critique et bibliographique, contenant les vies des hommes illustres, célèbres ou fameux de tous les pays et de tous les siècles . . .* (30 vols., Paris, 1821–23).
Dictionnaire historique de la Suisse	*Dictionnaire historique & biographique de la Suisse* (7 vols. and supplement, Neuchâtel, 1921–34).
DNB	*Dictionary of National Biography.*
Doniol, *Histoire*	Henri Doniol, *Histoire de la participation de la France à l'établissement des Etats-Unis d'Amérique. Correspondance diplomatique et documents* (5 vols., Paris, 1886–99).
DS	Document signed.
Duane, *Works*	William Duane, ed., *The Works of Dr.*

	Benjamin Franklin . . . (6 vols., Philadelphia, 1808–18). Title varies in the several volumes.
Dubourg, *Œuvres*	Jacques Barbeu-Dubourg, ed., *Œuvres de M. Franklin* . . . (2 vols., Paris, 1773).
Dull, *French Navy*	Jonathan R. Dull, *The French Navy and American Independence: a Study of Arms and Diplomacy, 1774–1787* (Princeton, 1975).
Ed.	Edition or editor.
Edler, *Dutch Republic*	Friedrich Edler, *The Dutch Republic and the American Revolution* (*Johns Hopkins University Studies in Historical and Political Science,* ser. XXIX, no. 2; Baltimore, 1911).
Elias and Finch, *Letters of Digges*	Robert H. Elias and Eugene D. Finch, eds., *Letters of Thomas Attwood Digges (1742–1821)* (Columbia, S.C., 1982).
Etat militaire	*Etat militaire de France, pour l'année* . . . (36 vols., Paris, 1758–93). Cited by year.
Exper. and Obser.	*Experiments and Observations on Electricity, made at Philadelphia in America, by Mr. Benjamin Franklin* . . . (London, 1751). Revised and enlarged editions were published in 1754, 1760, 1769, and 1774 with slightly varying titles. In each case the edition cited will be indicated, *e.g., Exper. and Obser.* (1751).
f.	florins.
Fauchille, *Diplomatie française*	Paul Fauchille, *La Diplomatie française et la ligue des neutres de 1780 (1776–1783)* (Paris, 1893).
Ferguson, *Power of the Purse*	E. James Ferguson, *The Power of the Purse: a History of American Public Finance* . . . (Chapel Hill, N.C., 1961).

Fitzpatrick, *Writings of Washington*	John C. Fitzpatrick, ed., *The Writings of George Washington* . . . (39 vols., Washington, D.C., 1931–44).
Force, *Amer. Arch.*	Peter Force, ed., *American Archives: Consisting of a Collection of Authentic Records, State Papers, Debates, and Letters and Other Notices of Publick Affairs* . . . , fourth series, March 7, 1774 to July 4, 1776 (6 vols., [Washington, 1837–46]); fifth series, July 4, 1776 to September 3, 1783 (3 vols., [Washington, 1848–53]).
Ford, *Letters of William Lee*	Worthington Chauncey Ford, ed., *Letters of William Lee, 1766–1783* (3 vols., Brooklyn, N.Y., 1891).
Fortescue, *Correspondence of George Third*	Sir John William Fortescue, ed., *The Correspondence of King George the Third from 1760 to December 1783* . . . (6 vols., London, 1927–28).
France ecclésiastique	*La France ecclésiastique pour l'année* . . . (15 vols., Paris, 1774–90). Cited by year.
Freeman, *Washington*	Douglas S. Freeman (completed by John A. Carroll and Mary W. Ashworth), *George Washington: a Biography* (7 vols., New York, 1948–57).
Gaz.	*Gazette.*
Gaz. de Leyde	*Nouvelles extraordinaires de divers endroits,* commonly known as *Gazette de Leyde.* Each issue is in two parts; we indicate the second as "sup."
Gen.	General.
Geneal.	*Genealogical.*
Gent. Mag.	*The Gentleman's Magazine, and Historical Chronicle.*

Hays, *Calendar*	I. Minis Hays, *Calendar of the Papers of Benjamin Franklin in the Library of the American Philosophical Society* (5 vols., Philadelphia, 1908).
Heitman, *Register of Officers*	Francis B. Heitman, *Historical Register of Officers in the War of the Revolution . . .* (Washington, D.C., 1893).
Hillairet, *Rues de Paris*	Jacques Hillairet, pseud. of Auguste A. Coussillan, *Dictionnaire historique des rues de Paris* (2nd ed.; 2 vols., [Paris, 1964]).
Hist.	Historic or Historical.
Idzerda, *Lafayette Papers*	Stanley J. Idzerda *et al.*, eds., *Lafayette in the Age of the American Revolution: Selected Letters and Papers, 1776–1790* (5 vols. to date, Ithaca, N.Y., and London, 1977–).
JA	John Adams.
JCC	Worthington Chauncey Ford *et al.*, eds., *Journals of the Continental Congress, 1744–1789* (34 vols., Washington, 1904–37).
Jefferson Papers	Julian P. Boyd, Charles T. Cullen, John Catanzariti, *et al.*, eds., *The Papers of Thomas Jefferson* (25 vols. to date, Princeton, 1950–).
Jour.	*Journal.*
JW	Jonathan Williams, Jr.
Kaminkow, *Mariners*	Marion and Jack Kaminkow, *Mariners of the American Revolution* (Baltimore, 1967).
L	Letter unsigned.
Landais, *Memorial*	Pierre Landais, *Memorial, to Justify Peter Landai's Conduct during the Late War* (Boston, 1784).
Larousse	Pierre Larousse, *Grand dictionnaire uni-*

	versel du XIXe siècle . . . (17 vols., Paris, [n.d.]).
Lasseray, *Les Français*	André Lasseray, *Les Français sous les treize étoiles, 1775–1783* (2 vols., Paris, 1935).
Laurens Papers	Philip M. Hamer, George C. Rogers, Jr., David R. Chestnutt, *et al.*, eds., *The Papers of Henry Laurens* (13 vols. to date, Columbia, S.C. 1968–).
Le Bihan, *Francs-maçons parisiens*	Alain Le Bihan, *Francs-maçons parisiens du Grand Orient de France* . . . (Commission d'histoire économique et sociale de la révolution française, *Mémoires et documents,* XIX, Paris, 1966).
Lee, *Life of Arthur Lee*	Richard Henry Lee, *Life of Arthur Lee, L.L.D., Joint Commissioner of the United States to the Court of France, and Sole Commissioner to the Courts of Spain and Prussia, during the Revolutionary War* . . . (2 vols., Boston, 1829).
Lee Family Papers	Paul P. Hoffman, ed., *The Lee Family Papers, 1742–1795* (University of Virginia *Microfilm Publication* No. 1; 8 reels, Charlottesville, Va., 1966).
Lewis, *Walpole Correspondence*	Wilmarth S. Lewis *et al.*, eds., *The Yale Edition of Horace Walpole's Correspondence* (48 vols., New Haven, 1939–83).
Lopez, *Lafayette*	Claude A. Lopez, "Benjamin Franklin, Lafayette, and the *Lafayette*," Proceedings of the American Philosophical Society CVIII (1964), 181–223.
Lopez, *Mon Cher Papa*	Claude-Anne Lopez, *Mon Cher Papa: Franklin and the Ladies of Paris* (rev. ed., New Haven and London, 1990).

Lopez and Herbert, *The Private Franklin*	Claude-Anne Lopez and Eugenia W. Herbert, *The Private Franklin: the Man and His Family* (New York, 1975).
LS	Letter or letters signed.
l.t.	*livres tournois.*
Lüthy, *Banque protestante*	Herbert Lüthy, *La Banque protestante en France de la Révocation de l'Edit de Nantes à la Révolution* (2 vols., Paris, 1959–61).
Mackesy, *War for America*	Piers Mackesy, *The War for America, 1775–1783* (Cambridge, Mass., 1965).
Mag.	*Magazine.*
Mass. Arch.	Massachusetts Archives, State House, Boston.
Mazas, *Ordre de Saint-Louis*	Alexandre Mazas and Théodore Anne, *Histoire de l'ordre royal et militaire de Saint-Louis depuis son institution en 1693 jusqu'en 1830* (2nd ed.; 3 vols., Paris, 1860–61).
Meng, *Despatches of Gérard*	John J. Meng, *Despatches and Instructions of Conrad Alexandre Gérard, 1778–1780* . . . (Baltimore, 1939).
Métra, *Correspondance secrète*	[François Métra *et al.*], *Correspondance secrète, politique & littéraire, ou Mémoires pour servir à l'histoire des cours, des sociétés & de la littérature en France, depuis la mort de Louis XV* (18 vols., London, 1787–90).
Meyer, *Armement nantais*	Jean Meyer, *L'Armement nantais dans la deuxième moitié du XVIIIe siècle* (Paris, 1969).
Meyer, *Noblesse bretonne*	Jean Meyer, *La Noblesse bretonne au XVIIIe siècle* (2 vols., Paris, 1966).
Morison, *Jones*	Samuel E. Morison, *John Paul Jones: a Sailor's Biography* (Boston and Toronto, 1959).

Morris, *Jay: Peace*	Richard B. Morris *et al.*, eds., *John Jay, the Winning of the Peace: Unpublished Papers, 1780–1784* (New York, Cambridge, London, 1980).
Morris, *Jay: Revolutionary*	Richard B. Morris *et al.*, eds., *John Jay, the Making of a Revolutionary: Unpublished Papers, 1743–1780* (New York, Evanston, San Francisco, 1975).
Morris Papers	E. James Ferguson, John Catanzariti, Elizabeth M. Nuxoll, *et al.*, eds., *The Papers of Robert Morris, 1781–1784* (8 vols. to date, Pittsburgh, Pa., 1973–).
Morton, *Beaumarchais Correspondance*	Brian N. Morton and Donald C. Spinelli, eds., *Beaumarchais Correspondance* (4 vols. to date, Paris, 1969–).
MS, MSS	Manuscript, manuscripts.
Namier and Brooke, *House of Commons*	Sir Lewis Namier and John Brooke, *The History of Parliament. The House of Commons 1754–1790* (3 vols., London and New York, 1964).
Naval Docs.	William B. Clark, William J. Morgan, *et al.*, eds., *Naval Documents of the American Revolution* (9 vols. to date, Washington, D.C., 1964–).
Neeser, *Conyngham*	Robert Walden Neeser, ed., *Letters and Papers Relating to the Cruises of Gustavus Conyngham, Captain of the Continental Navy 1777–1779* (New York, 1915).
NNBW	*Nieuw Nederlandsch Biografisch Woordenboek* (10 vols. and index, Amsterdam, 1974).
Nouvelle biographie	*Nouvelle biographie générale depuis les temps les plus reculés jusqu'à nos jours . . .* (46 vols., Paris, 1855–66).
Pa. Arch.	Samuel Hazard *et al.*, eds., *Pennsylvania*

	Archives (9 series, Philadelphia and Harrisburg, 1852–1935).
Palmer, *Loyalists*	Gregory Palmer, ed., *Biographical Sketches of Loyalists of the American Revolution* (Westport, Ct., 1984).
Patterson, *The Other Armada*	A. Temple Patterson, *The Other Armada: the Franco-Spanish Attempt to Invade Britain in 1779* (Manchester, Eng., 1960).
Phil. Trans.	The Royal Society, *Philosophical Transactions.*
PMHB	*Pennsylvania Magazine of History and Biography.*
Price, *France and the Chesapeake*	Jacob M. Price, *France and the Chesapeake: a History of the French Tobacco Monopoly, 1674–1791, and of Its Relationship to the British and American Tobacco Trade* (2 vols., Ann Arbor, Mich., 1973).
Proc.	*Proceedings.*
Pub.	*Publications.*
Quérard, *France littéraire*	Joseph Marie Quérard, *La France littéraire ou Dictionnaire bibliographique des savants, historiens, et gens de lettres de la France, ainsi que des littérateurs étrangers qui ont écrit en français, plus particulièrement pendant les XVIIIe et XIXe siècles* . . . (10 vols., Paris, 1827–64).
Rakove, *Beginnings of National Politics*	Jack N. Rakove, *The Beginnings of National Politics: an Interpretive History of the Continental Congress* (New York, 1979).
RB	Richard Bache.
Repertorium der diplomatischen Vertreter	Ludwig Bittner *et al.*, eds., *Repertorium der diplomatischen Vertreter aller Länder*

xlix

	seit dem Westfälischen Frieden (1648) (3 vols., Oldenburg, etc., 1936–65).
Rev.	*Review.*
Rice and Brown, eds., *Rochambeau's Army*	Howard C. Rice, Jr., and Anne S.K. Brown, eds., *The American Campaigns of Rochambeau's Army, 1780, 1781, 1782, 1783* (2 vols., Princeton and Providence, 1972).
s.	*sou.*
Sabine, *Loyalists*	Lorenzo Sabine, *Biographical Sketches of Loyalists of the American Revolution . . .* (2 vols., Boston, 1864).
SB	Sarah Bache.
Schaeper, *Battle off Flamborough Head*	Thomas J. Schaeper, *John Paul Jones and the Battle off Flamborough Head: a Reconsideration* (New York, Bern, Frankfurt am Main, 1989).
Schelle, *Œuvres de Turgot*	Gustave Schelle, ed., *Œuvres de Turgot et documents le concernant* (5 vols., Paris, 1913–23).
Schulte Nordholt, *Dutch Republic*	J. W. Schulte Nordholt, *The Dutch Republic and American Independence* (trans. Herbert M. Rowen; Chapel Hill, N.C., 1982).
Sellers, *Franklin in Portraiture*	Charles C. Sellers, *Benjamin Franklin in Portraiture* (New Haven and London, 1962).
Sibley's Harvard Graduates	John L. Sibley, *Biographical Sketches of Graduates of Harvard University* (17 vols. to date, Cambridge, Mass., 1873–). Continued from Volume IV by Clifford K. Shipton.
Six, *Dictionnaire biographique*	Georges Six, *Dictionnaire biographique des généraux et amiraux français de la Révolution et de l'Empire (1792–1814)* (2 vols., Paris, 1934).

l

Smith, *Letters*	Paul H. Smith *et al.*, eds., *Letters of Delegates to Congress* (23 vols. to date, Washington, D.C., 1976–).
Smyth, *Writings*	Albert H. Smyth, ed., *The Writings of Benjamin Franklin* . . . (10 vols., New York, 1905–07).
Soc.	Society.
Sparks, *Works*	Jared Sparks, ed., *The Works of Benjamin Franklin* . . . (10 vols., Boston, 1836–40).
Stevens, *Facsimiles*	Benjamin F. Stevens, ed., *Facsimiles of Manuscripts in European Archives Relating to America, 1773–1783* (25 vols., London, 1889–98).
Taylor, *J. Q. Adams Diary*	Robert J. Taylor *et al.*, eds., *Diary of John Quincy Adams* (2 vols. to date, Cambridge, Mass., and London, 1981–).
Trans.	Translator or translated.
Trans.	*Transactions.*
Van Doren, *Franklin*	Carl Van Doren, *Benjamin Franklin* (New York, 1938).
Van Doren, *Franklin-Mecom*	Carl Van Doren, ed., *The Letters of Benjamin Franklin & Jane Mecom* (American Philosophical Society *Memoirs*, XXVII, Princeton, 1950).
Villiers, *Commerce colonial*	Patrick Villiers, *Le Commerce colonial atlantique et la guerre d'indépendance des Etats-Unis d'Amérique, 1778–1783* (New York, 1977).
W&MQ	*William and Mary Quarterly,* first or third series as indicated.
Ward, *War of the Revolution*	Christopher Ward, *The War of the Revolution* (John R. Alden, ed.; 2 vols., New York, 1952).
Waste Book	BF's accounts described above, XXIII, 19.

li

WF	William Franklin.
Wharton, *Diplomatic Correspondence*	Francis Wharton, ed., *The Revolutionary Diplomatic Correspondence of the United States* (6 vols., Washington, D.C., 1889).
Willcox, *Portrait of a General*	William B. Willcox, *Portrait of a General: Sir Henry Clinton in the War of Independence* (New York, 1964).
WTF	William Temple Franklin.
WTF, *Memoirs*	William Temple Franklin, ed., *Memoirs of the Life and Writings of Benjamin Franklin, L.L.D., F.R.S., &c . . .* (3 vols., 4 to, London, 1817–18).
WTF's accounts	Those described above, XXIII, 19.
Yela Utrilla, *España*	Juan F. Yela Utrilla, *España ante la Independencia de los Estados Unidos* (2nd ed.; 2 vols., Lérida, 1925).

Note by the Editors and the Administrative Board

As we noted in volume 23 (pp. xlvi–xlviii), the period of Franklin's mission to France brings with it roughly two and a half times as many documents as those for the remaining seventy years of his life. In the present volume once again we summarize a portion of his incoming correspondence in collective descriptions; they appear in the index under the following headings: commission seekers; emigrants, would-be; favor seekers; intelligence reports; offerers of goods and schemes.

As we noted in volume 30 (p. lx), Franklin's new French secretary Jean L'Air de Lamotte was responsible for keeping the official letterbook. Many of the copies produced by L'Air de Lamotte are severely flawed. They contain errors of spelling, punctuation, and syntax that could not have been present in Franklin's originals. Regrettably, however, these copies are the only extant versions of much of Franklin's official correspondence dating from this period, and we publish them as they stand.

A revised statement of textual methodology appeared in volume 28 and is repeated here. The original statement of method is found in the Introduction to the first volume, pp. xxiv–xlvii. The various developments in policy are explained in xv, xxiv; xxi, xxxiv; xxiii, xlvi–xlviii.

This is the twentieth volume of *The Papers of Benjamin Franklin* that includes the name of Edmund S. Morgan as a member of the Administrative Board. He has been Chairman since 1990. Sterling Professor Emeritus of History at Yale and one of the nation's most distinguished historians of colonial America, Ed has quietly helped to define and lead the Franklin edition for almost three decades. He has offered perceptive counsel and moral support to each of the project's four editors.

No challenge is too daunting to put before Ed, no task too small to warrant his full attention. With wisdom, grace, and unfailing energy he undertakes whatever needs to be done to encourage, sustain, and promote this edition of Franklin's papers. In recognition of all that he has done for us and in celebration of his eightieth birthday we dedicate this volume to him.

Introduction

Franklin was in good health, energetic, and occupied with a variety of important ministerial tasks and private pursuits in the spring of 1780. He went about his customary business of ruling on prize cases, working for a general prisoner exchange, assisting escaped prisoners, drafting passports, and honoring bills that were presented to him for payment. His letters home to prominent military and political leaders (carried by Lafayette when he departed in early March) resounded with positive assessments of and high expectations for the ensuing campaign and with hopes for "soon a good peace."[1] These letters were certainly intended to put the best possible face on America's position but they also reflect Franklin's general optimistic outlook in the early spring.

In contrast to Franklin's hopes and assessments for the future of the war effort, prospects at home were dim and morale was low. The winter of 1780 was the longest and most severe America had seen in forty years or more. On May 2, wrote Sarah Bache to her father, "we are sitting by the fire . . . the Snow remains on the ground in many parts of the back Country." At Morristown, New Jersey, Washington's troops endured a bitter and difficult encampment, with 10,000–12,000 soldiers facing possible starvation; in late June they were still in winter headquarters.[2] The grimness of that winter seemed to mirror the desperation of allied military operations in America. At the beginning of 1780, victory appeared more elusive than it had at the end of 1777.[3]

The stalemated military situation was exacerbated by a near-catastrophic deterioration of the currency, a situation that Congress attempted to remedy in March by devaluing the currency

1. To Horatio Gates, March 5. See also his letters to the chevalier de La Luzerne and George Washington of the same day.

2. Mark Mayo Boatner III, *Encyclopedia of the American Revolution* (New York, 1964), pp. 747–8; Freeman, *Washington*, v, 139–73.

3. For an analysis of 1780 as the year of Britain's "wasted opportunities" see Dull, *French Navy*, pp. 187–94.

at 40 to 1. The worthlessness of continental money and the collapse of public credit made it impossible for the Quartermaster and Commissary departments to provision the army, and although Congress attempted to transfer to the states the responsibility of providing commodities and supplies (and eventually the soldiers' pay as well), substantial help from France was more important than ever in providing the personnel, financial resources, and supplies requisite for victory.[4]

Franklin was vitally important in conveying to French Foreign Minister Vergennes and Naval Minister Sartine a statement of America's pressing requirements. He even wrote directly to the King, urgently requesting the use of a warship to carry supplies for which "Les troupes americaines ont le plus pressant Besoing."[5] The American minister plenipotentiary also communicated to Congress the limits of French aid. The disposition of the court was "as favourable as ever," he reported, but France simply could not meet all of America's needs.[6]

Franklin's efforts to fill the congressional order for supplies, which he had begun in December, 1779, are a major theme of this volume. Although he had assigned Jonathan Williams, Jr., the job of assembling and shipping the enormous order for clothing, Williams still wanted his great-uncle to make final decisions on a bewildering number of details, from choice of fabric to arranging for insurance and customs duties, about which Franklin knew nothing. He also found himself having to soothe relations between Williams and French businessman Jacques-Donatien Le Ray de Chaumont—the other party responsible for contracting the order. The two men were rivals for control and competitors for their own private, profit-making trade with America.

Some of the goods were to be sent to America with the French squadron preparing to sail from Brest and the rest Franklin in-

4. See E. Wayne Carp, *To Starve the Army at Pleasure: Continental Army Administration and American Political Culture 1775–1783* (Chapel Hill, N.C., and London, 1984), p. 72; Ferguson, *Power of the Purse*, pp. 48–50; William C. Stinchcombe, *The American Revolution and the French Alliance* (Syracuse, 1969), p. 134.
5. To King Louis XVI, [March, 1780].
6. To Samuel Huntington, March 4.

tended to ship on the *Alliance* under the command of John Paul
Jones. Throughout March and April supplies were carried onto
the *Alliance* at Lorient and sent to Brest, but by the time they arrived, the ships at Brest were so full that only a small portion
would fit. Franklin was grieved, and at a loss for what to advise.[7]
(Jones suggested purchasing and outfitting the *Serapis* or borrowing the sloop of war *Ariel* from the French government.)[8]
The fleet, unable to carry all that was intended for it, departed
from Brest on May 2; the *Alliance*, having been taken over by
Captain Pierre Landais, sailed in early July, half empty. Franklin's March hopes for an expeditious dispatch of the badly
needed supplies were dashed. He was helpless at such a distance
to see to all the details of fulfilling the order, and he was power-
less to prevent Landais from seizing command of the *Alliance*.

Landais was, said Franklin, an "exceedingly captious and critical" individual, and he had incited what was in Franklin's opinion a mutiny.[9] On the grounds that Congress had commissioned
him to command the *Alliance* he refused the American minister's
order to accept his demission while awaiting court martial in
America, and he enlisted the support of a number of the *Alliance*'s officers and sailors, who were restive over the delay in
receiving their wages and prize money. Angry and blunt, Franklin ordered Landais in early June not to create a disturbance on
the ship, "as you will answer the contrary at your Peril."[1] The
captain ignored the warning, seizing the ship a week later. With
the ship's officers Franklin was somewhat milder, but still firm:
take the "friendly Counsel of an old Man, who is your friend. Go
home peaceably with your Ship."[2]

Behind Landais' mischief was the perennial thorn in Franklin's side, his former fellow commissioner Arthur Lee, "restless
Genius, [who] wherever he is, must either find or make a Quarrel."[3] In early March Franklin directed Jones to provide Lee with

7. From jw of May 6, and BF to him of May 10.
8. See American Gentlemen in Nantes to BF, [March, 1780] and our annotation of BF to Sartine of May 30.
9. To Jones, March 1.
1. To Landais, June 7.
2. To the Officers of the *Alliance*, June 7.
3. To William Carmichael, June 17.

passage on the *Alliance,* but in June, having received information from several sources that Lee was probably stirring up trouble behind the scenes, Franklin rescinded those orders, leaving the matter to Jones's discretion.[4]

Another former fellow colleague, John Adams, had arrived back in Paris in February. The nature of his mission was a mystery to Franklin, who had not yet received any dispatches from Congress announcing that Adams had been appointed to negotiate a peace and commercial treaty with Great Britain and who was told nothing by Adams. Franklin was, therefore, in "utter Ignorance." Adams did, however, reveal the purpose of his mission to Vergennes, who was puzzled by Adams' behavior.[5] The news of Congress' devaluation of the currency, which arrived in France in May, precipitated a dramatic quarrel between Adams and Vergennes that eventually led to Adams being *persona non grata* at the French Court. Vergennes supported the interests of French merchants engaged in trade with America, who stood to suffer severely from the devaluation. Adams staunchly defended Congress' actions.

Franklin was caught in the middle. He was a friend of such traders to America as Chaumont, and he was a confidant of Vergennes, who was eager to discredit Adams. On the other hand, Franklin had often expressed fears for the state of American credit in Europe and, like Adams, knew that some action needed to be taken. June ended with the situation unresolved.[6]

Franklin's scientist friends feared that troublesome politics would distract him from the world of natural philosophy.[7] Although he had no time to carry out experiments, he designed a method to determine the conductivity of metals. He also communicated at length with Jan Ingenhousz about electrical phenomena, formulating detailed answers to Ingenhousz' queries.[8]

4. To Jones, June 17.
5. See BF to Huntington, March 4, and to Carmichael, March 31 [–April 7]. See also our annotation of JA to BF, March 2.
6. From JA, June 23 [*i.e.,* 22] and June 29; to Vergennes, June 24, and from Vergennes, June 30.
7. See, for example, XXXI, lxii, 128, 246–7, and Ingenhousz to BF, May 3.
8. From Ingenhousz, May 3, and BF's answers to Dr. Ingenhousz' queries, [after May 3].

Franklin and Le Roy submitted to the Académie des sciences a lengthy memoir on lightning rods for the Strasbourg Cathedral, in response to the Académie's request the previous year for their opinion. The report endorsed the findings of Barbier de Tinan, *commissaire des guerres*, on the best means of protecting the cathedral. It also vindicated Franklin's own scientific conclusions: pointed rods are to be preferred, and they could be gilded to preserve them from the weather and create an effect pleasing to the eye.[9]

The period between March and June, 1780, saw intense activity at the Passy press. Hémery and his workers continued to manufacture type at a steady pace, building up an impressive supply of fonts.[1] In early May, Franklin bought the entire foundry. He also purchased two presses from Fagnion, the royal engraver, from whom he continued to buy punches and matrices.[2] Franklin conferred with Fournier about the script type that he had commissioned, he received shipments of type from Caslon, and he reviewed the offers of printing supplies and services from a variety of important European houses.[3] As for his own printing activity, he reset his passport form sometime before May.[4]

One bagatelle probably dates from the period covered by this volume. What Franklin regarded as a frivolous mathematical prize question proposed by the Royal Academy of Brussels prompted him to pen a jocular answer—a little essay on "inflammable air." Hitherto undated by scholars, the piece could not have been written before May 19, the date on which the

9. Franklin and Le Roy, Report on Lightning Rods for the Strasbourg Cathedral, May 12.

1. Hémery and BF took inventory of the shop on July 22, 1780 (APS). BF sent three boxes of brevier to JW, to be shipped to an American printer: JW to BF, March 7.

2. For these purchases see our headnote on accounts.

3. These include the Dutch firm of Enschedé, who used Dumas as their spokesperson, and the Société typographique de Neuchâtel as represented by Ostervald and Bosset Deluze.

4. The first known example of the second passport form is dated May 23; see our annotation of BF to Ferdinand Grand of that date.

announcement of the prize question went on sale.[5] In June, William Carmichael asked for a copy of one of Franklin's earlier bagatelles, "The Ephemera," which "several people of Distinction" in Spain wanted. Franklin obliged the request.[6]

"The French are convivial, live much at one another's tables, and are glad to feast travellers," Franklin wrote in March.[7] But we catch only glimpses of his feasting and conviviality during the spring of 1780. Old friends invite him to visit: the duchesse de Deux-Ponts wants him for Easter; the comte de Sarsfield offers a choice of days so that Franklin and Temple can choose the most convenient; he promises to accompany Madame Helvétius to Octavie Guichard de Meinières.[8] Madame Brillon, on the other hand, apparently is not a lively companion. Although she assures Franklin that he is her "meilleur ami," she is depressed for many weeks and keeps to her room.[9]

Much of Franklin's recorded social life during these months had a public cast to it, and many of the occasions centered around John Paul Jones's six-week visit to Paris. Franklin took him to meet Sartine, hosted a dinner for him at Versailles, and was invited to the gala celebration for the famed naval captain's induction into Franklin's own masonic lodge.[1]

Tales of British military activities in South Carolina and Georgia and of the whereabouts of General Henry Clinton pervade Franklin's incoming correspondence. For the Americans, the military situation in the south was critical: Britain was concentrating her efforts on reestablishing control over North and South Carolina, and d'Estaing had failed to recapture Savannah the previous October. Almost until the end of June, however, reports that Franklin received from America were upbeat—although inaccurate. The reality was that the British fleet had ini-

5. To the Royal Academy of Brussels, [after May 19].

6. From Carmichael, May 22 and to him, June 17.

7. To Cyrus Griffin, March 16.

8. From the duchesse de Deux-Ponts, March 25; from Sarsfield, April 8; from Octavie Guichard de Meinières, April 23.

9. From Mme Brillon, [May] 11.

1. See our headnote on accounts and the letter of [before May 1] from the abbé du Rouzeau.

tiated a close blockade of Charleston on March 20 and begun siege works twelve days later. On May 12 the city was captured. The news appeared in London newspapers on June 16, and shortly afterward Franklin wrote to the American agent in the Netherlands: "I am grieved at the Loss of Charleston."[2] What had seemed promising in the early spring turned sour by mid-June: there was no great American victory.

Despite the arrival of the grim military and financial news from home, the unpleasantness of the various disputes in which he was caught in the middle—Jones and Landais, Jonathan Williams, Jr., and Chaumont, Adams and Vergennes—and the frustration at seeing his efforts to dispatch the supplies thwarted, two positive prospects cheered and encouraged Franklin. The first was the potential diplomatic isolation of Great Britain and the beginnings of the implementation of the principle that "Free ships make free Goods." On March 10 Empress Catherine II of Russia had not only announced her support of it but invited the other neutral powers of Europe to help her enforce the principle on the belligerents. This "League of Armed Neutrality," welcomed by the French, began to take shape later in the year.[3] Franklin's support for the concept was philosophical in nature and practical in application. He believed that merchants should be allowed to carry on their business without interruption in time of war and he even proposed extending the principle to fishermen and farmers, "as working for the common Benefit of Mankind."[4] Putting it into practice, he ordered privateer owner John Torris to bring in no more Dutch ships unless they carried contraband goods.[5]

The second promising development was the French expeditionary force under the comte de Rochambeau that was approved by the French government in February, part of which sailed in early May. Franklin was asked to provide letters of introduction, financial help, and—to some of those French officers

2. To Dumas, June 22.

3. Isabel de Madariaga, *Britain, Russia and the Armed Neutrality of 1780: Sir James Harris's Mission to St. Petersburg during the American Revolution* (New Haven, 1962), pp. 156–84.

4. To Robert Morris, June 3.

5. To Torris, May 30.

stirred up by the news of troops gathering at Brest—commissions in Washington's army.[6] He had referred to it as early as mid-March, calling it a "grand Convoy" and "of great Importance to the United States."[7] The knowledge of it may have bolstered Franklin's spirits throughout the difficult weeks in May and June. Certainly the news of this expeditionary force was the most immediately promising development that he could offer to counter the defeat of Charleston and, indeed, it was a turning point in the war.

6. See the chevalier de Kéralio's letter of March 14, our headnote to François-Marie d'Angeleÿ and other commission seekers, March 25, and Condorcet's letter of March 26.
7. To Jones, March 18.

Chronology

March 1–June 30, 1780

March 5: Cartel ship sails from Plymouth with 100 American prisoners from Old Mill Prison.

March 7: BF accompanies JA to his presentation at court.

March 10: Empress Catherine II of Russia issues declaration of neutral shipping rights.

March 13: Arthur Lee arrives in Lorient.

Before March 14: Arrival of exchanged prisoners on cartel.

March 15: Former Minister to the United States Gérard returns to Versailles.

March 18: Congress devalues currency at ratio of 40:1.

March 19: Return of privateers *Black Prince, Black Princess* from cruise.

March 20: Lafayette departs for America from Rochefort; British fleet initiates close blockade of Charleston.

March 24–May?: Cruise of the privateer *Fearnot*.

Before March 28: Cartel ship returns to Plymouth empty and prisoner exchanges cease.

April 1: British begin siegeworks at Charleston.

April 3: States General of the Netherlands receives Russian invitation to make common cause in defending neutral shipping rights.

April 6–10: Cruise of *Black Prince* ends in shipwreck.

April 17: Battle off Martinique between Admirals Rodney and de Guichen.

April 17–June 2: John Paul Jones visits Paris.

April 24: States General of the Netherlands votes unlimited convoys, approval of Russian proposals.

April 28: Lafayette welcomed in Boston.

April 29: BF takes Jones to meet Sartine.

May 2: Rochambeau's army sails for America from Brest.

May 12: Surrender of Charleston by Gen. Benjamin Lincoln.

May 15: Battle of St. Lucia Channel between Rodney and de Guichen.

May 23–June 1: First individual cruise of privateer *Black Princess*.

May 23: BF receives second of four installments of 3,000,000 *l.t.* French loan.

May 31: Congress resolves that BF be directed to accept drafts of JA and Francis Dana to the amount of their salaries.

May: BF purchases hemlock juice for a skin ailment.

June 2–9: Gordon Riots convulse London.

June 13: Landais takes command of *Alliance*.

June 21: BF receives third of four installments of 3,000,000 *l.t.* French loan.

June 23: French government purchases *Serapis;* Landais moves *Alliance* to Ile de Groix.

June 29–July 18: Second cruise of *Black Princess*.

THE PAPERS OF
BENJAMIN FRANKLIN

VOLUME 32

March 1 through June 30, 1780

Editorial Note on Franklin's Accounts

Two new accounts begin during the period covered by this volume:[1]

XXV. Account of Postage and Errands, April 1, 1780, to May 31, 1783: American Philosophical Society, 237 pages. A collection of monthly statements and bills which are all marked as having been paid by order on Ferdinand Grand. For the months under consideration in this volume the statements, in French, were submitted by the cook, Coitmet. They consist mostly of postal expenses, about half of which are for mail sent by *la petite poste,* meaning that they originated from the district to which they are delivered.[2] Coitmet also kept track of a vast number of what he calls *comistions pour paris,* without explaining what kind of errands he means. They cost 1 *l.t.* 4 *s.* each. The same sum is charged for washing the *cabriolet* (gig), an activity that occurred three times in April and once in May.

The only other expenses indicated, all of them in May, are 1 *l.t.* for sawing wood for the masters, 3 *l.t.* for Mr. Franklin's wigmaker (this must refer to William Temple Franklin), 1.4 *l.t.* to pay for a bath, and 1 *l.t.* for sweeping the kitchen chimney.

XXVI. Franklin's Account with Chaumont, March 19, 1780, to December 22, 1780: Historical Society of Pennsylvania, 8 pages. These sheets, in the hand of Jean L'Air de Lamotte, are part of Franklin and Chaumont's efforts to reconcile their differences through the arbitration of Ferdinand Grand, and they frequently duplicate the items appearing in Account XIX (xxviii, 3). Made up mainly of disbursements by Chaumont to fill the congressional order of supplies entrusted to Jonathan Williams, Jr., this account also contains other expenses, including Chaumont's statement for rent due him. When this account was drawn up and signed on July 9, 1782, he proposed a figure of 20,000 *l.t.* for five years' retroactive rent to Franklin and the other commissioners.

The entries that apply to this volume are a sum of 250,000 *l.t.* that Franklin put in the hands of Grand on March 19 and 193 *l.t.* 10 *s.* for a courier to go from Passy to Nantes.

Two accounts are here identified whose entries begin during an earlier period:

1. The following other accounts still apply: VI, VII, XII, XVI, XVII, XIX, XXII, XXIII, XXIV (for which see xxiii, 21; xxv, 3; xxvi, 3, 4; xxviii, 3–4; xxix, 3; xxxi, 3).
2. Account VI (xxiii, 21) indicates that in the year beginning Oct. 4, 1779, BF paid 383 *l.t.* 15 *s.* for stationery.

Account XXVII. Accounts of the Public Agents in Europe, 1777–1787: National Archives, 1,020 pages. A fully indexed and cross-referenced group of accounts of the American and European agents who represented the United States. These include salaries, bills of exchange drawn for supplies, foreign loans, interest accounts, payments for American prisoners, war supplies from the French royal storehouse and the arsenal at Nantes, accounts of various ships, and sundry other expences incurred by the American ministers. While containing many entries that can be found in accounts cited previously in our edition, these are the most complete records that we have found for Franklin's official expenditures, handled through Ferdinand Grand. For the period covered by our present volume, those entries not cited elsewhere in our annotation include a payment to Bancroft on May 9 for newspapers (320 *l.t.*, 16 *s.*), to Moutard for books on June 22 (470 *l.t.*), and 300 *l.t.* on May 22 for transporting prisoners from Dunkirk to Paris.

These accounts have been microfilmed (National Archives Publication M1004) but unlike most of the records from the National Archives cited in this edition, including Account XXVIII, they are not part of *The Papers of the Continental Congress*.

Account XXVIII. Abstracts of Ferdinand Grand's Accounts with the United States, February 28, 1777–March 1, 1783: National Archives, 266 pages. On May 10, 1783, Ferdinand Grand told Franklin and his fellow peace commissioners that the previous month he had submitted his accounts to Superintendent of Finance Robert Morris (Library of Congress). Abstracts in English of these accounts were made in Philadelphia and are now in the National Archives, 210 pages bearing the date, "Register's Office, May 31, 1783," and 56 pages undated. Several sections relate to Franklin, including a seven-page abstract of Grand's account with him (September, 1777, to August, 1781), and a separate three-page abstract of his account with him (January, 1781, to January, 1782). There are also three-page abstracts of Grand's account with Commissioners Franklin, Deane, and Lee (March, 1777, to April 1778) and Commissioners Franklin, Lee, and Adams (April to July, 1778). Numerous sections also record payments Grand made on Franklin's behalf.

While these accounts are more readily available than Account XXVII, they are less reliable. Translated by someone unfamiliar with the names mentioned and unskilled at reading French handwriting, misspellings abound.

We also offer a summary of entries from Franklin's accounts which have not found a place elsewhere in our annotation but which provide insights into Franklin's private and public life between March 1 and June 30, 1780.

Account XVI (Cash Book, xxvi, 3).

The expenses connected with Franklin's press in Passy are, as usual, one of the prominent items. The staff (Hémery, Bieuville, Rocque, Garre—as he is now spelled—and Madelon) remain the same, at the same salary as indicated in xxxi, 3. Almost 400 *l.t.* were spent in March on lead and 30 *l.t.* on silver. On April 27, two presses were bought from Fagnion for the use of the secretary's office, at a cost of 300 *l.t.* Franklin noted: "As I purpose to keep them after my Mission here is finish'd, they must be put to my private Account." A large disbursement of 5,000 *l.t.* was made on May 7 for the purchase of Hémery's foundry, as well as more lead and antimony for 373 *l.t.* and on the 17th Fagnion received 144 *l.t.* for punches and matrices.

Assistance to prisoners recurs frequently: substantial contributions to Thomas Digges and William Hodgson for that purpose are indicated in our annotation, below, as well as loans to Baron de Wulffen. A "poor Frenchman" who had served on the *Boston* and been long a prisoner in England received 48 *l.t.*,[3] and Franklin advanced a louis to Thomas Kearl, a Virginian returning to America (xxxi, 556–7).

A few sundry items were purchased: tea for 9 *l.t.* from the abbé Morellet, books, a pocket glass and other glass from Ciceri, and an *écritoire.*[4]

Brunel the joiner was paid for his work, and Miss Chaumont was reimbursed 360 *l.t.* for her account, the rest to be paid by an order on banker Grand.

Account XVII (Franklin's Private Accounts with Ferdinand Grand, xxvi, 3) records the purchase, on March 9, of one share from the *Caisse d'Escompte,* and the sum of 644 *l.t.* 2 *s.* on May 29 for Benjamin Bache's schooling.

Account XXIII (William Temple Franklin's Accounts, xxix, 3) provides, as always, some insight into the family's life. The chevalier O'Gorman is paid 150 *l.t.* on March 11 for a cask of burgundy. Cabaret the stationer and Pissot the bookseller both receive payment for their wares. The new secretary, L'Air de Lamotte, really settles into the household, since a bed is bought for him and no longer hired. An English penknife is purchased for Franklin. The various servants, Coitmet the cook and Joseph Bogey (Bogay) the kitchen boy, receive their

3. For problems raised by the *Boston* see xxx, 401, 424–5, 470.
4. Ciceri has been identified in xxxi, 4. The *écritoire* must be the one BF presented to Geneviève Le Veillard (xxxi, 382–3).

wages,[5] while François and Arbelot are also reimbursed for their own food when they serve their masters at dinner parties. Money is advanced to Robert Drybrough (for whom see Jones's letter of March 14) and Pomier de l'Etang (who presented a note on John Torris).

Finally, a somewhat exotic note on April 19: 240 *l.t.* "Advanced to M. Secleback, a Maltois to assist him in returning to his own Country, he being taken by the English in going to serve in America and confined in Prison for two Years."

Editorial Note on Promissory Notes

Now that Franklin was distributing printed promissory note forms to prisoners receiving assistance, we will no longer publish individual promissory notes as sample documents.[6] Instead, in this and subsequent editorial notes, we will take notice of each person, the date on which he received a loan, and the sum.

Printed forms survive from thirteen escaped prisoners for the months covered by this volume. On March 11, Franklin gave three *louis* apiece to Benjamin Ashton and George Girdler. Two days later he gave six *louis* apiece to Nicholas Bartlett and Peter Duhard, both from Marblehead, Francis Robins, from Boston, and Capt. William White.[7] The baron d'Arendt received 25 *louis* on May 18.[8] On May 23, Franklin gave one *louis* to James Tille (or Tilee), and on May 27 (or

---

5. Coimet's monthly salary as cook amounted to 25 *l.t.* plus 9 *l.t.* for wine. Bogey (who sometimes also spelled his name "Bojay," thereby confusing WTF, who referred to him as "Bogay") received 6 *l.t.* per month plus a 6 *s.* daily allowance for wine. (Wages were paid every six months.) Coimet's bill, dated June 15–Dec. 15, and Bogey's, April 15–Oct. 15, are at the APS. Also at the APS is a bill from ———— Guiard, apothecary, which was not submitted until Dec. 28, 1781, but whose first item is dated May, 1780: a gross of purified hemlock juice.

6. For the first printed form, and a discussion of its subsequent variants, see XXXI, 497–8. All promissory notes, both printed and handwritten, are at the American Philosophical Society.

7. Geographical information, when given, has been supplied from the Alphabetical List of Escaped Prisoners, which recorded these dates and sums. Bartlett and White had been recommended by Digges on Jan. 9: XXXI, 355.

8. See his certificate printed under that date.

possibly the 23rd) he gave two *louis* to Frank Foster of Portsmouth, Virginia. On June 8 the baron de Wulffen signed a note for 20 *louis*,[9] and on June 25 William Hammond and Benjamin Hyland each received two *louis*.

Five men signed notes handwritten for them by L'Air de Lamotte. Jeremiah Peirce, of Rhode Island, received four *louis* on March 22.[1] On April 3, Franklin gave David Gardner, of Boston, two *louis*. John McFarland, of Boston, and Redmond Conningham Henderson, of Philadelphia, received a joint sum of five *louis* on April 26. On May 4, Nathaniel Harrington received the same amount.

The Alphabetical List of Escaped Prisoners records sums given to two men whose promissory notes have not survived.[2] On April 6 Franklin gave four *louis* to Benjamin Robert Chew. Elias Ellwell, on April 14, received a mere 12 *l.t.*, half a *louis*.

From Henry Coder   LS:[3] American Philosophical Society

⟨[before March, 1780], in French: I feel sorrier every day that my suggestions of two years ago were not accepted. Had we been allowed to attack under the American flag the English sailing in the Mediterranean, as I proposed, we would have destroyed their commerce.[4] If Sartine had given me the twelve hundred deserters for which I had asked, I would have created an auxiliary corps allegedly financed by Congress—in truth by me—and together with Captain Jones we would have landed near Exeter, raised immense contributions, and burned some important port. We could

9. The money was paid in two installments, for which see Wulffen's letters of before June 1 and of June 10, and BF's reply of June 11.

1. He wrote to BF on June 8, 1779: XXIX, 646–8.

2. Conversely, the List, a running account kept by a number of different secretaries, did not record all sums for which promissory notes do survive.

3. In the hand of Jean L'Air de Lamotte who briefly worked for Coder. Lamotte had acted as secretary for him in preparing this memoir. It was probably written somewhat before Feb. 7, 1780, when Lamotte, on Coder's recommendation, became BF's secretary (XXXI, 250–1, 331n), and certainly was composed before March.

4. A plan proposed by Coder and his friend Jacques Barbeu-Dubourg in the spring of 1778: XXVI, 655–6.

have captured 300 or 400 rich people who come to bathe at Britinston [Brighton] and used their horses to seize the principal residents of Sussex in order to bring them to Passy as hostages. We could have forced the King of England to recognize American independence and also captured Jersey and Guernsey, but instead Sartine gave the men to the Prince of Nassau, with humiliating and expensive results.[5] Lafayette's proposed expeditions to the very places I had suggested also came to naught.[6]

About a month ago I sent Sartine a note to suggest that our Channel fleet be placed under the joint command of d'Orvilliers and du Chaffault. If instead of risking the fleet in the Channel this late in the season[7] they put it in a position to intercept British commerce and menace Ireland, they can draw the British into battle. We could then use a squadron of four ships of the line, four frigates, and two fire ships under the command of Captains Jones and Cornix[8] to escort a landing party of 4,000 men to Sussex. After luring the British there, they could reembark in forty-eight hours and capture Plymouth. Meanwhile other forces could capture Jersey and Guernsey and then attack Portsmouth. This would compel the English to sign whatever peace we want. If the neutral powers object we could pretend that the ships were yours; no one could blame you for making reprisals. Sartine merely sent his thanks via his secretary, M. de La Croix,[9] and that is that.)

5. The Prince de Nassau-Siegen (XXVI, 558n) led an unsuccessful attack on the Channel island of Jersey in May, 1779: XXIX, 12; Patterson, *The Other Armada*, p. 104.

6. In March, 1779, Lafayette had proposed raiding the British coast, but the plans were cancelled in late May: XXIX, 549n, 561–2; Idzerda, *Lafayette Papers*, II, 239.

7. An indication that Coder's note was sent to Sartine in the late autumn of 1779; earlier that fall the comte d'Orvilliers for reasons of health had turned his fleet over to the comte du Chaffault de Besné (XXVII, 212n): Patterson, *The Other Armada*, pp. 210–11.

8. Probably Charles Cornic (1731–1809), a celebrated captain in the French navy: *DBF*.

9. *Almanach Royal* for 1780, p. 233.

To John Paul Jones

LS:[1] National Archives; two copies: Library of Congress

Dear Sir,   Passy March 1st. 1780.

I received the Letter you did me the Honour of writing to me the 25. & 28th past.[2]

I am glad to learn that you can take a Quantity of the Cloathing and Arms: and that you can accommodate the 4 Gentlemen I had mentiond to you.[3] M. De Sartine desires also a Place for a Passenger that goes on some Business from him: I make no doubt of your Willingness to oblige that Minister. I could wish also that you would find Room for Mr. Brown of S. Carolina, who is about returning there.[4]

I do not know that I have Authority to give the Order you desire to Lieutenant Rhodes.[5] But if you and he agree in the Transposition proposed I have no objection to it.

Capt. Landais has demanded of me an Order to you to deliver

1. In WTF's hand.

2. The former is printed in XXXI, 524–5; the latter is missing.

3. The clothing to be carried aboard Jones's command, the continental frigate *Alliance*, was uniforms that JW was assembling for the American army. The arms were those which French Foreign Minister Vergennes and War Minister Montbarey had promised to provide through the marquis de Lafayette. Both are discussed in BF's March 2 letter to Lafayette, below. The merchants John Ross and Samuel Wharton and the former commissioners Arthur Lee and Ralph Izard desired passage on the *Alliance:* XXXI, 499–500.

4. Joseph Brown, Jr., apparently was a good friend of WTF; in an undated letter to him (APS) he signs himself "yours Affectionatly"; see also XXX, 131n; *Adams Correspondence*, III, 302, 402, 408–9. He was one of fifteen passengers who arrived in Boston on Aug. 16 aboard the *Alliance;* the others were Arthur Lee and his nephews Thomas and Ludwell, Lafayette's aides Major Charles-Albert de Moré, chevalier de Pontgibaud, and Capt. Louis-Saint-Ange Morel, chevalier de La Colombe, and his secretary Joseph-Léonard Poirey (for whom see Idzerda, *Lafayette Papers*, III, 164), John G. Frazer (XXVIII, 408n), Michael Comyn (XXVII, 10–11n), Capt. Musco Livingston (XXVI, 256n), Duncan Ingraham, Jr. (XXVIII, 144n), two other South Carolinians, John Middleton (*S.C. Hist. and Geneal. Mag.*, I, 236–7) and Joseph Wilkinson, and two residents of Philadelphia, Henry Ash (Elaine Forman Crane, ed., *The Diary of Elizabeth Drinker* [3 vols., Boston, 1991], III, 2111) and E. Brush: *Boston Gazette*, Aug. 21, 1780; *Lee Family Papers*, reel 6, frame 717; John Ross to WTF, Feb. 19, 1780 (APS).

5. XXXI, 525.

9

him his Trunks and Things that were left on board the Alliance.[6] I find him so exceedingly captious and critical, and so apt to misconstrue as an intended Injustice every Expression in our Language he does not immediately understand, that I am tired of writing anything for him or about him, and am determined to have nothing further to do with him. I make no doubt however, that you will deliver his Things to any Person he may impower to receive them, and therefore think such an Order unnecessary.

I have not as yet received an Answer to the Memorial I sent to the Court of Denmark, reclaiming the Prizes sent into Norway, and deliver'd up unjustly by that Court to the British Consul. I have not heard that they have yet left Bergen. I hope we may yet recover them or their Value.[7]

There is a Mr Lockyer, who has served 22 Years in the British Navy as a Master, and having met with some Injustice would go to America, in hopes of finding Service there.[8] He wishes to go with you, and if you can give him any Employment on board it will be very agreable to him.

Dr Bancroft being by this time with you will take all the Steps possible to promote your Refiting, and forward the Payment of the Prize Money.[9] I do not comprehend what the Weight of Metal has to do with the Division unless where Ships are fitted out by different Owners.

I hope your Indisposition will soon be over, and your Health restablished, being, with sincere Esteem Dear Sir, Your most obedient & most humble Servant.   B FRANKLIN

Hon Capt. Jones.

Notation:[1] From his Excellency Dr. Franklin Passy March 1. 1780

6. XXXI, 560.

7. The prizes were from the cruise of the *Bonhomme Richard* squadron. They had been sent into Bergen, Norway, then a part of the Danish monarchy, where the British consul had reclaimed them, prompting BF's protest: XXX, 336–7, 591–4; XXXI, 261–5.

8. On March 3 a Mr. B. Lockyer wrote WTF to discuss the education of his children, whom he had decided to send into the country (somewhere near the coast) for their education. APS.

9. Bancroft appears to have first gone to Nantes, where he delivered letters to JW (for which see JW to BF, March 7); on March 13, below, Jones reported he had not yet arrived at Lorient.

1. This notation and one of the copies are in the hand of Thomas Hutchins.

To Pierre Landais

Copy: Library of Congress

Sir, Passy, March 1. 1780

I receiv'd the Letter you did me the honour of writing to me the 28th. past.[2]

Inclos'd I send you the certificate I gave you the last time I saw you to justify your stay in Paris till the Time of its Date,[3] You left it on my table.

As I do not understand that Capt. Jones has refused to deliver your Things, or that any Application has been made for them, an Order to him from me seems unecessary. I am persuaded that if you send an Inventory of Them to any friend you may have among the officers of the Ship, or in L'Orient, impowering him to receive them, you may have them without difficulty.

I suppose that Besides the money you received in Holland, and the 50. Louis here, you have since had 100. Louis more to defray your Expences in coming from Holland,[4] Staying here, and going to America, which I imagine is sufficient. As to your Prize Money and Wages, the Payment of them does not belong to me.

It is not in my Power to give you a Passage to america. Many Vessels are now going, and if you have a desire of rending your self there to obtain a Trial, you may doubtless easily find a Passage among them.

I have the honour to be, Sir, &c.

Capt. Landais.

From Jacques-Donatien Le Ray de Chaumont

AL: American Philosophical Society

[March 1, 1780?][5]

M. de Chaumont a L'honneur d'envoyer a S. Ex. la depesche cy

---

2. XXXI, 559–61.

3. XXXI, 484.

4. To answer charges that he had fired on Jones's *Bonhomme Richard* during the battle off Flamborough Head in September: XXX, 539–40; XXXI, 105–12. For the money Landais had received see XXXI, 474–5.

5. On that date Landais wrote Chaumont asking him to forward BF's response concerning Landais' trunks (APS). BF did respond on March 1, immediately above, perhaps prompted by this letter from his landlord.

Jointe de M. Dumas, et La Lettre de M. Landais pour Scavoir Ce que S. Ex. veut qu'il Reponde.
M. De Chaumont Croit que M. Jones n'a lair de Chercher a estre employé en france que pour pouvoir dire en amerique qu'il ne Couroit pas après Le Commandement de L'alliance.[6]

Notation: M. de Chaumont.

From David Hartley[7]   ALS: American Philosophical Society

My Dear friend   London March 1 1780
Having been very much chagrined with the delay of the Cartel I writ some time ago a very pressing letter to the admiralty earnestly requesting them for the sake of humanity to quicken the ceremonious forms of office.[8] They have sent me notice of their compliance & that another vessel is under sailing orders; probably by this time sailed. They add in their letter to me "We shall be much obliged to you for endeavoring to have an equal number of British prisoners taken by American vessels assembled at that place (viz Morlaix) to be returned in her."— Having received yours of the 2d of febry.[9] I consider that point as secured and let us understand once for all tht the prisoners will always be found at Morlaix. The forms of office are intolerable when they aggravate the Miseries of war to Extremity— For instance when my patience is worn out beyond enduring, I write

6. Jones had taken command of the frigate *Alliance* and returned to France from the Netherlands (via Spain) on Feb. 18, 1780: XXXI, 507n. Chaumont had been Jones's liaison with the French government when he commanded the *Bonhomme Richard* squadron in 1779: XXIX, 240n.
7. Hartley's letter was forwarded by Digges on March 3.
8. For the past several months Hartley and BF had been working to effect a continuation of the exchange of prisoners, but the cartel met with delay after delay. For its progress see, in particular, XXX, 376, 518; XXXI, 80, 98, 195, 418, 468–9, 550–1. See also Elias and Finch, *Letters of Digges*, pp. 148–50, 155–7. Hartley may be referring here to his correspondence with the Commissioners for Sick and Wounded Seamen, which was communicated through them to the Admiralty: XXXI, 114, 349. A cartel ship had been expected to sail from Plymouth in mid-February: XXXI, 550.
9. XXXI, 435–6.

to the Board of Sick & Hurt to beg & entreat that they will proceed. In a fortnight perhaps I receive an official answer— "We
have referred your letter to the Lds of the Admiralty & have
their Lps. [Lordships'] order to proceed & to request that you
will procure for us the precise Number" &c &c. There go 3
months more. Let me therefore explain to you that untill you ad-
vertise me to the Contrary I shall always understand that any
Cartel ship of ours will find 100 prisoners at Morlaix; upon that
ground I may prevail; but when they can say to me, "What you
told us *two months* ago may not be so *now*" I am baffled in the importunity with wch I wish to press forward the deliverance of my
friends and fellow creatures from captivity.

There is nothing that gives me so much pain as to see any
cases in which Nations think themselves compelled by what are
called the Laws of war to supercede the feelings of humanity. I
have at length received an answer to the proposition of the parole Exchanges at Sea in the negative.[1] The argument is stated to
me thus. That the proposition gives a greater advantage to an
American Captor than to a British, (a competition wch it shocks
me even to recite) because an american by discharging prisoners, may in one cruize take half a dozen prizes, whereas a British
Captor not being justified under the laws of his Country to discharge prisoners cannot have the same advantage of accumulat-
ing prizes. This is the argument. I grieve for the Consequences
as augmenting the miseries of mankind in war. I have on the
other side urged the arguments of humanity, and I shall still continue to represent them viz the Laws of god & the rights of humanity versus the horrid Laws of war—

As to other parts of your letter of the 2d of febry. I shall take
some future opportunity. But mark one word now. There is no
man in the world so fully convinced as I am or who can give such
full testimony as I can do of your principles, as well for effecting
a safe and honorable peace, as for an inflexible integrity and ad-
herence to engagements. Weigh these words. Take them as my
testimony. It is possible that at some time hereafter they may be

1. Americans had released on written parole large numbers of English
prisoners in the expectation that the Admiralty would release in exchange an
equal number of Americans: xxx, 246, 370, 488; xxxi, 396–8, 438, 446–7,
553.

more fully explained.— Now mark another word. I have studied very much in my letters to you to convey the *principles* wch guide my thoughts & conduct; viz reconciliation upon principles of humanity equity honour and the Strictest justice to all parties. Fiat justitia et ruat cœlum.[2] Let justice be sifted out to the nicest scruple of equity & honour, & let that justice [*torn:* be] the foundation of peace. Verbum sapienti. Your affecte   DH

From ——— Du Marquet and Other Applicants
for Emigration   ALS: American Philosophical Society

The first applicant for emigration during the months covered by this volume, whose letter is printed below, is torn between his patriotism and a desire to provide his children with an upbringing appropriate to their birth.[3]

On March 4 a discalced Carmelite friar named Father Paulus writes in Latin from Saint Peter's Church in Marseilles, wishing to emigrate to the "most blessedly united provinces" where he will offer ecclesiastical services to Catholics and whatever is required to those of other faiths, either now on the battlefield or later when peace returns. He is thirty years old, healthy and robust enough for any kind of service. Originally from Würzburg where he did his studies, he has spent three years in Mannheim, and is in Marseilles to serve the German nation and learn French. With a favorable reply from Franklin, he will obtain leave from his superiors in Germany.

A group of well-off people calling itself "la société requerante," writes on May 9 to request Franklin's protection and advice concerning the plan they have formed to establish a colony in America. They ask Franklin if their conditions can be met:

1. Complete freedom of conscience.

2. A geometric square mile of fallow land in a temperate, fertile, healthful region.

3. The privileges enjoyed by other inhabitants.

4. The administration of their domestic affairs without the intervention of any legislative authority except in cases of life or death.

2. Let justice be done, though the firmament fall to ruin.
3. Unless otherwise indicated, all the letters discussed are in French and at the APS.

For their part the members agree to submit to the general laws of the republic not in conflict with articles 1, 2, and 4. They direct Franklin to respond care of Monsieur de Kemtenstrauss, chevalier du St. Empire, poste restante at Munich.

On May 14 Fontaine writes from Fribourg to ask what inducements will be offered to people of talent who wish to emigrate to America. In a postscript he adds that if Franklin wishes to know who is writing him, he may obtain information secretly from Augustin Forestier, treasurer of the Swiss Guards at Paris.[4]

Nicholas Barth Reimers, a subject of Catherine the Great, writes in English on June 16. Twenty-seven years old, he was trained as a merchant. After a stay of four years in London and various travels in Germany, he settled at Riga where he quickly lost all his money and had to leave the country. For the past eighteen months he has been in Orleans where trade is slack because of the war. He has no occupation, no prospects, and many debts. He begs Franklin's help in procuring a place in the service of America. He has a good command of English and German, understands Dutch and French, and can be useful in any department on either side of the Atlantic.

On June 17 Englehard, a surgeon, writes from Brumath, just north of Strasbourg, where he was educated. He has spent thirteen years away practicing his profession. He was many years in Switzerland and in Paris as assistant surgeon in the Swiss Guards of the King. He also knows obstetrics and could be useful in any circumstances. Surrounded by peasants, he is unappreciated and unhappy. He has resolved to go to America if Franklin will assure him of a position, paid travel expenses, and a safe port. He must have an answer by the end of the month, when he is due to leave for Russia.

Bollene—par le pont st. esprit. Ce 1er. mars. 1780.
Monsieur

Quoique je n'aye pas l'honneur d'etre Connû de votre excellence vos talents, et vos vertus qui ne Sont ignorées d'auc'un francois m'enhardissent a avoir Celuy de vous ecrire avec la plus entiere confiance.

Je ne Connois l'amerique septentrionale que par les diverses relations que j'en ay lû; le discours (surtout) philosophique et politique de l'etablissement des européens dans le nouveau monde

4. Forestier, a burgher of Fribourg since 1776, was quartermaster and treasurer of the regiment, captain in the infantry and chevalier de Saint-Louis: *Dictionnaire historique de la Suisse.*

ma donné des etats unis dont vous etes le representant, Monsieur l'idée la plus avantageuse: et me fait desirer de pouvoir un jour aller m'y transplanter avec ma famille. J'ay l'honneur d'etre né gentilhomme; mais ma fortune est si modique que je me verray dans l'impossibilité de pouvoir elever des enfans cheris, (et dont le nombre augmente chaque année) d'une maniere relative a leur naissance. Ma tendresse pour eux, que partage avec moy une femme qui a tous egards merite le tendre attachement que j'ay pour elle m'engage a chercher de reparer par un moyen honnete l'injustice du Sort qui sembloit m'avoir fait naitre pour jouir d'une Situation heureuse.

J'aime ma patrie; je partage avec la nation l'amour merité, et le juste enthousiasme ou elle est pour notre jeune monarque digne descendant d'henry quatre. Mais Ces precieux sentimens la doivent ils me faire rejetter les moyens qui pourroient Contribuer a procurer un sort plus heureux a Ce que la nature, et mon Cœur me disent que j'ay de plus cher? J'en appelle a vous Monsieur vous etes Citoyen, mais vous etes père.

Si votre excellence Croit que mes idées de transplantation puissent se realiser avec avantage j'ose la prier de me dire son avis la dessus. Quelque occupation que puisse vous donner le poste que vous occupés, ne restil pas toujours un moment de loisir a l'homme de bien pour s'occuper du bonheur d'autruy? Si la reponse dont j'ose me flatter que vous voudrés bien m'honorer devenoit pour moy un encouragement a suivre mes projets, je serois flatté de meriter par quelque chose d'utile la bienveillance des nouveaux Compatriottes qui m'adopteroient, et pour Cet effet je proposerois a votre excellence quelques idées dont la reussite que je Crois infaillible procureroit un jour de grands avantages aux etats unis. J'ay pensé qu'il ne me falloit aucun moyen intermediaire pour m'adresser a vous; persuadé que je Suis qu'il est plus digne de vous, et de moy-meme de n'interesser que la sensibilité de votre ame, et l'utilité peutetre dont je pourrois devenir.

Je me reserve Cependant Monsieur lorsquil en seroit tems de me faire presenter a votre excellence par des personnes de Consideration qui ne puissent laisser chès vous aucune idée de mefiance envers moy. Je Crois la chose indispensable si en voulant bien repondre a ma Confiance je dois etre dans le Cas de vous proposer quelques idées.

J'ay l'honneur d'etre avec respect. Monsieur. votre tres humble et tres obeissant Serviteur   DU MARQUET

Notation: Morket Mars 1st. 1780

To the Marquis de Lafayette   Copy: Library of Congress

Dear Sir,   Passy, March. 2. 1780.

I receiv'd with Pleasure the Letter you honour'd me with of
the 29th. past, and am infinitely obliged by the zeal and Assiduity
with which you have forwarded our affairs at Versailles. The
15000. Arms and Accoutrements are a great article.[5]

I had written to Capt. Jones that Besides the 122. Bales of
Cloth,[6] we hoped for that quantity Arms which it was suppos'd
he might take as Bellast. I think the Cloathing 4000. suits was
also mentioned to him by Mr. de Chaumont. In his last letter to
me he says he will take as much as possible and hopes he may be
able to cram in the whole.[7] If not your ship[8] can take the rest. I
wish much to know where the arms are and when they can be
render'd at L'Orient.

Mr. Williams I hear is indefatigable in preparing the Cloathing,
and hopes to have the whole 10,000 suits ready by the End of the
Month.[9] I wish they could go with you, but that being impossi-

5. Lafayette had informed BF (XXXI, 565–6) that Foreign Minister Vergennes and Army Minister Montbarey had assured him of the delivery of
these arms for the use of the American army. Lafayette had been pressuring
Montbarey for them: XXXI, 358–9, 370.

6. Which the merchant John Ross proposed to send to America for making into uniforms. BF had left Jones the option of carrying them on the *Alliance* when she returned home: XXXI, 499, 501.

7. The previous December BF had placed with JW an order for 10,000 uniforms for the American army, to be purchased with a loan from the French
government, and JW was soon at work on it: XXXI, 267–8, 328–9. BF turned
to Chaumont, with his extensive business experience and government con-
tacts, to organize the assembling and shipping of the uniforms: Lopez,
Lafayette, pp. 186–7. Chaumont ordered JW to have as many uniforms as possible ready by the beginning of March. Jones, in turn, promised to carry to
America "a great part if not the Whole" of them: XXXI, 375–6, 524.

8. The French frigate *Hermione* was selected to take Lafayette to America
to announce the coming of a French expeditionary corps: XXXI, 370–1n,
519n.

9. XXXI, 504.

ble. I hope we shall get another ship of force to carry them. They are made precisely according to the Directions of the Commitee.[1]

If on seeing the accounts I find I can add a proportion of Cloaths for Officers, which you urge so earnestly, I Shall do it with Pleasure. But from the large and unexpected Drafts often made upon me by Congress, I am become timid. I must take Care of their Credit, and my own, and cannot take hazardous steps, as protesting or not praying [paying] one of their Bills would be attended with great Mischief on both sides the Water. And when I consider the vast Expence occasioned to this nation by the War, I am asham'd to be repeatedly worrying the Ministers by applications for more money.

I ought to let Capt. Jones know as soon as Possible whither the arms are to go with him, as he would Stow them low to serve partly for Ballast. If a Ship can be obtain'd for them and what shall remain of the Cloathing, perhaps it may be as well to excuse the alliance from that article, and let her take more of the Cloathing.

I am told the 122. Bails of Cloath to be shipt by Mr. Ross for the Congress, will by Computation make 7 or 8000 suits. These will be in Addition to the 10,000 making by Mr. Williams. Those Suits will be compos'd of Coat waste coat, Breeches, Overalls, 2 pair of Strokings, 2 pair of shoes, two shirts, two stocks, and a Hat for each man. I think there will also be Buckles. If there be any farther information that you want, let me know, and I will give what I can.

With The sincerest Esteem and affection, I am Dear sir, &c.

Mr. De La fayette.

From John Adams

AL: American Philosophical Society

Passy March 2d. 1780.

Mr Adams's respectfull Compliments to Dr Franklin. Informs him that Monsieur the Comte De Vergennes has appointed him

1. On orders of Congress the Board of War had drawn up the specifications for the uniforms: XXXI, 268n, 329n; Idzerda, *Lafayette Papers*, II, 354n; Lopez, *Lafayette*, pp. 184–5. Lafayette, however, had made his own suggestions, such as making the officers' uniforms of superior quality: XXXI, 504–5n.

next Tuesday to be at Versailles in order to be presented to the King and Royal Family.[2] Mr Adams will have the Honour to breakefast at Passy with Dr Franklin, at an hour early enough to go to Versailles, which he supposes will be 8 o Clock.

His Excellency Dr Franklin

Addressed: His Excellency / Benjamin Franklin Esqr

From Charles-Guillaume-Frédéric Dumas: Two Letters

(I) ALS: American Philosophical Society; AL (draft): Algemeen Rijksarchief; (II) AL: American Philosophical Society; AL (draft): Algemeen Rijksarchief

I.

Honoured & dear Sir,   the Hague March 2d. 1780.
    The Letter I send you a Copy herewith[3] I have just received. The Autor of it having always professed himself a friend to the

2. JA was presented the following Tuesday, March 7: *Adams Papers*, IX, 24. The presentation was not announced officially, however, as Vergennes had told JA it would be: Butterfield, *John Adams Diary*, IV, 251–2, 254n. This was the result of a misunderstanding which would contribute to the eventual rift between the two. When JA informed Vergennes of his selection as commissioner to negotiate peace and a commercial treaty with Great Britain, he asked the French foreign minister's advice about informing the British court and the public about his mission: *ibid.*, IV, 243–5. He did not explain, however, the purpose of making such an announcement; as he himself later admitted, his going to England "would have been a just cause of jealousy to our ally": Mass. Hist. Soc. *Coll.*, 5th ser., IV (1878), 384. JA's motives apparently puzzled Vergennes. He told La Luzerne, the French minister in Philadelphia, that the new commissioner had given him occasion "to judge he does not know the whole nature and whole object of his commission": James H. Hutson, *John Adams and the Diplomacy of the American Revolution* (Lexington, Ky., 1980), p. 58. JA in turn asked why his presentation had not been officially announced: Butterfield, *John Adams Diary*, IV, 254n. It appears the cause of JA's *faux pas* was his concern that BF would attempt to take over any peace negotiations: Hutson, *John Adams and the Diplomacy of the American Revolution*, pp. 52–9.
    3. It was a Feb. 25 letter (APS) from the Dutch aristocrat and well-known American sympathizer Joan Derk van der Capellen tot den Pol, which advised Dumas and BF to take better security precautions when writing him.

American cause, though not a more powerfull one than many others, deserves to be managed; & therefore I shall write to him very politely, & offer him, If he has some good ouvertures to make for the credit of America, to convey them, by my correspondence, to you, Sir, & to Congress. His circumstances are now very good, having not long ago got a considerable succession from a relation of his.

Be pleased, dear Sir, after having read my Letter, here inclosed, for Capt. Jones, to close it with a piece of wafer, & send or give it him when you will see or know of him.[4]

I think him too much exasperated against 784 & 166, & not enough aware of the fair promises 64 has made him. I am sure the latter is but an indifferent friend to the two former, to 338 & to 65.[5]

I am ever with a most respectfull attachment Honoured & dear Sir yr. Very humble & obedient servant DUMAS

Passy, his Exc. B. Franklin

Addressed: His Excellency / B. Franklin, Esqr. Minr. / Plenipe. of the United States / &c. / Passy ./.

Notation: Dumas, la haie March 2d. 80

II.

The Hague March 2d. 1780 in the Evening.
This moment *our friend*[6] tells me in great confidence, that 873. 30[7] has at last made one principal Step they expected from him,

---

4. Dumas to Jones, March 2: Bradford, *Jones Papers,* reel 5, no. 999.

5. The numerical code used here by Dumas had been composed by John Paul Jones: XXXI, 345–7. BF interlined the decoded words above the numbers: "784 & 166" were Sartine (who had provided the funds to outfit the *Bonhomme Richard* squadron) and Chaumont; "64" was the Ambassador (*i.e.,* the duc de La Vauguyon, French ambassador to the Netherlands, with whom Jones had been in frequent contact during his November, 1779–January, 1780, Dutch stay); "338" was Franklin and "65" was America.

6. Pensionary of Amsterdam Engelbert-François van Berckel. In addition to number codes Dumas used particular expressions and code names to designate important political figures (*e.g.,* "Le grand facteur" for La Vauguyon); a list of these is given in XXIX, 6n.

7. "The Stadholder" (William V of Orange).

by 705, 26. 884. 873. 783. 64. to sound 394. 274. about an 61.
MPGPPX. 880. & 873. 598 PBX. CDLDPC. 322. 795, 26. 873.
183. 610. 578, 28.[8]

388. 236, 27. 935. 388. 385. 884. 787. 884. 873. 783. 64. as a 960
man 601. 581. used to 842. 537. But 833. 388. 236, 27. 470. and 873.
783. 64. has 802. 880. very 214. an 304. 884. 665. 618. 880.
PBBLO.[9]

Our friend has this from 873. 783. 64.[1] himself; And 62. 341.
873. 362. 657LBI.[2] They are sure that 867. & OPXWLBN. 942.
39. 884. 873. 541.[3] And a negociation is set on foot for a body of
600. 531, 28. which 878. 262. 601. 878. 942. 606. 322. 874. 560.[4]

This Letter cannot go till to morrow. If there is some other
news, I shall add it on the other side of this sheet.[5]

Notation: Dumas la haie March 2d. 80

8. " . . . proposing to the Russian Ambassador [Prince Dmitrii Golitsyn]
to sound his Empress [Catherine II] about an alliance between this & the
northern states for securing the commerce of neutrals."
9. "He delivered what he had to say to the Russian ambassador as a young
man not much used to such matter. But still he delivered it and the Russian
ambassador has sent this very day an express to Petersburg on this errand."
William V was born in 1748.
1. " . . . the Russian ambassador."
2. " . . . also from the Grand Pensionary [Pieter van Bleiswijk]."
3. " . . . Sweden & Denmark will accede to the measure."
4. " . . . Norway marines which they doubt not they will obtain for their
money."
BF decoded Dumas' letter through "61. MPGPPX, (Alliance between)"
and thereafter decoded only scattered numbers and letters. Its subject, that
of obtaining Russian help in protecting neutral shipping rights, was of considerable interest to the Netherlands, given the recent seizure of Dutch merchant ships by the British. Meanwhile, the Russian Empress on March 10 issued to the courts of Britain, France, and Spain a declaration of neutral
shipping rights. She wrote separately to Denmark, Sweden, Portugal, and
the Netherlands, the leading neutral maritime states of Europe, inviting them
to cooperate in protecting such rights. This was the genesis of the League
of Armed Neutrality: Sir Francis Piggott and G.W.T. Omond, eds., *Documentary History of the Armed Neutralities 1780 and 1800* (London, 1919),
pp. 198–9; Isabel de Madariaga, *Britain, Russia and the Armed Neutrality of
1780: Sir James Harris's Mission to St. Petersburg during the American Revolution* (New Haven, 1962), pp. 140–84.
5. Also filed with the present letters at the APS is a two-page "Extrait
d'une Lettre que je viens de recevoir" in Dumas' hand. This extract blames

To John Paul Jones ALS: Yale University Library

Sir   Passy, March 3. 1780
    This is to authorize & require you to receive & accomodate
in your Ship as Passengers the honourable Arthur Lee & Ralph
Izard, Esquires, late Ministers of the Congress at the Courts of
France & Toscany.[6] I am, Sir, Your most obedient humble Servant   B FRANKLIN

To the honourable J.P. Jones Esqr. Commander of the Alliance—

Notations in different hands:[7] Dr. Franklin's order for our Passage / March 3d. 1780

From Thomas Digges ALS: Historical Society of Pennsylvania

Dr. Sir   London 3d Mar. 1780
    I recd your favrs. of the 2d. & 9th. Feby[8] very safely, and by
a Country man (Capn. Ben Carpenter of the Cartel ship lately
from Boston to Bristol)[9] I take the opportunity to forward you a

---

a Robert Tuite and a Macquefoy [McEvoy] for the Danish government's returning to the British the prizes from the *Bonhomme Richard* squadron's
cruise. Robert Tuite (d. 1813) was the son of the West Indian planter Nicholas
Tuite (1702–1772), for whom see the *Dansk Biografisk Leksikon* (16 vols.,
Copenhagen, 1979–84). Dumas' extract also inquires about a Mr. "Guillon,"
actually Alexander Gillon of South Carolina who was currently in Amsterdam trying to buy frigates for his adoptive state's navy (XXVII, 47n; XXX,
36–7; XXXI, 183–5, 450–1). An undated document in Chaumont's hand,
"Nottes pour M. franklin," addresses the former subject. One of the guilty
is a certain Jameson, but Robert Tuitten deserves most of the blame. Both
men are currently in London. University of Pa. Library.
    6. Two weeks earlier BF had agreed to make this request for the two for-
mer commissioners, now planning their return to America. Although Lee did
return on the *Alliance*, Izard found passage on another ship: XXXI, 500–1.
    7. The first of which is in Lee's.
    8. XXXI, 435–6, 462–3.
    9. The cartel ship was the *Polly;* her owner, Henry Mitchell, was also on
board and Digges had referred to him as the captain: XXXI, 365, 418. Benjamin Carpenter (b. 1751) was originally from Medford, Mass.: William

letter from Mr DH which will explain the state of the Cartel; I am in hopes before I seal my letter to also get one from Mr Hodgson; & not unlikely one from Mr Banks about the medal, and also a line from Mr B Vaughan.[1]

Captain Carpenter goes on the same errand with Belt, who is arrivd safe, & will go soon.[2] It may be necessary to inform you that the vessel in which Capn Carpenter came from Boston has been seizd as a prize, & it is yet doubtful whether the owner of Her Cap Hy. Mitchell who is also an inhabitant of Boston, & came in His vessel for the purpose of getting over Rigging Cordage & stores for two vessels He has building in Boston, will get any gratuity made Him for His ship, which He values at £2000.— Capn. Carpenter will be a supplicant to you for a pass for the Brigantine Adventure, Himself Commander, of abot. 160 Tonns & men answerable, which Mr Mitchell will immediately push forward from Ireland to Boston with the above mentiond articles, sail Duck, Tent Canvass, usefull stores, & Provisions. Mr Mitchells friends and Connexions in Ireland will enable him quickly to do this; and as His schemes bear a manifest tendency to do good for Ama, & that He may be in some measure riembursd his loss's on the Cartel business, I back His Solicitations & request to you, that another pass may be given for the Ship in which He will go himself. He would personally apply to you for it & go thro the necessary forms, but his attendance at the Admiralty every day with His Lawyer & in some hopes of getting a gratuity for the loss of the vessel, prevents Him. If the pass could express this last *an armd* vessel, it will be the better, & he might do something on his way from Corke. The vessel is calld the ship James Heny Mitchell Commander about 200 Tons

---

Leavitt, "History of the Essex Lodge of Freemasons," *Hist. Coll. of the Essex Institute* III (1861), 133; Charles H. Lincoln, comp., *Naval Records of the American Revolution 1775–1788* (Washington, D.C., 1906), p. 475.

1. William Hodgson, Sir Joseph Banks, and Benjamin Vaughan wrote BF later in March or in April. For the medal see below.

2. Capt. Walter Belt had executed a bond with BF to deliver clothing to the United States: XXXI, 417, 462n, 548. BF had expressed suspicion that passports which he issued might be used to engage in illegal trade: XXXI, 548. Belt's ship, the *Brighton*, did slip away from its British convoy and sell its goods in Boston at a great profit: Elias and Finch, *Letters of Digges*, p. 356–7.

Burthen & would be found & fitted as a letter of Marque, *provided it is proper*, and a Commn can be given by you for Capt Mitchell to act as such. If it can be done I see some good may arise from the scheme to our Country. I have been much with Capt Mitchell on the Business of the Cartel &ca. and also with Captain Carpenter, & I find them persons every way qualified to be trusted & whom I would wish to serve. Capt. Carpenter will immediately return to me in London & proceed on to Ireland, & will take charge of any thing you may have to send.

Capt B——t got back near the same period with Mr B——r——r,[3] the latter of whom I have not yet seen tho he carefully calld & left your Letters. He is an intelligent good sort of Man, but so buried in ship Business in the City that It may be some time before I can get a sight of Him. As yet I am not acquainted by Mr H——y whether or not he was successful in the persuit He went upon, & wch indeed was so complicated that I did not clearly understand. In B——ts adventure you may rely there is none but Am——ns & those of the right sort, concernd they are chiefly indeed all of them placd in this Country at present by the accidents of war, some prisoners—some left out of Bread by the stoppage of the Fishery &a. &a. but being six or seven in number & not without friends to lend them money, they will carry out full 10,000£ worth of Goods.

I have recd & placed to your Credit the 100£ remittd me. Some days before I got it I had written to my friend at Plyo. to supply Capt Ma——y, to the amot. of 16 or 18 Guins that he might bribe some individual to give up his place to Him in the next Cartel. I think this or something else may be effected for Him & he never has, nor shall he want my aid. The 28.1.10 was paid to Brown & Collison & you have a Rect. inclosd.[4] I have also bought the Dicy & Gramr Cost 35/6 & they will go in a box with other books from Mr Vaughan to Ostend. They are directed to the Care of Monsr. Francois Bowens (Mr Whartons friend) &

3. Barber, a business associate of David Hartley's cousin Samuel: XXXI, 353–4.

4. BF had sent £100 with which he wished Digges to pay the bankers Browns & Collinson and assist John Manley (for whom see XXXI, 418–19n), using the remainder of the money for other prisoner relief: XXXI, 463n.

He has orders to forward them on to you.[5] I employd my friend Mrs. Vaughan to procure the peice of Irish stuff calld independence, at least as much as would make a Ladys suit.[6] I fear by her not sending it to me to day that it cannot be had in London (but must be orderd from Ireland); but if it comes this Evening Capt Carpenter will take charge of it to you. If not, I will send it in an ostend trader to Mr Bowens for forwardance. There will also go with the p s/s(?) stuff the six trios of Augustar, wch Mr B.T.F wrote to me some time ago for.[7]

I am sorry I cannot give you a better accot about the contract for Exche. of Prisoners by the two Cartel ships to Falmo & Bristol.[8] Two of the Passengers in them made some little stir at first but their mouths seem to have been since shut. The two Capns. of the Packets Hill, & Boulderson, did what they could with the board of sick & hurt, but it seems the Exchange as agreed on by the Prisoners could not be complyd with because it was *unusual* & *unofficial*, & because a Cartel for that purpose actually existed between Boston & new York. But I beleive this answer will not satisfy the Yankees if ever any of the Prisoners are again catchd in Ama. The Bearer will carry you a list of names & the written agreement instead of complying with which only *partial* releass are given to four or five out of the 130 wch came in the two Ships— The releases are simply thus a letter to the Commander in cheif at N York to release one person or Gentn., for Mr. Jno Jackson; (this Mr Jackson is a talking sort of a forward lawyer who came in Mitchell) and also other similar letters to a Mr. Barry (an under secy to Govr Dalling) & to the Capns Hill & Boulderson these last are appointed again to Packets and are Kings Commissiond Officers, & Barry very soon after his arrival was sent back with Dispatches to Govr Dalling.[9] The rest are all

5. Perhaps the books were for BFB; see XXX, 586. François Bowens was an Ostend businessman of Digges's acquaintance: XXXI, 155n.

6. Possibly for Mme Chaumont: XXXI, 463n.

7. For Astorga's trios see XXXI, 193n.

8. The *Polly* put into Bristol; the other cartel, the *Bob*, put into Falmouth: XXXI, 418. They brought passengers from two captured British packets in hopes of exchanging them for American sailors held prisoner.

9. Barry's and Jackson's parole is given XXXI, 365–6. Sir John Dalling was the governor of Jamaica.

following their avocations & seem to be quite easy, nor do I find the admiralty have ever thought it requisite to write to New York that an equal number for them should be releasd there. This shall be properly enquird into & you shall know the issue.

I have sent you 10 or a doz news papers by which you will gather the present news & disposition in Parliat Lord N does not seems to hold the majority he used to do in his divisions of that House. The people do not seem at all elated with the success's & present state of Rodneys fleet. They think it at risque from Don Gastons Squadron. I find only 4 of his ships are to proceed on to the Wt Indies, & but 3 or four to go with Walsingham as Convoy to the Wt Inda. fleet wch will sail abot. the 15th or 20th. but probably 8 or 10 others will see them some distance from the Lands end.[1] There are many fears too abot. the French having the majority of Ships on the Wt Indies next summer & fears are revivd about the safety of Jamaica. The Associations get more & more seriously formidable every day & the ministry are hurt exceedingly with them.[2] If there is not a general reform gone

1. Adm. George Rodney's fleet of twenty-three ships of the line relieved Gibraltar after smashing a Spanish squadron blockading it: XXXI, 407n. Commodore Miguel Gastón brought a Spanish squadron from Brest, raising the strength of the fleet at Cadiz to twenty-five of the line: XXXI, 480n. Rodney was able to sail unmolested from Gibraltar, however; detaching most of his fleet to return to England he proceeded to the West Indies with four ships of the line. Commodore Robert Walsingham's five ships of the line and their Jamaica convoy were detained in Torbay by contrary winds until June: Elias and Finch, *Letters of Digges*, p. 164n; Mackesy, *War for America*, pp. 323, 325, 328–30. For Walsingham (1736–1780) see Namier and Brooke, *House of Commons*, III, 603–5.

2. The Associated Counties movement was launched in late 1779 by discontented country gentlemen from Yorkshire under the leadership of the Reverend Christopher Wyvill. Attracting the support of metropolitan radicals, the group drafted a broad program of "economical" reforms, *i.e.*, fiscal and economic measures that would reduce the cost of government. The Yorkshire petition was presented to the House of Commons on Feb. 8. On Feb. 24 delegates from Westminster and eight counties began meeting at the St. Alban's Tavern in London to debate the association's future program: Eugene Charleton Black, *The Association: British Extraparliamentary Political Organization 1769–1793* (Cambridge, Mass., 1963), pp. 32–51; Edward Royle and James Walvin, *English Radicals and Reformers 1760–1848* (Brighton, Eng., 1982), pp. 28–9; Cobbett, *Parliamentary History*, xx, 1370–83.

into I make no doubt but there will be soon some capital Rumpus. The Irish are farther than ever from being satisfyd & their
parliament seem resolvd to Repeal Poinings Law—[3] to put an
end to all appeals to England—to render their judges indepen-
dant of the Crown—to have a habeas Corpus act—to confine
their votes for supplys to the apportionment of New Dutys
only—to give bountys on their own Manufactures—to have a
mutiny Bill &ca. &ca. all which is very clever for us & must in
the end hurt poor old England as she is now generally calld, very
much.

Mr Jones being on a Circuit Mr Paradise deliverd yr. Certificate about the orders to Amn. Cruisers not to molest Capt
Cooke, to Mr Banks who quibbled & shuffled all he could—by
saying it was not an act of Congress, but meerly from yr. own
humanity that it was granted, that it expressd but one Ship when
there was two, that it was dated a year after the order issued by
France &ca. &ca. He has promisd Mr. Paradise a letter for you
wch I expect this Evg. & said that a Silver Medal should be certainly given you (gold ones only being given to sovereigns) &
that could there be proof that such orders were the deed of Congress they should have a gold medal.[4]

I do not hear or discover the least signs of any troops meant
to be sent to Ama there are some going & gone to the Wt Indies
the amot not more than 5,000. It is thought Wallace will command a small squadron of frigates and conduct the trade to N
York & Quebec wh will likely sail together abot. the 20th. Inst.
not unlikely with the Wt India ships.[5] I wish you a large share of
health & happiness & am with very high Esteem Dr Sir Yr.
obligd & Ob Serv   TD

I send you also a Letter from Mr Taylor of Bath.[6]

3. Poyning's Law (1494) subordinated the Irish legislature to the British
crown; it was repealed in 1782.

4. The Royal Society medal honored BF for his granting of a passport to
the explorer Captain Cook: XXXI, 448–9.

5. The British were in the process of sending more than 7,000 troops to
the West Indies: Mackesy, *War for America*, p. 323. Wallace probably is Sir
James Wallace, formerly the captain of a 50–gun ship captured by d'Estaing:
DNB.

6. XXXI, 439–41.

Since writing the within, I have seen Capt Mitchells letter to you[7] as well as one to the Council of the State of Massachusets, and they are so explanatory of His business that I need not add a word on that head.

The Letter I expected from Mr Banks, Mr Hodgson, or Mr Vaughan has not come to hand, but I have Recd from Mrs. V the peice of Stuff (Durant) as near the pattern as could possibly be got. It Cost 40/— and the ShopKeeper who brought it me says He could not cut the peice wch. Contains 30 yds.

I do not recollect I have any thing further to say than that I am with the greatest regard Dr Sir Yrs &c &c

The Dicy. and Grammar goes via Ostend with other books from Mr V——n. I shall write to Mr Bowens by the Bearer & if they are arrivd at Ostend & can be forwarded by the bearer they will be sent by Him in the Carriage or Dilligence.

Addressed: His Excelly. / Benjamin Franklin / Passy / pr. favr. / Cap Carpenter

Endorsed: Mar 3. 80

From John Jay

Copies: Library of Congress, Columbia University Library

Dear Sir,   Cadiz 3d. march 1780.

On this Day I gave the House of Messrs. Jaques, Louis And Laurt. Le Couteullx of this Place,[8] a Set of Bills on you for two Thousand five hundred and Sixty four Livres Eighteen Sols and ten Donrs. [deniers] payable ninety Days after the Date.[9]

---

7. Missing.

8. For this firm's prior services to Americans see XXVI, 467n. On March 20 Jay informed BF he had drawn bills of 3,596 *l.t.*, 13 *s.* on him with the same firm and Jay expressed his obligations to them: Library of Congress.

9. The third time the minister-designate to the court of Spain had drawn on BF for funds since leaving America: XXXI, 286–7, 409–10. Since Jan. 22 the Jay party had been in Cadiz, where Sarah Jay found herself "very agreeably accommodated": XXXI, 409; Morris, *Jay: Revolutionary*, p. 692. On March 8, finally assured that he would be welcome at the Spanish court, Jay began preparations for their trip to Madrid: *ibid.*, pp. 742–4.

I am Dear Sir with great Regard & Esteem your most Obedient Servant   (signed) JOHN JAY.

His Excellency Dr. B. Franklin.

From John Paul Jones

AL: American Philosophical Society; AL (draft) and transcript: National Archives

Honored and dear Sir,   L'Orient March 3d. 1780.

I had the Honor to write to your Excellency the 21st: & 25th: Ulto.—[1] We have hitherto had no Assistance from the Port and I now hope to get the Alliance ready with out them.— The Arms for the Continent if I am to take them on board the Alliance will be wanted soon as they cannot so well be Stowed after we begin to fill Water.

I wish for the determination respecting the Wine Brig that was taken last Summer bound from Bourdeaux for Dublin for I find that this long Suspence gives great uneasiness and hurts the Service.[2]

It gives me pain to Complain of any man, but you will Judge whether I have not reason when I tell you that M. Schweighauser refuses to settle with Mr: Williams for my part of the Rangers Prizes that have been *22 months* in his Hands.—[3] And for which I have not to this instant received any payment.— Whoever behave in that manner deserve a harsher Name than I shall now give them.—

The Conduct of M C. requires at least an explanation. M S—— as I understand Writes that the monies for Settling the Affairs of the Armament lately under my command has been lodged in the hands of a Banker at Paris ever since the begining of November at the disposal of M C.—[4] M C—— has impow-

1. XXXI, 507–8, 524–5.

2. The *Three Friends*, captured in June, 1779, by Landais while cruising with Jones: xxx, 12–13, 101, 137–8, 171–3, 224.

3. Schweighauser had handled the prizes made by Jones's sloop of war *Ranger* during an April 10–May 8, 1778, cruise: xxvi, 500, 665, 673.

4. "M C" is Monsieur Chaumont; "S——" is Sartine. The armament was the *Bonhomme Richard* squadron.

ered no person here to act in that Business.— He writes this Note in French to Mr: Gourlade by last post—"When you have need of Money draw on me at Four Usances."—without saying a Single Word to explain for what purpose the money is to be applied:— Besides, no Man I believe can raise Money on M C's Bills without further Security and a discount.— Why not therefore draw Bills on the Banker with whom the funds are Lodged? And why has he not given Orders to do this much Sooner?— As the Men engaged to serve with me they naturally look to me for their Right and I naturally demand it on their behalf.

I beg Pardon for giving you this trouble.— I would write to M C.— but he has not Answered my last.— I hope however that he will immediately make the necessary and Just arrangements and so acquit himself of the Duty he has Undertaken that I may not be reduced to the necessity of mentioning his Name a Second time to his Superiors.—

Unless you disapprove of the within letter to the Countess of Selkirk[5] I must beg you to forward it by the Surest Conveyance.—

With the highest esteem and Respect I am your Excellency's most Obedient and most hum Servt.

N.B. As there is a dispute about the Cannon that M: Bonfield sent here from Bourdeaux for the Bon H Richard;[6] and as they were bought very Cheap and are well adapted for the Ships now Building in America, I could take them on board instead of a Quantity of Shingle ballast—If you Can make the necessary Arrangements. The Eighteen pounders are of a good length and Quality and Cost me much pains to procure them.

His Excellency B. Franklin Esqr: &c. &c.

Notation: J.P. Jones. L'orient. March 3. 80

5. In this March 1 letter (Bradford, *Jones Papers*, reel 5, no. 996) Jones told the countess that her family plate, taken during the *Ranger*'s cruise (XXVI, 502; XXVIII, 500, 599; XXIX, 66–7, 118–19) would now be returned to her. It was lodged with the firm of Gourlade & Moylan, who would forward it to her by whatever conveyance she wished. The return, however, was apparently delayed until after the end of the war: Morison, *Jones*, pp. 154–5.

6. XXIX, 628n.

From Mancet & Cie. and Other Offerers of
Goods and Schemes   ALS: American Philosophical Society

A number of people had concrete goods to offer the Americans and some others hoped Franklin would collaborate with or promote their pet project or plan for the new republican states.[7]

The Brest shipowners Mancet & Cie., whose letter is published below, want permission to give Franklin's name to their new privateer.

Also in the maritime line comes a project on May 6. Eager for revenge on the British for the bad treatment suffered at their hands, Alexandre Morisse submits his plan for the building and outfitting of a privateer to be named *La Jeune Dunkerquoise,* for which he asks Franklin's sponsorship. The printed enclosure specifies that instead of equipping this ship the European way with a dozen cannon and three-pound balls, the American system will be adopted: five cannons with six-pound balls and five guns throwing one-pound stone projectiles.[8] Such an arrangement will give attacking power to both sides of the ship and completely hide the sixty-member crew, of which Morisse will be the captain.

Writing from Paris on June 19, the firm of Chrestien & Cie. relates that they have been approached by the deputy of "Machachuset," who is desirous to procure ninety pieces of cloth from their manufactory in Sedan.[9] Eager as they are to oblige and create ties with Massachusetts, Chrestien would appreciate a conference with the worthy representative of the United States in whom he has the utmost confidence.

The large cloth manufacturing firm of Coulougnac & Cie. (XXXI, 289n) informs Franklin on May 15 that they are now at the head of a consortium of twenty textile-producing firms created solely to facilitate reciprocal commercial dealings between France and North America. Their two main seats, in Lyon (where their letter comes from) and Nantes are ready to handle all the orders that Congress or the States may place either for war purposes or private needs. Payment can be made through accepted drafts on Paris or by exchange for tobacco, indigo, rice, or furs. The goods will be delivered within six months and

---

7. Unless indicated otherwise, the following documents are in French and deposited at the APS.

8. Stone-throwing guns were still in use in the eastern Mediterranean: Jan Glete, *Navies and Nations: Warships, Navies and State Building in Europe and America, 1500–1860* (2 vols., Stockholm, 1993), I, 25.

9. The textile firm of Charderon *père & fils,* & Chrétien appears in the *Almanach des Marchands,* pp. 375 and 447.

are guaranteed to be of the best quality. They beg to be recommended to Congress and for their offer to be publicized through the newspapers. Their house in Nantes will easily sell all the goods sent from America. Thanks to their immense resources, they feel able to fulfill governmental wishes on both sides of the ocean.

A Paris wigmaker by the name of Chaumont encloses a printed circular advertising his product on June 14: a naturally curled hairpiece that truly mimics real hair and is held in place by a special pomade that comes in two-ounce sticks. The wigmaker's innovations have received the approval of the Royal Academy of Sciences.

Writing on May 21 to "Monseigneur de Francklin" from Dieuze in Lorraine, Collignon, a lawyer, member of the academies of sciences of Naples, Munich, Lisbon, and others, announces that the book he has written on clearing uncultivated land has been extremely well received all over Europe.[1] He is now submitting it to Franklin's "profondes lumieres." He is also sending a package made up of several copies meant for Congress since he is convinced that the topic of his work will be of the greatest use to the Americans. Please forward it as early as possible.

A rather grandiose scheme—a poem made up of eight cantos of four hundred verses each—is announced by the abbé de Boisrenard, writing on May 5 from Lorges, near Beaugency on the Loire. His enthusiasm for America sustains him but he needs Franklin's help to settle a few historical points. Who were the first men to conceive the notion of independence? Which American and British generals fought in Lexington and where is Lexington, which he cannot find on a map? Where exactly did General Gates capture Burgoyne? Where was General Lee made a prisoner? Did General Montgomery leave a son?[2]

1. His letter is at the University of Pa. Library. The date on it looks like 1785 but this has to be a slip of the pen since two other letters from him, clearly alluding to this one, are dated Dec. 11, and Dec. 26, 1780 (both at the APS). In the first one, Collignon wonders whether Franklin received the package he had sent him; if not, he will send a duplicate. He adds the names of the scientific and agricultural societies to which he belongs. BF endorsed it: "Acknowledge the Receipt of this Letter, & request to know the Subject of the Packet, as it is not mention'd and I receive many." Collignon's reply re-stated the contents of his book and asked the Doctor to let him know whether the new package should be sent by public conveyance. Claude-Boniface Colignon's book is *Essai de bien public, ou Mémoire raisonné pour lever à coup sûr tous les obstacles qui s'opposent à l'exécution des défrichements et desséchements* . . . (Neuchâtel, 1776).

2. BF may have been overwhelmed by all those questions: the proposed poem has not been found.

The castle of the Montgomerys still stands and should be bought for that child if he exists.

Still in the literary line, an anonymous correspondent addresses Franklin on April 19.[3] In his enthusiasm for the cause of Franklin's "compatriottes devenus nos frères," he has written a memoir "Pour la Gloire du Roy, l'avantage et Lhonneur de ma Patrie," but he fears that the copies he is sending to Maurepas, Montbarey, and Sartine will never reach those ministers' eyes—the reason being that his ideas are not expressed in a stylish way. He hopes that Franklin, focusing on the memoir's substance, will manage to get it published. Seeing it in full or in part, in the *Mercure de France,* would delight the author.[4]

Equally eager to see his musings appear in the *Mercure de France* is Talamuth (a pen name?), who fulminates against General Benjamin Lincoln. In an undated letter,[5] he accuses the general of having been corrupted by gold and marvels that a man as enlightened as Franklin should not have foreseen his treason. A lawyer prone to Delphic style and prophetic pronouncements, Talamuth predicts America's early enslavement unless his counsel, inspired by Reason, is heeded. Only after Franklin gets his "petite dissertation" published in the *Mercure de France* will he reveal the secret to which he alone possesses the key.

Two Germans, both using Gothic script, have elaborate financial plans for the United States.

Bühring, who writes from Berlin on March 3, wants to be paid for his idea.[6] For the sum of twenty thousand pounds sterling or a piece of land of equivalent value in America where he could settle with his family, he will reveal the plan he conceived to raise money for the

3. His letter and memoir are at the Hist. Soc. of Pa.

4. The ten-page memoir, found among BF's papers, advocates a massive invasion of England by at least 300,000 Frenchmen who would carry out the destruction of the island's ports and war machine over a one-year period. It then proposes the elimination of the British forces from the American continent. After that, in 1781, 30,000 Americans coming to Europe would help in the revolt of Scotland and Ireland, following which the English possessions all over the world would fall by themselves. The memoir's projection of the means for raising the necessary funds makes it sound easy. Its last page, in the margin of which Franklin wrote, "to prevent Desertion," advises the universal and obligatory use of passports, without which individuals may not travel, buy food, rent a room, etc., with severe penalties for those who do not denounce the suspected deserters.

5. We are dating it [after June 16] because it was on that day that news of Gen. Lincoln's capture in Charleston reached Europe: *Courier de l'Europe,* VII (1780), 391–4.

6. Someone wrote a brief French résumé of his proposal for BF's benefit.

United States, money on which no interest will have to be paid. What he has in mind is paper money he would put in circulation; but instead of falling below its value, as the current paper money is doing, his would be equal to real money, or almost. One condition, though: he has to be present to carry out the plan, for the slightest mistake could be very harmful. If the plan fails he asks no compensation.

The other German scheme, presented by Reyhermann, originates on April 7 in Apold, Saxe-Weimar.[7] It describes the alchemistic discovery of a never-ceasing source of gold. This discovery will allow the government to provide, at no expense, for pensioners and widows. The author claims to have sent his manuscript and printed dedications one and a half years ago; they must either have been received or purloined by his enemies. He asks for 6 or 10 Louis d'or in order to pursue his work.[8] In addition to this, there is an undated printed sheet soliciting subscriptions for the publishing of the project.

A man who does not give the slightest inkling of his purpose but merely tells Franklin "que j'ai quelque chose a vous communiquer de tres interessant et tres satisfézant pour vous" is the chevalier de Vosmon who writes from Paris on April 26. He asks very politely for an appointment. Franklin endorsed the note the following day and indicated "That I shall be at home on Wednesday morning, ready to receive him, if he thinks proper then to call upon me." But there must have been some mixup, for the endorsement continues on May 4: "Wrote again appointing saturday the 6th at 11 or to call on him about 1 the same day." This May 4 letter is missing but undoubtedly written in response to a May 2 letter from Vosmon renewing his request for an appointment. An undated letter by an unnamed third party reminds Franklin that Vosmon wrote a week earlier and gives his address.

Finally, inventions. A Parisian by the name of de Servandony, writing on March 29, has designed a contraption that allows a battery of canons to be raised twenty to thirty feet above the ground or the sea without much difficulty or expense. He will be glad to present a model of it any time at Franklin's convenience.

Another bellicose machine is proposed from London, in shakily spelled English, on May 30. The "Ingenious Ingineer" who thought up the deadly systems described therein is called John Cross but the

7. This scheme is expounded in three letters written on this day, each of them in duplicate.

8. There are two manuscript copies (one seventy-four pages long, the other sixty-one) of the introduction to the work and of the dedication. Each one has a preface dated Oct. 4, 1779, and a title page bearing the mention Leipzig, 1780.

34

people who recommend him (possibly Cross himself?) simply sign themselves "Your ould Friends in Broadstreet"—Broad Street being where William Hewson and his wife Polly lived.

These recommendations endorse Cross's invention, meant to preserve their country from a naval descent, and assert it has been tested and found to work. Still, they admit, it did not win the approval of General Williamson, was considered too cruel by Sir Charles Frederick, and was not even studied by General Conway.[9] But Franklin well knows the narrow-mindedness of English placemen who value recommendations over merit. Two broadsides are enclosed, one for his own inspection, the other for the King of France. They both are still among his papers, leading one to believe that Louis XVI did not receive his copy. The ten grimly prophetic engines of death enumerated by the author consist mostly of mines to be positioned in various ways in the sea or within the earth, to be exploded either from contact or at a distance. He also devised a moving battery drawn by horses for the protection of fifty men against a whole army, and a cannon secured in such a way that the greatest enemy force cannot dislodge it.

Monsieur,   Brest Le 3 mars 1780.

Le desir dont nous Sommes animés de partager les Succès et les travaux de tant de Braves Marins qui Se distinguent Contre Nos Ennemis Par les plus Beaux traits de courage et d'intrepidité, nous Engage a recourir à votre Excellence Pour la Supplier d'être favorable à L'armement d'un Corsaire de 22 Canons que nous nous Disposons a mettre en Course contre les Ennemis communs de la france et des états unis de L'amérique.

Nous osons Donc Recourir à votre Excellence pour lui demander la faveur de faire porter à Cette Corvette le Pavillon Américain, et de nous accorder des lettres de marque qui en Secondant nos vues, nous mettent à même de Remplir nos projets. Votre Excellence ajoutera a notre reconnoissance Si elle nous permet de Donner a ce Corsaire le nom de franklin. Ce Nom aussi Cheri que Respecté parmi le peuple Republicain dont vous êtes le representant, n'est pas moins En vénération Chez tous les français qui Savent rendre hommage aux vertus et aux talents qui

9. Gen. Sir Adam Williamson (1736–1798) is most famous for having commanded the royal artillery at the 1758 capture of Louisbourg: *DNB*. As surveyor general of the ordnance, Sir Charles Frederick had had contact with BF: XIX, 265, 424; XX, 122. For Gen. Henry Seymour Conway see XII, 209n. He was currently a member of Parliament.

vous caracterisent. Nous Sommes avec Respect, Monsieur, De Votre Excellence Les très humbles et Très obéissants Serviteurs

MANCET ET COMPE.
armateurs à Brest

Notation: Mancet & Compe. le 3 mars. 1780. à Brest.

To Edward Bancroft

Copy: Library of Congress

Dear sir,   Passy, March 4. 1780.

You will see by the enclos'd that a Demand is made of replacing the Things belonging to The Serapis which Comme. Jones borrowed from her and took on board the Alliance when he changed ships.[1] I request you to manage this affair with him in your usual Prudence. I am ever, my Dear friend, Yours most affectionately.

Dr. Bancroft L'orient.

To Samuel Huntington

LS and AL (draft):[2] National Archives; copy: Library of Congress; transcript: National Archives

Sir,   Passy, March 4. 1780.

M. Gerard, under whose Care I understand the Dispatches

1. When Jones, on BF's orders, turned over his prize, the 50-gun warship H.M.S. *Serapis,* to a French officer he took many items with him on board the *Alliance:* XXXI, 147n. Among them were thirty bushels of sea coal, a stove, eighty muskets, a dozen oars, twenty-nine pistols, sixty cutlasses, and four hen coops: "Exact Account of all the Articles taken out of the Prize Ship Serapis," Franklin Papers, University of Pa. Library. The *Serapis* reached Lorient on Feb. 6, four days before the arrival of the *Alliance* at the nearby Ile de Groix: XXXI, 476n, 482.

The enclosure is probably the letter of this date from Chaumont asking that BF write to Jones to restore all the *Serapis'* effects that he had taken and return them to the officer charged by the *commandant* at Lorient with responsibility for that ship. He also requests BF to demand a receipt from Jones. Library of Congress.

2. The LS is in WTF's hand. In preparation for drafting his letter BF drew up a list of topics to be covered and then assigned each its place (APS):

from Congress to me, were forward'd, is not yet arrived here, and I have not received them.[3] I cannot therefore at present answer any thing that may be contained in them. He is however expected next Week, and I may afterwards have time to write farther by the Alliance. Mr Adams is come but did not bring Duplicates of those Dispatches. I have in Obedience to the Order of Congress which he produced to me, furnish'd him with 1000 Louis d'ors.[4] I have also given a Credit to Mr Jay, upon the Correspondent of our Banker at Madrid for an equal Sum. I have not yet heard of his Arrival there. His Letter to me was of the 28th. Jany. from Cadiz.[5]

In my last I gave some Account of the Success of our little Squadron under Commodore Jones.[6] Three of their Prizes, sent into Bergen in Norway, were at the Instance of the British Min-

---

"3. Prizes in Bergen. Memorial. [*lined out:* Demand] Instructs / 4 Jones and Landais. / 11 Arms, Cloathing, &c. Immense Demand. / 10 Disposition of the Court / 12 Money obtain'd. Expence of this Nation. Desire of doing without new Taxes. / 6 Medal for Fleury. Price / 7. The others / 15 Holland.— Divisions there. / 16 Ireland.— / 17 Protestants in England. Associations of Counties Committes &c / 1. M. Gerard & the Dispatches with him not arriv'd / 2. Mr Adams ariv'd. I know nothing of his Business. have furnish'd him with 1000£ Shall [attd. hs Prt. Ty.?] Have given a Credit to Mr Jay. / 13. Have sent the Vote of Congress to M. Johnson, & desired & have had an Answer that he will undertake the Service. / 14. Thanks for / 18 Complain of having no Answers to sundry Points / 8 Exchange of Prisoners— Escapes. / 9 Paroles not regarded— / 5 Intreat that no more Cruises may be sent here, Or that some other Person may be appointed to take Care of them. [*lined out:* Our Pain for the Confederacy relieved] / 19 Secretary. / 20 Marquis de la Fayette." The letter as sent makes no reference to the points raised in numbers 14, 18, and 19.

3. Conrad-Alexandre Gérard, the former French minister to the United States, returned to Europe on the same ship as John Jay and at present was en route from Cadiz: XXXI, 224, 407. Ten days before they sailed from Philadelphia, President of Congress Huntington had written to inform BF of Congress' recent diplomatic appointments: XXX, 542–4.

4. JA's salary, like BF's, was £2,500 per annum: XXX, 543. BF converted his own salary (and presumably JA's) to *livres tournois* at a rather favorable exchange rate of twenty-four to one, *i.e.*, 60,000 *l.t.* or 2,500 *louis* per annum, retroactive to the day the salary was approved, Oct. 4, 1779: Account VI (described in XXIII, 21).

5. XXXI, 409–11. The letter actually is dated January 26.

6. XXX, 463–74.

ister, seized by Order of the Court of Denmark, and deliver'd up to him. I have, with the Approbation of the Ministry here, drawn up and sent to that Court a Memorial reclaiming those Prizes. It went through the Hands of the French Minister residing there, who has deliver'd it; but I have yet no Answer. I understand from the French Consul at Bergen that the Prizes remain still in that Port,[7] and it is said there is some hope that the Order may be revers'd. But this is doubtful, and I suppose the Congress will immediately consider this important Affair, and give me such Instructions upon it as they may judge proper. With this I send a Copy of the Memorial.

During the Cruise a mortal Quarrel arose between the Commodore & Captain Landais. On their Arrival in Holland, M. De Sartine, Minister of the Marine, proposed to me the sending for Landais, in order to enquire into his Conduct.[8] I doubted the Propriety of my meddling in the Affair,[9] but Capt. Landais' Friends conceiving it a Measure that might be serviceable to him and pressing it, I complied, and he came accordingly to Paris. I send the Minutes of the Enquiry[1] for the Consideration of Congress. These will go by the Alliance. I have not presum'd to condemn or acquit him, doubting as well my own Judgment as my Authority. He proposes to demand a Court Martial in America. In his Absence from the Ship, the Commodore took the command of her, and on quitting the Texel, made a Cruise thro' the Channel to Spain, and is since returned to L'Orient, where the Ship is now refitting in order to return to America. Capt: Landais has not applied to me to be replaced in her, and I imagine has no Thought of that kind, having before on several Occasions express'd to me and others, his Dissatisfaction with his Officers, and his Inclination on that Account to quit her. Capt. Jones

7. The consul, Jean-Etienne de Chezaulx, had been in contact with Chaumont as well as BF: XXXI, 334–5. The French minister in Copenhagen was Mathieu de Basquiat, Baron de La Houze. BF's memorial is printed in XXXI, 261–5.

8. XXX, 535. See also XXX, 539–40.

9. Originally drafted as, "He came accordingly to Paris. I doubted my having any Authority to try him."

1. XXXI, 105–12.

will therefore carry her home, unless he should be prevail'd with to enter another Service, which however I think is not likely. Tho' he has gained immense Reputation all over Europe for his Bravery.

As Vessels of War under my Care create me a vast deal of Business, of a kind too that I am unexperienced in, and by my distance from the Coast is very difficult to be well executed, I must repeat my earnest Request[2] that some Person of Skill in such Affairs, may be appointed in the Character of Consul, to take Charge of them. I imagine that much would by that means be saved in the Expence of their various Refittings and Supplies, which to me appears enormous.—

Agreable to the Order of Congress, I have employed one of the best Artists here in cutting the Dies for the Medal intended for M. De Fleury.[3] The Price of such Work is beyond my Expectation being a thousand Livres for each Die. I shall try if it is not possible to have the others done cheaper.

Our Exchange of Prisoners has been for some time at a Stand, the English Admiralty refusing after long Consideration to give us any Men in return for those who had been dismiss'd by our armed Vessels on Parole, and the actual Prisoners we had being all exchanged. When the Squadron of Comme Jones arriv'd in the Texel with 500 English Prisoners, I proposed Exchanging there; but this was declined, in Expectation, as I heard from England, of retaking them in their Way to France. The Stay of our Ships in Holland, thro' the Favour of the States being prolonged, and the Squadrons stationed to intercept us, being tired of Cruising for us, the British Ministry consented at length to a Cartel with France, and brought Frenchmen to Holland to exchange for those Prisoners instead of Americans. These Proceedings have occasioned our poor People to be kept longer in Confinement; but the Minister of the Marine having given Orders that I should have as many English, another Cartel charged with Americans is now daily expected, and I hope in a few Months to see them all

2. To the committee for foreign affairs: XXIX, 555–6.
3. For Fleury's medal see XXX, 416–17; XXXI, 422–3, 489–91. BF contracted with Pierre-Simon-Benjamin Duvivier; see his letter of April 20, below.

at Liberty.[4] This for their Sakes, and also to save us Expence; for their long and hard Imprisonment induces many to hazard attempts of escaping, and those who get away through London, and Holland, and come to Paris in their Way to some Seaport in France, cost one with another I believe near 20£ Sterg a Head. The Delays in the Exchange, have I think been lengthen'd by the Admiralty, partly with the View of breaking the Patience of our People, and inducing them to enter the English Service. They have spared no Pains for this purpose, & have prevail'd with some. The Number of these has not indeed been great, and several of them lost their Lives in the blowing up of the Quebec.[5] I am also lately informed from London, that the Flags of Truce with Prisoners from Boston, one of which is seized as British Property, will obtain no Americans in Exchange; the returned English being told that they had no Authority or Right to make such Agreements with Rebels &c.[6] This is not the only Instance in which it appears that a few late Sucesses have given that Nation another *Hour of Insolence*. And yet their Affairs upon the whole wear a very unpromising Aspect. They have not yet been able to find any Allies in Europe; Holland grows daily less and less disposed to comply with their Requisitions, Ireland is not satisfied but is making new Demands, Scotland and the Protestants in England are uneasy, and the Associations of Counties in England, with Committees of Correspondence, to make Reforms in the Government[7] all taken together give a good deal of Apprehension at present, even to their mad Ministers; while their Debt, on the Point of amounting to the amazing Sum of 200 Millions, hangs as a Milstone upon the Neck of their Credit, and must ere long sink it beyond Redemption.

4. This summary of developments relating to the exchange of prisoners largely parallels that sent a week earlier to the Rev. Thomas Wren: XXXI, 553–4. A cartel ship with American prisoners sailed from Plymouth in the first week of March.

5. H.M.S. *Quebec*, 32, burned and sank after a ferocious battle with the French frigate *Surveillante* on Oct. 6, 1779; only 66 of her crew of 195 survived: William Laird Clowes, *The Royal Navy: a History from the Earliest Times to the Present* (7 vols., Boston and London, 1897–1903), IV, 40–4.

6. XXXI, 469. See also Digges to BF, March 3.

7. See Digges to BF, March 3.

The Disposition of this Court continues as favourable as ever, tho' it cannot comply with all our Demands. The Supplies required in the Invoice sent me by the Committee, appear'd too great and numerous to be immediately furnished.[8] Three Millions of Livres were however granted me, with which after deducting what will be necessary to pay the Interest Bills and other late Drafts of Congress, I could not venture on ordering more than 10,000 Suits of Cloaths:[9] With these we shall have 15,000 Arms and Accoutrements. A good deal of Cloth goes over in the Alliance, purchased by Mr Ross, which it is computed may make 7 or 8000 Suits more. But altho' we have not obtained that Invoice of Goods, this Court being at immense Expence in the Preparations for the next Campaign, I have reason to believe that a Part of those Preparations will be employed in essential Assistance to the United States, and I hope effectual, tho' at present I cannot be more particular.

I have sent to Mr Johnson, the Vote of Congress relative to the Settlement of the Accounts. He has express'd his Readiness to enter on the Service.[1] Mr. Dean is soon expected here, whose Presence is very necessary, and I hope with his Help they may be gone through without much Difficulty.[2] I could have wished it had suited Mr Lee to have been here at the same time.

The Marquis de la Fayette, who during his Residence in France has been extreamly zealous in supporting our Cause on all Occasions, returns again to fight for it. He is infinitely esteem'd and beloved here, and I am persuaded will do every thing in his

8. BF had forwarded the request to Vergennes: XXX, 110n, 359n. See also XXXI, 267–9.

9. Chaumont drafted a proposal for spending the 3,000,000 *l.t.* over four quarters which took into account Congress' outstanding debts. He itemized the expenses of uniforms for 10,000 men, projected over the course of the year, which came to a total of 120,000 *l.t.* This one-page memorandum is undated, but was drafted between the receipt of the first and second installments of 750,000 *l.t.* each (for which see XXXI, 267n). University of Pa. Library.

1. Joshua Johnson recently had accepted an appointment to audit the accounts of the commissioners and commercial agents serving Congress in Europe: XXX, 544n; XXXI, 514, 564–5.

2. In late December, 1779, former commissioner Silas Deane had written that he was awaiting passage for Europe; he did not find one, however, until the following summer: XXXI, 272.

41

Power to merit a Continuance of the same Affection from America.

With the greatest Respect I have the honour to be, Sir, Your Excellency's, most obedient and most humble Servant.

FRANKLIN

The honble. Sl. Huntington Esqr. President of Congress.

Notations in different hands: From Docr. Franklin March 4. 1780 read May. 15. / B. Franklin Esqr March 4th: 1780 Read May 15. 1780—

From the Marquis de Lafayette

AL: American Philosophical Society

saturday Morning [March 4, 1780][3]
I am for the last time Going to Versaïlles, My Good friend, and Any Command from You on this occasion will be very well Come— As I am in a great hurry for My departure, Be so kind as to let me know if You want me to Come to Your lodgings to Morrow at ten o'clock or if you choose Better to Call here.

If it is equal to you, I'd thank you for your dispatches for to Night, as I sett off to morrow By twelve o'clock.

Notation: La Fayette

From ———— Briqueville de La Luzerne and Other Favor Seekers

ALS: American Philosophical Society

Franklin received a large number of requests for favors during the four months covered by this volume.[4] Heading them chronologically is Briqueville de La Luzerne's plea for Franklin's help in obtaining his release from jail, which we publish below.

A prisoner of another kind, captured at war, tries to obtain his freedom on March 20 through the intercession of a merchant from Le

3. The Saturday before Lafayette departed to join the *Hermione;* he left on the 6th: Idzerda, *Lafayette Papers,* II, 373n.

4. Unless otherwise indicated, all the documents discussed here are written in French and deposited at the American Philosophical Society.

Havre, Pierre Dumenil. He is an unnamed Irish captain, willing to serve under the U.S. flag if given a cargo and the protection of warships. Dumenil hopes that this will be politically possible and that he will be honored with an answer.

Still another aspect of freedom is solicited on March 18 for the Englishman John Kitchen, now a naturalized French citizen. Penned by a professional scribe, the petition is signed by "catherine hocquet famme de jean kitchine." It explains that the supplicant has turned down British offers of a brilliant fortune in exchange for what he considers perfidy. But now, afraid of atrocious British vengeance should he ever fall into their hands, he begs to be dispensed from service at sea for the King of France and allowed instead to stay at home. Rather than working, as he has for the last eight months, as *maître d'équipage* on the frigate *Fine* in Paimboeuf and Brest, he could support his indigent family by exercising his own *métier*.[5] In a postscript, the subdelegate of the *intendant de Bretagne,* in Paimboeuf, J. O'Dea, certifies that the above-mentioned facts are true and attests that Jean Kitchin, through his knowledge of English, plays a useful and essential role in helping the Americans.

Another Englishman, Richard Holroide, writing in English on April 24 from Dunkerque, also has a request concerning his personal freedom. He wishes to be allowed, along with his niece, to reside once again in Boulogne-sur-Mer where he had lived for years before moving to Dunkerque, Bruges, Ghent, and Brussels because of "the present disturbances." He is over seventy and disgusted with England's tyranny. His loyalty is to France where he desires to reside for the rest of his life.

Money, as usual, was on the mind of most of those who sought Franklin's help, either because they needed guidance in handling their own or because they simply wanted him to give them some. Of those who request a handout, the earliest in date is de Raÿmond, a Frenchman captured by the British twenty-two months previously, while on his way to fight for American independence. He has just returned from England. He has lost his entire fortune, thirteen thousand *livres,* and everything but his last shirt. In the week since his return, he has offered his services to various *seigneurs,* but has been turned down everywhere. He is determined to reach some port and to embark for anywhere provided Franklin rescues him as he has rescued so many oth-

---

5. Which he describes as *Barger,* a non-existent word in French. It is unlikely that he meant *berger,* shepherd, since the petition is otherwise correctly spelled throughout. In English, a barger is a bargeman or bargemaster.

ers. His letter is undated and mentions no place of origin but since Franklin recorded in his Cash Book for April 14 a disbursement of 48 *l.t.* in Raÿmond's favor, his appeal must have been sent slightly earlier.[6]

On April 24, a group of Marseilles merchants, headed by E. Conte, relate their troubles. A cargo of various merchandise that they had sent to Boston in 1778 landed in Portsmouth, New Hampshire, where they sold it for the paper currency of the day. They invested part of this money in local goods and deposited the twenty-four thousand dollars left over with a French merchant in Boston, M. Lareguy. They hastened to Martinique to sell their goods prior to returning to Europe, but their ship, dismasted during a storm in September, 1779, was captured on October 26 and led to England. At this point they learned that their correspondents had neglected to insure the ship, in spite of their orders. Their only hope is that Franklin will help them validate the 24,000 dollars deposited in Boston as capital or *à titre de liquidation*, by becoming the arbiter on their behalf. This might enable them to pursue trade with the American continent, a commerce for which they have both experience and inclination.

William Finnie, of Williamsburg, Virginia, reports on May 12 that he had a continental loan office certificate for 600 dollars drawn in favor of Matthew Irwin by Thomas Smith, Commissioner at Philadelphia. As it happened, two bills of exchange on France for 36 dollars each, for interest on this certificate, along with the original certificate, were lost. He therefore requests that the American Commissioners in Paris, to whom his letter is addressed in English, should refuse payment in case those documents are presented to them.[7]

Writing from Rabastens (between Albi and Toulouse) on May 24, the chevalier Depotien Duboishalbrand, just back from Baltimore, wonders where he could exchange the 132 Pennsylvania dollars that he brought back, a meager result for twenty months of captivity in New York. He trusts Franklin will take care of the operation.

6. The entry reads: "To M. de Raymond a French Gentleman who has been 2 Years Prisoner in England taken in the Argenterie going to serve in Georgia with Capt De la Plaine." For the misadventures of Emmanuel-Pierre de La Plaigne and the *d'Argentré* see XXIV–XXVII, *passim*. As the ship had been captured at the end of April, 1778 (XXVI, 186n), the present letter must have been written during or slightly after February, 1780.

7. On Oct. 23, a Congressional resolution ordered Smith to issue two new sets of bills of exchange to William Finnie, as well as certified copies of this resolution: *JCC*, XVIII, 967–8. A copy is with BF's papers at the APS. Finnie was deputy quartermaster of Virginia: *Jefferson Papers*, III, 608.

Cossoul, the Nantes merchant in partnership with Elkanah Watson, also has problems concerning a loss. He informs the Doctor on June 15 that a number of bills of exchange drawn on Franklin by various American States had been lost in Boston on April 25 by Bossenger Foster. Franklin should now exercise great caution in seeing to it that those letters are paid to none other than Watson, whose signature has been filed with him.[8]

Sir John Lambert too reports a missing document. Writing from Paris in English on June 20, he informs Franklin that James Cuming, of Philadelphia, now settled at Lorient, wishes to request that payment be stopped on two bills that were lost or mislaid. The advertisement which he encloses confirms this.[9]

Tedious as these money problems sound, they may not have been as distasteful to Franklin as the appeals to his supposedly vast power to "protect." First, two distraught mothers. In the belief that the American minister could obtain whatever he wanted from the King, the baronne de Fontallard, writing from Versailles, describes her pitiful situation on March 19: after having lost their whole fortune through "accidents si communs dans le monde," her husband did not survive his grief and died twelve years ago, leaving her in sole charge of nine children. Three of her four sons have been accepted in the Royal Corps of Engineers and are currently building a fort near Brest;[1] but the fourth, due to poor eyesight, is reduced to teaching mathematics, Latin, and German to young noblemen in order to provide for his wife and daughter. Her hope is that Franklin will persuade the minister of war, Montbarey, to grant her son the position of holograph engineer. As to her daughters, three of them are married and she has to support the other two on a pension of 200 *l.t.* given her by the Queen's brother, the archduke of Tuscany. Should the King grant her 2,000 *l.t.* a year, she could retire with the girls to the provinces and survive. She has been endeavoring to obtain this pension for the last eighteen months but has no hope without Franklin's intercession. One more thing: the previous December she sent the comte d'Estaing the proofs of her high birth, along with a plea for 30 *louis* in order to re-

8. BF answered this letter on June 27, sending a list of the bills of exchange lost in Boston. This can be surmised from Cossoul's to BF of Aug. 12, in which he thanks him and says he has forwarded that list to Bossenger Foster. A few days later, on Aug. 19, Cossoul announces that the lost documents have been found and that all is well.

9. The English baronet who was a banker in Paris had corresponded with Cuming on financial matters: XXX, 556.

1. One of them, a lieutenant, is listed in the *Etat militaire* for 1780, p. 423.

trieve the possessions she pawned, but her letter was misaddressed and now she desperately needs those documents. Please ask the count to return them, please allow her to come to Passy, and please answer.

Madame de Longchamps' troubles, on the other hand, are never clearly stated. She refers to them on April 18 as the misfortunes of her age and nature's obligations, both so exquisite and cruel, and also of being *bien née.* She wishes to introduce her family to the American minister, who is implored to address his answer to the Péchigny pension in Passy where her son is being educated out of charity.[2]

Franklin's supposed influence on the French judicial system is invoked by a map and print seller on March 19. In a four-page letter from London, written in English, R. Haines explains his predicament. Somewhat over a year earlier he had become "acquainted" with the governess of the Izard family, living in the faubourg St. Germain. Warned off the premises by Ralph Izard, he complied, he says, but was summoned anyway by a commissary of police who told him he had disobeyed instructions, that the woman was with child, and that he should remit a sum of money for her support into the commissary's hands. Sensing a fraud, Haines refused but stated that he would give the woman (who, by the way, was married) some money, whether or not he was the cause of her predicament. He was then summoned by an *inspecteur de police* and forbidden again to enter Izard's house; Izard in the meantime allegedly had promised a reward to any servant who would murder him. One night in June the governess came to his house and as he had walked her back to her lodging, Izard's coachman dragged him inside and, along with other servants, used him "extremely Ill." As a result of the fracas, he was taken to the Petit Chatelet prison, detained there for eleven days, and ordered to leave France immediately. The pretext for his expulsion was that he had corresponded with Lord Stormont. Now he begs Franklin to consider the financial loss he suffered: he had an extensive trade but had to liquidate his stock in haste for one fifth of its value, and flee with his three small children (no wife being around). He is currently living with his sister, Mrs. Evans,[3] in Kensington but wants to prove that he has committed no crime against the state, return to France, reinstate himself in business, and save his family from ruin. All this, of course, provided Franklin guarantees him a fair trial.

2. M. and Mme Devillier Péchigny were the proprietors of the boarding school at Passy attended by JA's sons Charles and John Quincy: *Adams Correspondence,* III, 272–3n; Taylor, *J.Q. Adams Diary,* I, 34–5n.
3. Sarah Evans: XXIV, 195.

Franklin is also urged to wield his influence in America. Writing from Brunswick on March 7, A.C. Schüler reminds the Doctor that he addressed him previously about a young brother who had enrolled, against his parents' wishes, in the ducal troops.[4] He is presently renewing his efforts to procure the return of this headstrong sibling, whose prime motivation had been a desire to travel and who is currently a prisoner of war. Through his position as private secretary and councillor of Duke Ferdinand of Brunswick, brother of the reigning Duke, the writer has obtained orders to pull his brother, flag-bearer of the Specht regiment, out of the service, and to bring him home. But the American authorities have to give their consent, a serious obstacle that can only be removed by "un mot de la part de Votre Excellence."

A rather strange bid for Franklin's protection is sent on June 9 by a Welshman from Brecon named Jephne Powell. In his desire to learn French and see some of the world, he traveled through France and Italy. He did not feel like taking sides when the war broke out, but kept on the move, finally settling in Switzerland where he made a living by teaching English and became a naturalized citizen. But now he wants a more substantial profession in France and wishes to enjoy the same privileges as the other Swiss living there. He is afraid, however, that if his English origins are discovered he will be in serious trouble. In this predicament, Franklin is his only recourse.

Protection, of course, also extends to helping the petitioner obtain some coveted position. David l'aîné, who had already applied for the American consulship in Morlaix,[5] renews his plea on April 5, from Versailles. He feels that with so many American prisoners coming back from England at this juncture, an agent in Morlaix, well acquainted with English, could render great services, and he reminds Franklin of the verbal promise he had made the previous year, *i.e.*, to keep him in mind as soon as Congress took some measures in that regard.

A certain Even Duhil, writing in English from Nantes on April 14, needs Franklin's influence to procure him a passage on Jones's ship

4. See xxx, 78–9. At that time (Oct. 8, 1779) Schüler had referred to his brother as having been captured with Burgoyne. Von Specht's was one of Burgoyne's Brunswick regiments: J.G. Rosengarter, *The German Allied Troops in the North American War of Independence, 1776–1783* (Albany, 1893), pp. 126, 149; Philip R.N. Katcher, *Encyclopedia of British, Provincial, and German Army Units 1775–1783* (Harrisburg, 1973), p. 124.

5. Always presenting himself as a friend of Montaudoüin, David had written on March 29, 1779: xxix, 43n. He will write once again, to the same effect but in English, on Sept. 27, 1780. APS.

soon to depart from Lorient, or on any American vessel currently in Paimboeuf. He is, he says, a captain in the 1st South Carolina Regiment who went back to France on furlough because of his father's death and now desires to rejoin his corps.

Also requesting passage on the *Alliance* is de Montluisant who writes from Lorient on June 30.[6] On Lafayette's recommendation, he has obtained an infantry lieutenancy from the King and been included in the list of officers bound for America remitted to Chaumont. Having traveled in vain to various ports, he has discovered that he can sail only from Lorient with Landais or Jones, but they both feel unauthorised to grant him passage without Franklin's approval. Would Franklin please consent to his return to America? He will try to be worthy of it.

A number of people want news from their relatives, friends, or business partners. A M. Eudel, who signs himself *contracteur général des fermes du Roy* (*i.e.*, an administrator of taxes), inquires from Cherbourg on March 8 about his close friend M. Tardiveau,[7] from whom he has not heard in two years. He does not even know whether Tardiveau, who emigrated from Nantes to engage in commerce in the United States, currently resides in Boston or Virginia. Could Franklin, who certainly appreciates the bonds of friendship, find out where the man lives? And could he forward the two enclosed letters to him?

A former *sous-aide major des gendarmes de la garde du roy*, the chevalier Dieche, is worried about not having heard in two years—and neither has the family—about the chevalier de Villefranche[8] who sailed to America with du Coudray. Writing from St. Marthory-en-Cominge on March 23, Dieche reminds Franklin of the various occa-

6. Born in 1753, Dominique-Louis de Montluisant appears in Idzerda, *Lafayette Papers,* II, 363n, 496, 512. In March, 1780, Lafayette supported a petition in which Montluisant expressed his desire to serve in America as a lieutenant.

7. Barthélemi Tardiveau's American career is sketched in XXIV, 41n.

8. Jean-Louis-Ambroise de Genton, chevalier de Villefranche, held the rank of captain when he joined du Coudray. He became a major in the American corps of engineers on Jan. 1, 1778, and lieutenant-colonel on May 8, 1783. He returned to France and died in 1784: Bodinier, *Dictionnaire.* He had worked as a geographer and an engineer on numerous fortifications, including West Point, and has been called "one of the best mapmakers in the Corps of Engineers." R.K. Showman *et al.,* eds., *The Papers of General Nathanael Greene,* (8 vols. to date, Chapel Hill, 1976–), V, 44–5. Much appreciated by Washington, he was one of the founding members of the Cincinnati: Lasseray, *Les Français,* I, 229–31.

sions on which he has already asked him the same question, the last one being in June, 1779, when he met the Doctor at the war ministry building, coming out from a talk with Sartine. He is aware that Villefranche has become a major in the American engineering corps and that he has met Lafayette there. Could Franklin procure the necessary information for letters to reach his friend? Franklin answers on April 2, stating that he, too, has heard nothing from Villefranche in these two years but that if Dieche wishes him to, he will include his letters with the next dispatches for America. On May 8 Dieche sends Franklin a letter of his own and one from Villefranche's oldest son, along with an appeal to the American minister to take Villefranche under his protection and procure him a promotion.

Writing from Dieppe on April 28, M. Bion laments the lack of news from his son Wilfrane(?), and the difficult time the relatives of the boy's late mother are giving him. In 1778, thanks to his knowledge of mathematics, hydrography, and drawing, the young man was given, at age 22, the post of pilot. Two campaigns later, he obtained permission to embark as lieutenant on the *Chasseur*, freighted for the Americans and escorted by La Motte-Picquet and three Boston frigates. They sailed in April, 1779, their destination apparently Virginia, their cargo consisting of artillery and salt. Could Franklin possibly let Bion know the fate of this ship and whether his son is dead or alive?[9] And should the boy be living somewhere in North America, could Franklin honor him with his recommendation?

The query addressed to Franklin from Lachassaigne on April 22, from Paris, has nothing to do with news but aims at verifying someone's good faith. A certain M. de Contour, well turned out, went through Lille some months ago, presenting himself as a Breton gentleman in the service of the United States navy. Is this true? The writer is assailed by doubt and would much appreciate Franklin's lights on the subject.[1]

As usual, some people want their mail forwarded. Wilhelm Au-

9. BF certainly knew by then that whereas the *Governor Livingston* and the *Mary Fearon* (mentioned by Bion) had reached their destination, the *Chasseur* (*Hunter*) had been captured by the British and brought into New York. See XXIX, 330, 444n; XXX, 268.

1. A notation by WTF on this letter indicates that BF answered it on April 23, but the answer is no longer extant. It was certainly negative for when the abbé de St. Favre wrote him two years later, on March 31, 1782, to express his doubts about the claims of a "chevalier d'uvet de contour," supposedly sent to Beaumarchais by BF to receive a gratification (APS), BF replied by return mail that the man was a fraud: Library of Congress.

gustine von Steuben, who had asked Franklin on February 11[2] to forward a letter to his son, telling the general of his mother's death, now requests on April 10, in German, that another letter be sent on to that son. He is glad to have heard from him.

From Paris, on March 9, the vicomte de Vibraye forwards somebody's letter from Stuttgart, meant for Franklin, and asks that the answer be sent to his home in the faubourg St. Germain.[3]

Writing in English, J. Marky, the Superior of the Irish Seminary in Paris (lodged at the rue du Cheval Vert) asks Franklin on June 9 to please indicate to him the safest way to convey a letter to Charles County in Maryland. He has succeeded a man Franklin had honored with marks of attention, the late Doctor Cahill who died the previous December 10.[4] On June 18, Father Marky thanks Franklin for his gracious offer of help and sends him a packet of letters, with duplicates, as he had been instructed to do. Still another letter destined for Maryland is sent to Franklin on August 24, with duplicate.

M. Chavannes, who formerly worked on the staff of War Minister Montbarey, begs Franklin on March 28 to forward to America the enclosed letter from M. Olry, a government official in Toul. In case this request is indiscreet, please return the letter.

In an undated letter,[5] Jean-Baptiste Le Roy asks his "illustre ami" to forward to Philadelphia by the earliest possible conveyance a business letter from a friend of his, that may be opened for perusal. Now that his wife is feeling better, he hopes to settle in Passy very soon.

A whole package of letters from American prisoners in England is forwarded on June 10 by Dumouriez, *Commandant à Cherbourg*, of fu-

2. See XXXI, 474.

3. Charles-François Huralt, vicomte de Vibraye (1739–1828) was minister plenipotentiary to the duchy of Württemberg at Stuttgart from 1775 to 1784: *Repertorium der diplomatischen Vertreter*, III, 145.

4. BF had helped Father Cahill recover the books that Bishop Patrick Joseph Plunket had lost when Landais captured the ship they had been put on, in 1779, on their way back to Ireland: XXX, 12; Richard Hayes, *Biographical Dictionary of Irishmen in France* (Dublin, 1949), p. 269; Rev. A. Cogan, *The Diocese of Meath Ancient and Modern* (3 vols., Dublin, 1862–70), III, 13–16.

5. Since Le Roy mentions that he went to Passy on "Sunday the 18" to visit BF, but seeing him engaged with fellow-Americans promptly withdrew, we presume that Sunday to have been June 18, 1780. The other possibilities, in May, 1777, or August, 1782, are less likely: May seems too early and August too late for a move to the country.

ture revolutionary fame.[6] It has been remitted to him, he explains, by an English cartel ship captain who was escorting back some French prisoners. Dumouriez opened the envelope because the address on it was too vague for the post office to know where to send it, but the package itself is still sealed and Franklin—to whom he is delighted to pay homage—will know better whether some of those letters should arouse suspicion.

A cordial note on May 21 comes from a man named Hugounen, who commanded the *tartane Marc Antoine* that delivered powder and ammunition to the Congress in February, 1776.[7] He remembers having paid his respects to Franklin, in those days, in Philadelphia, and would like to do it again, now, in Paris, if the Doctor will allow.

Finally, John Butler[8] informs Franklin in English on June 7 that he tried to visit him the previous night, having just arrived from London, which he had left on May 31st. He was not admitted to the house, however, and now plans to try again the following day at ten o'clock sharp. He hopes the Doctor will "please to order your Servant, to shew me to you, unless you are otherwise materially engaged."

> de la prison de l'abbaÿe Ce 4 mars 1780
> Je prend la liberté Monsieur de vous adresser un de Mes Memoire touchamps la malheureuse affaire que jai depuis saize ans,[9]

---

6. Charles-François du Périer Dumouriez (1739–1823) was to become the commander of French troops during the Revolution, only to defect to Austria in the spring of 1793. *DBF.*

7. A *tartane* was a small two-masted ship, in use in the Mediterranean.

8. His identity eludes us. We can only venture that possibly he was the husband of the Mrs. Butler whose luggage, captured in September, 1779, by the *Black Prince*, gave BF and John Holker a good deal of trouble. See XXX, passim.

9. It was indeed in 1764 (on Feb. 18) that a dispute over a horse—worth about 150 *l.t.*—pitted this member of the Norman aristocracy against another Norman gentleman, La Maugerie, in St. Lô. La Maugerie accused Briqueville de la Luzerne of trying to murder him, with the help of the manservant Noël. At first, in 1765, La Maugerie was exonerated and Briqueville sent to jail for one year while the investigation was continued. Confirmed a year later, the decision was reversed by the Parlement of Paris on July 13, 1769. By Aug. 4, 1770, Briqueville was free and La Maugerie in jail for life. But on Feb. 21, 1780, the bizarre lawsuit started up again after a huge inquest and contradictory judgments. Noël, a central character in the affair, was now separated from his master and sent to Fort-l'Evêque. And, as appears from this document, Briqueville was once again in jail. See Bachaumont, *Mémoires secrets,* XV, 52–3, 63–4; XVIII, 232–3.

et qui ne Cest renouvellée qua la cassassion du parlement; je vous prie de le lire, dapres, Si vous me croiée inocent dun pareil Crisme je vous prie de vous interresser au maleur que jaiprouve. Mon Nom vous est plus Connu que Mon procest, etems le maime que Mr. le chevalier de Laluzerne qui est Sous vos hordres, Ce qui me fait prendre la liberter de vous adresser Mon Memoire, larrêt du parlement la Grande chambre assemblé qui Ma dechargé Comme vous le verrée de toutes accusations moi et le nommé Noël mon domestique.

Je vous auray Monsieur la plus Grandes obligation de me juger vous Maime et Si vous me Croiée digne de vos bonté de vous interresser a moy.

Soié persuader Monsieur du proffont respect avec lequel jai lhonneur dêtre Votre trés humble et trés obeissant Serviteur

BRIQUEVILLE DE LALUZERNE
Capitainne au Commissaire Général Cavalerie

Notation: Briqueville de La Luzerne de la prison de l'abbaye Ce 4 Mars 1780.

From Lewis Littlepage

ALS: American Philosophical Society

Sir   Nants March 4th 1780.

You will I hope excuse my neglect in not sooner answering the letter with which you honour'd me[1] and returning thanks for your generous and friendly advice I only waited to do it in person; but my journey has been daily pospon'd for the company of an American Gentleman, 'till I beleive we have both declin'd it. I am sorry to have no American papers for your perusal, and, unfortunately, all on board the Livingston were thrown into the Sea by falling in with the Alliance, whom they mistook for a British Frigate:[2] the disappointment, however, is of no great conse-

1. Arrangements had been made for this young Virginian to study in Spain while residing with American Minister John Jay. He had asked advice about leaving from Nantes for Spain, and BF had advised him to correspond with Jay first: XXXI, 476–7, 489. He joined Jay in Madrid in November: Morris, *Jay: Revolutionary,* p. 770n.
2. The two ships had met while the *Alliance* was returning to France from La Coruña: XXXI, 481, 485.

quence as you would not have been very agreeably entertain'd from Advertisements, of which they entirely consist, nothing of importance having happen'd since the affair of Savanah. The depreciation of our currency still continues; tho' the Wise and Politick Legislature of Virginia endeavour all in their power to increase its value by Taxes and other impositions: whether they will be successful, or not, time must determine: the British Fleet was expected in Chesapeake bay, intending (as was suppos'd) to take the Fendant; who was in no very agreeable situation on account of the mortality which raged among her men.[3] I expect to proceed in a short time from this to Bordeaux and there remain according to your advice till I hear from Mr Jay. I shall ever have the most grateful sense of your favours, and have the honour to be Sir, your Most Obt. & very humble Servt.

LEWIS LITTLEPAGE

P.S. Not having the address of Dr Boush[4] I have taken the liberty to enclose a small Pacquet to you—

Notation: Lewis littlepage. Mar 4 1780.

To Horatio Gates[5]   Copy: Library of Congress

Passy, March. 5. 1780.
I embrace this Opportunity of the Marquis de La Fayette's return to the Army, to Salute you, my dear old friend, and to present you with my best Wishes for your Health and prosperity.

He will deliver you a Book lately published by General Burgoyn to explain and account for his misfortune.[6] The perusal may amuse you to make the work compleat— Methinks he

3. The *Fendant*, 74, spent two months at Yorktown before proceeding to Martinique: XXXI, 272n.
4. Dr. William Bousch, an acquaintance of the Lees: XXX, 181n.
5. BF had last written Gates nine months earlier: XXIX, 604–5. At present he was on leave from the Continental Army: Paul David Nelson, *General Horatio Gates: a Biography* (Baton Rouge, 1976), pp. 213–18.
6. *A State of the Expedition from Canada as Laid Before the House of Commons* ... (London, 1780); Digges had sent BF a copy on Feb. 10: XXXI, 470.

ought to have given us in it his proclamation[7] contrasted with his capitulation.

We are making great Preparations here, intending an active, and hoping for a successful Campaign.

May God give us soon a good Peace, and bring you and I together again over a Chessboard, where we may have Battles without Bloodshed. I am ever, with the highest Esteem, Dear sir, Your most obedient most humble Servant

Gen. Gates.

To the Chevalier de La Luzerne

AL (draft): Library of Congress

Sir,   Passy, March 5, 1780

I received with great Pleasure the Letter you did me the Honour of writing to me from Boston.[8] I rejoiced to hear of your safe Arrival, and that the Reception you met with in my Country, had been agreable to you.[9] I hope its Air will suit you, and that you while you reside in it, you will enjoy constant Health and Happiness.

Your good Brother does me sometimes the Honour of calling on me, and we converse in English, which he speaks very intelligibly.[1] I suppose that by this time you do the same. M. de Malesherbes did me lately the same Honour. That great Man seems to have no Wish of returning into Publick Employment, but amuses himself, with Planting, and is desirous of obtaining all those Trees of North America that have not yet been intro-

7. Burgoyne's bombastic proclamation of June, 1777: XXIV, 468n.
8. XXX, 281–2.
9. For La Luzerne's reception see XXX, 199n.
1. César-Henri, comte de La Luzerne (1737–1799), *chevalier de Saint-Louis, maréchal de camp*, known for his wit and learning, shared his uncle Chrétien-Guillaume de Lamoignon de Malesherbes' passion for natural history. He became governor of St. Domingue (1786–87) and minister of the Navy (1787–90): Pierre Grosclaude, *Malesherbes témoin et interprète de son temps* (Paris, 1961), pp. 613–14, 621, 629; *Nouvelle biographie générale*. For the La Luzerne brothers see also Butterfield, *John Adams Diary*, II, 394.

duc'd into France.[2] Your sending him a Box of the Seeds, would, I am persuaded, much oblige him. They may be obtain'd of my young Friend Bartram living near Philadelphia.[3]

You will have heard that Spain has lately met with a little Misfortune at Sea, but the Bravery with which her Ships fought a vastly superior Force, have gain'd her great Honour.[4] We are anxious here for farther News from that Coast, which is daily expected. Great Preparations are making here for the ensuing Campaign, and we flatter ourselves that it will be more active & successful in scope than the last.

One of the Advantages of great States, is, that the Calamity occasion'd by a foreign War falls only on a very small Part of the Community, who happen from their Situation & particular Circumstances to be expos'd to it.— Thus, as it is always fair Weather in our Parlours, it is at Paris always Peace. The People pursue their respective Occupations, the Playhouse, the Opera, & other publick Diversions, are as regularly & fully attended, as in Times of profoundest Tranquility, and the same small Concerns divide us into Parties.— When you left us, we were Gluckists and Piccinists.[5] Within these few Weeks we are for or against Jeannot, a new Actor.[6] This Man's Performance, & the Marriage

2. Malesherbes displayed a keen interest in North American trees and plants: Grosclaude, *Malesherbes*, pp. 477–80.

3. John Bartram, Jr. (1743–1812), apparently assumed the responsibility for most of his father's nursery and plantation there in 1771: XVIII, 89. Marbois visited in October, 1779, and found the garden sadly neglected. By the early 1780's John and his brother William (XVI, 9n) had restored the garden and resumed the seed business: *DAB;* Edmund Berkeley and Dorothy Smith Berkeley, *The Life and Travels of John Bartram: From Lake Ontario to the River St. John* (Tallahassee, 1982), pp. 15, 301–2. On Oct. 2, 1780, Malesherbes asked WTF to ship three packets of seeds unknown in America, from his own garden. APS.

4. Rodney's fleet had outnumbered the Spanish fleet he defeated by twenty-one ships of the line to eleven: Dull, *French Navy*, p. 178.

5. The rivalry between the partisans of Gluck and Piccinni, which continued into 1780, has been described in XXVII, 432n.

6. Volange, a French actor, attracted a large following at the popular *théâtres des boulevards* in the role of Janot in *Les battus payent l'amende*. The royal family sent for him at Versailles. His bust was sculpted as Janot at Sèvres, and fashions, hairstyles, and soups were "à la Janot." Although Volange's debut at the Théâtre Italien was a success, in other roles his per-

of the Duke de Richelieu fills up much more of our present Conversation, than any thing that relates to the War.—[7] A Demonstration, this, of the Publick Felicity.

My Grandson joins with me in best Wishes for your Health & Prosperity. He is much flatter'd by your kind Remembrance of him. We desire also that M. de Marbois would accept our Assurances. I have the Honour to be, with the greatest Respect, Sir, Your &c,

M. de la Luzerne

To George Washington

ALS (draft)[8] and two copies: Library of Congress

Sir,   Passy, March 5. 1780

I received but lately the Letter your Excellency did me the honour of writing to me in Recommendation of the Marquis de la Fayette.[9] His Modesty detain'd it long in his own Hands. We became acquainted however, from the time of his Arrival at Paris, and his Zeal[1] for the Honour of our Country, his Activity in our Affairs here, and his firm Attachment to our Cause, and to you,

---

formance was not up to expectations, and he returned to the boulevards: Larousse. For contemporary appreciations of "Janot's" talent and descriptions of the controversy see *Jour. de Paris*, Feb. 23, 28, March 2; Bachaumont *Mémoires secrets*, XV, 54–7, 59–60, 81–2, 107; Maurice Tourneux, ed., *Correspondance littéraire, philosophique et critique par Grimm, Diderot, Raynal, Meister, etc.* (16 vols., Paris, 1877–82), XII, 379; Métra, *Correspondance secrète*, IX, 86–8, 288–9.

7. Louis-François-Armand de Vignerot, maréchal duc de Richelieu (1696–1788), married Jeanne-Catherine-Josèphe de Lavaulx de Sommerécourt, comtesse de Rothe (1738–1816), the widow of Edmond de Rothe, on Feb. 15. A military man and dedicated libertine, this friend of Voltaire had long provided matter for conversation: *Walpole Correspondence*, VII, 204n; Jacques Levron, *Un libertin fastueux: Le maréchal de Richelieu* (Paris, 1971), pp. 409–10. See also Bachaumont, *Mémoires secrets*, XV, 40, 41–2, 48–50, 61; Métra, *Correspondance secrète*, IX, 224–5.

8. BF made numerous changes to his draft, revising the language and interlining words and phrases. We take note of those that are recoverable.

9. XXVIII, 288–9.

1. He first wrote "Zealous Activity", then deleted "ous" and interlined the next seven words.

impress'd me with the same Regard & Esteem for him that your Excellency's Letter would have done, had it been immediately delivered to me.

Should Peace arrive after another Campaign or two, and afford us a little Leisure,[2] I should be happy to see your Excellency in Europe, and to accompany you, if my Age & Strength would permit, in visiting some of its ancient and most famous[3] Kingdoms. You would on this Side the Sea, enjoy the great Reputation you have acquir'd, pure and free from those little Shades that the Jealousy and Envy of a Man's Countrymen & Contemporaries[4] are ever endeavouring to cast over living Merit. Here you would know, and enjoy, what Posterity will say of Washington. For a 1000 Leagues have nearly the same Effect with 1000 Years. The feeble Voice of those groveling Passions cannot extend so far either in Time or Distance. At present I enjoy that Pleasure for you: as I frequently hear the old Generals of this martial Country, (who study the Maps of America, and mark upon them all your Operations) speak with sincere Approbation & great Applause of your Conduct, and join in giving you the Character of one of the greatest Captains of the Age.[5]

I must soon quit the Scene, but you may live to see our[6] Country flourish, as it will amazingly and rapidly after the War is over. Like a Field of young Indian Corn, which long Fair Weather & Sunshine had enfeebled and discolour'd, and which in that weak State, by a Thunder Gust of violent Wind, Hail & Rain seem'd to be threatend with absolute[7] Destruction; yet the Storm being past, it recovers fresh Verdure, shoots up with double Vigour, and delights the Eye not of its Owner only, but of every observing Traveller.

The best Wishes that can be form'd for your Health Honour and Happiness, ever attend you, from Your Excellency's most obedient and most humble Servant

Gen. Washington

2. Preceding six words interlined.
3. Preceding three words interlined.
4. Preceding six words interlined.
5. For a similar encomium see XXIII, 287.
6. He first wrote "your" and then deleted the "y."
7. Word interlined.

From Richard Neave & Son

ALS: American Philosophical Society

Passey. Sunday 5. March 1780.
Chez Le Roi Pattissier Grand Rue

Kind Sir

Convinced that His Excellencys time is too much (Just now) engrossed, than to Attend to the Complaint of Individuals Suffering— We beg the Favour of You to take an Opportunity soon of Briefly hinting to him the present Situation of Richd Neave & Son:— Who have been now near three Years in France, Upon a full assurance of a Passage to America wth. Mr. Wharton— As Well as Support from him— Untill Such his departure.— Now that time he Acquaints Us is very near at hand, And that he Cannot Support Us any longer wth. Money nor Can We or Either of Us have a passage to America wth. him.—[8] Now it is Well Known to his Excellency, That the House of Neave & Son have been the Support of the House's of Baynton & Wharton & Baynton Wharton & Morgan for Many Year's—from 1757 or 1767—That I Settled Accounts wth. Mr. Saml. Wharton in Augt. 1770.[9] When the Several Ballances due to Us from Them was Upwards of 30,000 [*one word illegible*] the Greater Part of wch. is due at this day beside's the Interest— We do Assure you Sr. We never did an Act in England that Should Cause Mr. Wharton's Embarrassmt. We Suffered much from Creditors whom Neither Mr. Wharton or Ourselves Could Satisfie As to the Safety of their Money—and after paying them 11/6 per £ left them and much property, Rather than Submit to An Act of Bankruptcy that Would not only Involve Us—But Mr. Wharton to their power.— Thus While We have been Ruined by Our

---

8. Neave and his son Richard had signed oaths of allegiance to the U.S. the previous summer. They planned to emigrate to Pennsylvania and were at Dieppe awaiting passage: xxx, 198. Wharton left Paris on March 17, expecting to sail for America with John Paul Jones: BF to Jones, March 18, below.

9. The Neaves acted as bankers for the mercantile firm of Baynton & Wharton (after 1763, Baynton, Wharton & Morgan) and were creditors of the firm. Wharton's financial situation had been adversely affected by his failure to obtain recognition for his claims to lands in Ohio: xi, 187–8n; xii, 151; xiv, 256; xx, 331–2n; xxxi, 547.

Favour to that House, They have been Raising Ample Fortune's—
Wherefore We may say Every Act of Honesty & Friendship is
due to Us—from Mr. Wharton— Knowing his Excellencys
Freindship towards him We Beg he will Use his Good Offices
wth. him, that may Incline him to so much Justice to Us before
his departure That We may not be Reduced to Beggery Here, or
become troublesome to Any One, Untill We Can meet wth. the
prospect of a passage to America. Your Favour herein will
Greatly Oblige Sr. Your most h'ble Serts. RICHD NEAVE & SON

We had thot. of Conveying this to You by the hands of young
Mr. Franklin— But on Secd. Thought Judged it more prudent
to put it into your Own hands—   RN

Addressed: His Excellency B. Franklin Esq— / &c &c &c

Notation: Rich: Nevve & Son 15 March 1780

From Juliana Ritchie[1]   ALS: American Philosophical Society

Sir.   Cambray. March 5th. 1780.
    Permit me to address You in the freedom of a friend, one who
has for many Years sincerely esteemed & respected you for your
singular Virtues—tho' I had never the happiness of a Personal
acquaintance with you, such I ever thought a real loss to me, &
in the present situation of affairs I find an assencial one. Suffering as I do incessant aggitation of mind without any resource
from wence I can derive a certain knowledge of those things that
cause my unhappiness.
    It is near two Years since I have received any intelligence on
the part of my husband—[2] Our letters to each other have been
intercepted—or by some other means have all miscaryed during
that interval of time by which I am in a state of suspence & in-
tire ignorance of every particuler respecting His situation, oth-
erways then that of His being with the American Troops—but

1. A former Philadelphian now residing in genteel poverty in France, she
had first corresponded with BF in January, 1777: XXIII, 162–3, 211–12.
2. William Ritchie.

how imploy'd—I know not. What I have suffered—& still *suffer* from this irksome suspence is not possible to be expressed— I have wrote *repeated* letters to my friends in England begging to be informed in this point, but they have *all* been answered in terms to the same purpose Viz. they know nothing respecting the Concerns of Mr. Ritchie— *This* circumstance has had an effect to increase my fears & apprehensions for His safety. Pardon sir the liberty I take in troubleing you with my concerns— A heart like yours best knows how to pardon an intrusion caused by such a motive. I shou'd not have thus precipitately addressed you— but from certain reports that are circulated here, mentioning a number of *officers* in the american Troops—that have fallen victims to the British Army, & that a gentleman of the name of Richards—or Ritchie was a mongst the *unfortunate*. My suffering heart, presages the *worst*—& my mind is incessently conflicted—in the sad alternative of hope & despair—the *latter*-most prevails when we know the certainty of any Misfortune. Religion & resignation to The Divine decrees—comes to our releif but during suspence—the heart knows no respite from turtures in you sir I rest my dependence for a certain information respecting the situation of my husband, you are too just & good—to deceive me on the part of His fate—be it of a nature to give me pleasure—or pain. I presume sir you have lists—regularly transmited to you, of all the occurrances that take place in the American troops, & if not so—'tis probable—that those Gentlemen who lately arrived at Paris, from America, are well informed of those events &ca. Let me intreat you sir—to make inquiries on the part of Mr. Ritchie's health—& situation at the time of those Gentlemen's departure from thence, pray do me the honor to write to me—as soon as possible an account of what information you receive on this head, you will thereby oblige me more then I can express. I beg at the same time—to be informed of the state of your health, which I hope is well, that you may long enjoy that Blessing—with every other you so strictly merrit—is my ardent wish.

I hope Your Amiable Daughter was well when you heard from Her— I fancy by this time she has a fine family of Children. Ah me, I often reflect upon past occurrances—with regret—for their loss— My heart is still in Philadelphia, & the hope of one Day returning to finish my *Days* there—is my greatest solace.

My time has been chiefly spent in a convent—since I first came to France, where the retirement & stillness has aforded me too much leasure for meloncholy reflections when my fears—pictured to me—the sufferings of those worthy Virtuous People whom I had had the happiness to see & know, under such pleasing circumstances now all involved in the Miseries of a sad warr. May Kind Heaven remove their afflictions.

I purpose leaving this country—& returning to England some time in the course of the next Month, where if I can render you any service, to know your Commands will give me real pleasure. Please to address me at Cambray—where your letter will come safe to her—who' has the honor to be—with real Esteem Sir Your sincere friend & humble servant.[3]

JULIANA RITCHIE

I am a shamed to forward to you—so incorrect a scrawl—but I am so afficted with a head ach that I scarce am able to hold my pen.

To Mr. Franklin.

Notation: Ritchie March 5. 1780

From George Scott   ALS: American Philosophical Society

Sir   Marseilles 5th. Mar: 1780

After a very cold & a very tedious Journey I arrived here on the evening of the 27th. Ulto.[4] & have been luckey enough to

3. She wrote again on March 29. BF has answered neither her letter of March 5 nor one of three years earlier. Her friend the Countess of Kenmor (Kenmure) has invited her to accompany her to Paris, but obstacles prevent it. The countess will deliver her letter to BF's house. Fear and anxiety for Mr. Ritchie are depriving her of her health. APS. Frances Mackensie (d. 1796) was married to John Gordon of Kenmure; after his death she resided chiefly in France: Sir James B. Paul, *The Scots Peerage* . . . (9 vols., Edinburgh, 1904–14), V, 131–2; VII, 511–12.

4. The British merchant and friend of Joseph Priestley had left Paris in mid-February: XXXI, 422, 433–4, 453–4.

find a Genoese Vessell here just upon the point of departure for Naples, the Captain says that we shall positively saill to day & I expect him sending for me every moment.

From Paris to Lyons I travelled in Company with a friend of yours, Monsr. L'Abbé Rozier who was particularly civil to me. From Lyons to Avignion I fell in Company with the Marquis de Cugny who shewed me great respect, & since my arrival here I have waited upon the Governor of this Town Le Duc de Pilles to pay my respects to him, he received me very kindly & politely offered me any assistance in his power.[5]

Should any thing occur which you would wish to communicate to me by letter, I should be pleased to be honoured with a line or two directed to me at Naples.

I have an opportunity to Send this without expence wch. induces me to write otherwise my intelligence would not be worth the expence of postage. I am with sincere esteem & regard Sir Your Mo: Obliged & mo: Obedt. hble Servt.   GEO: SCOTT

I beg my best compliments to your Grandson. I am now in a warm climate the Weather being now very pleasant & agreeable

Addressed: The Honourable / Benjamin Franklin Esqr. / Passy / near / Paris

Notation: Geo: Scott Mar 5 1780

From Jonathan Williams, Jr.

ALS: University of Pennsylvania Library

Dear & hond Sir   Nantes March. 5. 1780.

I beg leave to introduce to your particular notice my Friend Mr Mason of Virginia[6] a Gentleman of a respectable Family &

---

5. Scott's traveling companions were the abbé François Rozier (editor of the *Journal de Physique:* XXIX, 353n) and the marquis de Clugny, a lieutenant in the regiment of Beauvoisis stationed in Corsica (*Etat militaire* for 1780, p. 226). The governor of Marseilles was the marquis de Pilles: XXIX, 471.

6. George Mason, Jr., armed with letters of introduction from Washington, had sailed from America in April, 1779, in a ship bound for Cadiz. His father had given him credit on a house at Nantes, where he eventually entered the tobacco trade. See XXIX, 224; Pamela C. Copeland and Richard K. Macmaster, *The Five George Masons . . .* (Charlottesville, 1975), p. 199.

plentifull Fortune by showing him every civility & every mark of Friendship he may have occasion for you will very sensibly Oblige Dear & hond Sir Your dutifull & affectionate Kinsman
JONA WILLIAMS J

Addressed: The Hon. / Doctor Franklin / Passy

Notation: J. Williams mar 5 1781

Francis Hopkinson to the American Commissioner or Commissioners   Two ALS:[7] American Philosophical Society

Gentlemen.   Philada. March 6th. 1780
   Since my last of the 14th. of Jany.[8] the following Setts of Exchange have issued from my Office Viz

To Pennsylvania

					Dolls
150 setts	36 Dolls.	No.	2218–2367	=	5,400

To New Jersey

					Dolls
50 setts	30 Dols.	No.	2026–2075	=	1,500
50 —	36 —		2368–2417	=	1,800
					3,300

To Pennsylvania

					Dolls
100 setts—	30 Doll.	No.	2076–2175	=	3,000
100 —	36 —		2418–2517	=	3,600
					6,600

I have the Honour to be Gentlemen, Your very humble servt.
FRAS HOPKINSON
Treasr of Loan

7. The other of which is marked "Quadruplicate."
8. XXXI, 130n, the most recent in a series of lists of loan office certificates, compiled in an attempt to detect counterfeits. Treasurer of Loans Hopkinson sent similar lists on May 14 (of sets of bills issued by the loan offices of Massachusetts, Rhode Island, Connecticut, Pennsylvania, and New Hampshire) and June 27 (bills issued by the loan offices of New Jersey, Connecticut, Maryland, and North Carolina). On April 13 he sent a list of eight sets

(Original)

Honbe. Commrs. at Paris

(No. 15)

Addressed: To The Honourable / The Commissioner or Commissioners / of the United States of America / at / Paris / (On public service) / (Original) / To be sunk if in Danger of falling into the Hands of the Enemy

From John Paul Jones

ALS: American Philosophical Society; AL (draft): Library of Congress

L'Orient March 6th: 1780.

I inclose for your Excellencies approbation an extract of a letter that I have received from Sir R Finlay respecting an invention of Bombs that are Calculated to set fire to any Object against which they are discharged from a Cannon.—[9] If they answer the description that I have had they will be an Acquisition of some Consequence to our Marine.— The expence of the Drafts is but triffling and I shall not Scruple to pay it.— I wish you may find the inventor worth of further Attention.— If the Drafts should not reach you before I leave France, please to oblige me by forwarding them to the Care of Mr Morris[1] of Philadelphia.—

With profound esteem and Respect I am your Excellencies most obliged Servt: JNO P JONES

His Excellency B Franklin Esqr:—

Notation: J.P. Jones L'Orient. March 6. 1780

---

of replacement bills issued to Thomas McKean, for which see *JCC*, XVI, 331–2. Copies of all these documents are at the APS.

9. The enclosure, also at the APS, reveals that "the bombs, or rather hollow bullets" were invented by an impoverished Swedish artillery lieutenant named Floberg, who wished an advance of 200 to 300 *l.t.*, followed by employment either on Jones's ship or in America. Robert Finlay was a Bordeaux businessman; he was acquainted with Silas Deane and John G. Frazer, as well as Jones: *Deane Papers*, I, 246, and *passim;* Bradford, *Jones Papers*, reel 3, nos. 561–2, 567; reel 4, nos. 707, 843; Finlay to Arthur Lee, May 2, 1778 (APS).

1. Robert Morris.

From the Baron de Tott[2]   ALS: American Philosophical Society

Monsieur   [after March 6, 1780][3]
   M. De Lafayette en partant pour L'amerique m'a Confié La Surveillance dune gravure qui represente Le general Washington,[4] et Je crois ne pouvoir mieux repondre a Ses Vües qu'en madressant a vous pour Le choix et le titre des Bils qui presentent La partie historique, faites moy la grace de m'indiquer le moment ou je pouray aller Vous Consulter a cet egard Sans vous etre incomode.[5]
   M. De Lafayette devoit aussi, Monsieur, avant Son depart,

2. The son of a Hungarian refugee who was at the head of a regiment bearing his name, François, baron de Tott (1733–1793) served as Vergennes' secretary in Constantinople. After a consulship in the Crimea (1767–1769) he organized Turkish defenses against Russia, came back to Paris in 1776, and was sent on an inspection trip to the French consulates around the Mediterranean. He returned to France around 1779. He was then appointed commander of Douai, fled to Switzerland in 1790, and spent the end of his life in Hungary. In addition to his military and diplomatic career, the baron was a painter and an amateur musician. Larousse; *Jefferson Papers*, X, 159n; E. Bénézit, ed., *Dictionnaire critique et documentaire des Peintres, Sculpteurs, Dessinateurs et Graveurs* . . . (10 vols., Paris, 1976).

3. When Lafayette left Paris: *Lafayette Papers*, II, 373n.

4. Sometime in late 1779 Lafayette had commissioned Jean-Baptiste Le Paon to paint a full-length portrait of Washington which he would then have engraved. He must have contracted with the engraver, Noël Le Mire, shortly before leaving for America. Le Mire's commission was reported on March 19 in Bachaumont, *Mémoires secrets,* and on March 29 Le Mire, soliciting subscriptions, placed an announcement of the project in the *Jour. de Paris.* The engraving would be ready on November 1, it said, and portrayed Washington "tenant des papiers relatifs à l'Histoire de l'Amérique." It would appear from the present letter that Lafayette left Paris before specifying to the engraver which papers should be depicted.

5. The meeting has left no trace, but the well-known engraving shows fourteen papers (treaties, bills, maps, and notes), each one numbered and labelled in English. A French key, or translation of the titles, numbered one to fourteen, was printed on a separate sheet. For a full-page reproduction of the engraving see Wendy C. Wick, *George Washington, An American Icon* (Washington, D.C., 1982), p. 30. The key, a copy of which is at the Cabinet des Estampes at the Bibliothèque Nationale, is reprinted, and the engraving is described, in Jules Hédou, *Noël Le Mire et son oeuvre* (Paris, 1875), pp. 80–81. See also Charles Henry Hart, *Catalog of the Engraved Portraits of Washington* (New York, 1904), number 31 (p. 18). Le Paon's portrait has not been found.

m'aboucher avec vous pour un petit cathéchisme americain, dont il vous a Sans doute parle et Si vous persistés dans ce projet nous en causerons egalement.[6] Je Seray fort aise que cette Occasion me procure celle de vous offrir L'homage de mon admiration et celuy des Sentimens du tres parfait attachement avec Lesquels jay L'honneur detre Monsieur Votre tres humble et tres Obeissant Serviteur   LE B. DE TOTT

aux petittes ecuries de La reine rue de Varennes./

Notation: Rott le Baron de.

From Thomas Digges   ALS: Historical Society of Pennsylvania

Dr. Sir   London 7 Mar. 1780

I am to beg the favour of you to inform me by first post, If the following American bills of Exa. are good ones; They are lodgd in my hands by a Countryman who waits to know their fate; that is, whether others of the same tenor & date have, or have not been paid. A letter sent to the former direction by Post, W.S. C—— at N——os Coffee Ho.[7] with such information will greatly oblige Sr. Your Most Obt. Servant   WS. C

No. 27—For 30 Dolls.   dated feby. 23d 1779—Payle to Jona Warner countersignd Nicholas Gilman for State of N Hampshire—[8]

6. This is undoubtedly a reference to the schoolbook containing prints of British war atrocities that Lafayette and BF had been planning: XXIX, 590–3. We know that BF had at least one of those engravings made during the spring of 1780, and sent some copies to Samuel Cooper: Cooper to BF, Sept. 8, 1780, APS. A reference in Account XXVI (Editorial Note on Accounts, above) may be related to this print: on April 9, Chaumont paid 63 *l.t.* on account of Congress for an engraving of "un sujet Americain." "600 exemplaires" of the print were struck, but none has yet been identified.
7. William Singleton Church, Nandos Coffee House.
8. Warner may have been the Jonathan Warner (d. 1803) who was a brigadier general of Mass. militia: Francis B. Heitman, ed., *Historical Register of Officers of the Continental Army during the War of the Revolution. . .*

26—For 30 Dolls.   dated, payable, & countersignd, as
                   above
25—For 30 Dolls   Do   Do   Do
166—For 24 Dollars dated Feby. 15. 1779—payable to
                   Jonan Warner, countersignd Nat
                   Appleton Massachusts.[9]
                   N.B. the above are all seconds—
No. 173   For 24 Dollars dated Feby 23 1779 payle to Peter
                   Boilston Adams,[1] countersignd by
                   Natl Appleton Massachusets bay.
                   N.B. this is a first bill.
      ___
      138 Drs.

Addressed: Monsieur / Monsieur B. Franklin / Passy

Notations: M. Digges 11. Mars. 1780. Londone. / March 7 1780
/ ansd 20. Mar 80[2]

From Jonathan Williams, Jr.

ALS: University of Pennsylvania Library; copy:
Yale University Library

Dear & hond Sir   Nantes March 7. 1780.
    Doctor Bancroft gave me your Favour of the 26 Feb.[3] & Mr
Chaumonts Letters desiring me to send as much as I could of
the Cloathing to Rochelle with the greatest Expedition. I ac-

---

(rev. ed., Baltimore, 1982), p. 569; Robert A. Feer, *Shays's Rebellion* (New
York and London, 1988), p. 323. Nicholas Gilman was commissioner of the
state continental loan office: Frank C. Mevers, ed., *The Papers of Josiah
Bartlett* (Hanover, N.H., 1979), p. 154.

    9. Nathaniel Appleton (1713–98), son of the Rev. Nathaniel Appleton
(XXI, 226n), was commissioner of the continental loan office for Massachusetts: *Sibley's Harvard Graduates,* XII, 355–9.

    1. Peter Boylston Adams (1738–1823), JA's younger brother: Butterfield,
John Adams Diary, I, 66n.

    2. On that date BF wrote Digges that all of Warner's other bills had been
presented by Mr. Knox (William Knox, XXX, 97n) and paid on Sept. 24, 1779.
Bill No. 173, however, had not yet arrived. Library of Congress.

    3. Missing.

cordingly went to Work to Bale up what was ready & had loaded two Waggons after a deal of Trouble & Difficulty with the Custom House. When the Waggons went to the Barrier there was a Demand of ¹/₃₀th of the Whole value for *les Droits dominal* of the Duc de Fitz James[4] this would have been a Sum of near 2000 Livres only for those two waggon loads. I consulted with Doctor Bancroft & we determined to prefer water Carriage rather than submit to this exorbitant Demand. I was obliged to allow a Dedomagement to the Waggoners for their expences & loss of Time. I have now got those & a few Bales more on board a small Vessell which goes away to night & I hope will be at la Rochelle in Time.[5] I have done all that was possible to do & have got away but a small quantity at last but I expect it will be as much as the Frigate will take, for Ships of War have in general but little Room. I am convinced of the old proverb "the more haste the worst Speed."[6] This hurrying away a Part of the Supplys delays the remainder. It is in general best to give reasonable Time for An Operation & I believe in the End it turns out more expeditious.— I did not mistake Socks for Stocks for it is mentioned in the Order *"of the same Quality with the Feet of the Stockings."* Being in suspence about the Buckles & knowing the necessity of Dispatch I had ventured to order them. I have since countermanded the Order but I have agreed to take all that are ready, which is reasonable. I have issued but few Bills yet & those only to procure Cash to replace the advances I had made for the Shoes Linnen & workmanship which all require Cash: you have inclosed a List of what I have hitherto issued.—[7] I will keep on the

4. Charles, duc de Fitz-James (1712–1787): *DBF.*

5. After paying the wagoners 268 *l.t.*, JW shipped 48 casks, bales, and trunks on the *Union*, Capt. Bureau, who was given 100 *l.t.* to "depart directly." Bureau later sued JW when orders came to redirect the goods to Brest; they were relanded at Paimboeuf (see JW's letter of March 27). Account XXIV (XXXI, 3); JW to the Committee for Foreign Affairs, March 7 (Yale University Library).

6. A proverb that Poor Richard never uttered, but that BF undoubtedly had heard. Introduced by Plato, it was first rendered in English in the fourteenth century and became commonplace thereafter. John Heywood used it in *Proverbs* (1546): Burton Stevenson, ed., *The Home Book of Proverbs, Maxims and Familiar Phrases* (New York, 1948), p. 1085.

7. Missing.

shoemaking but as it goes slowly, when it goes on well I will have Leather ready for the Time of Shipping. I inclose you a Letter for Mr Poulze as you desire it is a Copy of my last, but I have altered the Date.[8]

I will take care of the Boxes of Types as you direct as soon as they arrive.[9]

Mr Gridly one of my arbitrators had desired me to request you to order him a Passage in the Alliance as his Health requires his immediate Return.[1] I told him I would write to you & I wish you may oblige him but I wish more that you may favour my uncle with a Passage out. I have many Reasons for wishing he was with his Family but his long absence is of itself a sufficiently strong one.[2]

I have a few Pounds of Babery or myrtle Wax of which I will send you some by the return of Doctor Bancroft. I shall be obliged to you if you will give me a Receipt how to make Crown Soap of it,[3] I want to try the Experiment & it may serve to make this Wax an Article of Commerce here, at present it is not known.

I am ever with great Respect Your dutifull & affectionate Kinsman JONA WILLIAMS J

My Wife joins in Duty & Love to you. Bien des Excuses a M.

---

8. JW had written to Farmer General Jacques Paulze requesting that he not charge duty on the goods being shipped for the army. JW sent the letter to BF on Jan. 10, asking him to write a supporting note and deliver it. Having heard nothing, JW asked BF on Feb. 19 whether or not it had ever been forwarded: XXXI, 376, 506.

9. This was a font of brevier cast at BF's foundry at Passy for the American printer James Watson, and packed in three boxes. It was to join the two boxes of type for him that JW had placed on the *Alliance* in May, 1779: XXIX, 347; JW to "the commanding officer on board the Alliance," April 23, 1780, Yale University Library.

1. Joseph Gridley reminded BF of his request on March 28, below.

2. John Williams had been in France for sixteen months: XXVIII, 136. By the end of March, his travel plans changed; see Gridley's letter of March 28.

3. Crown soap was a Franklin family secret. BF had given the recipe to Jane Mecom, and at the end of 1778 had advised her son-in-law to make it. BF did not have the recipe with him in Paris, and JW would have to wait until 1785, when he visited Jane Mecom in Boston, for the recipe and a demonstration: I, 348; XXVIII, 364; XXX, 149–50; Van Doren, *Franklin-Mecom*, p. 242 *et seq.*

Chaumont pour n'avoir pas repondu ses derniers par ce Courier. Je le ferois par l'ordinaire prochain.

Notation: J Williams Mar 7. 80

Intelligence from Paris and Other Places

D: National Archives

The chevalier de Kéralio forwarded only seventeen intelligence reports to Franklin during the months covered by this volume.[4] After the first one, dated March 7 and printed below, the flow ceased almost completely until late May. When it resumed, the reports were generally quite brief in comparison to those of previous volumes. The other items were the following:

(I) Cadiz, May 28: Eight ships of the line have arrived from Ferrol; the fleet of twenty-eight of the line here was awaiting only their arrival before sailing.[5]

(II) Flushing [in the Netherlands], [June?] 5:[6] The tambour is beating in order to recruit ships' crews in all our towns. We believe there will be war unless the British (who are detested by 7/8 of the republic) honor their treaty. We have stopped fitting out whaling ships in order not to expose the crews to capture. Crews are so rare that the *Jeune Cornélie* has not been able to find three sailors here or in Middelburg.

(III) Amsterdam, June 8: Empress Catherine II of Russia has not yet responded to the States General.[7] We hope for more from our own

4. Kéralio had been providing reports since January, 1778: XXV, 469–72. For the latest examples see XXXI, 65–8. All of the present ones are at the National Archives; none are in Kéralio's hand.

5. Admiral Luis de Córdoba y Córdoba's fleet did not sail, however, until July 31, when it left Cadiz to protect incoming convoys. During the summer France stripped du Chaffault's Brest fleet of most of its ships of the line to reinforce Córdoba: Dull, *French Navy*, pp. 192–3, 366–8.

6. By which time the search for crews for the Dutch Navy was at its height; see Dumas to BF, May 19. The British had provoked the crisis by seizing a Dutch convoy: XXXI, 369n.

7. On April 24 the States General of the Netherlands decided to negotiate with Russia about joining Catherine II in defending neutral shipping rights: Dumas to BF, April 24, below. The report from Amsterdam also mentions the arrival of several ships from America. It is unusual in that it is specifically addressed to BF.

efforts. Everything possible is being done to put the Dutch Navy on a respectable footing. Several vessels have arrived from America bringing news of Lafayette's arrival.

(IV) Brest, June 8: A convoy left yesterday; its destination is believed to be the West Indies. Another convoy sailed for the Indies from the Ile d'Aix. Work is still proceeding on sending a second division of troops to Rochambeau, but the time of their departure is unknown.[8] At the beginning of the month three ships put to sea; one, from Lorient, is thought to be bound for the East Indies. The destination of the other two is unknown.

(V) Brest, June 12: It is said the two convoys for the West Indies will be combined. Another one is expected to sail tomorrow.

(VI) St. Malo, June 13: A ship from Baltimore at Cadiz reports Congress has reduced $200,000,000 in currency to a fortieth of its former value.[9] Several warships from Lorient and Rochefort have arrived at Brest. Construction of a frigate has begun.

(VII) St. Malo, June 15: Two British frigates are in view but they have not prevented the arrival of a convoy of fifteen sail; two cutters built for Spain are in the roadstead.

(VIII) Dieppe, June 15: The privateer *Comte de Maurepas* arrived yesterday with a prize. The Le Havre privateer *Stanislas* has put into Ostend for repairs after a fierce engagement with three British frigates.

(IX) Paris, June 16: All but one ship from a twenty-one-ship convoy from St. Domingue have reached here safely. Also arrived is the *Négresse* with dispatches from La Luzerne reporting that the siege of Charleston has been lifted, the British army is in retreat, and General Clinton has been killed. Lafayette has reached Boston. The riots in London have ended after causing £1,200,000 damage.[1]

(X) Paris, June 17: Letters written at Martinique on May 5 report

8. For the genesis of Rochambeau's expeditionary force see XXXI, 370–1n. The regiments of Bourbonnais, Soissonais, Saintonge, and Royal Deux-Ponts sailed for America from Brest on May 2. Once it found more transports, the government intended to send the regiments of Neustrie and Anhalt as a "second division." Because of the danger of interception by the British Navy, however, these regiments remained in France: Rice and Brown, eds., *Rochambeau's Army*, I, 117–18, 225n; Dull, *French Navy*, p. 190n.

9. Congress approved the devaluation on March 18: *JCC*, XVI, 263–6; Ferguson, *Power of the Purse*, pp. 51–2.

1. The American garrison at Charleston surrendered on May 12. Lafayette arrived at Boston on April 27: Idzerda, *Lafayette Papers*, III, 3. The Gordon Riots convulsed London between June 2 and 9: Digges to BF, June 10, below.

Rodney's squadron has been badly damaged in an April 17 battle and is now undergoing repairs at St. Lucia; Guichen will attack Antigua or St. Christopher.[2]

(XI) Le Havre, June 18: Six men have been killed and twenty-nine wounded aboard the privateer *Stanislas* during a five-and-a-half-hour fight with a British frigate.

(XII) Brest, June 19: Four British privateers have been captured by French warships. All the ships here except the *Northumberland* are in the roadstead. The departure of a convoy has been delayed for fear it will encounter the British fleet.

(XIII) Lorient, June 21: The frigates *Vénus* and *Magicienne* have brought here four captured privateers and 400 prisoners.

(XIV) Brest, June 22-23: Two India Company ships arrived recently. Orders have been given to the various workshops to hold in readiness enough materiel for forty ships of the line.

(XV) Paris, June 23: News of May 10 from Martinique is that Rodney has refused to fight Guichen and is moored at St. Lucia. Clinton is said to have returned to New York with part of his troops.

(XVI) Dunkirk, June 27: The privateer *Union Américaine* arrived yesterday with a ransom and a prize; five other privateers are preparing to sail.

Paris, Le 7. mars

Depuis cinq Couriers, on ne reçoit aucune nouvelle de Brest et l'on ignore absolument ce qui S'y passe. Mais en même tems on sait que les Régiments de Bourbonnois, Soissonois, Neustrie, Saintonge, anhalt et Royal-Deux ponts (on nomme encore Boulonnois et Royal Corse) ont reçu ordre de se tenir prêts à S'embarquer. Le Commandement de ce Corps de Troupes est donné, dit-on, à M. de Rochambeau, mais Sa destination est tres inconnue. Jusqu'à présent l'Escadre destinée à le convoyer n'étoit que de six Vaisseaux; on dit qu'elle sera renforcée de six autres et que le tout Sera aux ordres de mr. du Chaffaut.[3] On part [parle] du

2. The battle off Martinique between Admirals Rodney and Guichen was inconclusive: W.M. James, *The British Navy in Adversity: a Study of the War of American Independence* (London, New York, and Toronto, 1926), pp. 198–204, 441–2. The French admiral subsequently attacked St. Lucia, precipitating another naval battle on May 15: *ibid.*, pp. 208–11. The present intelligence report includes a list of the ships in the convoy discussed in the preceding one.

3. The escort for Rochambeau, comprised of seven ships of the line plus smaller warships, was entrusted to Charles-Louis d'Arsac, chevalier de Ter-

départ vrai ou faux de ce Général pour donner le Commandement de l'armée navale à M le Cte. d'Estaing. On parle encore
d'une Escadre de trois Vaisseaux confiée à M de Bougainville, et
M de la Clocheterie doit en commander deux autres pour des ex-
péditions Séparées et Secretes.[4]

Si l'on ignore ce qui Se passe dans nos ports, on n'est pas plus
instruit des opérations des Espagnols. On sait Seulement que
l'amiral Rodney appareilloit dans la Baye de Gibraltar, le 13
fevrier à 5. h. ½ du soir, et que le 15. à la même heure la flotte Es-
pagnole faisoit des dispositions dans la rade de Cadix pour mettre à la voile; on la dit à la mer et depuis trois semaines on n'a de
nouvelles ni des uns ni des autres.

M. franklin a eu des nouvelles de Boston. Deux armateurs
américains ont pris Sept batimens chargés de vivres et de munitions de guerre et un Sloop de guerre qui les escortoit. Ce Con-
voi alloit de hallifax à Penobscot.

M de la fayette devoit partir hier matin: il S'embarque, dit-on,
Sur la frégate *l'hermione* et porte l'habillement et l'armement
complet de 4000 hommes.

Le Roi vient de faire dans l'armée de terre une promotion
considérable d'officiers Généraux et de Brigadiers./.[5]

To ——— Caccia

ALS: Albert M. Greenfield, Philadelphia, Pennsylvania (1958)

Sir   Passy, March 8. 1780
  I unfortunately mislaid M. Cavalliers Letter, & have totally

---

nay (1723–1780): Dull, *French Navy*, p. 193; Rice and Brown, eds., *Rochambeau's Army*, I, 117, 329.

4. Jean-Isaac-Timothée Chadeau de La Clocheterie (XXVII, 608n) commanded the *Jason*, 64, in Ternay's squadron: *Les combattants français de la
guerre américaine 1778–1783* (Paris, 1903), p. 199. *Chef d'escadre* Louis-An-
toine de Bougainville (1729–1811: *DBF*), the celebrated explorer, had served
in America with d'Estaing's fleet and would return in 1781 with de Grasse.

5. On March 1 the French army promoted approximately 100 men to the
rank of lieutenant general, 250 to *maréchal de camp*, 220 to brigadier of infantry, 100 to brigadier of cavalry, and 40 to brigadier of dragoons: *Almanach
Royal* for 1781, pp. 147–62.

forgotten the Subject of it, or I should have answer'd it long
since.[6] If you can make me recollect the purport of it, I will send
you an Answer immediately. I have the honour to be Sir, Your
most obedient & most humble Servt.   B FRANKLIN

M. Caccia

Addressed: A Monsieur / Monsieur Caccia / a Paris

Notation: Passy franklin du 8. Mars 1780

To John Paul Jones

LS[7] and transcript: National Archives; copy: Library of Congress

Dear Sir,   Passy March. 8. 1780
    I received your Favour of the 3d Inst. I find the Arms are to
be sent in one of the Kings Ships.[8] I inclose an Order for the Cannon which you say You can take as Ballast. The other Particulars
of your Letter I shall endeavour to answer to morrow. With
great Esteem I am, Dear Sir, your most obedient & most humble Servant.   B FRANKLIN

A muster Roll of the Bonhomme Richard will be wanted, I understand, in order to divide the Produce of the Prizes.
    Mr. Ross having wrote me word that he shall go in the
Luzerne,[9] I request you to take in his Stead Capt. Hutchins a very

6. Cavallier had written on July 22, 1779, seeking BF's help in emigrating
to America. Caccia, a banker, forwarded his request: XXX, 34.
    7. In WTF's hand, except for the paragraph beginning "Mr Ross," which is
in BF's.
    8. Sartine wrote Lafayette on March 6 that all the uniforms, arms, and
other effects that BF delivered would be received without difficulty aboard
the warships or transports taking Rochambeau's expeditionary corps to
America: Idzerda, *Lafayette Papers,* II, 371. Presumably he told BF the same
thing.
    9. Ross had told WTF on Jan. 25 that he planned to sail to America on this
ship (the *Chevalier de La Luzerne,* Capt. Bell): XXXI, 501n. He must have recently reconfirmed his decision, although ultimately he chose instead to
travel on the brig *Duke of Leinster.* This vessel sailed on Oct. 7 in the company of Jones's new command, the *Ariel:* Jones to BF, Oct. 13, 1780, Bradford, *Jones Papers,* reel 6, no. 1231; Morison, *Jones,* p. 304.

worthy American, who has suffered much for his Attachment to our Cause—[1]

Honble Comme Jones—

Addressed: A Monsieur / Monsieur le Capitaine / Jones chez M. Gourlade / Negt / à L'Orient

Endorsed: From his Excellency Dr. Franklin Passy March 8th 1780

Notation: an order for the Cannon &c The BH: Richards muster Rolls wanted

From Count Andreas Peter von Bernstorff

ALS: Library of Congress; copies: Columbia University Library,[2] National Archives; press copy:[3] Library of Congress; transcript: National Archives

Monsieur   Coppenh. ce 8 Mars 1780.

Si Vous etiés un Homme moins connû et moins consideré, j'aurois eté fort incertain au Sujet de la Lettre que jai eu l'honneur de recevoir de votre part,[4] et qui ne m'est parvenue qu'au 31. du Mois de Janvier. J'aurois pû la regarder comme une demarche calculée à nous mettre dans un nouvel Embarras aussi penible que le premier; mais on ne craint et on ne risque rien avec un Sage tel que Vous, Monsieur generalement respecté par cet Univers que Vous avés éclairé, et connû par cet Amour dominant pour la verité, qui caracterise l'Homme de bien et le vrai Philosophe. Ce sont ces Titres qui feront passer votre nom a la posterité la plus reculée, et auxquels je m'interesse particuliere-

1. On March 6 Hutchins took an oath of allegiance to the U.S. A signed copy of that oath, certified by BF, is at the APS; a copy of the certification, signed by BF but lacking the oath itself, is at the Hist. Soc. of Pa.

2. With the papers of John Jay. A notation in his hand indicates it was enclosed with BF's June 13 letter to him, below.

3. With the papers of Thomas Jefferson. His secretary William Short made press copies of a number of documents relating to the prize case to which the present letter alludes; see xxx, 336n.

4. BF's memoir complaining to the Danish foreign minister about the return of Landais' prizes to the British: xxxi, 261–5.

ment dans un Moment, ou la Situation des Affaires m'impose la Loi de me depouiller en Vous ecrivant, de tout Caractère public, et de n'aspirer qu'a Vous paroitre ce que je suis bien veritablement, l'ami passionné de la Paix, de la verité, et du merite. Cette Maniere de penser decide non seulement de mes Sentiments personnels à votre Egard, mais aussi de ceux que j'ai relativement a l'Affaire facheuse Sur laquelle Vous avés bien voulû me parler, et qui dès Son Commencement m'a fait la peine la plus sensible. Vous conviendrés sans peine avec moi, Monsieur, qu'il y à des Situations epineuses, dans lesquelles il est impossible de ne heurter personne. Vous estes trop equitable pour ne pas entrer dans la nôtre. On ne se consoleroit pas de s'y trouver, et on ne pardonneroit pas a ceux qui les ont amené, si elles ne fournissoient aussi pas quelquefois l'occasion de s'entendre et de prevenir tout ce qui pourroit faire naitre à l'avenir des Embarras aussi essentiels.[5] Mr. le Baron de Blome[6] Vous parlera sur ce Sujet avec la Confiance et avec la franchise la plus entiêre, et si mes Souhaits peuvent estre remplis, je serai dedommagé de toutes mes peines, et il ne m'en restera que le Souvenir agreable d'avoir eu la Satisfaction de Vous assurer de ma main de cette Estime superieure et parfaite avec laquelle j'ai l'honneur d'estre, Monsieur Votre tres humble et très obeissant Serviteur.[7]   A. BERNSTORF

Endorsed: Danish Minister's Letter in Answer to my Memorial

5. Bernstorff had already told the French minister in Copenhagen that the Danish authorities would not examine the papers of any American ship camouflaging her identity by flying a French or Spanish flag: xxxi, 261n.

6. Baron Otto von Blome, the Danish envoy at the court of France: xxviii, 59n.

7. Bernstorff, although he adopts a conciliatory tone here, opposed American independence: Soren J.M.P. Fogdall, *Danish-American Diplomacy 1776–1920* (Iowa City, 1922 [University of Iowa Studies in the Social Sciences viii, no. 2]), 17, 152–3.

From Jacques-Jean Besongne[8]

ALS: American Philosophical Society

Monsieur   Rouen le 9 mars 1780

J'ai un assortiment assez considerable des meilleurs ouvrages francois concernant L'histoire La morale & les Arts, mon but etant de Quitter Le Commerce de la Librairie,[9] j'ai cru devoir vous demander vos avis et votre protection pour un dessein ou je suis resolu si Vous L'agrez de Risquer une vingtaine de mille Livres ce serait de faire passer aux provinces unies de l'amerique partie de cet assortiment, et d'y Former une maison de corespondance pour les livres du meilleur genre de La Librairie francoise,[1] Si cet essai me reussit je continuerai, s'il ne me reussit pas, je me bornerai La attendant votre decision, et L'honneur de Votre reponse.

J'ai celui d'etre avec respect Monsieur Votre très-humble et tres obeissant serviteur   J J Besongne

impr. Lib. a Rouen

From J.F. Frin & Co.[2]

LS: American Philosophical Society

Monsieur   Paris 9 mars 1780

Nous avons remis chez M Grand dès le 23 du mois passé 19 effets du congrès sur vous passés à notre ordre ensemble Drs. [Dollars] 648., plus un autre de Drs. 300 no. 247 ce der. à l'ordre

---

8. Jacques Besongne is listed in the "Tableau des libraires et imprimeurs du royaume" for Rouen: Antoine Perrin, *Almanach de la Librairie* (Paris, 1781; reprint ed., Aubel, Belgium: P.M. Gason, 1984), p. 70. He belonged to an important family of printer-booksellers dating back to the first half of the seventeenth century: Jean Quéniart, *L'imprimerie et la librairie à Rouen au XVIIIe siècle* (Paris, 1969), p. 24.

9. He continued in business at least until 1784, when he went bankrupt: Quéniart, *L'imprimerie*, pp. 163, 240.

1. Besongne had commercial ties with booksellers throughout France and Europe: *ibid.*, pp. 159–61, 163, 165, 167.

2. A Parisian banking firm: xxxi, 269n.

de Mr Daniel Crommelin & fils d'amsterdam à qui nous devons le renvoyer quand il sera accepté.[3]

Comme voici 15 Jours que vous avez ces effets, nous présumons, Monsieur, que vous aurez eu le tems de les examiner & que vous etes aujourdhui en etat de nous les faire passer en regle, c'est ce que nous vous prions de faire en réponse, si non ceux passés à notre ordre au moins celui de Drs 300 à renvoyer à nos correspondans d'amsterdam pour leur donner le tems de le négocier ou de nous l'endosser pour le toucher à son échéance.

Nous avons lhonneur d'être avec respect Monsieur Vos tres humbles obéissans serviteurs   J.F. FRIN ET COMPE.

Nous avons encore remis d'autres effets sur vous à m Grand, aussi passés à Notre ordre, mais comme c'est depuis peu nous n'en parlons pas.

Addressed: A Monsieur / Monsieur Le Docteur / Franklin / A Passy

Notation: Frin & Company 9 mars 1780

From Madame Brillon   AL: American Philosophical Society

ce vendredi matin 10 [March, 1780][4]

D'aprés l'attachement que l'on me connoist pour vous mon aimable papa on me tourmente sans césse pour vous demandér des léttres de recomandations pour l'amérique; la crainte de vous importunér me fait refusér asses constamment ces sortes de commissions, je n'ai cependant pûë ne pas me chargér de vous en demandér une pour un homme qui appartient et intérésse des gents de mes parents; la petite notte cý jointe vous instruira de ce dont il est chargé la bas et s'il vous est possible de le recomandér á quelqu'un de vos amis de philadelphie, vous rendrés un grand sérvice a qu'élqu'un qu'on m'assure en estre digne il me faudroit

3. For the Amsterdam correspondents of J.F. Frin see *ibid.*
4. There was a Friday the 10th in March, 1780, on which day BF wrote to Robert Morris along the lines that Mme Brillon wished. See the following document.

cétte léttre aujourd'hui s'il est possible parceque le jeune homme part lundi ou mardi:/:

Je ne pourrai pas vous donnér le thé demain, seriés vous assés aimable pour le venir prendre ce soir ou dimanche, un mot de réponse me feroit grand plaisir surtout s'il m'assuroit qu'en pérdant un des jours que j'ai le bonheur de passér avéc vous vous voulés bien me dédomagér en m'en donnant un autre; mon bon papa tout le monde vous honore vous aime, mais croyés en votre fille, tous ces amours réunis ne font pas la somme du mien, je vous l'ai dit, vous remplacés dans mon coeur un pére que j'adorois; ce coeur trop sensible pour éstre jamais parfaitement heureux vous a choisi, adopté, qui donc jamais óh mon ami vous aimera comme moi? Moi:/:

Addressed: A Monsieur / Monsieur Franklin / A Passy

Notation: Mr. Dillion[5] des gayeres chargé du service des vivres pour les subsistances des trouppes en Amérique.

To Robert Morris   AL (draft): Library of Congress

Dear Sir   Passy, March 10. 1780

The Bearer M. Billion des Gayeres goes to America in some Employ relative to the Provision for the Subsistance of the French Troops. His Friends have requested of me a Letter of Introduction to some Friend of mine in Philadelphia.[6] As I know of no one so well acquainted with, & so capable of advising in such Affairs as yourself, I take the Liberty of recommending him to your Civilities, as a Person who bears here a very worthy Character. With sincere and great Esteem I am ever, dear Sir, Your most &c

Mr Morris

5. In another hand. The notation is on a separate sheet of paper.
6. The only request of which we know is that of his relative, Mme Brillon; her letter on his behalf is immediately above.

From Thomas Digges ALS: Historical Society of Pennsylvania

Dr Sir   10 mar 1780

Your favr. of the 26th. ulo. got safe to hand,[7] & I have consulted with Mr. H—— on the mode of distributing your benefactions to some unhappy sufferers— A vessel saild from Plyo. with 100 on the 5th. Int. There remains there but 86 and what is rather singular there is pardons lodgd for 68 of that number agt. the return of the vessel.[8] Means are taking to get the remaining 18 (of wch M——n——y[9] is one) to have pardons also, that there may remain none in that prison after another Embarkation takes place; but the Lord knows when this will take place, as the next Cargoe by the rotine must go from Portso. I have done the requisite for Capt M, and had aided him at least wrote to my friend to do so above a month ago. The Revd Mr Heath—has been a second Wren to those people.

My two friends who first movd the affair in the Rl Society, will do the necessary business as to the medal for the Governor of Picardy.[1]

No news yet from Ama. but it is generally reported Clintons Southern Expedn. has been renderd abortive on accot of a violent gale wch seperated his fleet & has driven one of the Transports wth Hessians on board to St Ives.[2] A packet is arrd. from

7. XXXI, 548–9. H—— must be William Hodgson, who wrote BF about prisoner relief on the same day as the present letter, below.

8. The numbers Digges gives for the prisoners who sailed on the cartel ship and those remaining in Mill Prison are confirmed by an accounting that Joshua Johnson sent to Samuel Huntington on April 12, 1780: "State of American Prisoners in England," National Archives.

9. Capt. John Manley; see Digges's letter of March 3. He was not exchanged until much later: XXXI, 418–19n.

1. The duc de Croÿ, whom BF had recommended for a medal from the Royal Society for his work on behalf of Capt. Cook: XXXI, 548–9. The friends were William Jones and John Paradise: XXXI, 448.

2. Clinton's expedition of 8,700 troops was hit by a storm while sailing to attack Charleston: XXXI, 420. The damaged transport *Anne* with 200 Hessians aboard found her way to St. Ives in Cornwall: *London Courant, and Westminster Chronicle*, March 6. Most of the vessels were able to reach a rendezvous off Tybee Inlet, Ga., and on Feb. 11 Clinton's army landed on an island south of Charleston: John A. Tilley, *The British Navy and the American Revolution* (Columbia, S.C., 1987), pp. 174–5, 178.

Jama. wh saild 29 Jany. The homeward bound fleet of abot 40
vessels saild from thence the 24th. with a Convoy of abot 2 fifty
gun ships & as many frigates—[3] The treasure taken at Omoa
comes in that fleet. That fort has been retaken by the spaniards
who have lost a man of War bound thither with stores, peircd for
60 Guns but had only 50 mounted.[4] I am yr. very obt Sert

ALEXR. MCKINLOCK

Addressed: A Monsieur / Monsr B. F——n / Passy

Endorsed: Mar 10. 80

From William Hodgson   ALS: American Philosophical Society

Dear Sir   London 10 March 1780
I have to acknowledge the reception of your Letters of the 14
& 26 Ultimo,[5] & also one from Mr Grand with bill enclosed £100
to be applied to the relief of such prisoners as may be in the
greatest distress—[6] The Inclosures by the same conveyance
were forwarded— I am very glad you have taken Notice of Mr
Wren,[7] his Zeal his Activity & Diligence are great beyond your
Conception,— I have & shall consult with Mr Digges about the
distribution of the Money you have remitted & I have desired
Mr Wren to have his Eye upon those particular occasions that
may occur at Forton & require Interposition, keeping from the
prisoners the knowledge of your having sent a Sum of Money,
as I have reason to apprehend the purposes for which it was sent
wou'd be defeated by Publication—every Prisoner wou'd form

3. This convoy's safe arrival was reported in the March 15 issue of the *London Courant, and Westminster Chronicle.*
4. On Oct. 16, 1779, the British captured the rich Spanish port of Omoa, Honduras; they abandoned it on Dec. 28: Mackesy, *War for America*, pp. 275, 335; Mark Mayo Boatner III, *Encyclopedia of the American Revolution* (New York, 1966), pp. 509–10.
5. XXXI, 483–4, 550–2.
6. An entry in BF's Cash Book under March 11 notes that he furnished Hodgson with "another 100£ Sterling for the Assistance of Prisoners."
7. BF had written to the clergyman, who handled relief efforts for Americans confined to Forton Prison, on Feb. 26 (XXXI, 553–4).

one pretention or other & by that Means it wou'd soon be exhausted, in giving these directions as well to Portsmt as Plymo., I hope I meet your Ideas, if otherwise please to signify your pleasure & it shall be mine to Conform— The Agents for our Fund at Plymo are Mess Heath & sawrey both very worthy Zealous Friends—[8] As I presume you see our public prints you will have observed, that we have begun again, to collect Subscriptions,[9] they come in rather slowly, but still we have something in Bank to make a small weekly payment to the prisoners & it is but Justice to the board of Sick & Hurt to assure you that they have allways paid attention to my representations & furnished Clothing (after the failure of our Funds) to such prisoners as were in want— I have been twice with the Board of Sick & Hurt since I last wrote you, the prisoners from Plymo they assure me were embarked & woud sail the first fair Wind— I hope you will assemble all the Men you possibly can to send back by that Vessell. If I might presume to give an Opinion, I wou'd recommend the sending back double the Number & my reason for such an Opinion is this— They have got the Idea that you have not in France a sufficient Number of English prisoners taken by Americans to exchange for those of your people now here & perhaps there may be some objections to sending another Cartel if that supposition shou'd be realized; I suspect from their little Minds every possible Evasion— but if the Prisoners come over & the Credit is given by you, they will not I think, *Dare* to refuse returning an equal Number—& you will be sure not to omit furnishing me with the English officers receipt for the Men taken on board as they almost allways run away before they make their destined port obliging the Master to put them on Shore to avoid being prest—

You have been wrote so fully about the scandalous Conduct of our Ministers in the non-complyance with the paroles from Boston, that it is needless to say more than that their partizans are ashamed for them— As to the receipts given at Sea they

8. For whom see XXXI, 551–2n.

9. Within the last ten days alone the committee for relief of American prisoners had published appeals in, for example, the March 2, 4, 7, and 9 issues of the *London Courant, and Westminster Chronicle*. For Hodgson's participation in the committee see XXXI, 143n.

stand upon different ground & there is something like a reason
when they alledge that the Men thus discharged, were discharged
by the Captors for their own convenience & that perhaps they
wou'd many of them have been retaken if detained either in the
Privateer or her Prizes— Be assured my good sir that if in this
Cause of Humanity any Zeal or Diligence on my part can Avail
neither the one nor the other shall be wanting. I feel as much as
any American in this Struggle, for it has long been a settled principle in my Breast, that English & American Liberty must stand
or fall to gether, If I had room I woud have added a few Words
of our old acquaintance Williams the priest, he has been desired
to absent himself from our Society[1] I am very respectfully Dr sr
your most Obedt Hle Sert   WILLIAM HODGSON

Addressed: A Monsieur / Monsieur Franklin / à / Passy

Notation: William Hodgson London March 10. 1780

From Landais   ALS: American Philosophical Society

Please Your Excellency   Paris March 10, 1780.

I received the letter you did me the Honour of writing to me
The 1st Inst. and the inclosed Certificate, it might have been
upon your table When I was at your house but I d'ont recollect
of having Seen it at all. I must observe that long before that time
I had ask your Excellency for Some money,[2] having Spent what
remained of the 50 Louis d'or I first received for my expenses,
after I had reimboursed my Self of what money I had took of my
own for my Coming to Paris.

I have no officers, on board the frigate Alliance, now under
my Command, nor friends enough for to ask them to take the
trouble to have my trunks &c. delivered to my direction, and be-

---

1. David Williams of the Club of Thirteen (XXI, 119–20) had quarreled
with friends like Hodgson and Thomas Bentley and had been expelled: J. Dy-
bikowski, *On Burning Ground: an Examination of the Ideas, Projects and Life
of David Williams* (Oxford, 1993), pp. 58–60.
2. Landais and BF had twice exchanged letters about additional funds for
the captain: XXXI, 471–2, 474–5, 559–61; BF to Landais, March 1, above.

side they d'ont know, nor my Self at present, what they Contens, all I know is that all the Ship's papers were in them, and I want [won't] make my Self accountable for the Ship Expenses, when I may be deprived of them; besides all my own things may have been plundered, and nothing but the trunks left: but all, Capt. and officers are under your orders and will obey them as Soon as your Excellency will take the trouble to write them to have the Said trunk &c. Sealed up and delivered at the agent at L'Orient, where I expect to go peruse and See weither they are all as I left them (for I have to deal with people which have not the best Character in England according to their papers: I was not so either in England or france before your Excellency, Grand Sun, and nepheu had a false letter from Cap Jones printed, against mine:[3] for my part I d'ont judge in the present Circumstances but will not Confide any more) if your Excellency had wrote to me at Texel that the Command of the frigate was to be taken from me, and given to another, I would have Speared you, and my Self, those troubles; but I came as you directed me Confiding in your justice.

As to the Dutch Money I Received in Holand and Since I am in Paris, I am going to make a Short account of what I have Spent out of it Vizt. To go from The Helder to Amsterdam and once to go back at the helder and traveling through Holland I Spent all the money I had had in that Country (my expenses in Amsterdam included), to travel in Flander and france I Spent nineteen Louis d'or out of my own money, So remain But thirty one of the fifty first Louis dor I first received for my dayly Expenses here, I have been here four month, and Compelled to go to Passy at least twenty times and had a Coach what Expense come about fifteen Louis d'or: now my expense for my Self, a Servant, for living, firing, loging, &c for four month amount to Sixty louis d'or; I find that I have Spent ten Louis dor for other Small expenses So I have now left only Sixty four Louis d'or, out of which I will Spent about twenty five to go where to embark, then

3. Perhaps this is a reference to a letter of Jones in the *Gaz. de Leyde* blaming Landais for the supposed failure of the *Alliance* to aid the *Bonhomme Richard* (XXXI, 149n), but more likely it is a reference to a printing of Jones's Oct. 3, 1779, letter to BF; see XXX, 443n.

it will remain twenty nine louis d'or for my expense while I Shall wait the Ship departure & for my provisions &c! So I beg as a favour, Your Excellency would be So good to tell me what I must do for my Passage if I find one, what I have wrote for; for all I believe it Should be procured me by Your Excellency's order, as it is usual amongst all nations to provide with proper means to have an officer go to be tryed, when accused even if he has been punisched (without proper method taken) before hand, for what he is accused of.

I am Sorry to See Your Excellency Say tis not in his Power to give me a passage for America; I Beg your Excellency to Consider your Power and recollect that by it you had me drawn by your order from the Ship which the Honourable Congress trusted me with, and that you gave it and leave it to my accuser, who is accused him Self by a letter from Capt. Cottineau which you have had into Your hand;[4] Recollect also if you please that I have Shewd you my Commission, and naturalisation, from America, where I then must be Juged:

If your Excellency will not procure me a passage, I must at Least give You my humble thinks for Your advice upon the many vessels You Says are bound to America.

As to my prize money I wish Your Excellency would be So obliging as to lett me know whom I must Aply to for to receive it, that I may reinbourse what money I have Spent, Since I am Come back to Europe. I do'nt imagine Your Excellency would have [me] receive in America in paper money what Come to my Shear, for the Prizes Sold in Europe for hard money, it Should be a poor trade, and I doubt my friends would accept it in return for what money I have drawn upon them. Excuse my error, if you please, but I was told that the Bon homme Richard &c. were belong to Congress, accordingly I imagined that the Congress and crew Shear money was at your Command.

When I have ask'd your Excellency for my monthly pay I thought it just as I have receive none nor any money, not even the postage of letters, since my arrival, and what I have mostly

4. A Nov. 15, 1779, letter and accompanying memoir from the captain of the frigate *Pallas* to Chaumont, which Landais had earlier cited in his justification; see XXX, 443n, 457–8n, 580n; XXXI, 133–4, 380n.

Spent has been when being upon the Ship Duty, but your excellency do'nt judge it proper to grant it.

I Beg as a favour Your excellency would Honour me with an answer as Soon as possible and Sent me by the bearer the reception of this letter.

I am With Respect Your Excellency Most Obedient & most humble Servant   P: LANDAIS

Excellency Bn Franklin Minister Plenypotentiary of the United states of America.

Endorsed: Capt. Landais March 10. 1780 no Friends on board the Alliance

From Richard Bennett Lloyd

ALS: American Philosophical Society

Dear Sir,   London 10th. March 1780

I have had the honour of your two favours dated the 3d. and 26th of last month—[5] I beg you will accept my most sincere thanks for them and be assured I shall ever have a grateful sense of the trouble I have given you—. The Affair which I wish to communicate, is as follows— An American some time ago informed me that he thought it probable that among other complaints your Enemies mean to lay against you is that a Mr. Alexander (said to be an enemy to America) was frequently passing from Paris to London— and that you was upon such a close intimacy with that Gentleman as to give great room for suspicion—[6] I am well convinced of the paltriness of this accusation, shd. it ever be made, and I pity the Person whoever he may be— However I think it but right you should know the above. I pro-

5. XXXI, 441–2, 552.
6. Arthur Lee made accusations of this nature to James Lovell on Jan. 5, 1780 (National Archives), and President of Congress Samuel Huntington on the following Dec. 7 (Wharton, *Diplomatic Correspondence*, IV, 184); he criticized William Alexander more obliquely to JA: *Adams Papers*, VIII, 169. Unknown to BF, his friend Alexander in fact did receive money from the British government: XXVI, 189n.

pose to leave England some time in April and shall be glad to hear you have received this safe—[7] Mrs. Lloyd unites with me in best complts. to yourself & your Grandson— Believe me to be, Dear Sir, with the greatest esteem your obliged obt. humble Servant

RICHARD BTT. LLOYD

Be pleased to make my complts. to Mr. Adams. I wrote to him some months ago,[8] which Letter Mr. Grand promised to deliver—.

Addressed: The Honorable / Benjamin Franklin / &c. &c. &c. / Passy

Notation: LLoyd Richard B. London 10. March 1780.

From Leonard Lafitte[9]

LS: American Philosophical Society

Monsieur   à Bordeaux Le 11e. Mars 1780.

Enhardi par L'accueil honnête et gracieux que vous m'avez fait L'année derniere chez vous, ainsi que vos marques de bonté particuliere, j'ose prendre La liberté de m'adresser à vous à l'occasion d'une Lettre que mon frere Jean Lafitte Cadet et mon associé dans Le Commerce a reçue de Mrs. Jean et Mathias halsted Négociants de La Jersey actuellement rèsidents à Philadelphie, par laquelle ils Lui annoncent L'Envoi de Six Lettres de Change tirées Sur Les Commissionnaires du Congré résidents à Paris dont la notte est ciJointe.[1] Les quelles nous n'avons point reçues quoiqu'on nous Les ait envoyé par Triplicata; C'est pourquoi j'ai L'honneur Monsieur, de vous prier ne Connoissant point à Paris

---

7. This is the last extant communication between BF and Lloyd. On April 7 he wrote WTF that he and his family planned to embark for America in early May; his next two extant letters to WTF, dated Oct. 10, 1781, and July 15, 1782, were written from Annapolis. All three are at the APS.

8. *Adams Papers,* VIII, 306.

9. This Bordeaux merchant and his brother Jean Lafitte cadet had written BF earlier seeking letters of introduction for their nephew: XXXI, 14.

1. An undated document at the APS lists the Continental Loan Office bills of exchange endorsed to John Lafitte cadet: four bills dated Nov. 12, 1778, and two from February, 1779.

des Caissiers du Congré, de vouloir prendre des informations pour raison de ces Lettres de Change et Savoir Si on ne Les auroit point présentées pour en demander le paiement, ce qui ne pourroit être que par des ennemis du Congré qui les auroient trouvées dans les vaisseaux pris. Veuillez Monsieur Je vous Supplie me faire part le plutôt possible de Ce que vous pourrez en apprendre, afin que nous puissions faire réponse à nos amis, prèsumant par les mouvemens actuels que nous ne tarderons point d'avoir de bonnes occasions pour ecrire dans Le Continant.

Mr. Brillon à qui j'avois adressé une petite Relation de La fête donnée par le Commerce de Bordeaux à l'occasion de lheureux retour de Mr. Le Comte D'Estaing,[2] pour vous La Communiquer, m'a appris par Sa Lettre du 24 Janvier dernier que vous etiez retenû chez vous par un gros Rhume; Je Souhaite que vous en Soyez entierement delivré et que vous jouissiez de la meilleure Santé.

J'ai L'honneur d'Etre avec Respect Monsieur Votre très humble & Très obèissant Serviteur   LEONARD L LAFITTE

Oserai-je vous prier, Monsieur, de vouloir faire agréer mes hommages à Monsieur votre petit fils qui Comme vous m'a Comblé dhonnêteté et dont je conserve toujours Le doux Souvenir & La plus Sincere reconnoissance./.

Monsieur francklin

Notations in different hands: Lafitte Bordeaux le 11 Mars 1780 / Ansd. 20 Mar 80

From Landais   ALS: American Philosophical Society

Please Your Excellency   Paris March 11. 1780.

You Called me by your Order from the Commend of the American Frigate Alliance which The Honorable Congress had

2. While d'Estaing's conduct of the siege at Savannah was not considered a success, he was popular among the merchants of the Bordeaux *Chambre de Commerce* who appreciated his efforts to regularize the status of auxiliary officers drawn from merchant ships and now serving on the King's ships: Jacques Michel, *La Vie aventureuse et mouvementée de Charles-Henri, comte d'Estaing* (n.p., 1976), pp. 165, 279–80.

Pierre Landais

Confided the Commend off, to me; upon Some Accusations that none but a Court Martial Can judge, and you have given the Said Commend to my accuser, You have kept me here these four months past I d'ont know what for as it Could be Said in America, t'is my fault if I had not the Same Commend A'gain by not having not ask'd it Should be given me back, may be that it was offered to me; I therefore Beg as a Right Your Excellency Give me the Commend of the Alliance again, or give me your refusal of doing of it in writing from your hand, that I may have it to Show to Congress. I know the Officers and crew of the Alliance wishes for me and hate their present unlawfull Commander.[3]

I Beg as a favour you'll be So good to Send me a positive and Clear answer upon the Subject.

I am with Recpect Your Excellency Most Obedient & most humble Servt   P. LANDAIS

His Excy Bn Franklin Minr Plenipotentiary of the united States of America At Passy

Endorsed: Capt Landais March 11. 1780 demanding to be re-plac'd in the Alliance

To Landais   Copy: Library of Congress

Sir   Passy, March. 12. 1780.

I received this Day the Two Letters you did me the honour of writing to me dated the 10th. and 11th. Instant.

Having already twice answered very clearly and explicitly your demand about your Things, it seems unecessary to say any thing further on that Head. I have written long since to Capt. Jones to deliver them to any Person you may authorise to demand and receive them.[4] If you please you may give that authority to the agent you mention. I have also already often an-

---

3. For corroboration of Landais' statement see the letters of April 12, May 31, and June 7 from the officers of the *Alliance*. Even Jones's sympathetic biographer Samuel Eliot Morison admits that the recent cruise of the ship had not been a happy one, and that Jones's faultfinding and perfectionism made him disliked by many who served with him: Morison, *Jones*, pp. 271–2.

4. He had written Jones on March 1, above.

swered your demand of my procuring for you a Passage to america.

M. de Chaumont having had the Payment of all Expences in
Equipping the Squadron, will I suppose have the Payment of the
Prize Money. None of it will pass thro' my hands.

After the continual Quarrels between you and the People of
the Alliance from the time of your taking the Command of her
at Boston; after the repeated written complaints made to me by
you of the officers,[5] and by the officers of you during all the
Time from your arrival in Europe to your Departure on your last
Cruize; after having acquainted me in Writing with your Resolution not to Continue in the Command with such Officers, and
expressing the Same Disposition in discourse to Mr. Chaumont,
after being as you say 4. Months in Paris in all which time you
never gave the least Instruction of a Wish to return to her, nor
desired any thing of me relating to her but to have your things
out of her it is really surprising to be now told that the officers
and Crew like you for their Captain and that they hate their Present Commander (of whom however they have not made to me
the least Complaint) and to have now for the first time a demand
from you of being replac'd in that ship, made only when you
know she is just on the Point of Sailing. The demand however
may perhaps be made Chiefly for the sake of obtaining a Refusal,
of which you seem more earnestly desirous, as the having it to
produce may be of service to you in America. I will not therefore deny it to you, and It shall be as positive and clear as you require it. No one has ever learnt from me the Opinion I formed
of you from the Enquiry made into your Conduct. I kept it entirely to myself. I have not even hinted it in my letters to America, because I would not hazard giving to any one a Bias to your
Prejudice. By communicating a Part of that Opinion privately
to you It can do you no harm for you may burn it. I should not
give you the pain of reading it, if your Demand did not make
it necessary— I think you then so imprudent, so litigious and
quarrelsome a man even with your Best friends, that Peace and
good order and consequently the quiet and regular subordination so necessary to success are where you preside impossible.

5. *E.g.*, XXIX, 24–6.

These are matters within my observation and comprehension, your military Operations I leave to more capable Judges. If therefore I had 20 ships of War in my Disposition I should not give one of them to Captain Landais, The same Temper which excluded him from the french Marine[6] would weigh equally with me, of course I shall not replace him in the Alliance.

I am Assur'd however that as Captain of a merchant ship you have Two very good Qualities highly useful to your owners— viz Oeconomy and Integrity for these I esteem you, and have the honour to be sir, &c

P.S. I have passed over all the charges made or insinuated against me in your Letters and angry Conversations because I would avoid continuing an altercation for which I have neither Time nor Inclination. You will carry them to america where I must be accountable for my Conduct towards you, and where it will be my Duty If I cannot justify myself, to submit to any Censures I may have merited. Our Correspondence, which cannot be pleasant to either of us, may therefore if you please, end here.

Honble. Capt. Landais.

To J.F. Frin & Co.[7]

Copy: Library of Congress

Gentlemen   Passy, March 13. 1780.

I beg pardon for detaining your Bills so long. It was occasioned by the greatest number we happened then to have upon hand, and the time necessary to examine them all. Yours are now sent to Mr. Grands, accepted as of the Day on which they were presented; excepting the Two drawn in favour of Nath. Terry for 18. Dollars, and nath Brown for 36. Those Gentlemen, cannot regularly be paid by me, unless you will indemnify me in

---

6. Landais later produced evidence he had left the service voluntarily in 1773; it is part of a point-by-point rebuttal to this letter published in Landais, *Memorial*, pp. 93–6. A sketch of Landais' service in the French Navy appears in Six, *Dictionnaire biographique*.

7. In answer to theirs of March 9, above.

Case of any future Demand.[8] I have the honour to be, with respect, Gentlemen, Your most obedient and most humble servant

BF.

Messrs. J. J. Frin and Compe.

From William Carmichael

Copy: Library of Congress

Dear Sir, Madrid 13 March 1780.

I did myself the Honor of writing to you from Cadiz and since by M. Girard and therefore shall not repeat the information which those Letters and that Gentleman will have given you;[9] on the 25th. of last month I transmitted to Mr. Jay the King's Determination which was communicated to me by his Excellency the Count de florida Blanca & to himself in a Letter from the above mentioned minister;[1] the manner in which the Communication was made was very polite and I was informed that altho' it did not suit the King Dignity or that of Congress, that M. Jay should appear in his public Character until the object of his Mission & the Interests of Spain had been fairly discussed and decided on, yet that we should be received and treated as Strangers of Distinction and as such might appear at Court, Accordingly I have made use of that Permission and was present at the basamanos on Occasion of the Birth of the Prince[2] & ranged myself in the Circle of foreighn Ministers. I have seen nothing but what appears to be reasonable in the Conduct of the Minister with whom I have had the Honor to converse, yet I cannot help laminting every Circumstance which retards the Business on

8. Two days later they wrote to acknowledge receipt of the accepted bills from Grand and to assure BF that both they and Daniel Crommelin et fils would guarantee the two bills not endorsed. APS.

9. XXXI, 406–8, 502–3.

1. For Chief Minister Floridablanca's letter to Jay see XXXI, 502n. Carmichael's covering letter is printed in Morris, *Jay: Revolutionary*, pp. 742–3.

2. Prince Carlos (who had some twenty other names) was born on March 5: *Courier de l'Europe*, VII (1780), 211. He was the son of the Prince and Princess of Asturias and grandson of the king. For the "kissing of hands" on the occasion of his birth see the *Gaz. de Leyde* of March 24 (no. XXIV), sup. Like most of the couple's many children he did not survive to adulthood.

which we are sent. This is the Present State of affairs here on which I intreat your advice, in order that I may communicate it to M. Jay as early as Possible, I must also intreat you to give me such Information of the Situation of Affairs in your Department as may be necessary for us to know. I am informed that Considerable Perparations are making for an Expedition to the West Indies or America or both from Spain,[3] my mode of conveyance doth not allow me to enter into particulars, of which I have however had an Opportunity of advising Congress, I do not know where or how to address M. Adams or otherwise I should do myself the Honor of writing to him, both from a Principle of Duty and Inclination. Altho' it is not my good fortune to be immediately under your Direction, I flatter myself that you will add one other obligation to the many already conferred on me, by honoring me with your Advice while I remain here, I beg you to mention me in the proper manner to Monr. Gerard and to others who think well of me and to believe me with much respect. Your Obliged & most humble Servant

(signed) WM. CARMICHAEL.

P.S. As I know you will have the safest Opportunity of Writing to America *Shortly* in case my Letters to Congress may miscarry you may not think it improper to communicate the Contents of this Letter.

his Excellency Benjn. franklin Esqr.

From Dumas

ALS: American Philosophical Society; AL (draft): Algemeen Rijksarchief

Monsieur,   La Haie 13e. Mars 1780
     Le certificat dont il est question dans ma Lettre ci-jointe à Mr. le gd. Pre. d'Hollde. est celui dont je vous envoyai copie en son

3. The Spanish government planned to send 8,000 to 10,000 troops and twelve to fourteen ships of the line to the West Indies: Dull, *French Navy*, pp. 179–80.

temps de la part de Mr. Jones. Ainsi il est superflu d'en joindre
ici une autre.[4]

Hier il arriva un Exprès d'Angleterre, avec la nouvelle que
les cargaisons des navires Hollandois chargés de chanvre &
goudron & autres provisions navales de cette espece, escortés
par le Contre Amiral de Byland, & saisis par les Anglois sous
Fielding,[5] ont été déclarés de bonne prise, & confisqués par conséquent en Angleterre & qu'on délibere encore Si [*torn:* les
vai]sseaux mêmes ne seront pas aussi confisqués.[6] Voilà donc à
la fois la piraterie & l'insulte complete.

D'un autre côté, Mr. Swart Résident de la Rep. à Petersbourg
vient d'écrire à L.H.P. une Dépêche, qui fut lue hier à l'Assemblée & trouvée si intéressante, qu'on l'a faite Commissoriale,
pour délibérer sur le contenu, qui apprend à L.H.P., que la Cour
de Petersbourg voit avec indignation les excès que les Anglois
commettent sur mer, ceux en particulier qu'ils se sont permis
dernierement contre une flotte Hollandoise en violant mani-
festement le Droit des gens, & les mensonges qu'ils débitent partout, comme si la Russie étoit portée pour eux; tandis que le contraire est vrai, & que Sa Maj. Russe non seulement désapprouve
hautement leur conduite, mais est disposée & inclinée de plus à
entrer avec tous les neutres dans les mesures les plus propres à
rendre les mers plus sures, & la navigation commune à tous plus
respectée.[7]

4. On March 11 Dumas sent Grand Pensionary van Bleiswijk a copy of
Jones's Nov. 15, 1779, certificate concerning the pilot John Jackson; he here
enclosed one of his covering letters. (He also sent Jones a copy: Bradford,
Jones Papers, reel 5, no. 1012.) Dumas had already sent BF a copy of the certificate itself: XXXI, 253. For the accusation that he was answering see his April
11 letter to BF, below.

5. For the seizure of the Dutch ships on Dec. 31, 1779, see XXXI, 369n.

6. The British Admiralty decided on March 4 and 6 to confiscate some of
the ships but not others depending on the cargo they had carried: Edler,
Dutch Republic, pp. 131–2; *Gaz. de Leyde*, March 14, 1780 (no. XXI), sup.

7. Johan Isaac de Swart served in St. Petersburg in 1764–65 and from 1773
to 1794: *Repertorium der diplomatischen Vertreter*, III, 268; Isabel de Madariaga, *Britain, Russia, and the Armed Neutrality of 1780: Sir James Harris's
Mission to St. Petersburg during the American Revolution* (New Haven, 1962),
pp. 192–3n. On Feb. 15 he wrote the secretary of the States General of the
Netherlands ("Leurs Hautes Puissances") that the British seizure of Bylandt's convoy had caused great astonishment and was generally regarded as

Je tiens tout cela de notre Ami: ainsi, Monsieur vous pouvez compter dessus.

Ceci, & l'entretien du St. avec le Pce. de Gallitzin Envoyé de Russie, & le Courier dépêché à Petersbourg en conséquence, nous promet quelque changement de scene important; mais, dit notre Ami, 873. OEUP ZQMBEXCGTNU,[8] fait ici tout ce qu'il peut (& il peut beaucoup) pour soutenir ici les Anglomanes; sans lui qui retient le St———, & lui fait faire triste figure, on auroit déjà pris des mesures vigoureuses.

Je suis avec tout l'attachement respectueux que vous connoissez, Monsieur Votre très humble & très-obéissant serviteur

DUMAS

Paris à Son Exce. Mr. Franklin,

Mr. Carmichael m'a écrit le 25 Janvr. dernier de Cadix, avoir remis un paquet pour moi à Mr. Gerard. Je ne l'ai pas encore reçu. Si Mr. Gerard est à Paris, voudriez-vous bien avoir la bonté, Monsieur, de lui faire demander les papiers qu'il peut avoir pour moi?

Addressed: à Son Excellence / Monsieur B. Franklin Esqr. / Min. Plenipe. des Etats-Unis / &c. / Passy./.

Notation: Dumas, la haie March 13. 80

From John Paul Jones

ALS: American Philosophical Society; AL (draft) and transcript: National Archives

Honored and dear Sir,   L'Orient March 13th, 1780.

I am honored with your letter of the 8th.— I hope to send

entirely derogatory both to the treaty obligations and the right of nations: Fauchille, *Diplomatie française*, pp. 319–20. Soon thereafter Empress Catherine II invited the Dutch and others to help her protect neutral shipping rights; see our annotation of Dumas' letter of March 2.

8. "The Duke of Brunswick." Louis, Duke of Brunswick-Wolfenbüttel (1718–1788), an advocate of good relations with Britain, was one of the stadholder's chief advisors: *NNBW*, x, 155–7; Schulte Nordholt, *Dutch Republic*, p. 15.

on board some of the Cannon tomorrow.— As we have no Assistance from the Port our repairs do not advance as fast as I could wish: In making the new Sails we are much at a loss for hands.—[9]

Mr: Lee arrived here the Evening before last, and Mr: Lockyer presented me your letter of introduction of the 2d. this morning.[1] As far as depends on me I hope both the Gentlemen will be satisfied.— Doctor Bancroft has not yet appeared here, and the hourly expectation he has given me of seeing him has prevented me from acknowledging the honor done me by your Letter of the 1st: in Course of Post.— The Minister need not doubt of my willingness to oblige his Majesty and this Nation.— I shall yet perhaps have Opportunities of proving this after the Credit of the Cabal has passed its Meridian? I shall do my best to make the passage agreeable to Captn: Hutchings and Mr. Brown.—[2]

Captain Landais things were never entrusted to my Care.— I understand they were left with Mr: Blodget the purser who will have my Orders to deliver them.

I am ever with the highest and most affectionate Esteem Your Excellencies most Obliged and most hum Servt: JNO P JONES

His Excellency B. Franklin Esqr:

Notation: J.P. Jones L'orient, Mar. 13. 80

From M. Pulawski[3]   ALS: American Philosophical Society

Monsieur   à Varsovie le 13 de Mars 1780.

Sans avoir l'honneur de connoitre personnellement Votre Excellence mais plein de confiance en la bonté de son cœur, que je

9. For a daily record of the work aboard the *Alliance* in March see John S. Barnes, ed., *The Logs of the Serapis-Alliance-Ariel under the Command of John Paul Jones 1779–1780* (New York, 1911), pp. 71–7.

1. BF had also recommended him in his letter of the 1st, above.

2. Capt. Thomas Hutchins and Joseph Brown, Jr.

3. Although the writer calls Casimir Pulaski "mon frere" he does not seem to resemble the late American general's only surviving brother, Antoni (1747–1813) for whom see the *Polski Slownik Biograficzny* (33 vols. to date, Warsaw and elsewhere, 1935–).

connois de réputation, j'ose m'adresser à elle dans une affaire, qui n'interesse pas moins ma Famille, que le peuple généreux dont Vous étes le digne Representant en Europe.

Casimir Pulawski mon Frere, après avoir constamment lutté contre les ennemis de la liberté de notre commune Patrie,[4] et avoir été contraint de ceder enfin a la force réunie de nos Puissances Voisines, crût devoir chercher hors de son païs la liberté, dont il étoit si jaloux, et qu'il venoit de perdre; il la trouva chez vos vaillants Compatriotes, il l'embrassa, lui consacra son bras, et son épée, et s'il en faut croire les bruits publics, il ne l'a pas mal servie, je lui en sçai bon gré, je voudrois être à meme de le remplacer, ne fut-ce que par reconnoissance vis-à-vis d'une Nation, qui l'a si bien acceuilli.

Aujourd'hui j'ai la douleur d'apprendre, qu'il n'est plus, j'en serois inconsolable, si la malheureuse affaire de Sawanach, qui a terminé sa carriere,[5] n'avoit mis le comble à sa gloire. Sans doute qu'en mourant, il n'a eu d'autre regret, que celui de ne pouvoir contribuer plus long-tems aux succés, & au bonheur d'un peuple aussi valeureux. Mais comme les nouvelles publiques n'annoncent pas toujours la verité, voudriez Vous bien Excellence, prendre [*la peine*] de m'informer du fait, et au cas qu'il soit tel, qu'on le debite, de me marquer si notre Famille peut espérez quelque chose de sa succession, et quels moyens il faudrait employer pour réaliser nos prétensions; elles ne sont pas sans fondement, il nous écrivoit un jour, que la Fortune secondant toujours mieux son zele dans ses entreprises formées pour la gloire des Americains généreux dont il éprouvoit les faveurs, il se trouveroit en état ou durant sa vie, ou aprés sa morte de contribuer à relever notre famille abbatue dans les dernieres revolutions de notre patrie. Si Vous daignez Monsieur satisfaire à ma demande, comme je l'espere fondé sur vos généreux sentimens d'équité, et d'humanité, Vous acquerrez des droits à ma reconnoissance, et

---

4. Pulaski, his father, and his brothers were leaders in the 1768–72 Confederation of Bar, the Polish uprising against Russian domination: Wladyslaw Konopczynski, *Kazimierz Pulaski* (Krakow, 1931).

5. Pulaski was mortally wounded during d'Estaing's Oct. 9, 1779, assault on the British lines at Savannah and died two days later: Leszck Szymanski, *Casimir Pulaski: a Hero of the American Revolution* (New York, 1994), pp. 273–7.

à celle de toute notre famille, mais Vous n'ajouterez rien aux sentimens de respect, et d'éstime, que nous avons deja pour Votre Excellence, et avec les quels j'ai l'honneur Monsieur de Votre Excellence le très humble, et très obeissant serviteur

M. PULAWSKI JUN.
Staroste de Warka. En masovie.

From the Comte d'Estaing   AL: American Philosophical Society

Paris ce 14. Mars 1780.

Les occasions de faire sa cour á Monsieur franklin, et de profiter de ses bontés, sont trop precieuses a M d'Estaing pour en perdre aucune; il a l'honneur de l'assurer de son respect, et qu'il rede-viendra demain avec grand plaisir Citoyen de Passy[6] pour diner avec lui.

Notation: M. D'Estaing Paris ce 14. mars. 1780.

From Henri-Maximilien (Henry) Grand

ALS: American Philosophical Society

Monsieur   Paris ce 14 Mars 1780

Le désir bien vif que j'ay d'aller au devant de tout ce qui peut vous être agréable, m'a fait prendre en considération les moyens qu'il y auroit d'applanir les Obstacles qui se présentent pour vous empecher d'eprouver dans cette partie qui vous regarde personellement, de la Gestion des Fonds du Public, la même satisfaction qui resulte pour vous de pouvoir compasser, & vous rendre raison à chaque instant de vos autres Operations; comme celle ci n'est malheureusement pas entierement votre Ouvrage, elle ne scauroit avoir les memes agrémens.[7]

---

6. Since returning from his unsuccessful attack on Savannah (XXXI, 65n), the admiral had been recuperating from his wounds at his country house at Passy: Jacques Michel, *La vie aventureuse et mouvementée de Charles-Henri Comte d'Estaing* (n.p., 1976), pp. 237, 247–8. He seems to have known BF since before the American moved to Passy: XXIII, 67.

7. Henry Grand must have been given the task of reviewing BF's accounts in advance of Johnson's audit (see XXXI, 564–5.) The style of this paragraph

Il s'agiroit d'extraire de cette gestion touttes les Opérations où vous avez participé: mais come ouvrage épisodique, comme partie dont les raports sont engagés d'une maniere particuliere avec celle qui a precedé; la chose est, je crois, impraticable.

Il y avoit à vôtre arrivée plusieurs comptes de Fournisseurs de commencés; plusieurs marchandises d'expédiées, plusieurs payements de faits; & les Mandats que vous signates alors, soit individuellement ou conjointement, en faveur de ces Fournisseurs, ne servoient pas à acquitter uniquement de nouvelles Fournitures, mais étoient le rembours des précédentes, en tout, ou en partie; ce qui vous lie par là avec touttes les operations qui ont pu précéder, & qui s'enchainent de cette maniere les unes dans les autres.

Ce n'est donc que par la Reddition du compte général que vous pouvez opérer votre décharge particuliere, ce qui ne dependra pas de mes Soins & de mon assiduité d'accelerer; l'arrivée de Mr. Dean abrégeroit de beaucoup ma tâche, & cette raison de retardement peut servir pour engager Mr. Johnson à differer son voyage a Paris.

Je suis avec Respect Monsieur Vôtre très humble et très obeisst. Servr.   Hy. Grand

Monsieur votre petit Fils voudra bien me faire scavoir par la Petite Poste si je dois neanmoins me rendre a Passy jeudi.

Addressed: a Monsieur / Monsieur Le Docteur / Franklin / Passy

Notations: H. Grand 14 mar 1780 / H Grand

---

reflects the embarrassment in which the young man found himself. We think he means that he would like to help BF disentangle his individual accounts from those in conjunction with others (*i.e.*, Deane).

From John Paul Jones: Two Letters

(I) ALS: American Philosophical Society; AL (draft): Library of Congress; (II) ALS: New Hampshire Historical Society

I.

Honored and dear Sir   L'Orient March 14th. 1780

Inclosed is a Copy of the Only Bill of Ransom with which I have ever been concerned.[8] I have this day given Mr. Dryburugh a letter for you and I believe he embarks this Evening in the dilligence for Paris.— That Poor Man was of Singular Use to me as a Pilot on the British Coast and always gave me due advice of whatever he knew respecting the Enemies Situation.— I had no other motive for Ransoming his Vessel but Compassion for his helpless Family and to give him the Money as a reward for his Zeal and faithful Services.— He has given his Obligation to pay a part of it to another Man who acted as Pilot on board the Pallas. I hope your Excellency will not disapprove of my having given him such expectation; for I considered his Vessel only as an incumbrance and had given directions to Sink her.

Mr. Ross writes me the 12th.[9] proposing that I should go to Noirmoutier[1] to take on board the Alliance the 120 Bales of Public Stores, but I fear there is not Sufficient Water nor Safety before that Island. I hope however that an American Vessel may be found to bring them to the Alliance at Groa.— If I find that Ross's proposal can be Adopted with Safety I shall for my Own Part have no Objection.

Dr. Bancroft is not yet appeared here. Some Americans are

---

8. Dated Sept. 17, 1779, and in L'Air de Lamotte's hand, it is signed by Robert Drybrough of "West Weemyss North britain" and Andrew Robertson, who replaced him as master of his ship, the *Friendship* (which Jones had captured three days earlier). As ransom, Drybrough (whose name is spelled in the bill of ransom as Jones does here) promises to remit within 60 days at BF's residence at Passy £200 to Jones's order. In guarantee of the payment he agrees to serve as a hostage. Jones has made a notation on the document that the bill should be paid to Gourlade & Moylan for BF's use. APS. The *Friendship* was a collier from the Scottish port of Kirkcaldy: Morison, *Jones,* p. 216.

9. Bradford, *Jones Papers,* reel 5, no. 1013.

1. The island of Noirmoutier, off the mouth of the Loire.

this moment arrived from England, having been landed by the Cartel at Morlaix.[2]

With the highest esteem, I am Your Excellencies most Obliged and most humble Servant   JNO P JONES

His Excellency B. Franklin Esqr. &c &c.

Notation: J.P. Jones L'orient Marh. 14. 80

II.

L'Orient March 14th. 1780

Mr. Robert Dryburugh will have the honor to present this letter to your Excellency. He rendered me very Essential Services in the Firth of Edinburgh and on the East Coast of England by his knowlidge of that Navigation.— It was my intention to have Sunk the Small Coal Ship of Which he was Master and part Owner; but in consideration of his faithful Services and advices I at last accepted of his Bill of Ransom for two hundred pounds Sterling meaning to assign it over to him as a recompence.

Your Excellency will I hope approve of the measure, especially as the poor Man has a large and helpless Family.— I have the honor to be with profound respect Your Excellencies most humble Servant   JNO P JONES

His Excellency B. Franklin Esqr. &c &c.

From the Chevalier de Kéralio

ALS: American Philosophical Society

Monsieur.   à L'Ecole Rle. mre.[3] Le 14e. mars, 1780.

En ma qualité de Secretaire intime de notre céleste amie,[4] j'ai l'honneur de vous rappeller de sa part la promesse que vous Lui avés faite de Lui procurer pour ses enfants[5] des Lettres de crédit

2. The first news sent BF of the arrival of the prisoners from Mill Prison.

3. The Ecole Royale Militaire, at which Kéralio was subinspector: XXV, 413n.

4. The duchesse de Deux-Ponts: *ibid.*

5. Her sons Christian and Guillaume, soon to leave for America with Rochambeau: XXVIII, 539n.

sur la nouvelle angleterre. Dans ce cas elle desireroit une Lettre de 24,000 *l.t.* pour chacun d'eux; elle en a déja Sur Les isles; mais ou je suis bien trompé, ou L'Escadre de Brest n'ira point dans ces parages.

Notre bonne amie vous prie encore, Monsieur, de lui assigner un jour pour venir diner avec elle.

J'ai eu aujourd'hui des nouvelles de Brest en date du 8e. On a ajouté à L'Escadre *Le césar* de 74 et *L'ardent* de 64; il ÿ a eu aussi ordre d'armer plusieurs fluttes de la marine royale qui valent mieux que des batiments de transport.[6]

Une Lettre de cadix du 17e fev. dit qu'il falloit encore 7 à 8 jours aux Espagnols, avant de pouvoir sortir. *Festinant lenté.*[7]

Rendés toujours justice, je vous en supplie, à la Tendre Vénération avec laquelle je suis, Monsieur Votre très humble et très obéissant serviteur.   LE CHR. DE KERALIO

Notation: Keralio—Mars 14.80

From the Comte de Vergennes   Copy: Library of Congress

Versailles le 14 mars 1780.

J'ai l'honneur de vous envoyer, Monsieur, une Lettre qui a été écrite à M. Amelot Secretaire d'Etat par M. de Blossac Intendant du Poitou, au sujet du Sr. William Campbell qui demande la permission de resider a Poitiers;[8] Les details que donne M. de Blossac sur ce qui regarde cet étranger et les Certificats joints à la Let-

---

6. The *Ardent*, but not the *César*, sailed with Ternay to Rhode Island: Dull, *French Navy*, pp. 366–7. His convoy included two *flûtes* (armed transports): Rice and Brown, eds., *Rochambeau's Army*, I, 117, 118n.

7. The Spanish fleet did not sail from Cadiz for months; see our annotation of the intelligence from Paris provided by Kéralio, March 7. The Latinized Greek proverb can be translated as "Make haste slowly." See also JW to BF, March 7.

8. Secretary of State for Household Affairs Amelot had oversight of certain provinces and *généralités*, including Poitou: *Almanach Royal* for 1780, pp. 200–1. Paul-Esprit-Marie de La Bourdonnaye de Blossac was intendant for Poitou from 1751 to 1784: Vivian R. Gruder, *The Royal Provincial Intendants: a Governing Elite in Eighteenth-Century France* (Ithaca, 1968), p. 249.

tre, me portent a croire de même que lui, qu'il ne sauroit y avoir d'inconvenient a accorder cette Permission; Je n'ai cependant pas voulu répondre à la demande, sans savoir ce que vous en pensez; Comme le dit S. William, Campbell, Irlandois de Nation, se dit attaché aux Etats Unis de l'Amerique, qu'il a obtenu le droit de bourgeoisie à New York ainsi qu'il le justifie et que dans ces derniers tems il a fait un domicile d'environ deux ans à Paris où vous vous avez peut-être eu Occasion de le connoitre, Je vous prie en ce cas de me marquer ce que vous pensez de son personnel et de l'objet de sa demande et de me renvoyer les Pieces cy-jointes, pour me mettre en état de repondre a M. Amelot.

J'ai l'honneur d'être tres parfaitement, Monsieur, votre très humble et très obeissant Serviteur.   (signé) DE VERGENNES

M. Franklin.

To Thomas Digges
Copy: Library of Congress

Dear sir,   Passy, March. 15. 1780.

In compliance with your Recommendation, which I very much respect, I have given the Passports desired by Captains Mitchel and Carpenter.[9] All these Businesses give me trouble for which I charge nothing; I hope there fore that the Gentlemen will in return do some thing on my Recommendation, and that is, to

9. Digges recommended the two men in his letter of March 3, above. Benjamin Carpenter's passport, in WTF's hand and signed by BF, is at the Mass. Archives. Dated March 14, it describes him as having purchased the *Adventure*, a 160-ton brigantine, to carry to the U.S. a cargo of coarse woolens, canvas, cordage, etc. At the same repository is Digges's May 10 certification that, contrary to what is stated on the passport, the *Adventure* was principally the property of Henry Mitchell (see XXXI, 365n). Henry Mitchell's passport, drafted by WTF and dated March 14, is at the APS. It states that Mitchell has purchased the ship *James* of about 200 tons to transport to America coarse woolens, canvas, cordage, etc. Mitchell's passport also served, with the particulars of names and places revised, as a draft of a Dec. 4, 1780, one for Capt. Benj. Joy of the brigantine *Swallow*. Also at the APS are a March 14 bond executed by Carpenter for £2,000 and his March 15 oath of allegiance to the U.S. sworn before BF and attested by him.

let me see their Names in the list of Subscribers for the Relief of their poor Countrymen Prisoners in England.

Please to acquaint Mr. Hartley that I have received his favour and shall answer in a few Days.— The Cartel expected is not yet arrived; I have already written that the English to exchange will be at Morlaix.— I can now only add, that I am ever, with much Esteem, Dear sir, y. m. o. h. Servant

Mr. Digges.

To the Eastern Navy Board

Copy: Library of Congress

Gentlemen,   Passy 15. Mar. 1780

I acquainted you in a former Letter, that there were great Misunderstandings between Capt. Landais and the other Officers of his ship.[1] These Differences arose to such a Height, that the Captain once wrote me, he would quit the Command rather than continue with them.[2] Some of them leaving the Ship, that Disturbance Seem'd to be quieted. But there has Since arisen another violent Quarell between him and Captain Jones.— These Things give me great trouble, particularly the latter, the Circumstances of which I am under a Necessity of Communicating to you that Measures may be taken for putting properly an End to it by a Court martial, If you find that step necessary.

Soon after the arrival of our little Squadron in the Texel, I had a Letter from Commodore Jones complaining highly of Capt. Landais, and mentioning that he was advised to put him under Arrest in order to his trial by a Court Martial (for which however there was not a sufficient number of Officers in Europe) but he would do nothing in it till he heard from me,[3] I had another from Captain Landais complaining of Come. Jones, and begging me to order Enquiry into the Matter as soon as Possible.[4] I

1. BF had so informed the committee for foreign affairs (XXIX, 549–50), but we have no record of a similar notification to the Eastern Navy Board, which had dispatched the *Alliance* to France (XXVIII, 255–6).
2. XXIX, 497–8.
3. XXX, 461.
4. XXX, 507–8.

received also a letter from the Minister of the Marine, of which the following is an Extract, viz.

Je suis persuadé, Monsieur, que vous n'aurez pas été moins touché que moi de la perte du grand nombre de volontaires françois qui ont été tués dan le combat du Bonhomme Richard contre le vaisseau de Guerre Anglois la Serapis. Cet evenement est d'autant plus facheux, qu'il paroit que si la fregate americaine L'alliance avoit secondé le Bonhomme Richard, en combatant en même tems, l'avantage remporté par le Commodore Jones auroit été plus prompt, auroit couté moins de monde et n'auroit pas mis le Bonhomme Richard dans le cas de couler bas trente six heures après le combat. Le Capitaine de cette fregate ayant tenu une conduite très extraordinaire, je ne doute pas, Monsieur, que vous ne lui mandiez de se rendre aupres de vous pour en rendre compte, et que dans le cas où vous reconnoitrez que c'est par sa faute que la Victoire a couté tant de sang, vous ne jugiez à propos d'en informer le Congress, a fin qu'il fasse rayer Ce Capitaine de dessus la liste des Officiers de sa marine. &c.[5]

Upon this, & with the advice of a very respectable friend of Capt. Landais Mr. De Chaumont who thought sending for him to come to Paris in order to [*hold*] an Enquiry in to his Conduct, would prevent many inconveniencies to the Service that might attend a more public Discussion. I wrote to him, Oct. 15. acquainting him with the principal heads of the Charges against him, and directing him to render himself here, bringing with him such Papers and Testimonies as he might think useful in his justification.[6] I wrote at the same time to Comme. Jones, to send up such Proofs as he might have in support of the Charges against the Captain, that I might be enabled to give a Just account of the affair to Congress.[7] In two or three Weeks, Capt. Landais came to Paris, but I received no Answer from Come. Jones; After waiting some Days, I concluded to hear Capt. Landais on the 15 of November without longer Delay. And that the Impartiality of the Enquiry might be more clear I requested the above named a friend of Capt. Landais, and Dr. Bancroft a friend of Comme. Jones, to be present.

5. xxx, 535.
6. xxx, 539–40.
7. xxx, 537–8.

With this I send the Minutes that were taken on that Occasion.[8]

The Justification Capt. Landais offers in Answer to the Charge of Disobedience of the Commodore's Orders, seems to call on me for an Explanation as what relates to these I had given Capt. Landais. The Armament was made at l'Orient. Mr. De Chaumont was present there and had the Care of it. I was necessarily at a great Distance, and could not be consulted on every Occasion, and I was not on the following. A convoy being wanted for some Merchant ships to Bordeaux, and our Squadron being ready and there being time sufficient, it was employ'd in and performed that Occasional service. The Alliance and Bonhomme Richard afterwards at sea, ran foul of each other in the Night, the latter receiv'd great Damages, and all returned to L'Orient.[9] The state of the Crew as well as that of the ship making it at first doubtful whether the Bonhomme Richard, might not be long detained in Port, I was apply'd to for the Conditional Order I gave on the 28th. of July to Capt. Landais.—[1] I could not foresee that he would think a Cruise, for which he was to take on Board six Months provisions, and during which he was to be under the orders of comme. Jones, was accomplish'd by the little trip to Bordeaux and the Return abovemention'd and that he was therefore no longer under those Orders,[2] Nor could I imagine that a Conditional order for cruising alone, in case the Bonhomme would not be ready in time, would if She was ready and they sail'd together be construed in to an Exemption from that subordination, in a Squadron, which regular Discipline and the Good of the service requires, otherwise, I should certainly have removed those misapprehensions, by fresh and very explicit Orders. How far Capt. Landais is justifiable in those Interpretations and his Consequent Conduct, must be left to his proper Judges.

The absence of Commodore Jones, and of all the Witnesses, so that none of them could be cross-examin'd, have made this Inquiry very imperfect. You will perceive that Contradictions

8. XXXI, 105–12.
9. XXIX, 617n, 709n.
1. XXX, 154–5.
2. Landais' original orders are printed in XXIX, 388.

appear in the Evidence on both sides in some very material Points. Those with my Ignorance in the manoeuvring of Ships engag'd and their possible operations under all the Variety of Circumstances that wind, Tide, and Situation afford, make it as impracticable for me to form, as it would be improper for me without authority to give, a Judgment in this affair. I will only take the liberty of Saying in favour of Capt. Landais that, notwithstanding the mortal Quarrel that arose betwen them at sea, it does not appear to me at all probable he fired into the Bonhomme Richard with Design to kill Capt. Jones. The Enquiry tho' imperfect, and the Length of it, have however had one good Effect, in preventing hitherto a Duel betwen the Parties, that would have given much Scandal;[3] and which I believe will now not take place, as both expect Justice from a Court Martial in america, I have the honour to be, Gentlemen &c.

Honble. the Navy Board for the Eastern departmt.

To Conrad-Alexandre Gérard

Copy: Library of Congress

Dear Sir,   Passy, Mar. 15. 1780.

I congratulate you most Sincerely on your safe arrival after so many fatigues and Perils and on your happy Meeting with your family and friends.[4] I long to embrace and Welcome you in Person but have been prevented, partly by an unwillingness to intrude on Those first hours, which you might wish to Spend with your nearer Connections, and Partly by Accidental Business. Please to let me know by a line when you can see me with the least Inconvenience. I am ever with the sincerest Esteem and Respect, Dear Sir, y. m. O. & m. h. S.

Mr. Gerard

3. During the cruise itself Landais had challenged Jones to a duel when they returned to port. He challenged him again in an Amsterdam tavern: XXX, 445n, 507n.

4. Gérard arrived at Versailles on the 15th and Vergennes presented him to the King: *Gaz. de Leyde*, March 24, 1780 (no. XXIV). His trip from Cadiz took so long because he stopped in Madrid for several days: Meng, *Despatches of Gérard*, pp. 905–7.

To Joseph-Mathias Gérard de Rayneval

Copy: Library of Congress

Sir,   Passy, March 15. 1780.

I thank you for your Care in sending my Packet which I received. I congratulate you most cordially on the safe return of your good Brother. The American News papers will give you the honourable Sentiments & Testimonies of Public Bodies with regard to him; inclos'd I send you those of my friends and Correspondents which I have extracted from their Private Letters to me imagining they might afford you some Pleasure.[5] With great Esteem I have the honour to be, Sir &c.

Mr. De Renneval,

To Vergennes

Copy: Library of Congress

Sir   Passy, March 15. 1780

I received the Letter your Excellency did me the honour of writing to me yesterday, & have perused the Papers inclosed with it relating to William Campbell. They are undoubtedly genuine Papers, but I know nothing more of the Person, having never seen him, or heard any thing of him during his residence in Paris that I can recollect. I return the Papers, and am, with the greatest Respect. Your Excellency's most obdt. and most humble servant

Mr. De Vergenes.

From Samuel Cooper

ALS: American Philosophical Society

My dear Sir,   Boston March 15th. 1780.

As it is uncertain when this Letter will be delivered to you, or whether it will ever reach you, and as I write you more directly

---

5. We have not located the extracts praising Gérard de Rayneval's brother, Conrad-Alexandre Gérard. It is likely, however, that they included comments by RB, Robert Morris, John Jay, and possibly Cyrus Griffin: xxx, 366, 372, 402–3, 421.

by a Vessel just going to Bilboa,[6] I shall now only mention, That the Desire of my Countrymen of good Families who go abroad is so ardent to have the Honour of an Introduction to you, that I often find it irresistable. Your Benevolence I know will lead you to indulge such a Desire, not only as it flows in a good Measure, from that uncommon Respect for your personal and public Character with which They are impressed, but may also serve to promote some valuable national Purposes.

Mr. Appleton to whom I give this Letter[7] is the Son of Nathaniel Appleton Esqr of this Town, Director of the Continental Loan Office in this Place, and highly esteemed among us for his public and private Virtues. The Son is no Dishonour to his Family, and few young Gentlemen here have established a Character equally amiable. I hope his Behavior abroad will answer the Expectations of his Friends.

With every Sentiment of Respect & Affection, I am Sir, Your obedient humble Servant   SAMUEL COOPER.

His Excellency B. Franklin Esqr.

Addressed: His Excellency Benj: Franklin Esqr / Minister Plenipotentiary from the / States of America / at the Court of / Versailles.

Notation: Dr. Cooper Mar 15 1780

From Thomas Digges   ALS: Historical Society of Pennsylvania

Dr Sir   London 15 Mar. 1780

I expect this will be handed to you, in the course of a few weeks, by a particular Friend of mine, Mr Willm Burn of the house of Messieurs Burn & sons of Lisbon:[8] He is the Gentle-

6. Cooper's other letter is missing.

7. John Appleton (1758–1829) came to Europe for business reasons: *Adams Correspondence,* III, 390n.

8. Founded in or before 1764 as Edward Burne & Son, the firm had done business earlier in the war with the secret committee of Congress: David R. Chesnutt *et al.,* eds., *The Papers of Henry Laurens* (14 vols. to date, Columbia, S.C., 1968–), IV, 220n; Elizabeth M. Nuxoll, *Congress and the Munitions*

man, whom in two late letters[9] I solicited the favour of You to procure a Passport for (to be sent under cover to Messrs. Freres Aubert Tollot & Co. Turin) that would enable Him to travel in France & stay a short time in Paris; which place He is desirous of seeing before He finishes a Tour He has been some months upon.

As I have mentiond Mr Burn to You in my former letters, I need only at present recommend Him to your usual civility and attention. You will find Him a good friend to the Liberties of mankind in general, & a Well-wisher to the cause of America;— In some instances He has been servicable to that Country, and in a particular manner friendly to those Citizens of it, who have accidentally visited Lisbon; among whom I am a grateful example.

I am with great regard Dr Sir Your Obligd & Obt Servant

THO DIGGES

Addressed: His Excellency / Benjamin Franklin / at Passy / near / Paris

Endorsed: Mar 15 80

From Conrad-Alexandre Gérard[1]

ALS: American Philosophical Society

Monsieur   A Versailles le 15. mars 1780.

Si j'eusse eté maitre de disposer de mon tems, je n'aurois pas differé jusqu'ici à aller vous donner des preuves de mon empressement à vous presenter mes hommages. Le desir que vous montrés de me voir l'augmente encore et j'espere le satisfaire avant la fin de la semaine en vous allant faire une visite à Passy. En attendant je joins ici une lettre de M. Carmichael[2] et je suis

---

Merchants: the Secret Committee of Trade during the American Revolution, 1775–1777 (New York and London, 1985), p. 136. See also Digges's letter of March 17.

9. Not found.

1. In answer to BF's of the same day.

2. Dated Feb. 19: XXXI, 502–3.

avec la plus respectueuse consideration Monsieur Votre trés
humble et très obeissant serviteur   GERARD

Notation: Gerard 15 Mars 1780

From M.A. de Sonnemaens   LS: American Philosophical Society

Son Excellance   Venlo[3] le 15 mars 1780
    Nous prenont la lieberté d'Ecrire a votre Excellance pour
nous informer appre notre frere jean hanrÿ Barron de Wolff,[4]
Sortan du Service de Sa Majesté Prussien, par la Reduction que
Sa Majesté a fait, et par la Recommandation de votre Exellance[5]
il a ou le Bonheur de venier aide Camp chez Monsieur Le gen-
neral de vassenton, et comme nous trouvon a faire le partagé de
la famille nous auron bessoin de Savoir ou il ce trouvé. Nous
avon bien Recu de lettre daté de Nantes du 2 de Novembre 1777
quil Est parti et un lettre daté du 29 avril 1778 de Niebor de Nord
Carrolien mais depeu nous avon aucune Nouvelle de luÿ, priant
votre Excellance de faire le plessier a notre famille dinformer
pour que nous luÿ pouvont luÿ Ecrire au Suget du partage de la
famille que nous vouderon faire et a qui nous pouront remetter
Sa portion, votre Exllance nous randera le plus grand Service du

3. Now part of the Netherlands, it was then located in the Holy Roman
Empire.
4. Her brother called himself the Baron de Wulffen; see his letters to BF,
the first of which we print before June 1. We do not know whether he was in
fact a member of the Prussian military family of that name, and much about
him remains suspicious. According to a committee report presented to Congress he had appeared in America without credentials and was found un-
qualified by von Steuben, but was nominated for a lieutenant's commission
in the "Marechassé Corps." (This was Capt. von Heer's Provost Troop of
Light Dragoons, assigned the task of picking up deserters and stragglers:
Fred Anderson Berg, *Encyclopedia of Continental Army Units: Battalions,
Regiments and Independent Corps* [Harrisburg, 1972], pp. 132–3.) Congress
refused to confirm the commission and gave von Steuben $200 to send him
back to Europe. Once there, he presented to Jean de Neufville & fils a bill of
exchange drawn on the president and members of Congress. To avoid em-
barrassing the Dutch bankers, Congress honored the draft: *JCC,* XVIII,
1179–80; Fitzpatrick, *Writings of Washington,* XV, 127, 206n.
5. If true, we have found no record of it.

mond, nous recommandan notre frere et a nous a votre Exellance
Votre tres humble et tres obeissant Servant
M: A: DE SONNEMAENS NÉE BARONNESSE DE WOLFF

From [Pierre] Richard[6]   AD: American Philosophical Society

[after March 15, 1780]
Notes qu'a l'honneur de présenter le Sieur Richard, à Son Excellence Monsieur L'Ambassadeur des Etats-unis.

Son Excellence voudra bien accompagner la Lettre que j'ose
lui remettre pour Mr. Bingham, d'une recommandation pour
qu'il veuille terminer toutes les affaires dont il a eu la bonté de se
charger pour moi; c'est un ami dont la négligence ne doit être attribuée qu'aux malheurs des circonstances, & qui ne mérite, je
pense, aucun reproche.[7]

Puisque son Excellence veut bien envoyer mon mémoire au
Président du Congrès,[8] ne pourroit-elle pas demander l'acquit

6. In a March 15, 1780, memorial addressed to the president of Congress,
which we discuss below, Richard identifies himself as a director general of
the post office, printer to the King, and editor of the *Gazette de la Martinique*.
He is also identified as *imprimeur du roi et du Conseil supérieur* in Liliane
Chauleau, comp., *Conseil Souverain de la Martinique (Série B) 1712–1791: In-
ventaire analytique* (Fort-de-France, 1985), p. 148. The present document was
written sometime after that memorial.

7. William Bingham was returning from Martinique to the U.S.; he sailed
on March 30: XXXI, 558n. There is no indication in the index to the *Papers of
the Continental Congress* that Bingham, who had his own claims to settle with
Congress, ever presented Richard's memorial: *Morris Papers*, I, 238–9; Margaret L. Brown, "William Bingham, Agent of the Continental Congress,"
PMHB, LXI (1937), 80–3; Robert C. Alberts, *The Golden Voyage: the Life
and Times of William Bingham* (Boston, 1969), pp. 86–7, 104–5.

8. Richard apparently drafted the original of his memorial at St. Pierre on
March 15, 1780, and entrusted it to Bingham to deliver to Samuel Huntington. A copy, now in BF's papers at the Library of Congress, was made at some
later date, probably after Richard arrived in Paris. At various times since 1776 Richard sent cargoes of arms, powder, salt,
and rum to America. He was to be reimbursed with congressional promis-
sory notes, and the interest credited at Paris. Instead, the money was deposited in the Bank of Congress, with the principal redeemable in three
years. The collapse of paper money has meant a loss of three fourths of his
capital. Now he plans to rejoin his children in Paris, and some 300,000 *livres*

en entier des 16600 Dollars, comme un objet qui m'étoit dû depuis la fin de 1777, & que mes Correspondans ont gardé dans leurs mains, jusqu'en janvier 1779: elle pourroit en meme tems faire valoir mon Zele & les services importans que j'ai rendus à la Martinique aux Américains.[9] Dans le cas où l'on auroit égard à la recommandation de Son Excellence, on pourroit, pour plus de facilité, convertir cette créance en un contrat à constitution de Rente dont l'intérêt seroit payable à Paris; S'il en étoit autrement, Son Excellence voudroit bien alors prier le Président du Congrès d'ordonner le remboursement de ce qui me sera alloué entre les mains de M Bingham porteur de ma procuration, qui m'en fera la remise de suite.

Si son Excellence jugeoit à propos de charger M Bingham de Sa lettre pour le Président du Congrès, il seroit plus à portée d'en solliciter le résultat.

Dans le cas où son Excellence auroit besoin de moi, ma résidence est chez M de Courcelles, rue Vantadour, bute St. Roch. [*in another hand*] à Paris[1]

From ——— Bidé de Chavagnes[2]

ALS: American Philosophical Society

[before March 16, 1780][3]

Laccueil favorable et les bontés que jay eprouvé dans votre patrie, mont penetrés de la plus vive reconnoissance envers vos

---

are owed to him. Will the Congress put his funds in bonds, the interest payable at Paris? Bingham will testify to the truth of the memorial.

9. The Martinique *Gazette* (presumably Richard's), according to Bingham, published the most authentic details of military operations in America: Alberts, *The Golden Voyage*, pp. 459–60.

1. The only other piece of extant correspondence between Richard and BF is a letter Richard writes from Paris, rue de Menars, on May 28, 1783. He still has not heard from Bingham and asks BF to forward another letter to him. APS.

2. Captain of the French frigate *Sensible*, which in 1779 had taken JA to Boston and then back to Europe: see XXX, 524; Asa B. Gardiner, *The Order of the Cincinnati in France* . . . (n.p., 1905), p. 143.

3. The date on which BF wrote Samuel Cooper, below, that he had received a letter carried by Chavagnes. On the same day JA sent Chavagnes' respects to Abigail Adams: *Adams Correspondence*, III, 304.

compatriottes nos bons alliés, je desirerois pouvoir avoir lhonneur de l'exprimer dans toutte sa force a votre excellence et que les circonstances pussent me permettre de vous presenter moymême mes respects et les voeux sinceres que je forme pour la prosperité de votre nation, et faire connoissance avec leur illustre chef a qui jay lhonneur dassurer que je me suis trouvé trop heureux de pouvoir faire parvenir lettres, paquets, et une petite boette que l'on ma remis a boston pour son excellence et dont monsieur de vallois veut bien se charger. Jignore si monsieur johns adams, sa famille, mr. denas et allain sont de retour a versailles[4] et si ils ont etés aussi contents de moy que je lay eté de les posseder et passer en france, leurs estimes et amitiés me sont cheres ainsi que celles de messieurs le general *ancohks*, le docteur *couppa*[5] de tous les habitans et habitantes de boston, et si dans le courant de cette année il se trouvoit dans les operations combinées de la cour de france une mission pour l'amerique septentrionalle je serois bien jaloux den estre chargé ou de my joindre, les circonstances me mettroint peut estre a même de vous estre utile et de contribuer a la prosperité de vos armes, tels sont mes veritables sentiments pour votre nation dont je ne cesse de chanter les louanges. Je prie votre excellence d'en estre bien persuadé ainsi que du profond respect avec lequel jay l'honneur d'estre de son excellence Le tres humble et tres obeissant serviteur   BIDÉ DE CHAVAGNES
capne. des vaux. du roy de france.
Cy devant commandant la fregatte la sensible qui a eté 3 mois ½ a boston

4. "Vallois" presumably is Joseph de Valnais, the French consul in Boston (*Adams Correspondence*, III, 225n); "Denas" is JA's secretary, Francis Dana, and "allain" is Jeremiah Allen (xxx, 536), another American passenger aboard the *Sensible*. The reference to Versailles may refer to JA's March 7 presentation at court.

5. Gen. Hancock and Dr. Cooper; John Hancock was a major general of militia and Samuel Cooper had an honorary doctorate of divinity from the University of Edinburgh.

To Sarah Bache

ALS: American Philosophical Society

Dear Sally,   Passy, March 16. 1780.

I received your kind Letters of Sept. 14. and 25th.[6] You mention the Silk being in a Box with Squirrel Skins, but it is come to hand without them or the Box. Perhaps they were spoilt by the Salt Water & thrown away; for the Silk is much damag'd and not at all fit to be presented as you propose. Indeed I wonder how having yourself scarce Shoes to your Feet, it should come into your Head to give Cloathes to a Queen. I shall see if the Stains can be cover'd by Dying it, and make Summer Suits of it, for myself, Temple & Benny. I send some of Ben's Letters inclosed to his Father.[7] He is well taken Care of, and well contented. But I fancy you had rather he should be with me. Perhaps I may therefore recall him. Tho' I really think he is better at Geneva for his Learning. Many Persons of Quality here, send their Sons there, for the same Reason tho' the Religion is different.

I am glad to hear that Weaving Work is so hard to get done. Tis a Sign there is much Spinning. All the Things you Order will be sent, as you continue to be a good Girl, & spin & knit your Family Stockings.[8]

My Health & Spirits continue and I am ever, Your affectionate Father.   B FRANKLIN

Mrs. S. Bache

Addressed: To / Mrs Bache / Philadelphia[9]

6. xxx, 332–6, 397–8.

7. BFB's most recent extant letters to BF were dated Oct. 25 and Dec. 25, 1779: xxx, 586–7; xxxi, 279.

8. xxx, 334.

9. Figures on the address sheet apparently unrelated to the letter subtract 15 from 49 for a remainder of 34.

To Thomas Bond

Reprinted from William Temple Franklin, ed., *The Private Correspondence of Benjamin Franklin LL.D. F.R.S. &c. . . .* (2nd ed.; 2 vols., London, 1817), I, 59–60.

Dear Sir,   Passy, March 16, 1780.

I received your kind letter of September the 22d,[1] and I thank you for the pleasing account you give me of the health and welfare of my old friends, Hugh Roberts, Luke Morris, Philip Syng, Samuel Rhoades, &c. with the same of yourself and family. Shake the old ones by the hand for me, and give the young ones my blessing. For my own part, I do not find that I grow any older. Being arrived at 70, and considering that by travelling further in the same road I should probably be led to the grave, I stopped short, turned about and walked back again; which having done these four years, you may now call me 66. Advise those old friends of ours to follow my example, keep up your spirits and that will keep up your bodies, you will no more stoop under the weight of age than if you had swallowed a handspike. But it is right to abate a little in the article of labour; and therefore as your demonstrations of midwifery "are useful, and it is a pity you should give them up, for *want of subjects* in the lying-in wards," I advise you to get some of your young pupils to help you.

I am glad the Philosophical Society made that compliment to Mr. Gerard. I wish they would do the same to Mr. Feutry, a worthy gentleman here;[2] and to Dr. Ingenhausz, who has made some great discoveries lately respecting the leaves of trees in improving air for the use of animals: he will send you his book.[3] He is physician to the Empress Queen. I have not yet seen your piece on inoculation.[4]

---

1. Probably Bond's of Sept. 24, 1779, which gives news of BF's old friends and raises the other subjects discussed in the present letter: XXX, 394–6.

2. The poet Aimé (Amé)-Ambroise-Joseph Feutry, who had composed an ode for BF's 1779 Independence Day banquet: XXX, 45.

3. Jan Ingenhousz in November, 1779, had sent BF his *Experiments upon Vegetables . . .*, which explained his discovery of photosynthesis: XXXI, 122n, 140n. Ingenhousz was elected to membership in the APS, but not until 1786. Information kindly supplied by Whitfield J. Bell, Jr.

4. See XXX, 395.

Remember me respectfully and affectionately to Mrs. Bond, your children, and all friends. I am ever, Yours,   B. FRANKLIN.

P.S. I have bought some valuable books which I intend to present to the society; but shall not send them till safer times.[5]

To Dr. Bond, *Philadelphia. Letter of Friendship.*

To Samuel Cooper   LS:[6] Henry E. Huntington Library

Dear Sir,   Passy March 16. 1780.

I received your kind Favour by Capt. Chavagnes, which I communicated to the Minister of the Marine, who was much pleased with the Character you give of the Captain.[7] I have also yours of Nov. 12. by your Grandson, who appears a very pretty promising Lad, in whom I think you will have much Satisfaction. He is in a Boarding School just by me, and was well last Sunday, when I had the Pleasure of his Company at Dinner with Mr Adams's Sons, & some other young Americans.[8] He will soon acquire the Language; and if God spares his Life, may make a very serviceable Man to his Country.

It gives me infinite Satisfaction to find that with you, the wisest and best among our People are so hearty in endeavouring to strengthen the Alliance.[9] We certainly owe much to this Nation, and we shall obtain much more, if the same prudent Conduct towards them continues. For they really and strongly wish our

5. Possibly the nine volumes of the *Arts et Métiers*, for which BF had paid the abbé Morellet 126 *l.t.* on Nov. 7, 1779: XXXI, 4; Cash Book.

6. In WTF's hand.

7. Missing.

8. Samuel Cooper Johonnot had delivered his grandfather's letter (XXXI, 85–6). He attended the *pension* academy of M. and Mme Péchigny: Taylor, *J.Q. Adams Diary,* I, 34n.

9. Cooper's efforts included contributions to the pro-French Boston *Independent Ledger.* They may have been motivated in part by the nearly $1,000 per annum he was secretly receiving from the French: Charles W. Akers, *The Divine Politician: Samuel Cooper and the American Revolution in Boston* (Boston, 1982), pp. 256–7; William C. Stinchcombe, *The American Revolution and the French Alliance* (Syracuse, 1969), pp. 119–20.

Prosperity, and will promote it by every means in their Power.[1] But we should at the same time do as much as possible for ourselves, and not ride (as we say) a free horse to Death. There are some Americans returning from hence, with whom our People should be upon their Guard,[2] as carrying with them a Spirit of Enmity to this Country. Not being liked here themselves, they dislike the People. For the same Reason indeed they ought to dislike all that know them.

With the sincerest Respect & Esteem, I am ever, my dear Friend, Yours most affectionately   B FRANKLIN

Dr. Cooper

To Cyrus Griffin

Reprinted from William Temple Franklin, ed., *The Private Correspondence of Benjamin Franklin, LL.D F.R.S. &c. . . .*, (2nd ed.; 2 vols., London, 1817), I, 61.

Sir,   Passy, March 16, 1780.

I have just received the letter you have done me the honor to write to me,[3] and shall immediately deliver the packet it recommends to my care. I will take the first opportunity of mentioning to Mr. Gerard what you hint, relative to our not entertaining strangers so frequently and liberally, as is the custom in France. But he has travelled in Europe, and knows that modes of nations differ. The French are convivial, live much at one another's tables, and are glad to feast travellers. In Italy and Spain a stranger, however recommended, rarely dines at the house of any gentleman, but lives at his inn. The Americans hold a medium.

I have the honor to be, &c.   B. FRANKLIN.

To C. Griffin, Esq.

1. For an analysis of BF's "diplomacy of gratitude" see Gerald Stourzh, *Benjamin Franklin and American Foreign Policy* (2nd ed., Chicago and London, 1969), pp. 164–6.
2. Presumably a reference to Arthur Lee and Ralph Izard.
3. XXX, 421-2.

To Francis Hopkinson

Reprinted from William Temple Franklin, ed., *The Private Correspondence of Benjamin Franklin, LL.D F.R.S. &c. . . .,* (2nd ed.; 2 vols., London, 1817), I, 58–9.

Dear Sir,   Passy, March 16, 1780.

I thank you for your political *Squibs,* they are well made. I am glad to find you have such plenty of good powder.[4]

You propose that *Kill-pig,* the butcher, should operate upon himself. You will find some thoughts on that subject in a little piece called *"A merry Song about Murder,"* in a London newspaper I send herewith.[5]

---

4. Hopkinson had sent two political ballads, one of which was "The Battle of the Kegs," with his letter of Sept. 5: XXX, 298.

5. BF evidently enclosed a copy of the *Westminster Courant* of Jan. 25, 1780, which the *Pennsylvania Packet* cited as the source for this ballad when it reprinted it on May 2, 1780. The ballad then spread throughout New England: Ellen R. Cohn, "Benjamin Franklin and Traditional Music," in J.A. Leo Lemay, ed., *Reappraising Benjamin Franklin: A Bicentennial Perspective* (Newark, Del., 1993), pp. 311–12. A copy of the song, in L'Air de Lamotte's hand and corrected by BF, is at the APS. That text is as follows:

A merry Song, about Murder.

There was, and a very great fool,
who fancy'd all Subjects were Slaves,
who endeavoured at absolute rule,
by the help of a parcel of knaves:
now, *cutting of throats* was his joy,
and making red rivers of blood,
a *fine button* his favourite toy,
tho' his habits were not very good,
                    Toroddle, toroddle, toroll.

Swords, hatchets, and knives, he prepar'd,
to Slaughter his people like sheep;
Man, Woman, or child, he ne'er spared,
which makes even Savages weep:
then, like a great lubberly Calf,
on his marrow-bones down he did fall—
"I have kill'd of my people but half,
Lord! help me to murder them all!"
                    Toroddle &c.

So then the fool fasted and pray'd,
and *ba'ad* like an innocent lamb;
pursuing the while his old trade,

The greatest discovery made in Europe for some time past is that of Dr. Ingenhausz's relating to the great use of the leaves of trees in producing wholesome air; I would send you his book if I had it. A new instrument is lately invented here, a kind of telescope, which by means of Iceland chrystal occasions the double appearance of an object, and the two appearances being farther distant from each other in proportion to the distance of the object from the eye, by moving an index on a graduated line till the two appearances coincide, you find on the line the real distance of the object. I am not enough master of this instrument to describe it accurately, having seen it but once; but it is very ingeniously contrived.[6]

----

for his *piety* was but a sham;
but his measures so bloody were grown,
that some of his time-serving elves,
for their share in his crimes to atone,
did cut their own throats their own Selves.
Toroddle, &c.

The first was a Lawyer from *York,*
Cajol'd by his coaxing and art;
But who, rather than do dirty work,
Chose out of the world to depart;
Next Cl——ve, and like Br——ds——w the bold,
Last St——, with cynical grin;
Shew'd the folly of treasuring gold,
When the heart has no treasure within.
Toroddle, &c.

Now, let but the frolic go round,
take, ye Courtiers, your knives from the Shelf;
make each in his wind-pipe a wound,
'Till it come to the Blockhead himself!
But, I fear, he'll ne'er join in the fun,
for to all men 'tis very well known,
that he'd rather, ten thousand to one,
Cut a million of throats, than his own.
Toroddle, &c.

6. BF was describing a micrometer invented by the abbé Rochon, who had presented two models to the Academy of Sciences in 1777. It could measure, with great precision, the diameter of celestial bodies, and the distances between them. See Alexis-Marie Rochon, *Recueil de mémoires sur la mécanique et la physique* (Paris, 1783), pp. 172 *et seq.;* the instrument is also described in G. Touchard-Lafosse and F. Roberge, *Dictionnaire chronologique et raisonné des découvertes . . . en France . . .* (17 vols., Paris, 1822–24), XI, 402–4.

Remember me respectfully to your mother and sisters, and believe me ever, my dear friend, Yours most affectionately,

B. FRANKLIN.

F. Hopkinson, Esq. *Philadelphia.*

To Samuel Huntington

LS,[7] copy and transcript: National Archives; copy: Library of Congress

Sir, Passy, 16 March 1780.

The Bearer of this Capt. Hutchins, a Native of New Jersey, but many Years in the English Service, has lately escaped from England, where he suffer'd considerably for his Attachment to the American Cause. He is esteem'd a good Officer and excellent Engineer, and is desirous of being serviceable to his Country.[8] I inclose his Memorial to me,[9] great Part of which is consistent with my Knowledge, and I beg leave to recommend him to the favourable Notice of Congress, when any Affair occurs in which his Talents may be useful.

I have the honour to be with great Respect, Your Excellency's most obedient & most humble Sert. B FRANKLIN

BF brought one of Rochon's micrometers back with him to Philadelphia. Rittenhouse borrowed it in 1786 and explained to BF its mechanics, and it remained in BF's house until he died. Rittenhouse to SB, Nov. 22, 1786 (Dartmouth College Library); Rittenhouse: Explanation of Micrometer (undated, APS); Inventory of BF's Estate, April 26, 1790 (APS); *Jefferson Papers*, IX, 356.

7. In WTF's hand.

8. On March 15 Thomas Hutchins wrote JW, asking him to forward BF twelve of his maps and pamphlets on the interior of North America. APS. (Some of these described his military service there; see his entry in the *DAB*.)

9. Hutchins' Feb. 27 memorial (XXX, 291n), details his imprisonment for treason, resignation of his commission in the British army, impoverishment, and arrival in France. He requests service as an engineer in the American army. BF here forwards a signed copy (National Archives) to Huntington in his capacity as president of Congress. BF also gave him 480 *l.t.* on March 15: Account XXVII. Hutchins did eventually sail from Lorient (although not on the *Alliance*) and enjoyed a distinguished career in America, including appointment by Congress as geographer of the United States: *DAB*.

His Ex. Sam Huntington Esq.

Notation: Letter from Doct Franklin with Meml. T. Hutchins March 16. 1780 Read Feby 23. 1781 Referred to Mr McDougal Mr Ward Mr Bland[1]

To James Lovell

LS[2] and transcript: National Archives; ALS (draft) and copy: Library of Congress

Dear Sir,   Passy, March 16. 1780.

·The Marquis de la Fayette, our firm & constant Friend, returning to America, I have written a long Letter by him to the President, of which a Copy goes by this Ship.—[3]

M. Gerard is since arrived, and I have received the Dispatches you mentioned to me but no Letter in answer to mine, a very long one, by the Chevr de la Luzerne, nor any Acknowledgement that it came to hand.[4]

By the many News Papers & Pamphlets I send, you will see the present State of European Affairs in general. Ireland continues to insist on compleat Liberty, and will probably obtain it. The Meetings of Counties in England, and the Committees of Correspondence they appoint, alarm a good deal the Ministry; especially since it has been proposed to elect out of each Committee a few Persons to assemble in London; which if carried into Execution will form a kind of Congress, that will have more of the Confidence and support of the People than the old Par-

1. *JCC*, XIX, 187. The committee appointed to consider Hutchins' petition consisted of delegates Alexander McDougall of New York, Artemas Ward of Massachusetts, and Theodorick Bland, Jr., of Virginia. Congress concurred in their recommendation to appoint him geographer to the southern army: *JCC*, XIX, 339; XX, 475–6.

2. In WTF's hand.

3. To Huntington, March 4, above. BF probably expected the *Alliance* to carry this letter: to Jones, March 18, below.

4. Originally drafted as, "the Dispatches you mentioned to me, in a Letter by Mr Adams"; we have located no such letter. BF's own letter, directed to the committee for foreign affairs, of which Lovell was a member, is printed in XXIX, 547–61.

liament.[5] If the Nation is not too corrupt, as I rather think it is, some considerable Reformation of internal Abuses may be expected from this; with regard to us the only Advantage to be reasonably expected from it is a Peace, the general Bent of the Nation being for it. The Success of Admiral Rodney's Fleet against our Allies, has a little elated our Enemies for the present, and probably they will not now think of proposing it. If the approaching Campaign, for which great Preparations are making here, should end disadvantageously to them, they will be more treatable;[6] for their Debts and Taxes are daily becoming more burthensome, while their Commerce, the Source of their Wealth, diminishes; And tho' they have flatter'd themselves with obtaining Assistance from Russia and other Powers, it does not appear that they are likely to succeed; on the contrary they are in Danger of losing the Neutrality of Holland.

Their Conduct with regard to the Exchange of Prisoners has been very unjust. After long Suspence, and affected Delays for the purpose of wearing out our poor People, they have finally refused to deliver us a Man in Exchange for those set at Liberty by our Cruizers on Parole.— A Letter I inclose from Capt. Mitchel will show the Treatment of the late Flags of Truce from Boston.[1] There is no gaining anything upon these Barbarians, by Advances of Civility or Humanity.

Inclosed I send for Congress the Justification of this Court against the Accusation publish'd in the late English Memorials.[2]

5. Representatives of the Associated Counties movement continued their meetings at St. Albans Tavern in London, as more representatives arrived: Eugene C. Black, *The Association: British Extraparliamentary Political Organization 1769–1793* (Cambridge, Mass., 1963), pp. 51–2. See also Digges's March 3 letter.

6. First drafted as "they must seek for Peace".

1. A now-missing letter mentioned in the postscript of Digges's March 3 letter, above.

2. "Observations sur le Mémoire justificatif de la cour de Londres," which was distributed by Vergennes on Feb. 9 to the various foreign diplomatic representatives at Versailles: *Gaz. de Leyde*, Feb. 25 (no. XVI). Extracts were printed in the Feb. 25 to April 25 issues of the *Gaz. de Leyde*, and the work as a whole was published in 1783. Gérard de Rayneval was the author: Antoine-Alexandre Barbier, ed., *Dictionnaire des ouvrages anonymes* . . . (3rd ed., 7 vols., Paris, 1872–79), VI, 628.

With great Esteem, I have the honour to be, Sir, Your most obedient & most humble Servant.   B FRANKLIN

Honble. James Lovel Esqre.

Notation: March 16. 1780 Doctr. Franklin to J L recd. Feb. 18 1781

From Thomas Digges   ALS: Historical Society of Pennsylvania

Dr. Sir   17 Mar 1780

This will be handed you by a Capn. Jno Snelling a native of Boston tho for many years past He has been employd in the Streights Trade to & from London. He is well recommended to Me as an honest Amn. meaning to push out to his Home thro France, & as he wishes to take yr. advice about proceeding to Nantes &ca. I have given him a seperate introductory line to you.—[3] He knows nothing of former plans. Since Capt C——r left me, I have wrote you a few lines by post the 7th & 10th Ints. and am in dayly expectations of Capt C——rs return; His Employer Mr. M——ll is gone to Ireland & has done nothing. As far as I have recommended the granting some late favors from You, I have not the least doubt the transactions are *bona fide* intended for the purposes mentiond—ie getting home property. I dont mean by saying this, that *some* of the partys did not carry more than they had property to purchase. In the two instances wch. I lately recommend they were various persons (*every one natives & Citizens of A——a*) concernd. I would not on any accot be aiding to any other set of Men to obtain similar advantages for illicit trade. I never had, nor ever shall have, (without I am reducd to such necessity for getting out myself) the least con-

3. In this letter, dated March 20 and also at the Hist. Soc. of Pa., Digges describes Snelling as a Levant trader from London to the Mediterranean who has sold his effects and is willing to engage himself in his line of profession for the service of his country. He also mentions that Snelling has told him he is acquainted with BF's relative, Mr. Williams: Elias and Finch, *Letters of Digges,* pp. 180–1. Digges in the present letter gives shortened forms of the names of several persons to whom he had previously referred: Carpenter, Mitchell, Church, Hodgson, Manley, Hutchins, and Banks. The identity of Mr. L——th of Baltimore eludes us.

cern directly or indirectly in these adventures, but meerly recommended them to benefit some deserving A——ns who could not easily get out other ways, & from thinking such measures rather beneficial than other ways to my Country. They were people whom I had proofs were honest, & having a few hundreds of their own got credit for a few hundds more, & so pushd out four or five in a Ship. Mr. L——th of Bale. was an exception to this he came purposely to Europe to recover a debt of upwds. of 3,000£ due his Father— He got it & carryd out double that sum from having an extensive Credit. You know the circumstances of the *last* recommendations; If it succeeds there will go two or three honest men out with Capt. C——r, & these will be all that I know any thing of, for I beleive there will be then left here none others who deserve such oppertunitys.

I hope the box of books forwarded abot a fortnight ago has got safe. They were seemingly well packd & forwarded to order. An acquaintance Snor Ma——ll——n took that oppertunity of forwarding to you a brown paper parcel wch. also containd books.[4]

If you have not already done it please to ansr. my letter of the 7th Int. on the subject of the Bills of Exa. as I want to know whether or not they are good before I forward them on. A line by Common post to Mr Wm. S. C——h (as you once before directed or if under cover to Mr. H——gs——n) will oblige me. Their tenor & dates are as follow

No. 25—23d Feb '79	a first bill to Jona Warner Esqr. 30 Dollars Countersignd Nichs. Gilman for New Hampshire
No 26—do—	Do— to Do.— 30 D—
No 27—do—	second bill to Do— 30— Do
No 166 15 Feby. 79	second bill to Do.—24 Counterd Natl Appleton Massachuts
No.173.23d Febr 79—	first bill to Petr. Boilston Adams 24 Dolls—Do—Do—

138 Dollars

4. Probably his friend [Señor] Jean-Hyacinthe de Magellan or Magalhaens for whom he had earlier forwarded a packet: XXXI, 367.

I wish to know if these bills are good or not as they are left with me by a poor man for that purpose.

Nothing new since the Cartel saild the 5 relative to the Prisoners there are 86 left at Plyo. 68 of whom have pardons ready agt. the return of the Ship to that place & by that time the pardons for the 18 others (among whom Capt M——y is one) will be forwarded down.

I have nothing yet decided abot. the medal for the Duke de Croy my friends Mr. Jones is on a circuit & Mr Paradise is sick & has no ansr. since the affair was stated to Mr Banks.

Those Gent. who came over on Parole in the two last Cartels seem quite easy under their breach of that parole, & seemingly now give themselves not the least trouble about procuring or abiding by the terms of their agreement. It is singular with what ease & facility an Englishman can break his parole to Americans, & how lavish they are of the words scoundrells & villains, when there is the least appearance (wch I beleive there never has been) of Americans doing the like by them. Surely those lately returnd parole Prisors., 139 in numr., should be in some measure calld upon to abide By their parole Agreement, wch was a written one & cannot be misunderstood; I think the mode of requiring by publick advertisement, the People so releasd, to render themselves to you accordingly, would not be an improper one. The two Capns of the Packets (*the Kings Officers*) and the Mr. Barry a Secy to Govr. Dalling are long since returnd to their occupations the latter gone to Jama. & the two Capns. got other packets for that station. Should the *Yankies* once more take them, I think their chance would be but a shabby one. I am on all occasions Yr. very Affect & obt Servt.   P. DROUILLARD

If you can with propriety oblige me in procuring a French Passport for Mr. Wm. Burn of Lisbon, now on a tour in Italy, & who wishes to see some parts of France & Paris, *meerly as a Traveller;* It woud be a very singular obligation to Him & me. He does not want to go to any Sea Ports, or where he may be suspected, but, I beleive, meerly the common route from Turin to Paris or any other capital Town worth visiting. The Pass to be inclosd in a letter to Him, and put under Cover A *Messrs. Messrs. Freres Aubert Tollot & Co. Turin,* where Mr. Burn will be in the course of a fortnight or 3 weeks.

Mr. Burn is a principal in the House of Messrs. Burn & Sons at Lisbon, & is taking that tour meerly for his pleasure. He is a very worthy man whom I intimately know. He has done much business with Messrs. Willing & Morris, Cunningham & Nesbin, J Wharton, and others of the principal people in Phia & other parts of Ama.——[5] Is a *good* friend to the cause of that Country & the *only* house in Lisbon whh. has, since the disputes, openly acted in favour of Ama. In one instance, to my solicitation, He sent some Cargoes of salt at the period it was most essentially requisite. He will be on any other occasions servicable to Us, and as He deserves much from me & my Country, I have not only askd this favour of you but given him a seperate line of introduction should he obtain his wish of being permitted *as an Englishman* to visit Paris. If such pass can be got, I should be obligd to you to forward it on as soon as is convenient by Post as his stay in Turin will not be very Long. The House of Messrs. Burn & Sons is a well establishd & very substancial one in Lisbon; should you or any friend want to make use of one in that place I know of none more fit.

Please to forward the inclosd to Capn. H———ns, as it may be very satisfactory to him to hear What has been transacted since his departure & that his baggage is *all* arrivd safe at ostend.

Since writing the inclosd, Mr Paradise has been with me; He says Mr. Banks on receiving the paragraph of yr. Letter relative to a medal being given to the Duke de Croy, said He could not possibly recommend the giving one to that Gentn., as it would lead to a variety of similar requests &ca. Mr. B——— read to Mr. Paradise a letter wch I am to receive in a day or two & forward to you.[6] He has couchd it in very handsome & liberal terms to you, & speaks properly of the Congress, but persists in his old opinion that a gold medal cannot be given to that body without additional proofs, that it was by their order or Recommendation that orders were given to the American Cruisers to shew favor to Cap Cook &ca &ca. You will be a better judge when you receive Mr Banks's Letter which I hope will be in a few days, if not by this conveyance.

5. See our annotation of Digges's letter of March 15. Digges has misspelled the name of the firm of Conyngham and Nesbitt, for which see XXXI, 119n.
6. Presumably Banks's of March 29, below.

Addressed: Monsieur Monsieur / B. F——n / Passy

Endorsed: March 17. 80

Notation: Mar 17. 80

From Dumas

ALS: American Philosophical Society

Monsieur   Lahaie 17 Mars 1780

Je n'ai qu'un instant pour profiter de l'occasion d'un Exprès que Mr. Gillon envoie à Paris, & vous envoyer la belle & rare copie de l'Acte original de l'Union d'Utrecht,[7] dont j'ai eu l'honneur de vous parler à Paris que je le destinois pour les Archives du Congrès, auquel je serois bien aise qu'il pût parvenir promptement mais sans trop risquer: car il est très-difficile de se procurer des copies de cela, ayant été imprimées aux dépens de L.H.P., qui n'en ont fait la distribution qu'entre eux.

Les épreuves de caracteres m'ont été remis pour vous par Mr. Enschédé.[8]

Les deux Dialogues socratiques *Sophyle,* & *Aristée* sont de la façon d'un de mes Amis; j'en suis l'Editeur; & j'espere qu'ils vous plairont.

I 475. 621. 873. 134. 610. 193. 17. & I 942. 807. 470. if I can.[9] My 1st. Letter will tell you more of it.

7. Probably the elegant reprinting of the 1579 Union of Utrecht (which established the United Provinces of the Netherlands) and supporting documents entitled *Extract uyt de resolutien de Edele Mogende Heeren Raaden van Staate der Vereenigde Nederlanden...* (Haarlem, 1778); a copy is at Yale University Library.

8. The Haarlem firm of Johannes Enschedé and Sons was the premier typefoundry of Holland. They undoubtedly sent BF a copy of their latest specimen book, *Proef van letteren ...* (Harlem, 1768). An earlier edition (1757) had been translated into French, but BF, in his answer to Dumas of March 29, identified the fonts that interested him by their Dutch names. For a history of the firm, which still exists, see Harry Carter's chapter, "A Short History of the Firm," in Johannes Enschedé en Zonen, *The House of Enschedé 1703–1953* (Haarlem, 1953), pp. xxxi–lxi.

9. "I know now the Breast of Capt. Guillon & [I] will serve it if I . . . " BF first decoded this sentence on the notation sheet, mistaking Dumas' scrawly second "I" for a "3," which stood for Van der Capellen. He realized his mistake, and interlined an accurate translation above the numbers on the ALS.

Je suis avec un très respectueux attachement Monsieur Votre très humble & très obéissant serviteur DUMAS

P.S. Ayant su de Mr. Gillon, que Mr. Jones va partir incessamment de l'Orient pour l'Amérique avec l'*Alliance*, je prends le parti de charger ce même Exprès d'un paquet que je vous prie de faire passer à Mr. Jones: C'est un de mes paquets pour le Congrès.[1]

Passy à S. E. Mr. Franklin

Notation: Dumas la haie, March, 17. 80

To John Paul Jones

L:[2] National Archives; incomplete copy:[3] Library of Congress

Dear Sir, Passy Mar 18. 1780.

I received your Letter relating to the Bullets of the Engineer in Denmark, and shall write thither accordingly.[4] I have also just received yours of the 13th. Mr Ross writes to me, that he finds a Difficulty in passing the Goods to you, from l'Isle Noirmoutier.[5] I do therefore now desire you, if practicable, to call at or off that Island, in order to take them on board; their speedy and safe Arrival in America being of the greatest Consequence to the Army.

I have sent my Dispatches by Mr Wharton, who set off Yes-

1. Dumas undoubtedly included a covering letter for Jones (Bradford, *Jones Papers*, reel 5, no. 1023) and a March 15 letter to the committee for foreign affairs in which he enclosed a draft Dutch-American commercial treaty on which he had been working for the last year and asked for diplomatic powers to negotiate on behalf of the United States: XXVIII, 551 (and frequent subsequent mentions); Wharton, *Diplomatic Correspondence*, III, 549. The packet is discussed further in Dumas' letter of March 23, below.
2. In WTF's hand; he enclosed with it a note explaining that the letter was an exact copy of his grandfather's draft. Being obliged to go out before the copying was finished, BF had directed WTF to sign for him. Library of Congress.
3. Beginning with "take Time" in the third paragraph.
4. Jones to BF, March 6, above.
5. Missing, but see Jones to BF, March 14, and BF to Ross, March 19.

terday Morning.[6] When they arrive, and you have got the Cloth on board, I know of nothing to retard your proceeding directly to such Port in North America, as you shall judge most likely to be reached with safety. If in other Respects equal, Philadelphia is to be preferr'd.

I wish the Prize Money due to your People could be paid before they go. I have spoken often about it. As to the Prizes sent in to Norway, you know they were deliver'd back to the English by the Court of Denmark. I have reclaim'd them by a strong Memorial, but have yet received no Answer, and it is doubted whether we shall recover any thing, unless by Letters of Marque and Reprisal from the Congress, against the Subjects of that Kingdom, which perhaps in the present Circumstances, it may not be thought proper soon to grant. The Ship of War that you took, are I hear to be valued, the King intending to purchase them.[7] And the Muster Roll of the Bonhomme Richard is wanting, in order to regulate the Proportions to each Ship. These Things may take Time: I have considered that the People of the Bonhomme, may want some little Supplies for the Voyage; and therefore if these Proportions should not be regulated and paid before you sail, and you find it necessary, you may draw on me as far as, twenty four thousand Livres, to advance to them for which they are to be accountable; but do not exceed that Sum. I do this to prevent as much as in me lies, the bad Effects of any uneasiness among them; for I suppose that regularly all Payments to Seamen should be made at home.

A grand Convoy I understand sails from Brest about the End of this Month or Beginning of the next.[8] It is of great Importance to the United States, that not only the Alliance, but the

6. On the 16th BF provided Wharton with a signed certificate stating that during Wharton's years in London he had been "a good and faithful Citizen of the United States, and been *very* serviceable to their Cause, by the *constant* Correspondence he has kept up with their Ministers here, and the Intelligence he has communicated." A copy is at the Library Company of Philadelphia. It bears a notation dated Sept. 10, 1780, and is signed by Jones, Thomas Hutchins, and Thomas Read attesting that the original is in BF's hand and that the copy is accurate.

7. The public sale of the *Serapis* was ordered on April 22, but the local French navy officials were warned on May 8 not to buy the warship if it was priced above its value: Archives de la Marine, B² CDXIX, 7.

8. Undoubtedly a reference to the Rochambeau expedition.

Merchant men that may sail under her Convoy, should safely arrive there. If it will be convenient and practicable for you to join that Convoy, and sail with it 'till off the Coast, I wish it may be done. But leave it to your Discretion and Judgment. I have no farther Instructions to give, but committing you to the Protection of Providence, I wish you a prosperous Voyage, & a happy Sight of your Friends in America, being with great Esteem & Regard, Dear Sir, Your most obedient & most humble Servant

W. T. FRANKLIN for B. FRANKLIN

Honble Comme. Jones.

Endorsed: From his Excellency Dr. Franklin Passy March 18th 1780—No. 20.

To John Bondfield

Copy: Library of Congress

Sir,   Passy, March. 19. 1780.

I received yours offering the Govr. Livingston and mary fearon for the service of the United States. Understanding little about shipping, I leave those Matters to Mr. de Chaumont and Mr. Williams. I have spoken to the former, and given him your letter.[9] He is gone to Versailles to Day, where some Points are to be considered relating to The transport of the Goods, and he will be able to give you an Answer to morrow.

I have the honour to be &c.

Mr. Bondfield

From William Alexander

Copies:[1] Historical Society of Pennsylvania, University of Pennsylvania Library, Library of Congress, Pendleton Satterthwaite, East Orange, N.J. (1955)

Dear sir   [March 19, 1780]

I send you adjoined the Certificate you desire, and am perfectly convinc'd from Conversations I have since had with Mr.

9. Chaumont forwarded the now-missing letter to JW later in the month: JW to BF, March 27, below. Bondfield's ships had recently returned from America: XXXI, 517n.

1. Each copy of the letter has adjoined to it a copy of the certificate (dated

131

Pultney that no body was authorised to hold the Language which has been imputed to him on that Subject;[2] and I have a high Opinion of his Candour and Worth. I know it must be painful to him, to be brought into question in Matters of fact with Persons he esteems. I could wish that this Matter may receive no farther Publicity than what is necessary for your Justification.

To Joseph Reed: Three Letters

(I) LS:[3] New-York Historical Society; copies: Library of Congress, Pendleton Satterthwaite, East Orange, N.J. (1955); (II) LS:[4] New-York Historical Society; (II) and (III) copy: Library of Congress

I.

Sir,   Passy Mar. 19. 1780.

I have just received the Pamphlet you did me the Honour to send me, by Monsr Gerard,[5] and have read it with Pleasure, not

---

March 19) which Alexander mentions below. The ones owned by the Library of Congress and Pendleton Satterthwaite are adjoined to BF's March 19 letter to Joseph Reed, immediately below. Those at the Hist. Soc. of Pa., the University of Pa. Library, and the Library of Congress are in L'Air de Lamotte's hand.

2. William Alexander in March, 1778, had served as an intermediary for William Johnstone Pulteney, a correspondent and business associate, when Pulteney twice traveled to Paris to try to persuade BF that conciliation was still possible. For the abortive mission see XXVI, 94–5, 173–4, 188–90. Alexander's certificate attests that he was present during a conversation between Pulteney and BF. The American minister disapproved of the Englishman's proposals and doubted they would be agreed to in America. He offered, however, to communicate them to his colleagues and the French ministry. Pulteney opposed this and asked that his propositions not be mentioned and that the whole business "might be buried in Oblivion, agreable to what had been stipulated and agreed to by Dr. Franklin, before the Propositions were produced, which Dr. Franklin accordingly promised."

3. In WTF's hand.

4. In WTF's hand. The signature has been cropped, undoubtedly by an autograph collector.

5. Probably Gérard carried Reed's *Remarks on Governor Johnstone's Speech in Parliament* . . . (Philadelphia, 1779). The pamphlet was a documented defense of Reed's relations in 1778 with Gov. George Johnstone, former mem-

only as the clear State of Facts, do you Honour, but as they prove the Falsehood of a Man, who also shewed no regard to Truth in what he said of me, viz. that I approved of the Propositions he carry'd over. The Truth is that his Brother Mr Poultney came here with those Propositions & communicated them to me, after stipulating that if I did not approve of them, I should not speak of them to any Person. I told him frankly, on his desiring to know my Sentiments that *I* DID NOT *approve of them, and that I was sure they* WOULD NOT *be accepted in America.* But, says I, there are two other Commissioners here, I will if you please, shew your Propositions to them, and you will hear their Opinion. I will also shew them to the Ministry here, without whose Knowledge & Concurrence, we can take no Step in such Affairs. No, says he; as you do not approve of them, it can answer no Purpose to show them to any body else; the Reasons that weigh with you will also weigh with them: therefore I now pray that no mention may be made of my having been here, or my Business. To this I agreed; and therefore nothing could be more astonishing to me than to see in an American News Paper that direct Lye in a Letter from Mr Johnstone joined with two other Falshoods, relating to the Time of the Treaty, and to the Opinion of Spain. In Proof of the above I inclose a Certificate, of a Friend of Mr. Pultney's, the only Person present at our Interview; & do it the rather at this time, because I am informed that another Calumniator (the same who formerly in his private Letters to particular Members, accused you with Messrs. Jay, Duane, Langdon & Harrison of betraying the Secrets of Congress, in a Correspondence with the Ministry)⁶ has made this Transaction with Mr

---

ber of the Carlisle Commission (and William Pulteney's brother) who was accused of attempting to corrupt and bribe members of Congress. Johnstone resigned from the commission as a result of Congress's charges. See XXVII, 627n, 630; Smith, *Letters*, x, 93–102, 311, 559–60.

6. The names BF gives make only partial sense. Arthur Lee wrote to Silas Deane in 1776 warning against Sir James Jay, Dennys De Berdt, [John] Langdon from New Hampshire, and William Molleson, a Maryland merchant. In the same letter he referred to Reed as "a dangerous man": Stevens, *Facsimiles*, v, no. 467, pp. 2–3. See also Smith, *Letters*, x, 457–8; Louis W. Potts, *Arthur Lee: a Virtuous Revolutionary* (Baton Rouge and London, 1981), pp. 134–5. Duane was James Duane (1733–1797), a New York jurist and

Pultney, an Article of Accusation against me, as having approved those Propositions.[7] He proposes, I understand to settle in your Government. I caution you to beware of him; for in sowing Suspicions and Jealousies, in creating Misunderstandings and Quarrels among Friends, in Malice, Subtility & indefatigable Industry, he has I think no Equal.

I am glad to see that you continue to preside in our new State, as it shows that your publick Conduct is approved by the People. You have had a difficult Time, which required abundance of Prudence; and you have been equal to the Occasion. The Disputes about the Constitution seem to have subsided. It is much admired here and all over Europe, and will draw over many Families of Fortune, to settle under it as soon as there is a Peace.[8] The Defects that may on seven Years Trial be found in it, can be amended, when the Time comes for considering them.—

With great and sincere Esteem & Respect, I have the honour to be, Your Excellency's, most obedient & most humble Servant.

B FRANKLIN

His Exy. Jos. Reed Esqre.

Notations in different hands: Dr. Franklins Letter May 19. 1780 / Passy.

---

member of the Continental Congress whom Lee described in a Nov. 5, 1779, letter to James Lovell as a "secret, treacherous & dangerous Enemy to the United States" (National Archives). He was an early defender of Deane: Jack Rakove, *The Beginnings of National Politics: an Interpretive History of the Continental Congress* (New York, 1979), pp. 250, 253, 260; *DAB*. Harrison probably was Va. congressional delegate Benjamin Harrison, who was linked to the Lees' political enemy John Robinson: H. James Henderson, *Party Politics in the Continental Congress* (New York, St. Louis, and San Francisco, 1974), p. 95n.

7. Lee made his remarks on BF's conduct during the Pulteney mission in a Sept. 24, 1779, letter to JA (*Adams Papers*, VIII, 169), who may have revealed the accusations to BF. Lee made even more pointed allegations in a May 1, 1779, memorial to Congress (National Archives), about which Gérard may have known.

8. BF is repeating the praise for the Pennsylvania constitution that he had expressed to Reed some months earlier: XXXI, 6. For the controversy over the state's 1776 constitution see Douglas M. Arnold, *A Republican Revolution: Ideology and Politics in Pennsylvania, 1776–1790* (New York and London, 1989), *passim*.

II.

Sir   Passy, Mar 19. 1780.

I beg leave to introduce to your Excellency's Acquaintance and Civilities, Monsr le Chevalier De Chastellux; Major General in the French Troops, now about to embark for America, whom I have long known & esteem'd highly in his several Characters of a Soldier, a Gentleman, & a Man of Letters. His excellent Book on Publick Happiness shews him the Friend to Mankind, and as such intitles him wherever he goes, to their Respect and good Offices.[9] He is particularly a Friend to our Cause & I am sure your Excellency will have great Pleasure in his Conversation.

With great Esteem & Respect

His Ex. Jos. Read Eq. Prest. of Penna

Notations in different hands: Dr. Franklin Passy. May 19. 1780 / Introducing Marquis De Chastellux

III.

Sir,   Passy, March 19. 1780.

The Chevalier D'Oyré Captain in the Royal Corps of Engineers, being about to embark with The Troops for America,[1] and as possibly the Operations of War may lead or Permit him to visit Philadelphia, I beg leave to recommend him to your Excellency's Civilities as a Gentleman of Excellent Character in this Country, and a friend of our Cause. With the highest Esteem and Respect, I have the honour to be, Your Excellency's most obedient and most humble servant.

His Excelly. Joseph Reed Esq. President of the state of Penn.

---

9. The chevalier François-Jean de Chastellux was given the rank of *maréchal de camp* in March, 1780, and assigned to serve with Rochambeau's army. He sailed from Brest at the beginning of May and remained in America until January, 1783: XXIII, 273n; François-Jean de Chastellux, *Travels in North America in the Years 1780, 1781 and 1782* (Howard C. Rice, Jr., ed. and trans., 2 vols., Chapel Hill, N.C., 1963), I, 14–15. In 1775 BF had been sent Chastellux's *An Essay on Public Happiness*, the English translation of *De la Félicité publique:* XXI, 505–6.

1. Chevalier François-Ignace d'Oyré (1739–1799) came to America with Rochambeau: Bodinier, *Dictionnaire;* Rice and Brown, eds., *Rochambeau's Army,* II, 116n, 159.

To John Ross

Dear Sir, Passy, March 19. 1780.

I received yours (without Date) in which you mention a Desire that the alliance could come off Nourmautier to take in the Cloth.[2] I have written to Captain Jones to do it if practicable.[3] Perhaps the Mary fearon or Govr. Livingston or both may be taken up for the Publick service. I shall know to morrow, and if so shall write to you to ship the other Things in those Vessels. The Money is impossible. I am with much Esteem, Dear sir, &c.

Mr. Ross.

To George Washington: Two Letters

(I) LS[4] and copy: Library of Congress; (II) copy: Library of Congress

I.

Sir, Passy Mar 19th. 1780.

I beg leave to introduce to your Excellency's Acquaintance & Civilities, Monsr. le Chevalier De Chastelleux; Major General in the French Troops, now about to embark for America, whom I have long known and esteem'd highly in his several Characters of a Soldier, a Gentleman, & a Man of Letters. His excellent Book on Publick Happiness shews him the Friend to Mankind, and as such intitles him wherever he goes to their Respect & good Offices. He is particularly a Friend to our Cause, and I am sure your Excellency will have great Pleasure in his Conversation.

I have the honour to be, with great Respect Your Excellency's most obedt & most humble Servant B FRANKLIN

His Ex. Genl. Washington.

2. Missing. Ross asked Jones directly to come to Noirmoutier: Jones to BF, March 14, above.

3. On March 18, above.

4. In WTF's hand. The LS is in the Washington Papers, the copy in BF's letterbook.

Endorsed: His Excelly. B. Franklin Minr Plenipoty. 19th. Mar 1780

II.

Sir   Passy, March 19. 1780
   Count Christian and Count William de Deux Ponts Colonel and Lieutenant Colonel of the Regiment of that Name are now about to embark for America. As Possibly they may before their Return visit your Army, I beg leave to introduce them to your Excellency and to Recommend them to your Civilities as young Gentlemen well known to me, of Excellent Character and zealous Friends to our Cause and Country, With the highest Esteem and Respect, I have the honour to be, Your Excellency's &c.

Gen. Washington, and the same for Prisidend Reed.[5]

From Samuel Ross *et al.*   ALS: American Philosophical Society

                                          Lorient Marh. 19th 1780
The Humble Petition of three Men late belonging to the Continential Ship Reprisal Lambert Weeks Esqr. Commr. Humbly Sheweth
   That your Petitioners has just arrived from Mill Prison in Plymo. being Exchanged in the Adventure Carteel upon our Arrival at Morlaix we received thirty two Livres to bear our Expences to Lorient and now we are arrived here we are destitute of money & Cloaths.
   And now Sir to Convince You we have Prize Money and Wages due to us for several Cruizes I shall now relate to your Excellency the Number of Prizes we have assisted to take in the said Ship—
   In the first Place we all Entered in the Reprisal in the Month of April 1776 at Philadelphia we lay at Cape May and thereabouts for the Space of two months then we Carried Mr. Byngham to Martinica where we had an Engagement with the Shark

5. The letterbook copy of (I) also bears the notation that the same recommendation is to be sent to President Reed.

Sloop of War upon our Passage to Martinica we took three Prizes and they arrived safe at Philadelphia for those Prizes I dont Expect to receive any Money in France, from Martinica we then returned to Philadelphia again and in the Month of September 1776 we sailed for France with your Excellency on board said Ship on our Passage we took two prizes and Carried them into Quibberoon Bay where your Excellency Landed from thence we went to Nantz and refitted our Ship and Cruized off the Land's End of England and took three Briggs a Ship and the Swallow Packett which we fought for all those arrived safe at Lorient here we cleaned our Ship and sailed to Nantz and joined Company with the Brige. Lexington Henry Johnson Esqr. Commander also the Dolphin Cutter ——— Nicholson Esqr. Commander after making up the Squadron we all sailed together to Cruize in St. Georges Channell where we took several Prizes in one of those Prizes taken by the fleet we your Petitioners were put on board the Prize John and Thomas the 21st. June 1777 and was retaken 29th of the same Month nigh to the Penmarks on the Coast of France by the Hawk Letter of Mark Capt. Gribble Commander Mr. Thos Norwood was our Prize Master who made his Escape with several others from Prison Saml. Ross Prize Master's Mate Thos. Dwyer and Joseph McMullen Mariners there were ten in Number of us some entered on board an English Man of War some ran away from Prison and there is but us three Vizt. Saml. Ross Thos. Dwyer and Joseph Mac-Mullen the latter is quite deaf occasioned by sickness in the Prison where we were Confined two years eight Months and upwards.[6]

6. For the ten members of the prize crew captured on June 29, 1777, by Capt. John Gribble's *Hawke* see Clark, *Wickes,* pp. 252–3, 375–6; Ross, a mate on the *Reprisal,* was from Bristol, Norwood from somewhere in England, and Dwyer and MacMullen from Ireland. The three men also signed a March 23 petition asking for a small sum of money, which could be deducted from their wages and prize money. The other exchanged prisoners from Mill Prison who signed were John Hopes, Henry Lawrence, George Thayer, John Chester, James Dick, Philip McGlaughlan, William Ryley, William Lee, Thomas Bradley, Jacob Crawford, and John Harvey, formerly of the *Lexington* (for whom see Clark, *Wickes,* pp. 377–80) and Paul McGee, formerly of the brig *Cabot.* APS.

I have been informed by one of my Acquaintance that came from Philadelphia lately that one of the Reprisal's Crew that was retaken in a Prize and Carried to Forton Prison and made his Escape from thence and got to Philadelphia he petitiond to the Congress for his Prize Money that the Prizes were sold for in France and he Received for Answer he must apply to his Excellency Doctr. Franklin in France where the Prizes were condemned.

I was informed that Mr. Gour Lattee was Agent for the five Prizes brought into Lorient[7] and inquiring for him I found his Cheif Clark and he told me that the whole of the Business was put into Mr. Morris's[8] Hands at Nantz. Now that your Excellency would be pleased to Order the Agent to pay us our Prize Money that is due to us for the Prizes sold in France and render us an Account of what we have and what we are to Receive in France to satisfy the Agents at Philadelphia.

And that you would take this Matter into your Consideration is the earnest Desire of your most Humble Servants

SAMUEL ROSS

THOMAS DWYER X HIS MARK

JOSH. MCMULLEN X HIS MARK

Notation: Petition of three Men belonging to Capt. Weeks L'Orient March 19. 80

To Leonard Lafitte

Copy: Library of Congress

sir,   Passy 20. mar. 1780.

I received The Letter you did me the honour of writing to me on the 11th. Instant. The loan office Bills of which you send me a List, have not as yet been presented for acceptation, when they appear, I Shall give particular attention to the Indorsements in order to prevent their being paid if they should not have come through the proper Channel.

7. The Lorient firm of Gourlade & Monplaisir was sent some of Wickes's prizes: XXIV, 278; Clark, *Wickes,* p. 205.

8. The late Thomas Morris (XXII, 544n), to whom Wickes also directed prizes: Clark, *Wickes,* p. 205.

My Grandson is very sensible of your kind Remembrance of him and desires me to present you his respectful compliments.

With great Esteem I have the honour to be &c.

Mr. Lafitte Negt. Bordeaux.

To Antoine-Raymond-Gualbert-Gabriel de Sartine

LS:[9] Archives de la Marine; copy: Library of Congress

sir,   Passy, March 20th. 1780.

In compliance with your Excellency's Opinion, express'd in the Letter you did me the honour of writing to me on the 14th. of October last,[1] that I should send for Capt. Landais to Paris, to give an account of his Conduct respecting the late Engagement with the Serapis, where in it had appear'd to your Excellency, "that if the Frigate Alliance which he commanded had seconded the Bonhomme Richard by engaging at the same time, the Advantage gaind by Commodore Jones would have been sooner obtain'd, have cost fewer lives, and not have left the Bonhomme Richard in such a Condition, as to sink in 36. Hours after the Combat": I immediately wrote to the Said Capt Landais, acquainting him with that and other Charges against him, and directing him to render himself here, and to bring with him such Evidence as he could obtain and should think proper for his Justification: and I wrote at the same time to the Commodore acquainting him with this step, and directing him to send me the Evidence he had, to support the Charges against Captain Landais contain'd in his Letters.[2] Capt. Landais who had also himself desired of me to order an Enquiry,[3] was necessarily detain'd some time after in Holland, Sundry Accidents such as the Delay of Commodore Jones's expected Proofs, and the indisposition at different Times of my Self and Capt Landais, have

9. In the hand of L'Air de Lamotte, except for the postscript, which is in BF's hand and is not present in the letterbook copy.

1. XXX, 535.

2. XXX, 537–8, 539.

3. XXX, 507–8.

drawn the Enquiry to a Length unexpected;[4] and after all, I find so much Contradiction in the Declarations of the Parties, and the written Evidence adduc'd in support of them; and such an Insufficiency of marine knowledge in my self, when all the Possibilities are to be considered of this or that Manœuvre of a Ship under the various Circumstances of Wind, Tide and situation; that I cannot presume, even if I had authority for so doing, to condemn the Conduct of Captain Landais, or to advise the Congress to cross his Name from the List of their Sea Officers. His regular Trial will be before a Court Martial consisting of a competent Number of Such officers, which can only be found in America; and to that I must therefore refer him. That Court will judge how far he is chargeable with Disobedience to orders, Delay in coming to the assistance of the Commodore, or Neglect of taking the Merchant Ships. I will only venture to give your Excellency one Opinion of mine in his favour, that his firing into that ship instead of the Serapis, if that fact should be found clear, could never have been the Effect of Design, but merely from accident occasioned by the Night, or the natural spreading of Shot. For tho' it appear'd in the Course of the Enquiry; that a mortal Quarrel had arisen during the Cruise between the Commodore and him, Human Nature is not yet so depraved, as to hazard the killing of many, for the Chance of hurting one; nor is it probable that if Captain Landais had given such Orders, his People would have obey'd them.— All I can farther do, is to transmit to Congress Copies of the Minutes of the Enquiry; with the Papers produc'd, and to leave Capt. Landais at Liberty to return to America in order to a Trial. The Enquiry, imperfect as it is, has however had one good Effect, the preventing a Duel in Holland between those Officers, which might have proved fatal to one or both of them, and would at best have occasion much inconvenient Rumour, Scandal, Dispute and Dissention prejudicial to our Affaires. With the greatest Respect I have the honour to be, Sir, Your Excellencys, most obedient and most humble servant

B FRANKLIN

4. The inquiry was adjourned from Nov. 15 until Nov. 24, when it was finally suspended: XXXI, 110–12.

I have found your Character of Landais very just une bien mauvaise tête.

M. de Sartine.

From the Marquis de Lafayette

ALS: American Philosophical Society

Dear Sir   on Board the hermione 20h March 1780

We are Again Going to Sail,[5] But no News about our cloathing— What is Become of it, I Cannot Guess, and am extremely sorry that they are not Arriv'd— I hope the Whole will be soon Sent to America, and this intelligence will I dare Say Be very Agreable to the Army.

In Wishing You A Good health, and the accomplishment of any thing You May desire, in Wishing for Myself the Continuation of Your Much esteem'd frienship, I have the honor to be with the Most perfect Respect and tendrness Your affectionate

LAFAYETTE

I Beg You Will present My Compliments to Yr Grand Son and mr de Chaumont.

Notation: Marqs. La Fayette 20 mar 80

From John Holker

ALS: American Philosophical Society

Dear Sir   Rouen 21 of March 1780

I did not faill Informing my Self of the Preseis of laid as Sould in this Marquit which youl find here inclosed, which my friend Garvey Sends me, and I know no one more Capable of making the Purchas as he chifly buys all with Redy mony, having a Considerable Capital in hand, & In caise you send me any further or-

---

5. Storm damage had forced the *Hermione* back to port, but her second sailing was more successful; the French frigate reached Boston on April 27: Idzerda, *Lafayette Papers*, II, 379–80; III, 3.

ders on this head I certinly shall apploy to him, who I am sure will serve you to the outmost of his pouar.[6] My wife I found much better, and She mends apease by my presence &c we bouth desire and wish to see you here. No one Living woud be More wellcom or doe us more pleaseure, so See and make a trip here with Our friend Mr. Choment this Summer & wee shall strive to make you happey. I ever am Dear Sir your most Obedt & very humble servt   J HOLKER

From Dumas   ALS: American Philosophical Society

Honoured & Dear Sir   at the Hague 23 Mar. 1780.

Mr. Gillon will bring or forward you two packets; in one of which is the rare, elegant & authentic copy of the Utrecht Union, destined for the records of Congress, with some philosophic books for your entertainment. The other is for Captain Jones, & contains a packet for the honourable Robt. Morris, which I beg the favour to be forwarded before the sailing of the Alliance. If Mr. Gillon himself, or his man, will go there. This would be a good occasion.

I must beg another favour of yr. Excy. Viz. to let me know, as soon as possible, if You have received, in a Letter from me dated febr. 25, another Letter of mine for Mr. Carmichael,[7] & what is become of it; has it been sent away to Madrid. I am extremely uneasy on account of this Letter, & Shall be so till I receive your Answer.

153. 17. 134. is to 135. the 812. 873. 433.[8]

6. Holker had mentioned Garvey to BF the preceding October: xxx, 436n. See also our headnote to Clark & Cie.'s bill of June 3–4, below. BF had petitioned the French government on behalf of Maryland for various military supplies, including twenty tons of lead: xxix, 416.

7. See xxxi, 523. Dumas had recently received a warning from Carmichael about letters criticizing him to Congress: Dumas to Jones, March 18, Bradford, *Jones Papers*, reel 5, no. 1023.

8. "Captain Gillon Brest is to bribe the ship the Indian." Dumas probably made a coding error; he must have meant that Gillon intended to buy the ship. Gillon eventually did lease it for the South Carolina navy: xxxi, 184n.

I am with great respect, Honored & dear Sir your most obedient & humble servant   DUMAS

Addressed: His Excellency / B. Franklin, Esqr., / Min. Plenipe. of the / United States, &c. / Passy./.

Notation: Dumas, la haie March 23. 80

From François-Marie d'Angelÿ and Other Commission Seekers   ALS: American Philosophical Society

As Rochambeau's army was gathering at Brest in the spring of 1780, Franklin received several letters from officers seeking to join "Washington's army."[9] D'Angelÿ (d'Angély), whose letter is printed below, wants permission to raise light infantry and cavalry troops in America to complete General Washington's army.[1]

De Flaghac, writing from Strasbourg on March 26, is a captain in the dragoons but without appointment. He has asked Montbarey for a three year leave and permission to join "Wagginston's" army. He would prefer the rank he has in France but if necessary will serve as a volunteer. He asks Franklin's help in obtaining a favorable reception. He does not flee a failed business, nor does he go for his own advantage; he is motivated by honor and a desire for instruction. He is writing to Sartine for passage but will even take a merchant ship, French or Dutch. The slightest delay is contrary to his desire to make the most of this very interesting campaign.

Three days later Captain baron de Gaisberg and Lieutenant Ferdinand de Stahel write from Baborz, near Mohács, Hungary. There they serve the Empress Queen in a regiment of light cavalry, but yearn for

---

9. Unless otherwise noted all letters discussed are in French and at the APS.

1. Col. d'Angély (1735–1808), from an old Burgundian family, was born in Perpignan. He began his career as a page at the court of Anhalt in 1751 and, as he states in his letter, entered the service of Frederick II in 1755. He joined Rochambeau's expedition, serving as aide-de-camp to Antoine-Charles du Houx, baron de Vioménil (1728–1792): *DBF;* Bodinier, *Dictionnaire;* Gilbert Bodinier, *Les Officiers de l'armée royale combattants de la guerre d'Indépendance des Etats-Unis: De Yorktown à l'an II* (Vincennes, 1983), pp. 66, 126, 247, 257. See also Rice and Brown, eds., *Rochambeau's Army,* I, xxi, 34, 131–2; II, 136.

the liberty only partially present in their native country and look to America whose promise of happiness for the many includes the prospect of military advancement, which the peace at home has closed to them. They ask Franklin to secure for them positions in the army and they enclose a letter to Washington. Gaisberg, twenty-eight, is from a distinguished family but is a younger brother. Stahel is a young man and during a stay in Paris met Sainte-Foy, who will surely give His Excellency the necessary information.[2]

On April 15 the chevalier de Baillivy writes from Paris to request a meeting for himself and his brother, both about thirty years old. They have served in France thirteen or fourteen years and have good certificates. He mentions briefly a plan to go to the United Colony to obtain employment.

The sieur de Pommereuille is more specific about de Baillivy's plan.[3] He writes in English from Paris on May 18, apologizing for not having made use of the permission Franklin gave him last year to call on him. He asks for a letter to John Paul Jones recommending de Baillivy, "an ancient disbanded muskeeteer without the least fortune," of noble extraction,[4] and with a highly favorable certificate from the Earl of Montboissier, his former commander.[5] De Baillivy wishes to accompany Mr. Jones, regardless of rank, provided he be employed.

2. While Claude-Pierre-Maximilien Radix de Sainte-Foy (1736–1810) was a man of many titles and positions, it was probably as superintendent of finances for the comte d'Artois, from 1776 to 1781, that he met Stahel. For a coherent account of Sainte-Foy's career see André Doyon, "Maximilien Radix de Sainte-Foy 1736–1810," *Revue d'histoire diplomatique*, LXXX (1966), 231–74, 314–54.

3. Pommereuille had earlier sought a commission for himself: XXVIII, 82.

4. The *Dictionnaire de la noblesse*, II, 214–5, lists an Alexandre-François, *Mousquetaire du Roi*, and his brother, Ignace; their parents, the chevalier Nicolas de Baillivy and Barbe de Hault-de-Sancy, were married Jan. 7, 1744, making it likely the sons were about thirty in 1780.

A Christian Francis Alexander Baillivey appears in Heitman, *Register of Officers* as ensign in the 15th Massachusetts, 1777; he resigned Jan. 9, 1778. Baillivy is identified as a musketeer, discharged in 1775, of noble extraction dating back to the sixteenth century, 29 years old: Bodinier, *Les Officiers*, p. 267.

5. Philippe-Claude de Beaufort-Canillac-Montboissier, comte de Montboissier, was lieutenant-captain of the second company of musketeers: *Dictionnaire de la noblesse*, XIV, 124; *Etat militaire* for 1776, p. 159. On Sept. 21, Pommereuille writes again from Paris in English, this time with a fuller account of Baillivy's circumstances. He acknowledges BF's answer (now missing) that Congress had ordered no encouragement be given to military offi-

M. Nartus writes from the Hôtel de Toulouse in Paris on May 17 to inquire about M. Pommier de L'Etang. Enchanted with Pommier's stories of the sea and his country, Nartus resolved, perhaps precipitously, to quit a station for which he felt no strong disposition, and to follow Pommier. Nartus has quarrelled with his family over the haste of his actions, and so asks Franklin to help him with his goal of serving in the United States.

M. Duclos, retired after fifty-seven years in the Light Cavalry of the King's Guard as first *maréchal des logis* and *mestre de camp*, writes from Corbeny near Laon on May 24.[6] He recommends for service in the American army his relative Davesne, twenty-nine years old, *réformé* from the same company. Davesne "est de la plus belle figure possible, et a De Lesprist beaucoup." Franklin "peut sans faire informé a Monsieur de Mongardé," major of the company, who will surely recommend him too.[7]

Writing from Buda (Budapest), on June 7, Baron Janus Zreny would also like to serve in America, preferably as an officer. He claims no military experience but encloses six pages of his reflections on the likelihood of America's winning the war and his advice for a political and military victory. He speaks French, German, Latin, Italian, Polish; he will quickly learn English as he has some knowledge of it already. If Franklin judges him capable of an officer's rank, he is to write "au plus vite"[8] care of the abbé Zinner, *préfet* at the Académie royale

---

cers seeking passage to America. As enclosed certificates prove, however, Baillivy was already serving in America when Lafayette advised him to return to France so that he might procure for him a more advantageous position. He was taken prisoner on his way back, was exchanged only after Lafayette's second departure for America, and now wants to rejoin him there. Pommereuille suggests that BF would "do a pleasure to Mr. de la Fayette" in providing this gentleman with letters of recommendation for "the men of note who live in the main harbours of America where he may land," thereby facilitating Baillivy's reunion with the marquis. Lafayette himself began his career in the second company of Musketeers, the same company in which Baillivy served under Montboissier: Balch, *French in America*, II, 153; Idzerda, *Lafayette Papers*, I, 13n.

6. He is listed as *maréchal des logis* in the *Etat militaire* for 1767, p. 159.

7. Montgardé is listed as *aide-major* with the rank of *brigadier: État militaire* for 1780, p. 134.

8. Zreny writes from Cassau (Kosice) on Jan. 9, 1781, complaining that BF has answered neither an early letter (no longer extant), nor the present one sent care of Mr. de Blumendorff, *secrétaire chez l'ambassadeur imperial à Paris:*

thérésienne in Vienna.[9]

Closer to home two *gardes du corps* of the comte d'Artois write from Versailles on June 13. De Potot and Desgrange, currently in the service of His Royal Highness, ask Franklin to recommend them to Congress for military service as lieutenants, the rank they have enjoyed for five years. Since their only desire, however, is to be of service to the allies of their august sovereign and to acquire experience in the military art, they will gladly accept whatever employment is judged suitable. They do require an advance for their travel costs or at least the promise of a reimbursement. They will produce certificates from their commanders and obtain leaves of absence.

Monsieur   Paris ce 25e Mars 1780

Si j'eusse cru qu'il me fallut des protections pour parvenir jusqu'a Votre Excellence, j'en aurois eu certainement. Je me presente a vous avec confiance pour offrir mes services aux etats unis d'amerique; les circonstances reveillent un desir que j'ay formé depuis le commencement de la guerre et je desire que vos vues puissent favoriser mon zele.

Je Suis entré en 1755 officier au service du Roy de Prusse en 57 J'etois Capitaine d'un Bataillon d'Infanterie de troupes legeres; J'ay fait toute la guerre en cette qualité, et quoyque j'eusse alors peu de theorie de mon metier, je passois pour un bon officier. Le prince d'anhalt Bernbûrg avec qui j'etois fort lié m'engagea vers la fin de 1761 a passer avec luy en Dannemarc ou il etoit general Major. Je fus fait Chef d'escadron et Major d'un Regiment de hussards qui fut levé cette meme année. Cinq ans aprés, Mr de St germain trouvant la Cavallerie danoise trop pesante me tira du Regiment ou j'etois pour me mettre dans la meme qualité dans le

---

"Jamais Themistocles etoit si troublé de nuit et de jour par des trophées de Miltiades, comme moi par vos entreprises." A word from BF and he will resign his charge and bid farewell to his friends. On Oct. 5, 1781, he writes from Paris following a meeting with BF, who has turned down his offer to fight for America. His situation is awkward since he has resigned his office, and while he acknowledges that BF is not at fault, he does take him and the Congress to task for refusing to commission foreigners. He vows to dedicate the work he is writing to Washington and closes with the dedication, twenty-three lines newly composed in Latin verse.

9. Zinner himself had written on Oct. 26, 1778, from Budapest, to offer his services and ask for information about America for a planned book: XXVII, 646–8.

Regiment Royal Cuirassiers afin d'introduire dans ce Regiment des evolutions plus souples et plus legeres.[1] En 1769 l'Imperatrice de Russie ayant demandé au Roy de Dannemarc quelques officiers qui eussent fait la guerre, le Roy me mit du nombre des volontaires qui luy furent envoyés. Ayant appris la langue du pays a mon arrivée a l'armée Russe, je fus fait le 1er Janvier 1770 Lieutenant Colonel du Regiment de siberie Carabiniers. On detacha a l'entrée de la Campagne un escadron de chaque Regiment de Cavallerie de l'armée dont on me confia le Commandement et je me trouvai avec 12 escadrons de 175 hommes chacun a l'avant garde de l'armée, sous les ordres du general Bauer.[2] Le bonheur suivit si bien mes entreprises, que l'Imperatrice crut faire une bonne acquisition en m'attachant entierement a son service, elle me decora elle meme de l'ordre Militaire, elle m'offrit un Regiment de Carabiniers, une terre en livonie, une place de page pour mon fils qui n'avoit encore que neuf ans,[3] et une somme d'argent Considerable pour amener ma femme et mon fils en Russie: Je ne pus accepter ces propositions qu'après avoir été en Dannemarc prendre le consentement du Roy, il me l'accorda avec des marques de sa satisfaction. Je revins en Russie, j'entrai en possession de ce qui m'avoit eté promis, et je fis de mon mieux pour meriter l'opinion qu'on avoit conçue de moy.

J'etois commandant d'une partie des nouvelles acquisitions de l'Imperatrice dans la Lithuanie, lorsqu'on m'y amena les officiers françois faits prisoniers a Cracovie. Les services que je leur rendis exciterent la reconnoissance du Cardinal de Rohan alors ambassadeur de france a Vienne. Ce prince me flata de l'espoir de jouir en france d'un sort heureux. J'avois besoin de

1. In 1762, following a quarrel with *maréchal* de Broglie, Saint-Germain entered Danish service as field marshal and was charged with reorganizing the army: Larousse.

2. Friedrich Wilhelm von Bauer (1731–1783), born in Hesse, distinguished himself during the Seven Years' War under the Duke of Brunswick, with whose support he organized an engineering corps. He entered the service of Russia in 1769 and was much decorated during the Russo-Turkish War, after which he took over the administration of Russia's waterways. He died at St. Petersburg. *ADB*.

3. Gérard-François d'Angély, born in 1761, eventually served in Esterhazy's regiment of hussards in the French army: Bodinier, *Dictionnaire*, p. 8. *Sous-lieutenant* d'Angély is listed in the *Etat major* for 1780, p. 386.

148

prendre des bains pour me refaire des blessures et des fatigues de la guerre, j'en obtins la permission, j'eus l'imprudence d'aller a Vienne et a Paris pour m'assurer du sort que je pouvois esperer en françe en quittant la Russie. La somme que j'avois pretée aux officiers français m'ayant été adressée a Petersburg par le Cardinal de Rohan a Mr frederichs Banquier de la Cour, celuyci en fit part a l'Imperatrice: elle conçut des soupçons sur ma fidelité, et a mon retour en Russie je fus arrêté et mis en prison: après deux mois de detention, tous mes papiers ayant prouvé mon innocence; mais démontré en meme temps les vues que j'avois de rentrer en france, l'Imperatrice me depouilla de tout ce que je possedois, et je me trouvai après avoir perdu 70 mille livres de rente, sans autre ressource que celle que j'avois lieu d'attendre des bienfaits de la france. Elle m'a accordé un brevet de Colonel qui ne m'attache a rien et ne me donne aucune existence, avec une pension de 5000 *l.t.;* et Votre Excellence verra la verité de ce que viens de luy dire par la lettre de Mr le Mal. du Muy et par le brevet ci joints.[4]

N'ayant malgré les promesses du Roy aucune esperance de pouvoir etre employé dans ma patrie et ne pouvant supporter l'inaction dans laquelle je suis forcé de vivre Je desire servir ses alliés, et etre utile a la Cause commune. Vingt ans d'un service continuel, deux guerres difficilles dans lesquelles j'ay eu quelque succés me donnent l'esperance d'en avoir encore d'autres. Je suis fort et robuste, Je possede parfaitement l'allemand, passablement l'anglois, et si j'obtenois la permission de lever en Amerique un Corps de troupes legeres, moitié a Cheval et moitié a pied, espece de troupes qui manque je crois a l'armée du general Washington, j'oserois me flater d'etre utile a son armée. Je ne marchande point sur le grade, le titre sous lequel je pourrois remplir les objets, que l'ignorance des circonstances et

4. The enclosure is missing. Louis-Nicolas-Victor de Félix, comte du Muy (1711–1775), became minister of war in 1774 and *maréchal de France* in 1775: Larousse. When d'Angély returned to France in 1774 and was unable to find a position, du Muy granted him a pension of 5000 *l.t.* in recognition of his services to the French officers taken at Kraków during the Polish rebellion of 1768–73 against Russia: Gilbert Bodinier, *Les Officiers de l'armée royale combattants de la guerre d'Indépendance des Etats-Unis: De Yorktown à l'an II* (Vincennes, 1983), p. 66.

des lieux ne peut que me faire entrevoir, m'est parfaitement indifferent. Si Votre Excellence daigne accueillir mon zele, je la suplie de ne point s'en rapporter a moy sur les services que je suis
en etat de rendre et je luy demande la faveur de permettre a Mr
le Baron de Viomenil d'aller luy parler de moy.[5] Je prens sur moy
d'obtenir la permission de la cour de france de passer en
Amerique, je ne demande que votre protection pour ne point
aller dans ce paÿs la comme un homme sans aveu; mais soit que
Votre Excellence accepte ou refuse mes offres, je la supplie de
m'accorder un instant d'audience.

Je Suis avec Respect Monsieur de Votre Excellence Le tres
humble et tres obeissent Serviteur   D'ANGELŸ

Notation: D'angely Paris ce 25 mars 1780.

From Benjamin Franklin Bache

ALS: American Philosophical Society

Mon cher bon papa   Geneve ce 25 Mars 1780
   Je vous avouë qu'il y a Longtemps, que je ne vous ai écrit,
Mais il y a encore plus longtemps, que je n'ai eu de vos nouvelles;
j'aurois aimé que mon cher cousin ou mon ami Cochran[6]
m'eussent ecrit; si vos ocupations, comme je le pense, vous em-
pechoient de le faire Monsieur Marignac[7] et moi aurions été tres

   5. Vioménil, second in command of Rochambeau's army, was one of several of his family to serve in the American campaigns. Earlier Vioménil had
served in Poland and was one of those captured at Kraków: Bodinier, *Les
Officiers*, pp. 124, 126; Bodinier, *Dictionnaire;* Larousse.
   6. Charles Cochran was last heard from in XXX, 241, when he was supposed to provide BFB with the names of their four schoolmates in Passy who
had died from smallpox.
   7. Gabriel-Louis Galissard de Marignac, whose stylistic influence is heavily felt in this letter, was a regent of the Collège de Genève at which BFB
would remain until the summer of 1783. Born in Geneva in 1736, he had two
children by his first wife, and two by his second, *née* Suzanne Mallet-Genoud.
Marignac's teaching and personality were favorably noticed. Poorly paid, re-
gents frequently had to take in boarders. (Indeed, BFB moved in with the
Marignacs later in the spring.) Information kindly provided by Walter Zur-
buchen, archivist of state, Geneva.

en peine, si nous n'avions pas eu de vos nouvelles par les Gazettes & par madame arthaud, à qui Madame Grand en avoit
donné et chez qui je dinai lautre jour, elle me fait toujours beaucoup d'amitié ainsi que Madame Cramer, a qui j'ai les plus
grandes obligations, elle me tient lieu de mère;[8] si vous avès des
nouvelles de mon cher Papa, & de ma chere mama, je vous
prierois de men donner, & de les assurer, quand vous leur ecrirés
de mon respect, et de toute ma reconnoissance. Je fais tous mes
efforts, Mon cher bon Papa, pour vous conter [contenter?], aussi.
Je sens toutes vos bontés pour moi, & je ne cesserai d'être avec
gratitude et un profond respect. Votre tres humble et tres obeiant
serviteur et petit fils   BENJAMIN F B

Notation: B.F.B. to Dr. F—Geneva March 25. '80

A Monsieur / Monsieur Franklin Ministre / Plénipotentiaire des
Provinces unies de L'Amérique au près de / Sa Majesté très
chrétienne / recommandé à Monsieur Grand / Banquier rüe
Montmartre / A Paris

From the Duchesse de Deux-Ponts

ALS: American Philosophical Society

Samedis Saint [March 25, 1780?][9]

Je vient vous proposer mon cher et respectable amis de faire demain au soir Vos paques avec moi mes enfants le pere Caillot
Keralio fontenet &c &c.[1] Nous N'auronts que gens qui vous
Conviendronts, Nous boiront du thes Nous joueronts aux
echecs, tandis que Notre jeunesse a La tette de la quelle sera votre

---

8. Catherine Cramer, whose late husband, Philibert, had accompanied BFB
to Geneva, was the boy's landlady and temporary foster-mother. Agathe
Arthaud, Marie Silvestre Grand's sister, had become a special friend of BFB.
For these three Genevans see XXIX, 342n; XXX, 248n, 587.

9. The year 1780, when Easter fell on March 26, is the most plausible for
this invitation. The duchesse was moving into a new house in 1779 (XXIX,
171) and by 1781 her sons would be in America.

1. The actor Joseph Caillot appears in XXVIII, 215n. Fontenet was the
duchess' brother.

bon, et aimable fils a ce que jespere fera le train je serois bien
charmé mon digne amis si vous pouviez accepter ma proposition
ce ceroit une bonne oeuvre et Vous scavés quil en faut faire le
jour de paque.

Je Vous embrasse aussi tendrement que je Vous aime exelant
home et jembrasse aussi Mr Votre fils Mais pas si tendrement que
Vous parcequil est trop jeune   M: DOUAIRIERE DE DEUXPONTS

Addressed: A Monsieur / Monsieur francklin / Ministre pleini-
potentiare / des etats unie a La Cour / de france / a passis

From Jean Rousseau[2]   ALS: University of Pennsylvania Library

Monsieur   Genêve le 25. Mars 1780.

Le mémoire[3] que je prends la liberté d'addresser à Vôtre Excellence, a été composé comme Elle peut le voir par le contenu,
il y a bientôt deux ans: il n'est connu que de trois personnes dis-
tinguées à la Cour de France, à qui des Copies en ont été envoiées
depuis: peut être auront-elles êté communiquées à V. E.; dans
cette incertitude néanmoins l'Autheur[4] m'a chargé de lui en faire
l'envoi, la priant en même tems de favoriser Ses intentions, dans
le cas qu'Elle daigne approuver l'exposé en question, qui a èté
plutôt écrit, pour les Espagnols, que pour les autres intéressés.

L'Autheur offre Ses très humbles Services, pour être dans un
bureau, ou auprès d'un Ambassadeur, Envoié, ou Ministre, en
qualité de Secretaire &c. Il est d'un âge mur, puisqu'il a passé les
cinquante: ayant êté une trentaine d'années en Angleterre, il
écrit & parle familiérement l'Anglois, il parle Allemand, &

2. Rousseau, driven from Geneva, became a London merchant. He was a
cousin and correspondent of Jean-Jacques Rousseau: R.A. Leigh, ed., *Correspondance complète de Jean Jacques Rousseau* (50 vols., Geneva, Banbury, England
and Oxford, 1965–91), III, 136n; L, 425; Rousseau to BF, June 13, 1783 (APS).
3. An undated fourteen-page memoir in his hand, marked "Copie," which
claimed to demonstrate the advantages of American independence to
France, Spain, the other colonial powers of America, and the majority of European commercial states. Hist. Soc. of Pa. On May 16 Rousseau wrote to
ask BF if he had received it; it had been sent by Gabard de Vaux, the French
chargé d'affaires in Geneva. University of Pa. Library.
4. Rousseau himself, as he admitted on June 13, 1783 (APS). He also said
he had sent copies to Maurepas, Vergennes, and Necker.

l'écrit passablement, & a aussi quelque teinture de l'Espagnol. Accoutumé depuis longtems, de mener une vie active, l'oisiveté & l'ennui lui Sont insupportables: Si vôtre Excellence veut bien le proteger, soit pour l'employer Elle même, soit pour le recommander à d'autres: on peut être asseuré d'acquerir un Sujet Zélé, & affectionné à Ses Supérieurs, & qui jusqu'à présent, s'est toujours comporté avec honneur & probité, ainsi que des personnes très connues à Paris, & à Genêve peuvent le certiffier.

Je suis avec beaucoup de respect Monsieur De Vôtre Excellence Le très humble & très obeissant Serviteur

JEAN ROUSSEAU
Parent de feu Jean Jacques Rousseau

chez Messrs: De Tournes Lullin Masbou & Comp. Banquiers à Genêve.[5]

Notation: Rousseau.

From Peter Fowler[6]   L: Historical Society of Pennsylvania

Monseigneur   [after March 25, 1780][7]
Le Sr. Fowler, Chimiste, auteur d'une Poudre anti-hémorragiste expose très humblement, à Votre Excellence, qu'il a été

---

5. De Tournes, Lullin, Masbou et Cie. was in business from 1778 to 1784: Lüthy, *Banque protestante*, II, 282.

6. An Englishman who called on BF in December, 1777, carrying a medicinal powder that would stop bleeding: xxv, 267. His rival was Jacques Faynard, a Frenchman living in London. Faynard's claim to the anti-hemorrhaging powder had substance: the King of England had granted him a patent in 1773, after which Faynard printed a broadside listing the hundreds of nobles and physicians who had endorsed the medicine. Faynard visited Paris in 1779, demonstrated the powder to the academies of surgery and medicine, and was praised in the press: xxix, 34; *Courier de l'Europe*, v (1779), 55, issue of Jan. 22, 1779. Faynard was again in Paris in the summer of 1780. On July 27 the *Jour. de Paris* reported that his demonstration to the Société royale de médecine was so successful that Montbarey and Sartine ordered the powder to be used in hospitals both on land and at sea. Faynard warned the public that unless the bottles were signed by his own hand, they were counterfeit.

7. The date on which Fowler signed an oath of allegiance before BF (APS). He refers to himself in this letter as a "naturalisé américain." Why he wrote in French is a mystery.

mandé Le 22 Mars, Présent mois, par ordre du Gouvernement, pour répondre au Mémoire injurieux d'un Sr. faynard, qui L'accuse, entr'autre, d'avoir fait usage de sa Poudre pour le Succès de ses expériences, y alléguant, que dans une visite qu'il a eû L'honneur de vous faire, vous lui avéz dit Positivement, que le Suppliant n'avoit Jamais envoyé, à votre Connoissance, une Seule Boîte de la sienne en Amérique, laquelle imposture, si elle n'etait démentie, Serait d'une conséquence d'autant plus funeste au Suppliant, que le d. [dit] faynard, employe déja, depuis Longtems, tous les moyens possibles de surprendre la bonne foi de quelques Puissants Protecteurs qu'il s'est procuré, à force d'intrigues; de sorte que le Sr. fowler est menacé, malgré tous les Succès qu'il a obtenus avec sa Poudre, non seulement, de ne point obtenir la permission de la débiter en france, S'il ne prouve la différence qui existe entre la Sienne et celle de Son antagoniste, mais encore d'être poursuivi en qualité de Sujet de sa Majesté Britannique.

Le Sieur fowler naturalisé américain, reclame, Monseigneur, à ce Sujet, L'honneur de votre protection, vous priant d'informer M. Le Comte de Vergennes, des différents Envois que le Docteur Bancroft a faits, de sa Poudre, sous vos yeux pour L'usage des armées américaines, montant ensemble à plus de deux mille Boîtes, outre Les quatre Cent, dont le Capitaine Lockyer vient d'être chargé, Sous votre Protection immédiate. Ci Joint est le Mémoire instructif de tous les objects relatifs à cette affaire, Sur lequel le Sr. fowler vous prie de jetter un Coup d'oeil favorable.[8]

Le Suppliant ose espérer de votre Justice, Monseigneur, la grace qu'il Sollicite et il continuera ses Voeux au Ciel pour la Conservation des Jours de votre Excellence.

A Son Excellence, Le Docteur Francklin, Ministre Plenipotentiaire, des Etats Unis d'Amérique.

---

8. The memoir is missing, but Fowler succeeded in getting his powder shipped to America. It enjoyed a vigorous promotional campaign in the *Pennsylvania Gazette,* beginning on Sept. 20, 1780, where it was announced as "Balsamick Powders" endorsed by an unnamed faculty at Paris. Copies of the endorsement were available at the seller's.

From the Marquis de Condorcet

ALS: American Philosophical Society

Monsieur et très illustre Confrere,[9]   Ce 26. Mars. [1780]

Vous aviez eu la bonte de me promettre de m'envoier des lettres pour recomander a vos amis d'amérique le Prince Emmanuel de Salm.[1] Vous m'avez oublié. Cependant il part demain et je voudrais bien avoir Les lettres ce matin.

J'ai oublié de vous parler d'un point essentiel, du cheval de monture en trouve-t-on en Amérique de bien dressés, qui soient un peu grands (le P. de Salm a près de Six pieds) et qui aient la vigueur Convenable. On disait que le general Du Coudrai avait été noié par la faute de son cheval américain.[2]

Recevez mes excuses de la peine que je vous donne, et daignez agréer, Monsieur et très illustre Confrere, les sentimens de respect et d'attachement que je vous ai voués.

LE MIS. DE CONDORCET

Addressed: A Monsieur / Monsieur franklin

From Jonathan Williams, Jr.

ALS: University of Pennsylvania Library; copy: Yale University Library

This document alludes to Jonathan Williams, Jr.'s, relationships with two key figures in Franklin's life: Jacques Donatien Le Ray de Chau-

9. In the Académie royale des sciences, of which he was secretary: XX, 489n.

1. On March 25, 1780, BF wrote to Washington: "The Bearer of this, M. le Prince Emanuel de Salm, Colonel Commandant of the Regiment d'Anhalt, supposing it possible that the Operations of the ensuing Campaign may bring him near to your Excellency, has desired of me a Line of Introduction. He bears here an excellent Character, is highly esteem'd by all that have the Honour of his Acquaintance, and I make no doubt of your receiving great Pleasure in his Conversation." Anhalt, one of seven German infantry regiments in the French Army, was part of Rochambeau's second division and was unable to reach America; BF's ALS was never delivered and is now at the Archives Nationales.

2. Du Coudray accidentally drowned in the Schuylkill on Sept. 15, 1777: XXV, 220–1.

mont and Edward Bancroft. All three men were involved individually and with one another in private business ventures, Williams arranging for the shipping of thousands of *livres* worth of assorted goods to America.[3] But Chaumont, as becomes clear in the present letter, had now turned openly hostile to the American agent, accusing him of incompetence and intentions to mix private ventures with public business.

The reasons for this hostility seem to go beyond the men's rivalry for control of the Congressional order for supplies, evident in our published documents. They were also in competition over private business.[4] A French merchant reported that Chaumont was piqued with the *maison Williams* for charging him such steep commissions. Besides, sniped the writer, Williams had generally fallen out of favor as a result of his marriage, which was not widely approved.[5]

Williams knew that Chaumont suspected him of increasing his own profits at the Frenchman's expense.[6] But, as he told Bancroft, he charged Chaumont less than his usual commission: 7½ instead of 10 per cent.[7] For Bancroft, however, he charged a token 1 per cent for the shipment of two particular trunks.

At a moment when cargo space was at a premium, Williams and Bancroft had initially arranged for these trunks to sail with the military supplies. One of them was to go with Lafayette and the second with John Paul Jones on the *Alliance*. Their contents? Jewelry, gold and silver lace, black and white silk lace, thread lace, silk stockings, ruffles, embroidered buttons, silk handkerchiefs, and gloves, worth 22,225 *l.t.* 15 *s.*, in the first case, and 23,535 *l.t.* 12 *s.* in the second.[8] Ban-

3. In February, 1780, for example, jw's ship the *Tom Johnson* carried five bales of goods for Chaumont, consigned to Jean Holker in Philadelphia. jw to Holker, Feb. 10, 1780, Library of Congress. jw's business arrangements with Bancroft can be followed through jw's letterbooks in the Yale University Library.

4. Both supplying goods to Jean Holker, for example. See Matthew Ridley to Holker, Dec. 18, 1779, Library of Congress.

5. Unknown to Jean Holker, Jan. 20, 1780, Library of Congress. jw's marriage was not as universally scorned as the writer made it seem; John Holker, for example, reported to his son on Oct. 20, 1779, that Mariamne Williams ("Mlle Alexander Glascow") was "fort aimable et d'une très bonne fortune." Yale University Library.

6. jw to Ridley, April 16, 1780, Yale University Library.

7. jw to Bancroft, March 26, Yale University Library.

8. Bancroft gave the value of the first trunk in a letter to Jean Holker, March 13 (Library of Congress). The invoice of Trunk No. 2, signed by jw on March 18, 1780, is in the Yale University Library.

croft consigned both trunks to Jean Holker in Philadelphia, with strict instructions to sell them only when conditions favored making a substantial profit and to keep the entire operation absolutely confidential: some people might be malevolent, others might be jealous.[9]

The shipping plans soon changed, however. Williams told Bancroft, on the same day as he wrote the present letter to Franklin, that he had arranged to freight entirely on his own a schooner which would sail under convoy of the *Alliance*. It would carry a variety of goods that had been waiting for safe convoy, including packages for Chaumont and Bancroft's second trunk.[1] Trunk No. 1 would be shipped on the King's flûte *Barbue*, 20, part of de Ternay's squadron, and de Ternay himself had agreed to take charge of the key.[2]

Had Chaumont learned that Williams was involved in an ongoing scheme to profit by selling French luxury items in America? Was he one of those who Bancroft feared would be "malevolent"? It is possible that the Frenchman's recent threat, which Williams related to Bancroft (see our annotation, below), is an indication that he may have at least suspected that Williams was standing to profit handsomely in ventures from which he himself was excluded, ventures of which Franklin would certainly not have approved.

Dear & honoured Sir   Nantes March 26. 1780

My last Letters to Mr de Chaumont will show you the State of affairs here. I do all that man can do but nobody can do impossibilities and I ought not to be blamed for what I can't help. Mr de Chaumont has been a little severe with me and passed on me unjust and undeserved Reflections, but I am sure they do not come from himself so have already forgotten them. It is kind in Friends to state an accusation & give Room for exculpation, in-

9. Bancroft to Jean Holker, March 13. In that same letter, Bancroft reminded Holker that jw had previously shipped to him a bale containing ladies' gold- and silver-embroidered silk shoes, among other things, valued at 5290 *l.t.*

1. jw to Bancroft, March 26; see also his letter of March 27 (Yale University Library). jw was also shipping a large quantity of baled cloth for a variety of merchants, which was loaded on an anchored barge destined for Paimboeuf in early April when a sudden violent storm sank the vessel. He spent the days between April 6 and 11 dragging the river bottom for the bales, and the next month getting the goods dried, calendered, and rebaled. jw to John Holker, April 11 and May 11, Yale University Library.

2. Bancroft to Jean Holker, April 8, Library of Congress.

stead of drawing conclusions which must be erroneus when an accusation is False.[3]

I am afraid my Letter to Mr Paulze has not yet been delivered, as the Farmers have ordered me to be condemned to pay all the Duties & they state as a Favour that the Goods are not seized. I have written to Mr Chaumont fully about this matter & must beg you and him to see it properly arranged, for else I must pay Duties on what the Farmers themselves if they were properly informed would not desire to receive. I have recvd Mr Bondfields Proposition but he is at present at L'orient he is expected this Evening & my next shall inform further on this Subject.—[4] Capt Kendrick who has been long here from Prison[5] is desirous of going to America by an Opportunity which now offers but he cant get away without his Board is paid. Mr Schweighauser has done it in part but he declines paying the whole as he says you have been informed that Capt Kendrick might have gone away before. By Capt Kendricks Representation this does not appear to be the Case, & I shall be glad if you will order the whole of his Board to be paid as other Prisoners have been. I have advanced him for all his Cloths & other supplies he being an old Acquaintance. He commanded one of the Privateers which took the two West India men that were afterwards given up to the English.

I am ever most dutifully & Affectionately Yours

JONA WILLIAMS J

Doctor Franklin

3. JW was not so even-tempered when he was writing, on the same day, to Edward Bancroft: Chaumont had sent him the "most vexatious letter" he had ever received, blaming him for the goods' not having arrived at La Rochelle, and assuming that they had been taken. He also accused JW of having held up La Motte Picquet's squadron, the year before, by the delay in placing private business ventures on board one of the ships. Chaumont sharply warned JW that on this occasion he was forbidden to load any packages that were not on the public account, and threatened to inform BF if these orders were disobeyed. On March 30, JW quoted this part of Chaumont's letter to Bancroft, and asked him to explain again to BF the difficulties they had encountered with duties and customs. The correspondence between Chaumont and JW has been lost, but copies of JW's letters to Bancroft are at the Yale University Library.

4. See JW's next letter, March 27.

5. Following his captivity John Kendrick had made his way to Lisbon, where he wrote to BF in June, 1779: XXIX, 681–2.

Addressed: A monsieur / Monsieur Franklin / Ministre Plenipotentiaire / des / Etas Unis de l'Amerique / en son Hotel a Passy pres / Paris

Notation: Jona Williams May 26. 1780

From David Hartley   ALS: American Philosophical Society

My Dear Friend   March 27 1780

I send by this date another letter with enclosures relating to the Exchange of prisoners.[6] I hope in God that nothing will happen to interrupt that Exchange wch I look upon as a link of communication wch may by degrees lead us to farther pacific intercourses. The only object of my thoughts is by every possible means to soften animosities and to counteract by conciliatory mediation those harshnesses wch may alienate the parties from each other; more especially if any persons do exist who wish not any restoration of peace and good will. If any such persons do exist they will take their opportunities and advantage of acting their malicious work by mutual irritations in secret. Remember this wch is most true. The people of England are not alienated from reconciliation with america— You have asked me Why then will they seem to adopt by sufferance the acts of their Ministers—[7] They are deceived. Their eye does not reach to a distance of 3000 miles, and what the Eye doth not see, the heart doth not rue. Your ever affecte   DH—

Addressed: To Dr Franklin / &c &c &c

From Jane Mecom   ALS: American Philosophical Society

Dear Brother   Warwick 27 March 1780

I have red yrs of Octr. 25[8] & rejoyce you continue in helth & have so many Comforts about you the Agreable situation of yr

6. Missing.
7. In his letter of Feb. 2: XXXI, 439.
8. XXX, 582–4.

Dwelling, Beautifull Gardens, & yr choice of the best of company. I often form to my self an Idea of; & wish you could Injoy them hear with the same Benifit to yr Native country. You are happy in that you can never want friends go where you will, & as far as it is posable for any created being will Remain in Fashion but if the Artists that have taken yr Face have varied as much from each other as that affixed to yr Philosophacal Papers done in France some years ago from the coppy,[9] it will apear as changeable as the moon, however if it is call'd Dr Franklin it will be revered. In my last leter I wrote to beg a couple of those Prints, or Bustos, Ither which is thought most Like you & that can be Easest or saifest conveyd.[1] I seldom meet with any thing in the Newspapers but what is to yr honour, that of the mechanice Rust served only to make me Laugh.[2]

I understand your Commodore Jones has been ordred to Depart out of Holland with his Effects & Fleet. I hope he got off saif. Since the Enimie have Evacuated Newport we have Injoyd. peace & quietnes as to them, but the depreciation of our curency makes grat Dificulties & it seemes they cannot be Remedied while the war Lasts.

I have sent in the French Friggett that mr Adams went in a small box of soap containing but 2 Doz I thought I could have made a little more beter but I dont think I have suckceded. I have however sent another small box down to mr williams which I intend this Leter to go with you will be a Judg which is best when you git them & if Ither will be fitt to make presents of. I hope however to make another tryal when the wether Groes warm the second box contains 2 doz & seven.

I think I am fortunate that you have rec'd so many of my Leters. I hope the soap is also got saif to you. Shall be glad to know what you think on it when you have tried it. I was obliged

9. The engraving by François-Nicolas Martinet, copied from the Chamberlain print and used for the frontispiece to the *Œuvres de M. Franklin* (2 vols., Paris, 1773). BF had written to his wife that the copy had "got so French a Countenance, that you would take him for one of that lively Nation." The engraving is the frontispiece to our vol. xx; see also, in that volume, pp. xvii, 384.

1. That letter has been lost. Her last extant letter is above, xxx, 325–8.

2. See xxix, 723–4n.

to manage it in some Perticulars different from Useal method for want of convenience. Shall Rejoyce if it ansures the End you wishd. to have it for. Be it as it will let me know. Remember my Love to Temple & to Benny when you write to him. I am Ever yr very affectionate and obliged sister   JANE MECOM

Addressed: Doctr Franklin / at Passy near Paris / France

From Jonathan Williams, Jr.

LS: University of Pennsylvania Library; copy: Yale University Library

Dear & honoured Sir   Nantes March 27 1780

Mr De Chaumont has sent me Mr Bondfields Letter to you[3] with authority to freight his Ships on the same Conditions as the King Freights which Mr Bondfield supposes to be 25 *l.t.* pr Ton & Insurance *out* & *home* without Premium.

As it does not appear by Mr De Chaumonts Letter that he understands more than Insurance *out* & that at a certain Premium I did not think myself authorized to comply with Mr Bondfields Conditions, more especialy as the Terms the King allows are so various that no precedent can be fixed. I have therefore brought him to decisive Terms & put them in form of an agreement to which you will please to give your Assent or negative. If you approve of them please to sign the Approbation at the Foot of the Agreement in order to give me proper authority to execute the Conditions.— I do not know how you could do Better & was it not for the Insurance Back I should think the terms exceeding easy, the Insurance is however the only motive these People have to enter into such an Agreement for they really do not gain by the Price of the Freight their Outfitts are so exceeding heavy.

Mr De Chaumont ordered me to send all I could to Brest but not a Waggon was to be had all being taken for the King. I have however found 50 Mules which I have sent forward with two Bales each.[4] It is my Intention to ship in Pieces whatever may not be made up at the Time the Ships are ready.

3. See BF to Bondfield, March 19.
4. The mules apparently left on March 21, when JW drew up an invoice of

In order to save Time for every moment is now precious I send this by the Express half the Expence of which Mr Bondfield has agreed to Pay.

Please to remember the Affair with Mr Paulze for without an Order from the Farmer I cannot get the Cloaths cleared.—

I am ever Your dutifull & Affectionate Kinsman

JONA WILLIAMS J

Notation: Jona Williams March 27. 80

From the Board of Admiralty[5]

ALS: American Philosophical Society; copies:[6] Library of Congress, National Archives

Sir   Board of Admiralty Philadelphia March 28th. 1780.

By the annex'd list you will perceive the present disposition of the Continental Navy in North america.[7] The detachment of

---

clothing "forward'd by Land to Brest on the backs of Mules, of Aubin Coquart & Consort, & addressed to Mr. Bersolle, to be by him exported to America." The thirty bales included 400 coats, 500 waistcoats, 150 breeches, 1200 shirts, and 500 pantaloons. The invoice was enclosed in JW to the committee for foreign affairs, April 6 (National Archives). Before loading the mules, however, JW had been "obliged to Unbale and rebale smaller for a Mule can only carry a certain weight and that must be divided to carry half on each Side": JW to Bancroft, March 30, Yale University Library.

5. Which was now responsible for the administration of the Continental Navy: XXXI, 520–1n. It had one non-congressional member (ex-delegate Francis Lewis, for whom see XXX, 125n) and two congressional members (William Ellery and James Madison): *JCC*, XV, 1366; XVI, 277; XVII, 490.

6. The copy at the Library of Congress was made by Thomas Hutchins in August, 1780. The one at the National Archives is in L'Air de Lamotte's hand (except the dateline, which is in WTF's). BF enclosed it in his letter to Jones of June 1, below.

7. This enclosure (Harvard University Library) is labeled "List of the Navy of the United States March 1780." It lists eleven warships (including several still under construction) with their captains and their locations: *America*, 74, *Confederacy*, 36, *Alliance*, 36, *Bourbon*, 36, *Trumbull*, 28, *Deane*, 28, *Providence*, 28, *Boston*, 28, *Queen of France*, 20, *Ranger*, 18, and *Saratoga*, 18. Someone has crossed out Landais' name as captain of the *Alliance* and substituted Jones's.

four Ships to gaurd the Harbour of Charles Town[8] has subjected our Coasts to the depredations of the enemys armed vessels from New York who of late have frequently appeared in our Bays and made many Captures.

For these reasons the Board think it will be necessary that the frigate Alliance should be forthwith Ordered to proceed for this port, and should any Supplys for our Navy and Army be ready in France a part may be sent in the Alliance and the residue on other armed Vessels under her Convoy.

I have the honor to be Your Excellencys Most Obedt Hble servant   FRA: LEWIS by order

P.S. The board woud be highly obliged to your Excelly to send them a set of drafts of the New ships in the Royal navy of France for the use of our Master Builders.—

His Excellency Benjamin Franklin

From Dumas: Two Letters

(I) and (II) ALS: American Philosophical Society

I.

Monsieur   Lahaie 28e. Mars 1780
    Vous verrez, par l'avis ci-joint, que la Frise a accédé à la Résolution d'Hollande.[9] Je n'apprends rien encore du parti qu'ont pris les autres Provinces. Il est vrai qu'étant indisposé, je n'ai

---

8. Three of these ships, the *Providence*, *Boston*, and *Ranger*, were captured when the city surrendered on May 11 and subsequently taken into the British Navy. A fourth, the *Queen of France*, had been sunk in the Cooper River as an obstruction to the British: Gardner W. Allen, *A Naval History of the American Revolution* (2 vols., Boston and New York, 1913), II, 491–7.

9. The enclosure was Dumas' French translation of the province of Holland's resolution adopting unlimited convoys for Dutch shipping (including ships carrying naval stores and timber, like those intercepted with Adm. Bylandt): XXXI, 49, 524n. It was presented to the States General of the Netherlands on March 3, and Friesland, one of the other six Dutch provinces, recently had voted its concurrence: Fauchille, *Diplomatie française*, pp. 195–7.

pu m'informer, mais il paroît clairement, sur le tout, qu'on ne cherche ici qu'à pousser le temps par les épaules.

Mr. Y——— a présenté le 21e. un Mémoire où il presse L.H.P. de se déclarer;[1] ce qu'elles déclineront assurément. Il est long; & je ne l'ai qu'en Hollandois. Comme je ne doute pas qu'il ne paroisse dans la Gazette la semaine prochaine, je differerai de la traduire.

On m'écrit d'Allemagne les anecdotes suivantes "Il y aura vers la fin de May prochain en Lithuanie un phénomene politique. Ce sera la conjonction de Venus avec Saturne; ou, pour parler plus clair, le Salomon du Nord ira y rencontrer la Reine de Saba. Assurément vous ne soupçonnerez pas que ce voyage ait la galanterie pour objet."[2]

"Lorsque l'Impératrice de Russie apprit que le Chevalier Harris avoit été attaqué d'une fievre de bile, occasionnée par le chagrin d'avoir manqué son coup, *Oh*, dit-elle, *le pauvre Harris! Je ne me serois seulement pas doutée qu'il eût de la bile.*"[3]

Je suis avec mon respectueux dévouement, tant que je vivrai, Monsieur Votre très-humble & très-obéissant serviteur DUMAS

Je vous écris, Monsieur, une autre Lettre, par l'autre voie. Si vous ne la receviez pas, de grace faites la lui demander. Car il importe que vous l'ayiez au plutôt.

Passy à S. E. Mr. B. Franklin, Min. Pl. des Etats-Unis

1. British Ambassador Sir Joseph Yorke demanded that the States General respond satisfactorily within three weeks to Britain's claim for the military assistance promised in the 1678 Anglo-Dutch treaty of defensive alliance: *Gaz. de Leyde*, March 28, 1780 (no. XXV), sup.; Sir Francis Piggott and G.W.T. Omond, eds., *Documentary History of the Armed Neutralities 1780 and 1800* (London, 1919), pp. 146–8.

2. The implication seems to be that Frederick II of Prussia (the Solomon of the North) planned to visit Catherine II of Russia (the Queen of Sheba). In fact it was Frederick's rival, Emperor Joseph II, who was planning such a visit, scheduled for June: Isabel de Madariaga, *Britain, Russia, and the Armed Neutrality of 1780: Sir James Harris's Mission to St. Petersburg during the American Revolution* (New Haven, 1962), pp. 193–4.

3. In January Sir James Harris, the British minister at Catherine's court, had been rebuffed in his bid for a Russian alliance. During the same period he was ill with jaundice: *ibid.*, pp. 131–2.

Addressed: à Son Excellence / Monsieur B. Franklin, Esqr. / Min. Plenipe. des Etats-Unis / *Passy.*/.

Notation: Dumas la haie March. 28. 80

II.

Monsieur   A La haie 28e. Mars 1780

J'ai eu le malheur d'écrire une Lettre à mon cher Ami Mr. Carmichael, qui a été interceptée, & qui est entre les mains de S. Exc. Mr. l'Ambassadeur de France à La Haie. Dans cette Lettre (J'ignore si elle est signée de mon nom au long) j'ai commis une imprudence, une folie, impardonnable à un homme sage. Je n'en ai point gardé copie: mais, autant que je m'en souviens, j'y prie Mr. Carmichael de ne plus m'adresser des Lettres chez Mr. G. Grand à Amsterdam, parce que 1° sa qualité de Beau-pere du Genl. Prévôt, & 2° son intimité avec un certain Anglois à Amsterdam, le rendoient suspect; 3° qu'il n'avoit pas la confiance des amis de l'Amérique à Amsterdam; & 4° qu'il avoit tenu des propos qui pouvaient décréditer l'emprunt domicilié chez lui de la part des Etats-Unis de l'Amérique.[4]

Je suis affligé de ce que mon zele pour les intérêts des Etats-Unis, poussé à l'excès, m'ait fait prendre & donner l'allarme si inconsidérément, puisque cela peut nuire à Mr. G. Grand, qui ne m'a rendu que de bons Offices, comme vous le savez, Monsieur. Pour réparer le mal, je ne vois de meilleur moyen que celui de vous exposer le fait. Cela est humiliant, douloureux; il peut m'en coûter, avec la vie, l'affreux regret d'avoir à me reprocher la perte de mon Enfant & de sa Mere. Les trois premieres raisons qui m'engageoient à suspecter Mr. Gd., ont reçu du poids chez moi des insinuations d'un homme de confiance de certains personnages que vous connoissez,[5] lesquels m'ont con-

4. Dumas' letter to Carmichael repeated the suspicions he had expressed to BF a year previously: XXIX, 192–3. For such suspicions to become public was extremely impolitic, as Georges Grand was a close friend of Vergennes and had helped him plot the Swedish *coup d'état* of 1772: Price, *France and the Chesapeake*, II, 722.

5. The confidant probably was Johann Friedrich Stürler vom Altenberg (XXVIII, 353–4n) and the certain persons, Sartine, Chaumont, and Sartine's secretary Baudouin: XXIX, 461.

firmé ces insinuations. Je ne puis prouver aucune des choses qu'on m'a insinuées pour me prévenir contre Mr. G. Grand; & j'ai à craindre qu'on ne me laisse seul dans le danger. Aussi je n'ai nommé personne: c'est donc à moi que l'on s'en prend; & c'est moi que les uns voudront, & les autres laisseront perdre. Je crois donc inutile de nommer mes auteurs & leurs garants, excepté à Vous, Monsieur, Si vous me l'ordonniez. Mr. le Duc de la Vauguyon ayant ordonné que je lui donnasse une rétractation de ce que j'ai écrit à Mr. Carmichael, pour la remettre à Mr. G. Grand, j'ai préféré, toute réflexion faite, de la faire entre vos mains, Monsieur; & j'en donne connoissance à Mr. l'Ambassadeur, afin qu'il avertisse Mr. G. Grand qu'elle est entre vos mains, & que lui, ou Mr. son frere, pourront demander de l'y voir, & entendre lire.

J'ai, en vérité, la mort dans le coeur, & la cruelle tâche de cacher mon état à ma famille tant que je pourrai. Mais, jusqu'au dernier soupir, je serai avec le plus tendre respect, Monsieur De Votre Excellence le très-humble, & très obéissant serviteur   DUMAS

Il me paroît nécessaire, Monsieur, que Mr. de C—— & Mr. B—— voient la Lettre ci-jointe chez vous.

On exigera de *notre Ami* de ne plus me voir; On interessera Mr. De N—— apparemment dans l'emprunt qui est ouvert chez Mr. G——.[6] A la bonne heure. Mais serai-je completement la victime d'une telle combinaison? Je soupçonne celui qui m'a trahi & livré; et c'est affreux.

Addressed: à Son Excellence / Monsieur Franklin, Esqr. / Min. Plenipe. des Etats-Unis / &c. / *Passy.*/.

Notation: Dumas la haie March 28. 80

6. Dumas refers in this sentence to van Berckel, Neufville, and Grand; for Neufville's loan attempt on behalf of Congress see XXVIII, 629–31; XXIX, 101 and following; XXX, 465–6.

From Joseph Gridley[7]

ALS: American Philosophical Society

Sir   Nantes 28th March 1780.

It is some time since, I requested the favour of Mr. Jona Williams to write you for an Order, Pass, or some kind of paper in my favour, to enable me to obtain a passage to America on board the Frigatte Alliance; which Mr Williams judged with me was a Necessary & regular application, but he has received no Answer.[8]

There are other Vessells going to America, in which I can take a passage, but as I have for a long time been in a bad State of Health, I think the Alliance most to be preferr'd, as there is a Doctr. on board, which the other ships have not, & I possibly may be in great want of one, without which, I may prehaps suffer, altho I have the greatest reason to think the Sea air will be of infinite Service to me.

Mr John Williams who intended going in the Alliance, has alter'd his plan & is going to Carolina,[9] his Birth on board her, will be therefore Vacant, and if your Excellency will do me the favour, to expedite me a paper of the kind, you will infinitely oblige him, who has the Honor to be Your Excellencys Most obedt. & Very Humble Servant   JOSEPH GRIDLEY

His Excelly. Benja. Franklin Esqr.

Addressed: Benjamin Franklin Esqr. / Plenipotentiary at / Passy

Notation: J. Gridley March 28. 1780

From William Hodgson

ALS: American Philosophical Society

Dear sir   London 28 Mar: 1780

I wrote you on the 10th Current to which I beg to be referred— Since when I am much concerned to find that the Car-

---

7. The last extant letter from this merchant, who may have died in France: XXVII, 658n.

8. See JW's letter of March 7.

9. He sailed during the summer: XII, 193n; JW to WTF, July 27, 1780 (APS).

tel Vessell is returned from Morlaix without a single prisoner in Exchange— I heard this from Plymo & have since been desired to go to the Sick & Hurt office who confirmed the Acc't. They appear to be very much disgusted at the proceeding & say it is a breach of Faith— It was out of my Power to give any other Answer than a general one— that I imagined it was some mistake or neglect of office that I was firmly persuaded it was not your Intention, or consistent with your Character to deceive, the French Commissary of Marine at Morlaix gave the master of the Vessell a Certificate purporting that he had Rec'd 100 American Prisoners, but that he had no English prisoners in his power to return but that an Acct shou'd be kept with Monsr de sartine qui en avoit Conferré avec Mr Franklin— Those are the words. I hope Sr you will furnish me with such an explantion of this Affair as shall be satisfactory and expedite future exchanges at present untill the Affair is cleared up all further progress in this business must be put a Stop to— I am with great Respect Dr sir your most obedt sert   WILLIAM HODGSON

Addressed: A / Monsieur / Monsieur Franklin / à / Passy

Notation: William Hodgson London March 28. 80.

From John Paul Jones

ALS: American Philosophical Society; AL (draft) and transcript: National Archives

Honored and dear Sir,   L'Orient March 28th. 1780.

I have received your Orders of the 18th. and have written to Nantes for particular information respecting the Anchorage off Noirmontier that I may take measures accordingly.—[1] I am very glad that Doctor Bancroft who has been an Eye and Ear witness to the Situation of Affairs onboard the Alliance can explain to you every Circumstance. In the meantime I shall do my utmost either to go or send for the Bales of Cloth.— The Cannon are

1. Jones to John Ross, March 23, 1780, Bradford, *Jones Papers,* reel 5, no. 1026.

all on board;[2] and you may depend on my best endeavours to fulfil your final Directions.

I beg leave in particular to refer you to Doctor Bancroft for a representation of some Circumstances that respect myself you will I am persuaded soon see the necessity that Obliged me to take the Steps I did in Holland—and I am afraid you will find the Busy Body C—— less worthy[3] than you had formerly imagined.—

With the most sincere and affectionate Esteem and respect I am Dear Sir, Your most Obliged and most Obedt. Servt.

JNO P JONES

N.B. I understand there is a Quantity of Sheathing Copper belonging to the Continent at Nantes.[4] I wish it could be Ordered to be Ship'd with the Shott for the Alliance.—

His Excellency B. Franklin Esqr. &c: &c:

Notation: J.P. Jones. L'orient March 28. 80

From Richard Peters

ALS: American Philosophical Society

Sir   Philadelphia March 28th. 1780.—

I was yesterday honoured with your Letter of the 25 Octr 1779 being the only Letter I have been favoured with from you these two Years past.[5] I cannot express my Gratitude & Thanks for your obliging Favour which has relieved my Mind from much Anxiety on my Father's Account. I send you a Bill for thirty Guineas[6] & the Bill you mention shall be paid as soon as I can find Mr Trecesson or it is presented. I hear he has left Col Ar-

2. See BF to Jones, March 8.

3. Deleted in the draft: "of confidence"; he is referring to Chaumont.

4. This may be the copper that BF told Schweighauser to ship in September, 1779: XXX, 324.

5. The Oct. 25 letter is printed in XXX, 584–5. BF had also written in July: XXX, 95.

6. A bill of exchange for 720 *l.t.* (30 guineas), signed by La Luzerne and payable to BF at 60 days sight, is with BF's papers at the APS. He endorsed it "Remitted by W Peters in part of what he owes me. BF—".

mand & gone to the W. Indies to join his Regt.[7] If so I will have the Money remitted there as no Doubt it will be equally agreeable. If finally I cannot find that Gentleman, I shall send the Money to you & will take the earliest Oppertunity of remitting the Ballance which I yesterday thought I should have been enabled to do, but an unfortunate Accident prevented my recieving a Sum of Money the purchase Monies of two Houses of my Father's which I agreed to sell but the Bargain was not perfect & the Houses caught Fire & were consumed.[8] Not having heard from you I thought you had either not recieved my Letters or had not been able to effect the Purpose I troubled you about. I am therefore unprepared suddenly to fulfill your Request, but shall not fail both on Motives of Gratitude & Justice to do it & I hope it will soon be in Power. Both my Father's & my own Estate have suffered so much by the Enemy & the Depretiation that it is with no small Difficulty any Revenue is raized either from his Estate or mine tho we have Property of considerable Value. This I mention to you as I would not tresspass on your Goodness to make any farther Advances 'till I enable you from hence so to do, & it hurts my Feelings that you should lay a Moment out of your Money longer than the public Circumstances delay its being sent. Nothing shall impede my reimbursing you, but the Bills you mention for Interest Monies are engross'd by the Merchants whose Profits enable them to give enormous Exchange & indeed the Certificates drawing this Interest are chiefly bought up by the Traders. I beg the Favour of your forwarding the enclosed Letter to my Father. I have avoided in it the subject of politics. It relates to his private affairs which considering *his Situation* ought to be settled & I could wish if thro' your Correspondent you could do it that you would be pleased to drop a Hint of the Necessity of his making a Settlement on his Family here who have taken a decisive part on the American Side of the Question.

I trouble you with a Letter to Mr Carmichael which I pray You to forward.

I enclose you a Reciept for a Sum of Money I was obliged to

7. Trécesson had rejoined the Armagnac regiment in May, 1779: xxx, 585n.

8. Shortly after writing the present letter Peters advertised for sale or lease the remains of two dwelling houses at and adjoining the corner of Front and Pine Streets: *Pennsylvania Packet*, April 8, 1780.

pay for a Mr Girard who was recommended by you to me at the Instance of a Monsr du Bourg.⁹ He left me without the Means of Defence after having told me that he had left a Monsr Buard to adjust the Matter. Whether he is a Fool or a Knave I cannot tell but rather incline to think his Conduct proceeded from Folly. Buard however denied his having any Means of Payment but as he was interested in the same Business he left me also in the Lurch. They have both used me extremely ill as I became their Bail from mere Motives of Civility to Strangers. I had the priviledge of settling the Matter at 4 for 1 as my Case was hard. Exchange between Specie & Currency was from 10 to 12 for 1. The Demand against Girard was near £19. in Specie or 6 & ⅓d half. If you can find Girard or can obtain it from his Friends I pray the Favour of you to do it & place what you get to my Account. The principles of Settlement I leave entirely to you. I dont mean that this shall interfere in the least with the other Affair. I beg your Forgiveness for the Trouble I am obliged to give you & am with every Sentiment of Gratitude & Esteem your obliged & obedt Servt   RICHARD PETERS

Dr Franklin

Addressed: His Excellency / Benjamin Franklin / Minister Plenipotentiary of / the United States of america / Passi / near Paris / Hond by Mr Meyor¹

To Dumas: Two Letters

(I) and (II) Copy: Library of Congress; transcript: National Archives

I.

Dear Sir   Passy March. 29. 1780.
    I did receive the Letter you mention to have enclos'd for Mr. Carmichael in yours of the 25th. of february.² I had before re-

---

9. Girard (Gérard) came to the U.S. in 1777 with a letter of recommendation from Barbeu-Dubourg and a covering note by BF: XXIV, 519, 527–8.
    1. Pierre Meyer, Gérard's nephew and secretary. See RB's letter of March 29, below.
    2. Dumas had inquired about the letter on March 23, above.

ceived a Letter from him Dated at Cadiz, acquainting me that he was just Setting out for Madrid, and desiring I would send him a Credit there for 200 Louis.[3] Mr. F. Grand, our Banker here had undertaken to do this with his Correspondent a Banker there. I not knowing how to address your Letter to Mr. Carmichael at Madrid, sent it to Mr. Grand's to be put under his Cover to his Banker who might deliver it to Mr. Carmichael, as he would necessarily find out his lodging to acquaint him with the Credit. The Day after sir George Grand was gone for Holland his Brother[4] came to me and Expressing a great Deal of Concern and Vexation, told me, that sir George seeing that letter on his Desk, said this supercription is Mr. Dumas's Handwriting; and some time afterwards came to him with The Letter in his Hand open, Saying this Letter is full of ingratitude (or some Words to that purpose) and I will carry it to Holland and show it to the Ambassador; and that he had accordingly carry'd it away with him not withstanding all that was or could be said to the Contrary. That it gave him infinite Pain, to acquaint me with this action of his Brother, but he thought it right I should know the Truth. I did not mention this to you before hoping that upon Reflection sir G. would not show the Letter to The ambassador, but seal it up again and send it forward; and I was desirous to avoid increasing the Misunderstanding between you and sir George. But as I understand by yours to Mr. Bowdoin[5] that he has actually done it, I see no reason to keep it longer as a Secret from you.

If I had known it to be a Letter of Consequence, I should nevertheless have taken the same Method of forwarding it not having the least Suspicion that any Person in that house would have taken so unwarrantable a Liberty with it. But I am now exceedingly Sorry that I did not rather send it to the spanish ambassador's.— Let me know in your next what you may think proper to communicate to me of the Contents of it.

I am, with great Regard, Dear sir &c.

M. Dumas.

3. XXXI, 406–8.
4. Ferdinand Grand.
5. Presumably Baudouin.

II.

Dear Sir,   Passy Mar. 29. 1780.

It is some time Since I have written to you having nothing material to communicate: But I received duly your several Letters of Feb. 1. 18. 15. [*i.e.,* 25] March 2. 11. 13. 17. & 23.[6] and thank you for the Intelligence they contain. The last has this minute come to hand, & I shall answer it separately.

I pray you to assure Mr. FLX, OPB, NLZPAAPC[7] of my Respects, and that it was only on one Pacquet for him that I put my Name, when I thought to have sent it by a friend. The baseness of the Post-Office in opening it, surprises me. No other Letter for him has since pass'd thro' my hands.— If any others come to me for him, I Shall Send them under Cover to you.

The Tuite you mention is not a North american but a West Indian, i.e. a Native of one of the English sugar Islands. 17. is not 21. [*i.e.,* 54] of 196. X. P. acts only for 824. Ca.[8]

I forwarded your Letter to Capt. Jones. I do not know which of his English Pilots it was, that Is mention'd in yours of the 657.ry. I know he has been generous to an Excess with them. Explain to me if you please the fact that is the Subject of that Letter, and who Mr. Gordon is.—[9]

I am curious to know what the states will do about the Confiscation of the Goods taken in Pryland's [Bylandt's] Convoy.

I received your large Packets, that for Capt. Jones Shall be carefully sent him. I thank you for the Philosophial Pieces,[1] which I will read attentively as soon as I have a little Time.

6. The three February letters are published in XXXI, 430–2, 460–1, 523–4. The March letters are above, except for the now-missing one of the 11th.

7. Van der Capellen, whose warning was enclosed with a March 2 letter from Dumas to BF; it and another enclosure to Dumas' letter are discussed in our annotation of it.

8. "Gillon is not agent of Congress. He acts only for South Ca." For both Tuite and Gillon see our annotation of Dumas' March 2 letter.

9. "657ry" stands for "Pensionary." Dumas had written Pensionary van Berckel about Jones's treatment of a captured pilot, enclosing a copy with his March 13 letter to BF. Gordon, whom Dumas mentioned in his letter to van Berckel, had accused Jones of mistreating Jackson: Dumas to BF, April 11, below.

1. The Socratic dialogues Dumas mentioned to BF on March 17.

MARCH 29, 1780

Please to present my thanks to Mr. Enchidi for his curious specimen of Characters, and request him to send me the Price of the following Articles, by the pound weight, and what is the Proportion between the Holland and the English Pound Weight.

Non parel (Fr. Mignonne) Romein and Curiyt[2]
Caractere de Finance.
    Dubbelde Descendiaan Geschreven Schrift—
    Dubbelde Garmond Geschreven Schrift.
Descendiaan Duits N. 1.
Garmonts Duits.
Brevier Duits.—

M. Dumas

---

2. BF's secretary Lamotte mistranscribed the terms "Romein" and "Cursyf," meaning roman and cursive, or italic. One of the smallest sizes made, this *non parel* (non pareil, 6–point) was the only roman font BF expressed interest in, probably because it had not yet been cast in his foundry, and because Enschedé's specimen no doubt reminded him of the order he had received from Congress in 1777 to supply America with 20,000 Bibles. At the time, he had inquired about the possibilities of either purchasing non pareil type in Holland, or having the Bibles printed there, and he received a specimen of the non pareil available from Enschedé's typefoundry. BF seems to have dropped the matter until now, however, when, in addition to this inquiry, he soon investigated the cost of having pages of non pareil typeset and printed. See Hémery's Inventory of July 22, 1780 (APS); xxv, 74–6, 317–18; xxvi, 410, 569; Ostervald and Bosset Deluse to BF, April 23 and 31, below.

The remaining types about which BF inquires in the present letter were script (*caractère de finance*), and black letter (*duits*). All these fonts had been cut by Johann Michael Fleischman (1701–1768), one of the most celebrated punchcutters of the age. For specimens see Charles Enschedé, *Typefoundries in the Netherlands from the Fifteenth to the Nineteenth Century* (rev. ed., Harry Carter, trans., Harlem, 1978), figs. 178, 193, 271, 270, 225, 210, and 205 (in order of BF's listing), and for exact dimensions see p. 455. See also Daniel Berkeley Updike, *Printing Types, Their History, Forms and Use* (2 vols., Cambridge, Mass., 1922) II, 37–9, fig. 214.

Certification of a Signature[3]

AD (draft): University of Pennsylvania Library

[March 29, 1780]

I do hereby certify that the Signature P Henry[4] to this Instrument is truly the Hand-writing of the Governor of Virginia. At Passy, this 29th Day of March 1780.

MINISTER PLENIPOTENTIARY OF THE UNITED STATES
AT THE COURT OF FRANCE

From Richard Bache

ALS: American Philosophical Society

Dear & Hond: Sir   Philadelphia March 29th. 1780.

Yours of the 29h. Octr. last came to hand only a few days ago, and is the only one I have had from you for some Month's past—[5] I embrace this opportunity of Mr. Gerards Nephew[6] who goes

---

3. Most probably written on behalf of Louis-Pierre Penot Lombart de Laneuville, a brigadier general in the American army who was now lobbying for the rank of lt. col. in the French army (which he received on June 24): Laneuville to WTF, March 2, 1780 (APS); Bodinier, *Dictionnaire*, p. 379. (BF had performed similar services for Laneuville's younger brother: XXXI, 391.)

Laneuville used WTF, with whom he shared a lively social life, as a go-between to request help from BF in his quest for advancement. The ten letters written to WTF during the period of this volume (APS) ask a variety of favors, including securing a passage with John Paul Jones (which he then turned down), attesting documents, and intervening on his behalf at Versailles. On April 14 BF drafted an attestation of Laneuville's signature on a power of attorney; that draft, written to "whom it may concern" and initialed by BF, is at the University of Pa. Library. On the same sheet is an apparently unrelated address in an unknown hand, "M. Hope au bain D'orleans rue de Richelieu."

4. BF first wrote "Thomas Jefferson". He interlined "P. Henry" above and deleted "present" before "Governor". Henry had been governor from 1776 to 1779 while Laneuville was serving with the American army. We can only conclude that BF did not have the signature in front of him when he drafted this certificate.

5. The Oct. 29 letter is missing. BF's most recent extant letter to his son-in-law was that of Oct. 1, 1779: XXX, 423.

6. Gérard's nephew, who also served as his chief secretary, was Pierre Prothais Meyer: Smith, *Letters*, X, 440; Meng, *Despatches of Gérard*, p. 225n.

175

Via Virginia to hand to you 3d. Bills of the Setts sent you by Mr. Gerard[7] who I hope has got safe home at last— My Love to Temple, tell him, I thank him for his care in distributing Bache & Shee's circular Letters, & for the list he has furnished me with;[8] he has my thanks too, for his care in sending me Ben's Letters.

Sally and the Children are well they join in affectionate Love & Duty with D. sir Your ever affece. son   RICH: BACHE

You will receive herewith two Letters that came to my hands not long since but where from I know not the one for yourself, the other for the Marquis De laffayette.

Addressed: Dr. Franklin

Endorsed: Bache all answer'd Oct 4. 1780

Notation: Rüe Chateau Burbon a l'hotel d'Angleterre

From Joseph Banks   ALS: American Philosophical Society

Sir   Soho Square March 29 1780

By the hands of Mr. Paradise I have receivd a copy of the instructions for the Protection of Captn. Cooke which you circulated among the Armd Vessels of your Friends in N America. I perus'd the paper with the Greatest pleasure for having never doubted my self that the liberal & enlargd sentiments I had always admird in your mind remain there in full lustre. I could not but rejoice at the triumph which such an indisputable proof afforded me over those who warp'd by politicks or party wish'd to entertain a different opinion of your character.[9]

Give me leave then as the Friend of disinterested discovery & of Captn. Cooke, to return you my warmest thanks.

Permit me also as President of the Royal Society to thank you

7. For the first and second sets of bills for the annual interest on BF's investment in the loan office see XXX, 363; XXXI, 19.

8. Advertisements for the newly-formed merchant firm of Bache & Shee: XXVIII, 552; XXIX, 273; XXX, 193, 364–5. The list is described in XXIX, 273n.

9. See Digges's letters of Feb. 4 (XXXI, 448–9) and March 3 (above).

in the names of many of our most valuable members who abstracting themselves from all less general considerations fix their whole attention upon the great Object of Science & would take the most publick method of conveying to you their acknowledgements were they not sensible that such an act might be wilfully misunderstood.

Some Medals are preparing to be struck in memory of our late Friend the Royal Society will intreat the King of France to accept one at their hands as a testimony of the high sence they entertain of his Generous orders in favor of that excellent navigator[1] it would give me pleasure to learn that the Congress issued similar orders if they did I shall rejoice in the opportunity of transmitting to America the like permanent token of our regard & gratitude.

Adieu my Dear Sir beleive my Mind incapable of being Led astray by the influence of political opinions. I respect you as a Philosopher & sollicit the continuance of your Friendship in full Persuasion that all your actions are conformable to your most Conscientious Ideas of rectitude whatever my wishes may be as a native & inhabitant of a country with which you are at war. Your Faithfull & affectionate Hble Servant   Jos: Banks

From William Carmichael   Copy: Library of Congress

Dear Sir,   Madrid 29 Mar. 1780
     The Count De Montmorin[2] is so obliging as to offer me an Occasion of writing to you by a Courier which I am loth to

1. Medals were given to Louis (as well as to Catherine II of Russia, George III, Queen Charlotte, and Prince George) "in testimony of the humane and liberal orders those potentates gave to their navy officers and Cruizers for the protection & safety of Captain Cooke." A subscription was opened to pay for them: William Bell Clark, "A Franklin Postscript to Captain Cook's Voyages," APS *Proc.* xcviii (1954), 402–3.
2. The French ambassador to the Spanish court had been providing information to Carmichael: xxxi, 502n. Recently, he had been sent orders, however, to refrain from an active role in Spanish-American negotiations: Vergennes to Montmorin, March 13, 1780 (AAE).

177

refuse for fear of betraying a Want of Respect to you or give Reason to others to suspect that I have no Share in your Confidence. I have nothing material to communicate unless the uneasiness I feel in being left here ignorant of the Situation of our affairs in any other Part of the World and without any Sources of Credit or Intelligence but what I disire from my self be a communication that I ought to make to you. M. Jay is on the Road from Cadiz which Place he left the 21st. inst. I expect him here the last of the Week.[3] I cannot help repeating the Satisfaction I feel in the candid Conduct of Ministers of this Court, which will enable M. Jay immediately on his arrival to enter upon the Execution of the Business on which he is sent. The Court Seems determined to prosecute the War and is taking measures to provide the funds necessary to support it. It appears to be however rather a War of the Court than of the Nation. There is Reason to suspect that our Enemies are not idle here and that their Communications pass by the Way of Lisbon.[4] Should you have an Opportunity of obtaining any Information on this Head. M. Jay will be much obliged to you for it. Should any Letters from America or Elswhere be addressed to your Care you will oblige us in sending them hither by one of the Couriers dispatched to the Ct. De Montmorin whose Politeness & friendship is the only Consolation I have here. I beg you to present complements to Dr. Bancroft and your Grandson and to believe me. With great Respect your obliged & Humble Servt.   (signed) WM. CARMICHAEL.

His Excellency Benjn. franklin.

3. John and Sarah Jay reached Madrid on April 4: Richard B. Morris, *The Peacemakers: the Great Powers and American Independence* (New York, Evanston, London, 1965), p. 47.

4. The British naval commander on the Portuguese station was George Johnstone. Spending much of his time in Lisbon, Johnstone tried to arrange peace terms between Britain and Spain; he was repudiated by the British government but Floridablanca continued the negotiations by other means: Samuel Flagg Bemis, *The Hussey-Cumberland Mission and American Independence: an Essay in the Diplomacy of the American Revolution* (Princeton, 1931), pp. 24–40, 89, 145–7.

From Charles Collins[5]

ALS: American Philosophical Society

Sir   Shearburg March the 29 1780

As you are the gentleman orethersed to hear and Redress the Complants of those americans who has Bin presners In England I make Bold to Rite to your honer as a Child wold to a father for I hop Sir you wold Be a father to me at this presant time. I wold Informe your honer that I was taken the 9 of September In the yer 1778 In a Contenantle Brig Resestance mounten 18 guns William Burk Capten. I was In Compasity of a mid shipman on Bord Bound with Exprest for Counde Eastin [Estaing] who Being at that tim at Rhodisland the 14 day I was put in Rhodisland preson with 9 pepole with me the 22 day I was taken out on Bord the Culloden an English 74 gun Ship while I was on Bord wee tuck Sevrel Verseles and one the Brig Standley Mr. degrass Capten. In Sight of the french fleet I was on Bord till wee arive at milford haven and the 15 Day of december wee was put on Shore In pembrock prison wile I was on Bord I was used very Barbrosly and always Intisening me to Enter But I Refused after Being In preson 12 months and 6 day I and 20 americans Brok out of preson tuck a Small Sloop 7 mile up the Rever past By Sevrel firgets and tenders and Came Safe to france after Being at Sea 3 days without water or pervisens and as ther Being no Contenantle Ship as I Cold go on Bord of for I had not money to last me to aney plase ware thear was aney for I had no more then what I Sold the prise for I thought proper to go on Bord the Black prences Cuter I wold Be glad to Informe your honer of my transaxanes But I have not time when I Came to france I had no Clothes I hope your honer will Be Pleased to let me have a little money for what little I had I Bought Clothes with and if your honer Shold Command me to go on Bord of a Contenantle Ship I am at your Sarves.[6] The Black prences is holed up and I am

---

5. Collins had written from Pembroke Prison in Wales the previous summer on behalf of several Americans who were confined there. He came to Cherbourg to sail with Edward Macatter on the new *Black Princess:* XXX, 71–2; Clark, *Ben Franklin's Privateers*, pp. 108–9, 131; Kaminkow, *Mariners*, p. 42.

6. Collins wrote again on April 26, acknowledging BF's letter of April 20

partley agred to go with Capten Wile In another Cuter of 20
guns at Shearburge In Compasity of thir leutanent. Sir I am your
most obedant humble Sarvent   CHARLES COLLINS

To the Right honoreble Docter fraclen

Addressed [*in another hand*]: To / His Excellency Doctor Franklin / at Paris

Notation: Collins Charles March 29. 1780.

To Rodolphe-Ferdinand Grand   Copy: Library of Congress

Dear sir,   Passy 30. Mar. 1780.
    M. Dumas has written a Long letter to M. Bowdoin [Baudouin]
Acquainting him, that the Ambassador had sent for him, produc'd and read to him his Letter to Mr. Charmichael cover'd him
with reproches, and menaced his Ruin he has also written to me
disiring to know how I dispos'd of that letter he having sent it under Cover of a Letter to me dated Feb. 25. which last was inclosed
in one to Mr Bowdoin. All this has made it necessary for me to
write to him[7] the whole truth as you related it to me, otherwise either myself or you would have been suspected of having opened
that letter, and sending it to the Ambassador. M. Bowdoin sent me
Dumas's letter to him by Mr. Chaumont open having acquainted
him also with the affair. Mr. Chaumont imagined the Letter had
been stolen from among my Papers. As this might occasion suspicion of Treachery in my Secretaries, I was obliged to acquaint
him also with the Truth, mentioning to him, as I have done also
in my letter to Dumas, the extream Concern and Vexation this action of sir George had given you. Thus the whole Blame will rest
on him where it ought to be. For If after gratifying his unjustifi-

---

(missing). Since there is no continental vessel in France that he can board for
America he will content himself with serving on the *Black Princess.* Will BF
mention his name in letters to Boston so that his former captain and parents
will know he is free? Torris is at Cherbourg and expects to go to Paris soon.
APS.
    7. On March 29, above.

180

able Curiosity, he had Sealed the Letter again and sent forward, the Censure he will now suffer might have been avoided. But as he has manag'd so imprudently as to let it be made known to Mr. Dumas, that his Letter was intercepted and opened by the Ambassador's showing and reading it to him, it is not fit that you or me or any one else should lay under the least suspicion of being concern'd in the Transaction. I thought it right to acquaint you with all this, as I suppose the affair will now be talk'd of, and you might otherwise wonder how it came out.

With great Esteem I am ever, Dear sir, &c.

M. Ferdinand Grand.

From Peter Blackit

ALS: American Philosophical Society

Hond: Sir   Dunann Prison the 30the: of March 1780

This is to acquaint you that I was lately Boatswain of the Princess Privateer belonging to america. I must give to understand that about two month ago we took a Prize, a brigg belonging to Wales the mate of which was brought on board the Princess Privateer & about forty or fifty prisoners more being on board; & about three weeks after the taking of the Said Brigg when I was on shore at Risco [Roscoff] refreshing myself whilst we were cleaning the bottom of the Sd. Princess, the Capn: Sent a Guard of Soldiers to take me up who did so, & conducted me to the common prison where I was detain'd one day & the next was remov'd to St: Pauls [St. Pol-de-Léon] where I was confin'd in the Common Prison among Theives & Murderers for the Space of nine days with very little to Subsist on, & from thence was remov'd to Morlax where I was confin'd to the Common Prison. About three weeks after that was march'd to Dunann with the English Prisoners where I now remain in the Common Prison & all for no other cause against me that that a fals report that the mate of the Said brigg should say that I had agreed with the Prisoners on board the Said Princess privateer to take her away from the Capn: & the rest of the crew & carry her into England which was a fals report & the Said mate of the Brigg namely Mr: Phillips Denies that any such thing was ever talk'd of by me who is with me ready & willing to prove to the Contrary— Therefor Hond. Sir I shall not only Esteem it a favour but likewise a particular mark of friendship if you would be so kind as to stand my friend & let me have a Lawfull Tryal, & if anything shall be prov'd against me I am ready & willing to be convicted as the Law shall direct & prevent my being sent to England in a Transport where I have no business which favour will greatly Oblige Sir your most Obet: & very Humble Sert.

PETER BLACKIT Boswn.

P.S. I have about ten Thousand Livers prize money Due to me

Addressed: To / the Honl: Docr: Frankling / American Ambassidor / at / Paris / or elswhere

Notation: Blackit Peter, Prison, 30. march 1780.

From Pierre Roussille[8]   LS: American Philosophical Society

Monsieur   a paris 30 mars 1780

Je me trouve malgré moi dans La nécessitte demprunter une plume etranger pour réclamer vos bontés, quelque jours avant mon depart pour me rendre a bordeau il m'est Survenu une indisposition qui ma totalement privé de Cet avantage pour une maladie qui Sest déclaré, dans Le principe est très Serieuse Ce qui me retient encore au Lit. Mes jours ont été pendant quelque tems en danger. Heureusement que Levenement n'a point justifie Les Craintes du Chirurgien je me trouve dans une état des plus tristes par Le dérangement de ma Sante privé de tout moyens pour me procurer Ce qui m'est Le plus nécessaires; j'ay fait

8. Roussille had met BF in January, 1777: XXIII, 128. As he will explain on Dec. 27, 1780, and in an undated letter written around September 1, 1784, he sailed on May 22, 1778, on the *Boston*, Capt. Tucker. While aboard one of her prizes, he was captured (on July 8 of that year), not to be released from England until Feb. 26, 1780. Both letters are at the APS. Upon his return to France he learned that the *Boston* had subsequently taken other prizes, and his correspondence with BF revolves around his efforts to obtain what he considered his fair share of that prize money.

écrire a Mr. Monfil,[9] votre Corespondant pour qu'il vous informe de Ce dont jay eu L'honeur de vous entretenir, vos bontés a mon egard M'enhardisent a vous prier Monsieur de vouloir bien avoir quelqu'egard dans La Situation présente, ou je me trouve, Comme ayant apris par un de nos Mrs. que La dite fregattes avoit fait des prisses Considerables qui ont été Conduites a L'orient, vous M'aves donné des Marques distingués d'une ame bienfaisante dont j'espere que vous voudrés bien me Les Continuer en me faisant passer quelque peu d'argent pour fournir aux frais de ma maladie, je vous en tienderai Compte Sur Ce qui peut me revenir ainsi que des deux Louis dor que vous m'avés avancé pour fair ma route.

J'ay Lhoneur d'etre avec Le plus profond respect Monsieur votre très humble et très obeissant Serviteur   ROUSSILLE

Mon adresse est a Mr. rousille au Caffé de L'empereur rue vielle Monoye a paris

Addressed: A Monsieur / Monsieur de franquelin / deputé du Congrets chés / Mr. De Chaumont en / Son hotel a passi

Notation: Roussille

From Jonathan Williams, Jr.

ALS: University of Pennsylvania Library; copy: Yale University Library

Dear & honoured Sir   Nantes March 30. 1780

I informed you in my last that the Farmers insisted on the payment of the Duties, & even made a merit of not seizing the Goods. I am sure this is because they do not understand the nature of my Request for it is not an exemption from any Duty which I ask, but I ask not to pay a Duty which I am only liable to by having employed one or two hundred of poor People. I have written another Letter to Mr Paulze which I inclose you will see by it how reasonable my request is & if they understand it I

9. Presumably John Bondfield, who did indeed write to Roussille on June 3. APS.

am sure it will not be refused. I have been already obliged to pay 600 Livres duty and if it is paid on all the Cloathing it will I suppose amount to 10,000.

I am ever most dutifully and affectionately Yours

JONA WILLIAMS J

Doctor Franklin

P.s. My Uncle is going out to America, as I do not know how he may be received having been a Kings Officer before the War, I shall take it is a great Favour if you will favour him with a short introduction to the President of Congress, meerly to express that he has not been employed by the English King since his Commn in America 10 Years since, that he has been in France 18 months, & that you wish him to be receivd by his Countrymen. This Letter I dont mean to be delivered unless there be occasion but having it with him open it will be a sort of Certificate. I hope you will see no impropriety in my Request and kindly grant it.—

Notation: J Williams March 30 80

To William Carmichael   Copies (two): Library of Congress

Dear sir,   Passy, March. 31st.[–April 7] 1780.

I received by M. Gerard your kind Letter written at Philadelphia.[1] His safe Return has given me great pleasure.

As soon as I received yours of Jan 25 from Cadix,[2] I order'd a Credit of 1000 Louis d'ors to be Lodg'd for Mr. Jay and you, by Mr. Grand with his Banker at Madrid. He wrote by the next post. It does not appear by yours of March 13, that you had then been acquainted with this, or received my Letter. This Surprized me, and I enquired of Mr. Grand about it, who tells me that a Letter from his correspondent of march 12. mentions the Receipit of the Order; and he supposes that Mr D'yranda[3] would soon find you out.

1. Missing.
2. XXXI, 406–8.
3. A Madrid banker associated with Ferdinand Grand: XXXI, 512n, 513.

The Ms. De Lafayette is gone again to America. He took leave at Court in his American Uniform. He carries with him a warm heart for our Cause and Country. Dr. Bancroft is just returned here from L'Orient, Where he has been to assist in getting one of our Frigates out, the alliance. He will probably write to you by next post.

I thank you for your Intelligence of the state of affairs at home, and for the Extracts of Mr. Lee's Philippics against me. Such they were intended. But when I consider him as the most malicious Enemy I ever had (tho' without the smallest Cause) that he Shews so clearly his abundant Desire to accuse and diffame me, and that all his Charges are so frivolous, so ill founded, and amount to so little. I esteem them rather as Panegyrics upon me and Satyrs against himself.

I am glad to understand by yours of Feb. 19 and Mar 13.[4] that you had met with so agreable reception at madrid. The more so as I once imagined that the long Delay of that Court in acceding to The Treaty had a dubious Appearance. Here I have every Proof of the utmost Cordiality, and the sincerest Good will to us, and our Cause. It is true I do not obtain all I have been directed to ask for. The Committee of Commerce sent me over an Invoice of Goods amounting I guess to more than twelve Millions of Livres.[5] I have been obliged to abridge it greatly, the Sum granted me not sufficing. I Send however some of the most necessary articles, viz 15,000 compleat Dresses for Soldiers 15000 new fusils, and 1000 Barrels of Gun powder. If Mr. Jay can obtain a Sum from Spain it may help to Supply the Defficiency. You have reason, as you say, to pity my Situation. Too much is expected from me, and not only the Congress draw upon me often unexpectedly for large Sums, but all the agents of the Committee of Commerce in Europe and America, think they may do the same when pinch'd alledging that it is necessary to The Credit of the Congress, that their particular Credit should be supported. From the Desire here of carrying on the War without levying new taxes, and the Extraordinary Expence of the

4. XXXI, 502–3, and above.
5. See XXX, 110n, 359n.

Navy,[6] so much money cannot be spared to us as is imagined in America, but essential aid will be given us this Campaign either by an actual Junction of force or Concert of Operations in the United States, or by a powerful Diversion in the West Indies, a very considerable armament of Ships and Troops being on the point of departure for those Countries.[7]

Mr. Adams is at Paris, with Mr. Dana. We live upon good Terms with each other, but he has never communicated anything of his Business to me, and I have made no Enquiries of him, nor have I any Letter from Congress explaining it, so that I am in utter Ignorance.[8] Indeed the Congress seem very backward in writing to me. I have no answer to a Long Letter I wrote by the Chevalier de la Luzerne, nor even an Acknowledgement that it came to hand; Pray can you tell me the reason?

Friday April 7 Having met with some Interruption I did not finish my Letter in time to go by the last Post. Mr. Grand has Since read me part of a Letter from Mr. Le Marquis d'Yranda in which he mentions his having seen you; and his Willingness to serve Mr. Jay and you, but that you appear'd somewhat reserved. We concluded that you had not received M. Grand's Letter which went at the Same time with mine[9] (of which Latter I inclose copies) because he had acquainted you with his having recommended you to The Marquis, and had given you Such a Character of him as would have induced you to have conversed freely with him. We could not imagine how these Letters could miscarry: But since Mr. Grand left me, I have Thought that you may possibly have forgotten that you advised me to direct for you under the name of Mr. Clement, to be left at the Post office, and perhaps you have not asked there for a Letter so address'd. I am concerned lest your not receiving the Credit contained, might have incommoded you.

I did not imagine Mr. Jay would have Staid so long at Cadiz, or I should have written to him there. After some Doubts

6. By now, more than 150,000,000 *l.t.* per year: Dull, *French Navy,* p. 349.

7. The ships and troops for the West Indies were already en route: *ibid.,* p. 187.

8. Congress had informed BF in general terms of JA's mission, but BF had not yet received the letter and JA, distrusting his former colleague, provided little information: XXX, 542–3; XXXI, lx.

9. XXXI, 512.

about the manner of our future Corresponding, I am inclined to Think the best way will be to convey our Dispatches with those of the respective Courts, the fidelity and honour of the People managing the Post Offices not being so much to be rely'd on, and we shall probably have no Secrets that our friends may not safely be acquainted with, and not proper to be known by others.[1] M. De Vergennes informed me the other Day, that Mr. Jay was on his Way to Madrid and I therefore now write to him there. I wish it had so happen'd that he had first called at Paris, and if he could spare you a few Weeks to take a Trip hither, to visit your old friends, it would besides the Pleasure of seeing you be a great Satisfaction to me, who am at present very ignorant of the true State of America, and I am persuaded such an Interview between us would be useful in many respects.

Dr. Bancroft yesterday read me a Letter he had received from you, in which you express your surprize at not having heard from me. You will now find that I had written by the very first Opportunity after the Receipt of yours from Cadiz. He will write you by next Tuesday's post.

Messrs. Lee and Izard are gone to L'orient in order to embark in the alliance together, but they did not Travel together from hence. No Soul regrets their Departure: They separately came to take leave of me very respectfully offering their services to carry any Dispatches &c. We parted civilly, for I never acquainted them that I know of their writing against me to Congress. But I did not give them the Trouble of my Dispatches. Since Mr. Lee's being at l'orient he has written to Mr. Grand requesting a certificate from him in Contradiction to some thing you had said of him in a Paper delivered to Congress. I suppose Mr. Grand will explain this to you. There has been a fracas between our friends Sir Geo. Grand & Mr. Dumas, in which both have been to blame, and each ought to forgive the other. It relates to a Letter from Dumas to you which had been intercepted. I suppose he will acquaint you with the affair, and if you should not fully understand it from his acct. I can give the Explanation.

I retain my health *a merveille;* but what with Bills of Exchange, Cruizing Ships, supplies &c.— besides the proper Busi-

1. An echo of a comment BF had made at the beginning of his mission to France: XXIII, 211.

ness of my Station, I find I have too much to do. Your friend Billy (who presents his Respects) is a great help to me or I could not possibly go through with it.

With sincere Esteem and affection I am, Dear Sir Your most obedient and most humble servant.

William Carmichael Esqe.

To [Dumas]²

ALS: Boston Public Library; transcript: National Archives

Dear Sir,   Passy, March 31. 1780

I wrote to you yesterday³ relating to the Affair of your Letter to Mr Carmichael that you might know exactly the Truth of the Transaction. On Reflection I think it proper to add, that what I wrote was for your Satisfaction only; and that as the making it publick would give infinite Pain to a very worthy Man, Mr. F. Grand, who would then appear in the Light of *Delateur de son Frere;* & it can serve no other Purpose but that of Vengeance on Sir George, and be of no Advantage to you, I must insist on your Generosity in keeping it a Secret to yourself. In this you will also very much oblige me, who would by no means have my Name publickly mention'd on this Occasion; and I depend on your Compliance. With great Esteem, I am ever, Dear Sir Your most obedt. huml Servt   B. FRANKLIN

Endorsed: Passy 31e. Mars 1780 S.E. M. Franklin

To John Paul Jones

L⁴ and copy: Library of Congress

Dear Sir,   Passy, March 31st. 1780.

I received yours of the 14th by Mr Dryburugh. I had also another from Mess. Gourlade and Moylan acquainting me that they

2. Identified by his endorsement.
3. Actually on March 29. BF probably drafted the present letter on the 30th.
4. In WTF's hand and signed by him on behalf of his grandfather.

188

had received the Ransom Money about 200£ sterling, as paid to me, agreable to the Bill of Ransom; and had given my Acct. Credit for that Sum.[5] This lays me under a Difficulty, for I am thus become accountable for that Sum to the People of the whole Squadron that was under your Command; and if I give it to him, as you seem to desire, I am liable to repay it out of my own Pocket, which I cannot afford. If you had given him what you thought he merited, and satisfied the People with regard to it, I should have made no Objection. As it stands, I can do no other than pay the Sum received into the Mass that is to be divided among the Captors. I furnish'd him however with Ten Pounds more than you had advanced to him, to help him home; and it may be right, if you think fit, to recommend him to Congress.

I think the Copper that was at Nantes, is gone for America, but if any remains, I shall be glad that you can take it, and will write Accordingly.

When in mine of the 18th I mentioned 24000 *l.t.* Livres to be advanced for the Accommodation of the People of the Bonhomme Richard, I meant it also for those of the Alliance, and desire it may be so understood.[6]

I understand that Orders are gone down to value the Prize Ships the Serapis and Countess of Scarborough. I shall endeavour to procure another for dividing the Sum they amount to among the Squadron. But this will I fear occasion such delay, that you will not be ready to sail with the Convoy. As the usual Forms of Examination of the Ships and Stores &ca and the Evaluation of each Article, may take some Weeks; during all this time too, an enormous Expence is going on in maintaining so many People. These Things perplex and chagrin me exceedingly and I earnestly wish to have nothing more to do with Ships, being quite a Novice in such Business.

There is now a Proposition of sending by you besides the

5. Gourlade and Moylan's letter is missing.
6. Jones's friend Jacques-Alexandre Gourlade later told him that he had encouraged BF to double the amount. BF supposedly pleaded financial embarrassment for not doing so; the only money he had received was from the French government and he regretted having to ask it for more. Bancroft for his part claimed to have asked BF to add 12,000 *l.t.* to the amount: Bradford, *Jones Papers*, reel 5, nos. 1035, 1048.

15,000 small Arms, 1000 Barrels of Powder. The Powder is already at Port Louis, and two thirds of the Arms. I shall be able to write more precisely about this tomorrow. I am sure of your Willingness to take all you can: but I doubt more is expected of you than is possible.

With great Esteem I am, ever, Dear Sir, Your most obedt and most humble Servant.   W.T. FRANKLIN for B.F.

Honble Comme Jones.—

Notation: Wm/B. Franklin Per B Franklin No. 30 mar 31— 80

To Jonathan Williams, Jr.   Copy: Library of Congress

Dear Jonathan   Passy, March. 31. 1780.

I have received yours of the 26th. I am promised an Answer from Mr. Paulze this Morning and If I receive it shall send it to you by tomourrow's Post. This Soliciting of Interested People to forgive Duties they think their Right, is an odious Task to me. I had rather at any time, If I could afford it, pay 'em myself.

Mr. Chaumont thinks Mr. Bondfield's Propositions too high and advises me not to accept them. Having no Judgment in such Business my self, I wish much to have nothing more to do with it. I am heartily tired of Ships, and Cruizes, & &c.

Mr. Scheweighauser having long had the Care of Supplying what was needful to The Americans at Nantes, I must necessarily either confide in him or appoint some body else. The latter I am not inclined to do, as I daily expect the Congress will put their port affairs on a new footing, by establishing Consuls. I can therefore do nothing more for Capt. Hendricks.[7]

I have no doubt of your doing every thing in your Power and for the best, in the affair of the furniture. People some times demand more Expedition than they expect in order to obtain all that is possible. Mr. Chaumont is eager to dispatch Business but he respects and loves you, as does, Your affectionate Uncle BF.

7. JW reported this to Kendrick on April 16: Yale University Library.

If there is any Sheathing Coper belonging to The Congress in the hands of Mr. Scheweighauser, obtain it from him by showing this, give him a Receipt for it, and send it to Capt. Jones.

Mr. Jona. Williams.

From Dumas

ALS (draft): Algemeen Rijksarchief

Monsieur,   La haie 31e. Mars 1780

J'eus la satisfaction, mardi au soir, de voir *notre Ami* au moment de son arrivée. Il m'a reçu très-cordialement. Je lui avois écrit deux jours auparavant, pour lui demander cet entretien; & je l'avois régalé du Rendez-vous de Salomon chez la Reine de Saba, & de la bile de H [*deleted:* arris] ce qui lui avoit fait grand plaisir.[8] Je lui communiquai une longue Lettre de Mr. Carmichael, où il entre dans le détail de l'état présent de l'Amérique confédérée, de l'exclusion & chûte entiere des amis du Dr. Berkenhout & de Temple, & de l'adhésion, plus ferme que jamais, du Peuple Américain à l'Alliance avec la France, après quoi je lui parlai de la Lettre interceptée, & de la colere du g—— F—— contre moi.[9] J'ai vu qu'à tout ceci il est parfaitement neutre. Ainsi je continuerai de le voir paisiblement, tant ici qu'à Amstm.; & je serai toujours prêt, quand il y aura quelque chose qui doive être communiqué au g—— F——, ou qui puisse lui faire plaisir personnellement, de le faire, dès que je le trouverai disposé à me bien recevoir.

Quant à la Lettre Déclaratoire que je vous écrivis dernierement, ils n'en savent rien encore ici; & le g—— F—— ne me fait rien dire à ce sujet. Ainsi je ne crois pas qu'on vous parle, Monsieur, de rien de pareil. Lorsque je l'écrivis, j'avois tout le

---

8. For the stories which entertained van Berckel see Dumas to BF, March 28 (which was the preceding Tuesday).

9. Dr. John Berkenhout and John Temple were advocates of a negotiated settlement with Britain: XXIV, 300n, 554; XXV, 165–6. Both met a cold reception and the former was jailed: Lewis Einstein, *Divided Loyalties: Americans in England during the War of Independence* (London, 1933), pp. 90–2. The "g—— F——" is the Grand Facteur, French Ambassador La Vauguyon.

systême nerveux en commotion après les violentes scenes que j'avois soutenues. Je crois m'appercevoir, qu'une grande partie de cette colere est destinée à me prendre par la terreur, connoissant l'impression que cela fait chez moi.

Je viens de voir encore notre Ami, qui est toujours le même pour moi. Lui ayant observé que ce que j'avois écrit en confidence seulement à un Ami, ne pouvoit faire le même tort, au bout du compte, a Mr. G. que les discours du fils de Mr. G———, qui a parlé à tout venant & à moi-même comme un vrai Tory; il m'a dit qu'il l'avoit entendu parler sur le même ton à Heemstede Campagne près de Harlem.

Je desire & redoute, Monsieur, votre Lettre en réponse de mes dernieres. Je sens combien mon imprudence est digne de votre censure; & ce sentiment me poignarde à touts moments, quand je pense qu'elle peut vous occasionner le moindre trouble. Si vous trouvez, avec Mr. De Ch——— et Mr. B———, qu'il faille donner quelque satisfaction au frere de Mr. G——— de la Rue Montmartre,¹ je ferai & signerai ce dont vous serez convenu avec ce dernier, que j'aime & honore beaucoup.

Notre Ami m'a assuré qu'il ne se passe, ni ne se passera rien ici, que le Courier, envoyé à Petersbourg, pour savoir si l'Imperatrice veut entrer avec la rep. dans certaines mesures, ne soit de retour.

On dit depuis quelque temps, que Mr. Laurens, ancien President du Congrès, est désigné pour venir ici,² d'abord incognito, & qu'il déploiera son caractere quand il en sera temps. J'en serois charmé. Je crois que cela fera un bon effet. Mais il seroit nécessaire que je le visse avant qu'il vît personne, pour lui faire connoître la Carte du Pays. Les uns disent qu'il est parti d'Amérique, & en chemin: les autres, qu'il est déjà en Europe. Notre Ami m'a demandé ce qui en est; comme je l'ignore moi-même, je n'ai pu

1. Ferdinand Grand's business address: *Almanach des marchands*, p. 373. The abbreviations represent Chaumont, Baudouin, and Grand.

2. Henry Laurens, elected by Congress to negotiate a loan and make a commercial treaty with the Netherlands, went to Charleston to take passage to Europe: XXXI, 412n. The British attack on the city delayed his departure, however; he finally sailed from Philadelphia in mid-August: Smith, *Letters*, XV, 160, 533n.

le satisfaire. Vos avis à cet égard, & vos lumieres, me seroient bien nécessaires, & par conséquent doublement précieuses.

Je suis avec le plus respectueux attachement, Monsieur Votre tres humble & très obeissant serviteur   D

La Lettre interceptée, ne peut être que celle, Monsieur, que j'avois enfermée dans une pour vous. Si vous l'avez reçue, je comprends qui a trouvé quelque moyen de s'en emparer, & de l'apporter lui-même ici au g—— F——.

J'ai compris clairement par les discours du g—— F—— que Mr. G—— prétend, que mes appointemens ne me sont accordés que sous condition que je les tirerois toujours de lui, de 6 en 6 mois. Mais ma fidélité pour les Etats-unis est, & doit être, indépendante de l'or et des caprices d'autrui.

Passy à S.E. Mr. Franklin

Addressed: His Excellency / B. Franklin, Esqr. / Min. Plenipo. of the United States / &c. / *Passy./*.

Notations in Dumas' hand: Lettre qui m'a été renvoyée par Mr. B. dans la sienne du 6 Avr. / N.B. Mr F—— n'a pas reçu cette Lre. Elle m'a été renvoyée par Mr B—

From Robert Morris: Two Letters

(I) ALS and LS: American Philosophical Society; (II) ALS: University of Pennsylvania Library

I.

Dear Sir   Philada. March 31st 1780

I have just recvd by the hands of our mutual Friend Mr Holker your favour of the 22d Octr last recommending the affairs of Monsr De la Freté with Mr. Roulhac of Edenton to my assistance.[3] I had already engaged in that service and you may depend that every recommendation of yours has the Force & effect on my mind that you wou'd wish for. I shall ever feel myself pleased in the execution of Your Commands. I beg to trouble You with

3. XXX, 571. See also XXVI, 290n; XXVIII, 566n.

a letter for your Friend Monsr Dumas in Answer to one from him[4] & with sincere attachment & Esteem I remain Dr Sir Your most obedt hbl sert   ROBT MORRIS

His Excy Benjn. Franklin Eqr.

Addressed: To / His Exelly. Benjn. Franklin Esqr. / Minister Plenipotentiary / of the United States of America / at the Court of / Versailles / [*in another hand:*] per the Fier Rodrigue / Cap Monteau

Notation: Robt. Morris Philadelphia March 31. 1780

II.

Dear Sir   Philada. March 31st 1780

I do not know that what I am now going to write is in the least degree necessary or that Mr. Deane will thank me for it but the thought has just struck me, that as he has constantly & invariably manifested a Warm attachment to your Person and Character, in his examination before Congress in his Publications, & in all his private Conversations at which I have been present, it might be some satisfaction to you & him, to have a testimony of this kind from a Friend to you both,[5] who having nothing to seek or ask for himself can mean nothing but to promote that Harmony & Friendship which he wishes to continue in existence between two Worthy Men; I consider Mr. Deane as a Martyr in the Cause of America after rendering the most signal & important Services he has been reviled & Traduced in the most shamefull manner. But I have not a doubt the day will come when his Merit shall be universally acknowledged and the Authors of those Calumnies held in the detestation they deserve.

My own Fate has been in some degree Similar, after four years

4. Undoubtedly Morris to Dumas, March 24 (National Archives), in which he apologized for his delay in answering a Jan. 7 letter and promised to support Dumas' interests wherever he could. Most of the letter, however, concerned the attacks of Morris' political enemies.

5. Morris had rallied support for his business associate Deane during the lengthy congressional hearings into Deane's finances: Edmund S. Morgan, "The Puritan Ethic and the American Revolution," *W&MQ*, 3rd ser., XXIV (1967), 30; Ferguson, *Power of the Purse*, pp. 81–94, 102–4.

Indefatigueable Service, I have been reviled & traduced, for a long time by whispers & insinuations which at length were fortunately wrought up to Public Charges; which gave me an Opportunity, to Shew how groundless, how Malicious these things were, how Innocent & Honest my Transactions, My Enemies ashamed of their persecution have quitted the pursuit and I am in the peaceable possession of the most Honourable Station my Ambition aspires to, that of a private Citizen of a Free State.[6] Yourself my Good Sir have had a share in these Calumnies but the Malice which gave them Vent was so evident as to destroy its own Poison, they coud not cast even a Cloud over your justly & much revered Character. These things have taught me a lesson of Philosophy that may be of Service. I find the most usefull members of Society have most Enemies because there are a number of Envious beings in the Human Shape and if my opinion of Mankind in general is grown worse from my experience of them, that very circumstance raises my veneration for those Characters that justly merit the applause of Virtuous Men, in this light I view Doctor Franklin & Mr. Deane and under this View of them, I assert with an honest Confidence, that I have a just & equitable title to a return of that Friendship which I think it is honourable to profess for them with that degree of truth & affection which impresses me to it. I am Dr Sir Your most Obedient & very humble Servt.   ROBT MORRIS

His Excy Benjn. Franklin Esqr Minister Plenipotentiary Paris

From the Comte de Sarsfield

ALS: University of Pennsylvania Library

Dear sir   Paris le 31 mars 1780
    Pouves vous me dire ou Est un mr d'orbrais qui, allant en amérique chargé de quelque Commission de votre part, a Eté fait

6. Attacked by Thomas Paine, Daniel Roberdeau, and others and defeated for reelection to the Pa. Assembly, Morris retired from public life in November, 1779: William G. Sumner, *The Financier and the Finances of the American Revolution* (2 vols., New York, 1891), I, 223–35. He returned to public service a year later.

prisonnier?[7] Il doit Etre a present de retour en france. Il S'est chargé de quelques bagatelles pour moy, Je Suis surpris de ne pas en entendre parler.

En relisant la lettre ou on m'en parle Je vois que Jay mal traduit ce n'est pas une commission que vous lui aviez donné but he had a Commission from you.

Si vous n'en avez pas entendu parler depuis son retour, vous savez au moins ce qu'il etoit avant Son depart. Je vous prie d'avoir la bonté de me le dire cela pourra m'aider a le retrouver.

Vous connoisses les sentimens avec lesquels Jai L'hr detre my dear sir votre tres humble et tres obeist serviteur[8] SARSFIELD

Addressed: A Monsieur / Monsieur franklin ministre / plenipo-tentiaire des Etats / unis d'Amerique / A Passy

Notations in different hands: Sarsfield 31. mars. 1780 / hotel de sarsfield

From John Torris

ALS: American Philosophical Society

Honnd. Sir   Dunkerque 31st. march 1780.

I have Recd. the Letter your Excellency did me the Honnour to write me the 21st. Feby., with the Judgement for the owner's adventure, which I have sent to Quimper corantin, & am thank-full for same.[9]

The Papers relating to the Betsey, have been sent by the admi-ralty of Brest, to Mr. De Grandbourg Secretary to S. A. S. the Duc

7. This D'Orbray was mentioned on Nov. 1, 1777, in a letter sent by James Cole, writing from the Ile de Ré. Cole explained in it that he was trying to reach Philadelphia along with two friends, O'Meara and D'Orbray, and that they needed free passage; see XXIV, 29n, where D'Orbray's name was inad-vertently left out. The three men presumably joined De La Plaigne's ill-fated expedition to Georgia (XXV, 234n; XXVI, 185n, 688–9) and were soon cap-tured.

8. BF answered Sarsfield on April 5. He can recall nothing of a Mr. Dor-brais or of hearing his name. Has Sarsfield mistaken it? Library of Congress.

9. BF's latest letter to the principal owner of the privateers *Black Prince* and *Black Princess:* XXXI, 465n. BF provided commissions to the ships in hope they would capture prisoners who could be exchanged for captive American sailors. St. Corentin is Quimper's patron saint.

De Penthievre, by Error, & it Is in vain I have Sollicited till now, they Shou'd be Transmitted to your Excellency.[1] I Imagine they are sent to M. De Sartine; & I beseech your Excellency, to make an enquiery after them, to expedite forthwith the Judgement. Messrs. Diot & Co. my Correspondants at Morlaix, are very anxious to get forthwith the Judgements for the Last 3. Prises to our Black Prince, of which the Papers have long ago been sent to your Excellency Viz. Brig Philip, Capt. Geo. Hoare, from St. Lucia to London Schooner Peter, Capt. Thos. Byrne, from London to Madeira Brig Friendship Capt. Pretty John from Lisbon to Dartm[*torn*][2]

I Beseech your Excellency will dispatch me these Judgements Immediatly, as we cannot Sell without, & the Merchandizes are spoiling.

I am with gratitude & greatest respect Honnd. Sir Your Excellency's Most Humble & most obedient Servant   J. TORRIS

His Excellency Dr. Franklin

Endorsed: Mar. 31.

Notation: Torris 1780

To King Louis XVI

L:[3] Archives du Ministère des affaires étrangères; copy: Historical Society of Pennsylvania

[March, 1780][4]

M. franklin attendoit L'arrivée de la fregatte La Confederation,[5] pour envoyer a Philadelphie des Munitions de guerre, et L'ha-

1. These papers had been missing since early February: XXXI, 465n. Grandbourg had been involved in earlier prize cases (XXIX, 215, 368); Penthièvre as admiral of France had oversight of such matters.
2. These three ships had been taken during the second joint cruise of Torris' privateers, Feb. 24 to March 19: Clark, *Ben Franklin's Privateers*, pp. 109–10.
3. In the hand of Chaumont.
4. Based on the notation. It likely was written after BF received Lafayette's letter of March 20, above, stating that the supplies for America had not arrived in time to go on the *Hermione*.
5. The *Confederacy*, which had carried Jay and Gérard as far as Martinique: XXX, 358n; XXXI, 226n, 286.

billement Complet de quinze mils Soldats, qui en Sont absolument Depourvus.

Cette fregatte etoit destinée a porter M Gerard en france, elle a été dematée de tous Mats Sur le Banc de terre Neuve, et est en Relache a la Martinique; ou elle Sera employée a des Correspondances entre la Martinique et L'amerique Septentrionale, ou a Convoyer en france les Navires Marchands.

M. franklin ne peut Supléer au deffaut de Cette fregatte, qu'en implorant au Nom des etats unis de L'amerique Septentrionale, les Bontés de Sa Majesté très Chretienne; pour accorder incessamment un vaisseau de Guerre, dans lequel il puisse faire Charger Les Munitions de guerre et Les habillements, dont Les troupes americaines ont le plus pressant Besoing.[6] Il est d'autant plus essentiel que Ce Vaisseau Soit d'unne marche et d'unne force Superieure, que rien ne pouroit Remplacer la perte des dits aprovisionements. Il est a desirer que Ce Vaisseau Soit pris dans Le port de Rochefort parceque les habillements Se font a Nantes.

Le Dit vaisseau peut Se Rendre a L'amerique Septentrionale avec trois mois de Vivres parcequ'il en trouvera abondament a Philadelphie, ou de Memoire d'homme on n'a jamais fait de Si Bonne Recolte que la derniere, ainsy que dans tout Le Continent.

Au deffaut d'Equipages francais on poura y Supléer par des Equipages americains, qui attendent leur Echange en angleterre Contre Les Prisonniers que L'Escadre Jones a fait Sur les anglais.

Le Vaisseau de Guerre qui Sera accorde Sera a mesure S'il est destiné ensuitte pour les Colonies francaises, de proteger les Navires Marchands qui Sont en grand Nombre et qui porteront des vivres de toutte Espece.

M. franklin Suplie Sa Majesté très Chretienne, de luy accorder avec Bonté unne prompte Reponse Sur Sa demande, attendu qu'il ne peut Retarder les avis a faire passer au Congrès Sur les Secours qu'il est Chargé d'envoyer.

Notation: fin mars 1780.

---

6. An alternative was the *Alliance*, but BF had doubts about how much more she could carry; see his March 31 letter to Jones.

From American Gentlemen in France

LS: Yale University Library; draft[7] and transcript: National Archives

Sir, [March, 1780][8]

The Glory acquired to the American Arms and the injury done to the Common Enemy of France and America, by the Squadron lately under Commodore Jones have afforded us very great Satisfaction, and this would be sensibly increased in our minds and advantageously Communicated to our Countrymen on the other side of the Atlantic, with other very beneficial Effects there should His most Christian Majesty be graciously pleased to add the Serapis Ship of War to the infant American Navy.

Deeply & gratefully Sensible of the Obligations already Conferred on our Country by the King and his Ministers we should not venture to sollicit this new favour did not particular Circumstances at this time encourage us to do it.— On one hand the great and increasing number of French Ships of War, will as we are informed afford Sufficient Occupation for the Seamen of this Kingdom and on the other, we see many American Seamen, who have escaped or been lately released from English Prisons now waiting at L'Orient and other French Ports, where no American Vessels are in need of their Services; many others as we understand are likely soon to arrive and fall into Similar Circumstances of whom a Considerable number may probably be lost to our Country, unless the means of preserving and employing them can be Obtained.—

We think therefore that the Serapis having Surrendered to the Flagg of the United States, might under the same Flagg be most speedily and advantageously manned and employed against the Common Enemy so as effectually to serve the Cause and promote the Interests of our illustrious Ally as well as of the United States.— We therefore beg that you Sir will be Pleased to Com-

7. In John Paul Jones's hand. He later wrote on it, "This Letter was Signed by a great Majority of the American Gentlemn in France." Undoubtedly he circulated this letter among American merchants, mariners, and ship owners, 29 of whom signed it.

8. The dateline of the draft reads "L'Orient march 1780." It probably dates from the latter part of the month, after Jones received BF's March 18 letter, above, telling him that Louis XVI intended to purchase the *Serapis*.

municate to the Kings Ministers these our Sentiments and Wishes, and to give them such Countenance and support as they in your Superior Judgment may appear to deserve.—

We have the Honor to be with great Respect, Sir Your most humble and most Obedient Servants

JOHN BONDFIELD	RICHARD CHAMBERLAYNE
WILLIAM HAYWOOD	HENRY ASH
EDWD BANCROFT	DANIEL LORING
JOHN WILLIAMS	GEO: MOORE JR
JONATN: NESBITT	PETER AMIEL
JAS CUMING	JONA. COLE
THOS: BELL	CHRISTN. WILK
JAMES MOYLAN	JOHN KENDRICK
JONA WILLIAMS J	JOHN COGGESHALL
JOSHUA JOHNSON	MOSES GRINNELL
JNO. ROSS	NICHOLAS BARTLETT
JNO GREEN	FRANCIS ROBINS
JOS MEREDITH	WM WHITE
JOHN GALE	NAT. CUTTING
SAML SMITH	

The Honble: Benja: Franklin Minister Plenipotentiary of the United States of America, at Paris.

From François-Louis Teissèdre de Fleury

ALS: American Philosophical Society

Sir   paris, March 1780

Obliged to joign immediately My Regiment at Brest I can not possibly Receive Myself, the Medall, which you was so good, agreable to the dezire of Congress, to have struck for me, but my father will be proud to Receive it in my absence.[9]

If you thought proper to send it, (with a Letter for me) to *Mr. L'abbé gibelin, hotel de sabran, Ruë fauxbourg st. honoré;* he would forward it to my father, & I would be very gratefull of your kindness.

9. For Fleury's silver medal see XXXI, 422–3, 489–91.

The medall voted for me by congress, is a silver one; but I could wish, besides, to have one of gold struck at my own expences. It will not hurt the dies; I leave the money for that purpose in the hands of the medaillist. He will keep the gold medall for me till my Return.[1] I hope you will not have any objection.

I have the honor to be with great Respect of your excellency, the most humble servant. L. Fleury

Franklin and Chaumont to Arnauld de La Porte,[2] with La Porte's Reply

ALS:[3] Bibliothèque du Port, Brest

Monsieur Versailles ce 1er. avril 1780—

M. de Sartines m'a autorisé en mettant L'apostille au memoire cy Joint de vous Confier L'objet dont il Sagit. M. William Neveu de M. franklin doit envoyer de Nantes de L'orient et de Morlaix L'habillement Complet pour dix mil hommes, et M. de Beaumé[4] a envoyé de Paris douze Caisses de Medicaments,[5] Le tout

1. Fleury's regiment, which had fought with Rochambeau, arrived in Brest in June, 1783. BF presented Fleury with his medal shortly thereafter, on Aug. 15. See XXXI, 490n.

2. On April 1, BF paid 60 *l.t.* to a courier from Versailles "going to L'Orient & Brest with Orders about shipping the Clothes, Arms, &c." Cash Book. This letter, along with the memoir from Sartine mentioned in the first sentence (now missing), must have been part of those orders.

3. In Chaumont's hand.

4. Antoine Baumé (1728–1804), celebrated chemist, apothecary, and member of the Academy of Sciences. He had done extensive work on dosages of pharmaceuticals and had also been involved in the manufacture of chemicals and experimentation with new methods of manufacturing porcelain. He drafted more than a hundred of the technical entries for the *Description des Arts et Métiers. DBF.*

5. At some point after the congressional order for uniforms and supplies reached France (XXX, 359), two pages' worth of medicines and surgical instruments were added to the end of the list. We presume that these were what Baumé had assembled. The list of medicines appears only on one copy of the congressional order (Hist. Soc. of Pa.), which differs in several additional ways from Congress' original invoices: the quantities for most of the articles were reduced by half, estimated prices were given for each item (totalling 353,088 *l.t.*, 2 *s.*, 7 *d.*), and supplies that had evidently been procured were checked, with the actual quantities written next to the requested figures, if

a L'adresse de M. Bersole a Brest pour estre Embarqués par vos ordres et estre Remis a M. holker Consul de france et agent de la Marine a Philadelphie, pour les tenir a la disposition de M. le Marquis de lafayette. J'ecris en Consequence, Monsieur, a M. Bersole de prendre vos ordres Sur ces objets, pour quil fasse Marquer les Balots de la Marque que vous luy indiquerez afin qu'on puisse les Reconnoistre et les Remettre a leur destination par tout ou ils arriveront.

La Majeure partie de Ces Balots doivent, Monsieur, estre arrivés a Brest ou y arriveront dans Les Dix premiers Jours de ce mois, et Je prends La Liberté de vous observer qu'il est Bien essentiel qu'ils soyent embarqués, on Les avoit destinés pour L'hermione et unne gaucherie en a privé M. le Marquis de lafayette. Je vous Suplie en graces d'en proteger L'embarquement, ils Sont destinés a vêtir des Soldats qui Sont Nuds. Je Crois vous en dire assez pour que vous Jugiez de leur veritable destination.

Je Suis avec Respect et attachement Monsieur votre tres humble et tres obeissant Serviteur   LERAY DE CHAUMONT

M. le Docteur franklin, Monsieur, me Charge de vous temoigner toutte Sa Reconnoissance des Bons Services que vous Rendez a Son Pais.   B FRANKLIN

M. de la Porte intendant de la Marine a Brest

Vls [Versailles?] ce 5. avril

Le temps ne me permet pas, mr, de repondre au long à la lettre que vous m'avez fait l'hr. de m'ecrire de Versailles le 1er. de ce

---

they differed. This annotated copy was at some point sent to America; it bears a note about artillery by Henry Knox, dated Jan. 5, 1781. We conjecture that it was meant to let Congress know what they could expect to actually receive.

Unbeknown to BF, Chaumont had recently financed two other shipments of medicines to be sent to America in care of Jean Holker. The first was delivered to Gen. Lincoln at Charleston; the other sailed on the *Hermione* (which left on March 20). The total value of these medicines was approximately 70,000 *l.t.*, for which Holker sought reimbursement (unsuccessfully) from Congress. The invoice he subsequently sent to Chaumont (APS), which the latter presented to BF, became part of the dispute between the two when they were settling their accounts in 1782.

mois. Je n'ai que celui de vous informer que j'ai pourvû à l'embarquement des Ballots que vous avez à Faire passer à mr. holker pour les tenir à la disposition de m le mis. de lafayete. Les 100. ballots adressés par m Williams à m Bersolle s'embarquent actuellement. Les 12. caisses de medicamens ne sont point encore arrivées, elles le seront egalement dès qu'elles seront rendûes Msr, Si toutefois elles le sont à temps. J'aurai l'honneur de vous adresser la facture; Elle sera adressée de maniere à cacher la destination, et en même temps à assûrer la remise des effets à Mr. holker.

En me pretant en ce qui depend de moi à cette expédition Je remplis le service du Roi, et j'execute les ordres de mon ministre. Je serai très flatté que mr. Le Dr. franklin veüille bien voir de plus dans l'empressement que j'y mets mon devoüement pour les Etats unis de l'Amérique et mon respect pour sa personne.

To John Paul Jones

Two copies: Library of Congress;[6] transcript: American Philosophical Society

Dear Sir,   Versailles, April 1. 1780

Enclosed is the Order from the Prince de Montbarey, for the Delivery to you of the Arms and Gun powder mentioned in Mine of Yesterday, which you will receive per Post.—[7] This Courier carries also from me a Pacquet directed to you from Mr. Dumas, enclosing one for Congress to your Care.—[8] By the

6. One copy, made by L'Air de Lamotte, is in BF's letterbook. The other, from which we print, is in Thomas Hutchins' hand and is located in the Peter Force Collection.

7. Both copies include a marginal note: "15000 Fusils / 100,000 lb. Gunpowder." The enclosure probably was Montbarey's letter to BF of this date (Library of Congress) saying that he had given orders for the artillery arsenal at Port Louis to deliver to Captain Jones 100,000 lbs. of powder and 15,000 new fusils. He asked BF to tell Jones to give a full receipt to the director of artillery there, M. Minard Désaleux (for whom see *Etat militaire* for 1779, p. 261). In a postscript Montbarey added that he was enclosing a letter to Désaleux and asked BF to forward it.

8. The packet Dumas mentioned in his March 17 and 23 letters, above.

Post M. de Chaumont has written to his Correspondent M. Monplaisir at L'Orient, to advance 100,000 Livres for the Americans of the Alliance & Bonhomme Richard on Account.— My best Wishes ever attend you.

Your most obedient humble Servant (Signed) B FRANKLIN

A True Copy taken at L'Orient in August 1780 by THO: HUTCHINS

Notation: (No. 3) From his Excellency Dr. Franklin Versailles April 1st. 1780— No. 45. Copd.

From William Dorsett ALS: American Philosophical Society

Sir April 2th 1780

This Comes to Let You know that I am one of Maryland Who Saild from Alexadria and had the misfortune to Be taken the Day after we Left the Capes of Virginnea they Being Scarse of Provisions Sent all the men a Shore On perroal Except me only they Carried into Newyork the Prize Master Being a friend to a Maricah Gave me Liberty to Make my Escape if I Could I found that it was Impossible to Get to Maryland I was Resolv'd to keep Clare of the Prison Ship so I met with Capt Alexandria Kenniday who Toald me that he was of Virginnea and that he Intended the first Oppotunity to Go into Virginnea after he made another Voige to london to which I Thought it would be the Best Chanse I Should meet with So I Embraseed that Opportunity and Saild for London and was taken and Carried into fackum [Fécamp] and then I was in Some Hopes of Geting to amaricae so much the Soonner as I had fell into the hands of them that are Uniteed with amaricae but I find it to the Contrary I will not go into England unless I am foursd against my will I think it a very unjust thing to be Treated in the manner that I am; to be a prisner among friends as I Exspected them; I Sent a Line to the Commeserys and He Sent word Back that he Could Not Let me have my Liberty without your Consent I Shall Take it as a Particular favour If you will Send a Line or too that I may Get my Liberty

to go to amaricae and in So Doing You will Grately Oblige Your
humble Sert[9]   WILLIAM DORSETT

Addressed: A / Monsieur / Monsieur Franklin Plenipotentiaire
/ Des Etats unis de Lamerique / A Passy proche / Paris

Notation: Dorset Wm. April 2. 1780.

From Mary Hewson   ALS: American Philosophical Society

Dear Sir   Craven Street April 2.[–5] 1780
It is long since we had a line from you,[1] but we have sometimes heard of you; to hear you are well gives us pleasure.
Though you do not write I trust you do not forget us, nor wish
us to forget you, therefore I take this favourable opportunity of
sending you a long letter, such I intend it to be, for I fancy I have
a great deal to say, as it is so long since we have had any communication.

You know that my affairs are settled in a manner that affords
me a competent income.[2] My mother and I continue upon the
same plan we entred upon when we went to Cheam, and I have
no thoughts of altering it, for, by not extending the plan, I shall
be rich enough to indulge myself, and my children, in any occasional expences that will essentially gratify me, or benefit them.[3]
Thank God! We are all in good health; my mother had an alarming attack about three months ago, but is now quite recovered.
William is a boarder at Cheam School, which is my chief in-
ducement for residing in that place.[4] Many people say it is a dis-

9. Dorsett sent another plea, undated, which largely repeats this one and
reports that he was captured by the frigate *Trace.* If a Frenchman fell into the
hands of the Americans "they Could have their Liberty to Go to any part of
america they Choose," and he expects the same. APS.

1. She apparently had not received BF's letter of Jan. 10: XXXI, 360–2.

2. She had finally received her inheritance from her aunt: XXX, 515–16;
XXXI, 55.

3. Polly and Mrs. Stevenson had moved to Cheam, Surrey, in the summer
of 1777: XXV, 215; XXVI, 91.

4. Over a year earlier she had written of her decision to send William off

advantage for a school-boy to be within sight of his home, but I am conceited enough to think I know better, and that, as I never take him from the school when any business is going on, I do not impede his progress in learning, but add a little to his stock of knowledge, and sow some seeds of virtue which he could only by chance catch from those who have not my interest in the harvest. He is a very good boy, and I hope not dull, though I cannot boast much of his scholarship; whether the fault lies with him or his master I will not determine, perhaps more rigourous methods would quicken his speed, for he is indolent, but it is the maxim of that school not to flog except for offences which their laws deem criminal, and a deficiency in learning is not in the catalogue of those offences. I approve the principle, therefore must abide by the consequences, and give up my son's proficiency in latin for the sake of what to me appears more important. I am not without ambition, and a mother's cannot be so highly gratified as in her son's rising to distinction, but I would not sacrifice one worthy principle of his mind for the highest honours that learning can attain. William learns anything with great facility, but he does not make it his own, notwithstanding his memory is retentive. During the christmas holidays I employed him in getting by heart passages in verse which he did with great precision, and repeats them with propriety. I likewise exercised him a little in addition & substraction, which he is fond of. You know I am a bad arithmeticien, but I am proficient enough for my pupil at present, and it gave me pleasure to observe how readily he took my instructions. I was his writing-mistress too. You may laugh if you please, but I sent him to school writing a better hand than when he came home. The retirement of our situation gives me time to do many things for my children, which in the bustle of the world I could not do. My two little ones can now read very well;[5] that

---

to school: xxviii, 366–7. William Gilpin (1724–1804) served as the school's headmaster for almost thirty years instituting numerous progressive reforms during his tenure. He substituted fines and isolation for corporal punishment, for example, and added exercise and gardening to the boys' routine. William D. Templeman, *The Life and Work of William Gilpin (1724–1804)* . . . (Urbana, Ill., 1939), pp. 58–65, 148; *DNB*.

5. Her two younger children were Thomas and Elizabeth: xx, 318n; xxi, 318; xxii, 590; xxvi, 360; xxviii, 367.

is the whole of their scholarship, and much patience it cost me. Few people consider the acquisition so wonderful, as, to a reflecting teacher, it appears. How much did I wish that your alphabet & orthography were established! For I was perpetually told: "It does not sound so, Mama."[6] Thomas is very quick & very inquisitive. Notwithstanding his extreme volatility he will stop to investigate anything that excites his curiosity. His soul overshoots his body; indeed I apprehend his perpetual activity wears him, and prevents his growth. He is healthy & well proportion'd, but extremely diminutive. Elizabeth is much taller & stouter. I think she will be tolerably handsome, and as I leave her form to Nature I flatter myself her whole figure will be pleasing. Her understanding is no way deficient, and as I shall do my utmost to qualify it properly I hope to see her a truly agreeable woman. I am thankful for the great blessing of three children with sound constitutions, perfect forms, good understandings, and amiable dispositions. I flatter myself that you will have some pleasure in reading this account though perhaps it will prove no more than that I love my children, and that I love you, two truths you were not unacquainted with; as to the evidence I meant to give, you may not depend upon it as it is a mother's. William just now asked me if I should ever go to you.[7] His sister, who stood by him, immediately said "*I* shall." I can assure you she depends upon being your grand-daughter. I asked her what I should say to you for her. She could think of nothing but how you do; of her own accord, she said ask how Temple does, & Mr Bache. Those were her own words, so pray tell Mr Bache that she paid him more respect than she paid his cousin, for she gave him the title of Mr which she did not bestow upon Temple. My friend Temple will forgive the omission. I asked Tom what he had to send. *"Duty"* was his reply, "and my love to Temple." William was asked next, and he said "Duty to my Godpapa & love to Temple." Having filled almost five pages with myself and my children, it is time to turn to something else. I write this at

6. Polly had expressed a keen interest in BF's phonetic alphabet when he sent it to her in 1768, and she later urged him to work for its adoption: XV, 173–8, 215–20, 249; XXII, 299–300.

7. Mrs. Hewson had contemplated a trip to France but later decided against it: XXVI, 657–8; XXVIII, 164, 366.

Mr Whitefoord's by whose favour this conveyance is procured.[8] He desired me to make his best respects to you, and to say he does not despair of seeing you here, an event much wished for by many, though, I fear, not by those who can bring it about. I think you are all in the wrong, it is only we who have nothing to do that are quite right. My mother & my daughter dined at Mr Theobald's[9] last friday, at which time your health was drank; my daughter reminded me to tell you so. All our friends in this street are well, my family occupies the two opposite houses; the inhabitants on the other side are much your friends, and very kind to us. We have another between this & Charing Cross who lately sent you an account of our welfare. I do not recollect any event among our acquaintance, but the death of Mrs Henckell, my friends truly estimable mother.[1] A tedious, hopeless illness rendered desireable that event which she looked to with fortitude & resignation.

I received a letter from Mr Williams of 12th Octr. which I answered in Jany. I have not heard from him since. I hope he & his lovely wife are well. I was much pleased with that event, for I think him too amiable to remain unmarried, and Mariamne well deserves a good husband, so I hope they will enjoy all the happiness which such a union promises. I hope you will find some way to send us a line when you or your secretary have time to write it. I see no objection to the conveyance by post. I do not recollect whether I told you that Mr Collinson[2] declined the charge of our letters.

April 5th.

As Mr Strange has not called I kept my letter open till now that we return to Cheam.[3] We take back with us Mr Whitefoord's

8. The merchant, newspaper essayist, and wit Caleb Whitefoord lived next door to the Stevenson family during BF's London stays: X, 171–2n.

9. James Theobald, a London acquaintance of Mrs. Stevenson and Polly: XXV, 143n; XXVIII, 346.

1. She was the mother of Elizabeth Henckell, an old friend of BF and Polly: XIX, 152n; XXIX, 159.

2. Probably Thomas Collinson, BF's former banker, who had forwarded BF's letters to Mrs. Hewson: XXVIII, 165.

3. The engraver Robert Strange traveled between Paris and London and carried letters for BF and his friends: XXXI, 404n.

daughter whom he now publickly introduces as such, and is very fond of.[4] She is a fine girl, but wants tuition, which my mother & I have undertaken to give her; between us we hope to make her useful and agreeable; without such friendly assistance she would stand no chance of being qualified to fill an honourable station.

Our friend Mrs Wilkes has just established a house at Richmond in which she now has six young ladies whose education she superintends, and has £100 a year from each. She acquits herself as you would expect, and I dare say you will rejoice at her success.[5] Mr W. is gone to Algiers. The eldest son was well provided for at New York but was obliged to come home on account of his health. Charles is a fine youth, but not yet in any way of acquiring a subsistence. Fanny is with her mother: Mrs Montague very kindly patronizes her.[6] Do you know Mr Barrow is dead?[7]

I must now finish my letter. Adieu!

Your ever affectionate   MARY HEWSON

From Sartine
Copy: Library of Congress

A Versailles le 2. Avril 1780.

J'ai l'honneur, Monsieur, de vous envoyer ci joint un mémoire imprimé qui m'a été adressé par les armateurs du Corsaire François qui faisoit partie de l'Escadre du Commodore Paul Jones. Ils réclament leur Part dans la totalité des Prises faites par cette Escadre combinée; Ils établissent leurs prétentions sur des faits qui paroissent mériter votre attention; Je vous prie de

4. Whitefoord was unmarried until 1800; he and his wife had four children: x, 173n.

5. Elizabeth Wilkes (xiii, 537n; xv, 238n) established her school the previous year when her husband Israel went to Africa in search of business opportunities: xxix, 579. For her daughter Fanny see xxii, 595.

6. We presume she is the famous bluestocking writer Elizabeth Montagu, whom BF met possibly as early as 1767: xiv, 70n; xix, 38.

7. Probably Thomas Barrow. He and his wife knew BF in London in 1766 and were residing in New York City when the Revolution began. He joined other Tories on a British ship in the harbor, and some time after that may have returned to England: xiii, 537; xxiii, 297–8; xxvi, 90n.

vouloir bien me faire part du Jugement que vous en aurez porté.[8]

J'ai l'honneur d'etre, Monsieur, avec la Consideration la plus distinguée, votre tres humble et très obeissant Serviteur.

(signé) DE SARTINE

M. Franklin.

From Patrick Dowlin   ALS: American Philosophical Society

Excellent Sir/   Roscow [Roscoff], Apl. 3d. 1780

Yrs. I Recd. the 27th ult, wherein you were pleased to Inform me of my future Conduct in Regard of Prisoners,[9] which I wou'd be glad to know Sooner as I have been destressed so far as to Set 21 Men at Liberty[1] they Signing Proper Duplicates for the Same and I being on the Enemies Coast Short of Provisions &c. caused me to do the Same, has took two of the Enemies Packets, who threw their Dispatches over Board, very near taken a third, but Was hinderd by being too near a Sand Bank Close to Dublin Bar, so was Obliged to Tack Ship and Stand to the Southwd. On the 19th. Ult. the Princess our Consort and me Came to Ancher in Morlaix Road. I am Sorry to Inform yr. Excellency of the Bad Usuage Recd. by the French Men Entertained in my Vessell, who have Acted neither as Sailors or Soldiers, and Contrary to the Contract between France and the United States, I have, always, being denied the Priviledge of said Contract as in any port I Have put into they, the sd. French hath found favour from the Commissary's of sd. Ports. Contrary to the Interests of United States, being Disabled of our Crew by

8. The French privateer probably was the *Grandville*, one of two which had accompanied the *Bonhomme Richard* squadron: XXX, 444–7. In a Sept. 21, 1780, letter to Edme-Jacques Genet, Jones called the *Grandville*'s claims absurd and complained that BF had refused to become involved: Bradford, *Jones Papers*, reel 6, no. 1216.

9. XXXI, 463–4.

1. During the recent cruise of his *Black Prince* and Edward Macatter's *Black Princess*. The cruise is detailed by Clark, *Ben Franklin's Privateers*, pp. 109–15, 128.

the Departure of the French who left me I am Constrained to go to Dunkirk when propperly Cleaned and Provisions got on board, here at Roscow, but hopes that with the few Country Men I have to bring the Cutter Safe and if any thing Offers I hope to Annoy the Enemy on our Passage to Dunkirk, the full copy of our Journal you shall Receive if fortune favours me so far as to Arrive at Dunkirk, yr Commands will be Agreeable to Me, when you Receive another Letter from me as I mean to Sail at the first Opportunity for sd Port. Give my Respects to yr. Excellency's Nephew, and the rest of American Gentlemen at Paris of yr Acquaintance, I Remain Sr. Yrs Sincerely[2] PAT DOWLIN

Addressed: his Excellency / Benjamin Franklin at / Passy near / Paris

Notation: Capt. Dowling. April 3. 1780

To ——— Rinquin: Three Letters

(I), (II) and (III) Copy: Library of Congress

I.

sir Passy, april 4. 1780

I received the Letter you did me the honour of writing to me the 22d. past inclosing the Pieces relating to The Prize Brigantine the Papillon.[3] I do not recollect that Those Pieces were sent to me before. Inclosed you have the Judgment upon that Prize.[4]

With great Regard, I have the honour to be sir, your m. o. h. S.

M. Rinquin.

---

2. This is Dowlin's last letter to BF. He survived the war and received a commission in the French navy, but was discharged in 1788 for bad conduct: Clark, *Ben Franklin's Privateers,* p. 175.

3. The *Papillon* probably was the prize which Capt. Patrick Barry had sent to Morlaix a year earlier: XXIX, *passim.*

4. Missing, as are the documents and letters enclosed or discussed in (II) and (III). The *Friendship, Peter,* and *Philip* were recent prizes of the *Black Prince* and *Black Princess:* Torris to BF, March 31, above.

II.

sir   Passy, April 4. 1780.

I received the Letter you did me the honour of writing to me the 20th. past with the Rapport d'entrée du Brigantin, l'amitié et le proces Verbal du scellé. As none of her Papers are brought in, I do not see sufficient Grounds for Judgement or Condemnation. She may for any thing that appears be a neutral Vessel.

I have the honour to be, sir y. m. o. h. S.   BF.

M. Rinquin.

III.

sir   Passy, april 4. 1780.

I received the honour of yours dated the 8th. of march, with the Proces verbal et les Interrogatoires relating to the Philip of London. Enclosed is the Judgment of that Prize. As to the Pierre of London. There being no Examinations of Prizoners taken in that Vessel, nor any Papers produced to prove that she belong'd to the Enemy, I cannot proceed to give Judgment upon her, lest she should hereafter appear to be a neutral or friendly vessel.

If we were to condemn Vessels on the bare Declaration of the Captors without farther Proof, Piracies might be by that means encouraged.

I have the honour to be, sir, y. m. ob. h. s.

Mr. Rinquin.

To George Washington   Copy: Library of Congress

Sir,   Passy April 4th. 1780.

If by any Operation of War in the ensuing Campaign, the Regiment of Neustrie should happen to be near your army, the Chevr. Le Veneur,[5] Lieutenant Colonel of that Regiment, will probably have the honour of paying his Respects to your Excel-

---

5. Alexis-Paul-Michel le Veneur, vicomte le Veneur (1746–1833): Lewis, *Walpole Correspondence*, VII, 50n; *État militaire* for 1779, p. 159. It apparently was through his mother-in-law that he procured this recommendation. On April 1 Marie-Louise-Madeleine de Brémond d'Ars, marquise de Verdelin, a

lency. He is recommended to me by Persons of Worth, as a Gentleman of Excellent Character, highly esteemed by all that know him. As such I beg leave to introduce him to you, and to request for him those Civilities which you afford with Pleasure to strangers of merit.

With the greatest Esteem and Respect, I have the honour to be, y. Ex. m. o. and most h. S.

His Exy. Genl. Washington.

From John Paul Jones

ALS: American Philosophical Society; AL (draft): National Archives

Honored and dear Sir,   L'Orient April 4th. 1780.

I have received yesterday yours of the 1st by Express from Versailles and went immediately down to Port Louis where I was told that the powder is ready but that a considerable part of the Small Arms are not expected there before the 15th.— The necessary Arrangement to receive them will in the meantime be made on board the Alliance.[6] I fear that you will now find that M. C——— has imposed upon you by promising what he has had no intention to perform—[7] He has given no means of advancing money here—and if the people remain much longer dissatisfied I tremble and *let him tremble too* for the Consequence! Besides the

---

friend of Mme du Deffand and Jean-Jacques Rousseau, wrote an unnamed correspondent asking her help in obtaining BF's recommendation for him (University of Pa. Library). For the marquise see Lewis, *Walpole Correspondence*, III, 214n. BF's recommendation proved pointless, however; the regiment of Neustrie, part of Rochambeau's ill-fated second division, never made it to America.

6. Deleted in the draft at this point: "I have this day by post had the honor to receive Your".

7. On April 4 Jones went to Chaumont's correspondent Pierre-André Montigny de Monplaisir for the 100,000 *l.t.* BF had said Chaumont would provide. Monplaisir could not honor the request; his written explanation is dated April 5: Bradford, *Jones Papers*, reel 5, nos. 1037–8. A week later Jones called on Gourlade and Moylan for 800 *louis* (19,200 *l.t.*) to distribute among the crew of the *Alliance* and on the 22nd they were given a month's pay: Bradford, *Jones Papers*, reel 5, nos. 1044–5; John S. Barnes, ed., *The Logs of the Serapis-Alliance-Ariel under the Command of John Paul Jones 1779–1780*

Affairs mentioned in the within letter he has made another proposition that an Honest Man would be Ashamed of—[8] I wait for something further by the Next post—for I am very loth to expose his Conduct and willing to give him time to repent.

I am ever with the most Affectionate Esteem, Dear Sir truly yours in haste.   JNO P JONES

His Excellence B. Franklin Esqr. &c &c.

Notation: J.P. Jones, L'orient. April. 4. 80

From Thomas Ridout[9]   ALS: American Philosophical Society

Sir   Bordeaux 4th: April 1780—

On my embarking at Annapolis, in the Ship Buckskin of Baltimore, the 26th of December last, Mr: Carroll committed to my Care the Letter herewith enclosed for yr. Excellency—[1]

An intense Frost detained the Ship near two Months in the River Potuxent, & it was not till yesterday She arrivd at this City—

Some Mercantile affairs at this place, deprives me at this time of the Honor of Personally paying my respects to you—

I am Your Excellency's most obedt: & very Hble: servant
                                                    THOS. RIDOUT

a l'Hôtel D'Angleterre

His Excellcy: Benjn: Franklin Esqr

Addressed: His Excellency / Benjn Franklin Esqr:

Notation: Thomas Ridout 4 April 1780

(New York, 1911) p. 81. Bancroft told Jones on April 15 that Chaumont had given the excuse that the French government was in arrears with him; from this letter we also learn that BF had given Jones permission to pay the crew the 24,000 *l.t.* BF had authorized: Bradford, *Jones Papers,* reel 5, no. 1048.

8. Perhaps what Monplaisir reported to Jones on the 5th: Chaumont supposedly told him that BF had decided to pay the crew of the *Bonhomme Richard* in France, but to make the crew of the *Alliance* wait for their pay until they returned to America.

9. For this young man see XXXI, 238n.

1. XXXI, 198–202.

To Juliana Ritchie

Copy: Library of Congress

Madam   Passy April 5th. 1780.

I have received the Letters you did me the honour of writing to me the 5th. and 29th. of last Month. I have never learnt any thing of Mr. Ritchie since I left America in 1776. The officers that left that Country last year are scarce any of them now at Paris, nor do I know where they are at present, but I will make what Enquiries I can, and if I learn any thing important for you to know, I shall communicate it to you, either at Cambray or in England, when I know your address. My family at Philadelphia which you so kindly enquire after, was well in september last. The communication between the two Countries is so interrupted and so many Letters are taken or sunk for fear of being taken, when the Vessels that have threw them are chased, often when they are chased by friends, that I do not wonder at your not hearing from Mr. Ritchie, who perhaps writes but seldom, being myself sometimes near a year without Letters from those who have written frequently.

With great Regard, I have the honour to be, Madam Your most obedient and most humble servant

Mrs. Ritchie.

From Puchelberg & Cie.

ALS: American Philosophical Society

My Lord,   L'Orient Apr 5th. 1780

We have the honnour to inform Your Excellence, that the Kings officer appointed for the affairs of the marine having given his orders for the transportation of all the English prisoners, all those made by the american privateers which were yet behind, have been transferred likewise to Dinan, except a single Boy, who being sick is in the hospital.[2]

Several of the american officers on Board of the alliance, being in want of Money, have applyd to us for it, because the Repartition of the prices, [prizes] made by them, has not yet been

---

2. Seven weeks earlier, BF had ordered the firm, acting as American agents in Lorient, to turn over the privateers' prisoners to the French: XXXI, 478.

done. So we beg Leave to ask on this point Your Excellency's Commands, whether we may fournish them with any thing they stand in Need of.

We have the honnour to Remain with due Respect My Lord Your Excellency's Most obed. humb. Servants

PUCHELBERG & CO

Notation: Puchelberg, L'orient 5. Avril 1780.

From the Abbé Guillaume-Thomas-François Raynal[3]

AL: American Philosophical Society

a paris rue neuve st Roch le 5 avril [1780][4]

L'abbé Raynal a eté plusieurs fois a passy pour avoir l'honneur de voir monsieur le docteur, sans pouvoir le joindre. Il le supplie de vouloir bien recevoir ses hommages, et de lui renvoyer ses livres et ses papiers. L'amerique est devenue si interessante pour toutes les nations quon ne peut instruire trop tot le public de ce qui la regarde.

Addressed: A Monsieur / Monsieur le docteur franklin / a passy

---

3. The abbé (XX, 447n) had last written in February, 1779: XXVIII, 459.

4. A plausible date (although it might have been written a year earlier) since the work to which Raynal alludes in this letter, the third edition of his *Histoire philosophique et politique des établissements et du commerce des Européens dans les deux Indes,* was announced for publication in the spring of 1780: Friedrich Melchior Grimm *et al., Correspondance littéraire, philosophique et critique,* Maurice Tourneaux, ed. (16 vols., Paris, 1877–82), XII, 347–8. An enlarged and bolder version of a six-volume edition that he had first published anonymously in Amsterdam in 1770, it did not appear until the very end of 1780, due to a delay caused by the engravers of the illustrations and maps. Raynal worked on the manuscript into the summer and visited his Genevan publishers that fall: Bachaumont, *Mémoires secrets,* XV, 208; Grimm, *Correspondance,* XII, 442; Anatole Feugère, *Un précurseur de la Révolution. L'abbé Raynal (1713–1796). Documents inédits* (Angoulême, 1922), pp. 265–6, 273.

From Pierre-Jean-Georges Cabanis

ALS: American Philosophical Society

Monsieur   Auteuil Le 6 avril [1780?][5]

Je vous Renvoye L'Epreuve Corrigée. Vous pouvez actuellement La tirer; je La crois Correcte. Je me sais bien bon gré de pouvoir vous être bon à quelque Chose. Ne m'Epargnez pas, je vous prie. Vous savez Combien nous avons de plaisir à penser à vous à Auteuil, et par Conséquent Combien nous Desirons que vous pensiez un peu à nous. La bonne Dame & L'abbé de La Roche vous font mille Complimens pleins D'amitié. Agréez Les sentimens de veneration et de Respect tendre que vous m'avez inspirés.

Je suis Monsieur votre très humble & très obeissant serviteur

CABANIS

Addressed: a Monsieur / Monsieur franklin / a Passy

Notation: Cabanis

From Thomas Digges

ALS: Historical Society of Pennsylvania

Dr. Sir   London 6 April 1780.

I wrote you a few days ago by Capt Snelling, and sent a few news papers & books. I now embrace the oppertunity by capn. Cozeneau[6] to send you the news papers of the day & a few political publications, which tho in the lump may not be worth your reading, will in some measure shew the disposition of the times, which seem to be galloping fast on to some serious rumpus

5. This letter may refer to the page proofs of "The Whistle," for which see XXXI, 69–77. On the other hand, it might also belong to 1784 when, on April 8, BF sent Mme Brillon a group of printed bagatelles (APS). Cabanis may well have read proofs for one or more of those pieces, and indeed, "The Whistle" might even have been printed at that time.

6. Isaac Cazneau, according to his signatures on an April 16 oath of allegiance signed and certified by BF (APS) and on a bond of the same day (described below). Quite likely he had carried a 1772 letter from JW to BF: XIX, 157. In 1776 he had been named captain of a Continental Navy frigate, but did not take command: *JCC*, IV, 290; Claghorn, *Naval Officers*, p. 52.

among the People— Many go so far as to talk of a Revolution— a great majority of the People seem bent upon a reform in the Constitution, to reduce the power of the Crown, to have a better Representation, & to alter the duration of Parliament to triennial; I do not apprehend there will be another septennial Parliat in this Country.

Among the Pamphlets I send, You will see "A Memorial addressd to the Sovereigns of Europe on the State of Affairs between the old & new World." I wish you to look at it, & should be glad to be at yr. elbow during the reading, because it is the work of Pownall, who I am very sure frequently acts & writes under the beaming influence of Ministry—tho it has a specious appearance of being written to favour America, I do not like the manner he draws the attention of the Sovereigns of Europe (particularly the Dutch when talking of the Spice Islands) towards my Country.[7] The other things are all on the score of Plans for Assosiations— Resolves of Committes Reports of the Deputation which may be calld the Congress—&ca. &ca. They will convince you of the distracted state of this Country, but to what good end these movements among the People may lead cannot at present be assertaind. They cannot fail however of doing good for America, however biasd the minds of the leaders may be (from pride, resentment, or former follys) against the giving america Independence or doing what is honorable & just towards Her. I am sorry to say it, but there does not appear among the People, those Assosiations, or Committees, any common principle of Union which can be made the foundation of Union, & bind them together against both the terrors & allurements of the Court.[8]

The Petitions now before Parliamt are to be read today[9] & it is supposd a considerable concourse of People will attend the av-

7. "The Dutch will hear of them [the Americans] in Spice Islands, to which the Dutch can have no claim": [Thomas Pownall], *A Memorial, Most Humbly Addressed to the Sovereigns of Europe, on the Present State of Affairs, between the Old and New World* (London, 1780), pp. 85–6. Pownall predicted that the rise of American power would produce great changes in world trade and urged the maritime powers of Europe to convene a congress to form "some general laws" to reform commercial relations: *ibid.*, pp. 118–27.

8. See BF's letter to James Lovell of March 16, above.

9. On April 6 the House of Commons resolved itself into a committee of

enues to the Ho. If these petitions & the clamours of the People who attend them operate in the manner which many foretell England is still a free Country; if not— then may we pronounce that spirit to be evaporated, by wch alone the sacred flame of liberty can be nursd.

The papers sent, & the Bearer of them (who is known to you) will give you all the publick news— We have yet nothing from America on Genl. Clinton since the 26. Decr.; but the *report* or rather the *lye* of yesterday was that He had arrivd with abot.⅓d of His fleet & had made a landing in Georgia. There is to be no troops or even Recruits sent to Ama.[1] & it may be satisfactory to that Country to know there will be no offensive Campaign this year to the *noward*. Discovery having been very lately made, that a fleet & army are going or gone from Brest, for Canada or Halifax six sail of the line or seven are getting ready with all speed to go under the Command of Graves to Ama. 15 to 20 days will be the soonest they can sail.[2] The West Inda. fleet is still detaind by contrary winds upwds. of 200 sail of Ships convoyd by Comme. Walsingham whose squadrn. consists of four of the line, one frigate, one twenty, and three fire Ships, most likely they will sail as to day. When this fleet gets out to the Wt Indies, it is supposd the force of the fleets for the Summers work will stand as 30 or 31 of the line English to 35 french exclusive of Spanish.

Captain Jos: Cozeneau is the Captain of the Cartel from Boston to Cornwall. His vessel is *now* calld the Penelope and has got round to Liverpool from whence she is meant to proceed homewards with some useful Articles. Mr. Dunkin the owner of Her & a Citizen & residt of Boston[3] will write you the particu-

---

the whole to consider some forty petitions for economic and fiscal reform: Cobbett, *Parliamentary History*, XXI, 340.

1. Clinton was not sent any new regiments, but the government did intend to send him some German and British recruits. Not until October, however, did 3,000 of them arrive in New York: Mackesy, *War for America*, p. 338; John A. Tilley, *The British Navy and the American Revolution* (Columbia, S.C., 1987), p. 202.

2. Rear Admiral Thomas Graves (*DNB*) was preparing to sail for America with eight ships of the line: Tilley, *British Navy*, pp. 190–3.

3. Edmund Dunkin had come to Falmouth aboard the packet when she was still called the *Bob:* XXXI, 418.

lar state of the vessel and of those parole Prisoners whom He brought over. He with Capt. Cozeneau is a supplicant to you for a pass to convey their property in safety. They are good men & true, & I hope it will be in yr. power to grant what they request. Capt Cozeneau will explain every thing to you, and as He is personally known to you, I need not here add any thing in His favour.[4]

I am to offer you Mr. T——es [Temple's] Comps. & best wishes— We often drink your health, & as we wish for a prolongation of yr. Eye sight, we are to beg you will send over by the Bearer a Spectacle glass that will sute your sight— A Gentleman here is possessd of a remarkable bright Cristal which was found in the Cherokee Country & He wishes to make you a present of a pair of spectacles from it.

Inclosd you have Mr Banks ansr. to you about the medal for Capt Cook.[5] I do not like his letter very much— He can never convince me that He is a friend to the Liberties of mankind or that his mind is not biasd by political opinion. I wish much to contrive the getting a gold medal for Congress, & will lend my aid here for doing so in any mode or manner you may point out. He has in ansr. to yr. Letter to me about getting a medal for the Duke De Croy, said that it could not with propriety be given as it woud open a door to various other applications for similar presents.

I have taken the liberty to inclose you a letter for Mr. Carmichael which I am to beg a forwardance of.

When you have read the News papers & pampts you will oblige me to let Mr J Adams see them which may save me an expence of sending duplicates— My present finances obliges me to be thus œconomical.

I am with the highest esteem Dr Sir Yr obligd & obt Servant
TD

I should be thankful for any Amn. News papers or intelligencs that may be worth publishing in the Remembrancer or News Papers—

4. On April 16 Cazneau signed a bond for £2,000 before WTF and L'Air de Lamotte that the *Penelope* would deliver her cargo in the United States (APS); oddly enough, on June 8 Digges reported her en route to British-held New York: Elias and Finch, *Letters of Digges*, p. 216.

5. Above, March 29.

I hope the Box of Books & psls of Stuff has got safe to hand.

I forward to You under another Cover two Letters from Mr D. H to the Chairman of the York Committee which He begs me to forwd. to you—[6] The Inclosd has been some days in my possession.

Addressed: His Excellency / Benjamin Franklin Esqr / Passy

Endorsed: April 6 80

Notation: April 6. 80

From Van de Perre & Meÿners[7]

ALS: American Philosophical Society

⟨Middelburg, April 6, 1780, in French: Monseigneur, we beg you to help us obtain the restitution of our ship the *Berkenbos,* Capt. Arÿ de Neve, captured by Capt. John Paul Jones in early January, on its way from Liverpool to Leghorn with a cargo of herring and lead. The ship was sent to Boston or Philadelphia under the false pretext that the cargo was English property,[8] after the captain had made that statement under duress, as we heard from a witness just returned to this city. Would Your Excellency see to it that we obtain 1. the return of the ship; 2. the return of the cargo as belonging to neutrals—the lead to us and the herring half to us and half to T. Violetti from Leghorn—; 3. reimbursement of the expenses and damages caused by this unjust capture; 4. the release of that part of the crew that Paul Jones kept on his board. We have full trust in your willingness to help us since our cause is just.[9]⟩

6. Hartley's *Two Letters to the Committee of York* (n.p., [1780]).

7. According to Dumas, one of the most influential firms in Zeeland; van de Perre was a nephew of van Berckel: Dumas to BF, May 26, below. Dumas defended their honesty to Jones: Bradford, *Jones Papers,* reel 5, no. 1088.

8. See XXXI, 389–90.

9. BF endorsed the letter "Answer'd."

From Jonathan Williams, Jr.

ALS: University of Pennsylvania Library; copy: Yale University Library

Dear & hond Sir.   Nantes April 6. 1780

The Courier having passed by L'orient I did not receive your Favour of 31 March 'till yesterday.

The Permission I ask of Mr Paulze is no exemption from a Duty which is a Right and if the Farmers choose to understand the Matter they will see it is not. I have declined Mr Bondfields proposition & shall send Goods to Brest as fast as I possibly can agreeable to Mr de Chaumonts orders.— Mr Schweighauser informs me that all the Sheathing Copper he had was shipped in the Providence.—

I suppose you have Letters by the Buckskin which is arrived at Bordeaux.[1] I shall be glad to know if you have any interesting news. I am informed that the State of Maryland has taken some notice of me about the management of their Funds in England, but I do not well understand what it is. If you have any account of it please to let Billy drop me a Line.[2] I am ever your dutifull & affectionate Kinsman   JONA WILLIAMS J

Doctor Franklin

Notation: Jona Williams Apr 6. 1780

To John Jay

LS:[3] Columbia University Library; copies: Library of Congress (two)

Dear Sir,   Passy, April 7th. 1780.

I have been sometime in Suspense about Writing to you, not knowing whether you were at Cadiz or Madrid. But being inform'd a few Days since[4] that you had set out for the latter, I now

1. See MacCreery's letter below, April 8.
2. See JA to BF, April 19, and BF's reply of April 21. BF never answered JW on this point, and JW asked WTF about it on May 9 (APS).
3. In WTF's hand. The address sheet is in BF's. He also made a few interlineations, noted below.
4. Probably by Conrad-Alexandre Gérard.

acknowledge the receipt of your several Favours of Sept. 26. from Philadelphia. Decr 27. from Martinique, Jan 26th. & 28th and March 3d from Cadiz.[5]

The Account you give of the prudent & pleasing Conduct of M. Gerard, agrees perfectly with my Opinion of him. I communicated it to his Brother, who is Secretary to the Council of State.[6]

Your Bill drawn in favour of Mr. Bingham for Livres 3379.8.o. came to hand and was immediately accepted.[7]

In a former Letter[8] which I hope you have by this time received, I acquainted you that your Bill drawn at Cadiz for 4079 Livs Tournois, had been presented and accepted; and tho' payable at only sixty Days from the Date, I order'd it, as you requested, to be paid immediately.

I thank you for the Communication of the Letters you had written to the Ministers. They are extreamly well drawn. I shall be glad to see also, if you think proper, the Answers you received. In my next I shall in return give you some Account of a Secret Negociation I am engag'd in with Denmark, on occasion of their delivering up 3 Prizes to the English that had been taken by the Alliance.

The Reports you tell me prevail at Cadiz that the Loan Office Bills payable in France have not been duly honour'd,[9] are wicked Falshoods. Not one of them duly endors'd by the original Proprietor was ever refused by me or the Payment delayd a Moment. And the few not so indorsed have been also paid on the Guarrantee of the Presenter or some Person of known Credit. No Reason what ever has been given for refusing Payment of a Bill, except this very good One, that either the 1st, 2d, 3d or 4th of the same Set had been already paid. The Pretence that it was neces-

---

5. The latest of these is above; the others are published or summarized in XXX, 402–3; XXXI, 286–7, 409–11, 410n.

6. On March 15, above. Since 1776 Gérard de Rayneval had held the title of "secrétaire du Conseil d'Etat": Jean-Pierre Samoyault, *Les bureaux du secrétariat d'état des affaires étrangères sous Louis XV: administration, personnel* (Paris, 1971), p. 289.

7. XXXI, 286–7. BF inserted the word "Livres" in this paragraph.

8. XXXI, 513.

9. XXXI, 410.

sary for the whole Set to arrive before the Money could be paid, is too absurd and ridiculous for anyone to make use of who knows any thing of the Nature of Bills of Exchange. The unexpected large Drafts made upon me by Congress and others, exclusive of these from the Loan Office, have indeed sometimes embarrass'd me not a little, and put me to Difficulties; but I have overcome those Difficulties, so as never to have been obliged to make the smallest Excuse, or desire the least Delay of Payment from any Presenter of such Bills. Those Reports must therefore have been invented by Enemies to our Country, or by Persons who proposed an Advantage to themselves by purchasing them at an under Rate. Inclosed I send you a Certificate of our Banker in Refutation of those Calumnies.[1]

The Letters you mention having for me,[2] if they were not those brought to me by Mr Gerard, you will be so good as to send me by Post. As to the Packets, please to open them, and if they contain only Newspapers, retain them 'till you have an Opportunity by some private Hand, as the Postage (they being old) will exceed their Value.

Your Bill for 4564. Livrs 18 s. 10 d. has been presented and accepted and will be duly paid. I hope you are before this time acquainted with the Credit I long since lodg'd for you at Madrid, with M. le Marquis d'Yranda, for 1000 Louis,[3] which will make the Trouble of drawing on me unnecessary; I hope also you will be able to obtain some Aids of Money from that Court for the Congress, to be sent out in the Goods I have been obliged to omit for want of Money. If that should be the Case I will send you Copies of the Invoices.[4]

This Court is hearty and steady in our favour. A considerable Armament is going out, from which we have reason to hope great Advantages in the ensuing Campaign.

1. Copies of a March 15 statement by Ferdinand Grand are at the Library of Congress, the National Archives, and the Henry E. Huntington Library (with extracts of the present letter). Grand testified he had paid all bills promptly and had returned only those which had already been paid.

2. XXXI, 410.

3. See XXXI, 513.

4. BF interlined this sentence. He also added "Livrs," "s.," "and "d."in the first sentence of this paragraph.

I wish to hear of your safe Arrival at Madrid. Be pleased to make my Respects acceptable to Mrs Jay, and believe me to be with the sincerest Esteem & Respect Dear Sir, Your most obedient & most humble Servant.   B FRANKLIN

His Exy J. Jay Esqre.

Addressed: A son Excellence / M. Jean Jay / Ministre Plenipotentiaire / des Etats Unis de l'Amerique / à Madrid

Endorsed: Doctr. Franklin 7th. Ap. 1780

To Richard Peters

Copy: Library of Congress

Dear sir   Passy, April 7. 1780.

I assure all the Officers who apply to me to be introduced in to our service in America, that our armies are fully officered; that there is no vacancy in which they can be plac'd, that a great Number of good Officers who had been here to offer their service, are actually returned to france for want of Employ, and that this must be their Case if they go over. But I have the misfortune not to be believed by some of them who determine to go notwithstanding and run all risques. I hope however that I shall be beleived on your side the water when I assure you that I do not give them the least Encouragement or Expectation knowing too well the Embarassment the Congress was Subjected to by the recommendations extorted by Importunity from Mr. Deane, and the Expence it occasion'd.[5] The Gentleman, M. d'Angely who is the bearer of this, is one of Those who countrary to my advice is resolved to make the Voyage.[6] His Goodwill to our Cause will merit your Civilities and Counsels. It is to those only that I take the liberty of recommending him. With sincere Esteem, I have the honour to be, Dear sir,

Richard Peters Esqe. Member of the Board of War.

---

5. Which led to Deane's recall by Congress: xxv, 361n, 572n; xxvi, 470.
6. See his March 25 letter, above.

From Dumas

ALS: American Philosophical Society; AL (draft): Algemeen Rijksarchief

Monsieur   Lahaie 7e. Avril 1780

J'ai l'honneur des trois vôtres, deux du 29 & une du 31e. Mars. La terreur & la ruse, jointes au désespoir de ma famille, qui avoit découvert (je ne sai comment) ce qui se passoit, & qui se croyoit perdue avec moi, m'avoient fait tourner la tête, & extorqué ma Lettre lâche du 4e Avril. Selon ce que l'on m'avoit fait entendre, & à notre ami aussi, nous devions croire que la Lettre avoit été ouverte & envoyée à Mr. l'Ambassadeur ou par le département des affaires étrangeres, ou par le Me. d'E——[7] Et notre Ami m'avoit exhorté à appaiser, comme je pourrois, Mr. l'Amb. qui se trouvoit offensé (& avec raison) de ce que l'humeur du moment m'avoit fait dire dans la Lettre interceptée, *qu'il protégeoit Sir G—— je ne Savois pourquoi, ni ne voulois le savoir, & que je ne le croyois pas grand ami des Am——*. J'avois donc écrit & envoyé cette Lettre du 4. Le soir du même jour je reçus vos Lettres, Monsieur, avec celle de Mr. F—— Gd., comme aussi celle de Mr. B——.[8] Quoiqu'il fût tard, j'écrivis néanmoins une 2de. Lettre à Mr. l'Ambr., pour lui dire que ma Lettre du matin ne devoit point sortir de ses mains, & que le moindre usage indiscret qu'en feroit Sir G——, lui seroit plus pernicieux qu'à moi. Le jour suivant je lui écrivis la Lettre, dont voici copie.——[9] Vous comprenez, Monsieur, qu'après la foiblesse que je venois d'avoir, je ne pouvois garder entierement le silence, & que la Lettre du 5, qui révoque cette foiblesse, étoit nécessaire pour mon honneur. La vengeance, que je vous sacrifierois toujours volontiers (& le sacrifice ne seroit pas grand) n'y entre pour rien. J'espere que cette derniere Lettre

7. Probably "Ministre [or Ministère] d'Espagne" as Carmichael, the letter's intended recipient, was in Spain.

8. Probably Baudouin. The preceding abbreviations refer to Sir Georges Grand, the Americans, and Ferdinand Grand.

9. Dumas enclosed a copy in his own hand of his April 5 letter to La Vauguyon informing the ambassador that he had discovered the instigator of the "procédé infame et punissable" and asking him to hush up the affair for the sake of BF's repose, since the publicity would only trouble and afflict him.

engagera Mr. l'Amb—— à mettre fin à tout cela. Je me tairai. Mais il est nécessaire que Mr. F—— Gd. oblige son frere à se taire aussi, & qu'il lui écrive très fortement pour le lui enjoindre. Ayez la bonté, Monsieur, de lui en faire sentir la nécessité absolue.

I write to day to the Gentleman you know according your orders, as well as to Mr. Enschede at Harlem for the prices of such of his characters as you wish for. I shall give yr. Excy. the Explanation you desire respecting the subject of my last Letter to the 657y.[1]

Le Mémoire Russe pour inviter L.h.p. à faire cause commune avec l'Imperatrice, afin de protéger le Commerce & la navigation des neutres, & la Déclaration de la même remise aux Ministres des Cours de Versailles, Madrid & Londres à Petersbourg, paroissent ici généralement approuvées. Nous verrons ce qui en résultera de cette approbation du public.

La bigarrure des 4 lignes Angloises ci-dessus, au milieu de mon françois, est l'effet de ma distraction. Il m'étoit venu une visite. En reprenant la plume, je croyois avoir commencé en Anglois.

Je suis avec un grand respect, Monsieur Votre très-humble & très-obéissant serviteur   D

Vous trouverez, Monsieur, le Mémoire Russe à L.h.P., & la Déclaration aux Cours, dans le Supplément à la Gazette de Leide No. XXVIII.[2]

Passy à S. E. M. F—

Addressed: à Son Excellence / Monsieur B. Franklin, Esqr. / Ministre Plenip. des Etats-Unis / d'Amérique / *Passy./.*

Notation: Dumas, la haie April. 7. 1780

1. "Pensionary."
2. The issue of April 7 (sup.), which included both the Empress' declaration to the belligerents on her interpretation of neutral rights and an April 3 letter from Russian Envoy Golitsyn inviting the States General of the Netherlands to make common cause with her in protecting those rights. Both documents are printed (in English translation) in the April 11 issue of the *London Courant, and Westminster Chronicle.*

From Jean Conrad Zollickoffer

ALS: American Philosophical Society

Monsieur!   Bordeaux le 7. Avril 1780:

Pendant Mon Séjour à Philadelphie[3] J'ai eû l'Honneur de faire
la connaissance avec Madame vôtre Fille, & Monsieur Hillégas
Trésorier Général des 13. Provinces Unis. Touttes ces deux Personnes que J'ai l'aissé en parfaitte santé m'ont chargé des Lettres
pour vous Monsieur,[4] dont J'ai l'Honneur de vous les Envoÿer
par Monsieur De Freÿ Capit. de Cavalerie au servises des Etâts
Unis.[5]

Je souhaitte qu'il aÿe le Bonheur de vous trouver Monsieur
dans une santé parfaitte pour le Bonheur de l'Etât, & que ces Lettres vous donnent bien de la satisfaction.

J'eûsse désiré que le tems m'eût permit de vous les rémettre
Moy même, c'eût été pour Moy la plus grande satisfaction, mais
comme Je suis bon Républiquain (Etant suisse de Nation) Je Suis
bon ameriquain. Je m'occupe de faire icÿ, un, ou plusieurs ar-
mements, de même quà Nantes, pour que les Habitants de
L'amerique ne soÿent pas dans le Cas d'Etre depourvû de ce
dont Ils pourront avoir besoin.

Comme pour completter mon Entreprise Je pourrois avoir
besoin de quelqu'Interessés, par conséqt. Mon voyage pour Paris
pourroit dévenir Indispensable, Je me réserve allors l'Honneur
de vous présenter Monsieur mes très humbles devoirs, & Celuÿ
de vous assurer de Bouche que Je suis avec la sousmission la plus
réspectueuse Monsieur Vôtre Tres humble & Tres obéist. serviteur   J. C. ZOLLICKOFFER
                Chez Mr. Deneker Riedy & Comp. à Nantes

Comme J'ai apporté avec Moy pour une Certaine Somme des
Billets de Loon office, voudriez vous Monsieur me faire la Graçe

---

3. For which see XXV, 61n.

4. Only a fragment of SB's letter survives and nothing of Hillegas': XXXI,
96n.

5. On Oct. 4, 1779, the baron de Frey, a captain in Pulaski's Legion, had
been granted eight months leave by Congress: *JCC*, XV, 1139; Lasseray, *Les
Français*, I, 222.

de me faire marquer à Nantes s'il y a Moÿen de les Négotier à Paris, & Comme Il faut m'y prendre.[6]

à Monsieur Le Docteur Francklin Ministre de l'amerique Septentrionale

Notation: Zollikoffer Apr. 7. 1780

From Kéralio   ALS: American Philosophical Society

8e. Avril, 1780.

Messieurs des Deux-ponts, Monsieur, m'écrivent du 2e. et me chargent de vous parler de leur bien tendre vénération et de Leur reconnoissance. Vous devés avoir reçu une Lettre de L'ainé:[7] ils avoient Leurs ordres pour s'embarquer le 4e, et le 8e tout devoit être prêt à mettre à la voile. Ils passent L'un et L'autre à Bord du vaisseau L'éveillé de 64 Canons.

On m'assure que Suivant des Lettres de Londres, nommément adressées à M. de Sartine, Le feu ayant pris au Magasin à poudre au Port-röyal de La jamaique, ce magasin qui étoit Le plus grand et presque le Seul dépôt avoit sauté et presque ruiné Le Fort et endommagé beaucoup de vaisseaux dans le port.

Vous connoissés Le tendre respect avec lequel je suis Monsieur Votre tres humble et très obéissant Serviteur.

LE CHR. DE KERALIO

Notation: De Keralio 8. Avril 1780.[8]

6. Zollickoffer wrote again on April 29, hoping that de Frey had delivered the packets from Philadelphia and asking the best way of cashing his loan office certificates. APS.

7. The elder of the duchesse de Deux-Ponts' sons was Christian (XXVIII, 539n); we have not located his letter. See also Kéralio's letter of March 14.

8. Kéralio twice wrote WTF within the following six weeks, after which his personal correspondence with both BF and WTF apparently ceased until October. On April 10 he forwarded a copy in his own hand of an April 4 intelligence report from The Hague about Catherine II's proposed league of neutral powers, adding that Golitsyn had invited the States General to join. On May 14 he reported that a returning frigate had seen Adm. Ternay's fleet clear

From William MacCreery[9]

ALS: American Philosophical Society

Sir   Bordeaux 8 April 1780

I had the pleasure of addressing you by last Tuesdays Post, & forwarded some Maryland News Papers, which hope you received.[1] The News Papers and Journals of Congress which I received for you from mr. Lovell I now send by Captain Fray who will have the Honor to wait upon you on his arrival at Paris.

The Barron de Thuiliere who has just arrived from America, will do himself the pleasure to wait upon you also. He is Captain of the Regiment *Royall deux-ponts,* one of those ordered out to America (as I have here been informed) and I beleive he is not unknown to you.[2]

From the acquaintance which I have had with both these Gentlemen, [*as*] well in America as here, I think they have much merrit, and are attached to us. I can not say as much for a Barron

---

of the French coast. He announced his impending departure for his annual inspection tour of French military schools (for which see XXIX, 11–12) and gave a forwarding address. Both letters are at the APS; copies do not seem to have been forwarded to Congress, so we have not included them among the intelligence reports summarized above, March 7.

9. Apparently this Maryland merchant had sailed to Baltimore on the *Buckskin* (XXIX, 334) and then back to Bordeaux on the same ship. While in Baltimore he sold cargo for its owners (Lesage & Cie.) for $130,000, with which he purchased 24 loan office certificates. He deposited these with Martin Oster, the French vice-consul in Philadelphia. Oster's Dec. 8, 1779, declaration to this effect and a Dec. 18 financial statement are at the Yale University Library; so, too, is supporting documentation, including three March 12, 1781, signature attestations signed by BF.

1. Only the last page of a covering letter, probably written on the same Tuesday (April 4), is extant. In it MacCreery refers to what must be d'Estaing's recent American campaign, in which "every Friend to America" feels the admiral's only fault was exposing himself to too much risk. (D'Estaing was wounded in the unsuccessful attack on Savannah.) He looks forward to Lafayette's "Joyfull arrival" in America and promises to send by Capt. Fray (Frey), who will be leaving for Paris in a day or two, newspapers and congressional journals received from James Lovell. Will BF either give his respects to JA or tell MacCreery where he can write to him? APS.

2. Thuillières had written BF before leaving for America, and BF warmly recommended him to Washington: XXIV, 147–9.

Bonstellen, who came passenger in the Buckskin.[3] He is our most inveterate Enemy, & gave out in America that he expected to be sent for to England, for the information he is capable of giving there. He purposes going to England, having had a Sister married there since his departure for America— He intends going to Paris shortly, by the way of Nantes: Shou'd he wait upon you, hope you will not be deceived in him.

I have the Honor to be with the greatest Respect Sir Your most Obedient and very humble Servant   WILL MacCREERY

Addressed: To The Honorable Doctor B. Franklin / M.P. from the U.S. of A. / at the Court of Versailles / at Passy / Favor'd by The Barron de Thuiliere.

From Sarsfield
ALS: American Philosophical Society

samdi 8 avril [1780][4]

Jay Eté tres faché Monsieur que Mr Votre petit fils et vous vous Soyez trouvés Engagés mercredi mais vous pouvez m'en consoler aisement en me donnant Jeudi ou Samedy. Je vous offre ces deux Jours afin que vous Choisissiez celui qui vous sera le plus commode. J'ay Eu si peu lhonneur de vous voir cet hiver que Je desire infiniment que vous ne me refusiez pas.[5] J'espere que Mr De Malesherbes y pourra venir.

Vous Connoissez les sentimens avec lesquels Jay Lhr DEtre Monsieur votre tres humble Et tres obeissant Serviteur

SARSFIELD

Addressed: a Monsieur / Monsieur franklin Ministre / plenipotentiaire des Etats / unis d Amerique / A Passy

Notation: Sarsefield

3. The baron de Bonstellen came to America in search of an army commission; Congress refused but did pay for his return passage: *JCC*, xv, 1298.

4. The only year during BF's stay in France when April 8 fell on a Saturday.

5. Whether this dinner party took place or not, Sarsfield invited BF and WTF once again to a dinner on May 4. The invitation is dated May 1. APS.

From Samuel Andrews and Alexander Shaw

ALS: Historical Society of Pennsylvania

Hond: Sir   Dunann Prison the 9th. of Aprill 1780

I am under the disagreeable necessity of acquainting you of my present Situation which is that of being confin'd in the Castle at Dunann amongst the English Prisoners. & am inform'd that notwithstanding I am an american born, that I shall be Transported to England with the English Prisoners, a thing very unjust— I must inform you that a few weeks ago I was in the French Service say belonging to the Concord Frigate Six months & [*torn:* one?] day last month being in Brest, I went to the Prison to see an acquaintance say an amerin: who gave me a Letter to carry to Mr. Le Guin mayor of Coventry & owner of a Privateer that my friend had been a Cruize in & had taken a Valuable Prize, by a moderate computation my friends Shair would amount to not less than 4 or 500 Livs: & put in amongst English Prisoners on purpose to cheet him out of his prize money— I sent the Letter by my Land Lady to Mr: Le Guin he asked her how she came by the sd. Letter she told him that an Englishman gave it to her & was then at her house Le Guin sent a guard of Soldiers to the house who Guarded me to the Commissary who orderd me to the same Prison where my friend Lay with the English Prisoners & the next day was march'd off for Dunann where I now remain & your humble Petitioners humbly crave that you would be so kind as to get us out of Confinement & pave the way for us to Obtain a passport in order to go to our native Country once more which favour will greatly Oblige your Most Obet. & Very huml. Serts   SAML. ANDREW

ALEXANR: SHAW

Addressed: To / Dr: Franklin / Ambassidor for the United states / of America / at / Paris / or else where / [*in another hand:*] a paris

Notation: Prisoners in Dunanor Prison April 9—1780

From Philippe de Delleville   ALS: American Philosophical Society

Monsieur   Bayeux le 10 Avril 1780

Ayant été informé que Sept étrangers étoient debarqués a Aromanches parroisse Maritime de mon ressort, Je m'y Suis rendu, Suivant le devoir de ma place, et après les informations prises par la voye d'Interprete Je les ay reconnus pour des Americains presque tous de la Province de Rod Island et l'un d'entre eux pour éstre de Boston meme et Capitaine de prise, un autre du meme grade deux matelots et trois Charpentiers de Navire, et tous prisonniers évadés de Portsmouth.[6] Ils en ont du partir Jeudy dernier, Sur les dix heures du Soir, aprés avoir corrompu la Sentinelle, et Sont arrivés, Sans gouvernail ni voiles autres qu'une mauvaise planche et de la toille de leurs paillasses et hamacs qu'ils avoient cousuë, dans une trés petite et trés foible chalouppe, après prés de Quatre Jours de navigation et au milieu des plus grands dangers; Je les ay logés chez moy leur ai donné et leur donnerai tous les Secours qui en dependront. Ils desirent de retourner en Amerique le plutost possible.

Quoyque J'aye Sur le champ informé M. de Sartine ministre de la Marine, de ces details dès hier et que Je luy envoye aujourdhuy une Coppie du Proces-verbal que J'en dressai, Je n'ay pas cru faire une demarche deplacée et qui vous fust désagreable, en vous en informant vous meme, ainsi que du plaisir veritable que J'ay eu et que J'aurai toute ma vie a faire quelque chose d'agreable a votre nation et a vous prouver le vray respect avec lequel J'ay l'honneur d'estre Monsieur Votre trés humble et trés obeissant Serviteur   PHILIPPE DE DELLEVILLE
                                            Lt. gl. de l'amirauté

Notation: Neville Phillippes de Bayeux 10. Avril 1780.

6. For these escaped prisoners see Theobald Jennings *et al.* to BF, immediately below.

From Theobald Jennings *et al.*

ALS: American Philosophical Society

Honourd. Sir.   Bayo April the 10. 1780

This to Inform your Excellency of our Safe Arrival from forton prison Which Place We had been Confined for the space Of
Six or Seven Months and no hopes Of A Cartel Which Was our
Occasion of Runing away[7] took a small boat and on the 8 Ultimo We Arrived Safe Within Six Miles of this place Where We
was Received with great kindness by the Inhabitants,[8] to Acquaint and Let your Excellency Know that We Are Very Desti-
tute of Almost Every Nessessary of Wearing Apparal the three
Undernamed persons Taken in Capt. Manly by the Surprize
Frigate and Carryd. to England[9] Theobald Jennings Draper
Tomar prize Masters, Jarvis Sammis Carpenter, Johannis Lun-
blood & Robert Fowler, taken in the Mary and Elizabeth Benjamin Wicke Commandr.[1] John Tuck in the Rambler John
Stephens of Marblehead[2] Joshua Woodman taken in the General
Glover Nicholas Bartlett[3] We Mean to go for America the first
Opportunity and as soon as We Receive An Ansr. from your Ex-
cellency We Shal Set out for Brest there to Embark for America
And Would Be glad your Would Order Something for to bear
our Exspences there as We are very Destitute of any hard money

---

7. While at least one of these prisoners, Joshua Woodman, had been par-
doned for exchange (see Kaminkow, *Mariners,* p. 211), the exchanges themselves had been halted after the cartel ship returned empty to Plymouth in
March: Hodgson to BF, March 28, above. On April 14, below, Digges mentions the discontent at Forton, attributing the escape of prisoners to the
empty cartel.

8. See Philippe de Delleville's letter of this date, immediately above.

9. The *Jason,* Capt. John Manley, was captured in Sept. 1779: XXXI,
418–19n.

1. The *Mary and Elizabeth,* Capt. Benjamin Wickes (Weeks), was captured by the *Hussar* in December, 1779: Kaminkow, *Mariners,* p. 229. For
Wickes see XXX, 286n.

2. John Stevens commanded the brigantine *Rambler,* of Salem, which was
captured in October, 1779: John A. McManemin, *Captains of the Privateers
during the Revolutionary War* (Spring Lake, N.J., 1985), p. 250.

3. The *General Glover* was captured in September, 1779: XXX, 26; XXXI,
175.

and We the Undernamed persons doth Remain Your Ever And
Obedient Countrymen   THEOBALD JENNINGS
                                                 DRAPER TOMAR
                                                 JARVIS SAMMIS
                                                 JOHANNIS LUNBLOOD
                                                 ROBERT FOWLER
                                                 JOHN TUCK
                                                 JOSHUA WOODMAN

Benjamin Franklin Esqr.

From Jonathan Nesbitt   ALS: American Philosophical Society

Sir!   L'Orient April 10th: 1780
    The Two Bills which I have the honor to inclose you for Ac-
ceptance were sent me by Edward Bird Esqr: of Philada: with
orders to procure payment for the same, unless I had advice that
Major Peter Scull was arriv'd in France.—⁴ The firsts of these
Bills were deliver'd to Major Scull & the seconds were forwarded
by the Diana, which Vessell I understand is unfortunately Captured by the Enemy.—⁵ You will observe that through neglect
or mistake, Mr. Bird has not Indorsed the Bills which I now inclose you, but I hope Sir, that Circumstance will not prevent
their being duly honor'd.— I must request that you will take the
trouble to return me these Bills as soon as possible.—⁶ I have the
honor to be with Sentiments of great respect. Sir! Your most
Obedt. humble Servt: JONATN: NESBITT

The honble: Benjn: Franklin Esqr:—

    4. Peter Scull, the secretary of the Continental Board of War, was nomi-
nated as BF's secretary, but instead John Laurens was elected. Scull decided
to travel to Europe for his health, but died at sea: Smith, *Letters*, XIII, 511,
581, 586; Morris, *Jay: Revolutionary*, p. 714.
    5. The snow *Diana*, commanded by Joy Castle (for whom see XXVI, 669),
was captured by the *Alert*: Claghorn, *Naval Officers*, p. 51.
    6. BF returned the bills for 390 *l.t.* accepted. As they were not regularly en-
dorsed he feared that he might inadvertently cash another of the four sets; if
that should happen he would rely on Nesbitt's honor for reimbursement. BF
drafted his reply, dated April 19, on the back of Nesbitt's address sheet. A
letterbook copy is at the Library of Congress.

Addressed: The honble: Benjn: Franklin Esqr. / at his Hotel at / Passy

From Jeremy Bentham[7]   AL (draft): University College, London

[after April 10, 1780][8]

C

Afran[9]

This book (if ever it should reach your hands)[1] was written for the use of leading men: nor to any but leading men has it been sent. As such a copy of it comes to you. My notion of you is such that if there be any thing good in it, you will not fail making a good use of it for the benefit of those for whom you act.

If at this or any more distant period any of the ideas which are contained in it should be the means of adding to the prosperity of *your* country (since the unhappy distinction is now made) it will be some consolation for the miseries you have been a means of bringing upon *mine*.

I am Sir with all the respect that is due to an eminent benefactor of mankind and all the regard which can be due to the destroyer of my country's peace.

To William Hodgson   Copy: Library of Congress

Dear Sir,   Passy April 11. 1780.

I received your favours of the 10th. and 28th. of march. The Method you propose of managing the Money for the Prisoners

7. Bentham (1748–1832) was a jurist, political philosopher, and member of Lord Shelburne's circle at Bowood: *DNB*. In spite of his efforts he seems never to have met BF.

8. On that date Bentham sent his brother Samuel the draft of a covering letter to Catherine II which was to accompany a copy of his work on penal law. Five months earlier he had told his brother he was considering sending copies to BF and to the *philosophe* d'Alembert. This work was now about to be printed. It was not published until 1789, however, and was then entitled *An Introduction to the Principles of Morals and Legislation:* Timothy L.S. Sprigge *et al.*, eds., *The Correspondence of Jeremy Bentham* (9 vols. to date, London, 1968–), I, xxviii–xxxi; II, 334, 411, 414–20.

9. Bentham's shorthand for "To Franklin": *ibid*, II, 334n.

1. Bentham sent a printed quarto copy of the work via Francis-Xavier

is perfectly agreable to me. You desired in your last that I would explain how it happen'd that no Prisoners went back in the last Cartel. I did not till this Day well understand it myself; or I should have answer'd sooner. When our Little Squadron brought near 500 English Prisoners into The Texel, I would have exchanged them there for Americans, but I was told that would not be agreed to in England, as there was a Chance of retaking them in their Passage to france. But a Cartel being treated of as I understand, by the ambassadors of England and france at the Hague, The french ambassador applied to Commodore Jones for those Prisoners to be exchanged there, who would not deliver them up without my orders, and a promise of Exchanging them for americans. The ambassador thereupon wrote to me requesting such orders,[2] which I sent accordingly, expressing my Reliance that an Equal Number (472) of other English would be deliver'd to me at morlaix to be exchanged there for americans.[3] After this at the Instance of Mr. De sartine I gave orders to our agent at L'Orient, to Deliver a Number of other Prisoners we had there, to The Captain of the happy Cartel, in Exchange for so Many french Men,[4] with the same Reliance as above mentioned. As soon as I received your Information that the Cartel was sailed from Plymouth with 100 americans, I applyed for 100 English to be rendered at Morlaix for the Exchange[5] and was told that orders should be that Day given; to march them thither from saumur for that Purpose. I imagined it had been done; and the Exchange made till I heard the contrary from you. To Day I learn that they were not arrived while the Cartel was there. And I have now desired of M. De Sartine that two hundred may be immediately sent over. One to pay for the 100 Americans re-

Schwediauer or Swediaur, a medical writer and friend of Jan Ingenhousz. Schwediauer delivered it, but, to Bentham's disappointment, BF made no observations on it: *ibid.*, I, xxviii–xxix; II, 183; John Bowring, ed., *The Works of Jeremy Bentham* (11 vols., Edinburgh and London, 1843), x, 88.

2. XXXI, 150–1.
3. XXXI, 203–4.
4. XXXI, 477–8, 483–4.
5. In fact BF requested English prisoners be provided in exchange for *every* group of Americans arriving at Morlaix until all 410 were free: XXXI, 479. Cartel ships brought a hundred Americans at a time.

ceived and the other to Exchange a fresh Parcel. His verbal Answer is, that the request is just, and shall be complyed with, and he will write a Letter to me to morrow, which I may send over to be shewn to The board of Sick & Hurt, that will explain the matter, and clear me from any Charge of bad Faith. He added that he would also take the first opportunity of Sending the Remainder to equal the Number deliver'd in Holland; in order to Exchange for americans; having no Scruple of doing this by advance, the Board having Shewn the greatest Honour and Exactitude in all their Proceedings.[6] I am sure it has been my Intention to do the same; and I shall always act accordingly. Tho' I am not insensible of the Injustice towards us in the Instance of the Boston Cartels formerly mentioned[7] I shall write to Mr. Hartley (from whom I have just received Copies of the french Certificates &c)[8] per next post after I receive the Letter from Mr. De Sartine. In the mean time I wish you would be so good as to communicate to him the Contents of this, with my Respects.

I should be glad to hear some more particulars about Mr: W.[9] and the Reasons of discarding him. I hope the rest of that worthy society are well and happy.

With great Esteem, I am, Dear sir, Your most obedient and most humble servant.

Mr. Hodgson

6. Also, British officials were ordered to be conciliatory and obliging to the French: Olive Anderson, "The Establishment of British Supremacy at Sea and the Exchange of Naval Prisoners of War, 1689–1783," *English Hist. Rev.* LXXV (1960), 83.

7. The *Polly* and the *Bob:* XXXI, 418.

8. Probably enclosures to his letter of March 27, above.

9. David Williams. See Hodgson's March 10 letter.

From Jean-Etienne de Chezaulx[1]

ALS: National Archives; press copy:[2] Library of Congress

⟨Bergen, April 11, 1780, in French: I have received both of your letters of February 21st and am extremely grateful for them.[3] I wish I could have done more to serve American interests, but my efforts were not totally fruitless since the Danish government has agreed to bear all expenses incurred by your people here, both before the restitution of the prizes and since then. The needs of the crews have been more than fully met. M. Danckert D. Krohn,[4] a man of goodwill, who advanced the necessary monies, has been reimbursed. Your sailors who currently have no ship will sail for Dunkirk next Thursday on the chartered Danish ship *Fortune,* weather permitting.[5] The prize captains—whose conduct has been exemplary—have received money from the government for extraordinary expenses. The local governor, M. Bager, has shown them much kindness, so that all ended well and the only unresolved point is how much damage you will obtain from the Danish court. I hope Congress will be satisfied.[6]

The *Governor Johnson,* a merchant ship of yours loaded with Virginia tobacco, entered this port on March 4. I had its captain, Michel Baudee, raise the French flag in order to obtain the same privileges as French shipping and he obtained permission to sell his cargo. I reported my actions to Naval Minister Sartine and Ambassador La Houze. I have asked M. Krohn to act as its commissary, under my guidance. P.S. Enclosed is a letter from your officers.[7]⟩

1. The French consul at Bergen had been assisting the crews of the three prizes brought there from Jones's cruise, and had tried unsuccessfully to block the return of the ships to the British: xxx, 336–7, 340, 342–3, 591–4; xxxi, 261–5, 334–6, 506.
2. Made by William Short.
3. One of BF's letters of that date was to the prize crews: xxxi, 506, 507.
4. A local banker: xxx, 342–3.
5. They sailed from Bergen on April 19, reaching Dunkirk on May 4: Charles Herbert, *A Relic of the Revolution* . . . (Boston, 1847), p. 240.
6. The body of the letterpress copy ends here.
7. From White *et al.* of this date, below. The letterpress copy has a different postscript asking BF's consent to Chezaulx's arrangement with the stranded crewmen by which they could choose to return to America aboard

From Dumas

ALS: American Philosophical Society

Monsieur   La Haie 11e. Avril 1780

Puisque dans l'honorée vôtre du 29 Mars vous me demandez de vous expliquer l'affaire du Pilote Anglois avec Mr. Jones, je dois supposer que Vous n'avez pas reçu la copie du Certificat qu'à la requisition du dernier je vous avois envoyée dans une de mes Lettres du Texel ou d'Amsterdam:[8] Ce qui ne seroit pas surprenant, vu l'état de confusion & d'anarchie où nous étions là pendant quelque temps. Quoiqu'il en soit, pour vous épargner la peine de chercher, j'aime mieux joindre ici une autre Copie de ce Certificat. Quant à Mr. Gordon, si j'ai bien compris ce qu'on m'en a dit, il doit être Consul de cette Rep. dans le Nord de la Gr. Br. Ce qui est sûr, c'est qu'il avoit écrit une Lettre à L.H.P. pour réclamer ce Pilote Jackson de Hull, comme pris & retenu illégalement, contre les conventions, selon lesquelles on ne doit point enlever les Pêcheurs & Pilotes côtiers. Cette démarche de Mr. Gordon ayant donné lieu à des discours fort injurieux, non seulement pour Mr. Jones, mais aussi pour les Américains en général, j'ai pris le parti de faire parvenir une copie du Certificat au G—— P——, et de lui écrire la Lettre dont vous avez copie,[9] afin que L.H.P., & Mr. Gordon, & l'Angleterre, pussent savoir au vrai l'histoire de ce Pilote, comment on en avoit agi envers lui, & ce qu'il étoit devenu.

Notre Ami m'a promis de me raccommoder avec le gd. Facteur. Il m'a dit aussi que l'on délibere aux Etats d'Hollde. sur l'invitation de l'Impe. de Russie faite à cette Rep.; que notre O E N O P M B E X C G T N U T N T P D C P C Z L B D T C L X C[1] traversent cela tant qu'ils peuvent; mais qu'ils ne reussiront pas.

---

the *Governor Johnson* without forfeiting their rights to prize money from the *Alliance*'s cruise with Jones.

8. On Dec. 17, 1779, Dumas had sent BF a copy of a Nov. 15 John Paul Jones certificate regarding the pilot John Jackson: XXXI, 253. The copy of the certificate enclosed with the present letter is now at the APS.

9. Dumas had enclosed a copy of his covering letter to Grand Pensionary Van Bleiswijk with his March 13 letter to BF, above.

1. "Duc de Brunswick ici et ses partisans."

Je suis avec mon respectueux dévouement pour toujours Monsieur Votre très humble & très obéissant servit   D

Passy à Son E. M. Franklin

Addressed: à Son Excellence / Monsieur B. Franklin, Esqr. / Min. plenipe. des Etats unis / *Passy./.*

Notation: Dumas, la haie April. 11. 80

From ———— Ricot   ALS: American Philosophical Society

Monsieur   St Valery S: S. Le 11 avril 1780.

Je prends la liberté de vous informer que le Corsaire Nommé le Prince Noir de 22 Canons a Eté forcé de faire Côte a Berk [Berck] distant de quatre lieües de ce port, par la chasse que Lui a donné une fregatte angloise, le Neuf de ce mois; interessé par plus d'un motif au Bien des Etats unis, jÿ ai depeché Sur le Champ un de mes affidés pour offrir des secours au Capitaine Et a L Equipage.

Si vous me chargéz dordre Relatifs a ce Navire, je Les Exe-cuterai avec autant de zele qu'il Soit possible de le faire a tous Vraÿs françois Envers Ses amis.

Jai L'honneur dEtre avec Respect Monsieur Votre tres hum-ble Et tres obeissant serviteur

RICOT Receveur de Mgr. Lamiral Et Capne de port

Notation: Mr. Ricot. April 10. 1780

From Thomas White *et al.*[2]   Press copy: Library of Congress[3]

May it please your Excellency   Bergen April 11th. 1780

We received your kind letter of the 21st. of Febry.[4] with the greatest pleasure as you have therein approv'd our conduct

2. The same spokesmen for the prize crews at Bergen who had written BF several months earlier: xxx, 340n; xxxi, 340–1.
3. In the Thomas Jefferson Papers.
4. xxxi, 507.

whilst in this place & given us orders to proceed immediately to France, if the ships were not restored. We shall therefore in consequence of the King of Denmark's, as well as your Excellency's orders sail for Dunkirk the first wind. All proceedings with respect to our affairs have been regularly settled, for which we refer to the copies of accounts already forwarded to your Excy. by the French Consul. Our expences whilst on board the ships were paid by the English Consul & those since by the King of Denmark, which enables us to proceed without drawing bills upon France.

The kind reception we met with from the Governor, Consul & Mr. Khrone deserves the greatest approbation as they have done every Thing in their power to serve us in all exigencies; we accordingly waited upon those gentlemen with your Excellency's thanks in respective letters, & received public assurances of their readiness to serve us or our countrymen upon any future occasion.— The Governor Johnson with tobacco from Maryland having put in here in distress; & her men having put themselves under the English protection, Monsr. Chezeaux as well as ourselves thinking it for the benefit of America to supply them with 5. or 6. men we shall do it with pleasure.

We have the honor &c.　　　(Signed) Thomas White
　　　　　　　　　　　　　　　Thomas Fitzgerald
　　　　　　　　　　　　　　　Alexr Moore
　　　　　　　　　　　　　　　James Hogan
　　　　　　　　　　　　　　　Nathl. Marston

His Excy. Dr Franklin Esqr. Passy.

(Copy W: Short, Secy)

From Richard Bache　　　ALS: Public Record Office, London

Dear Sir　　　　　　　　　Philadelphia April 12th. 1780

This will be handed you by Captain McPherson, who intends visiting Paris Via Amsterdam as you are already well acquainted

with him, an Introduction of him to you is the less necessary—[5]
He is upon a plan of business I am totally ignorant of, but should
he require your good Offices, you will not I dare say withhold
them— Sally & the Children are well, the youngest is just got
thro' the small Pox—[6] I am ever Hond. sir Your Affectionate son
RICH. BACHE

Dr. Franklin

Addressed: His Excellency / Dr. Benjn. Franklin / at / Passy /
Favored by Capt. Mc.Pherson

From Officers of the *Alliance*

ALS:[7] University of Pennsylvania Library

Sir   Ship Alliance Road LOrient 12 April 1780
We the Officers of the Frigate Alliance under the Command
of the honourable John Paul Jones Esqr: beg Leave to Represent
to your Excellency that our circumstances are Really Nesessi-
tous, and that we are alarm'd at having Received neither wages
or prize money since the Ship is so nearly prepared for Sea.
We have waited with all possible patience in Expectation they
would be paid us, from the propriety of it and some favourable
Reports. Now as your Excellency is the person Authorised to Interfere on our part we flatter ourselves from your known benevolent disposition, that your Excellency will do every thing in your
power to Obtain for us Justice and froward the Ship's sailing.
Our situations are such in the town that we should be very unhappy to Leave it before we Receive our wages & prize money
to enable us to discharge our Debts Contracted through mere necessity: it is of great Importance to us all especially to a number
of men half naked, which is absolutely the case with two thirds

5. Possibly John Macpherson, a Philadelphia merchant and ex-privateer:
XXII, 250n; Claghorn, *Naval Officers*, p. 192.
6. Louis, born in October, 1779: XXX, 550–1; XXXI, 96.
7. In Degge's hand.

of our Crew, many of them have families in America who are also in want.[8]

We think it unnessesary to trouble your Excellency with a Detail of every particular, Assuring ourselves that your Excellency will take it into Consideration and Indulge us with an Answer— In the mean time we wish you health and every Blessing and are with the greatest Respect & Veneration Your Excellencys Most Obedient and most devoted Servants   JAMES DEGGE 1 Lieut
                                            JAMES LYND do
                                            JOHN LARCHAR JUNR
          FITCH POOL   M PARKE Capt Marines
          SAMUEL GUILD   JAMES WARREN
          ISAAC CARR   THOMAS ELWOOD
          ARTHUR ROBERTSON   THOS. HINSDALE
          JAMES DALY   JAMES BRAGG
          JNO. JARVIS   BENJAMIN PIERCE
          N BLODGET   JOHN DARLING
          A WINDSHIP   CHIPN. BANGS

L'Orient: 12 April 1780—

To his Excellency Dr. Benja Franklin Minister plenipotentiary to the United States at Passy, near Paris

Addressed: To his Excellency / Dr. Benja Franklin / Minister plenipotentiary to the thirteen / United States / at Passy / near Paris

Endorsed: Officers of the Alliance April 12 1780

From Jonathan Trumbull   ALS: American Philosophical Society

Sir!   Lebanon Connecticut. April 12th: 1780
    This will be deliver'd to you, by my youngest Son Colo. John Trumbull, whose Ambition of gaining a more extensive knowl-

8. On April 14 ninety-three of the *Alliance*'s crew sent their own petition, prompted by a report that the former crewmen of the *Bonhomme Richard* were going to be paid their wages and prize money. They asked the same privilege so they could furnish themselves with necessities and assist their

edge of foreign Nations, leads him to Europe.—[9] I have to beg your notice of Him, while He may remain in Paris, and your Advice and Assistance in whatever He may request.—in fine I wish you to be his patron.—and I assure you, that nothing can give me more pleasure than to hear from you, that his manner of improving his Time.—and his Companions, meet your Approbation.

I have likewise to beg you to give him Credit, in Case of any Accident, as being made a prisoner &c.—and promise the most punctual Attention to his Bills drawn in your favor, for whatever Amount.

Of the News political or military, I cannot give you a better State in writing, than my Son will give in person.— I beg leave therefore to refer you to him, & am Sir, with every sentiment of Respect & Esteem Your most Obedt: Humble servant

JONTH: TRUMBULL

His Excelly B Franklin Esqr

Addressed: His Excelly. / Benjamin Franklin Esqr. / Minister Pleni: from the U. States of / America, at the Court of France

---

former countrymen exchanged from prison. They complained that many of them had been long absent from their wives and families and confined in prison. They had been told they would receive their wages and prize money before sailing. They asked BF to consider the matter and send an answer as soon as possible. In two postscripts they explained that the remainder of the ship's company was on duty but consented to the petition and requested that BF direct his answer to Benjamin Pierce, gunner of the *Alliance.* On June 1 the crewmen (115 this time) wrote again, warning they would not sail until they had received their prize money and six months' wages. They also asked that Landais be returned to command and defended his conduct at the Battle off Flamborough Head. Both petitions are at the University of Pa. Library.

9. John Trumbull (1756–1843), had resigned from the Continental Army in 1777 after a dispute with Congress over the date of his commission. Thereafter he went to Boston to study art: *DAB.* On May 7, 1780, he sailed from New London on the armed French ship *Négresse.* After a five-week voyage to Nantes he proceeded to Paris. Discarding plans for a commercial venture he procured a now-missing introduction from BF to the painter Benjamin West: Theodore Sizer, ed., *The Autobiography of Colonel John Trumbull, Patriot-Artist, 1756–1843* (New Haven and London, 1953), pp. 58–61. See also Irma B. Jaffe, *John Trumbull Patriot-Artist of the Revolution* (Boston, 1975), pp. 44–6.

From Dumas   ALS: American Philosophical Society

Monsieur   Lahaie 13e. Avril 1780
  Depuis le Mémoire présenté par le Plénipe. de Russie à L.h.P.,
dont voici copie,[1] ainsi que de la Déclaration de la même Cour
aux Puissances belligérantes, les Etats Provinciaux d'Hollande
déliberent sur l'invitation de l'Impératrice; & il n'est pas douteux
(je le sais de notre Ami) que la Résolution que la Province prendra là-dessus la semaine prochaine, ne soit conforme au voeu
général, qui est pour que cette Republique entre dans les vues de
l'Impératrice. Or comme les Résolutions de cette Province sont
ordinairement adoptées par les autres, on s'attend à voir cette rep.
prendre un parti qui accélerera la pacification générale. Les plus
outrés du parti Anglois, voyant qu'ils ne peuvent empêcher la résolution sans se rendre absolument odieux, cherchent, tant qu'ils
peuvent, à l'énerver par l'insertion d'expressions obscures & am-
bigues, qu'ils y veulent faire mettre: mais le bon parti s'occupe à
balayer cette poussiere à mesure qu'on la jette en son chemin.
  Quant aux deux autres objets qui occupent cette République,
savoir aux Convois illimités & aux secours demandés par l'Angleterre, la Province d'Hollande a déjà, depuis plusieurs semaines, unanimement résolu les premiers, & décliné les derniers, comme ne tombant point sous le *casus foederis* en cette
guerre. Les Provinces de *Frise*, d'*Overyssel* & d'*Utrecht* ont successivement accédé à cette Résolution; & l'on s'attend à la même
accession de la part des trois restantes.[2]
  On dit, depuis quelque temps, que Mr. Lawrens, ancien Président du Congrès, est désigné pour venir ici, d'abord incognito,
pour ne déployer son caractere de Plénipotentiaire que lorsqu'il
en sera temps. Avec cette précaution sa venue pourra faire un
bon effet. Mais il seroit très-nécessaire que je le visse avant qu'il
vît personne, pour lui faire connoître la Carte du pays. Les uns
assurent qu'il est parti d'Amerique, & en chemin; les autres qu'il

---

1. Dumas enclosed a copy of the page of the *Gaz. de Leyde* to which on
April 7 he had called BF's attention; see above.
  2. The three remaining provinces were Groningen, Drenthe, and Zeeland.
La Vauguyon told the stadholder that if they voted for unlimited convoys
and if the Dutch response to the Russian proposals was favorable France
would grant the Netherlands full trade privileges as neutrals: Fauchille,
Diplomatie française, pp. 494–5.

est déjà en Europe. *Notre Ami* me demande ce qui en est; & je ne puis le Satisfaire. Vos avis, Monsieur, & vos lumieres sur son sujet, me seroient bien nécessaires, et par conséquent doublement précieuses.

J'ai pris la liberté de tirer sur V. Exc. à une usance à l'ordre de Mrs. J. De Neufville & fils les £2700 qui me sont alloués pour ma subsistance & fraix d'Agence ordinaires de la demi-année courante.[3]

Je suis avec un très-grand respect, Monsieur Votre très-humble & très obéissant serviteur   DUMAS

Notre Ami se proposoit hier de voir Mr. l'Ambr., & de le réconcilier avec moi. Il me dira demain le succès de ses bons offices.

Passy à Son Exc. M. Franklin

Addressed: à Son Excellence / Monsieur B. Franklin / Esqr. Min. Plenip. des Et. Un. / &c. / *Passy ./.*

Notation: Dumas, la haie April 13. 80

From Anton Georg Eckhardt[4]

ALS: American Philosophical Society

Monsieur!   Utrecht 13 Avril 1780

Je proffite du voyage de Monsieur Le Comte du Pac[5] a Paris, et de ces offres Obligeants a veuiller vous remettre celle ci, pour

---

3. Dumas' salary as American agent was 5,400 *l.t.* (225 *louis*) per annum: XXIX, 101, 257.

4. A Dutch inventor who had lived in London for many years, and whom BF had supported for membership in the Royal Society in 1773: VIII, 359. With fifteen patents between 1771 and 1809, he was the most prolific "quasi-professional" inventor in late eighteenth-century England. During the present period, however, he had returned to his native Holland and was working on improvements to water wheels. Christine MacLeod, *Inventing the Industrial Revolution: the English Patent System, 1660–1800* (Cambridge, 1988), p. 142; *NNBW*, VI, 465–6. Among BF's papers at the APS is a printed description and engraving of Eckhardt's rolling parallel rule, manufactured by P. and J. Dolland in London, which was patented in 1771: Bennet Woodcroft, comp., *Alphabetical Index of Patentees of Inventions* (reprint ed., London, 1969), p. 174.

5. Gabriel-Marie du Pac, comte de Bellegarde (1754–1849): Jules Villain,

vous accuser Monsieur La Reception de votre gracieuse Lettre,[6] a laquelle jaurois dabord répondu ci je navois crû devoir premierement attendre la lettre que Vous me annonciez de Monsieur L'academicien Le Roi, que je nai cependant pas recû jusqu'a present. Je Suis Chagrin Extremement ainsi que mon frere d'apprendre l'Etat dIndisposition ou vous vous trouvé Monsieur que nous Esperons cependant naura pas de Suitte; et que la belle Saison dans laquelle nous allons Entrer Contribuera a un prompt et Entier Retablissement.[7]

Nous sommes on ne peut plus Sencible Monsieur de loppinion avantageuse que vous veuillez avoir de nos applications et de la bonne volonté d'aider a lEtablissement que nous desireriont de pouvoir faire dans qque [quelque] Paÿis oû ces applications et nos divers objets pouroient Etres Utiles, et jose nous Récommander de nouveau a votre Digne Protection a cet Egard: nous desirerions Infiniment que Monsieur Le Comte du Pac qui prend tout l'interest a notre sort pouroit apprendre qques nouvelles desirables de votre Pard, et ci vous nous Conseilleriez de faire un tour a Paris avec quelque Esperance de Succes a i réussir pour un Etablissement ou celui de lun ou lautre de nos principaux objets, quand nous Seriont bien Charmés de pouvoir vous presenter nos Devoirs Monsieur: néanmoins nayant recû aucune nouvelle de Monsr Le Roi de l'accademie des Sciences, et ayant apris par Monsr: Lavocat Le Roi (qui vous remi notre premiere Lettre) que vous Etiez dIntention dEcrire pour nous a Londre, nous prenons la Liberté de vous remettre que ce en Cas vous pensiez quil ne nous Serois pas Conseillable daller en France mais plustot en Angleterre, que nous sommes prets a Suivre votre Conseil Monsieur mais que nous osons desirer allors cette bonté de votre

comp., *La France moderne. Grand dictionnaire généalogique, historique et bio-graphique: Haute-Garonne et Ariège* (2 vols., Montpellier, 1911–13; reprint ed., Marseilles, 1982), II, 1770.

6. Missing. No letters from BF to Eckhardt are extant, and the only earlier one from the inventor appears in XXV, 195.

7. BF may have written to them the previous November, when he was indisposed: XXXI, lxiii, 140, 280. Eckhardt's brother was Francis Frederick, who was granted two English patents in 1793 for methods of preparing and printing designs on paper and fabric: *Alphabetical Index of Patentees of Inventions*, p. 175 of second pagination.

Digne Pard de vouloir nous accorder qque Recommandation a Celui ou ceux que vous i Croiriez le plus a meme d'aider a notre Etablissement et celui de nos objets ûtiles, ce qui nous encoûrageroit dont a i faire un tour, quand nous avons lieu dEsperer quavec de tels Recommandations, et en demontrant lutilité de nos objets principalement celui de notre Fabrique, que nous avons Perfectionné de beaucoup depuis que vous en avez vu les Echantillons, nous pourrions i Reussir. Jose dont remettre ceci a votre meillieur avis et Conseil Monsieur, et appres nous i avoir Recommandé et vous avoir assurer de notre vive gratitude et des Sentiments d'attachement les plus Devoues.

Jai Lhonneur dEtre avec le Respect et la Consideration la plus Distinguee Monsieur Votre Tres Humble et Tres Obeissant serviteur   A: G: Eckhardt FRS

p.s. Je prend la liberté de Joindre ici qque Memoires de nos principaux Objets, que je crains monsieur Le Roi ne vous aura pas Remis, ne les ayant peut Etre pu trouver chez un ami ou je lavois addressé et qui en avoit des Exemplaires. Je me flatte que vous i trouverez deduit clairement les avantages de ces machines.[8]

Notation: Le Comte de Bellegarde, rue des Maçons sorbonne, no. 9

From Thomas Digges   ALS: Historical Society of Pennsylvania

Dr. Sir   London 14. Apl. 1780

Since my last to you I have recd a few lines from your Relation by the hands of Mr. L——g——n, & am very much surprisd to hear that the maps &ca. forwarded to amstermdam have not yet got to hand.[9] They went very early in Jany by the Ship Lady Elizabeth Klaas Doorn Commandr, the box markd B F and a Card naild to it with the Direction For Messrs. Fizeau Grand

8. The memoirs have been lost, and we cannot be sure which of the inventor's projects are being discussed here.

9. L——g——n is George Logan; see his April 15 letter. The relation must be WTF, who had been an intermediary in obtaining maps from Digges for Lafayette: XXXI, 356–7.

& Co Amstermdam. I shippd it myself & long ago forwarded the Capts Rect and the bill parcells for it— I think it may be better got at by Mr. F writing a line to Mr. Grand at Amsterdam about it.

We have an arrival from St. Kitts the 5 March an Expedn. (of abot 4,000 Men) was then talkd of as nearly ready to rendevous at St Lucie from the quarter of Antigua. That part of the French fleet wch. was reported to be *blockd up* in Guardaloupe very easily found its way to Martinico & after the junction the latter end of Apr. formd a fleet of 14 sail of the line &ca. We are given to understand here that when Monr. Guichens Squadn. gets there, & the other five which went before him, the French will have 36 sail; There is not much boasting of superiority & I beleive there will not be more than 31 English of the Line.

The Wt. Inda. Fleet saild the 8th 200 Sail Of merchantmen under convoy of 4 of the line, one frigate, one 20, & 3 fire ships. Adml. Graves (whose destination is generally said to be to America) was to have gone with 7 Ships but the Crews of several of them mutinyd, and one ship the Invincible remains so refractory as to have cut away all her boats & the Crew have confind their officers to their Cabins.[1] Most likely by this day it is all right, & the Ship on Her voyage— This fleet was hastily got ready in consequence of some advices that A fleet with troops on board was going from Brest to Ama. some say to Canada. We have yet no accots. of Clinton & Co. The general opinion is, that He has got to the Coasts of Georgia (some say to Beaufort) but the storms have left him in such a situation as to make it very improbable He can succeed against Chas Town— The Ship from St. Kitts brings an accot of another of His fleet being wreckd on the Rocks of Bermudas that vessel had foreign troops & some horses on board. Mr. Jonathan Loring A——s——n has been with me a few days.[2] He left B——n the 24th. Jany. & was un-

---

1. The mutiny was suppressed, but Graves was further delayed and finally sailed for New York in mid-May with only six ships of the line: John A. Tilley, *The British Navy and the American Revolution* (Columbia, S.C., 1987), pp. 192–3. The West Indies convoy was delayed even longer; see our annotation of Digges's March 3 letter.

2. In January Jonathan Loring Austin had been selected by Massachusetts to negotiate a European loan. On his way from Boston to France, he was cap-

lucky on His voyage to F—— in a small unarmd vessel The
Zephir. There was nothing particular in the news way when He
left that place. You will hear more of him soon. The new Pro-
tector was to take Her departure abot the 1st. Mar & will likely
bring Mr. A——s——n a packet to yr. care. Another packet
would sail in abot. 3 weeks or a month after the Zephyr.

Mr. H——n [Hodgson] is rather anxious to hear from You
he not having a letter since the arrival of the Cartel without any
passengers. This causes much murmuring at Forton & several
have forced their way out since the vessel returnd & continue
flying up to L——n. On the 13th. Int. the numbers were 227 at
Fort——n and abot 85 at P——h— Mr Drouillard[3] wrote to his
friend at that place to supply Capt. M——y [Manley] with the
sum some time ago orderd. Whether this has Enabled him to take
a journey or not I cannot yet learn but I apprehend it has for silence is always the Ansr. to letters when things go well.

I fear Capt. C——m is again taken with 4 others.[4] The Capn.
of the Privateer who took the vessel from F. writes "she was a
small vessel loaded with salt wine &ca. on board her were five
Passengers among them the celebrated Capt. C——" the Passengers are kept on board the Privateer still on a cruise, but the
Prize is arrivd.

This Day in the Commons the Petitions of the People are to
be debated. Some of the late Petitions & all the subsequent Resolves at the adjournd meetings, declare the mischief done the
Country by the war is intollerable & the people do not seem en-
clind to bear it longer. Most of them declare openly that the evil
is in the prosecution of the war in America & pray it may be
given up. Mr. D H moves the house this day on that theme, &
many people think the debate of to day will evince a disposition
in the House *even on the treasury side of it,* to give up the principles of the Amn. war. The voice out of doors is universally for

tured by a Jersey privateer and briefly imprisoned, but reached France in
May: *Sibley's Harvard Graduates,* XVI, 306.
3. One of Digges's aliases.
4. Indeed, Conyngham recently had been captured: Gourlade & Moylan
to BF, May 8, below. He was confined to Mill Prison until his exchange in mid-
1781: Neeser, *Conyngham,* p. l.

accomodation with Ama. & many of those who were violent a Year or two ago for the prosecution of it with severity & rigour now go so far as to openly wish peace with Ama. on the terms of avowd & declard Independence.

I am with the highest esteem Dr sir Your very Obt. Servt

W Ross

I will keep this open as long as I can in order to give You any news that may come out from the quarter of the House of Commons. J. T—— [Temple] often desires me to mention Him to You & I think it will not be long before you see him.

The Speaker was taken ill & all business of course stopt to day many say it was a political illness & that some moves in Admn. will be the consequence— By his speech, it would seem He wishd to resign & most likely He will not be speaker very long—[5] The House wishd to have an adjournment for some days. & monday week they are to meet agn.

Addressed: A Monsr. Monsr. B. F— / Passy

Endorsed: April 14 80

Notation: April 14. 80

From John Jay

Copy: Library of Congress

Sir, Madrid 14. April 1780.

On the 26th. Jany. last at Cadiz, I did myself the Honor of wrinting to your Excellency a Letter,[6] by M. Gerard, enclosing one for the honorable Arthur Lee Esqe. and Copies of others I had written to the spanish and french ministers, and among other things informing you, that several Letters or rather large Pacquets directed to you were in my Possession, with which I was

---

5. Cobbett, *Parliamentary History,* XXI, 492–4. When Parliament reconvened on April 24, Sir Fletcher Norton (1716–1789) attempted unsuccessfully to regain the post he had just resigned; thereafter he was in opposition to the government: Namier and Brooke, *House of Commons,* III, 214–17. For further discussion see *Adams Papers,* IX, 139n.

6. XXXI, 409–11.

much at Loss what to do, and requesting your directions. I have also written to you other Letters of Later Date from the same Place, advising you of Bills I had drawn upon you viz, the 28th. Jany., 3d. march and 20th. March.[7]

As the Receipt of other Letters carried by M. Gerard from hence to Paris has been acknowledged, there is no Room to Apprehend that mine to you by him, has miscarried—I find it therefore difficult to account for my not having been favored with a single Line from you since my arrival.

Your Letters should immediately on my arrival have been sent by the Post, but it being well known that all Letters whose Contents there is Reason to suppose interesting, are inspected in the Course of that Conveyance I would not prevail upon myself to expose yours to that Treatment especially as there are indorsements on some of them being sunk in Case of Captaine [Capture]. Nor did it appear to me more prudent to send them by a Special Express, because being a Stranger I knew not whom to trust or in whose Recommendations to confide.

But as between two and three months have already elapsed without my receiving any orders or advice from you on the Subject I should Expose myself to Censure were I longer to forbear transmitting them in such manner as appeared to me least hazardous. I shall therefore deliver them in a Bag Sealed and directed to M. Joshua Johnson at Nantes this Evening, to Monsr. Henry Bouteiller a young french Gentleman,[8] who will set out for that Please [Place] to morrow, and who travelled from Cadiz here in company with me. From the Character which I received of him there as well as my own observations of his Conduct since I am induced to confide both in this Honor and his Care. I shall enclose this Letter to Mr. Johnson and request the favor of him to send it to you together with the others by the first safe Convoyance and I shall apprise him of my Objections to their going by the Post. Among them are some directed to Persons of Suspicious Character in Britain, and were all delivered to me by

7. The first of these three letters is described in XXXI, 410n; the other two are above.

8. Henri Bouteiller, son of Guillaume Bouteiller, one of the richest merchants of Bordeaux: Jean Meyer, *L'Armement Nantais dans la deuxième moitié du XVIIIe siècle* (Paris, 1969), p. 183n.

the officers of the Confederacy at martinico, except the one directed to Mesrs Mary Brown at Trees Bank Scotland, which was committed to my Care by her Sister, a Daughter of Peter Van Brugh Livingston Esqe. of Baskindridge—[9] The Contents of it are perfectly unexceptionable, and would give more Pleasure to an American than a Briton.

As not only a good understanding but also a constant Interchange of Intelligence and attentions between the public Servants at the different Courts are necessary to procure to him [his] Constituents all the advantages capable of being derived from this Appointment, it would give me very sensible regret in [if] my Endeavours to cultivate the one and engage the other should prove abortive.

I this moment recd. a Note from the Marquis d'Yranda, informing me that M Grand of Paris had desired him by his Letter of the 22d. feby. to hold at my Disposition the Net Produce of Nineteen thousand nine hundred and twenty one Livres Tournois which I might receive when I thought proper—from the Particularity of the Sum I conjecture this to be in consequence of your Order.

I have the Honour to be Your Excellency's most obedient and most humble Servant   (signed) JOHN JAY

P.S. I have just rec'd from M. Lee an answer to the Letter I took the Liberty of sending inclosed to you by M. Gerard.

His Excellency Benjn. franklin.

From Sartine   Copy: Library of Congress

à Versailles le 14. Avril 1780.

J'ai lu, Monsieur, avec beaucoup d'attention la Lettre que vous m'avez fait l'honneur de m'écrire le 20. mars dernier au Sujet de l'Enquête que vous avez fait faire sur ce qui s'est passé entre le Commodore Jones et le Capne. Landais. Puisque vous avez

9. Mary Livingston Brown (b. 1746), the wife of a British army officer, was Sarah Jay's cousin and had two sisters in America: Morris, *Jay: Revolutionary*, p. 748n.

trouvé beaucoup de Contradiction dans les Declarations des parties, et dans les preuves Ecrites qu'elles ont produites pour les appuyer, Je pense comme vous que le seul Parti a prendre est d'assoupir entierement cette affaire qui, Si elle étoit renvoyée à
l'Examen d'un Conseil de Guerre en amerique, ne pourroit faire
que le plus mauvais Effet.[1]

J'ai l'honneur d'etre avec une parfaite Consideration votre
tres humble et tres obeissant Serviteur,   (signé) DE SARTINE.

M. Franklin.

To Delleville   Copy: Library of Congress

sir   Passy, April 15. 1778, *i.e.*, 1780
    I received the Letter you did me the honour of writing to me
the 10th. Instant, relating to the seven Americans who had Escaped in a boat from England, and arriv'd on your Coast. I beg
you to accept my thankful Acknowledgements for the hospitality you have shown them—. I hope they will be allow'd to sell
the Boat to furnish themselves with necessaries. Monseigneur
l'amiral has always been so good as to permit such application of
the property. If more should be wanting to enable them to travel
to Brest, in order to obtain a Passage thence to America. I beg
you would furnish them therewith, and I will immediately reimburse you by paying your Draft upon sight.[2] With great Respect
I have the honour to be sir

Mr. Philippe De Delleville Lieut General de l'Amirauté a
Bayeux.

1. BF had said Landais *would* be subject to a court martial in America.
2. Delleville replied on May 5. He confirms that the government allowed
the sale of the rowboat in which the seven escaped from Portsmouth. He is
sending the proceeds, 68 *l.t.*, to his colleague at Nantes, who will remit that
sum to the Americans. To enable the seven men to travel to Nantes more
comfortably and to provide for their future needs, he has supplemented what
the *commissaire* of the French navy furnished them, the same amount the
King provides his own subjects in similar circumstances. Remuneration is not
necessary; his expenditure should be considered proof of the devotion the
French feel towards the Americans and their cause. APS.

From B. Barbier   ALS: American Philosophical Society

⟨Nantes, April 15, 1780, in French: Monsieur, please interest yourself in the dishonesty with which one of your fellow Americans, John Green, has been treated. Last April he obtained the command of the brig *Patriote*, owned by M. Gruel, on condition that he invest 10,000 *l.t.* in the venture, which he did.[3] On Jan. 6, having settled all his affairs, Capt. Green hired a pilot and sailed but the ship soon ran aground and was lost.[4] He managed to save most of the cargo, unpacked it to dry, and discovered he had been abominably cheated. Gruel offered him a compensation of 50%, which is far from covering the discrepancies between the prices charged and the cargo's real value. I, too, have a financial stake in the ship and together we presented our case to the Admiralty court. We have the greatest confidence in the integrity of the judges, but you know how prejudicial to affairs judicial delays can be. In particular they have become an obstacle to the business of Capt. Green, who has obtained a ship at Lorient.[5] He has been there a week, and I am the only Frenchman ready to assist him. You are the support of Americans, particularly in France. We ask you to expose our complaints to the chancellor of France, so that he can have the *procureur général* of the Parlement of Brittany intervene with the admiralty judges. The honor of the Nantes business community and the interests of your compatriots require that we expose Gruel's unfaithfulness and dishonor. M. Penet can testify as to the manner in which he has abused the confidence of Americans who addressed themselves to him.[6] Messrs. D'Acosta frères[7] can bear witness to my honorable conduct.⟩

3. Actually Green was in Philadelphia in April, 1779, preparing to sail to France. He was given command of the *Patriote* (by John Ross) in November: XXIX, 737; XXXI, 121.

4. XXXI, 121n.

5. Not until March, 1781, did he sail from Lorient for Port-au-Prince aboard the *Lion*, 18: Philip Chadwick Foster Smith, *The "Empress of China"* (Philadelphia, 1984), p. 53. The ship was newly launched and Green may have been given her command while she was still under construction.

6. Penet and Gruel were former business associates: XXII, 545n.

7. Present business partners of Penet: XXXI, 188.

From ——— de Chantereyne[8]

ALS: American Philosophical Society

Monsieur,   Cherbourg le 15. Avril 1780

Je suis chargé de Larment [l'armement] de la Black Princesse capne Edward maccatter, pour M. Torris.[9] Nous avons besoin de votre Protection auprès de M. Mistral & de M. deshayes[1] comres. de la marine au havre & a Cherbourg, tant pour obtenir des matelots irlandois quètrangers qui Sont en diverses prisons, ou viennent dans des Prises. Si vous voulliès bien, Monsieur, leur ecrire une lettre de recommandation, Je suis tres persuadé que ces Messieurs auront tous les egards que votre excellence merite a juste titre.

Jai lhonneur detre avec un profond respect Monsieur Votre tres humble & tres obeissant serviteur   DE CHANTEREYNE

M. Le Dr. francklin

Notation: Chantereyne. Apr. 15. 1780

From George Logan[2]

ALS: American Philosophical Society

Dear Sir   London April 15th: 1780.

I have the pleasure of informing you of my safe arrival here last Friday. The Letters you intrusted to my care have been delivered. Dr: Fothergill, & Mr: Barclay are very happy in hearing of your good state of health. The latter who has the care of

---

8. He had already written BF on other matters: XXVI, 211; XXXI, 465–6. BF forwarded a letter to Sartine on April 24, probably the present one, with a note asking him to act favorably on the request. Yale University Library.

9. A new and better *Black Princess* to replace the old one, which was left at Morlaix. Macatter marched some Americans to Cherbourg to man her, but there were not enough of them: Clark, *Ben Franklin's Privateers*, p. 131.

1. Who had assisted Americans at Cherbourg: XXIX, 354, 381, 385.

2. Dr. George Logan: XXXI, 302n. He returned to the U.S. in the autumn of 1780. His distinguished later career included a term in the U.S. Senate: Frances A. Logan, ed., *Memoir of Dr. George Logan of Stenton . . .* (Philadelphia, 1899), p. 42.

my affairs,³ thinks they may be settled in about four or five weeks, but wishes me to return to America by a Dutch vessel, which is expected to sail about that time to St: Eustatia. If possible I should be happy to have your opinion on this subject. Should there be no safe opportunity immediately from France, I should prefer Mr: Barclay's advice, as I am anxious to be in America.

With respect to Public affairs, I must refer you to Mr: Diggs, who will write by this opportunity. I may inform you that the Minority are daily gaining strength; & that the American affairs bear an agreeable aspect; though many, & even some of the present Minority, are not as yet convinced of the necessity of acknowledging the independence of the United States. I had the pleasure of spending yesterday morning with Mr: Hartley he will make a motion tomorrow with respect to America, & which I expect will oblige the ministry, to come to some explanation with respect to their future prospects of this unhappy war. America has only to pursue the plan of conduct, which she has commenced with so much reputation.

There are no publications of any consequence, except what Mr: Diggs has already sent you. Should any thing appear within two weeks I will do myself the pleasure of sending you [*torn: one word missing*] by a Gentleman, who I expect [*torn: will?*] leave London about that [*torn: one or two words missing*] Paris.

I am with great respect Your much Obliged Frd. & Hble: Serv: GEO LOGAN

Addressed: To / His Excellence / Benjamin Franklin / Passy near / Paris. / pr favour of Dr Plunket⁴

Notation: Logan Geo. London April 15. 1780.

3. His father William Logan (II, 376n) had recommended him to David Barclay (IX, 190–1n) and John Fothergill: Logan, *Memoir,* pp. 33–4.
4. Plunkett also carried an April 22 letter of introduction from Digges, below.

From John Torris
ALS: American Philosophical Society

Honnoured Sir   Dunkerque 15th. April 1780.

With inexpressible grief, I have the Honnour to acquaint Your Excellency with the Loss of our poor Black Prince Captn. Dowlin. She has Suffered all the hardships She ever cou'd, from the French, these Few weeks past. The Self-Conceited & Weak Commissary of Morlaix[5] has forced my Correspondants there, to disembark the 22d to 25th. ulto., all her men that wou'd Cruise no longer, altho.' they had 32 days more to Compleat their engagement; the Crew was reducd to 53. men, which hinder'd Mr. Dowlin to Venture North about. He sailed from Roscoff for this Harbour the 6th. Instant. The 7th. He took & Sent for Cherbourg, the Flora Dutch Brigg Hendrick Rondenberg master, because She appears by her Bills of Lading & the Said Captain's report, her Cargoe of flaxseed &a. Belonged to Merchants in Dublin. The 8th. She Came up with an English King's Cutter but was obliged to Leave her off, Being Close Chaced by two Large frigates. The 9th. She Came up with a Brig when Chaced by a frigate Stretching out from the Land, which forced her to Leave the Brig. The 10th. She was again close chaced by the Same frigate under English flagg, Little or no Wind, at 2 PM. Came under the Land at Estaples [Etaples], hoisted French Colours & fired Signals of destress for the assistance of the Forts, at 4. PM, being within pistol Shot of the Frigate (which still kept up her English Colours) the Fort of Berk [Berck] Fired on her, then the Poor Black Prince Stranded, & the Frigate, in 2 ½ fathom watter, brought down her English Colours, Shewed french Do. & Sheerd off. All the Crew & matterials are Saved. I went on the Spot & had the mortification to See the recke of our poor privateer, which deserved a better fate! I am back late last night with the Men & the Brave Captn. Dowlin. On my arrival, I Learnt that it was The Calonne[6] Commanded by the Ignorant Captn. Guilman, on the first of his Command, that had run our poor

5. His name was Boucault: Sartine to BF, April 24, below; Diot & Co. to BF, Aug. 16, 1780 (APS).

6. A Le Havre privateer with a crew of two hundred commanded by François-Joseph Guilleman: Henri Malo, *Les derniers corsaires. Dunkerque (1715–1815)* (Paris, 1925), p. 141.

Black Prince a Shore. He made a report here on the Subject, fit to Justiffy him Self, but the guard of the Fort that fired on his frigate, & thousands people on the Shore, who saw every thing of this Stupid & Villanous Chace, will Certiffy The above account; & that, She Shewed her Self Clear to every body, to be an English Frigate, & that, Captain Dowlin had fired three Leward guns under French Colours, at different times, an hour before he was forced to run on Shore, or be Taken; & that the Frigate kept up English pendant & flagg all a Long & untill She was fired upon from the Shore. I Beseech Your Excellency to make Complaints on these matters of the Commissary of Morlaix, & of the Ignorant Captn. Guilman, to the Minister of the Navey, Because, The Conduct of both is no Way Tollerable, requires punishment & damages. I wou'd Sooner Sell my Last Shirt, than not procure Soon a Large Cutter for the Intrepid & Clever Captn. Dowlin & I Imagine Your Excellency will readily Back him the Same Commission he has from Congress?

I am going Soon to Cherbourg about the dutch Vessell & the Fitting out of the New Large Cutter for Captn. Edward Macatter, & as She has the name of the Black Princess, his Commission will Serve? The Old & unfit princess is Laid up at Morlaix. I Shall have the honnour to write Your Excellency from Cherbourg, & beseech you will favour me with your answer There.

I have the Honnour to be with Gratitude Honnoured Sir Your Excellency's Most Humble & most Obedient Servant

J. TORRIS
at Mr. De Chantereyne's Cherbourg

Endorsed: April 15

Notation: Mr. Torris April 15. 1780—

From Edward Bancroft   ALS: American Philosophical Society

Honour'd & Dear Sir   Monday Morning 17. april 1780.

This morning at about 4 O'Clock I was awaked by the arrival of Capt. Jones & Mr. Montplaisir from L'Orient. The Latter went forward to Paris, but Capt. Jones not having stopped since he Left L'Orient is lain down for a little Sleep. I shall call him in about half an hour & as soon after as he can dress I suppose he will wait on you. He brought me the inclosed Letter from Mr. Wharton,[7] which will inform you of almost all that I yet Know except that the Kings officers at L'Orient have begun to cut up & Pull down a considerable part of the internal partitions &c of the Ship Seraphis, which has much increased the discontent of the Alliance's Crew.

I am ever with the utmost respect & Affection Honoured & Dear Sir Your most Humble & Devoted Servant

EDWD. BANCROFT

Addressed: A Monsieur / Monsieur Franklin / Ministre Plenipo-tentiare &c / en son Hotel / a Passy

Notation: Ewd: Bancroft 17, April 1780.

From Thomas Digges: Two Letters

(I) and (II) ALS: Historical Society of Pennsylvania

I.

Dr. Sir   London Apr 17. 1780

Dr. J. Harvey Pierce,[8] and Mr. William Sprague will hand you this. They are two professional & good men who mean to quit this Country for a better, & will I make no doubt carry over knowlege & political opinions which will be beneficial to any part of our Country where they may fix for life. Their particular intentions will be best explaind to you by themselves. They propose travelling thro France to Nantes and take their passage from that or some adjacent port for America. In the doing this your advice & help will be very beneficial to them, and I beg leave to ask it for them.

7. Missing.
8. John Harvey Pierce, a surgeon: P.J. and R.V. Wallis, eds., *Eighteenth Century Medics (subscriptions, licences, apprenticeships)* (2nd ed., Newcastle, Eng., 1988), p. 459.

I am with great truth & Respect Dr Sir Your Obedt Servt
Th Digges

P.S.—I gave you a line by Post the 14th. since which there is nothing new or any arrivals from the Wtward

Notation: April 17. 1780.

II.

Dr. Sir   London Apr. 17. 1780
    Mr. Saml Bailey (of Newberry Port) has been with me & I am trying to get him out in a direct road to his home. He has related His singular storey to me.[9] It appears manifest to me that the Privateer who took him had no right to commit such an act of hostility so near the shore of a Neutral Country; The People of Flores, particularly the Governor or Commandant, were openly hostile to the Americans & appeard to have given information to the English Privateer (calld the Achilles Capt Wm. Yawkins beloning to London) to come round from another part of the Island of Flores to seize the American Ship. Just before the period of their striking to the Cutter, seventeen of the Men belonging to the Bemus made their Escape in the boat to the Island and are left there in a miserable situation. Their names & discreption are below. Can any means be usd to get them away? There is no trade to the Island of Flores save in the summer time just after the Harvest. A few ships goes from Lisbon for the *only* produce of the Island *Wheat*. I am yr very Obt Ser   T.D

> Captain —— Pettice of Middletown Connecticut
> John Lewis Boatswain of the Ship Behmus
> Danl Ely Cooper to make the Hhds. for the Molasses
> Thos. Merrell ⎫
> Saml Foot ⎬ Seamen, all of Newberry Port
> Saml Long ⎭

    9. Digges enclosed a deposition of Capt. Nathaniel Harris of the ship *Behmus* (or *Behemus*) of Newburyport, which related the story of the capture of his ship at the island of Flores in the Azores; Harris and Bailey were taken to Falmouth: Elias and Finch, *Letters of Digges*, pp. 195–7. Bailey did return to Newburyport and in 1782 was part-owner of a small ship: Charles Henry Lincoln, comp., *Naval Records of the American Revolution 1775–1788* (Washington, D.C., 1906), p. 431.

———— Dorrington Seaman, an Englishman
———— Forgoson an Englishman
Enock Rolf—Newberry
two Boys
———— Young New berry Port
and five others names forgot

When the Vessel was taken She was within one quarter of a mile of the shore on the western part of the Island & near one of the two small villages of the Island. N.B. there is only two villages like *Whigwams* on the Island one to the Et. and the other to the Wt.

From Dumas

ALS: American Philosophical Society; AL (draft): Algemeen Rijksarchief

Monsieur   Amsterdam 17 Avril 1780.
Je suis ici depuis Samedi, chez Mrs. De Neufville,[1] qui me sachant accablé de chagrin à Lahaie, m'ont pressé de passer quelques jours chez eux pour le dissiper, s'il est possible. Si quelque chose est capable de produire cet effet, ce devra certainement être l'amitié de ces braves gens, qui viennent de me convaincre, non seulement que *amicus certus in re incerta cernitur*,[2] mais aussi, qu'ils sont & seront toujours attachés aux Intérêts des Etats-unis. J'ose donc avancer hardiment, que cette maison mérite leur confiance, & peut & veut leur être très utile. On m'avoit fait accroire, & à notre Ami aussi, que la Lettre avoit été interceptée tout autrement que par Sir G————. On étoit parvenu, Si ce n'est à me faire croire, du moins à craindre que l'on ne parvînt à détacher de moi & Mrs. De N———— & notre ami. Ma famille venoit de découvrir ce qui se passoit. Ses allarmes & la terreur m'avoit extorqué le 4e. une espece de palinodie dans une Lettre dont je me répentis d'abord, & que je révoquai énergiquement dans une autre Lettre peu d'heures après, & plus

1. Messieurs De Neufville were Jean and Leendert, his son and partner (XXIX, 566n).
2. "A sure friend is discovered in an uncertain affair": Cicero, *De Amicitia*, XVII, 64, quoting the poet Ennius.

fortement encore le lendemain 5e. Notre Ami a entrepris depuis de me réconcilier avec ————. Il me rapporta Vendredi ce qui suit: "On avoit reçu ma Lettre du 5e.: on ne ressentiroit point les expressions par lesquelles j'avois offensé personnellement dans la Lettre interceptée; on ne l'enverroit point en France; mais on persistoit à exiger que je fisse à Sir G—— une réparation dans les formes." J'ai dit à notre Ami que je ne le ferois jamais, parce que je ne pouvois parler contre ma conscience. Il a convenu que je ne devois pas le faire. Je lui ai demandé s'il avoit la moindre objection à ce que je le visse lui-même comme par le passé. Il m'a dit, qu'au contraire je lui ferois plaisir. Seulement, qu'il ne se mêleroit plus de ce qui se passoit entre ———— & moi. Je continuerai donc de vous rendre compte, Monsieur, & au Congrès, de ce qui se passe, de la part de notre ami: & si l'occasion se présente de faire plaisir à ———— je le ferai comme s'il m'honoroit de ses bonnes graces. Peut-être vaincrai-je par là son ressentiment: car quant à la réparation, je ne puis croire qu'il l'exige sérieusement, puisqu'il a dit à *notre ami,* qu'il désapprouvoit l'action qui lui a fait parvenir la Lettre.

Je finis, Monsieur, par vous apprendre, que Vendredi matin les Etats d'Hollande ont accepté unanimement les propositions de la *Russie;*[3] que personne ne doute que L.H.P. ne suivent cet exemple, & que les conférences avec le Plénipotentiaire Russe commenceront, selon toute apparence, incessamment pour les arrangemens à prendre. Je vous félicite de cela de tout mon coeur, Monsieur: car voilà un événement bien important pour l'Amérique. Vraisemblablement ceci nous amenera la paix. C'est le sentiment de notre ami. Je suis chargé de vous présenter les respects de notre ami & de Mrs. De Neufville. Vous connoissez, Monsieur, le respectueux attachement avec lequel je serai toute ma vie De Votre Exce. le très-humble & très obéissant serviteur   DUMAS

Passy à son Exc. Mr. B. Franklin

3. A French translation of the resolution is printed in Sir Francis Piggot and G.W.T. Omond, *Documentary History of the Armed Neutrality 1780 and 1800* (London, 1919), pp. 216–17, under the date of April 13, a Thursday.

Addressed: à Son Excellence / Monsieur B. Franklin, Esqr. / Min. Plenipe. des Etats-unis / &c. / à *Passy.*/.

Notation: Dumas. Amstm. April. 17. 80

From Louis-Guillaume Le Veillard

al: American Philosophical Society

samedy matin. [after April 17, 1780][4]
Mr. Le Veillard souhaite le bonjour a monsieur franklin et le prie de vouloir bien luy faire dire s'il peut le prendre en passant pour aller ensemble diner chéz mr. de Malesherbes, et si monsieur Jones y viendra aussi, mr. de Malesherbes ayant chargé monsieur franklin le petit fils de l'y engager.

Addressed: A Monsieur / Monsieur franklin ministre plenipo- / tentiaire des etats unis / Passy

From John Paul Jones[5] als: University of Pennsylvania Library

Hond. and dear Sir,   Passy April 18th. 1780
Before I sailed from the Isle of Groa on my late expedition I gave written Orders to every Captain under my command, with proper signals of Reconnoissance and three points of Rendezvous in letters sealed up one within another, to be Opened only in case of necessity.— After every necessary arrangement had been made for the departure of my proper squadron, the Com-

---

4. The date of Jones's arrival in Passy.
5. In response to the memoir Sartine had sent bf on April 2; see above. bf soon took Jones to meet Sartine in order to demand that the *Serapis* and *Countess of Scarborough* be sold according to the terms about prizes agreed upon before the cruise. Sartine agreed and promised to issue the necessary orders: Wharton, *Diplomatic Correspondence*, iv, 294. (This meeting probably occurred on the 20th; see bf to Sartine, April 22.) bf also took Jones to the King's *levée* and the following day the captain was presented to Louis: John Paul Jones, "Memoir of the American Revolution," reproduced in Bradford, *Jones Papers*, reel 9, no. 1920, pp. 77–8.

manders of the Privateers the Monsieur and the La Grandville came on Board the Bon homme Richard and asked my leave to accompany me. They had my permission to sail in company with the squadron; but as they had come under no agreement to continue in company and to act under my Orders, I neither gave them signals of Reconnoissance nor points of Rendezvous. I did not consider that I had any authority over them.

The Monsieur seperated from me immediately after I had passed the entrance of the Channel, & the La Grandville seperated from me a few days afterwards on the Coast of Ireland.— They have a right to share in the Prizes that were taken while they were present with the squadron; but any claim in behalf of the La Grandville &c. to prizes that were taken by the squadron after they had seperated from it appears altogether Unreasonable and cannot I believe be admitted by the Rules of any Flag whatsoever.

I am with great esteem and profound respect Sir Your most Obliged and most humble Servant   JNO P JONES

His Excellency B. Franklin Esqr. &c. &c.

Notation: J.P. Jones L'orient April 18. 80

From Juliana Ritchie   ALS: American Philosophical Society

Sir.   Cambray. April 18th. 1780.

The 7th. instant, I was favored with the letter that you did me the honor to write to me the 5th. I beg leave to offer you my sincere thanks—for that proof of your politeness & good nature. Tho' you have not been able to give me any intelligence respecting my husband, yet you have taken a weight from off my spirits, that I am not able to express—as, from your silence, my suffering heart had infered the last event that could befall Mr. Ritchie & that you declined to be my informer thereof.

In Early life, the affections take deep roots, *mine* have never changed. We were two giddy pated young fools, without reflection, judgment, or experience to guide us—free from those *difficulties*—that have proved a cause of bitter affliction to us both, I was sent home to my Father, to remain there 'till such time as Mr. Ritchie had settled His affairs & formed a plan for our re-union, soon as possible; but the event has proved, that I have never seen Him since; fifteen years—I have been left to tread the dangerous paths of life, in a base degenerate world *beset* with many snares— But Heavens Great Mercy has guided me safely through *them all,* without my having incurred one *real* or *imputed* flaw; but so many years spent in painful solicitude & fruitles expectation, successive disapointments—have greatly contributed to distroy my health; sorrows such as mine have been make sad havock in the human frame. The only prospect in which I could rest my hopes of a solace to My *ills* (for these lat-ter years) was the hopes of our passing the latter part of *Our lives* in quietness togather; but of *that* comfort I now despair. The American Warr, the dangers that Mr. Ritchie is exposed to, cast so many bars across my wishes—that I find small ground to An-chor my hopes upon; & the fears I feel for His safety, makes me very meloncholy. Hapily for me, I have some small fortune, set-tled upon my self, so securely in trust—as to admit of no inno-vation, & being reversionary after my death, I could never— (even my-self) convey any part *thereof* (only from *quarter* to *quarter*) to Mr. Ritchie. My yearly *income* is very *small;* yet with oeconomey—& attention, I make it sufficient for my support— without incurring either *debts* or *obligations.* These countries are much cheaper to live in, then any part of England, & as I have Relations here—(one an Abbesse to a Convent of English Bene-dictins[6])—I decided in giving *this* place the preference. I have resided here almost six years—in great retirement. I came first here with a party of Ladies of fashion, from England who stayed with me three years—since which time I have been alone, in a small house, that has a little garden to it that amuses me, & when I go to the Convent, which is Generally to pass the summer

6. The convent at Cambrai was established early in the seventeenth cen-tury. Members of the order devoted themselves to the education of young girls and translated into English a number of French spiritual tracts. Eugène Bouly, *Dictionnaire historique de la Ville de Cambrai* . . . (Cambrai, 1854), p. 449; *Mémoires de la Société d'Emulation de Cambrai,* LXXIV (1927), 139–42 144, 152–3.

months, I lock up the house, take my maid, my birds, my dog, & cat, & march off—all togather.

You see sir I write to you in the confidence of a friend, & I reley upon your known prudence, to not mention anything I have here related to you, 'tis to *your-self* only.

It has been my ardent desire to make you a visit at Paris to have the pleasure of seeing you, & chating with you about many things, but it has so happened that I could never obtain my wish in this respect, tho' I have had two favorable oppertunities offered to me, by most particuler friends—both in the Course of about six months, the first, Sir Patrick & Lady Bellew[7] who pressed me very much to accompany *them*, but I was to *ill* to venture, & last, was Lady Kenmor, who acts like a mother to me. I must now resign *that wish* 'till *happier* days & Climates. I trust firmly in your good heart, to give me any information you may gain on the part of Mr. Ritchie, please to address me at Cambray—(as in case I am gone to England) your Letter will be forwarded safe to me. But from some late accounts I have received from *thence* it appears probable that the concerns I have to *arange there* may be done without my going— I wait for another letter—e'er I decide.

I have real pleasure in knowing that your family were all well in Septr. last— I hope you are in good health, tho' you are silent to me on that head.

I have the honor to be with great respect sir. Your most obliged humble servant   J. RITCHIE

Mr. Franklin.

Mr. Franklin

Notation: Ritchi Cambray April 1780.

7. In response to a request by the Irish Catholic Sir Patrick Bellew BF had drafted a passport for him to return from France to England: xxx, 126, 320.

From Jonathan Williams, Jr.

ALS: University of Pennsylvania Library; copy: Yale University
Library

Dear & honoured Sir.   Nantes April 18. 1780.

I have by order of M. de Chaumont embraced every opportunity I could to send Cloathing to Brest to be thence exported by M. Bersolle to America,[8] and what I have hitherto sent amount to as follows . . . Vizt.

3260 Coats.
3260 Waistcoats
975 Breeches.
3300 Overalls
4530 pr Shoes
2022 Hatts
13032 Shirts
11000 Ells of Linnen for Shirts.
4500 Stocks.
2037 Blankets &c
11 Bales of Hosiery number unknown

These Cloathing are much more unsorted than I wished but as I was pressed in point of Time I thought best to send as much as I possibly could although the Quantities were not in proportion. If it had been possible I should have prefered sending an equal quantity of each kind.—

Mr Bersolle tells me the Fleet is all ready to Sail[9] but as the Wind is contrary I hope these Goods will arrive in time. What method of Conveyance is determined on for the Remainder? I am ever with the greatest Respect most dutifully & Affectionately Your   JONA WILLIAMS J.

Notation: J Williams April 18. 1780

---

8. Around April 16, JW sent to the committee for foreign affairs eleven invoices dating from March 21 to April 15 of all the goods he had sent to Brest. A copy of his letter, giving dates of the invoices, is at the Yale University Library.

9. Ternay's fleet and the transports carrying Rochambeau's army moved to the anchorage off Brest on April 15 and sailed for America on May 2: Rice and Brown, eds., *Rochambeau's Army,* 1, 118.

From John Adams

ALS: American Philosophical Society; copy: Massachusetts Historical Society

Dear sir   Paris April 19. 1780

I have been informed, that the State of Maryland, have named Mr Charmichael, Mr Johnson, Mr Williams, Mr Lloyd, and Mr Jennings, as proper Persons, out of whom they have desired, your Excellency to choose one, in order to draw out of the English Funds a Sum of Money, they have there, for which the Agent is to have two and an' half per Cent.[1]

Mr Charmichael, is otherwise employed, Mr Johnson, Mr Williams, and Mr Lloyd are all proper Persons, but perhaps they may be otherwise employed too, except Mr Lloyd, whose fortune, both by himself and his Wife is so ample that it may be no Object.

Mr Jennings, who is not less qualified than any of them, is a Gentleman of Learning, and Abilities, who has left his Affairs from a Love to his Country to whose service, he devotes his Time. He is now at Brussells. As he is a native of Mary land, perhaps his Pretentions may upon the whole, be superiour to those of others, or this Sentiment may be the Dictate of the Esteem and friendship I conceived for him on Account of his Candor, when I was here before.[2]

I intreat your Excellency, not to consider this, as a desire to dictate in a matter in which I have not right nor Colour, to interfere, and therefore ought to ask your Pardon, for presuming to advise.

If your Excellencys decision should fall upon, any of the other Gentlemen I shall be perfectly content and think no more

1. The governor of Maryland had empowered BF to appoint a replacement if the state's trustees in England failed to act on its instructions: XXXI, 336–8. JA learned about it from Edmund Jenings: *Adams Papers*, IX, 130.

2. JA's admiration for Jenings was so strong that he had recommended him to Elbridge Gerry as a secretary for the American mission in France: *Adams Papers*, VIII, 143. Jenings, who may have been a British agent, had his property confiscated by Maryland on the grounds he was a British subject (although the state later reversed this decision): James H. Hutson, ed., *Letters from a Distinguished American: Twelve Essays by John Adams on American Foreign Policy, 1780* (Washington, 1978), pp. xii–xiii.

of it. I have the Honour to be with, the greatest Respect, Sir your most obedient and most humble Sert   JOHN ADAMS

His Excellency Dr Franklin

Notation: J. Adams. April 19. 1780

From Nicholas George Möeballe[3]

ALS: American Philosophical Society

Middelburg in Zeeland this 19th. of April 1780.—
May it Please Your Excellency
To be reported by your most humble Servant the Subscriber having the Honor to be Known in person by your Excellency as former a Colonel in the American Service, Virginia Troupes,— how that a verry disagreable mormure, as well in the Province of Holland as here, do Compel me, as a thrue friend to the American Cause, to Trouble your Excellency with this present, in Hoopes of your Generous Pardon; and reflection that the only motive of me Writing this, arises from a Sincere attachment to both the united Provinces and united States.

A Vessel call'd the Berkenbosch, belonging to Several Gentlemen in the Province of Zeeland who do Leive here in Middelburg, viz. Messrs. van der Perre & Meÿnders etc. was in the Month of January Capturd bÿ the American Fregat the alliance, Commander Mr. P. Jones, the Said Vessel had Taken its Cargo at Leverpool and was Bound to Livorno, the Cargo consisting in Lead and Haring, the first Wholly belonging to the Gentlemen here, and part of the Haring To Mr. Thos. Violetti at Livorno; And the Vessel with Cargo after being Captur'd, is reported here, to have ben Sent, of for Boston or Philadelphia, all onder

3. Lt. Col. of the Virginia State Garrison Regiment from December, 1778, to August, 1779: E.M. Sanchez-Saavedra, ed., *A Guide to Virginia Military Organizations in the American Revolution, 1774–1787* (Richmond, 1978), p. 122 (where his last name is spelled Moëballé). He also wrote WTF on this date (APS), asking him to forward the present letter. He reported himself in better health, but still in debt, and announced plans to travel to the Dutch East Indies. When he was in Paris BF loaned him two *louis:* Möeballe to WTF, Dec. 12 and 29, 1779 (APS).

pretext that such Vessel & Cargo Should be English property; and Whereas the Honorable Gentlemen owners, perfectly well are Known by me, to be the most powerfull and most distinguished in Rank in this Province; and that the Same, before this disagreable inteligence ariv'ed here; by evry occasion deed assure me of their real attachment to America, as they actually, by Several Vessels, have fournish'd the American Correspondents in france with Such articles as America may be wanting, and whereas upon her(?) producing of me American Papers only, I have ben Honored and assiste'd by the Say'd Gentlemen; I have thought it me duty to enquire especially into this matters, at the Same Time assured those Honorable Gentlemen, that this Capture is a mistake only and by no means Consistent with the ordres of Congress; in a manner that the Vessel, Cargo & Crew will be resituted and dammages payd, by properly aplying to your Excellency. In the most Sanguine hoope to meet with your aprobatie for zo doing, and that it may please your Excellen'y, to report Such real fact to Congress, for a Speedy execution, in zo much more as this action otherwys'e might proove alienating both Countries each from another; especially those real owners, which were the most attagh'd to the American Cause, and unhappily own the first Vessel belonging to the united Provinces, that was Captured by the American Power.— It is reported here and in Holland, that the Captain of the aforementiond Vessel has been compelled to give a Certificate setting forth, that, the Cargo was English properties, which I do hope not to be the Thruth; and the Papers there about may be better Testimonies. This I have thought me duty to report your Excellency, as I have an oportunity, and am enable'd to give a thrue report viz. that both Vessel & Cargo do realy belong to the Honorable Mesr. van der Perre & Meÿnders etc: all residing In this Town, exept for as much of part of the Hareng, as do belong to Livorno.— I have the Honor to remain Your Excellencis! most obedient humble & Sincere Servant   NICS: GEO. MÖEBALLE

To His Excellency Doctor Franklin Minister Pleniptaire. for the united States, in France—etc etc etc

His Excellency The Ambassador for the united States of America by His most Christian Majesty & & &c.

From Pierre-Simon-Benjamin Duvivier[4]

ALS: American Philosophical Society

Monsieur   Ce 20 avril 1780.

La Médaille dont Votre excellence m'a chargé est gravèe[5] et je la regarde comme finie, je desirerois avant de faire tremper les coins avoir lhonneur de vous en montrer les Epreuves pour profiter de vos avis pendant quil en est encore temps. Pouriez vous me fixer un jour ou je pourois estre sur de vous rencontrer chez vous, ou bien en venant a Paris voudriez vous m'honorer de votre visite et m'en prevenir par un mot d'écrit. Vous verriez chez moy une grande quantité de mes ouvrages que je n'ai pas pu vous porter et qui vous donneroient Surement la confiance pour les autres mèdailles que vous devez faire graver et aux quelles je m'appliquerai comme a celle de Mr. le chevalier de fleury dont jespere que vous serez content.

Jai lhonneur d'estre avec respect de Votre Excellence Le tres humble et tres obeissant Serviteur   B DuVivier

Addressed: a Son Excellence / Son Excellence Monsieur / Franklin Ministre des Etats / unis d'Amerique près le Roy / de france / a Passy

Notation: B DuVivier ce Avril 20. 1780

From John Paul Jones

ALS: Archives du Ministère des affaires étrangères; copy: American Philosophical Society

Honored and Dear Sir,   Passy April 20th. 1780

It is now near two Years since I was honored by an invitation from the Court of Versailles to continue in Europe, accompa-

---

4. Known as Benjamin (1730–1819), he came from a family of numismatic engravers and was himself one of the most prolific in French history. Duvivier was named *graveur des médailles de Sa Majesté* in 1761 and was elected to the Académie royale de peinture et de sculpture in 1776. He engraved all the coins used during the reign of Louis XVI, in addition to innumerable medals. See Henry Nocq, *Les Duvivier*... (Paris, 1911); *DBF*.

5. The congressional medal for Fleury.

nied with a promise of being thereby the more usefully employed against the common Enemy.[6] This invitation I accepted with your and your Colleagues approbation, and my best endeavours have been exerted for the common Cause, as well as to manifest my Gratitude to the King, to his Ministers, and to this generous-minded Nation.— I have not as you will beleive served in this War for Riches, but for Glory and a Glorious Cause; and as I am now returning to my Duty in America[7] I should be happy to carry with me to the Congress of the United States such Testimony of his Majesties approbation as my conduct may be thought to have merited during my absence from that Country.[8]

I am with the most affectionate esteem and respect Dear Sir Your most obliged most obedient and most humble Servant

JNO P JONES

His Excellency B. Franklin Esquire Minister Plenipotentiary &c. &c. for America at the Court of France.

Notation: Le Commodore Paul Jones

From Antoine-François Prost de Royer[9]

ALS: American Philosophical Society

Monsieur   Lyon 20. avril 1780

Malgré vos grandes occupations et le tourbillon ou vous avez vécu, vous pourrez encore vous souvenir que J'ai eu l'honneur de vous faire ma cour chez vous en 1776 et 1777 Rue Jacob a l'ho-

6. An invitation solicited by Jones: XXVI, 237, 606–7.

7. Jones's return to the *Alliance* at Lorient was delayed, however; he was prevailed upon to remain in Passy with Edward Bancroft for six more weeks: Morison, *Jones,* pp. 275–9.

8. BF forwarded the present letter to Vergennes on April 23, requesting that he give it such attention as he judged proper: AAE.

9. Prost de Royer (1729–1784) was a jurist, public official, and member of the Académie de Lyon, who edited a four-volume *Dictionnaire de jurisprudence* . . . (Lyon, 1781–4): Larousse. This letter was not sent from Lyon, but brought to Paris by the chevalier de Pougens, who included it in his own of May 8, below.

tel d'hambourg, et de vous voir souvent chez M. Paulze et M. Elie de Baumont mon ami.[1] Je vous laissai même un mémoire des objets de commerce qui pourroient etablir des raports entre nos provinces et les Etats unis. Je Saisis avec empressement l'occasion de me raprocher de vous.

Mon premier objet dans cette demarche est de vous presenter M. le Chevalier de Pougens des Comtes de Riviere oudeville,[2] nom connu dans les trois Royaumes, puisqu'en 1474 cette famille a donné a l'angleterre une Reine dans la personne d'yzabeau femme d'Edouard IV. Les noms anciens ne sont rien pour vous comme pour moi. Lé Chevalier de Pougens a d'autres titres a un bon accueil de votre part. Ce sont ses vertus et l'etendue de ses connoissances.

Destiné a Jouer un Rolle dans le corps diplomatique, placé a Rome depuis 3 ans sous les yeux de M. le Cardinal de Bernis,[3] la même petite verole qui a mis au tombeau la Marquise de Puymonbrun sa niece et l'abbé d'aix secretaire d'Ambassade,[4] a privé le Chevalier de Ces bons yeux avec lesquels Il se delassoit en peignant si bien, et Il S'occupoit en parcourant les biblioteques de Rome, comme Il avoit connu celle du Roi.

Apres avoir fait ici pendant pres d'une année des remedes en partie inutiles, determinè a rejoindre sa patrie, et a y vivre dans la retraite, Il a formè la plus vaste entreprise de litterature. Il vous montrera sans doute, Monsieur, le prospectus qu'il a fait Im-

1. BF resided at the Hôtel d'Hambourg in January and February 1777: XXIII, 100. During this period he indeed was in contact with Jacques Paulze and Jean-Baptiste-Jacques Elie de Beaumont.

2. Marie-Charles-Joseph, chevalier de Pougens (1755–1833), an illegitimate son of the Prince de Conti, became one of the best known scholars of his day and published numerous works of philosophy, literature, and lexicography in spite of the affliction described below: Quérard, *France littéraire*. Royer here claims that Pougens was a descendent of Richard Woodville, first Earl Rivers (d. 1469), whose daughter Elizabeth married King Edward IV in 1464: *DNB*.

3. François-Joachim de Pierre, Cardinal de Bernis (1715–1794), a former foreign minister of France, served as the French ambassador in Rome from 1769 to 1791: *DBF; Repertorium der diplomatischen Vertreter*, III, 128. Pougens stayed with him from 1776 to 1779: Frédéric Masson, *Le Cardinal de Bernis depuis son ministère 1758–1794* (Paris, 1884), p. 380.

4. The abbé Deshaises died of smallpox on Feb. 13, 1779, the marquise du Puy-Montbrun on May 3, 1779: Masson, *Cardinal de Bernis*, pp. 380–1.

primer ici. En le lisant vous serez etonné de l'etendue des Connoissances qu'il Indique; vous le serez encore plus, quand vous saurez qu'il l'a dicté, et quil n'a pas Vingt cinq ans.

Vous aurez droit, Monsieur, a son hommage par vos vertus, par vos actions, par l'etendue et la bienfaisance de vos connoissances. Je ne fais que vous l'annoncer, et je ne doute pas que vous ne me sachiez gré de vous l'annoncer. Vous êtes le Platon de notre Europe; C'est un jeune philosophe que Je vous présente. Pourriez vous le repousser?

Le 2e. objet de ma lettre est de mettre sous vos yeux le prospectus d'un grand ouvrage que Je vais publier et qui est un dictionnaire de la Jurisprudence francoise.

Independament des choses vraiment Interessantes que Je rassemblerai Dans ce cadre sur l'administration, le droit public, la police, et la procedure criminelle, je dois y parler de quelques Etats, de leurs lois, de leur Jurisprudence. Or les Etats unis de l'amerique ne doivent être oubliés, ni a cause de leur excellente legislation, ni a cause de leur raport avec la france.

Le 2e. Volume que Je mettrai sous presse dans deux ou trois mois, contiendra le mot amerique, Etats unis de l'amerique.

Il ne seroit pas Indifferend, Monsieur, et Il Seroit digne de votre bienfaisance, de me mettre a portée de traiter a fond cet article.

J'ai bien le petit volume Imprimé en 1777 qui contient les differentes constitutions. Mais cela suffit Il?

Vous pourriez me donner ou me faire donner un tableau raccourci, bien Interessant. Vous pourriez me mettre a portée de critiquer ce qui vous paroitroit devoir etre changé. Et cela pourroit n'etre pas Indifferend pour la prosperité même de votre souveraineté naissante.

Ayez la bonté, Monsieur, de reflechir sur ma demande. Songez que mon grand ouvrage, attendu avec Impatience, sera classique, et pourra avoir beaucoup d'Influence sur les raports qui unissent les deux nations.

Si Je connoissois moins la sublimité de votre âme, je ne vous parlerois pas avec cette franchise mais votre bonté me rassure.

Je reviens a mon chevalier qui brule de vous voir. Je vous atteste que c'est l'homme le plus vertueux et le plus savant que Jaye vu a son âge. Jai vécu avec fontenelle, Montesquieu, haller, Voltaire, Rousseau, et Jai eu le bonheur de vous voir.

276

Il me reste a vous offrir ici mes services, mon zele, et tout ce qui est en moi; trop heureux, Si vous me mettiez en etat de vous y donner des preuves des Sentimens et de ladmiration que vous m'avez Inspirés.

Je Suis avec respect Monsieur Votre tres humble et tres obeissant serviteur   DE ROYER

M. franklin

From George Scott   ALS: American Philosophical Society

Sir   Naples 20th. April 1780

I arrived here safe on the Evening of the 13th. Currt. after a very dilatory & tedious Journey. On leaving Paris Monsr. L'Abbé Rozier happend to be one of the Company in the Coach & was particularly civil to me. He went no further than Lyons. Here I took the Coch D'Eau for Avignion, a great number in the Boat amongst the number the Marquis de Clugny shewed me great civillities, he was going to Toulon, & from thence to join his Regiment on Corsica. From Avignion I hired a Chaize for Marseilles: was 3 days upon the Road. Staid 4 Days at Marseilles & then went on board a Genoese Vessell departing for Naples— On this Vessell we were a month before we made Civita Vecchia, here staid a few days & hired a Chaize for Rome staid here 5 or 6 Days to see Curiosities & then hired a Chaize for this place & was 4 Days on the road— This is a very good Town & living reasonable.

I have been very kindly received by Sir Wm. Hamilton[5] who has treated me with all possible affabillity & yesterday delivered my Memorial to the Minister of State[6] & he will enforce it with all his power. I don't yet know the event.

5. British envoy to the Court of Naples: xx, 78n. For his residence there during the American Revolution see Brian Fothergill, *Sir William Hamilton: Envoy Extraordinary* (London, 1969), pp. 134–7.

6. Sir John Francis Edward Acton (1736–1811), a political ally of Hamilton. Of English extraction, Acton came to Naples in 1778 to reorganize the navy. A favorite of Queen Maria Carolina, he rapidly advanced to become prime minister. *DNB;* Fothergill, *Hamilton*, p. 176. Scott's memorial may have had to do with his trading ventures.

On my arrival here a Letter met me from our excellent friend Dr. P——; he desires me when I have the pleasure to see you again to deliver a message to you but as that is rather uncertain I have resolved to transmit you a copy of the whole letter here enclosed.[7] When I shall leave this place is at present uncertain. We have very warm weather, in short it is summer. Roads dusty & Sultry. Vegitables very forward & in very great plenty of all kinds— Very fine sallading Cabbages, Colliflowers, Green pease, Beans, Asparagus, Artichokes &c in abundance & very good Shambles Meat of all kinds, & plenty of Poultry & Fish— In passing thro' this Kingdom I percieved the Corn very forward. I saw many hundreds of Acres of Wheat with the ears fully shot. Grass is forward also. I desire my best compliments to Mr. Franklin Junr. & believe me to be with great sincerity & regard Dr Sir Your Mo: Obedt. Servant   GEO: SCOTT

We have wine both Red & White in great plenty & tollerably reasonable. I pay 6 Grains for a paris bottle & this is near 5 sous french money, but then I take a dozen together. In Taverns they charge 15 Grains.[8]

Dr. Franklin

Addressed: The Honourable / Benj: Franklin Esqr. / Passy / J.H. Myers

Notation: Scott, Naples 20. april 1780.

From James Turing & Son   ALS: American Philosophical Society

Sir!   Middelburg 20th. April 1780.
    We did Ourselves the honor of adressing your Excellency the 28th. October last, requesting Your Excellency would conde-

7. The enclosed letter, whose date (except for the year) is obscured by a tear in the manuscript, was from Joseph Priestley: Scott to BF, May 13, below. He thanks Scott for delivering two letters (as yet unanswered). Will Scott present his respects to their friend when he sees him and inform him that his letter (probably BF's of Feb. 8: XXXI, 455–7) was satisfactory? His greatest wish is to see him ambassador to England from the "free states of America." APS.
    8. The Neapolitan monetary unit was the ducat, containing 100 grani:

scend to forward Some Documents to Mr. J. Williams at Boston, tending to Empower him to Sue for & reclaim from Capt Babcock on his Sureties, Our Brigg the Brunetta late commanded by Capn Griffiey, about which your Excellency was pleased to Correspond with us at that time[9] and we trust Said Gentleman, will on Your Excellencys Recommendation & countenance, pursue in earnest the reclaim & procure an adequate Redress: And being told Some time Since, but with what foundation we cannot Say, that the Brunetta was arrived at Boston, We beg again to trouble your Excellency on the Subject, to inquire whether your Excellency has received any reports about the Said vessel, & what hopes we can form of Succeeding in Our aplications. We crave again Your Excellency's indulgence for this intrusion and remain with profound Veneration Sir Your Excellency's most Obedient & Devoted humble Servants   JAMES TURING & SON

To John Adams

LS:[1] Massachusetts Historical Society; copy:[2] Library of Congress

Dear Sir,   Passy, April 21. 1780.

The Letter your Excellency did me the honour of writing to me Yesterday,[3] gives me the first Information of the Resolution mentioned as taken by the State of Maryland relating to their

---

Franz Pick-René Sédillot, *All the Monies of the World* . . . (New York, 1971), p. 348. There were 20 sous in an *l.t.* BF had recently paid 150 *l.t.* for a cask (approximately 110 gallons) of burgundy: XXX, 632n; Ronald Edward Zupko, *A Dictionary of English Weights and Measures* . . . (Madison, Milwaukee, and London, 1968), p. 33.

9. XXX, 437–8, 510. The present letter is the last extant communication between the firm and BF.

1. In WTF's hand.

2. Dated April 22 in BF's letterbook. It has a postscript: "*Upon a separate paper.* Mr. franklin presents his compts. to Mr. Adams and requests he would send him by the Bearer the Book of Treaties, which he has just now occasion to consult, but will return it in a day or two." BF may have wanted it to find an Anglo-Danish treaty mentioned by Baron de Blome, the Danish envoy, for which see BF to Huntington, May 31.

3. Actually the 19th; the letter is above.

Money in England. If there is no Mistake in the Intelligence, (which I apprehend there may be) and such a Power as is supposed should come to my Hands, I shall then take your Excellency's Recommendation, (which has great Weight with me) into Consideration. At present I can only say that I shall not name my Nephew Mr. Williams. For tho' I have a great Opinion of his Ability, and Integrity, and think that by his early Declaration and Attachment to our Cause, and Activity in its Service, he has a good deal of Merit with the States in general, I know of none that he has with Maryland in particular; and as the other four are Natives of that State, I think the Choice ought to be from among them. Mr. Williams will however be very sensible of the Honour done him by being put into the Nomination.

With the greatest Respect, I have the Honour to be Your Excellency's most obedt and most humble Servant.   B FRANKLIN

His Exy. John Adams Esqr.

From James Hutton

ALS: American Philosophical Society

Dear Sir   Queens Row Pimlico. 21. April 1780.

Our last year's Voyage to & from Labradore was a safe one, the Eskimaux remain friendly, and our people at both Missions were well. Many thanks to you for the last year's Passport,[4] which I here return again, that you may be sure no ill use can be made of it by us. Our Captain Mugford is this year not in such a state of Health as to be able to perform the Voyage, so we take the Mate in his Room, He has beggd us if possible to get a Vessel with two masts, that in case one was damaged in hard weather, there might yet be a mast remaining, as in case of the Loss of the only mast, they might perish for want of succour in those unfrequented Seas. We have agreed to his Request & bought a small Brigg with two masts, very little bigger than the former, the Description of which, is, as under the Brigg, Amity, Captain, James Fraser, about 75 Tons, Square Stern'd, navigated by 7 men.

4. XXIX, 308–9.

I Should be much obliged to you, if you would be so kind as to send another Pass according to the above Description, so that it may be here before the twentieth of May at latest.[5]
We are all sorry for the Loss of Capt. Cooke. I hope the Papers that are on the way hither from Kamschatka will come safe.[6]
I know not whether you could procure us a Spanish Pass, or whether I should apply to Mr de Sartine. I shall mention it to Him, who will probably forward this.
We had two old Persons at our Labradore Mission one, an old Lutheran Minister, a Dane, Drachardt by name, who had been a dozen years employd by the Danes in their Mission in Greenland, He in his Heroic way, though He had been many years retired to Hernhutt, as soon as He heard of a Mission to Labradore, dedicated his Life & Labours freely and eagerly to that Service, and ended his Days there after a chearful laborious Life,[7] the other, was a Surgeon from Wurtemberg, very skilful & much respected in his own Country, his name was Waiblinger.[8] These two old men died about the same time and were buried at the same time, as these were much loved by the natives, many of them, all that were near, were at the burying, and many of them lost their horrur for Death.
Since then, a younger man, born & bred among us has offerd his Service, to succeed Waiblinger, his name is Kriegelstein, Son of one of our first Brethren[9] himself a Physician.

5. BF sent a passport, which was dated May 17: XXIX, 308n.
6. While in search of the Northwest Passage between the Pacific and Atlantic, Cook's ships, the *Resolution* and *Discovery,* visited the Kamchatka Peninsula of Russia in 1778. After Cook's death the ships returned to Britain with his journals, revisiting the Kamchatka area en route; they arrived at the Orkney Islands in August, 1780: Richard Hough, *The Last Voyage of Captain James Cook* (New York, 1979) pp. 158–68, 240–1.
7. In 1751 Lawrence Drachart had joined in suggesting the founding of the Moravian mission in Labrador: J. Taylor Hamilton, *A History of the Church Known as the Moravian Church* . . . (Bethlehem, Penn., 1900), p. 181. Herrnhut in Saxony was an early Moravian center: *ibid.,* pp. 26–48.
8. Perhaps a relative of John George Waiblinger (d. 1775), one of the early leaders of the church: *ibid.,* pp. 71, 237.
9. An early disciple named Krügelstein had been imprisoned in Russia (*ibid.,* p. 208); this may be an alternate spelling of the name.

Mrs Hewson's friend Mrs Dolly[1] is well, and will lend me the last volume, newly published of my friends Papers.

I am Dear Sir your most obedient & obliged humble Servant

JAMES HUTTON

If there be no other way of sending the Passport in time & with certainty, it may be sent by the Post directed to me No. 10. Nevil's Court Fetter Lane Fleetstreet. I have mentioned the 20th of May as the last Term, but it may be sent as much sooner as you please, if there be an opportunity. I hope Mr Wharton is well.

Addressed: Caro B. Fr.

Notation: Hutton 21. avril 1780

From Timothy Matlack[2]   ALS: American Philosophical Society

Sir,   Philadelphia April 21. 1780

To you as President of the American Philosophical society, I beg leave to enclose an oration delivered last month before that respectable society.[3] The revd. Dr Ewing had long ago been appointed to perform this annual duty; but he being chosen Provost of the University, and that seminary having greatly suffered during the war, his whole time and attention were required to reestablish its reputation—[4] he therefore declined the oration. The

1. Hutton had known Dorothea (Dolly) Blunt since at least 1770: XVII, 223.
2. Matlack (d. 1829), from whom BF at one time had held or rented property, was secretary of the Supreme Executive Council. In 1779 he became an *ex officio* member of the Board of Trustees of the College of Philadelphia. He was elected to the APS in 1780 and became an active member of the Society. See II, 351; XXII, 514–15; *DAB;* Douglas M. Arnold, *A Republican Revolution: Ideology and Politics in Pennsylvania, 1776–1790* (New York, 1989), pp. 310–11; *Jefferson Papers,* IV, 545n; *Early Proceedings of the American Philosophical Society* . . . (Philadelphia, 1884), *passim.* As far as we know, this is the only piece of extant correspondence between Matlack and BF.
3. Matlack was appointed on Feb. 17 to deliver the annual oration to the Society. His address extolled the benefits of agriculture and the republican virtues of industry and economy: Timothy Matlack, *An Oration Delivered March 16, 1780* . . . (Philadelphia, 1780); *Early Proceedings* . . . , p. 106. The copy he enclosed is missing.
4. Life at the College of Philadelphia was severely disrupted during the

short time which could be allowed to compose it, deterred those who were anxious to establish, or preserve, a literary character from the undertaking; but, as I had no wish to appear any thing more than I am, the task was very easy to me, and an apology for so crude a performance is only necessary on account of the society, not on my account.

I have the greater pleasure in enclosing this piece to you, as it affords me an opportunity of recommending to your notice a very worthy young Gentleman, Doctor John Foulke, son of Judah Foulke late of this city.[5] His abilities and application to his studies have gained him great respect here, and will recommend him abroad. He has undergone a regular examination before the Trustees of the late College; but by the change in that institution he is prevented from obtaining a diploma, the proper officers not being yet appointed. I know that your benevolent disposition renders it unnecessary to ask your favour toward so valuable a

---

Revolution. American troops were quartered there, and during the occupation of the city it was used as a British military hospital. Efforts of college officials to restore it were complicated by the reorganization that the Constitutionalist Party imposed upon it in 1779. The Pa. Assembly replaced the old board of trustees, renamed the institution the University of the State of Pennsylvania, and prescribed new oaths of loyalty to the state government. Dr. John Ewing, a Presbyterian clergyman and natural philosopher (XI, 526n; XVII, 11–13, 176–7, 211–12), was appointed to succeed William Smith as provost. See Edward P. Cheyney, *History of the University of Pennsylvania 1740–1940* (Philadelphia, 1940), pp. 116–32; Robert L. Brunhouse, *The Counter-Revolution in Pennsylvania 1776–1790* (New York, 1971), pp. 77–9; Arnold, *A Republican Revolution*, pp. 187–8.

5. Several prominent Philadelphians wrote on behalf of John Foulke (1757–1796), son of the Philadelphia Quakers Mary and Judah Foulke. He went to Europe to continue his medical training, studying at Paris, Leipzig, and, after the conclusion of hostilities, London: Foulke to BF, Oct. 12, 1781, and to WTF, April 12, 1783. APS. Upon his return to Philadelphia he became an active member of the APS, served on the staff of the Pennsylvania Hospital, and was a fellow of the College of Physicians. He delivered popular lectures on pneumatics and anatomy. See Horace M. Lippincott, "Dr. John Foulke, 1780, A Pioneer in Aeronautics," *Gen. Mag. and Hist. Chron.*, XXXIV (1931–32), 525–33; Whitfield J. Bell, Jr., "Philadelphia Medical Students in Europe, 1750–1800," *PMHB*, LXVII (1943), 3, 8, 20, 22, 23, 29; Lyman H. Butterfield, ed., *Letters of Benjamin Rush* (2 vols., Princeton, 1951), I, 250–2. Foulke and WTF became friends and corresponded throughout Foulke's European stay; their letters are at the APS.

young man; otherwise I should have warmly solicited your interest in his behalf.

The indians have made an attack on our Frontiers, which will distress the inhabitants of Northampton and Northumberland exceedingly.[6] The settlements in those counties being so widely spread, occasions very great difficulties and leaves nothing to be done for their defence, but by invading the indian country, which must be attempted if possible.

I am with the greatest respect Your Excellencys most obedient and very humble servant   T MATLACK

His Excellency Benjamin Franklin Esqr. Minister Plenipotentiary of the United states of America at the Court of France

To John Ross
Copy: Library of Congress

Sir,   Passy, April 22[–June 3] 1780.

I duly received your favours of the 14th. & 17th. Instant.[7] I am sorry to understand from you that the wollens are in such a situation as to endanger their being lost to the states: But do not see why it should be expected of me to point out a Vessel for them to be shipt in, or to approve or accept of any Contract you may make for the freight of them. The affair is yours, I never had

6. In the several months following Gen. John Sullivan's savage expedition against the Iroquois (May-November, 1779) small war parties went out to attack white settlements in New York and Pennsylvania, including the Wyoming Valley of the Susquehanna River in Northumberland County: Barbara Graymont, *The Iroquois in the American Revolution* (Syracuse, N.Y., 1972), p. 229.

7. Those are missing, but two letters to WTF survive, written from Lorient. The first, of April 17, concerned a small bill and order of Hopkinson's, and offered to carry letters to America. The second, dated April 19, began by apologizing for his April 17 letter to BF regarding the *Serapis*, which could be ignored. Ross had just received permission from Necker to transport the woolens at Noirmoutier to Lorient, to be shipped on the *Alliance* duty-free, but as that ship could not take them, would WTF ask BF to send instructions? If Jones received command of the *Serapis*, Capt. Green could take over the *Alliance*. APS.

any thing to do with it; I know nothing of it, and am quite sick of meddling as I have been too often induced to do with a kind of Business that I am utterly unacquainted with. If you like Messrs. Gourlade and Moylan's Vessel to send them in, and approve of their Terms, but want my assistance to pay the freight, I will help you so far. Your retaining the sail cloth Linnens, &c. as a Security for the Payment of your advances, is what I suppose you have a Right to do, I am sure I have none to make any objection to it, nor Should I make any if you thought fit to keep the Cloth also. The long and fruitless attendance you mention, without receiving relief from an order of Congress which you suppose in my Possession, was not occasioned by any fault of mine, since I never gave you any Expectation of paying your Ballance and have done all in my Power that the order requir'd of me. Indeed I cannot find among the Papers any orders relating to your affairs. I wish to see a Copy of that you mention. If I remember right, it was only an Order that you should settle your Accounts with the Commissioners here, which Is done; not an order that they should pay the Ballance. I thank you for your kind offer of carrying Letters for me, and Shall trouble you with a few, one to our common worthy friend Mr. Morris, and heartily wish you a prosperous Voyage.

I am excedingly griev'd at the Discontents that you mention among the People of the alliance. Unforeseen Accidents have occasioned Delays in procuring for them their Prise-money: but the exactest Justice will be done them as soon as possible. I know not what the Manoeuvres are that you mention, which every American will ever consider as an insult offered to the united States. I am sorry to see in some of our Countrymen a Disposition in all occasions to censure and exclaim against the Conduct of this Court towards us, without being well acquainted with facts, or considering the many & substantial Benefits we have received and are continually receiving from its friendship and Good will to us.

June 3. The above was written when dated, but not sent. I now understand that the Ariel is lent us, to help in carrying our Goods, and I hope you will be able to ship your Cloths without freighting any vessel. I have received several Letters from you containing Propositions relating to the Serapis, and demanding money of me;[8] all of which were impossible for me to comply with, and I have not answered them. I had often before assur'd you that I had not the means of complying with your demands, and I take it unkind of you that you still worry me continually with a Repetition of them. It tells me that you do not believe me. I am sorry I have so little Credit with you. My Conduct towards you, (give me leave to remind you) has been more friendly. When you had first embarrass'd your self with a Debt of 20,000 £ sterling in Europe, I interested my self with the other Commissioners, to engage their Consent to furnish you with that Sum. You had it on a Promise to replace it Soon. Instead of doing so, you made use of the fresh Credit it gave you to run in debt as much more. I have had that Tenderness for you, that I not only never dunn'd you for a Compliance with your Promise, but I never before even, hinted your Default to you; tho' often much embarrass'd for want of the Money. And you dunn me for 20,000 £ more, as if I really owed Such a Sum to you. Yet I beg you will consider this, and Spare me for the future.

Whether you proceed to america, or stay longer here, I wish you all Success and Prosperity in your affairs being with much Esteem (tho' put a Little out of humour) Your very sincere friend, and most obedient humble Servant

Mr. Ross.

(sent June 3d. 1780)

---

8. The only letters from Ross that survive from this period are directed to WTF (APS). On May 3 he sends thanks for having taken care of Hopkinson's order. The letter of May 10 concerns his plan for buying the *Serapis*, and urges BF to pay him what he is owed. WTF can quickly determine that sum by reviewing the accounts Ross left in his care. If cash cannot be immediately procured, then Ross will settle for a credit on Mr. Grand. Capt. Jones's delay in leaving Paris means that several vessels are detained, at great daily expence. On May 15, Ross sends bills arrived from America and mentions that several letters for BF are being forwarded that day.

To Sartine

Sir   Passy, April 22 1780.

The Bearer waits upon your Excellency for the order you were so good as to promise on thursday last, for the sale of the Prizes taken by the squadron under Commodore Jones.[9] He waits here for that order only and the ship must be detained at a great expence till it can be executed.

With the greatest Respect I am your Excellency's, most obedient and most humble servant.

His Exy. Mr. De Sartine.

From William Carmichael

Dear Sir,   Madrid 22d[–27] April 1780.

I have at length the pleasure of being relieved from much Anxiety by the Receipit of your Letter of the 31st. of March and 7th. of April. I endeavoured to recollect every Circumstance of my Conduct since I left france, and altho' I found in this Scrutiny that I had left many things undone which I ought to have done, I brought myself in not guilty biased perhaps by that sort of Partiality we usually feel for ourselves. Your Letters have undoubtedly met the fate of several Adressed to me here by others either under a fictitious or my real name. My Impatience to hear from you hurried me to the Post office every day the Courier arrived, and I carefully read the List of Letters there, but M. Clement[1] never made his Appearance. The Ct. de Montmorin soon after my arrival introduced me to the Marquis d'Yranda who has been very polite to me and to whom I am not otherwise reserved, than in forbearing to go so often to his House as he hath desired me. He informed me that he had received Directions to supply M. Jay, but not mentioning my name, I was constrained to make use

9. The previous Thursday was April 20, presumably the day BF took Jones to meet with Sartine about the sale of the *Serapis* and *Countess of Scarborough*. A French translation of the present letter is at the Archives de la Marine.

1. The name Carmichael used for receiving mail: XXXI, 408.

of other resources. I am afraid the gentlemen you mention left you with respect in their eyes and rancor in their Hearts, if this should be the Case, I hope the fable of the Viper and file will be renewed.[2] I Should be glad to know from M. Grand the nature of M. Lee's letter to him, because as the last mentioned Gentleman sometimes Sees things in a different Light from any one else. It is not improbable that M. Grand may be led into some error. I have not with me a Copy of the paper, which in Consequence of the Request of many Gentlemen in the House, I laid before Congress, but I recollect the Substance of it Viz that M. Lee has rendered himself disagreable to the Court and Individuals of the french Nation and even suspected by the former and that I derived my knowledge of this from these who were connected with the Court & named the Messrs. Grands on this Occasion.[3] This and much more M. Girard and M Holker confirmed by papers delivered either to Congress or Members of that body, which as well as that written by me are in private Journals or files of Congress. I have heard with much Satisfaction an Account of the generous Conduct which france continues to observe to us. Our Necessities are certainly great and our Reliance on our Ally is in proportion to these Necessities. I hope the articles you have sent will arrive in Safety, for they are much Wanted. Your Letter by the Chevalier de La Luzerne ought to have prevented future Drafts upon you. I was in Congress when it was read and I can assure you that It gave much Satisfaction.[4] I apprehend that you will receive an Aswer from M. J. Johnson at Nantes to whom M. Jay sent your papers and Letters all of which were intrusted to his Care, by a Private Hand last week. I am a little surprized that M Adams had not opened himself to you on the object of his Mission, because an Order of Congress directed all their Reso-

2. A cautionary fable attributed to Aesop about a viper unwisely biting a file; Carmichael hopes that attacking BF will do similar harm to Arthur Lee and Ralph Izard.

3. Carmichael had told Congress that he had learned through Ferdinand Grand, Georges Grand, and others that Lee was distrusted by the French court. Gérard leaked similar information to members of Congress: XXXI, 243n; Smith, *Letters*, XII, 417–21; Meng, *Despatches of Gérard*, pp. 116–17.

4. BF's letter of May 26, 1779, was read in Congress on Aug. 17: XXIX, 547n, 561.

lutions on that subject to be sent to you[5] and these you will also receive from M. Johnson which precludes the necessity of any Detail from me. I always wished to have it in my Power to revisit france and the obliging manner in which you express a desire to see me, hath increased my Wishes, perhaps if your Business should either advance rapidly or meet with unexpected delay. M. Jay may consent to spare me a few Weeks, In which Case I do assure you that I would most willingly ride post night and Day. Several Vessels have lately arrived from America in the ports of Spain and these being Boston News Papers to the 10th. of march from which It appears that the fleet which sailed from N-York on the 26. of December[6] had been totally dispersed by a violent gale of Wind our Cruizers had captured Several of the Transports which were dismasted and otherwise in a very distressed Situation. Some accts. say that many of them left New-York with provisions for 14 days only. I am informed from Bordeaux that Several Letters from America for me brought by the Buckskin were inclosed to me & forward to this City. I have received a packet of new papers from the Gentleman to whom they were instrusted with advice that he had sent my Letters by the same Post, but it appears that they have met the fate of a Letter which you mention from M. Dumas who is much distressed on that Account. I am not Well informed on this subject and am hurt that any difference should subsist between men whom I esteem. I write this by the post, because the Minister of france being at Aranjuez, I know not when he means soon to dispatch a Courier if Letters to me are intercepted either in france or this Country, I must expect that mine to america will run the same Risque, which Circumstance will totally disable me from Serving either my Country or the Common Cause. I approuve of the method of Correspondence you mention because I think our Interest is so much the same, that a knowledge of the designs of each ought to be reciprocal. I have not yet Received Dr. Bancrofts Letter. Pray present him my compliments as also to Billy, whose Copies

5. We find no record of such an order. BF initially was told only that JA had been elected to negotiate treaties of peace and of commerce with Britain: XXX, 542–3.
6. Clinton's invasion fleet for South Carolina.

set me an Exemple I am afraid I shall never be able to imitate. M. & Mrs. Jay are neither in the Best State of Health. They desire me to make the proper Compliments for them to you I am with much Respect Your Excellency most obliged & most Humble Sert.   (signed) WM. CHARMICHAEL

P.S. Madrid 27th. April 1780. Since writing the above I have received my Letters from Bordeaux 27 Days after their Date and with evident marks of their having opened. My last Letter is of the 25th. of December from M. Chase who desires me to present his Respects to your Excellency.[7] I find that the other Servants of the Public will soon be in the same Situation, that you have been, that is drawn upon for money before it is accertained whether they will be able to procure the necessary funds to Answer these drafts. M. Laurence ought to be in Holland at present.

The Executive hath transmitted M. Jay an act of their Legislature appointing you to nominate one out of five members chosen to sell certain funds appertaining to the State of Maryland in the Stock of G. Britain. In case their present Trustees do not chuse to execute that Business. I find that my Countrymen have done me the Honor to put me at the Head of this List. This is incompatible with my present avocation. Disposed I am to render my native States all the Service in my Power, I must in the Case of the Contingincy above mentioned, intreat you not to think of me as I am interested in every thing that Concern my State, I must intreat your Excellency to communicate to me the progress of this Business. Sir John Dalrimple whom perhaps you know personally has been here near three weeks, under the pretexte or in reality of Travelling with his Lady who is in a bad State of health. I have been able to trace most of his motions here, which wear a suspicious Apparance,[8] and having some Reason to think

7. Samuel Chase (XXII, 148–9n) had traveled to Montreal with BF in 1776; he, like Carmichael, was a former congressional delegate from Maryland.

8. Sir John Dalrymple (XXII, 81n) did present the Spanish government a detailed peace proposal (Wharton, *Diplomatic Correspondence*, III, 727–31), but appears to have been acting on his own. The Spanish government gave Jay a copy of the proposal: Samuel Flagg Bemis, *The Hussey-Cumberland*

that he means to proceed from hence to france, I think it my Duty to inform you, not from any Apprehension of what he may able to effect, because we have too many Proofs to doubt now, but that the Servts. of our Country should not neglect to give you that advice which I know you will receive from M. Le Comte de Vergennes in case this Philosophical Traveller should Visit Paris for his Health or that of his family at this Crisis, I have the Honor to be your Excellency's most obliged & most Humble Servt.

(signed) WM. CARMICHAEL

His Excellency Benjn. franklin Esqe.

From Thomas Digges   ALS: Historical Society of Pennsylvania

Dr. Sir   London Apl 22d 1780

I beg leave to recommend to Your usual civility and attention the Bearer of this my friend Docr. Plunkett, who means to take a journey in a few days to Holland & France; and should He return from Paris directly hither He will obligingly take charge of any thing you may have to send to this quarter. You will find him a good friend to the rights of mankind, & particularly attachd to the cause of Our Country, in the Armies of which, He has had a Brother who has very honourably distinguishd Himself.[9]

I am with very great regard Dr Sir yr obligd & Obt Servant   TH DIGGES

Notation: April 22 1780

Mission and American Independence: an Essay in the Diplomacy of the American Revolution (Princeton, 1931), pp. 62–4. He hinted that he knew BF personally, but we find no evidence of it.

9. Probably David Plunkett of Maryland, a former captain of dragoons: Heitman, *Register of Officers,* p. 331. For his heroism at the Battle of Long Island see Andrew C. Trippe *et al.,* "Battle of Long Island," *Maryland Hist. Mag.,* XIV (1919), 113.

From Gérard de Rayneval   AL: American Philosophical Society

a versailles ce 22. avril 1780.

Mr. Gerard prie Monsieur franklin de vouloir bien remettre le paquet cijoint pour L'amerique à Mr. le Capitaine Paul Jones qui a bien voulu lui promettre de s'en charger.[1]

Il l'assure en même tems de son respect et de son attachement.

From Francis Hopkinson   ALS: American Philosophical Society

Dear sir,   Philada. 22d. April 1780

This Letter will be presented by Mr. Foulk the Son of Judah Foulk of this City whom you may remember. I beg leave to recommend him to your Notice, he is a worthy young Man in his private Character—whether Whig or Tory I cannot say—his Connections are for the most part of the latter Denomination.— I wrote to you by Mr. Gerard who is I hope safe arrived at Paris long before this.—[2] We are very anxious here for the Fate of Charles Town—the present Time is probably the very Crisis of Decision respecting that City. The Southern Post arrived last Evening—the British had got their Ships over the Bar—the heavy ones I mean—which was deemed impracticable—& were making their approaches to the City—[3] We sanguine Whigs however are not without Hopes of Relief from the French or Spanish Ships in the West-Indias.— Affairs in Ireland look well for us—a Cork Paper of January has found its Way here, & revived our Hopes from that Quarter—[4] May God defend the

1. Jones may have encountered Rayneval during his recent visits to Versailles.

2. Gérard carried Hopkinson's letter of Sept. 5, 1779: XXX, 299.

3. On March 20 eight British warships, the heaviest lightened by transferring guns and cargo, made their way through the shallow ship channel: John A. Tilley, *The British Navy and the American Revolution* (Columbia, S.C., 1987), p. 179.

4. Hopkinson may be referring to an article datelined Cork, Jan. 10, 1780, which reported the refusal of the Earl of Buckinghamshire, lord lieutenant of Ireland, to receive an address of the Cork Union. The address, which offered to assist him in repelling the hostile attacks of his majesty's enemies against the kingdom, appeared in the April 4 issue of the *Pennsylvania Packet*.

Right, & defeat the wicked purposes of those who would op-
press & enslave their fellows!—
  Your Family & Friends are all well, as also are mine—
  I am ever Your truly affectionate   F. HOPKINSON

Addressed: address / Honourable / Doctor Franklin / favour'd
by / Mr. Foulk

From Jonathan Williams, Jr.

ALS: University of Pennsylvania Library; copy: Yale University Library

Dear & Hond Sir.   Nantes April 22. 1780.
  Capt McKirdy in the Dove is just arrived From Maryland[5] &
by him it appears that Clinton has at last appeared in So Carolina: I send you the only important Papers I have recvd by him.
Mr Lewis a Passenger assures me that our People are strong in
Force in that Quarter & do not fear the Enemy. I cannot find ei-
ther by Letter Newspaper or Information the smallest Acct of
the Mercury Capt Samson who carried your Dispatches in November last, & I apprehend he has suffered a harder Fate than
Capture.[6] The Winter for 40 Years Past has never been so severe.—
  I refer you to my last to M de Chaumont about the Cloathing,
By the Contrary Wind I have great hopes that what I sent to
Brest will arrive in Time. I do not continue sending because I
Fear to be too late & I wish for orders for the Cloathing I have
now by me. Mr Chaumont will tell you that the Farmers have ordered an arrangement to be made with me about the Duties. I do
not yet know what it will be but I am assured it will be reduced
to a trifle.—

  5. Capt. John McKirdy of Baltimore commanded the *Dove,* bonded on
March 13, 1780: Charles Henry Lincoln, comp., *Naval Records of the American Revolution, 1775–1788* (Washington, D.C., 1906), p. 276.
  6. For Capt. Simeon Samson and the *Mercury* see XXX, 170–1n, 618n. JW
soon learned that the ship had arrived in Plymouth, Mass. on Feb. 14: JW to
WTF, May 9, 1780, Yale University Library. (Clark, *Ben Franklin's Privateers,*
p. 92, cites the vessel as arriving at Martha's Vineyard on Feb. 16.)

I am with the greatest Respect Your dutifull & Affectionate Kinsman   JONA WILLIAMS J

Notation: J Williams April 22 1780

From Henry Grand   AL: American Philosophical Society

[before April 23, 1780?][7]
Mr. Hy. Grand's most respectfull Compliments wait on Doctor Franklin sends him according to his father's request the inclosed Letter, to which he will be pleased to honour him with an answer as soon as possible.[8] What his Excellency May have determined relative to his Account will also be very agreable as Mr. Grand will loose no time in winding of it up in that form, if it is approved.

Notation: Hy. Grand.

From John Paul Jones   Copy:[9] American Philosophical Society

Honored and Dear sir,   Passy April 23d. 1780.
In the Letter that I wrote you from Corogna, in spain,[1] I remember to have been particular respecting the Brigantine that I had met with off Cape finistere Under Dutch Colours. She appeared to be from Liverpool, having been taken from the Sub-

7. If our conjecture about the enclosure is correct (below), this letter would precede BF to Fizeaux, Grand & Cie. of April 23.
8. We believe the enclosure was a note (undated, APS) in the hand of M. Le Breton of Rouen: he has received a bill of lading for eight boxes of printing type sent by Fizeaux, Grand & Cie. for BF. Does BF intend to have it enter the country by passport? If so, he should send one right away. On the verso, the same hand wrote "reponce à Mr. Grand" and the note is endorsed "BF." A M. Le Breton is listed as one of the leading merchants of Rouen and "signataire" of an insurance company in the *Almanach des marchands*, p. 417.
9. In L'Air de Lamotte's hand, and prepared for BF's use in replying (on this same date, below) to Van de Perre & Meÿners' complaint of April 6, above.
1. XXXI, 388–9.

jects of America by a Liverpool Privater, and sent in a short time before.— The Alliance has very much the appearance of an English frigate, and as I then wore an English uniform, and had my marines dressed in the Uniform that was found on board the Serapis, it was natural for me to think the Master of the Brig Spoke the Truth, when he Said the Cargo was British property, and that he only hoisted dutch Colours, to protect him from the flags of france Spain and America.— It is well known that the dutch do not fit out their Ships in foreign ports and that the Vessel in question was never in holland.— But as the Master was not dispossessed of his Vessel, the property will not be altered by his going to America (unless the Legislature of that Country Should so determin it) and he will be at liberty to sell his Cargo at a Much better market than in any other Part of the world. As to *force* being used to obtain a declaration from the master it is absolutely false, and you will believe that it was Unnecessary had I even been *"Corsaire"* enough to have been capable of it.— If there are now any of the Men on board the alliance that belonged to that Brig, Unless they have entered for our service, they Shall not be detained.

The Men I put on board the Brig, had my Orders to assist the master and mate in the Navigation of the Vessel, and in the Pilotage on the Coast of America.—

With great Esteem and Respect I am always Dear sir Your most Oliged and most humble servant   (signed) J.P. JONES.

His Excellency B. franklin Esqr. &c &c.

Notations in different hands: From Capt. Jones to B. Franklin (Copy) / Cap. Jones to B. franklin Passy April 23 1780.

To Dumas   Copy: Library of Congress; transcript: National Archives

Dear sir,   Passy April 23d. 1780

I am Much pleased with the Account you give me, of the Disposition with which the Proposals from the Empress of Russia have been received, and desire to be informed from time to time of the progress of that interesting Business.

295

I Shall be glad to hear of your perfect Reconciliation with the   [2] Because a Continuance of your Difference will be extreamly inconvenient, Permit me to tell you frankly what I formerly hinted to you,[3] that I apprehend you suffer your self too Easily to be led in to personal prejudices by interested People, who would ingross all our Confidence to themselves. From this source have arisen I imagine the Charges and Suspicions you have insinuated to me against several who always declared a friendship for us in Holland. It is right that you should have an opportunity of Giving the *Carte du Pays* to Mr. Laurens when he arrives in holland. But if in order to serve your particular friends you fill his head with these prejudices, you will hurt him and them, and perhaps your self. There does not appear to me the least probability in your supposition that   is an Enemy to America. Here has been with me a Gentlemen from holland,[4] who was charged as he Said, with a Verbal Commission from divers Cities to enquire whither it was true that amsterdam, had as they had heard made a Treaty of Commerce with the united states and to Express in that Case their Willingness to enter into a Similar Treaty. Do you know any thing of this? What is become or likely to become, of the plan of Treaty, formerly under consideration?[5] By a Letter from Middlebourg to which the enclosed is an answer,[6] a Cargo seized and sent to america as English Property, is reclaimed partly on the supposition that free ships make free Goods. They ought to do so between England and holland, because there is a Treaty which stipulates it;[7] but there being Yet no treaty between Holland and america to that purpose, I apprehend that the Goods being declared by the Captain to be English, a neutral ship will not protect them the Law of Nations governing in this Case, as it did before the Treaty above mentioned. Tell me if you please your opinion.

With sincere Esteem and affection I am ever.

Mr. Dumas.

2. Dumas would know to insert "grand facteur," *i.e.*, La Vauguyon.
3. Perhaps XXXI, 413.
4. Named Westhuysen: BF to Dumas, June 5, below.
5. The draft American-Dutch commercial treaty on which Dumas had been laboring: *e.g.*, XXIX, 100–1.
6. His letter to Van de Perre & Meÿners of this date, below.
7. The Anglo-Dutch commercial treaty of Dec. 1/11, 1674.

To Fizeaux, Grand & Cie.

Copy: Library of Congress

Gentlemen Passy, 23d. April 1780

I received your respected favours of the Instant with your Acct of Expences relating to the Cases of Characters &ca. which I have desired M. F. Grand to discharge in my Behalf, and am much obliged by your Care in forwarding them to Rouen.[8] Plese to Accept my Thanks and belive me to be with sincere Esteem. Gentlemene Y. m. o. and M. h. S.

Mess. fizeaux Grand and Co.

To Octavie Guichard Durey de Meinières[9]

AL: American Philosophical Society

Passy, April 23. 80

It is certain that Mr. Franklin has promised Madame Helvetius that he will accompany her on Wednesday next to the Pavillions de Chaillot.[1] He has long desired to pay his Duty there, but was afraid to encounter the keen and fine Reproaches of Made de Meinieres, which he had before experienc'd, and which his Conscience told him he deserved. He resolved, however, to venture

8. These were the eight boxes of printing type that BF had ordered from Caslon in June, 1779. He had instructed Caslon to ship them to Fizeaux, Grand & Cie. in Amsterdam, and had then told the Amsterdam firm to forward them to Rouen, care of John Holker: XXX, 610–12. The type arrived in Rouen, but was addressed to M. Le Breton; see our annotation to Henry Grand's letter of [before April 23], and Holker to BF, April 26.

9. Octavie Guichard (1719–1804) was a *femme de lettres* of some repute. Well versed in English, she translated Samuel Johnson's *Rasselas*, David Hume's *History of England*, and several other works. After the death of her first husband, Bellot (or Belot), a lawyer, she married in 1765 Jean-Baptiste-François Durey de Meinières (1703–1787), president of the *seconde chambre des enquêtes du parlement de Paris*, himself a writer on legal matters. The couple belonged to Mme du Deffand's circle and to that of the Helvétius family. *DBF* (under Durey); Lewis, *Walpole Correspondence*, III, 351n; IV, 124, 130. Bachaumont has some biting comments about her love life: *Mémoires secrets*, II, 238, 271–2.

1. At the time of her death, Mme de Meinières still lived in Chaillot, then on the outskirts of Paris, near the Couvent de la Visitation Ste. Marie. Minutier Central of the Archives Nationales, MC, VIII, 1345.

sous la Protection de Notre Dame d'Auteuil, which he hoped might obtain for him some Clemency. And he is very happy to find, by their very kind and elegant little Billet, that this Arrangement will not be disagreeable to M. & Made. de Meinieres, for whom he has (in common with all that know them) the greatest Esteem & Respect imaginable.

Addressed: A Madame / Madame la Presidente de Meinieres / à Chaillot

To Van de Perre & Meÿners

Copy: Library of Congress

Gentlemen,   Passy, April 23. 80.

I duly received the Letter you did me the honour of writing to me the 6th. Instant: I took the first Opportunity of Communicating it to Commodore Jones, and I send you inclosed the Answer I have received from him,[2] by which you will perceive that he absolutely denies his having used any force to obtain from your Captain the declaration he made that the Cargo was English Property but asserts that the said Declaration was voluntarily made, the Captain supposing him and his ship the alliance to be English. However this may be, I shall communicate your demand to the Congress, and as we have good Laws and regular Courts of admiralty in all the states, for the trial of Such Causes, I have no doubt of your obtaining that Justice which your Cause shall appear to merit. You will see by the enclos'd papers an Instance of the Regard to Justice shown by the Congress to the subjets of portugal,[3] a Nation, which has been not only unfriendly to us, but whose king in the beginning of our troubles issued a very severe Edict against us.[4] There is there-

2. Jones's letter of April 23, above.

3. BF may have sent a copy of the May 18, 1779, issue of the *Gaʒ. de Leyde,* which carried a congressional resolution promising reimbursement to the owners of a captured Portuguese ship (see XXIX, 468n) or possibly the May 11, 1778, resolution itself. Several copies of the resolution are with BF's papers at the APS and Hist. Soc. of Pa.

4. XXII, 645n. Relations with Portugal had improved: XXX, 467–8.

fore no probability that like Justice will be refused to the subjects of their High Mightenesses[5] whom the United states highly respect, and with whom they desire to maintain a good Understanding with a friendly and free Commerce between the two Nations. I have the honour to be, with respectful Consideration, Gentlemen &c.

Mrs. Van de Perre and Meyners Merchants at Midleburg, Holland.

To Sartine

LS:[6] Archives de la Marine, copy: Library of Congress

Sir,   Passy April 23d. 1780
I thank your Excellency for expediting the Orders relative to the Sale of the Serapis.[7] I suppose similar Orders are gone to Dunkerque for the Sale of the Countess of Scarborough. If not I beg you would be pleased to send them by the Bearer; as the Daily heavy Charge that must arise on a Delay of Dispatching the Alliance, makes me anxious to see the Affair finished.

I am ever with the greatest Respect Your Excellency's most obedient & most humble Servant   B FRANKLIN
His Exy M. De Sartine.

Notation: Rep le 5 mai

5. The States General of the Netherlands.
6. In WTF's hand.
7. On April 22 Sartine sent orders to Port Commandant Thévenard and *Commissaire* Grandville at Lorient to sell the *Serapis* at public auction. Thévenard in turn promised to divide the proceeds among the crews of the *Bonhomme Richard* squadron but worried the Americans would try to bid up the selling price: Archives de la Marine, B²CDXIX: 7; B³DCLXXXII: 123–4. For Jean-Charles-Bernardin Charlot de La Grandville (1737–1804) see Didier Neuville, ed., *Etat sommaire des archives de la marine antérieures à la Révolution* (Paris, 1898), p. 137.

From Frédéric-Samuel Ostervald and Abraham Bosset Deluze[8]

ALS:[9] American Philosophical Society

Monsieur,   Paris le 23e. avril 1780.

Nous nous proposions de rendre encore une fois nos devoirs à Votre Excellence, mais la crainte de la détourner de ses importantes occupations, nous fait préférer cette voye pour La Supplier de daigner nous apprendre, Si l'offre que nous avons eu l'honneur de luy faire de nos très humbles Services pour quelque entreprise Typographique pourroit lui paroitre mériter quelque attention & nous procurer l'avantage de lui marquer notre Sincere dévouement. Comme nous ne devons plus passer que le reste de la Semaine dans cette capitale, nous desirerions de recevoir dans cet intervalle les ordres de Votre Excellence, au cas qu'il lui plut de nous en favoriser.[1] Nous irions avec empressement les prendre nous mêmes, Si elle le jugeoit à propos.

Nous avons l'honneur d'être avec un profond respect, Monsieur De Votre Excellence Les très humbles & très obéissants Serviteurs   OSTERVALD & BOSSET DELUZE

Rue Croix des petits champs Hôtel de Bretagne:

---

8. Frédéric-Samuel Ostervald (1713–1795), civic leader and man of letters, was one of the founders, in 1769, and directors of the Société typographique de Neuchâtel, the important Swiss publishing house. Abraham Bosset Deluze (c. 1731–81) joined in 1775 as director of finances. The firm, which specialized in reprinting works in a less costly format, had just finished publishing a quarto edition of Diderot's *Encyclopédie:* Robert Darnton, *The Business of Enlightenment: a Publishing History of the Encyclopédie 1775–1800* (Cambridge, Mass., and London, 1979), pp. 35, 39; Robert Darnton, "Le marché littéraire français vu de Neuchâtel (1769–1789)," Jacques Rychner and Michel Schlup, eds., *Aspects du livre neuchâtelois* (Neuchâtel, 1986), p. 61. In 1780 the STN was mid-way through publishing its quarto edition, revised and expanded, of the French Académie des sciences' *Descriptions des arts et métiers,* to which BF subscribed: XXXI, 4; Dorothy Medlin, Jean-Claude David, and Paul LeClerc, eds., *Lettres d'André Morellet* (2 vols. to date, Oxford, 1991–), I, 296, 419.

9. In Ostervald's hand.

1. See their letter dated April 31, below. Morellet addressed Bosset at his Paris hotel as late as the first week of June: *Lettres d'André Morellet,* I, 420–1.

From Benjamin Vaughan

AL: Library of Congress

My dearest sir,   London, April 23, 1780.

I write this simply to inform you that I sent you no less than three pacquets and a letter by Mr. Austin, to forward from Amsterdam. I hope they will safely arrive.— Your book is translating in two places in Germany; & Dr. Forster's son would have translated it himself, had not the advertisements from other quarters prevented him.[2]

This letter may perhaps be delivered to you by a Dr: Hamilton, a strict acquaintance and friend of Dr. Crawford and of whom Dr. Crawford speaks very honorably. He is an Irish gentleman, & having some little independency is upon a scheme of travelling for two years. I do not know that he will present this in person, but if he holds his intention of keeping company with *another* Irish physician to Paris (who is related to an American major,)[3] you will probably hear of or see him; and it is well you should know that he is trust-worthy: Besides that being on his travels, it can do no disservice to your country's cause that he should have seen *you*. When I first heard of the opportunity, I did not know *he* was the party,— He goes so quick upon my last, that I can only inform you in addition to what I say there, that the Speaker is really knocked up by his chair, and leaves the decision of his resignation entirely to Dr. Fothergill & Mr Pott:[4]

2. The advertisements were probably for G.T. Wenzel's three-volume *Des Herrn D. Benjamin Franklin's . . . sämtliche Werke . . .* (Dresden, 1780), a work based on Vaughan's recently-published edition and Jacques Barbeu-Dubourg's translation of BF's *Exper. and Obser.:* Robert L. Kahn, "George Forster and Benjamin Franklin," APS *Proc.,* CII (1958), 3. Johann Georg Adam Forster was the son of Johann Reinhold Forster, a German naturalist: XV, 147–8; XXVII, 181n.

3. Hamilton may be William Hamilton (who held an M.A., but was not a doctor), whom Priestley had introduced the preceding spring: XXIX, 99. Adair Crawford is the scientist whose work Vaughan had previously sent BF: XXX, 381–2; XXXI, 60. The "other" Irish physician is probably Dr. Plunkett.

4. Speaker of the House of Commons Sir Fletcher Norton had reported his illness, real or feigned, to the House on April 14: Digges to BF of that date, above. Fothergill had been in poor health himself since late 1778 and died later in the year: Betsy C. Corner and Christopher Booth, eds., *Chain of Friendship: Selected Letters of Dr. John Fothergill of London, 1735–1780*

The former thinks him gouty, the latter nervous; but he is always well, while following his hounds. Wedderburne will be Chief Justice of the C: Pleas, and as he cannot be in the Commons, if ministry choose not to lose his services in parliament, they must have him in the Lords.[5] If Sr. Fletcher Norton goes then, we shall have six lords made by the law. The County of Lancaster I believe will have a meeting; The dissolution of the Chester *committee* is a juggle & surreptitious, but the county will probably replace them with some warmth in June at the next County meeting:[6] York is very warm, but there are varieties of opinion from the remains of the *old* Rockingham system, and the scruples of Sr. G. Savile.[7]

I am, as *ever*, my dearest sir, yours most devotedly

You know that the Rockingham's accede with very little exception to Lord S———'s letter.[8]

(Cambridge, Mass., 1971), pp. 32–3. Percivall Pott (1714–1788) was a senior surgeon at St. Bartholomew's Hospital: *DNB.*

5. Lord North had promised Alexander Wedderburn the chief justiceship of the common pleas and a peerage, which he had long desired, to retain his support for the ministry. He became chief justice in June and was created 1st Lord Loughborough: Frank O'Gorman, *The Rise of Party in England, The Rockingham Whigs, 1760–82* (London, 1975), pp. 371, 616; Namier and Brooke, *House of Commons,* III, 620.

6. The Duke of Portland, a close political ally of the Marquis of Rockingham, had doubts that the reform movement would succeed in Cheshire, and indeed that county's representative attended only one of the joint association meetings in London: Eugene Charlton Black, *The Association: British Extraparliamentary Political Organization 1769–1793* (Cambridge, Mass., 1963), pp. 47, 51. George III personally supervised measures against a proposed meeting in the county of Lancashire: *ibid,* p. 48.

7. Sir George Savile (XI, 480n) was a political ally of Wyvill and a close friend of David Hartley.

8. Possibly Lord Shelburne's March 26 letter to the chairman of the Wiltshire Committee: *The Remembrancer; or, Impartial Repository of Public Events for 1780* (17 vols., London, 1775–84) IX, (1780) 270–2. In late March Shelburne and Rockingham achieved a tenuous unity in support of reform. Rockingham, however, disagreed with the demands of Shelburne and the county associations for shorter parliaments and more equal representation; by April the rift between the two men was open: Thomas W. Copeland *et al.,* eds., *The Correspondence of Edmund Burke* (10 vols., Cambridge, Eng., and Chicago, 1958–78), IV, 217–18; O'Gorman, *The Rise of Party in England,* pp. 414–15, 421.

From Dumas

ALS: American Philosophical Society; AL (draft): Algemeen Rijksarchief

Monsieur   Amsterdam 24 Avr. 1780

J'ai eu l'honneur de vous marquer dans ma derniere l'acceptation unanime des propositions de la Russie par la Province d'Hollande.⁹ C'est un Triomphe complet de *notre Ami* sur le coryphée du parti Anglois, Mr. Van der Heim Secretaire de l'Amirauté de la Meuse; celui-ci avoit minuté un préavis de l'Amirauté que le G——— P——— montra à *notre Ami,* qui fit si bien sentir au G——— P——— combien ce Préavis, obscur & chargé de superfluités capables de tout embrouiller, rendroit odieux ceux qui l'adopteroient, que le G——— P——— le remercia, & admit tous les changemens, additions & retranchemens que notre ami jugea à propos.

On vient de recevoir ici une Déclaration de la Gr. Bret. du 17e. de ce mois, déclarant les sujets de cette Rep. "déchus des privileges de Commerce & de Navigation dont elle jouissoit comme alliée de la Gr. Bret. selon les traités, & les mettant à cet égard sur le pied des autres Etats neutres."¹

Je viens de recevoir la réponse suivante de Mrs. Enschedé de Harlem, sur les prix que vous demandez Monsieur.

	argent d'hollde.	
Nonpareil rom. & cursif	£2. 6s.	
Caractere de Finance, ou double Médian écrit	1. -	
Double Descendian écrit	1. 2.	
Double Garamond écrit	1. 4.	⎫ la
Descendian Duits	-. 13 -	⎬ Livre
Garmond Duits	-.16.-	⎭ pesant
Breviaire Duits	1. 2.	

---

9. Above, April 17. The States General on April 24 voted the exact resolution as had the States of the Province of Holland. On the same day it also voted to extend convoy protection to ships carrying timber, masts, and other naval materiel. Still fearing Britain, however, the States General was not willing to issue its own declaration of neutral rights. Consequently it decided to conduct negotiations in St. Petersburg to procure a defensive alliance first: Fauchille, *Diplomatie française,* pp. 205, 495; Isabel de Madariaga, *Britain, Russia, and the Armed Neutrality of 1780: Sir James Harris's Mission to St. Petersburg during the American Revolution* (New Haven, 1962), pp. 192–3.

1. This Order in Council is published in Sir Francis Piggott and G.W.T.

La proportion entre le poinds d'Angleterre & celui d'Amsterdam dont il est question ici est de 107 ou 108 à 100. Ainsi le poids d'Amsterdam est de 7 ou 8 pour Ct. plus pesant que celui d'Angleterre.

Je suis avec un très grand respect, Monsieur Votre très humble & très obéissant serviteur   Dumas

Passy à S.E. Mr. Franklin

Addressed: His Excellency / B. Franklin Esqr. / Min. Plenipe. of the united States, &c. / *Passy* /.

Notation: Dumas Amstm. April 24. 1780

From Auguste Lesage[2]   ALS: American Philosophical Society

Monseigneur   Lille le 24 avril 1780

Jay eut L'honneur de vous Ecrire il y a quelque tems au sujet d'un pacquet que jay ches moy a vous faire passer pour que vous ayes La Complaisance de m'Indiquer la voye par ou vous voules le Recevoir, Je suis depuis privé de vos ordres obligé moy de me Les donner et elles seront executées a La Lettre ce qu'attendant Jay L'honneur d'Etre avec bien du Respect Monseigneur Votre tres humble & tres obeissant serviteur[3]   AUGT. LESAGE

Jay eut l'honneur de vous adresser un pacquet Dernierement par La diligence de paris J'espere qu'il vous sera bien parvenû.

Notation: Le Sage August. 24 Avril 1780.

Omond, eds., *Documentary History of the Armed Neutralities 1780 and 1800* (London, 1919), pp. 148–9.

2. Auguste or Augustin Lesage was a Lille merchant: Jean-Pierre Hirsch, *Les deux rêves du commerce: entreprise et institution dans la région lilloise (1780–1860)* (Paris, 1991), pp. 44, 156, 205–6, 212. We do not have his previous letter, to which he refers below, nor have we been able to discover the nature of the packet he mentions.

3. Lesage wrote again on May 5, this time requesting that BF give his answer to the bearer, M. Maujat. BF endorsed the letter: "To W.T.F. To go to Versailles and obtain Passports for this, & for the Paper & Printing Letters at Nantes." APS. BF had sent type to Nantes in April, instructing JW to ship it to America; see our annotation of JW's letter of March 7.

From Sartine

Copies: Archives du Ministère des affaires étrangères,[4] Library of Congress

Versailles Le 24 avril 1780.

J'ai vu, monsieur, par les deux différentes lettres qui vous ont été écrites de Londres par m. Hodgson,[5] que les Commissaires anglois chargés de l'Echange des Prisonniers n'ont pas interprété dans son sens véritable le certificat que le Commissaire de la marine a délivré au capitaine du Batiment Parlementaire qui a ramené cent Américains à Morlaix, où il espéroit recevoir un nombre égal de Prisonniers anglois conduits en France par les Sujets des Etats Unis. Vous voudrez bien vous rappeler la Négociation des Ambassadeurs de France et d'angleterre à la haie relativement aux Prisonniers conduits au Téxel par l'Escadre du sieur Paul jones.[6] Ces Prisonniers aiant été regardés comme pris en Mer par une Escadre Françoise, et leur Echange aiant été arrêté par les deux Ministres sous cette dénomination; il étoit politiquement impossible de contrarier une opération qui avoit souffert beaucoup de difficultés, en Faisant délivrer 400. Américains en angleterre, en Echange des 400 anglois échangés au Téxel; puisque dans le même tems que 100. américains arriverent à Morlaix, des Bâtimens expédiés de st. malo consommoient l'Echange convenu en hollande par les Ambassadeurs respectifs. Je donnai ordre à m. Boucault à Morlaix de certifier au Capitaine du Parlementaire anglois, qu'il n'y avoit dans ce Port aucun Prisonnier qui peut lui être remis, mais qu'il en seroit tenu compte à la Cour de Londres, et bien loin que l'on put Supposer dans cette conduite une infidelité, il me semble au contraire que la France devenoit alors garant de cet Echange et votre négociation ne devoit pas être interrompue sous ce prétexte. Ce seroit cependant avec grand plaisir, monsieur, que je proposerois au Roi de

4. Enclosed with a June 5 letter from Sartine to Vergennes.

5. Presumably Hodgson's of March 10 and 28, above. BF probably presented them to Sartine at or after the meeting described in his April 11 letter to Hodgson, above.

6. For which see XXXI, 120n, 150–1, 202–4, 240n. To prevent Jones's squadron from being expelled by the Dutch government, La Vauguyon had pretended that its ships and prizes had flown French colors.

vous Faire remettre 400. Prisonniers anglois pour procurer la liberté à 400. américains détenus en angleterre. Vous avez pu juger des égards que sa majesté a pour ses alliés par la Facilité avec laquelle elle a bien voulu Faire relacher et remettre à votre disposition tous les Sujets des Etats Unis pris par des François Sur des Bâtimens Ennemis et s'est ainsi privé d'autant de moiens d'Echanger ses Sujets. Mais le Cartel arrêté entre les deux Cours oppose un obstacle insurmontable à sa bonne volonté.[7] Tous les Prisonniers étant renvoiés respectivement, la Cour de Londres ne pourroit apprendre qu'avec Surprise et mécontentement qu'il vous Fut remis des Prisonniers pour consommer l'Echange des Américains qui doit être distinct de celui des François. Vous étes sans doute très persuadé qu'il ne seroit pas possible de l'abuser sur cette conduite qui n'auroit aucun Succès et Seroit d'ailleurs contraire à la Franchise dont le Roi a déja donné tant de preuves à Ses Ennemis. J'ai déja Fait repasser 28. anglois Faits prisonniers par les Etats Unis.[8] Je ne puis que desirer qu'il en arrive un assez grand nombre en France pour consommer l'Echange des 400. Américains auxquels vous ètes justement empressé de procurer la liberté.

J'ai l'honneur d'être avec la considération la plus distinguée, M.

Copie de la Lettre de m. de Sartine à m. Franklin.

From John Diot & Co.

ALS: American Philosophical Society

sir   Morlaix the 25th. april 1780

A severe illness has put it out of my power to Send you before now the abstract of the Journal of the Black Prince, Which I hope your Excellency will Excuse me for.

---

7. Sartine was right. The British insisted that sailors be exchanged according to the colors under which they fought, not wishing to send to France French-born sailors serving in the Spanish Navy: Olive Anderson, "The Establishment of British Supremacy at Sea and the Exchange of Naval Prisoners of War, 1689–1783," *English Historical Review*, LXXV (1960), 82–3; Wharton, *Diplomatic Correspondence*, III, 648–9.

8. On the cartel *Happy Return:* XXXI, 477–8n, 551.

Subjoined We have the honnour to forward it to you. Your Excellency has undoubtedly heard 'ere now the unlucky fate of that privateer, which cou'd not Escape being taken by two English frigates, but by Stranding and She is intierely Rackt on the coast of Normandy.

We are Very thankfull to Your Excellency, for the speedy Judgment of the Phillip[9] and wou'd Still be more So, if you wou'd do the like for the Schooner Peter and brig Friendship Notwithstanding there was no papers found on board said Vessells, which generally go with a Single Customhouse bill, which, without Wonder, might have been dispersed and lost on board the Privateer, in the hard Weather She bore afterwards.

We hope Your Excellency, will take the Case into Consideration, and by Sending Soon your Judgment of Condamnation, you'll do Justice, and will enable the owners of the Black Prince to fit out an other privateer to take Revenge on the desperate Ennemies of the Congress.

We are most Respectfully Your Excellency's Most obedient and Most Humble Servants   JN DIOT & CO

His Excellency Benjin. Franklin Minister for the United States of North america Passy

Endorsed: April 25

Notation: Diot 1780

From —— Lefrique

ALS: American Philosophical Society

Monsieur   Paris 25 Avril 1780

J'ay recu par la diligence de Bruxelles un paquet pour acquit a Caution contenant des Livres qui Sont restés a la douane pour Etre Envoyez à la Chambre Sindical. Si j'avois pu Les retirer Je Laurois fait cejour dhuy maïs si cetoit des Livres Equivoque ont ne me les remettroient pas et vous, Monsieur, le magistrat vous les feroit remettre.

---

9. Apparently BF kept no copy of his judgment of the *Philip*, as we find no other record of it (or of the *Black Prince*'s journal).

Je Suis avec respect Monsieur Votre tres humble et tres obeissant Serviteur LE FRIQUE
Directeur des diligences de flandre rue st Denis

Si Jeusse Eu Le paquet Je l'aurois remis a Madame Laboureau qui ma dit avoir L'honneur d'estre votre parente;[1] a qui J'ay promis de luy remettre le premier paquet qui viendroit pour vous se faisant un plaisir de vous le porter.

Addressed: A Monsieur / Monsieur Le Docteur flanklin / en Son hôtel / á Passy / Le 24 avril 1780. 5 heures du Soir Bureau de flandre

Notation: Le frique Paris 25. Avril 1780.

From Jonathan Williams, Sr.

ALS: American Philosophical Society

Hond. Sir—   Boston Apl 25th. 1780
The Bearer Col: John Tyler a Friend & Neighbour of mine[2] Comes to France partly on Business & partly On Pleasure your Civilities to him as a stranger in France will Oblige your Dutifull Nephew & Hble Servant   JONA. WILLIAMS

NB Col. Tyler has aquited himself with Honour in the American Service

Addressed: His Excellency Benja. Franklin Esqr / at Passy in / France / per Col: John Tyler

1. She even claimed "Franklin" as part of her name: XXVI, 343–5.
2. Lt. Col. John Steele Tyler (d. 1813), a veteran of the 1779 Penobscot campaign; he traveled to Nantes from New London on the same ship as John Trumbull: *Adams Correspondence,* III, 328n. In July the two arrived in London and lodged together on George Street. When an arrest order was issued for Tyler in November, he was forewarned and escaped, but Trumbull was arrested and imprisoned: *Political Magazine and Parliamentary, Naval, Military, and Literary Journal,* I (1780), 739–40; Theodore Sizer, ed., *The Autobiography of Colonel John Trumbull . . .* (New Haven, 1953), pp. 63–6.

To Samuel Ross

Copies: Harvard University Library, Library of Congress[3]

Sir/   Passy April 26. 1780

I received yours of the 17 Instant.[4] The prize money due to Capt. Wickes & the Officers & People of the Reprisal was I imagine received by him before he sailed for America, & in that case it is probable your share was received with the rest. But if any of the prizes remain unsold when he went away, which I do not remember, the produce of such prizes must have come into the hands of Mr. T. Morris or of Messrs. Morris & Lee, who are accountable for the same.[5] It never belongd to me to pay any prize money due to the captors, for none of it ever came into my hands, and what you received from Dr. Bancroft for which I am to repay him, was not as payment to you, but so much advanced in kindness to you, considering your necessities, which you are to refund when you receive your wages, & which I doubt not you will do on your arrival in America.

I am Sir, your most Humble Servant   (signd) B FRANKLIN

Addressed a Monsieur Monsieur Samuel Ross, a bord de l'Alliance recommandé aux soins de Messrs. Gourlade et Moylan Negts a L'Orient

From John Holker

ALS: American Philosophical Society

Dear Sir   Monteny 26 April 1780

The Vessel is arrived from Amsterdam with the different objects you Recomended to my caire,[6] but as they was consind to Mr Bretin Negt, of this please I have been obliged to let him unloud them, and to Lodge them in the Doyne,[7] than such time as

---

3. The latter of which is undated.

4. Missing, although see his March 19 petition.

5. In 1777 Thomas Morris and William Lee had been co-agents in France of the commerce committee of Congress: XXIV, 161–2n.

6. For this shipment of printing type see the annotation of Henry Grand to BF, [before April 23], and BF to Fizeaux, Grand & Cie., April 23.

7. Douane, or customs house.

you can send me a permission to Receive them duty free; youl observe that your Caricter at Court Grants you the liberty to Receive any kind of Goods free from Duty, so by your apploying to Mr. Vergen or to Mr. Necker they will give you an Order to the farmer Generalls to take them out of the Burot of Depoe which Order youl be so good as to send me and I shall take caire they air Lodged saife, than you can find a sure occasion to have them Shiped for Emereca.

Youl see I have write you too lines in french so as you may send my leter to the Minister which will saffise with a word from your Self, and by Joyning the Letter of Veteure[8] you ought to have Received from Amsterdam.

I find you had larnd the disagreeable account of the house my Son lived in being Burnd,[9] I am unesey and shall bee, than I can larne the affeare from him Self, the more so knowing the quantity of affears he is charged with, and being feirefull some of his peapers may be Burnd. If you larne anything Regarding this object youl greatly oblige me to let me have it, as allso If you have any Good News, for it wood seem wee have had no accounts that can be depended upon this long time.

My wife Joynes with me in every thing that is kind & Respectuse to you, and shall be happey you Injoye Good health, & that soon we may larne that everything is well, and Mr. Washington in posession of *New yourk* God send it, for wee shant be happey than wee get those accounts.

It is my oppinion that My Lord North having lost the megorety in the house, will bring about a pease, for I cant see how the Menestery can stand their Ground unless they doe it.

My kind Complements to Mr. franklin and your Grand Son, and ever am most sincerely and ever will be til Death My Dear Sir your Most Obedeant & very humble servt   J HOLKER

Notation: Holker J. 26. April 1780.——

8. Lettre de voiture, or consignment note.

9. His son Jean Holker, French consul living in Philadelphia, occupied a house on Market Street owned by Richard Penn that burned completely on Jan. 2, 1780: *PMHB*, xx, 73.

From ———— De Reine   ALS: American Philosophical Society

Monsieur lambassadeur   a versailles Le 26. avril 1780.

Les harricots que j'ai eu lhonneur de vous donner hier chez
Madame, Sont originaire du cap de bonne Esperance, ils ont étés
recoltés a versailles.[1] Ce un tres bon farineux, Surtout a l'huile et
au vinaigre, en verd et Sec.

Cette espece d'harricot, Monsieur, propagera beaucoup, et je
Suis tres persuadé quil reussira tres bien en amerique, ou ils de-
viendront d'un Secour, et d'une utilité interressante, Surtout
pour la mer.

J'ose en outre, Monsieur l'ambassadeur, me persuader que
vous voudrez bien me faire la grace de recevoir avec bonté la re-
cette de ce topique.[2] Qui mieux que vous aux yeux de qui rien
néchape, Surtout lorsque les choses ont pour principes de contribuer au bonheur de la foible humanité! Vous saurez apprecier
mieux que personne la valeur de cette decouverte, dont les effets
ont étés prouvés par l'experience.

Je ne Suis point, Monsieur, l'auteur de ce Secret, ce uniquement dans l'Esprit de contribuer a faire le bien! J'ai combattu
avec vigueur des prejugés d'autant plus dangereux que les gens
de l'art par un principe de cupidité ont interet a le détruire, et il
ni a Sortes d'horreurs que Madame toujan n'ai eprouvé.[3] Non
seulement j'ai encouragé l'ame honnete et deinteressée de cette
femme qui a en moi la plus grande confience mais encore je lui

1. In May of 1778, de Reine had sent a sample of these beans and directions for planting: XXVI, 386.

2. A three-page memoir entitled "Observations sur Le Caladaroû ou
Mozambron, Gomme des indes Arabiques" is among BF's papers at the APS.
It states that while *moʒambron* (defined in Larousse as aloes sap) includes the
aloe plant as one of its ingredients, it contains other, unknown drugs which
scientific study may reveal. *Moʒambron* can be obtained easily and cheaply in
Pondicherry or other establishments along the Coromandel Coast of India.
The author gives directions for an infusion of *moʒambron* in good wine
brandy and prescribes different doses according to the age, strength, and
temperament of the patient, as well as to the complaint. The remedy is particularly effective for falls, contusions, and fractures.

3. De Reine previously wrote about a topical remedy for fractures, urging
BF to invite the author, Mme la veuve Detoujan, to discuss its usefulness:
XXVII, 309–10.

ay dit que je nepargneroit rien pour mettre a portée de faire l'experience de Son topique, et pour empecher qu'il ne Soit perdu.

Quelle Epargne pour les Souverains, Surtout en tems de guerre, independenment de la precieuse conservations des hommes, mais encore Surtout les objets de consommations pour tous les pansements, qui, coutent des Sommes tres considerable.

J'ose vous Supplier, Monsieur, d'etre intimement persuadé, que nul Sortes de vues d'interets nentre pour rien dans mes principes. Et toutes les fois que j'ai Eté assés heureux pour par venir a Contribuer a faire le bien, j'ai toujours été Surpayé d'a-vance par la Satisfaction indicible que j'ai ressenti!

J'ay lhonneur d'Etre avec autant de considération que de Respect Monsieur L'ambassadeur Votre tres humble et tres obeissant Serviteur   DE REINE

ancien Cap. d'infanterie rue Sataury pavillon jourdain aux 4. bornes./.

Avez vous eu des nouvelles du Riz nababe que je vous ay donné pour semence./.[4]

Notation: Le Reine. Versailles 26 avril 1780

From Henry Grand   AL: American Philosophical Society

Mercredi [between April 26 and May 31, 1780?][5]
Mr. hy. Grand a lhonneur de présenter ses respects à Monsieur le Docteur franklin, il fut hier au soir a Passy pour lui demander de

4. He had sent the fine rice with the beans two years earlier. He writes again on June 20 (APS), to deliver a bottle of the raki he has mentioned. In the East Indies it is preferred over other spirits for making *punche.* If BF or his friends would like he can obtain eighty bottles more at three *l.t.* each. The letter and the raki he leaves with Mme Meunier at the hôtel de Jouy, the hotel Chaumont had recommended earlier: XXIX, 191. See also Jean Lagny, *Versailles, ses rues* (Versailles, 1990), p. 107.

5. The second Wednesday and the last Wednesday of Jones's triumphal Paris visit, during which he received numerous dinner invitations like the present one. (The first Wednesday, April 16, preceded his decision to prolong his visit.) One of his hosts was BF, who paid 63 *l.t.* for a dinner at Ver-

la part de Mr. Girardot[6] si il seroit engagé pour diner vendredi ou samedi, désirant beaucoup avoir lhonneur de sa compagnie celui de ces Jours qui lui sera le plus comode, avec Mr. Paul Jones.

Des que Mr. hy. Grand aura la reponse de Monsieur franklin il l'enverra à Monsr. Girardot, qui aura lhoneur de linviter a diner pour celui de ces deux Jours quil sera degagé.

Addressed: A Monsieur / Monsieur le Docteur / franklin / Passy

Notation: Hy. Grand

From Thomas Bond

ALS: American Philosophical Society

My dear Sir   Philadelphia April 27. 1780
   The young Gentlemen whom I wish to be so lucky as to be the bearers of this to you, Mr. John Foulke & Mr. George Fox are the sons of our worthy deceased Friends Judah Foulke and Joseph Fox.—[7] They have both had a liberal Education, and are now in the Laudable pursuit of further useful knowledge in Europe: and being desirous of your Advice and Patronage there, have requested me to introduce them to You, which I undertake

---

sailles to entertain "Capt. Jones & the Gentlemen from L'Orient": Cash Book.

6. Henry's father Ferdinand and Jean Girardot de Marigny were fellow bankers.

7. Joseph Fox died in 1779: VI, 284n. His son George (1759–1828) left Philadelphia the following spring and remained in Europe until the end of the war, residing most of the time in Saint-Florentin, Burgundy; by October, 1783, he was back in America (Fox to WTF, Oct. 1, 1783, APS). He was a member of the APS and the Society for Political Inquiries and a director of the Library Company of Philadelphia. He was also a trustee of the University of Pennsylvania and served in the Pennsylvania Assembly. Fox and WTF, who may have known each other when they were students at the College of Philadelphia, became great friends in France; a number of Fox's letters to him are at the APS. Anne H. Cresson, "Biographical Sketch of Joseph Fox, Esq., of Philadelphia," *PMHB*, XXXII (1908), 196–7, and information kindly provided by Whitfield J. Bell, Jr. When WTF departed for London in 1790 he left with Fox a large number of the manuscripts BF had bequeathed to him, and these eventually made their way to Philadelphia repositories: I, xxi–ii.

with Pleasure, as I have no doubt, all your Civilities to them, will meet with the most grateful Acknowledgement, and at the Same time afford you the agreable Opportunity of countenancing & encouraging Merit in your American Children; and directing them to the paths of Public Usefulness.—. Mr. Foulke has deservedly obtained in the Philadelphia University a Diploma of Batchelor of Medicine, where Mr. Fox from Education, Industry & Abilities, was equally Entitled to one in the Arts & may have it when required.

As Nothing can add more to the Wealth, Happiness & Commerce of a Country than the Knowledge of all its Productions, the nature of its Climate & the best Mode of Cultivation, it certainly is a great loss to this vast Continent that Agriculture, Natural History and the Arts, have not been objects of public Attention, amongst us, and as the Knowledge of them is a most delightful & Gentlemanly accomplishment, I have hinted to Mr. Fox, who is a Man of Fortune & Genius and proposes staying some Years in France, that I thought he might do honour to himself, and render very Essential Service to America, by embracing that Opportunity of being introduced to the knowing on these subjects, Especially on Botany, Mines, Fossils, Gardening, Propagation of Fruits, Fermentation of Wine, Beer, Cyder &ac. making Canals, Water Works, Machines &ac. If you find this hint agreable to his Inclination, as you can easily do it, I make no Doubt you will second it properly.— Nature has been very lavish in the distribution of Cold on North America this Winter, it has been the longest & severest, ever known & the most salutary to that part of the Animal Creation, that had Shelter & provision against it, but very destructive to Such as had not. What Effect it has had on Insects, Trees, Plants & Vegetation is yet uncertain. The Philosophical Society will publish an historical Account of it, which will probably be curious & Useful.[8] That Society is incorporated & has a prospect of becoming more Respectable, and

8. The APS appointed a committee to collect data from "the curious in every part of the continent" on the effects of the severe winter. The notice received wide publicity in Philadelphia newspapers and throughout the country: *e.g.*, the *Pennsylvania Packet* for March 23; David M. Ludlum, *Early American Winters, 1604–1820* (Boston, 1966), pp. 111–19. One report, from Lewes, Del., appeared in the APS *Trans.*, III (1793), 326–8.

have the Materials of Another Volume of Transactions ready for Publication, which is only delayed from the scarcity of Paper.[9] Your Family and Mine are well, & unite in the most Affectionate Compliments, to You with, Sr. your very respectful humble Servt.   T BOND

Doct. Franklin

From John Jay

ALS (draft): Columbia University Library; copy: Library of Congress

Dear Sir   Madrid 27 Ap. 1780
   Your Favor of the 7th. Inst. together with a Duplicate of that of the 22d Feby last[1] which I have never seen are come to hand, and give me all that Satisfaction which attends the Removal of Apprehensions of Neglect from those we regard & esteem.
   I am much obliged by the Readiness with which my Bills were accepted, and am happy to find that the Reports respecting the fate of others, are as false as they have been injurious. At Martinico the Loan Office Bills sold at a considerable Discount, and indeed it was no easy matter to sell them at all. I shall take the earliest opportunity of setting them and others right about that matter.
   On my Return from aranjues where I purpose to go tomorrow I shall transmit the Papers you mention with some others equally interesting. I can easily believe that your Difficulties have been great and various. They were often the subject of Conversation in America and I am sure your Friends as well as Country will rejoice in the late important Successes of your Ne-

9. A plan to incorporate the Society was ordered at the Dec. 17, 1779, meeting, and the state legislature passed an Act of Incorporation on March 15, 1780: *Early Proceedings of the American Philosophical Society* . . . (Philadelphia, 1884), pp. 105–6; APS *Trans.*, II (1786), xi–xvi. Fifteen years had elapsed since the publication of the first volume of the *Trans.*, in 1771. See also Edward C. Carter II, *"One Grand Pursuit": A Brief History of the American Philosophical Society's First 250 Years, 1743–1993* (Philadelphia, 1993), p. 15.
   1. XXXI, 513.

gociations. The French Court by continuing steady & true to the Object of their treaty with us will obtain those wh. induced them to make it their Conduct towards us hitherto, has I confess attached me to the whole Nation in a Degree that I could not have thought my self capable of ten Years ago.[2] In my Opinion Britain is to be conquered in America, and that it wd. be more for the Interest of her Enemies to confine their offensive Operations to that Point than enfeeble their Efforts by attention to many lesser Objects. Let america be supplied with Money Cloaths & Ammunition, and she will by expelling her Enemies & establishing her Independence do more essential Injury to those imperious Islanders than they have sustained for Centuries.

I have sent the Letters & Packets I brought for you from America to Mr. Joshua Johnson at Nantz by Mr. Boutillier a young Gent of that place and have desired Mr Johnson to send them to you by the first safe Conveyance.[3]

What Aids this Court may be pleased to afford us is not yet ascertained— I hope they will be such as may be proportionate to the common Interest their Dignity and Our Wants— The Minister[4] I am told is able and the King we know is honest. On this Ground I place much Dependence, for I can hardly suppose that either of them will omit embracing this golden opportunity of acquiring Glory to themselves, & Honor & advantage to their Nation by compleating the Division & Ruin of the british Empire, and that by Measures which will in so great a Degree conciliate the Affections as well as Esteem of America.

Mrs. Jay has enjoyed more Health within this fortnight than she has been blessed with for three months past—[5] She presents her Respects to you and begs that your next Letter to me may enclose for her one of the best Prints of your Self which we are told have been published in France but are not yet to be had

2. As late as 1778, Jay, the grandson of a Huguenot refugee, expressed a preference for a "liberal Alliance" with Britain to one with France: Morris, *Jay: Revolutionary,* p. 475.

3. See Jay to BF, April 14.

4. Chief Minister Floridablanca, no doubt.

5. She gave birth to their second child on July 9: Morris, *Jay: Revolutionary,* p. 703.

here— I believe there is no Man of your Age in Europe so much a Favourite with the Ladies.

I am Dear Sir with great Esteem & Regard Your most obedient Servant   JJ

P.S. I have not recd. the Letter to the Marquis DYranda, but have seen him & I given Mr. Carmichael an order on him for the Sum you mention—

His Excy Doct. Franklin

Notation in Jay's hand: Dr. to Doctr. Franklin 27 Ap. 1780

From Joseph Wharton, Jr.[6]   ALS: American Philosophical Society

Dear Sir   Philada April 27th 1780

The many marks of your esteem for me at Passy, at the same time that they are so many proofs of the kindness of your disposition, lays me under the agreeable necessity of acknowledging them with gratitude and thankfullness. And as that disposition is not confined, but with the most amiable generosity, seeks opportunities of doing good, it gives me peculiar pleasure, that I, even at this distance, can again participate of it, by desiring you to extend it to the bearer, my friend Dr John Foulke.— The Doctor is a Whig in his principles—has subscribed the Test to this State,[7] and though from the singularity of the tenets of the Quakers, he has not been active in the Field, yet, in the line of his Physical profession, has been usefull in the Hospitals. His in-

6. Samuel's brother, who had been at Paris from 1778 through 1779; XXVII, 463–4; XXIX, 261–2.

7. The Test Act of June 13, 1777, required all white male inhabitants to renounce allegiance to George III and swear (or affirm) loyalty to Pennsylvania. In October, 1779, the Constitutionalist majority in the Assembly passed a supplement to the test laws imposing a strict loyalty requirement thereby excluding their opponents from political participation: Robert L. Brunhouse, *The Counter-Revolution in Pennsylvania, 1776–1790* (New York, 1971), pp. 40–2, 49; Douglas M. Arnold, *A Republican Revolution: Ideology and Politics in Pennsylvania, 1776–1790* (New York and London, 1989), pp. 106–9.

tention in visiting France, is to improve himself in Surgery and
Physic; but being a perfect Stranger in Paris, will stand in need
of recommendations to the most eminent in the Medical
branches as well as for favorable introductions into the Hospitals.— Will you therefore my good Sir, as my friend is of unim-
peached Morals, and his Relations long known for good Citizens, take him by the hand, and recommend him to those
Gentlemen who can be most usefull to him? I know you will; and
in this happy thought, I subscribe myself Respectfully, Dear Sir,
Your most obed & most devoted hb Servant   JOS WHARTON

P.S. I beg my best compliments to the Honble Mr Adams &
Mr Jay.

His Excellency Dr Franklin

Addressed: His Excellency / Benjamin Franklin Esqr / Minister
Plenipotentiary from the / United States of America to the /
Court of Versailles. / Favored by Dr Foulke / to be thrown over
board in Case of Capture / private

From Thomas Digges   ALS: Historical Society of Pennsylvania

Lond. 28 april 1780

We have at length got some accots from Clinton. A packet which
left N York the 30th Mar is arrd.[8] There are no official dispatches
from Clinton himself, but it appears from what I can gather at all
quarters, His fleet after much buffiting about & the loss of four
or five transports, got to Tybee the beginning of Feby. there took
in one Regt, Refreshments &ca & got to the Bar of Chs Town
about the 10th or 11th. Mar. The Russell man of war & a packet
left the army & fleet there the 12 or 13th, when they had chiefly
landed all the troops & took post on James's Island, but at some
distance from the Town. One part of the army was at Stono

8. As was reported in the April 28 issue of the *London Courant, and Westminster Chronicle.* For Clinton's account of the siege and May 12 capture of
Charleston see William B. Willcox, ed., *The American Rebellion: Sir Henry
Clinton's Narrative of His Campaigns, 1775–1782* ... (New Haven, 1954,
reprinted Hamden, Conn., 1971), pp. 157–72.

ferry, but they had not taken or attempted to possess any posts or forts of the Americans— By accots from the quarter of ministry I am informd Lincolns army was between 5 & 6,000 well posted without the Town, that the neck of Land had been seperated by a Ditch from the Town, & that in it there were cross canals cut so as to prevent fire & to form barriers. When Clinton saild from N Y he had but 7,500 men upon paper, so that after his losses, & the Storm it is not likely he can act with more than 5,000 men effectives. I think from the feeble flat manner the whole story is told with in the New York papers, and as it is represented here, that this force is not equal to the reduction of Chs Town. One ship of the line & some transports are said to be lost on the Bar; If so he has but one other of the line & abot. 5 frigates to act against the forts Sullivan & James; There were five or six Amn & french Frigates within the port, & if Fort Sullivan is as Strong as it was in 1776 surely with the additional aid of the ships they may be able to give the English men of war a second dressing.[9] There are many particulars in the papers wch I shall refer You to because they will reach you as soon as this Letter can.

The House of Commons of Ireland, has on the two late important national questions producd a majority in favour of the Court of 39,[1] but it appears directly contrary to the wishes of a great majority of the People— The members of that House have been manifestly touchd by English Cash & they have proved themselves as corrupt as ours in this Country. The affairs of Ireland do not seem to rest upon the hinge of a Parliy [Parliamentary] vote, for the people seem quite ripe to right themselves. Both in that quarter & this every person seems heartily sick of the American War & cordially wish it was given up— The State of that war will be enterd into on tuesday next, when Genl Conway is to move the House about it, & intends as I learn to go into the non expediency of it & to make some proposals of getting

9. The first "dressing" was the repulse in June, 1776, of Clinton's first attack on Charleston.

1. An attempt to deny the power of the British Parliament to legislate for Ireland was defeated on April 19 by a vote of 136–97: *London Courant, and Westminster Chronicle*, April 27.

accomodation with Ama.[2] They are too secret for me to get at the terms on which such motion is to be founded or what lengths He means to go in his proposals for accomodation, but some say it is on the old score the preliminary to be a truce for a certain time. D H—— and the Genl. tho they do not frequently commune have I believe had some conversations about it, but I am not very sanguine as to expectations of good to arise therefrom.

I have not had any information that Capn. C—— is again taken & hope it is not true. Capt. M——y after making his escape, has been taken & reconfind.[3] No news about the Cartel & little appearances of her again getting afloat. The Cartel to B—— which was seizd[4] is likely to be paid for, but there is not the leas stir or hope about the release of the equal number of Amns. for those 130 wch came over in the two vessels from Boston. D H—— and Mr E——d B——n often express an inclination to hear from You, the Latter about the meddals.[5] Pray what is to be done further about the meddal I wrote to you upon.[6] For since the forwarding Mr. B——k's letter to you I have not had a line from you about it, nor do I know if the letter got safe, tho I think it was by Cap C——z——u that I sent it.

I am with great Esteem Yours   Wм. S C

Addressed: Monsieur Monr. B. F— / Passy

Endorsed: April 28. 80

2. On May 5 Henry Seymour Conway's bill was tabled by the House of Commons, 123–81: Cobbett, *Parliamentary History,* XXI (1780–1), 570–91.

3. John Manley tried to escape on at least three occasions during his December, 1779, to December, 1781, confinement: XXXI, 418–19n; John A. McManemin, *Captains of the Continental Navy* (Ho-Ho-Kus, N.J., 1981), p. 297.

4. The *Polly,* seized at Bristol.

5. The "medals" were copper blanks for coinage; for Edward Bridgen's proposal about them see XXX, 355–6, 429–31; XXXI, 129–30.

6. This medal was the one from the Royal Society about which Digges had last written on April 6, above, via Capt. Isaac Cazneau, enclosing a letter from Sir Joseph Banks.

From Franco and Adrianus Dubbeldemuts[7]

ALS: American Philosophical Society

Monseigneür   [c. April 28, 1780][8]
Come Le Navire nommé de goude Roos. Cape. Willem de
Wind. appartenant a des Habitans de Cette Province Suivant La
Declaration que nous Prennons La Liberté de vous Envoÿer Cy
Inclus, Sur Son voÿage de Hamboürg a St. Crüx [Croix] a Eté
pris par un Corsaire Anglois & apres Repris Par un Corsaire
Americain, & Conduit a New York, nous vous Prions de nous
faire la grace d'Ecrire a Vos amis aüdit Lieü, afin de Relacher Ce
navire & la Cargaison & de faire Poursuivre le navire son Voya-
ge a St. Crux, en Payant au Capne. Les fraix & pertes Occasionné par Ce delay. Ce que nous Esperrons Obtenir par votre
Intercession.
   Nous avons L'honneur dEtre avec une distinguee Consideration Monseigneur Vos tres Hl & ob Servts
                                        FR & A: DUBBELDEMUTS

From John Jay

Copy: Library of Congress

Dear Sir,   Madrid 28th. Ap. 1780.
   In your Letter of seventh Inst. the Receipt of which I yesterday aknowledged by the post, mention is made of a Bill drawn
by me upon you for 4564 *livs.* 18*s.* 10*d.* which had been persented
and accepted and would be duly paid. I did not Yesterday attend
to the Sum, but the fact is that none of the Bills drawn by me on
you are for that Sum, so there must either be a mistake in your
Letter, or unfair Dealing with Respect to the Bill. On the 3d.
march last I drew a Bill in favour of the House of Le Couteulx,
at Cadiz for 2564 *Liv.* 18*s.* 10*d.* of which I advised you by Letter
of that Date.— All the figures in these Sums being alike, except

7. Who had been writing to Passy on various matters since 1777: XXV,
122–4, and following.
8. The latest date on the enclosure, a series of notarized statements attesting that ——— Assendelft de Coningh and his father ——— Ary de Coningh of Dordrecht were the owners of the *Goude Roos.* APS.

the *4* instead of the *2* induces me to hope it may be a mistake of Yours. If it should not, the Bill ought not to be paid— I have consulted the Entries in my Books, and am certain I never drew such a Bill.

I am, dear Sir, with great Regard and Esteem, your most obedient Servant.   (signed) JOHN JAY.

His Excellency B. franklin Esqe.

From Richard Peters   ALS: American Philosophical Society

Dr Sir   Philada. 28th. Aprl 1780

A Disappointment in procuring a Bill which much chagrines me has prevented my sending you the Ballance of the Money you were so obliging to advance to my Father & for which I beg to repeat my most sincere Thanks.[9] I hope to be more fortunate the next Oppertunity which shall offer. The Difficulty of Remittance is so great that I cannot expect any farther Advances but shall trouble you only when my Remittances shall be sent for the purpose. I beg your Care of the enclosed Letters which I have sent to be forwarded by you. The Enemy had made no Attack on Charlestown the 8th. instant.

I have the Honour to be with the highest Respect & Esteem your very obed Servt[1]   RICHARD PETERS

Mrs. Peters's most respectful Compliments. Monsr Trecesson's Draft not yet presented. I hear he is gone to the W Indies where I have written to inform him I am ready to pay the Money when the Bill is presented.[2]

Dr Franklin

9. On March 28, above, Peters had sent BF 720 *l.t.* as a partial payment on what he owed.

1. Peters wrote another letter to BF on April 28. It recommended John Foulke, a worthy young man of promising medical abilities. On that same day Benjamin Rush also wrote Franklin on Foulke's behalf. He observed that Foulke carried with him "the good wishes of thousands." Both letters are at the APS.

2. He wrote Trécesson that very day: xxx, 585n.

Addressed: His Excellency / Benjamin Franklin / Minister Plenipotentiary / of the United States of America / Passi near / Paris / Hond by Dr John Foulke

From Bethia Alexander   AL: American Philosophical Society

This brief and cryptic message refers to one of the *causes célèbres* of the reigns of Louis XV and Louis XVI. Comte Thomas-Arthur de Lally, baron de Tollendal[3] (1702–1766), son of the colonel in command of the Irish Dillon regiment, was a fervent Jacobite and a brave soldier. Appointed commander-in-chief of the French expedition to India in 1756, at the beginning of the Seven Years' War, he fought valiantly, but antagonized almost everybody through his lack of political sense, his despotic manner, and fits of temper. Captured by the British in 1761 and sent to London, he obtained permission to return to France in order to defend himself against mounting accusations, especially on the part of his arch-enemy, the French governor of Pondicherry, Georges du Val de Leyrit. French opinion was so shaken by the almost simultaneous loss of Canada and India that Lally was made a scapegoat, condemned to death for treason by the parlement de Paris on May 6, 1766, and executed three days later in spite of pleas from the Dillon family and others.[4]

Lally was no traitor and his judiciary murder was soon denounced by Voltaire, "that Don Quixote of all illustrious rascals,"[5] whose *Siècle de Louis XV* was banned because of its anti-parlementary stance. Voltaire's last joy before dying in June, 1778, was to hear that the odious condemnation had been reversed and was to be re-examined by an open-minded commission appointed by Louis XVI.[6] Meanwhile, Lally's illegitimate son, Trophime-Gérard, comte then marquis de Lally-Tollendal (1751–1830), had taken up the cudgels in his father's defense and found himself embroiled for years in a legal and orator-

3. A gallicized form of Tullynadala, in County Galway.
4. See Tibulle Hamont, *La fin d'un empire français aux Indes sous Louis XV* ... (Paris, 1887); Richard Hayes, ed., *Biographical Dictionary of Irishmen in France* (Dublin, 1949); *DBF*, XII, 996–7, 1004.
5. As Bachaumont put it in the *Mémoires secrets*, IX, 134. In 1773 Voltaire published two collections of articles on India and France. Quérard, *France littéraire*, X, 363.
6. Schelle, *Œuvres de Turgot*, V, 556.

ical duel with Gov. de Leyrit's nephew, the *conseiller au parlement* Jean-Jacques du Val d'Esprémy énil. The battle between them lasted from 1778 until 1786, taking place first at the *parlement* of Rouen, where Lally-Tollendal was the loser (in 1780), although he was judged the more eloquent and was sustained by Condorcet.[7] Transferred to Dijon, the affair dragged from 1781 to 1783 and ended badly once again—so badly indeed that the memoir Lally had caused to be printed in Rouen was ordered to be shredded and burned, with absolute prohibition to booksellers and printers to distribute it.[8]

By the summer of 1786, Lally-Tollendal's appeal against the ruling in Dijon was to be heard at the *bureau des cassations* in Paris, and at some point in 1787 the initial judgment was irrevocably reversed.

We do not know whether Franklin complied with Bethia's request.

St. Germain April 29— [1780]

Miss Alexander presents her sincerest Compliments to Dr: Franklin, begs him as the most particular favor he can confer on her Father or her, to convey the packet of papers he will recieve along with this billet—to her Fathers lodgings Hotel D'yorck— The packet contains some papers belonging to Monsieur de Lally to whom Mr: Alexander has the greatest obligations—[9] As they have been printed at Rouen unless Mr: Franklin carrys them to Paris in his own carriage they will be stopt at the gate.

Miss Alexander begs the Doctor would present her Compliments to Madame Helvetius.

Addressed: A Monsieur / Monsieur Franklin / A / Passy

Notation: Miss Alexander St. Germain april 29.

---

7. See Elisabeth and Robert Badinter, *Condorcet (1743–1794): un intellectuel en politique* (Paris, 1989), pp. 170–3.

8. This is probably the document that Bethia is asking BF to deliver to her father. If so, it is entitled *Mémoires et plaidoyers présentés au Conseil d'Etat, pour la mémoire du général Thomas Arthur, comte de Lally, son père* (Rouen, Dijon, and Paris, 1779): Quérard, *France littéraire*, IV, 466. We are certain that Bethia's letter was written in 1780 since Alexander, who generally lived in St. Germain with his family, was in residence at the hôtel d'York on the rue Jacob at this time, as attested by a letter he wrote WTF on June 9 (APS).

9. We cannot tell what those obligations could have been. The families knew one another; the younger Lally, after his father died, was raised by the Dillons at the Château de St. Germain-en-Laye. Not long after the present letter (*c.* June), Bethia wrote BF on behalf of Countess Dillon, below.

From Richard Bache

ALS: American Philosophical Society

Dear sir   Philadelphia April 29 1780.

At the request of my Friend Mr. John Wilcocks,[1] I take the Liberty of introducing to your Notice & Civilities Mr. Fox, Son of the late Mr. Joseph Fox, with whom you was well acquainted; I have not the pleasure of knowing this young Gentleman, but from the Character I have of him, I trust you will find him deserving of your Countenance & protection— I am ever Hond. sir Your Affectionate son   RICH BACHE

Dr. Franklin

Addressed: His Excellency / Dr. Benjamin Franklin / Minister Plenipotentiary from the United States / of No. America at the Court of / Versailles / Favored by Mr. Fox

From David Rittenhouse

ALS: American Philosophical Society

Sir   Philadelphia April 29th. 1780

Amidst the many important objects of your attention I doubt not but you sometimes unbend your mind by an Excursion thro' the fields of Philosophy, I shall therefore make no apology for communicating to you a freak of Nature which seems to be new, at least it is so to us. On the 19th. of August last during a heavy Shower of Rain, not attended by any Thunder lightning or wind, a prodigious Torrent fell on the North or Blue Mountain 10 Miles from Carlisle, and Carried away every Rock and Tree however large that stood in its Course, it likewise tore up the Earth & Stones from 4 to 10 feet deep, and from two to 6 perchers wide, for upwards of 100 rod, that is from very near the top of the Mountain down to the foot of the first Steep Ascent.[2] I had

1. A Philadelphia merchant (XIX, 152–3n) whose bills of exchange had formerly been sent to BF in London: XIX, 330, 418; XX, 18, 65.

2. Later accounts of the "singular mountain freshet" recorded that the torrent had flooded the valley floor, depositing rocks and trees from the mountainside and causing extensive damage to livestock and dwellings. A bolt of lightning struck a tree in such a peculiar way that later Rittenhouse reportedly brought BF to see it. Rev. Conway P. Wing *et al., History of Cumberland County, Pennsylvania, 1731–1879* (Philadelphia, 1879), pp. 114–15, 271.

heard such wonderful accounts of the effects of this Cataract that I was induced to take a ride of 130 miles to view the Spot, and spent a whole Day there with satisfaction and astonishment. The facts I am perfectly convinced of by my own observation, and which appear to me most worthy of your notice are these. It was certainly a stream of water falling from the Clouds in a Spot not above 10 yards diameter, and not any Collection of waters falling in rain, on the surface of the Earth. The face of the mountain will not admit a possibility of supposing it to have been a collection of water already fallen in rain the common way, it being a very high narrow ridge, and the Soil, Stony, Sandy and sufficently porous to drink up rains falling in the common way. And tho' the Stream seems to have continued some time, certainly at least a few minutes, it nevertheless fell invariably in the same Spot, without moving to the right or left. I should be happy in having your opinion on this matter, my own Conjecture is that a Great Quantity of the Electric fluid, passing silently from the Cloud to the Mountain, carried the forming drops of rain from all quarters of the Cloud to one point, and by uniting them producd this prodigious Cataract—

I am, Dr. Sir, with the utmost respect and esteem, your sincere friend and most obedient humble Servant

DAVD. RITTENHOUSE

Dr. Franklin

Addressed: To His Excellency Benjamin Franklin Esqr. / Minister Plenipotentiary from the / United States to the Court of Versailles / Favor'd by Dr. Foulke

From Hugh Roberts[3]

ALS and ALS (draft): Historical Society of Pennsylvania

My Dr. Friend BF   Philada: 29. 4 mo [April] 1780
On revival of the memory of the many agreable hours I have formerly passed in thy Company; Joys of an elivating kind

3. Roberts had claimed the previous September that he was too old to write to BF: XXX, 394.

arise, and make them appear in prospect: yet to consider the length of time elapsed, it seems as if we had lived in a distant age, & risen to take a view of succeeding generations; where but little of the former appearances remain, or make any legible impression.

I frequently pass the length of a Street, without seeing a person with whom I have any acquaintance, for our old Friends are mostly departed; very few remain here but S: Rhoads, with whom I yet spend some agreable hours,[4] and often make thee, our old friend the pleasing subject of conversation.

I sometimes visit thy daughter Sally with her three fine Children, where in thy late place of Abode, many things around, renew a lively impression of my worthy Friend BF— My former labours in the building, planting and gardening way, begin to appear as Solomon has truely described, to be Vanity;[5] and no other conduct will give so firm a hope, as seeking that wisdom, that is from above—

I expect this will come by the hands of George Fox, a young man of our neighbourhood, of good Abilities and Literature, who now embarks for France, and I think intends to endeavour to improve in the Study of Physick; and if it should fall in thy way, to impart to him, some useful hints, for his conduct in a strange land, I shall accept it as a favour, and they may contribute to stimulate his Spirits to worthy Actions, when noticed by a Gentleman so much remarkt for a truely beneficent mind.

I remain with the greatest esteem for thee & thine

HUGH ROBERTS

To Benjamin Franklin

Addressed: To / Dr: Benjamin Franklin

---

4. XXX, 394–5.
5. "Vanity of vanities, saith the Preacher, vanity of vanities; all is vanity." Ecclesiastes 1:2.

From Ostervald & Bosset Deluze

ALS:[6] American Philosophical Society

Monsieur,   Paris le 31. Avril 1780.

Nous rendons nos très humbles actions de graces à Votre Excellence, de ce qu'Elle a daigné recevoir notre hommage respectueux & nous mettre à portée de voir celui dont toute l'Europe connoit les lumieres & les vertus. Envisageant comme une nouvelle faveur l'ordre que Votre Excellence nous donna relativement au prix de l'impression d'une fueille tirée du caractere appellé Nompareille;[7] nous l'aurions exécuté sans aucun délai, S'il ne nous avoit pas parû nécessaire de lui présenter en même tems, comme nous prenons la liberté de le faire, un essai du travail en ce même caractere exécuté exprès dans l'une des imprimeries de cette ville & qui le Sera mieux encore dans la notre. Quant au prix, nous croyons pouvoir le porter à Quatre vingt & deux Livres la fueille in 12° ayant vingt & quatre pages, et ce prix embrassera avec la fabrication, le collationnage & l'assemblage des fueilles que l'on fait payer à part ici. Si le papier de cet échantillon paroit convenable à Votre Excellence, nous en employerons de la même qualité & nous pouvons, comme nous avons eu l'honneur de le lui dire, le fournir à beaucoup meilleur compte qu'en France ne payant aucun impot. L'augmentation des frais de voiture Seroient peu considérables, puisque notre ville n'est qu'à cent lieues de cette capitale. Au reste, nous avons Supposé comme à l'ordinaire dans le prix cy dessus, que l'ouvrage Seroit imprimé au nombre de mille exemplaires. Le Second mille & les Suivants exigeroient Cinq Livres de plus chacun pour le tirage. Animes du plus vif desir de rendre notre établissement Litteraire & Typographique utile à Votre Excellence & à Ses respectables concitoyens, qu'il nous Soit permis de Saisir cette occasion pour lui présenter le tableau de nos prix selon les differents caracteres que l'on employe le plus communement avec quelques essais d'éditions Sorties de nos presses, dans lesquelles

6. In Ostervald's hand.

7. For BF's current interest in *non pareil* type see his second March 29 letter to Dumas, above.

nous cherchons à reunir la propreté dans l'exécution avec une correction exacte.[8]

Nous continuerons d'offrir à Votre Excellence nos services empressés. Des Helvétiens n'oseroient ils point aspirer à la Confiance de l'illustre représentant d'un peuple généreux qui travaille avec tant de Zêle pour obtenir le plus précieux de tous les biens. Nous Sentirions trop vivement le prix d'un tel avantage pour ne pas chercher constamment à remplir les devoirs qu'il nous imposeroit.

Nous supplions, Votre Excellence de vouloir nous apprendre le jour auquel nous pourrons avoir quelques nouveaux ordres à recevoir de sa part, & nous nous empresserons de nous rendre aupres d'Elle.

Nous avons l'honneur d'être avec un profond respect Monsieur De Votre Excellence Les très humbles & tres obéissants Serviteurs   Ostervald & Bosset Deluze

Rue Croix des Petits Champs Hotel de Bretagne.

From the Abbé Arnoux   AL: American Philosophical Society

[before May 1780][9]

L'abbé Arnoux prie Monsieur franklin de lui donner une lettre de Recommandione auprès de quelques uns de ses amis de Neuport de providence ou de Rhodisland pour M. Petry Secretaire de l'armée françoise aux ordres de M. de Rochambeau, et sous Lieutenant d'infanterie.[1]

---

8. On a separate sheet they list a half dozen types with prices, explaining that while the prices reflect a run of one thousand copies, they do not include the cost of the paper. Oversize formats and texts full of algebra are charged at a different rate. They contrast the cost of a ream of their paper with what it would cost at Paris. Their prices include production costs of correcting, gathering, and collating. We have found no evidence that BF ever placed a printing order with the STN.

9. When Rochambeau sailed for America.

1. Perhaps Jean-Baptiste Petry who in 1783 began his lengthy consular career as vice-consul at Charleston: Abraham P. Nasatir and Gary Elwyn Monell, comps., *French Consuls in the United States: a Calendar of their Correspondence in the Archives Nationales* (Washington, 1967), p. 567.

M. petry est très honnette, et on ne scauroit dire trop de bien de son esprit et de son Caractere. Les personnes à qui il sera recommandé seront surement bien aises de le Connoitre.[2]

Notation: L'abbé Arnoux.

The Abbé Thomas du Rouzeau to William Temple Franklin

Printed invitation:[3] American Philosophical Society

[before May 1, 1780]

VERITE∴ UNION∴ FORCE∴

T∴ C∴ F∴[4]

L∴ R∴ L∴ des Neuf Sœurs, Est convoquée pour le *Lundy 1er. du 3e.* mois de D∴ L∴ D∴ L∴ V∴ 5780.[5] à *11* heures précises. *Le très cher et très Illustre f∴ Paul Jones y assistera.*

2. According to an Oct. 15, 1781, letter from Petry's brother, BF had provided letters of introduction to Philadelphia, Boston, and other places. University of Pa. Library.

3. We assume that the invitation to this glamorous induction feast, held halfway through BF's *Vénéralat,* was extended to the grandfather as well as the grandson. Of the fifty-odd masonic convocations preserved at the APS (their dates go from April 9, 1779, through July 4, 1785), eleven are addressed to BF and another eleven to WTF for the same date. Of the remaining twenty-six, all for different dates, fourteen are addressed to BF and eleven to WTF.

Paul Jones, as the French called him, was the hero of the day. He had been received at Court and acclaimed wherever he appeared, especially at the Opera. See Maurice Tourneux, ed., *Correspondance littéraire, philosophique et critique par Grimm, Diderot . . .* (16 vols., Paris, 1877–82), XII, 394.

An extensive account of the ceremony appears in Bachaumont's *Mémoires secrets.* He relates that La Dixmerie's encomium of Jones was brief and sober as befitted the tribute to a man of action, and remarks that "before serving Mars, Jones had courted Apollo," *i.e.,* written tender and graceful poetry. La Dixmerie extolled the American's resourcefulness at the Battle off Flamborough Head, comparing him to a clever coquette: "On croit la prendre & l'on est pris." XV, 225–6. Further, the Lodge commissioned Jean-Antoine Houdon to make a bust of Jones: Morison, *Jones,* pp. 277–8.

4. Très chers frères.

5. La Respectable Loge des Neuf Soeurs . . . De l'année de la Vérité 5780. The masonic year began on March 1.

Vous êtes priés d'y venir augmenter les douceurs de l'union fraternelle.

Il y aura *Lectures, Banquet et Concert.*

Je suis, par les N∴ C∴ D∴ F∴ M∴ V∴ T∴ H∴[6] & affectionné Frere   L'AB. DU ROUZEAU

Secrétaire D∴ L∴ R∴ L∴ Des Neuf Sœurs, rue de la Bucherie.

Si vous ne pouvez pas assister au Banquet, vous en donnerez avis au Secrétaire deux jours avant l'Assemblée. N'oubliez point de vous munir de vos ornemens.[7]

Addressed: A Monsieur / Monsieur franklin fils / N∴ S∴./. A Passý.

From Amelia Barry

ALS: American Philosophical Society

My Dear Sir,   Legn. 1st. May 1780

In consequence of the letter I had the honor to receive from you, dated (Novr. 28th) I applyed to Govr. Pownal, concerning what you mentioned of his publication of the map of the middle Colonies, and of your generous concurrence with his declaration in the preface to the pamphlet that accompanied the new edi-

6. Par les noms connus des frères maçons votre très humble.

7. BF received three other invitations for Masonic meetings in the months covered by this volume. The first, from Rouzeau, [before May 29] announces a banquet to be held on May 29, and to include a working session for the nomination of officers. In the second he sends notice [before June 3] of a gathering for June 3, at which time Edward Bancroft, to be presented by Jones, will be received. A third invitation [before June 26] marks the first appearance of the second secretary of the Neuf Soeurs, Louis d'Ussieux (1747–1805), *homme de lettres,* agronomist, and an editor of the *Journal de Paris* (Larousse). An assembly to be held on June 26 will include readings, music, a banquet, and the introduction of two new members, Professor Pierre-Jacques Bonhomme de Comeyras and *Frère* Louis-Joseph Landry de La Hautaye, *avocats au Parlement.* For d'Ussieux and these two members see Le Bihan, *Francs-maçons parisiens.* On invitations where a banquet is included members are requested to give two days notice if they cannot attend the banquet.

tion:[8] but my letter not having been honored with notice, & my circumstances being realy pressing, I took the liberty to write a second letter, & yesterday received one from him which seems now (thank Heaven!) to let the matter rest with you, my revered paternal Friend.— I will trouble you Sir, to run over an extract from Govr. Pownall's letter, that you may see how he states the affair.

—"I was not silent to your application for any other reason but that I did not know what Answer to write, & having left the whole of the Publication & acct. of the Sale of the *Map & Topographical Description* to Mr. Almon the Editor, & desiring him (which he tells me he has done,) to write to Dr. Franklin & to send him an acct. of what Profits (all Charges deducted,) he can afford to remit on your account, for whose benefit I always intended such surplus profits. I was in hopes you would have heared from the Doctor on the Subject. I have this day since the reciept of your letter of the 27th of March, dated at Legn. spoken again to Mr. Almon, & desired him to write again to Docr. Franklin. He has promised me that he will. I will therefore beg of you to address yourself to Docr. Franklin for such ansr. as he in consequence of Mr: Almon's state of the acct. shall be able to give you & likewise you may address yourself to Mr. Almon Bookseller Piccadilly. Whether this Letter will reach you; Whether my Letter to Docr. Franklin (although I shewed it to Ld. G. Germaine, & beged of him to forward it if he saw nothing improper in it, or in my writing it, which he told me he had put into the post) ever arrived at Docr. Franklin's hand I do not know, & cannot guess never having recd. any acknowledgment of its reciept."

The above with a polite conclusion, expressing a respect for my Father's memory &c, is the substance of the Governor's letter: To you then my dear Sir, I must look up for direction in this affair:— Mr. Barry has been absent from me nine months, on business, & I am indeed in want of money.— Your humanity will I am persuaded, induce you to honor with a speedy ansr.

8. BF's letter of Nov. 28 is missing. Apparently it advised her to write to Thomas Pownall concerning royalties owed her for the reissuance of her father's (Lewis Evans) map: XXXI, 302n.

Most Dear Sir, Your Excellency's ever obliged & devoted
Humble Servt.   A. BARRY.

Your little God-daughter entreats me to present her dutiful
comps. to you.

His Excellcy. B. Franklin Esqr.

Endorsed: May 1. 80

Notation: A Barry May 1st 80

From James Bowdoin   ALS: American Philosophical Society

My dear Friend   Boston May 1st. 1780
   It gave me great pleasure to hear by the Marquis de la Fayette,
who arrived here three days ago that you continued to enjoy a
perfect State of health.
   The Snows of seventy winters seem to have had no other
effect on your constitution than to whiten your locks.
   It is for the credit of philosophy, when its adepts can so well
guard against the attendants of age. But what is age? If it be only
decay, it is not to be estimated by years, but a man's feeling. If a
man feels himself well and Sprightly, or is not sensible of decay,
he is young at a hundred: and the contrary sensations will de-
nominate him old at twenty. I wish the continuance of your
health, and that half a century hence, as well as frequently at
times intermediate, we may have the pleasure of taking a bottle
together, and drinking, et de bon goût—to the health, prosperity and long life of our illustrious ally his present most christian
majesty. When the title most christian, was given to the kings of
France, it was prophetic of the present reign: for what can be
more christian than to relieve the oppressed, and Support and
defend the liberties and happiness of mankind.— Buvons, buvons a la Santè du roy.— Whether this be good french or not, I
do not know: but the wish implied in it, is the wish of every honest American upon the Continent.

Having So good an opportunity by Mr. Guild,[9] I embrace it to inclose to you a copy of the Constitution of government lately agreed on by our State-Convention to be Submitted to the consideration of the people.[1] We shall Shortly know, whether they will accept it or not; or what alterations are to be made in it. It is time there should be a Supercedeas on the old Constitution: things being circumstanced as they are.

Mr. Guild's inclinations leading him to See Holland and France, he expressed a great desire of being introduced to Dr. Franklin. I beg leave to recommend him to you as a worthy Sensible gentleman, who will be able to give you information of the present State of things here. As he has testimonials from the President & Fellows of Harvard College relative to his character, I need not say any thing further on that head.— The bad state of my eyes makes writing painful to me. You will therefore have the goodness to excuse this short Scroll; and to believe that I am with great affection and regard dear Sir—Yr most obedt. hble Servt.   JAMES BOWDOIN

Honble Dr. Franklin

Addressed: The honble Benja. Franklin Esqr / at / Paris

From Condorcet   ALS: American Philosophical Society

Monsieur, et très illustre confrere,   le 1er Mai [1780?][2]

Permettez-moi de reclamer vos bontés pour un gentilhome francais nomé *M. de Beaulieu, officier dans la légion de Pulaski,*[3]

9. Benjamin Guild (1749–1792), a tutor in Harvard College. Upon his return from Europe he opened a bookstore, apparently having accumulated stock for it during the trip: *Sibley's Harvard Graduates,* XVII, 161–6.

1. Bowdoin, JA, and Samuel Adams had been appointed to draft a new constitution, the former constitution of 1778 having been rejected by the voters. The new one eventually was declared approved, although the result of the vote could have been read otherwise: Jackson Turner Main, *The Sovereign States, 1775–1783* (New York, 1973), pp. 178–83; *Adams Papers,* VIII, 228–71.

2. The first year of Beaulieu's parole and hence the earliest possible date.

3. Joseph-Louis d'Escudier de Beaulieu (b. 1753), a former captain in Pulaski's legion, had been wounded and captured during the 1779 Savannah

et actuellement renvoié Sur Sa parole à philadelphie. Je vous prie de vouloir bien le recomander à quelqu'un de vos amis, et en même tems vous imformer de la maniere dont il ne Se Conduit. Ce sont Ses parens[4] qui m'ont charge d'avoir L'honeur de vous écrire. Ils voudraient que leur fils ne soit absolument Sans connaissances à philadelphie, et en méme tems ils voudraient Savoir Si l'on y est Content de lui.

Vous connaissez, monsieur, mon cher confrere mon tendre et respectueux devouement   LE MIS. LE CONDORCET

Addressed: A Monsieur / Monsieur franklin

Notation: Parallel man 1781

From Jean de Neufville & fils

ALS:[5] American Philosophical Society

Honour'd and Dear Sir: Amsterdam the 1st. May 1780.
  May it please your Excellency
  That after a longer Silence then we could wish,[6] we take on now the liberty of recalling ourselfs to her remembrance, with assurance that we will be ever devoted to her, and to the American cause which we have the pleasure now, to see more and more of consequence in our Country; the Influence of the French Court the declaration of the Russian Empire and the Resolutions of our States in consequence,[7] give us great hopes that with a glorious Peace, the Connections of the Republicqs may now be soon realised.
  We received lately a letter from the worthy American Comodor J.P. Jones, by whoes directions we take the liberty of

---

campaign and subsequently went to Philadelphia on parole: Bodinier, *Dictionnaire,* p. 185; *JCC,* XVII, 750–1.

4. Capt. François-Louis d'Escudier de Beaulieu (b. 1704) and his wife Elisabeth Guiraud d'Escudier de Beaulieu: Bodinier, *Dictionnaire.*

5. In the father's hand, as are the other ALS from the firm in this volume.

6. For the latest extant letters from the firm see XXXI, 399, 568–9.

7. For which see our annotation of Dumas' April 24 letter.

troubling your Excelly: with the inclosed, we hope she will excuse our desire to have it forwarded.[8]

The Accounts of the despersed fleet of Clinton, who arrived at Georgia with a small rest of his force may prove again favourable to the Cause of the United States, but more so again as we hope to hear soon in its Consequences; and So may the end of this Campain fixe the Constellation, of the new Independent Republick in all her glory.

With the most extended and devoted Regard We have the honour to be Honourd & Dear Sir. Your Excellency's most obedient And most humble Servants   JOHN DE NEUFVILLE & SON

From Richard Bache   ALS: American Philosophical Society

Dear & Hond. Sir   Philadelphia May 2d: 1780.

Your last Letters to us were dated October,[9] but we have had the pleasure since of hearing you were well in January— I have wrote you repeatedly of late; By this Ship a Son of Mr. Jos: Fox, & another of Judah Foulke go Passengers, their Friends have applied to me for Letters of introduction to you. I have given them Letters, tho' I hesitated a while about it, because I was not well acquainted with the young Men's political Principles, and I knew that some of their most intimate connections were Tories. I hope however, that you will find them deserving your notice— I herewith send you three packets of Newspapers, which I have committed to Mr. Robert Mease's Care, he is Brother to Mathew Mease, who was on board Paul Jones' Ship the Poor Richard, when he took the Serapis; he is a good Whig & an honest Man— Should he visit Paris, he will deliver this himself; if not, he will forward it with the papers to you.—[1] Sally writes you by this op-

---

8. No correspondence between Jones and the firm during the preceding six weeks is extant.

9. We have found only one letter from BF to his daughter or son-in-law from October, 1779: XXX, 423.

1. The Philadelphia merchant Robert Mease was involved in a scheme to bring property from Ireland to America: *Adams Papers*, IX, 272n. He also carried packets from James Lovell: Lovell to BF, May 4, below.

portunity. Accept our Love & Duty—Remember us to Temple
& Ben & believe me to be ever Your affectionate son

RICH BACHE

Dr. Franklin

Addressed: His Excelly. / Dr. Benjamin Franklin / Minister
Plenipotentiary from the / United States of No. America at the /
Court of Versailles / favored by Mr. Mease

From Sarah Bache

ALS: American Philosophical Society

Dear & Honoured Sir   Philadelphia May 2d. 1780

I was willing to take the latest day of Mr Myer's staying to
write to you, as my little Boy was then in the small Pox, that I
might have it in my power to tell you it was over. It is and very
happily, I happened to miss the time of Mr M.'s going, so that he
only took a small letter of recommendation, which I had given
him before—[2] this will be handed to you by Mr Robert Meaze a
Gentleman at whose Brothers house I was at for four Months after I was drove out of Philadelphia, with all my Family, and
treated by them all as a Sister and a Friend, he was there at the
time and is a very worthy good young Man,[3] he will take care of
the news papers which we send, there goes in the same Ship two
of Temples old Friends, young Fox and Foulke, they have letters
from Mr B. to you, and will need none to Temple—

The Children are perfectly well little Betsy sings and is as gay
as a Bird,[4] much more so than they are at this time, for tho tis'
the second of may we are sitting by the fire, and I am told the
Snow remains on the ground in many parts of the back Country, by all accounts the winter in the year forty was not quit so
severe as this, tis indeed the first time I ever wished for Summer— Mr Bache is now writing please to remember me afec-

2. On March 29 RB sent bills of exchange via Pierre Meyer, Gérard's
nephew, above.

3. She probably had stayed with James Mease: XXXI, 20n.

4. Elizabeth Franklin Bache would turn three years old in September, and
Will was seven: XXVII, 602n; XX, 317n.

tionately to Temple, and to dear little Ben when you write, I dare
not indulge my wishes of seeing you all tho they are very strong,
and I hope the time will yet come when we shall all meet, being
as ever your Dutifull Daughter   S BACHE

Addressed: Dr Franklin

From Pelatiah Webster[5]   ALS: American Philosophical Society

Hond Sir   Philada. 2 May. 1780
    I hope you will excuse me, if I interrupt your attention for a
moment to the great objects which Engross your tho'ts by advices of particular things which are objects of genl Concern &
much conversation here, & tho' Important yet may not be the
subject of Publick Dispatches.
    The state of our Finances & Currency is the most alarming
circumstance which Engages the genl. attention at present. I
have devoted my time six months past to the study of that subject, & have wrote five Essays under the signature of "A Citizen
of Philada."[6] The Two Last I Inclose, shod. have sent the whole
set but I coud. not suppose you coud. have time to read them all.
If you shod. find time & think the Essays deserve so much attention shod. be greatly obliged for your Remarks, the Intricacy

5. A Philadelphia merchant and political economist (XI, 32–3n), Webster
published a succession of articles arguing for supporting the war by taxation
rather than loans, curtailing issues of paper money, and establishing a policy
of free trade. He calculated a scale of depreciation, or table of exchange, to
serve as a guide in all dealings involving paper currency and specie: *DAB;*
Anne Bezanson, *Prices and Inflation During the American Revolution, Pennsylvania, 1770–1790* (Philadelphia, 1951), pp. 24–5. This is the first of only
two extant letters from him to BF, and, as far as we know, BF never replied.
    6. Webster published five essays on the subject of free trade and finance
between July, 1779, and March, 1780; they later were collected in a volume
entitled *Political Essays on the Nature and Operation of Money, Public Finances, and Other Subjects; Published during the American War, and Continued
up to the present Year, 1791.* (Philadelphia, 1791), pp. 9–127. The two which
he says he encloses appeared on Feb. 10 and March 30: *ibid.*, pp. 74–127. At
least one of the earlier essays seems to have been well-received: Smith, *Letters,* XIV, 25.

of the subject, & the maze that Congress & all America are in concerning it, with the most alarming Effects, & the pressing necessity of Immediate action & attempt of Remedy, all prove that the attention of the ablest Genius, is Necessary to the Publick safety— In addition to what you will find in the Essays, I have observd, that every Publick department is Deeply in Debt that the Quota demanded by Congress from the several states are dilatorily paid, & if all paid wd. not be Equal to the Expenditures.— Inclose the Resolutions of Congress of 18 March, Least they Shod. not have Reach'd you.—[7] I subjoin the price Current of our market by which you will be able to Judge the State of our Trade & Currency.—[8] The County is yet full of Supplies & is very Little Exhausted, but our Currency [*MS faded*: is not?] a sufficient medium to Draw private property into publick use.— Please to make my best Compliments to Mr J Adams, & Shew him my Essay if you think proper.

I am, Sir, with all Esteem & Respect Your Most Obedt. Hum servt.   PELATIAH WEBSTER

price Currt. at Philada.
W. Ind. Rum £50 per Gall.
Musco. [muscovado] Sugars, £300 per hund.
Bohea Tea £30 per lb.
Bar Iron £2400 per Ton
flour £90 per hund.
Excha. of Hard Money
3 months past, 60 for 1.
Bills on Europe 45 for 1.

P.S. The Common News here is that on the 12 ult. Charlestown was Not Taken but very Closely invested, that the Enemies ships (20 from 64 down to small ones) had got over the Bar & passed Sullivans Island with some Damage & were anchord in the Bay off the point where Fort Johnson formerly stood. Their Land Forces were supposed 6000 men with a recruit of 2000 men Ex-

7. See our annotation of BF to Huntington, May 31, below.
8. The average monthly wholesale commodity prices in Philadelphia for 1780 are provided by Bezanson, *Prices and Inflation*, p. 337. For the ratio of the old continental currency to specie see *ibid.*, pp. 46–7; Ferguson, *Power of the Purse*, p. 32.

pected from N York from whence they saild several Weeks ago. Ours are not Inferior, & the president Huntington told me this Day, that by the Last advices, they were resolved to Defend the place to the Last, & were in fine spirits, & Confident of success.

Genl Washington has not yet moved from his Winter Quarters in N Jersey, his force is Eno' to Ballance that of Genl Kniphausen Who Commands in N York, but does not Seem disposed to action, Except sending out now & then a Forraging party to plunder &c[9] The Enemy keep their post at Penobscot otherwise N England is free. We have Great health Every Where thro' the Country Especially in the army,— We seem to have No Difficulties but in the finances, & they are Easily cured but perhaps the measure of suffering sufficient to procure the necessary Exertions, is Not yet full—. Mr. Laurens was not saild for Holland on 12th Ult, but was then at Wilmington N Carolina—[1] Our markets Are Very high, Beef 60/ per lb Butter 105/. Candles 90/. Hiccory Wood 3 to 400 Dollrs. Cheese 52/6 a 60/. Gammons 60/ a 75/. Sawing a Cord of hiccory Wood 15£ &c. &c.

honble Benja Franklin Esqr

From Jean-Jacques Caffiéri   ALS: American Philosophical Society

Monsieur,   Paris ce 3 may 1780

Permettes moi de vous inviter de me faire lhonneur de venir à mon atellier Du Louvres pour y voir La Statue en marbre de St Satyre destine pour etre placé Dans une Des chapelles de L'Eglise Royale Des Invalides.[2]

9. Baron Wilhelm zu Innhausen und Knyphausen (1716–1800) commanded British forces at New York until Clinton's return from South Carolina: *ADB;* Willcox, *Portrait of a General,* pp. 302, 322–3.

1. In a futile search for a ship to take him to the Netherlands: Richard B. Morris, *The Peacemakers: the Great Powers and American Independence* (New York, Evanston, London, 1965), p. 24.

2. The statue, destroyed during the Revolution, was one of several that Caffiéri executed for the church of the dome in the Invalides and part of a major project begun mid-century to replace with marble the fourteen statues originally sculpted in plaster: Carle Dreyfus, "Les statues du dôme des Invalides au XVIIIe siècle," *Archives de l'art français: Recueil de documents iné-*

St. Satyre etois frere ainé de St Ambroise et Célebre orateur il Se Distingua aux Tribune de Rome ou il plaida plusieurs Causes dans L'auditoire du Préfet Symmaque.

St Satyre est representé Dans Le moment quil harangue Le Peuple a une Tribune.

J'ay Lhonneur Dêtre tres Parfaitement Monsieur Votre tres humble Et tres obeïssant Serviteur   CAFFIERI

Notation: Caffiery, 3. May 1780. a Paris

From Jan Ingenhousz   ALS: Library of Congress

Dear friend,   Brussels May 3. 1780

I hope you are not so entirely involved in the troublesome business of the world Politic, as to have abandon'd entirely the world of Nature, whose laws, made by the supreme wisdom are as constant, and inalterable as its Legislator himself. It would, indeed, be hard to me to concieve, that a man, a Philosopher so often and so successfully employed in researches of the most intricate and the most mysterious operations of Nature, should have so far lost all feelings for those truly delightfull occupations of mind, as to be given over without reserve to the pursuit of systemes framed by men, and build upon foundations of so little solidity, as to be often overturned by mere changes and accidental circumstances.

I have so much the more reason to be persuaded that you are not lost to the world of Nature, tho many of your old friends thinck so, as I know by repeated experience, how[3] easy it is to induce you to the contemplation of nature, by reasoning upon philosophical subjects. Your reading with so much eagerness the result of my philosophical inquiries, your constant readiness to

---

dits, nouvelle période, II, (1908), 261–4, 267, 282–3, 292–3, 294–5. See also Luc-Vincent Thiery, *Le Voyageur à Paris* (Paris, 1790), part two, p. 40. The public viewing of the statue was announced in the *Jour. de Paris* on May 11. For a further description of it and details of its reception see Bachaumont, *Mémoires secrets,* XV, 151, 166–7, 171, 176–7.

3. Ingenhousz wrote "who". BF underlined the word and corrected it.

listen to the news of any discovery in natural knowledge and to give your opinion on questions which I proposed to you so often, when I had the pleasure of enjoying your company last winter,[4] encourage me to submit to your consideration some difficulties on Electricity, which some eminent philosophers thinck inexplicable by your allmost universaly recieved systems of positive and negative electricity.

I. If the electrical fluid is truely accumulated on the inside of a Lyden phial and expelled in the same proportion from the outside, why are the particles of glas not all thrown outwards, when the phial, being overcharged, breaks or is perforated by a spontaneous explosion?

II. When a strong explosion is directed thro a pack of cards or a book, having a piece of tin foil between several of its leaves, the electrical flash makes an impression on some of those metallic leaves, by which it seems as if the direction of the electric explosion had gone from the outside towards the inside, when on the other metallic leaves the impression is in such a direction, that it indicates the current of electrical fire to have made its way from the inside of the phial towards the outside: so that it appears to some electricians, that in the time of the explosion of an electrical phial, two streams of electrical fire rush at the same time from both surfaces and meet or cross one another.

III. When a flash of lightning happens to hitt a flat piece of metal, the metal has sometimes bien pierced by several holes, whose

---

4. For Ingenhousz's visit to Paris, and BF's interest in his recent work, see XXXI, 121–4, 140n, 360. We do not know for how many months Ingenhousz stayed, nor whether he accepted BF's offer of lodging, but the two men spent a considerable amount of time together. In addition to discussing electricity and the conductivity of metals, mentioned in this letter, they evidently also spoke about BF's idea for a new stove (Ingenhousz to BF, Oct. 2, 1782, APS; XX, xvii–xviii, 251; XXVII, 506–7), and his theories on the causes and cure of smoky chimneys (which he finally wrote at Ingenhousz's urging: Smyth, *Writings*, IX, 317, 413–43). At some time during 1780, perhaps inspired by a conversation at Passy, Ingenhousz invented his "new" electrical machine: inexpensive, portable, and constructed primarily of unbreakable parts. Ingenhousz, *Nouvelles expériences et observations sur divers objets de physique* (Paris, 1785), pp. 99–116, pl. I; W.D. Hackmann, *Electricity from Glass: the History of the Frictional Electrical Machine 1600–1850* (Alphen aan den Rijn, Netherlands, 1978), p. 140.

edges were turn'd some the one way, and some the other. So that
it has appeared to some philosophers that several streams of
electrical fire had rush'd in one way and some the opposit way.
Such an effect of lightning has been publish'd lately by father
Barletti.[5]

IV. Tho from the very charging of the Lyden Phial, it seems
clear, that electrical fluid does in reality not pervade the substance of glas; yet it is still difficult to concieve, how[6] such a sub-
til fluid may be forced out from one side of a very thick pane of
glass by a similar quantity of electrical fire trown upon the other
surface, and yet that it does not pass thro any substance of glass,
however thin, without breaking it. Is there some other fact or illustration, besides those to be found in your public writings, by
which it may be made more obvious to our understanding, that
electrical fire either does not enter at all the very substance of
glas and yet may force from the opposit surface an equal quantity; or that it enters realy the pores of the glas on the positive
side, and yet that it can not pervade the thinnest lamella of glas
without breaking it? Is there any comparative illustration or exemple in nature, by which it may be made clear, that a fluid
throw'n upon one surface of any body may force out the same
fluid from the other surface without passing thro this substance?

I should wish to be informed, how you account for these phenomena, and to recieve you answer upon one or other when you
have made up your mind about it, without waiting for the solution of the rest.

If you could communicate to me some short hints, which may
occur to you about the most convenient manner of constructing
gun powder magazines, the manner of preserving the powder

5. Carlo Barletti, *Analisi d'un nuovo fenomeno del fulmine ed osservazioni so-
pra gli usi medici della elettricità* (Pavia, 1780). Barletti, whose conclusions
were anti-Franklinist, analyzed the phenomenon of how a recent lightning
bolt had perforated the weather vane on a Cremonese church. Ingenhousz
had reviewed the work with BF during his visit at Passy (Ingenhousz to BF,
Aug. 20, 1782, APS). See Antonio Pace, *Benjamin Franklin and Italy* (Philadelphia, 1958), pp. 31–4; and for the scientific issues, J.L. Heilbrun, *Elements
of Early Modern Physics* (Berkeley, Los Angeles, and London, 1982),
pp. 213–18.
6. Corrected by BF from "who".

from moisture and securing the building in the best manner from the effects of lightning, you would oblige me. Whatever may occur to you on this head, will be very acceptable. It seems to me very imprudent to heap up immense stores of that terrifying ingredient in stony vaulted buildings in the time of piece, when there is no danger of any combustible matter being thrown upon it, and more so to place several of such storehouses so near one an other as may endanger them from being all blown up, when one should happen to be set on fire by what ever accident it may be. Mr. Le Roy did not keep his word in showing me your advise upon this.

You know, that his Imperial Majesty has intrusted me with the direction of such repositories for as far as regards the danger from lighning. Since this important trust was put upon me, I have thought it my duty to consider this matter with more attention as I used to do before. I have allready a good provision of reflexions, which I intend to lay before the public, as soon as I shall find my self disposed to the undertaking of putting them in good order.

Permitt me to trespass a little more on your time, and to beg you to lay aside, for a few hours, the heavy wight of public affaires, your country has entrusted you with, to fulfill your intended sceem to determine by a well adapted experiment, what metals are the best and readyest conductors of heat. You have allready entrusted me with the account of the method you imagined as decisive for the determination of this point. But, having no right to make any use of this knowledge I am impatient to be informed of its success.[7]

7. Back in Vienna several months later, Ingenhousz did perform this well-known experiment that now bears his name, although when he published the results he explained that it had been BF's idea entirely, and all the credit belonged to "ce grand homme." In early 1780, he wrote, BF had shown him all the preparations; he admired the experiment, and BF generously suggested that they perform it together. To Ingenhousz's disappointment, BF's "occupations continuelles" prevented their carrying it out. When Ingenhousz left Paris for Vienna, in July (he must have returned to France after writing the present letter), BF gave him all the equipment, telling him to perform the experiment at his leisure. See "Sur la différence de la célérité avec laquelle la Chaleur passe à travers les différens Métaux," published in *Nouvelles expériences et observations . . .* , pp. 385–6. Ingenhousz finished the experiment around Dec. 5, 1780, when he reported the results to BF (APS).

As you never refused me some hours of philosophical conversation, whenever I have the pleasure of being with you; I may with as much confidence sollicit you to bestow now and than an hour in answering by writing to some philosophical questions, and thus steal from your political occupations consecrated only to the service of your own country, some hours for the benefit of whole mankind. I can commit no indiscretion in endeavouring to prevent, that such of your philosophical notions, as never are or never would have be known to others, may not be lost to the world. Your ennemies even, I trust, would not grudge at my corresponding with you on such subjects, tho in the middel of that political convulsion, which continues still to shake the very foundations of the mightyest empire, which ever existed on the surface of the earth, and which embitters the minds of many against those, who happened to have a great share in this awfull revolution of human affaires.

Lettres directed to my name *au soins de mr. devroom marchand sur le marché au beur*(?) *a Bruxelles,* will come to right.

One of the best and most skillfull electricians I ever saw, is a young gentleman here, 19 years old, the son of a rich banker, whose name is *Walkiers.* He does scarce meddle with any thing but Electricity, and his father encourages this particular taste. His electrical machine far excells every one I ever saw, his battery is the strongest, that I ever met with. He has a genius for contriving new experiments, and understands thoroughly the theory. He has a most sensible conductor upon the house, which is affected very often by distant clouds or even without clouds. I expect great thinks from him, the more so, as I am [*torn: one word illegible*] natural knowledge can make but slow progress in the' hand of those, who doe not pursue one single object with ardour, and leave allmost every other object aside.[8]

I made some experiments with this young gentleman on purpose to discovre the law, by which are produced the direction of

8. Charles-Louis Walckiers de St. Amand (1760–1787) distinguished himself four years later by inventing a large and powerful endless-band electrical machine that was tested by the Académie royale des sciences to its satisfaction. He presented his memoir to the Académie on Jan. 31, 1784, and BF was appointed to the committee that investigated it: *Procés-verbaux,* tome CIII, fol. 3. See also Hackmann, *Electricity from Glass . . .* , p. 140.

the burrs upon cards and of the impressions and holes in leaves of tin foil, laid between cards, when a strong blast of an electrical explosion is directed thro them. I observed that those burrs and impressions had no regular direction, when the pack of cards was equaly pressed on bothe sides between the two nobs of metal which serve [to] convey the electrical explosion thro them. The stream was allso allways divided in different branches by passing thro these cards and pieces of tin foil, as on some there appeared two three or even more burrs and impressions, which had a contrary direction even on the same piece. Mr. Walkiers had allready made very accurate observations on this head, and found constantely that the direction of these burrs and impressions is allways towards that side where was the least pression. He produced realy these burrs and impressions on what ever side he pleased. This seems to demonstrate, that they produced by the explosion of the body happening at the moment this rapid fire makes its way thro it, the parts of the body taking the direction towards the weakest resistance.

I am with great esteeme Dear frend Your most obedient humble servant and faithfull frend   J. INGENHOUSZ

Endorsed: Dr. Ingenhauss Philosophy

Franklin: Answers to Queries from Dr. Ingenhousz

AL (draft) and copy: Library of Congress

[after May 3, 1780]
Queries from Dr. Ingenhouse, with my Answers, BF;[9]

Question I.

Answer

By the Circumstances that have appear'd to me, in all the Jarrs that I have seen perforated at the Time of their Explosion, I have

---

9. In the draft, BF inserted this title, and squeezed in Ingenhousz's questions, after the answers had been written out. We print only his answers here, and refer readers to the preceding document for the questions.

imagined that the Charge did not pass by those Perforations. Several single Jarrs that have broke while I was charging them, have shown, besides the Perforation in the Body, a Trace on both sides the Neck, wherein the Polish of the Glass was taken off, the Breadth of a Straw; which prov'd that great Part at least, of the Charge, probably all, had passed over that Trace. I was once present at the Discharge of a Battery containing 30 Jarrs, of which 8 were perforated and spoilt at the Time of the Discharge, yet the Effect of the Charge on the Bodies upon which it was intended to operate, did not appear to be diminished. Another Time I was present when twelve out of Twenty Jarrs were broken at the Time of the Discharge, yet the Effect of the Charge which pass'd in the regular Circuit, was the same as it would have been if they had remained whole. Were those Perforations an Effect of the Charge within the Jarr forcing itself thro' the Glass to get at the Outside, other Difficulties would arise and demand Explanation, 1. How it happens that in 8 Bottles and in 12 the Strength to bear a strong Charge should be so equal, that no one of them would break before the rest and thereby save his Fellows; but all should burst at the same Instant? 2. How it happens that they bear the Force of the great Charge till the Instant that an easier Means of Discharge is offered them, which they make use of, and yet the Fluid breaks thro' at the same time? My Conjecture is, that there has been in the Place where the Rupture happens, some Defect in the Glass, some Grain of Sand perhaps, or some little Bubble in the Substance, nearly void, where during the Charging of the Jarr the Electric Fluid is forc'd in and confin'd, till the Pressure is suddenly taken off by the Discharge, when not being able to escape so quickly, it bursts its way out by its elastic Force. Hence all the Ruptures happen nearly at the same Instant with the regular Discharge, tho' really a little posterior, not being themselves Discharges, but the Effects of a Discharge which pass'd in another Channel.

Question II

Answer

Those Impressions are not Effects of a moving Body, striking with Force in the Direction of its Motion; they are made by the

Burs rising in the neighbouring perforated Cards, which rise accidentally sometimes on one Side of a Card, sometimes on the other in consequence of certain Circumstances in the Form of their Surfaces or Substances or Situations. In a single Card supported without touching others while perforated by the passing Fluid, the Bur generally rises on both Sides, as I once show'd to Mr Symmer at his House.[1] I imagine that the Hole is made by a fine Thread of El. Fluid first passing, and augmented to a bigger Thread, at the Time of the Explosion, which obliging the Parts of the Card to recede every way, condenses a Part within the Substance, and forces a Part out on each side, because there is least Resistance.

Question III.

This will be answer'd in my Remarks on M. Barletti's Book which Remarks when finish'd I will send you.[2]

Question IV.

That the Electric Fluid by its repulsive Nature is capable of Forcing Portions of the same Fluid out of Bodies without entring them itself, appears from this Experiment. Approach an isolated Body with a rubb'd Tube of Glass; the Side next the Tube will then be electris'd negatively, the opposite positively. If a pair of Cork Balls hang from that opposite side, the Electrical Fluid forc'd out of the Body, will appear in those Balls, causing them to diverge. Touch that opposite Side, and you thereby take away the positive Electricity. Then Remove the Tube, and you leave the Body all in a negative State. Hence it appears that the Electric Fluid appertaining to the Glass Tube did not enter the Body; but retired with the Tube, otherwise it would have supply'd the Body with the Electricity it had lost.

1. For Robert Symmer see VIII, 417n; I. Bernard Cohen, *Franklin and Newton* ... (Philadelphia, 1956), pp. 543–6; J.L. Heilbrun, *Elements of Early Modern Physics* (Berkeley, Los Angeles, and London, 1982), pp. 213–14.

2. BF finally sent them on June 21, 1782: "An Attempt to explain the Effects of Lightning on the Vane of the Steeple of a Church in Cremona, August, 1777. Addressed to Dr. John Ingenhouss." The text is published in Smyth, *Writings*, VII, 88–97.

With regard to Powder Magazines

My Idea is,

That to prevent the Mischief which might be occasion'd by the Stones of their Walls flying about in case of accidental Explosion, they should be constructed in the Ground; that the Walls should be lin'd with Lead, the Floor Lead, all ¼ Inch thick & the Joints well solder'd; the Cover Copper; with a little Scuttle to enter, the whole in the Form of a Canister for Tea. If the Edges of the Cover scuttle fall into a Copper Channel containing Mercury, not the smallest Particle of Air or Moisture can enter to the Powder, even tho' the Walls stood in Water, or the whole was under Water.[3]

To Duvivier AL (draft): American Philosophical Society

Monsieur   à Passy ce 4 Mai 1780

J'ai montré les Epreuves de la Medaille à plusieurs Personnes, qui les ont trouvées bien, a l'exception des Lettres qui composent l'Inscription dans l'Exergue. Elles sont si irregulieres, que je vous prie de les corriger s'il est possible. J'ai l'honneur d'etre

A M. du Vivier, Graveur du Roi aux Galeries du Louvre

See Vote about the Medals—

To Simon-Pierre Fournier le jeune[4]

AL (draft): American Philosophical Society

Monsieur   à Passy ce 4 Mai 1780

Je parle si mal François que je ne suis pas surpris de trouver que vous ne m'ayez pas bien compris relativement au Portrait

---

3. This is an entirely different conception than was tentatively proposed to the Académie des sciences in March, 1779, by a committee that included BF: XXIX, 209–11.

4. In response to a letter now missing. The portrait Fournier is requesting was to be painted by Alexis Judlin (d. 1810), who had exhibited miniatures at the Royal Academy: Sellers, *Franklin in Portraiture*, pp. 135–6, 317–20.

que vous avez desiré. Quand j'ai fait Mention de M. du Plessis, c'etoit pour dire, qu'ayant fait un bon Portrait de moi en grand pour M. de Chaumont, votre Artiste pouvoit le Copier ce Portrait en Miniature pour vous. Mais comme vous aimiez mieux de le faire tirer d'apres nature j'ai consenti, pour vous obliger, de donner des Séances à tel Artiste que vous voudriez employer, quoique ce soit une chose trés ennuyante pour moi, & que je l'eusse déja refusé a plusieurs. Il me semble, par quelques Expressions dans votre Lettre, que vous entendez que je payera l'Artiste. Il faut donc que nous nous entendions mieux avant de commencer. Car quoique je sois très sensible a l'honneur que vous voulez me faire d'accepter mon Portrait Et en meme tems je ne crois pas qu'ils meritent que vous en fassiez la Dépense. Je vous dirai que je ne suis ni assez riche ni assez vain pour en faire tirer a 8 ou 10 Louis la piece pour les donner en Presents.

Je trouve l'N & l'& bien formés.[5] Je vous remercie de vôtre Pièce sur la belle Invention de Caracteres de Musique.[6] Je suis étonné qu'ils ne soient plus en Usage. Je n'ai jamais vu le Traité sur l'Origine de l'Imprimerie, & je suis bien curieux de le voir.[7] Avant que vous donniez vos Ordres pour le Moule a Lucien je serois bien aise de vous voir, & de conferer avec vous sur le Poids de la Fonte, & le Prix. Je suis, avec beaucoup d'Estime et de Consideration, Monsieur &

Presentez je vous prie mes Respects a Made Fournier.

5. A reference to the script type that Fournier was making for BF; see XXX, 346–7. The "N" and an ampersand can be seen in the specimen sheet reproduced in XXX, facing p. 347.

6. The piece was actually written by Fournier's father, Pierre-Simon: *Traité historique et critique sur l'origine et les progrès des caractères de fonte pour l'impression de la musique* . . . (Paris and Berne, 1765). It represented the successful conclusion of Fournier's struggle against the music-printing monopoly; see Harry Carter, *Fournier on Typefounding* (London, 1930), pp. xxii–xxxi.

7. A group of pieces by Pierre-Simon Fournier, collected under the title *Traités historiques et critiques, sur l'origine et les progrès de l'imprimerie* (Paris, 1758–61). BF bequeathed his copy to BFB.

From Dumas

ALS: American Philosophical Society; AL (draft): Algemeen Rijksarchief

Monsieur,   Lahaie May [4,][8] 1780.

Je ne manquerai pas de vous rendre compte de ce qui se passe ici. Vous avez bien raison d'appeller interessant ce qui S'y passe avec la Russie.[9] C'est un grand coup, entr'autres pour l'Amérique: car à présent il est sûr que la Rep. ne pourra être entrainée dans cette guerre en faveur des Anglois, qui, d'ailleurs, par leur Déclaration du 17 Avril,[1] ont, au moins provisionellement, renoncé à son alliance. Notre Ami est persuadé que cet événement va amener une paix générale, & je le crois aussi. En attendant on arme ici, mais lentement, comme à l'ordinaire. On ne manque pas de vaisseaux, mais d'hommes pour les monter. On vient d'en mettre en commission un de 76 canons, nommé *l'Amiral-général,* & l'on en a donné le commandement au Vice Aml. Hartsing[2] bon républicain, & grand ami de notre ami.

Comptez, Monsieur, qu'il ne tiendra pas à moi, que je ne sois réconcilié avec. . . . [Ambassador La Vauguyon], quoique d'autres trouvent que j'ai déjà trop rampé devant lui, & que c'est là ce qui me fait traiter avec plus de dureté, & même contre toute raison: car on a dit à notre ami, qu'encore qu'on désapprouvoit certaine action on exigeoit cependant que je justifiasse l'acteur: ce qui est—mais brisons là-dessus. Je ne veux plus vous troubler, Monsieur, par des accusations de qui que ce soit. Je n'ajouterai que ceci: c'est que la même main qui a ouvert ma Lettre à Mr. C——,[3] avoit ouvert précédemment celles que Mr. C——

8. We have supplied the day of the month from the draft. With the ALS Dumas enclosed extracts from the supplements to the April 21, 25, and 28 issues of the *Gaʒ. de Leyde* (nos. XXXII–XXXIV) concerning Dutch relations with Britain, Russia, and France.

9. The States General's decision to negotiate with Russia about joint action to protect neutral shipping rights; see our annotation of Dumas' April 24 letter.

1. The Order in Council suspending Dutch commercial privileges about which Dumas had informed BF on April 24.

2. Andries Hartsinck (b. 1720), who had become a vice admiral in 1776: *NNBW,* VIII, 698. The news about him appeared in the May 2 issue of the *Gaʒ. de Leyde* (no. XXXV, sup.).

3. Georges Grand, who had opened Dumas' letter to Carmichael.

m'avoit écrites, & que ce ne fut que pour engager mon Ami à m'écrire sous un autre couvert, que je lui ai dit trop cruement ce que je pensois; & ce que j'ai dit, se dit tous les jours en cent endroits à Amsterdam, non seulement de lui, mais aussi, à quelques circonstances personelles près, de plusieurs autres maisons comme des Hoope, des Muilman &c. savoir qu'ils anglicanisent. La vraie origine de cela, c'est qu'on veut se venger sur moi de n'avoir pas eu l'approvisionnement de l'Escadre. Dans l'affaire de la Lettre, on en a usé avec beaucoup d'artifice, on m'avoit fait accroire qu'on le tenoit de toute une autre maniere que de la vraie: on m'avoit même fait accroire que j'étois abandonné de tout le monde, même de ceux que vous appellez *mes amis particuliers* à Amsterdam.

Au reste, comme ce n'est que par le canal de ces derniers que je sais que Mr. L⸺ doit venir en ce pays, il y a grande apparence qu'ils le verront avant moi, & qu'ils n'auront nullement besoin que je les lui recommande. Je n'entendois par *la Carte du Pays*[4] que des généralités nécessaires à savoir à tout Négociateur.

Quant au Hollandois qui a été chez vous,[5] Monsieur, si je savois son nom & sa qualité, je pourrois vous en dire mon sentiment plus précisément. Ce qu'il vous a dit est plus que suspect, est faux. Il n'y a aucune ville, ni même aucune province de la rep. qui puisse conclure séparément un Traité avec une puissance étrangere. Quant au Plan que vous avez vu, & dont j'ai envoyé différentes copies en Amérique, Mrs. d'Amst⸺ n'y sont entrés que pour desirer que ce project puisse un jour s'effectuer entre les deux rep., & pour que le Traité, en ce cas, soit tout prêt, & que l'on gagne le temps qu'il faudroit pour le faire dresser, examiner, approuver &c. Vous avez, Monsieur, copie des Lettres de notre ami, où tout cela est clairement exprimé.

Puisque vous me faites l'honneur de me demander mon opinion sur le vaisseau Hollandois pris par Mr. Jones & envoyé en Amérique, je dirai, qu'il seroit juste peut être de le restituer, malgré la déclaration du Capitaine, qui dit que la propriété de la Cargaison est Angloise.

4. Which Dumas had wished to explain to Henry Laurens: Dumas to BF, April 13, above.
5. The next nine paragraphs are in answer to BF's April 23 letter, above.

1°. Parce que le Traité de commerce entre la France & l'Am. établit expressément la maxime de *free bottom free good*.

2°. Parce que ce Traité n'exclut aucune autre nation du même traitement de la part de l'amérique, à tous égards, que la France a stipulé pour elle.

On pourroit cependant alléguer d'un autre côté,

1°. que la Rep. n'a pas encore conclu un pareil Traité avec l'Amérique.

2°. Qu'en vertu de l'Acte de Navigation, les effets réclamés sont illégitimement chargés sur un navire non-Anglois. Il est vrai que les Hollandois repliqueront à cela, qu'ils n'ont jamais consenti expressément à cet Acte de Navigation.

Il résulte toujours de là, ce me semble, qu'on pourroit déclarer de bonne prise la propriété Angloise, mais dédommager scrupuleusement les Hollandois de tout ce qu'ils perdent & devoient gagner là-dessus.

J'ai acheminé la Lettre pour Middelbourg.

Pour revenir à Mr. L——, je me garderai bien de lui mettre dans la tête rien qui puisse faire du tort à l'Am—— ou à lui-même. J'espere même qu'il contribuera à me remettre bien avec certain Seigneur. Du reste, j'ignore quand il arrivera; & si je puis faire ma paix avant ce temps, sans blesser mon honneur & ma conscience, je n'y manquerai pas. Je suis avec tout le respectueux attachement qui vous est voué pour la vie, Monsieur Votre très-humble & très obéissant serviteur   D

Il est arrivé à Amst. un petit Navire Americain, Cap. Hedon consigné à Mrs. J. De Neufville & fils; parti de Boston le 28 fevr.[6] Il ne s'etoit rien passé de nouveau.

Passy à S. E. M. Franklin

Notation: Dumas la haie May 1780

---

6. Perhaps the brigantine *Hannah*, 8, William Haydon commanding: Allen, *Mass. Privateers*, p. 163; Claghorn, *Naval Officers*, p. 146.

From James Lovell

ALS: American Philosophical Society

Hond Sir   May 4th 1780

I cannot write with official authority nor have I time to enlarge now upon our public affairs owing to the particular Circumstances of the Mass: Delegation which forces me to attend in Congress[7] and the Vessel will probably sail before our Adjournment this Afternoon. I refer you to the Journals & Gazettes together with Mr. Robert Mease's Conversation. It is not necessary that I should recommend this Gentleman to your Civilities: your Knowledge of his Family, and his present Care to forward Pacquets to you,[8] both secure for him your Attentions.

We have had no Letter from you since one of Sepr. 30th. read Feb. 23d.[9] nor have we at any Time recd. a Copy of the Instrument annulling the 11th. and 12th. articles[1] the publication of which articles in our Newspapers make some public proceedg. here necessary in regard to the Annullment. It was some time in Novr. —78 as appears by the Copies of some Letters delivered by Mr Adams the originals of which did not come to hand.

Our Affairs at the Southward are to be judged of by the Gazettes. We 11. 14. 8. 12. 1. 3. 27. 13. 11. 17. 6.[2] We have a very good Prospect that the late War between 3. 6. 18. 23. 3. 4. 13. 6. 14. 24. 18. 13. 16. 26. 4. 23. 3. 4 is the last that will spring up between those Tribes. They have convinced each other by every

---

7. At the moment only two members of the Massachusetts delegation, Lovell and Samuel Holten, were in attendance: Smith, *Letters*, xv, xviii–xix.

8. He carried packets for JA as well: *Adams Papers*, IX, 270.

9. xxx, 420–1. In fact Congress had received and read a much longer letter from Franklin of Oct. 4 (xxx, 463–74): *JCC*, xvi, 226.

1. Of the Treaty of Amity and Commerce. Congress had exercised its option of dropping these two articles and in November, 1778, the commissioners and Vergennes exchanged declarations to that effect: xxvii, 330–2, 668.

2. Lovell was using the cipher he had sent to BF on Feb. 24: xxxi, 521–2. BF, correctly assuming that the key was still "cor," attempted to decipher it on the back of the address sheet. He became confused at number 13 (which was Lovell's mistake; it ought to have been a 1) and wrote out every permutation of possible letters for both this sentence and the phrase below. He never understood them. This numerical string should read "may not boast." The phrase in the next sentence should read "the merchant & farmer." Lovell sent JA an explanation of the cipher in a letter of this same date, but JA had no more luck with it than did BF: *Adams Papers*, IX, 272n.

Skirmish that they ought to be in perpetual Amity on the Ground of reciprocal Benefits.

I do not feel easy till I have my Pacquets on Board. If I have Time I will again write to you by the same opportunity more largely.

Be assured of my greatest Respect for your Character and my sincerest Wishes for your Prosperity being, Sir, your Friend and most humble Servant   JAMES LOVELL

Addressed: Honorable/ Doctor Franklin/ Minister plenipory./ of the United States/ of America/ in/ France/ favd by/ Mr. Mease

Endorsed: J Lovell May 4. 80 / Lovel

From Gabriel-Louis Galissard de Marignac: Bill for Benjamin Franklin Bache's Schooling

DS: American Philosophical Society

[May 5–September 5, 1780]

Monsieur Franklin doit pour la pension de Monsieur son petit fils depuis le 5e. May au 5e. 7bre 1780	£175.10."
Papier, encre plumes & cahiers	4. ". "
pr. racommoder ses bas	3. ". "
Une Médecine	1. ". "
pr. l'achat de 12. Mouchoirs	9.10."
pr. une ligne	".12."
comptes à Mr. Aval	10.10."
Prix des bonnes Notes	".10."
pr. differens ports de lettres	5.". "
Maitre de dessin	14. ". "
ovide, cornelius Nepos, appendix & autres livres	6.10."
pr. les fraix des promotions	4. ". "
Un chapeau & des gands	6. 5."
Rubans de queuë	".12."
pr. le Domestique à un gouter	".10."
blanchissage de linge 4. Mois	6. ". "
pr. une cage	1. ". "

355

pr. le maitre d'exercice	1. ". "
pr. 2. habits Cottone fournitures & façons de 3.	37.10."
pr. la comédie	3.13.6
pr. achapt de bas	4.10."
pr. le gouter, que son grand Papa lui a permis³	73. ". "
pr. le compte au Marchand Drapier	15.15."
Differens blanchissages d'habits, vestes, culottes & bas de soye	5. 5."
pr. ses Dimanches & argt: donné	9.10."
pr. le Maitre d'Anglois	14.12."
pr. le cordonnier	12. ". "
pr. racommoder des bas	2. ". "
pr. un ruban de queuë	". 6."

£427.10.6

427 *l.t.* 10 *s.* 6. le louis à 14 *l.t.* 10. 6. pr. 24 *l.t.* argt. de france
£706. 8."

pr. acquit MARIGNAC

Notation: BF. Baches Accts at Geneva.

From Sartine

Copy: Library of Congress

A Versailles le 5 May 1780.

J'ai reçu, Monsieur, la Lettre que vous m'avez fait l'honneur de m'écrire le 13. du mois dernier.⁴

D'après la Demande qui m'en a été faite par M. Le Ray de Chaumont, J'ai donné des ordres à Dunkerque pour faire remettre à la Disposition de son fondé de Procuration la Corvette La Cesse. De Scarboroug. Cette affaire est terminée depuis le 14

---

3. For the special treat BFB was expected to provide his schoolmates see Marignac to BF, published under June 19, and BF to SB, June 27, both below. BF paid this bill from Marignac on Sept. 6, by a draft on Grand: Sums Paid by B. Franklin for B. F. Bache, Dec. 27, 1776–Sept. 6, 1780 (APS); Account XVII (XXVI, 3).

4. Someone has mistranscribed the date of BF's letter; it should read 23.

Janvier dernier⁵ ainsi vous pouvez convenir avec M. de Chaumont de tout ce qui concerne la vente du Bâtiment dont il s'agit.

J'ai l'honneur, d'être avec la plus parfaite consideration, Monsieur votre tres humble et tres obeissant Serviteur

(signé) DE SARTINE.

M. Franklin

From Benjamin Franklin Bache

ALS: American Philosophical Society

Mon cher grand papa   ce 6e. mai 1780

Je Souhaiterois beaucoup d'avoir de vos nouvelles, mais je pense que les affaires vous empechent de m'écrire, car sans cela je serois fort en peine, mais du moins je voudrois que mon cousin me donnât de vos nouvelles, et en même temps des siennes, ainsi que mon ami Cockran, je voudrois aussi avoir des nouvelles de mon papa et de ma mama. Je me porte très bien, Je souhaite que vous vous portiès de même; je fais tout mon possible pour vous contenter, je voudrois bien revoir toute ma famille et tous mes amis, et avoir mon frère à Genéve avec moi Madame artaud, avec qui je dinai l'autre Jour, me donna de vos nouvelles, et cela me fit un grand plaisir; Madame Cramer qui a toujours beaucoup de bontés pour moi, se porte très bien; Je me trouve très bien chez Monsieur de Marignac, et lui et madame me traitent comme Leurs enfants. J'ai l'honneur d'être avec un prond [profond] respect Mon cher grand papa votre tres humble et tres obeissant petit fils   BENJAMIN FRANKLIN B

Addressed: A Monsieur / Monsieur Franklin Ministre / Plénipotentiaire des provinces unies / de l'Amérique auprès de sa Majesté / très chrétienne. Chez Monsieur / Grand Banquier ruë Montmartre / A Paris

Notation: B.F.B. to Dr. F Geneva May 6. '80

5. For these orders to transfer the ship to Chaumont's representative see Archives de la Marine, B¹XCIII: 149. For the sale of the *Countess of Scarborough* see BF's May 12 letter to the Dunkirk admiralty judges, below.

From the Board of Admiralty
ALS: National Archives

Sir   May 6th 1780

By the enclosed affidavits and protests[6] you will perceive that James Robinson Esquire late commander of the continental Sloop Fly being dispossed of that sloop by a Majority of the Crew at Sea, was together with his Docter and Pilot put on board a Schooner called the Daphne bound from Providence to New York[7] which schooner they also took possession of and carried her with her Cargo, to the french fleet then laying off Georgia, where the said schooner Daphne and Cargo was taken from them by the Captain of the french frigate Chimére.[8] Captain Robinson his docter and Pilot being by a resolved of Congress dated the 14th of October 1777[9] entitled to the Sole property of said schooner Daphne and Cargo applied to the Board for relief in the premisses, who immediately laid the enclosed Papers before His Excellency the Chevr DelaLuzerne Minister Plenipotentiary of France from whom the Board received the following written Message in the french language, "The Chevalier DelaLuzerne has the Honor to Send back to Mr. Holker the papers relative to the Capture of Captain Robinson, this Gentleman must direct three or four proved Copies of them to Docter Franklin who can follow the Affair to the greatest Advantage.

6. The now-missing enclosures probably included the Board of Admiralty's Dec. 31, 1779, letter to La Luzerne forwarding evidence on the incident discussed below: Charles Oscar Paullin, ed., *Out-Letters of the Continental Marine Committee and Board of Admiralty, August, 1776–September, 1780* (2 vols., New York, 1914), II, 146–7. In February Congress had ordered it to conduct a board of inquiry (*JCC*, XVI, 140–1), but we have found no record of one.

7. He first wrote "London", and then interlined "York". Apparently the crew of the *Fly* mutinied in order to turn the ship over to the British and put Capt. Robinson, the doctor, and the pilot on board a British ship bound for New York. For Robinson see Claghorn, *Naval Officers*, p. 261.

8. The frigate *Chimère*, Capt. de Saint-Cézaire, had been part of d'Estaing's squadron since it was sent to America: France, Ministère des Affaires Etrangères, *Les Combattants français de la guerre américaine, 1778–1783* (Paris, 1903), p. 65.

9. This congressional resolve (*JCC*, IX, 802), passed in retaliation for British encouragement of mutinies on American ships, rewarded the captains or crews who brought British ships into American ports or harbors.

Feby 29th 1780." Pursuent to the Chevaliers advice we have taken the liberty to trouble you with the enclosed papers in hopes that you may be enabled to Obtain for Captain Robinson some compensation for the loss of the Daphne and Cargo. I have the Honor to be Your Excellencys very Hble Servt   F LEWIS

His Excellency Benjamin Franklin Minister plenipotentiary at Paris

From Chantereyne   LS: Historical Society of Pennsylvania

Monsieur,   Cherbourg le 6 May 1780.

Jespere que votre excellence aura bien reçu par le dernier ordinaire, la procedure de MM. les officiers de lAmirauté de Cherbourg concernant la Prise hollandoise la flore Chargée pour Compte des Negts De Dublin, faite par Le Corsaire Americain le Black prince armé à Dunkerque, par M. J. Torris qui est parti depuis quelques jours pour Paris, & qui aura lhonneur de vous rendre compte des circonstances qui ont occasionné cette prise neutre.[1]

Je vous prie, Monsieur, de vouloir bien jetter les yeux sur un memoire d'observations que jai fait rediger par M. Groult docteur en droit jurisconsulte le plus eclairé sur les loix maritimes de leurope, dans lequel il fait voir la legitimité de larret de ce navire.[2] Je me flatte que votre excellence y fera toute lattention que merite cette affaire pour le bien des Sujets des etats unis.

Je suis avec un profond respect, Monsieur, Votre tres humble & tres obeissant Serviteur.   DE CHANTEREYNE

M. Le Dr. Franklin.

1. The Admiralty procedure from Cherbourg is missing. Torris had already informed BF of the capture of the *Flora:* above, April 15. The *Flora* was owned by a Rotterdam firm, her cargo (which was not contraband) by Dublin merchants; the case is discussed in Clark, *Ben Franklin's Privateers,* pp. 128–32, 137–41, 144–5.

2. Thomas-Pierre-Adrien Groult (1733–1814), among whose many publications was *Indication des ouvrages et pièces de législation relatifs à la saisie des bâtiments neutres* (Paris, 1780): *DBF.* His observations, six pages in length, are at the Hist. Soc. of Pa.

From Jonathan Williams, Jr.

ALS: University of Pennsylvania Library; copy: Yale University Library

Dear & honoured Sir.   Nantes May 6. 1780.

I wrote you the 18 April informing you of the Cloathing I had at different Times sent to Brest by M. de Chaumonts direction. I have since Advice that the said Cloathing arrived in Time but that the Transports were all full & Consequently but a small part is embarked.[3] This being the Case I concluded not to send any more 'till further Orders, for it is absurd to be at so great an Expence without at least a probability of having the Goods shipped. Please to let me know what method is to be adopted for the future Expedition of the Cloathing and I shall be obliged also if you will please to favour me with your approbation of what I have hitherto done.

I am ever most dutifully and affectionately Yours &c

JONA WILLIAMS J

Notation: Jona Williams May 6. 1780

From Gourlade & Moylan   ALS:[4] American Philosophical Society

Honord Sir   L'Orient 8th. May 1780

We have received a letter from Doctor Laurence Brooke late Surgeon of the Ship Bon Homme Richard, dated at Lisbon the 6th. ulto. extract of wch. we have the honor of transmiting you agreeable to his request.[5]

We are with the utmost respect Honord sir Your most obt. & most humble Servts   GOURLADE & MOYLAN

3. JW managed to place only 100 bales on the transport *Petit Cousin:* Lopez, *Lafayette,* pp. 193–4; Rice and Brown, eds., *Rochambeau's Army,* I, 118n.
4. In Moylan's hand.
5. Brooke came to Paris, where he stayed until 1783. He then returned to Virginia and established a medical practice in Fredericksburg: St. George Tucker Brooke, "The Brooke Family," *Va. Mag. of Hist. and Biog.,* XIX (1911), 321–2.

Extract from Doctor Laurence Brooke's Letter

"I saild from Curuna the 10 march with Cap. Cunningham and several other American passengers in a Tartan for Virga. and on the 24th. of that month had the misfortune of being taken by the General Edwards privateer between Madeira and the Western Islands.[6] Two days after we had been taken we were all except poor Cunningham put on board a portuguize Snow bound to Lisbon. He was detaind by means of a Scoundrel who had sail'd with him three months in his Cutter and made him known to the Crew of the privateer notwithstanding he had changed his name.

The reason they gave for not liberating him was founded on a false report that the Court of London had offerd a great reward for him either Dead or alive, I left him in very great distress and in a very bad state of health and unless something is don immediately for his releif he must infalibly fall a sacrafice to his misfortunes. I therefore request you will make his situation known to the Honorable Doctor B Franklin, that he may take such steps as will prevent the loss of so valuable subject to the united states of America."

Addressed: The Honorable / Doctor Benj. Franklin / Plenipotentiary Minister / from the United States of / America / at / Passy./.

Notation: Gourlade & Moylan L'Orient May. 8. 80

From the Chevalier de Pougens

LS: American Philosophical Society

Monsieur   Ce 8 Mai 1780
J'ai l'honneur de vous envoïer un paquet que je suis chargé de vous remettre. Le mauvais état de ma santé et de ma vüe m'em-

---

6. The captor of the tartan *Experiment* actually was a Dartmouth privateer named the *Admiral Edwards* and commanded by John Marden: Neeser, *Conyngham,* p. l; Digges to BF, July 12, 1780 (Hist. Soc. of Pa.); *Courier de l'Europe,* VII (1780), 225 (issue of April 7, 1780).

peche de venir vous le porter moi même, n'aïant pas la certitude
que vous Soiés visible, voulés vous bien me fixer le moment où
je pourrai Sans indiscrétion venir vous offrir mes respects et mon
admiration.

Je joins ici le plan d'un ouvrage dont je m'occupe depuis
plusieurs années; je ne publie pas encore ce discours, peut être le
but que je me propose vous interresserat-il, ne fut-ce même que
par son immensité?[7] J'attens vos ordres et Suis ainsi que toute
l'Europe avec le respect que l'on doit à la vertu Monsieur Votre
tres humble et très obeissant serviteur

                              LE CH. DE POUGENS
                    hotel royal place du Palais Royal

M. le Deur. franklin.

Notation: De Fougere 8 may 1780.

From Fournier[8]   ALS: American Philosophical Society

Monsieur   Paris Le 9 mai 1780
    Je Suis on ne Peut Plus Sensible au Cadot que vous voulez
Bien me faire de Permettre aux Peintre de Prendre deux a trois
Séances Pour avoir votre Portrait je me suis arrangé de Prix avec
luy: je n'ai jamais compté, monsieur, que vous me Le fériés faire

---

7. As he explained in a follow-up note of May 29, he was enclosing the *discours préliminaire* of his projected *Bibliographie encyclopédique.* Turgot had
also received a copy of this prospectus, and was less than enthusiastic about
it, as he wrote to Du Pont on May 27. For all his erudition, the young man
struck him as pedantic, confused, and too inclined to show off. Schelle, *Œuvres de Turgot,* V, 621. Pougens, who was eventually made a member of almost every academy in Europe, probably gave up on this particular project,
which appears nowhere in his long list of publications. His May 29 request
for an interview must have produced a favorable answer since Pougens wrote
happily on [May 31] that he would visit the Doctor the following day, June
1. Both letters are at the APS. No further letter between them has survived
but Pougens remained a lifelong friend and correspondent of WTF. In 1825,
he published in Paris a book of reminiscences entitled *Lettres Philosophiques
à Madame *** sur divers sujets de morale et de littérature,* in which he quotes BF
on various topics.
8. In answer to BF's of May 4, above.

LE FRANKLIN.

Les Sciences et les Arts que l'on cultive dans un Etat decelent le genie de la Nation et l'esprit du Gouvernement.

Ce Caractere a été gravé à Paris, pour M. FRANKLIN, en 1780, par S.P. *Fournier* le jeune.

Early Proof Sheet of "Le Franklin"

a vos Dépens, C'est Bien heureux Pour moi de L'avoir: quand il m'en couteroit 20. Louis je Les donnerais avec Plaisir. Ce n'est Point je vous jure flatterie de ma part; C'est Le Plus Beau Cadot que j'aurai eu de ma vie, et qui me fera honneur et même a ma Postérité. Le Peintre vous Remettra Cette Lettre, et je vous Prierai de lui donner une Séance Si votre tems vous Le Permet.[9] Je Pars mardy Pour Chartres, et dans un moi ou Six semaines je vous apporterez Lépreuve en Lettre de votre Caracteres ainsi que Le traité des observations Sur L'origine de L'Imprimerie fait Par mon pére, et que vous trouverez Surement Bien Ecrit. En attendant Lhonneur de vous voir je vous Prie de me Croire avec des Sentiments d'estime, et de Recconnoissance Monsieur, Votre très humble et très obéissant Serviteur   FOURNIER

Mr francklin a Passy.

Addressed: A Monsieur / Monsieur francklin / A Passy

Notation: fournier Paris le 9 may 1780

To Thomas White *et al.*   Copy: Library of Congress

Gentlemen   Passy, May 10. 1780.

I received yours of the 5th. Instant and am glad to hear that you are safely arrived at Dunkirk. But the Letter you mention of the 4th. April, is not yet come to hand,[1] Though I have one of the 11th. from the french Consul at Bergen.[2] He gives me such an Account of your good and prudent Conduct while there, as affords me great pleasure. I had complain'd in strong Terms to the Danish Court, of the Barbarity of turning you ashore in a strange Place without any thing to subsist on;[3] and I am glad to learn from the Consul, that you afterwards were treated with hospitality and kindness. I hope we shall also obtain Satisfaction

---

9. It evidently did not; Judlin gave up trying to see BF by July 15, when he requested a portrait to copy. Sellers, *Franklin in Portraiture*, pp. 318–19.
1. We have located neither theirs of May 5 nor April 4, but we do print one from them of April 11.
2. From Chezaulx, above.
3. XXXI, 263.

for the Prizes so improperly given up to the English. In the mean time my Instructions to you are, that you proceed immediately to L'Orient, in Order to join the Alliance now there under the Command of Capt. Jones, and about to depart for america. If you should want a little Assistance towards the Expence of your Journey or Voyage thither, Mr. Coffin will be so good as to supply you:[4] But as nothing has come in to my hands from her Cruises, and she has Occasioned me very heavy Charges which I am but ill provided to bear, you will require no more from him than is absolutely necessary. I am Gentlemen, Your most obedt.

Messrs. Thos. White, Thomas fitzgerald, alexr. Moore, Nath. Marston, &c. James Hogan. [*in* WTF'*s hand:*] Officers of the Alliance

To Jonathan Williams, Jr.

Copy: Library of Congress

Dear Jonathan   Passy, May 10, 1780.

    I received yours of the 18th. past and the 6. Inst. and approve of the steps you have hitherto taken to dispatch the Goods. It Grieves me to understand that the ships from Brest could not take them. At this distance from the Ports, and unacquainted as I am with such affairs, I know not what to advise about getting either that Cloathing, or the small arms and Powder at L'Orient, or the Cloth of Mr. Ross, transported to America; and yet every body writes to me for orders, or advice, or opinion, or approbation, which is like calling upon a blind Man to judge of Colours. I know those things are all wanted in America; I am distress'd much with the Thought of a Disappointment, and Mr. De Chaumont, the only Person here whom I could rely on for Counsel, has been ill these three Weeks, and incapable of attending to any Business. I must therefore desire you to find out some good means of conveying all these Goods and execute it in the best

---

4. Coffyn apparently did supply the men with 18 *l.t.* to see them to Paris. They arrived there on May 21, continued to Passy, "had a little conversation" with BF, and left for Lorient on the 24th: Charles Herbert, *A Relic of the Revolution . . .* (Boston, 1847), pp. 240–2.

manner you can, and with all possible Expedition. If you freight a Vessal, try to get her away under convoy of the Alliance; but if that cannot be done, she must wait for some other Convoy. I am ever your affectionate Uncle.

For what concerns Mr. Ross's Cloth I must leave that to his Discretion having really nothing to do with it. But it may be well that you should consult together.

Mr. Williams.

From Cabanis

ALS: American Philosophical Society

a Brive bas Limousin Route de toulouze Le 10 may 1780
Mon pere[5] qui me parle bien souvent de vous, Monsieur, ne Connait qu'une très petite partie de vos ouvrages, et voudrait avoir des Détails sur La Construction des Conducteurs pour garantir Les maisons de La foudre, et sur celle des *para-tonnerre* dont Les personnes se servent en Amérique. Je prends la Liberté de m'adresser à vous pour cela. Il m'est égal que Les details que vous m'envoyerez, soient écrits en français ou en Anglais: Ce que je desire C'est que vous ne perdiez pas beaucoup de tems à Les Ecrire, et que si vous avez des feuilles imprimées de La partie de vos ouvrages où ils se trouvent, vous me Les fassiez passer tout simplement. Si j'avais pensé que tous vos écrits traduits en français, ne fussent pas dans nos provinces, je Les aurais portés avec moi, et je ne vous importunerais pas aujourdhuy. Leur réputation et La votre surtout, y sont au moins bien répandues et bien établies: j'ose Croire que vous ne doutez pas du plaisir que j'ai à entendre tout Le bien qu'on y dit de vous, et à voir L'interet qu'on prend à La cause de La Liberté que vous défendez. Ayez la bonté de parler quelques fois de moi avec notre dame[6] et avec nos amis D'Auteuil: je parle souvent de vous tous, et j'y pense

5. Jean-Baptiste Cabanis (1725–1786), a former lawyer turned agriculturist, experimented widely on cereals, potato crops, silkworms, fruit trees, and sheep. In 1781 he published his *Essai sur les principes de la greffe*. He was a friend of Turgot: *DBF*.
6. Mme Helvétius.

encor plus. Je ferais ma Lettre bien plus Longue si je n'ecoutais que Le plaisir que j'ai à m'entretenir avec vous: mais vos momens sont précieux, et je dois Les respecter. Faites accepter à mr. votre petit fils et acceptez vous-même Les sentimens Distingués D'estime et d'attachement avec Lesquels je suis, Monsieur, Votre très humble & très obeissant serviteur   CABANIS FILS

a Mr. franklin

Notation: Cabanis fils, Brive 10 May 1780.

From the First Medical Society in the Thirteen United States of America Since Their Independence[7]

ALS: American Philosophical Society

Sir   New Fairfield State of Connecticut May 10th. 1780

A number of Reputable Physicians belonging to the States of Massachusetts, Connecticut, and New York, having in May 1779 formed a Society by the name of the first Medical Society in the thirteen United States of America Since their Independence, and having lately had information of a Royal Medical Society in France Constituted by letters Patent of his most Christian Majesty, of which Society we have the pleasure to find that Doctr Franklin is a member; Encouraged by that humanity, and love of Science, so Conspicuous in the French Nation, and relying on your assistance, and influence, we have presumed to Solicit of the Royal Medical Society the favor of a literary Correspondence; (with this) our letter to the Medical Society is inclosed, and Committed to your care; the letter is left open for your perusal, and if previous to its being laid before that Society, a French translation be necessary, we beg of you to perform that service (as there is not a Member of our Society so intimately ac-

7. A revival, perhaps, of an earlier group of doctors who had organized in Sharon, Conn., in 1767, also under the direction of Dr. James Potter. Potter's statement announcing this new society, presented on July 5, 1779, was published in the *Connecticut Courant and Hartford Weekly Intelligencer,* Oct. 26, 1779. See Richard Harrison Shyrock, *Medical Licensing in America, 1650–1965* (Baltimore, 1967), pp. 18–22.

quainted with the French Language as to make a correct and elegant translation)—[8] We conceive Sir that no Period in the Roll of Time ever opened so bright, and promising a prospect, of the Spread of Liberty, and Science, as this which now dawns in America, and that the all accomplishing hand of Time never erected so important, so Magnificent an Empire, as is now Rising in this new World. The known abilities, & integrity, of our Ministers of State, give us the greatest reason to expect from their foreign Negotiations, the most Important advantages (not only to the Political) but Scientific interest of America, and as you Sir are deservedly Seated at the head of all the American Patriots, we have no doubt of obtaining the favour we ask of the Royal Medical Society, Should our attempt, and design, merit your approbation, and assistance— The plan on which our Society is founded, and the Reason of our asking for a literary Correspondance, you will see in our letter to the Royall Medical Society. After wishing every Blessing to your Person, Compleat Success to all your Negotiations, and in due time a Safe return to this your Native Land we beg leave to Subscribe ourselves your most Obedient, and very humble Servants Signed by order and in behalf of the Society   JAMES POTTER President
Attest OLIVER FULLER Secretary

To his EXCELLENCY Benjamin Franklin Esqr. LLD and American Plenipotentiary at the Court of France—

Addressed: To / His Excellency Benjamin Franklin Esqr. LLD / And Plenipotentiary at the Court of France

8. That letter, dated May 10 and addressed "To the Illustrious Royal Medical Society of France," is among BF's papers at the APS. Decrying the "slaughter which is daily made amongst our fellow citizens by the barbarous hands of medicasters," they request a literary correspondence and explain their constitution and practices. Although not officially sanctioned by the state, they examine candidates and issue medical licenses to qualified individuals.

From Jonathan Williams, Jr.

ALS: University of Pennsylvania Library; copy: Yale University Library

Dear & hond Sir   Nantes May 10. 1780.

I have been applied to by Capt Thomas Molloney an english Prisoner whose Case seems a hard one[9] and in consequence of his earnest Sollicitations and the Desire of Messrs Galleweys of this Place[1] I have promised to lay it before you.

He was taken by Capt Jones off Ireland in a little Brig which he commanded, & he owned half of her himself; when Capt Jones sent the Cerf Cutter into Dingle Bay in search of his Boats this Man was put on Board as a Pilot, and the Cerf afterwards leaving Capt Jones brought him into this Port, where he was put in Prison. By some neglect in the Cartel or the peculiarity of the mans being a sole Prisoner, & brought in by the Cerf without its being properly declared whether he was taken under the french or the american Flagg, he has hitherto been left out of both Cartels, and has had the mortification of seeing his own People & many subsequent Prisoners exchanged & himself left behind. Messrs Galleweys have procured him his Parole & he is at large in the Town.

If you think proper I shall be glad if you will give an order to Mr Schweighauser to have this man released on his giving sufficient Security to return another man in his Place, and the Security to be discharged when the man so released appears with a proper Certificate in France. This I apprehend is the only way as

9. Malony had already written BF on April 4, relating in greater detail the story JW presents below. The captain had sailed from Limerick on the *Mayflower* with a cargo of beef, butter, quills, and porter bound for London. He had been taken by Jones on Aug. 20, and agreed to pilot the *Cerf* into Dingle Bay, thinking that he would return the following day. A storm sprung the cutter's mast and separated her from the fleet. Malony spent 14 days at sea, and was subsequently imprisoned at Nantes, wearing the same clothes he had on when he left Capt. Jones. He is the sole support of a wife, a widowed mother, two sisters, and a blind brother, and his only source of income was the ship he had just lost. APS. See also xxx, 444–6.

BF endorsed the letter, but we have found no evidence that he intervened on Malony's behalf.

1. Andrew and David Gallwey; see their letter of June 5.

he I understand is the only Prisoner remaining here taken under the american Flagg.

I hope there is no impropriety in giving you this Trouble & remain as ever with greatest Respect Your dutifull & affectionate kinsman JONA WILLIAMS J

Honble Doctor Franklin

Notation: Jona Williams May 10. 1780

From Madame Brillon   AL: American Philosophical Society

ce jeudi [May?] 11 [1780?] a passy[2]
Je voulois vous écrire avant hiér mon bon papa; mr votre fils vint me voir[3] et je le chargai de vous dire que je vous attendois hiér; hiér vos affaires vous ont empêchés de venir; aujourd'hui mon coeur Souffriroit trop s'il se refusoit au besoin de vous dire qu'il vous aime: aimér, le dire, avoir besoin d'éstre aimé, est d'une aussi grande nécéssité a l'éstre bien sensible, que l'air pour réspirér est nécéssaire a un astmatique: me voici contente de vous avoir répétté, ce que je vous ai dit mille fois, ce dont vous ne pouvés douttér—je radotte donc? óh non; l'amitié ne radotte jamais; elle a ainsi que son malin de frére, la faculté de répétter sans césse une chose qui paroist toujours nouvélle; élle a de plus que lui, une confiance plus entiére plus désintéréssée; tous nos secréts sont un bien acquis a l'ami (peut estre pas a l'amant): vous Sçavés mon bon papa a qu'él point vous pouvés lire au fond de mon coeur; vous sçavés par l'importance de la dérniére confidence que je vous ai faitte; que vous devés, que vous estes mon meilleur

2. Mme Brillon's statement that she is keeping to her room points to the spring of 1780, when she became seriously depressed. We do not know whether the secret she entrusted to BF still had to do with the Juppin affair (for which see XXIX, 450–2).

3. WTF may have already embarked on the courtship of Cunégonde Brillon—the older daughter—which would lead, one year later, to BF's proposal of a marriage between them: XXXI, 324; BF to Mme Brillon, [before April 20, 1781], (Library of Congress).

ami; puisse cétte certitude vous faire autant de plaisir, que j'en aurai toujours a vous l'assurér:/:
Comme je ne sors point de ma chambre; ne me rendrés vous pas la soirée que j'ai pérduë hiér?

Addressed: A Monsieur / Monsieur Franklin / a Passy

From Charles Millon[4]   ALS: American Philosophical Society

Tres respectable Docteur,   Ce 11. may 1780.

Je m'apercois dans le moment que ma memoire me servit bien mal avant hier mardy 9. lorsque, dans la rüe de la Pelleterie ou vous vous trouviez, pour lEssay ratté d'une Pompe,[5] je vous citay un passage de Diodore de sicille que j'estime appartenir a lElectricité. Je vous indiquois le XIIe. Livre de Cet historien, et Je me trompois. Cest le XIe. Livre, paragraphe XXXVI. ou a l'ocasion de la ville de Nées que Deucetius transporta dans la plaine et auprès du temple des Dieux Palicès. L'historien Diodore decrit quelqu'uns des phenomenes qui avoient procuré a ce temple et aux pretendus Dieux auxquels il Etoit Consacré,

4. A *conseiller* since 1750 at the Châtelet, or municipal courts of Paris, Charles-Blaise-Léon Millon (b. 1723) had written BF in 1777, enclosing an eight-page critique of sections of the 1776 Pennsylvania constitution: xxv, 301–2; *Almanach royal* for 1780, p. 371. He was an examining commissioner for the Société libre d'émulation, and had himself made discoveries useful to the science of mechanics: xxvii, 210. He was a freemason, a member of *Les Cœurs Simples de l'Etoile Polaire* since 1775: Le Bihan, *Francs-maçons parisiens,* p. 356.

5. The street, no longer in existence, linked the Pont au Change on the Ile de la Cité and the Pont Notre-Dame, the location of a suction and force pump to distribute water from the Seine to fountains around the city: Hillairet, *Rues de Paris,* II, 186, 210.

On May 10 the *Journal de Paris* had announced under the rubric "Hydraulique" that a sieur Chapus, *ingénieur-hydraulique,* had developed and was prepared to demonstrate a "machine durable, composée de fer & de laiton, qui se meut à tout vent ou par le moyen d'un cheval & qu'on peut appliquer au courant d'un ruisseau ou d'une riviere quelconque; elle en éleve une quantité d'eau considérable pour les arrosemens, les cascades ou autres embellissemens." Chapus was staying at a hotel on rue St. André-des-Arts, Millon's address.

la veneration et le respect dont il fait mention.[6] Or vous etes savant et surement honnête homme, sans quoy la phisionomie seroit traitreusement trompeuse; et a ce titre Je pense que si, Comme moy, vous soupçonnez les Pretres de ces Dieux avoir Connu Notre Electricité et en avoir tiré le party que les anciens Pretres tiroient de leurs Connaissances phisiques, pour rendre leurs semblables plus vertueux et plus Justes, vous direz avec Moy, *Nihil sub Sole novum*.[7] Et peut etre leur idée vüe et saisie par vous, pourra nous Enrichir de quelque nouvelle decouverte. Je suppose que vous avez ou que vous pouvez vous procurer aisement un Diodore de sicile, soit en Grec soit En latin, soit meme en françois ne sachant pas s'il a Eté traduit En anglois.

Je vous suis bien obligé du Cadeau que vous avez Eu la bonté de me faire du programe de la société Royalle des arts de Londres sur les poids et Mesures.[8] Jauroy l'honneur d'aller vous en reïterer le remerciment de bouche si mes affaires me permettent d'aller a Passy l'un de ces jours. En attendant agreez Je vous en prie Lassurance vraye et Loyale du Respect avec lequel Je suis Tres Respectable Docteur Votre tres humble et tres obeissant Serviteur   MILLON

Coner. [conseiller] au chatelet rüe st andré des arts vis à vis la rue Gilles-coeur

Addressed: A Monsieur / Monsieur Le Docteur franklin / A Passy

Notation: Millon Commissaire au Chatelet May 11. 1780

6. For the description of the geysers near Mt. Aetna and their power to change human behavior see *Diodorus of Sicily*, C.H. Oldfather *et al.*, eds. (12 vols., London and New York, 1933–67), IV, 353–7 (*Library of History*, book XI, chapter 89).

7. Nothing new under the sun.

8. BF may have given him the abstract of the five claims submitted to the Society for the Encouragement of Arts, Manufactures and Commerce and published at London, June 2, 1779.

From Vergennes

L (draft):[9] Archives du Ministère des affaires étrangères; copies: Library of Congress (two), National Archives; transcript: National Archives

A Versailles le 11. Mai 1780.

Mr. le Brn. de golz[1] a fortement desiré, M, que je vous recommandasse M. darendt, officier prussien attaché au Service des Etats-unis,[2] et je me porte d'autant plus volontiers à Satisfaire à La demande de ce Ministre, que vous vous ferez certainement un plaisir de l'obliger autant que cela Sera en votre pouvoir. M. d'Arend vous expliquera lui-même les differents objets pour lesquels il croit avoir besoin de votre appuy auprès du Congrès.

M franklin

To the Judges of the Admiralty of Dunkirk

Copy: Library of Congress

Gentlemen   Passy, may 12. 1780.

By the Declaration and report to me made by the honble. Captain Cottineau de Kerloguen who commanded the Pallas frigatte in the late Cruise of the American Squadron under the Orders of the honble. Commodore John Paul Jones Esqre, Commissioned by the Congress of the United States of America, a Copy of which Declaration, verified by the said commodore, I here with send you. It appears to me that the English Ship of War, called the Countess of Scarborough therein mentioned to be met with when convoying a fleet of the same Nation from the Baltick, and taken by the Pallas is undoubtedly a good

---

9. In the hand of Gérard de Rayneval, who as the *premier commis* responsible for American correspondence, drafted many of Vergennes' letters to BF. The present letter probably was enclosed with Arendt's of May 13, below.

1. Bernhard Wilhelm, *freiherr* von der Goltz, the Prussian minister plenipotentiary to the French court: XXXI, 37n.

2. Arendt had been on leave from the American army since August, 1778, spending part of the intervening time in Prussia: XXVIII, 298n; XXIX, 375–6, 501–3.

The Cathedral at Strasbourg

prize being taken from the Enemies of the United States of America. And I do accordingly hereby desire of you that you would proceed to the sale of the aforesaid Prize, in conformity to his Majestys Regulation of Septr. 27th. 1778.[3]

I have the honour to be &c.

To the Judges of the Admiralty at Dunkerque.

Franklin and Le Roy: Report on Lightning Rods
at Strasbourg   ALS (draft): Académie royale des sciences, Paris

Started between 1015 and 1028 in Romanesque style, the magnificent cathedral of Strasbourg underwent many transformations over the centuries. Around 1320, the intersection of nave and transept was marked by a Gothic construction resembling a bishop's miter, hence called the *Mitre*. By 1365 the twin towers of the façade had been erected, and were joined to each other some thirty years later by a platform meant to support a belfry. The belfry, however, was never constructed. Twin spires were then planned, only one of which was built by 1439. A little guardhouse replaced what would have been the other one.[4]

In 1759, the cathedral's lead-covered roof caught fire during a storm and the *Mitre*, destroyed, was rebuilt in the shape of a truncated pyramid. Twenty years after that catastrophe, on May 12, 1779, Barbier de Tinan, *commissaire des guerres* and member of the Academy of Dijon, presented to the Académie royale des sciences in Paris his

3. The declaration is missing. The sloop of war *Countess of Scarborough* surrendered to the *Pallas* during the Battle off Flamborough Head, although the *Alliance* also exchanged fire with the British warship: xxx, 627–8. Both the *Pallas* and the *Countess of Scarborough* arrived at Dunkirk on Jan. 2: Archives de la Marine, B³DCLXXIV: 8. On May 19 Officers of the Admiralty Coppens d'Hersin and Janssoone(?) replied that they had fixed a date for the sale of the *Countess of Scarborough* (APS); she was finally sold not as a warship but as a merchant vessel: Morison, *Jones*, p. 266.

4. See Georges Livet and Francis Rapp, eds., *Histoire de Strasbourg* (Toulouse, 1987), pp. 98, 107–8, 122. See also Bertrand Monnet, *Métamorphoses de la Cathédrale de Strasbourg du XIe. siècle à nos jours* (Paris, 1987).

translation of the abbé Toaldo's work on lightning rods as well as his own memoir on the best way to preserve the cathedral from damage by lightning. Franklin and Le Roy were appointed commissioners to study Barbier's memoir.[5]

Their twenty-page joint report, in Le Roy's hand but signed by both men, was read at the Académie exactly one year later, May 12, 1780.[6] The draft contains many corrections and several references to a *gravure* (now missing) which apparently was intended to accompany the report.

⟨May 12, 1780, in French: The Académie has asked us to report on a memoir by M. Barbier on the means of arming the Strasbourg cathedral with lightning rods.

Strasbourg is located in the middle of rather flat countryside dominated by the cathedral's very high spire—so high indeed that no attempt at devising a protective system for so tall a building has ever been made. Its exterior, furthermore, is studded with a large number of iron bars and clamps which add to the danger posed by the frequent storms. Those storms originate southwest of the city, in the Vosges, and proceed in a northeasterly direction.

The two crucial issues we shall discuss are the shape given to the lightning rods' ends and the means by which the lightning's fire is brought down to earth.

5. *Procès verbaux*, t. 98, fol. 158. In 1778, Giuseppe Toaldo (1719–1797), physicist and professor of astronomy at the University of Padua, republished in Venice a work that had originally appeared in 1772. Entitled *Dei Conduttori per preservare gli edifizi da' fulmini*, it contained an Italian translation of BF's Oct. 8, 1772, letter to Horace-Bénédict de Saussure (XIX, 324–7). Father Toaldo sent this volume to BF in homage. During the preparation of their joint report, presumably, Le Roy wrote BF a letter dated only "Tuesday morning" in which he asked for the loan of Toaldo's book (APS). Barbier de Tinan's translation of Toaldo's 1778 version, augmented by some of his own comments, appeared in Paris in 1779. In 1780 Barbier published in Strasbourg his *Mémoire sur la manière d'armer d'un conducteur la cathédrale de Strasbourg et sa tour:* Quérard, *France littéraire; Dizionario Enciclopedico Italiano* (14 vols., Rome, 1955–74). A copy of the *Mémoire*, bearing BF's notation on the title page, "De la part de l'Auteur à BF.", is at the APS.

6. *Procès verbaux*, t. 99. The report is included in a separate *pochette*. By June 30 it had already been printed; see BF's letter to Cabanis of that date, below.

On the first question, M. Barbier wisely prefers the rods with pointed ends[7] and suggests that they be gilded so as to preserve them from the weather, and also to create an effect pleasant to the eye. As to the second problem, about which one cannot be too cautious, it should be noted that the spire is divided into three parts. Starting from the top, they are a tier made up of cross, lantern, and crown; then a pyramid in the shape of an octagon consisting of eight small winding stairs and turrets; and finally, resting on the platform, a square construction flanked by an openwork turret containing a staircase.

M. Barbier proposes, for the top part, a scaffolding of vertical iron rods off the northeast and southwest sides—those most often hit by storms—to join a "necklace" of horizontal rods just below the crown. From this necklace there would jut four rods descending between the little staircases of the pyramid and corresponding to the four turrets. They would finally follow at a distance the outer walls of the turrets belonging to the lowest part, which rests on the platform.

Protruding from the long drop between the cross and the turrets, a number of secondary conductors, five or six feet long and ending in copper-covered joints, would have to be installed for extra security. More of the same should be placed at each angle of the platform.

One third of the way down between the platform and the ground there runs a circular gallery, and more rods could be placed there, as well as a protective system extending to the copper roof of the nave. For better safety still, lead washers should be inserted between the various screws.

The final step is to connect this protective framework to the ground.

M. Barbier's solution is to establish a tight metallic connection

7. For the controversy of pointed rods versus rounded ones, see XXIV, 163. The report specifies: "The most informed physicists argue today on the proper shape for lightning rods. The fears that M. Wilson tried to raise about pointed rods, through his equivocal experiments, have been laid to rest. The Committee of the London Royal Society declared that there was no reason to change the rods of the Purfleet magazines which, as one knows, are very pointed."

between the copper roof of the *Mitre* and the three adjacent copper roofs, two of which are well suited to attract lightning since they are garnished with very pointed pyramids.

Such a system would provide excellent protection against storms coming from the east. Since that part of the cathedral is so far removed from the tower, M. Barbier plans to give it extra safety by adding still sharper points to those of the pyramids. The next step is to take advantage of the two gutters situated right there, which can be made to communicate, through a leaden pipe, with an already established well. As usual, there will be a duplicate fallback system in case of accident, in the shape of metal rods constructed in the same way as those in the front of the cathedral. Both systems will be joined at the bottom by a thick iron bar pushed at least one foot into the ground at the bottom of the well.

Let us add, to complete this description, that M. Barbier proposes to secure the rods by flattening their extremities as well as those of the "necklace," then drilling a hole through these flattened parts and attaching them to each other by means of a square-headed screw tightly shut by two keys.

It is our opinion that M. Barbier's system would present still greater security if the *Mitre* were provided with more points and if the descending rods were made thicker. We agree with his observation that the work should proceed from bottom to top. We conclude by praising his plan and expressing the hope that, given the disastrous history of Strasbourg's tower, it will become a reality. Thus protected, the tower will be a model for the rest of the kingdom and a symbol of the progress accomplished by physics in France when it is considered that only fifteen years ago lightning rods were still viewed as dangerous.)[8]

8. BF's warm endorsement notwithstanding, nothing was done about protecting the cathedral's spire until 1834–35, when a lightning rod was finally installed: Fonds de l'Oeuvre Notre-Dame, Budgets, pp. 137, 138, 590. Information kindly sent by M. Roger Lehni, of the *Ministère de la Culture et de la Francophonie* for Alsace. See also Georges Delahache, "Le premier projet de paratonnerre pour la cathédrale," *Bulletin de la Société des Amis de la cathédrale de Strasbourg*, 1 (1925), 14, where the author mentions J.-B. Le Roy's suggestions of 1770 and 1773 that the Academy put into practice BF's brilliant discoveries.

From Gourlade & Moylan

ALS:[9] American Philosophical Society

Honord Sir   L'Orient 12th. May 1780

The inclosed letter for Captain Jones[1] contains a certify'd Copy of a delaration made by the Officers of the late ship of war Bonhomme Richard, at the Admiralty, regarding the Capture of the English ship Serapis, wch. he desird shou'd be immediately forwarded him.

As we think it possible said letter might not overtake him at passÿ, we take the liberty of forwarding it under this cover that you may do with it's inclosure what may be necessary, and for this purpose, we have left it unseal'd.

We have the honor to be respectfully Honord sir Your most hle sts   GOURLADE & MOYLAN

The Honble. Doctor B. Franklin

Addressed: The Honorable / Doctor Benj: Franklin / Plenepotentiary Minister / from the united States of / America / Passÿ./.

Notation: Gourlade & Moylan L'Orient May. 12. 80

From William Hodgson

ALS: American Philosophical Society

Dear sir   London 12 May 1780

I reced in course your favor of the 11th Ultimo, the Substance of which I communicated immediately to the Board of Sick & Hurt, but as what may hereafter be determined upon depends in a great measure upon the French Minister, the Board were of Opinion it wou'd be better to wait those further explanations

---

But France was not yet ready to take that step. For ecclesiastical and other resistance to lightning rods see I. Bernard Cohen, *Benjamin Franklin's Science* (Cambridge, Mass., and London, 1990), pp. 118–58. After a chapel of the basilica of St. Francis had been destroyed by lightning in 1791, Pope Pius VI, while seeing to its restoration, insisted that "electrical Franklin rods" be installed. Cohen, *ibid.*, p. 140. We thank Professor Cohen for his helpful suggestions on this document.

9. In James Moylan's hand.

1. A letter from Moylan of this date: Bradford, *Jones Papers*, reel 5, no. 1071.

(which you promised to send to Mr Hartley per first post after receiving them from Monsieur de sartine) & lay the whole before the Admiralty at one View, I have seen mr Hartley many Times & he is at this hour without a Line from you or any Intelligence on the Subject—here therefore it rests & must rest, untill you enable us by Monsr de sartines Letter to take some further Steps. I hope it will not be long e'er you can give us some Satisfactory explanations— I will just observe that there seems in the board a very great reluctance to accept French captured prisoners in leiu of American captured ones. I urged to them that to me it appeared as if they had first adopted the Idea in regard to the prisoners in Holland & that they cou'd not with propriety disclaim it elswhere, but you know much better than I that it avails little to urge any Arguments if there is not a previous disposition to hearken to them— As you express a desire to hear some further particulars about Williams I will as briefly as possible state to you the Affair— During Mr. Horne's confinement for the supposed Libel,[2] the Circumstances of which you are well acquainted with, I used frequently to spend the Evening with him—in Conversation he asked me If I coud convey to you a small parcell from a Literary Man— I said I believed I coud, he said there woud be nothing political nor any thing improper for the most Timorous person to take charge of & that the Letters were mere matters of Books & woud be left open—he never mentioned to me that it was for Mr David Williams that he made the request, however upon his sending me the parcell I found it was from Mr Williams with some of his proposals for printing his Lectures accompanied with two Letters one for you & another for Dr Bancroft both left open on purpose by Mr Horne, order that I might see there was nothing improper to be conveyed—all this Time Mr Williams was wholly ignorant that it was to me Mr Horne had applyed for the Conveyance— Upon reading the Letter to you, he stated the meeting at your Lodgings respecting the Liturgy & then added all those who so met him had Slunk off—conveying the Idea that he had been ill

2. John Horne (XXIII, 332) was imprisoned from 1778 to 1779 for seditious libel: *DNB* under Tooke; Minnie Clare Yarborough, *John Horne Tooke* (New York, 1926), pp. 85–97, 103–5.

treated & decieved— Now as this was a gross falshood allmost
every man (except Mr Whitehurst)[3] having subscribed to & supported him— I wrote him a Letter complaining of the misrepresentation & added that I coud not possibly forward that Letter
without forwarding at the Same Time such an explanation of the
Affair to you as woud not tend to his Credit or reputation, this
was a thunder Clap to him he was unable even to make an Apology, he withdrew however the first Letter & wrote another in
general Terms, which I forwarded by Mr Ridley—[4] This lay
brooding upon his mind & his spleen had Vent in an Abusive
paragraph or Letter in the Morning post which I inclose you as
a Curiosity[5] you will see that in order to blacken me you are introduced & others to whose Principles at least he professed attachment, but Revenge knocks down all these Barriers— You
will naturally ask how it came to be known that he was the Author—for Answer I can only say, there were traced home to him
such concurring Circumstances as left not a doubt in the Mind of
any one of the Club that he was the Author alltho it would not
amount to legal proof before a Jury. The consequence was he
was given to understand his presence wou'd be no longer agreable at Slaughters,[6] we are without any News for a long Time
from America. I am with great Respect Dr sir Yours sincerely

WILLIAM HODGSON

P.S. Mr Whitehurst desired me to ask you if his book was got to
your hands he sent it by some Compte or other whose Name I
forget[7]

3. The clockmaker John Whitehurst (IX, 42n) had been, like BF, an original member of the Club of Thirteen (XXI, 119–120), which was devoted to
creating a philosopher's liturgy: David Williams, *Incidents in My Own Life
which have been Thought of Some Importance* (reprint ed., Peter France, ed.,
Falmer, Eng., 1980), p. 16.
4. XXVII, 354–5.
5. The enclosure is missing. Josiah Wedgwood was also sent a copy: J. Dy-
bikowski, *On Burning Ground: An Examination of the Ideas, Projects and Life
of David Williams* (Oxford, 1993), p. 59.
6. Old Slaughter's Coffee House: XXXI, 143n.
7. On or about March 20, 1779, Whitehurst probably sent BF a copy of his
An Inquiry into the Original State and Formation of the Earth (London, 1778).
His covering letter is missing, but at the APS is another covering letter of
that date addressed to BF for forwarding. It enclosed a copy of his book for

Dr Franklin

Notation: W Hodn.

From Benjamin Vaughan

AL: Library of Congress

My dearest sir,   May 12, 1780.

Dr. Hamilton had a letter for you some weeks ago; but I find him still in Holland. The bearer of this is of his party, & as Dr. Crawford gives him a character, I inclose the Drs. letter in case you should meet with him.[8]

By the present opportunity you have two packets from Dr. Jebb.[9] The MS. he had prepared for another conveyance which he missed; and as I thought you *might* wish for an opportunity of saying something of a political nature, I not only did not discourge but rather encouraged his sending it.

I send a pamphlet Dr. Price has just sent to us; If Dr. Crawford forwards another, you know you have a duplicate to send abroad.[1]

---

an unnamed scientist who had conducted experiments on "the component parts of Mineral Substances." This letter and the book were carried by a Baron Waitz (XXIX, 214, 430), whom Whitehurst introduced.

8. See Vaughan's April 23 letter, above.

9. Dr. John Jebb (1736–1786) was an outspoken liberal in religion and radical in politics. At the February-March meetings of the county petitioning movement he represented Westminster. He was also a strong supporter of the American cause. *DNB;* Eugene C. Black, *The Association: British Extraparliamentary Political Organization 1769–93* (Cambridge, Mass., 1963), pp. 51n, 176–7. See also Caroline Robbins, *The Eighteenth-Century Commonwealthman . . .* (rev. ed., New York, 1968), pp. 370–3. The packets may have contained *An Address to the Freeholders of Middlesex, Assembled at Free Mason's Tavern . . .* , which he had delivered on Dec. 20, 1779, and published almost immediately afterwards: John Jebb, *The Works Theological, Medical, Political, and Miscellaneous . . .* , ed. John Disney (3 vols., London, 1787), I, 144–5. The 4th edition, revised and expanded, is printed in Jebb, *Works,* II, 453–90. If BF did indeed receive the parcel we have found no record of it.

1. Probably *An Essay on the Population of England and Wales from the Revolution to the Present Time,* which appeared in 1779 as the concluding essay to a volume by his nephew William Morgan and in 1780 was published as a

Dr. Priestley is very ill on the bed just now, with a violent pain in his stomach, which in one light is encouraging as it tends to make us think his disease is in the gall-bladder & its ducts, & not in the liver which is hardly capable of such serious pain.[2] Dr. Fothergill & Dr. J. Jebb have prescribed to day: Dr. Heberden & Sr. J. Pringle some days ago prescribed medicines which nature did not allow a favorable opportunity for taking,[3] & they will not it seems come into the *city* to our house where the Dr. now is, finding himself more at home than in Berkley Square now he is ill.[4]

As to politics, the Rockinghams & other aristocratic people hang off a great deal since the asociations have gone such lengths (owing much to Dr. J Jebb) but perhaps occasions may offer to work on the people without them. Much will depend on events. Ministry are very confident as to possession of their places, and not out of hopes as to the empire: So much do mens ruin depend on the *opinion* that they are ruined. Other people in their situation would have been ruined by *fears;* but providence has kindly given them insensible hearts & insensible heads to make them

---

separate work. It is advertised in the *St. James's Chronicle* for May 18–20: D.O. Thomas and W. Bernard Peach, eds., *The Correspondence of Richard Price* (3 vols., Durham, N.C., and Cardiff, 1983–94), II, 55–6; D.O. Thomas, John Stephens, and P.A.L. Jones, *A Bibliography of the Works of Richard Price*, (Aldershot, England, and Brookfield, Vt., 1993), pp. 101–5.

2. Priestley was recovering from a bilious disorder, and he had passed, with much pain, a gall stone: John T. Rutt, *Life and Correspondence of Joseph Priestley* . . . (2 vols., London, 1831–32), I, 334–5. See also Vaughan's letter of June 26.

3. An illustrious group of physicians attended him. For Fothergill see Vaughan's April 23 letter. Jebb had taken up the practice of medicine after he was denied permission to continue lecturing at Cambridge because of his liberal religious beliefs; he opened his medical practice on Craven St. in 1778, but his radical politics prevented his appointment as a physician to a London hospital. *DNB*. The distinguished Dr. William Heberden had been an acquaintance since BF's residence in London in the 1750's: VIII, 281n. BF's old friend Sir John Pringle had been the royal physician: X, 85n.

4. Priestley apparently was staying with the Vaughan family at their home and place of business on Mincing Lane. Samuel Vaughan and Priestley were old friends, and Benjamin had been Priestley's pupil at Warrington: XXI, 441; XXX, 379. The London residence of the Earl of Shelburne, for whom Priestley still served as secretary, was in Berkeley Square.

more fit for working its purpose. I am, my dearest sir, yours ever most devotedly,

From the Baron d'Arendt: Two Letters

(I) AL: American Philosophical Society; (II) ALS: American Philosophical Society

I.

Paris ce 13me May 1780.

Le Baron de Arendt a l'honneur de présenter Les trés humbles respects a Monsieur le Docteur Francklin et de Lui remettre une lettre de la part du Comte de Vergennes,[5] crajnant que M. le Comte L'aura deja prevenû. Le Baron a attendû ce moment de reïterer sa demande en quéstion a M. le Docteur, pour ne l'importuner point, et il Le sollicite de lui indiquer par la petite poste ou un expres au plutôt qu'il Lui plaira le moment, quand il Lui plaira de Le voir.[6]

Notation: Arendt le Baron de Paris 13. may 1780.

II.

Paris, Hôtel de Luines rüe de Colombier, F. St. G. ce 13me. May. [1780]

Je crains Monsieur d'avoir oublié dans ma lettre d'aujourd'hui matin, de Vous dire ou je suis logè, cè que m'engage de le faire par ces lignes en Vous repetant mes tres humbles respects.

LE BON D'ARENDT

Addressed: A Monsieur / Monsieur Francklin / Ministre Plenipotentiaire / des Etats unis de L'amerique / prés le Roi / Passy

---

5. Above, May 11.
6. On May 16 Arendt wrote again to ask for an appointment that afternoon or the next morning. APS.

From the Baron de Poellnitz[7]

ALS: American Philosophical Society

Monsieur   Bordeaux le 13 de Mais 1780

Arivés dépuis quélques Jours à Bordeaux je n'ais plûs Dissimule le Désir que J'ai d'etre Comptés parmis Les Hommes Libres De L'amerique, & dépuis içi J'ai renvoyés à S.M. Le Roy De Prûsse ma Commission, & la Clef de Chambelan—a present je n'attens plûs que La Paix, pour m'embarquer pour MarieLand, ou Nd Caroline.

En attendent, je prie Votre Exellençe de me Conserver les Dispositions favorables qu'Elle à bien voulû témoigner à moi, & pour mon Epouse,[8] qui est très Sensible aux Bontés De Votre Exellençe, & de croire que J'ai LHoneûr d'etre, avec La Considération La plûs Haute, & la plûs Distinguée, De Votre Exellençe, Le très hûmble, & très Obeissant Serviteûr[9] FKHB POELLNITZ

mon Adresse à Mr Le Baron De Poellnitz près de La porte D'albrêt Maison de L'architecte Bayle, à Bordeaux.

Notation: De Poellnitz Bordx. le 13. May 1780.

From George Scott

ALS: American Philosophical Society

Honourable Sir   Naples the 13th. May 1780

I did myself the pleasure to write you a few lines from hence on the 20th. Ultimo under cover to a friend of mine in Paris, in

7. Baron Friedrich Karl Hans Bruno von Poellnitz (1734–1801) was a former chamberlain at the court of Frederick II of Prussia: Charles Starnes Belsterling, "Baron Poellnitz of New York City and South Carolina," *New York Genealogical and Biographical Record*, LXXX (1949), 130; Don Higginbotham, ed., *The Papers of James Iredell* (2 vols. to date, Raleigh, N.C., 1976–), II, 349n.

8. Two months earlier he had married Lady Anne Stuart (1746– c. 1819), daughter of John Stuart, third Earl of Bute, and grand-daughter of Lady Mary Wortley Montague: Belsterling, "Baron Poellnitz," p. 132; *DNB*. The marriage was the third for Poellnitz and the second for Lady Anne, whose marriage to Hugh Percy had been annulled a year earlier: Higginbotham, ed., *Papers of James Iredell*, II, 349n; Lewis, *Walpole Correspondence*, XXII, 302–3n; *DNB* under Percy and John Stuart.

9. He wrote again from Bordeaux on Jan. 1, 1781, to offer his and Lady Anne's New Year's congratulations: APS. The letter is published in Belsterling, "Baron Poellnitz," p. 133.

which I enclosed you, copy of a letter I had received from our mutual & very worthy friend Dr. Priestley to whom I wrote lately. The Same I hope has come regularly to your hands.

I am in a very hopefull way of succeeding in my business here, but I find I shall be detained much longer than I expected; & I cannot say now with any degree of certainty when I shall be able to leave this place, as proceedings here are so very dillatory.— As this is the case, I find it will be impossible that I can accompany my Goods as I proposed, so I have given directions to Messrs. Crommelins[1] to send the whole, or such part of them as they think proper, immediately to Statia, to their friends there, to sell for my account.— Now as I am disappointed in this respect, I fear a prejudice will arrise to me, from the want of my personal attendance; & as my future welfare & that of my family much depends upon a prudent & advantageous disposal of these effects, because if the sales be managed with that proper care & attention wch. is requisite, my circumstances will be so restored, that I shall be as well, not to say better, in this respect than I have been; & will put me in such a sittuation that, I shall be able to assist friends that I am very desirous of assisting if need should require it.— In this sittuation I am of opinion a very little of your kind assistance would be of essential service to me, if you will be so obliging as to do it for me. What I require is only this, that you will please write messrs. Crommelins a few lines in my favour, to desire they will exert themselves in causing my Goods under their direction to be sold to the very best advantages. I know that such a reccommendation from you will have great weight & influence them much in my favour. Your ready compliance in this will infinitely oblige me.

I have the honour to be with great respect & esteem Honourable Sir Your mo: Obedt. & very humble Servant[2]

GEO: SCOTT

Honble. Benj: Franklin Esqr.

1. Amsterdam bankers: XXXI, 269n.
2. Scott wrote again on May 17. He repeated his request and reported that he had also written to J.F. Frin & Co. Hoping for BF's speedy compliance, he will remain at Naples until he receives an answer. Direct to him there care of Messrs. Hart & Wilkens. APS.

I beg the favour of my [*torn:* best sen]timents to Mr. Franklin Junr.

Addressed: The Honourable / Benjamin Franklin Esqr. / Passy

Notation: George Scott Naples May 13. 1780.

From John Torris
ALS: American Philosophical Society

Honnd. Sir   Dunkerque 13th. May 1780.

On my return Home I Paid Mr. Coffyn the 144 *l.t.* your Excellency has been so good to give the Bold De Letang.

I Beseech your Excellency will no more advance any money to the People of our Privateers, as they are mostly Paid before hand for their Cruise, they being very extravagant in their Expences.

I have Called at M: Le Duc De Penthievre's & found the *Proces* for the Aurora[3] was sent the same morning to your Excellency, who, on perusall, will see the flat Contradictions & bad faith in the reports of the Parjured Capt. Roodenberg, & that, these Circumstances, Together with the fraudulous form of the Bills of Lading, which, contrary to the Law of all Nations in war Time, do not mention the owner's Name, must Clearly prove that the Cargoe is in fact the Property of the *Consignataires* in Dublin; & were your Excellency to adopt the Ennemy's method to force the Neutral *Reclamateurs* to swear to the Property, you wou'd have no further doubt about it, not Presumeing that reputable Merchants woud ever Parjure themselves. The Memorial on the affair, which I daily expect from the Celebrated Mr. Groult, will satisfy your Excellency that, a Condamnation of the Cargoe must forthwith be granted to the Captor. I shall send this Memorial to Mr. De Maussallée my *Avocat aux Conseils,*[4] & he will Call on your Excellency for all the Documents, for to enable Himself to Convince, that, the Cargoe is Legally acquiered to the owners & Crew of the unfortunate Black Prince.

3. *I.e.,* the *Flora.*
4. XXX, 404n.

I have wrote yesterday to Morlaix for all the Papers that might have been found on Board of our Two unCondamned English Prises, Lying & spoiling there.

The Friendship Capt. Pretty John with salt from Lisbon to Dartmouth.

The Peter Capt. Thos. Byrne from London to Madeira with flour.

So soon these documents reaches, if any found, I shall forward them to your Excellency.

But in the Interim, Capt. Dowlin observes, that, your Excellency will run no kind of risk in ordering the admiralty at Morlaix to sell previously, Because, Besides the reports, the Prisonners Bills signed by both Crew when set at Liberty, wherein their stations on Board are mentionned, which he deliver'd to Mr. John Diot who sent them to your Excellency the 27th. March,[5] do explain & prove so well, that these Vessells were maned entierely with British Subjects, therefore were English Bottoms, & of Course good Prises, that your Excellency need no other proof to Condamn, & in argueing I never thought of these signed obligations of both Crews, Laying in the Hands of your Excellency. I am now Persuaded that on Peruseing them, your Excellency will remove all kind of objections & be enabled to grant Immediate Justice to the Captors in Condamning without further delay these Two Spoiling Prises, & endeed, these proofs wou'd be fully sufficient in our Tribunals.

I remain with all respect Honnd. Sir your Excellency's Most obedient & most Humble Servant   J. TORRIS

Endorsed: May 13

Notation: Mr. Torris May 13. 1780.—

5. Missing, although see Diot's April 25 letter to BF.

To Paul Bentalou[6]

Copy: Library of Congress

Sir,   Passy, May 15. 1780.
The Buckskin not belonging to the United States, but to private Persons, I have no authority to order a Passage for you in that Ship, as you desire. I have the honour to be, Sir, Your most obedient & most humble Servant

Captain Bentalon, chez Mr. Changeur[7] Negt. rue Rousselle à Bordeaux

From [Julien-Pierre] Allaire[8]

ALS: American Philosophical Society

On February 14, Peter Allaire had asked Temple Franklin to obtain from his grandfather a passport allowing him to leave for Brussels the following day. To Temple's query at the bottom of the document, Franklin answered a large "No."[9] On the following morning, Allaire was arrested and taken to the Bastille, where he remained confined until May 24 under the double accusation of having tried to poison

6. A captain in Pulaski's Legion and close friend of his, he was wounded at Savannah, came to France to recuperate, and was now planning his return to America: XXVIII, 298 (where we followed the *JCC* in mistakenly saying he was wounded at Charleston); Heitman, *Register of Officers*, p. 84; Bentalou to ———— Bessière, April 4, 1780 (APS). He eventually did return to the U.S., where he served in both the Quasi-War with France and the War of 1812: W.W. Abbot *et al.*, eds., *The Papers of George Washington: Presidential Series* (6 vols. to date, Charlottesville, 1987–), I, 191n.
7. One of the major commercial houses of the city: Paul Butel, *Les négociants bordelais, l'Europe et les Iles au XVIIIe siècle* (Paris, 1974), p. 308.
8. A relative of Peter Allaire who apparently had met BF on various occasions, Julien-Pierre (1742–1816) enjoyed a successful career in land and forest administration, interrupted by the Revolution and resumed after it. He did much to improve agriculture and the raising of a new kind of sheep in the Marne region. From a *Notice biographique* at the Bibliothèque du Jardin des Plantes (8e B 134–4), kindly forwarded by M. Maurice Déchery.
9. That document is at the APS as well as WTF's answer of Feb. 14 informing Allaire that BF "does not chuse to comply" with his request for a passport.

387

Franklin with his gift of madeira on January 31,[1] and of being a British spy. The following document is a plea for his release.

Monsieur   Paris le 15 May 1780.

Permettés que je vous rappelle par ecrit une priere que je vous ai desja faite de vive voix, et que je me serois empressé de vous aller reiterer, si je ne craignois pas de derober des momens precieux à vos importantes occupations. C'est en faveur d'un de vos compatriotes M. Allaire que des raisons que j'ai respectées des que vous avés bien voulu me les laisser entrevoir, ont fait detenir prisonnier à la Bastille. Lorsque j'eus l'honneur de vous voir, vous me repondites que les circonstances exigeoient qu'il fut detenu jusqu'au départ de la flotte qui etoit en armement à Brest.[2] Dans le premier moment de ce départ, je n'ai pas cru qu'il fut encore tems de vous importuner, aujourd'huy ou il y a tout lieu d'esperer qu'elle est passée et que celle de Cadix même est hors des atteintes de nos ennemis communs, il ma semblé que le moment des suspicions etoit passé ou qu'elles n'etoient plus à craindre, surtout en prenant les précautions que votre sagesse vous suggerera soit pour le départ de paris, soit pour la residence à assigner au prisonnier dont je sollicite l'elargissement.

Permettes que je vous rappelles aussi, les circonstances d'un procès considerable qu'il a en angleterre, à raison duquel sa liberté y seroit en danger et la necessité ou il est toutes fois de rester en europe pour en hâter la decision. Ce furent les motifs que je vous presentai quand je sollicitai la permission pour luy D'habiter la france, et par predilection Boullogne sur mer ou il a des correspondans auxquels il doit de l'argent et de la reconnoissance, et d'ou il pourroit suivre plus facilement son procès par l'entremise de sa sœur qui est à Londres depuis six mois.[3] Vous eutes la bonté de me repondre que vous seriés vous même son solliciteur des que les circonstances le permetteroient. J'ose vous le recommander aujourd'huy comme un sujet des etats unis

1. For which see XXXI, 428–9.
2. Rochambeau had sailed on May 2.
3. A surprising choice of residence, since Boulogne was a hotbed of spies. As it turned out, Allaire was expelled from France via Valenciennes, a safe distance from the coast. See [——— Charpentier], *La Bastille dévoilée, ou Recueil des Pièces authentiques pour servir à son histoire* (3 vols., Paris, 1789–90), III, 10–14.

que la necessité a contraint de Garder exterieurement une neutralité qui n'est pas dans son cœur et que j'ose vous assurer
n'avoir jamais vu dans ses expressions. Je l'y aurois apperçue
d'autant plus aisement que je suis plus sincerement le partisant
de la liberté, et l'admirateur de Celui qui lui erige dans le nouveau monde le plus beau temple que la main de l'homme lui ait
jamais consacré.

Permettés que je vous rappelles que j'ai eu l'avantage de vous
voir souvent chés feu M D'alibart, et chés M Brisson[4] mes amis
pour lesquels vous avés de la Consideration, et que ce dernier
seroit aupres de vous le Garand de ma sincerité ainsi que de l'admiration respectueuse avec laquelle j'ai lhonneur dêtre. Monsieur Votre trés humble et trés obeissant serviteur

ALLAIRE
administrateur General des domaines du Roy Grande
Rue du faubourg Montmartre No. 19

Notation: Allaire Paris 15. may 1780.

From Samuel Wharton   ALS: American Philosophical Society

Dear Sir   L'Orient May 15 1780
   As a News paper of the 8th of April was received by Captain
Montgomery,[5] after He left Philadelphia, in which is published
a curious, confidential Letter, dated the 30th of January, from
General Clinton to Lord George Germaine, and as it gives a
very agreable State of Facts, and Arguments, I send your Excel-
lency a Copy of it, taken in a hurry by Captain Hutchins, my
Son, and myself.[6] The News paper (one of Dunlap's) contain-

---

4. The botanist Thomas Dalibard, who died on March 14, 1778, was indeed a close friend of BF, as was Mathurin-Jacques Brisson (1723–1806), also
a botanist.
   5. Probably Capt. James Montgomery, who took command of the brig
George on April 7: Claghorn, *Naval Officers,* pp. 210–11.
   6. The copy that Wharton sent is missing. Clinton's supposed letter,
highly pessimistic about the possibility of British success over the rebels in
America, was published in the April 8 issue of John Dunlap's *Pennsylvania
Packet* and by the end of May had been reprinted in London (*e.g.,* in the May
31 *London Courant, and Westminster Chronicle*). BF was sufficiently interested

ing the above Letter, will be forwarded to Night by Mr. Nesbit to Mr. Jay, with some Bills drawn by Congress at six Months sight upon Him. There are also Bills in this Town drawn by the same honorable Body on Mr. Lawrence at the same Sight, at the Hague.[7] Captain Montgomery says, That the Markets at philadelphia were abundant, and reasonable, and as many Vessels in the Harbor, loading for different ports, as He remembers ever to have seen in Time of peace. He speaks of the last Winter, as uncommonly severe, But the price of Wood much cheaper than it had been, and adds, That the People in Power, and all Ranks of persons at Philadelphia, were under no apprehensions of Charles Town being taken. The post is just setting out, so that I cannot add any more,— But We are extremely impatient for Captain Jones's Return, and our Departure; For we are most heartily fatigued with our Residence in this unhealthy, dull place. May I ask the Favor of your Excellency to present my best Respects to Mr. & Mrs. Chaumont, & Family—Mr. Grand & Family and to your Grandson? With the sincerest Respect and Attachment I am dear Sir Your most Obedient & most humble Servant   SAML. WHARTON

His Excellency Dr. Franklin.

Notation: Warton Mr. Saml. May 15 1780.

From John Wheeler   ALS: American Philosophical Society

Denan Prison the 17th May 1780
May it Please your Excelence
    I was Born in Ireland, and brought up to the Sea. My Parents went to America & Setteled there, at the Commencement of this

---

to copy it in its entirety and have it translated into French (Hist. Soc. of Pa. and the University of Pa. Library, respectively); a French translation began appearing in the May 30 issue of the *Gaʒ. de Leyde* (no. XLIII, sup.). The letter, however, proved to be a hoax: Smith, *Letters*, xv, 24n; *Adams Papers*, IX, 331n. The copy BF made bears the notation "Pretendue Lettre de Clinton."
    7. Congress had resolved the previous December to draw on Laurens and Jay: *JCC,* xv, 1404–5.

present War, I was then Up the Streights And Never Could get an Opertunety to go to America Sience the War, being Mostley Employed in the Norway Trade from Newry in Ireland. I was lately Taken in a Vessell belongeing to Dublin by a French Priveteer & am Now in Denan Prison. I would be glad to go to America, to go in the Congress or Mercht. Service if your Excelency is pleas'd to get me out of Prison. I am Capeble of Any Station on board a Ship That the Congress, or My Friends Interest will please to Bestow on me. There is Some Clever young Men from Ireland in the Same prison who would be glad to go in the American Service with me. Your Excelence will please to Dispach your Orders as Soon as posseble as there is a Carteel Expected and I am Afraid I would be ordered on board her, as my Parents And Most of my Friends live in Pensilvenia and Near Philadelphia I shall from this Declare myself an American and with Gods Assistance I am in hope of being of Service to the Cuntrey.

Relyeing on your Excelency's Generosity I Remain your True Obedient And Humble Servt.   JOHN WHEELER

Notation: Wheeler John, Denan Prison the 17th. May 1780.

From Arendt   AL: University of Pennsylvania Library

⟨[before May 18, 1780],[8] in French: While in the service of the Americans with the rank of Colonel, baron Arendt gave full satisfaction. He received one year's leave to recover from an accident[9] and spent a good part of it nurturing the Prussian government's goodwill toward the American cause. Because [William] Lee detained him in Berlin on various errands, he worries about the bad impression his delay in returning might make on Congress[1] and begs Dr. Franklin to justify it and ensure his welcome in America. His many travels have entailed great expense and he

8. Dated by BF's certificate for the baron, May 18, below. He may have composed this letter before his first request for a meeting with BF (above, May 13).
9. He suffered a rupture when his horse fell: *JCC*, XI, 808.
1. His year's furlough had been granted on Aug. 18, 1778: XXVIII, 298n; *JCC*, XI, 809.

would appreciate the small sum of 25 louis promised by M. Lee as can be seen in the enclosed letter.[2] He also asks free return passage in the safety of a convoy.⟩

To the Judges of the Admiralty of Vannes[3]

Copy:[4] Archives de la Marine

gentlemen   Passy 18th May 1780
By the declaration and report to me Made By the honourable Commodore Jones, a Copy of Which Declaration I here With Send you. It appears to me that the British Ship of War the Serapis therein mentioned to be met With, When Convoying a fleet of the Same Nation from the Baltick & taken By the Bonhomme Richard Which Was Commissioned By the Congress and Commanded By the aforesaid Commodore, is undoubtedly a good Prize, Being taken from the Ennemies of the United States of America, and I Do accordingly hereby Desire of you, that you Would Proceed to the sale of the above Said Prize, In Conformity to his Majesty's Regulation of September 27th. 1778.
I have the honour to be &c.
Ainsy signé B. FRANKLIN
ministre Plenipotentiaire
Des etats unis De Lamerique a La Cour de France

2. Arendt enclosed a July 5, 1779, letter from William Lee. Arendt was planning to leave for Berlin to procure military supplies for Lee to deliver to Virginia. Lee agreed to the payment of a "genteel Gratification" if the baron were successful; if not, Lee promised to recommend that Virginia compensate him for up to 25 *louis* in travel expenses.
3. Having oversight of judicial matters at nearby Lorient where the *Serapis* was to be sold: T.J.A. LeGoff, *Vannes and Its Region: a Study of Town and Country in Eighteenth-Century France* (Oxford, 1981), p. 80.
4. In the hand of Jean-François-Marie Chanu de Limur, Lt. Gen. of the Admiralty of Vannes, who sent it to Sartine (see Sartine to BF, June 17). In a June covering letter (Archives de la Marine, B⁴CLXXII: 181–2), Chanu de Limur informed Sartine that the sale would be held on June 22. Obviously unfamiliar with the English language, he made several minor errors of transcription which we have silently corrected.

Copie De La Lettre de M. B Franklin aux officiers De L'amiraute de Vannes

Certifie Conforme a loriginal

CHANU DE LIMUR

Certificate for Arendt

Copy: Library of Congress

[May 18, 1780]

Colonel D'Arendt in the service of the United States of America, having had leave to come to Europe for the recovery of his health, and being about to return to his Duty, I do hereby certify at his request, such Captains or Owners of Ships as he may apply to for a Passage, that from his Character for Probity, and the Pay he must have due to him in America, I make no doubt of his Readiness and Ability to discharge punctually on his arrival there, any obligation he may enter into on Account of Such passage.[5] Given at Passy this 18th. Day of May 1780.

B.F.

M. Plenipoten. &c.

Certificate Given to M. Le Baron d'Arendt.

From Dumas

ALS: American Philosophical Society; AL (draft): Algemeen Rijksarchief

Monsieur,   La Haie 19e. may 1780

Quoique les Etats d'Hollande soient assemblés ici depuis 10 jours, il ne peut encore s'y passer rien d'interessant, jusqu'au retour de l'Exprès qui a porté à Petersbourg l'acceptation, faite par les Etats-Génx., des propositions de la Cour de Russie. En attendant l'on sait ici, par les Dépêches du Résident de la Rep. à Petersbourg, Mr. Swart, que la nouvelle de la Résolution de la Province d'Hollde., qui, comme on sait, donne toujours le ton

5. On May 18 the baron signed three copies of a promissory note for 25 *louis d'ors* (600 *l.t.*) loaned him by BF. Two of these copies are at the APS.

393

aux autres, y a causé des sensations fort agréables, non seulement à la Cour de Russie, mais aussi parmi les Ministres étrangers qui y résident, & que le Ministre de Prusse,[6] surtout, s'y est expliqué d'une maniere très-forte sur l'insolence des Angl., & sur l'indignité de leur procédé contre la rep.; enfin, que le système de la neutralité armée pour humilier l'Angl. prend force de plus en plus à la Cour & parmi les Puissances: ce qui est très-visible par les discours que tiennent leurs Ministres.

Ce qui suit ne doit pas encore être divulgué. J'écrivis il y a quelques jours à Amst. pour leur conseiller d'offrir le 5e Matelot de leurs navires Marchds. afin de pulvériser le prétexte de la rareté des Matelots pour la Flotte de la rep. & d'empêcher que les mal intentionnés ne presentent une contre-adresse.[7] Voici ce qu'on m'a repondu ce matin. "La Requête est dressée, sur laquelle on demandera aux Etats la prompte protection du Commerce, en offrant tout ce que les Etats jugeront à propos d'imposer au Commerce; que ce soit le cinquieme, & même le troisieme Matelôt, personne de bien intentionné ne s'y opposeroit. On a dressé la Liste de ceux à qui elle sera présentée pour signer, & nous ne croyons point, que, quand même ils ne la signeroient pas tous, personne ose s'y opposer." Ainsi je puis vous annoncer d'avance, Monsieur, que la semaine prochaine une telle Requête sera présentée. Ce qui n'est rien moins qu'indifférent dans ces circonstances.

Je prépare une nouvelle Lettre, très soumise, pour me remettre bien avec le G—— Facteur, & je lui redemande pour la troisieme fois formellement pardon des jugemens téméraires que j'ai pu porter sur ce qui le concerne. Je vous ai dejà dit, Monsieur, ce qu'il exige de moi, qui m'est impossible. Mais, de grace, si vous croyez que je puisse faire quelque chose de plus que ce que j'ai fait, expliquez-vous positivement, ordonnez-moi explicitement & nommément ce que vous desirez que je fasse pour le con-

6. Count Johann Eustach von Goertz (1737–1821): Isabel de Madariaga, *Britain, Russia, and the Armed Neutrality of 1780: Sir James Harris's Mission to St. Petersburg during the American Revolution* (New Haven, 1962), p. 115; *ADB*.

7. The Dutch eventually were able to man their navy by offering, as JA reported, "very great premiums for seamen, as far as sixty ducats a man": Wharton, *Diplomatic Correspondence*, IV, 29.

tenter; je vous obéirai, s'il m'est possible, avec la même promptitude, que je vous ai obéi en déposant sur le champ tout desir de Vengeance & de poursuite contre Sir G——. Je vous préviens seulement de ceci: c'est que je suis dans la plus forte persuasion que je dirois des faussetés, si je faisois la déclaration qu'on me demande par rapport au *fur litterarius.* Il faut considérer aussi que ce que j'ai fait n'est qu'une imprudence, que le besoin de faire adresser mes Lettres sous un couvert non suspect m'avoit arrachée; & ce que l'autre a fait est un crime. On veut qu'en justification & récompense de ce crime je sois *le délateur de moi-même:* ce qui est bien plus dûr encore que d'etre *le délateur de son frere.*[8]

Je suis toujours, & pour toujours, avec le plus respectueux attachement, Monsieur, Votre très-humble & très obéissant serviteur   DUMAS

Je suis aussi bien que jamais avec notre Ami.

Passy à Son E. M. Franklin &c.

Addressed: à Son Excellence / Monsieur B. Franklin, Esqr. / Min. Plenipe. des Etats-unis / etc. / *Passy./.*

Notation: Dumas la haie May 19. 1780

From James Milne[9]

ALS: American Philosophical Society

Sir,   Paris 19. May 1780. Chez Mr: Gregson Rue Dauphine

I shall be much obliged to you if you will allow me a moment for an audience, and to fix the day when I may present myself to you at Passy.

8. The last phrase refers to Ferdinand Grand. The thief of the letters was Georges Grand (see BF to Dumas, March 29). BF would certainly have remembered Alexander Wedderburn's use in 1774 of the appellation "homo trium literarum" indicting BF himself as a thief: XXI, 49. For a recent discussion of BF and the "fur" epithet see Keith Arbor, "One Last Word: Benjamin Franklin and the Duplessis Portrait of 1778," *PMHB,* CXVIII (1994), 183–208.

9. The *mécanicien* from Manchester, England (d. 1816), who had come to France in 1779, prepared to introduce new technology for carding cotton and

MAY 19, 1780

I have to solicit your attention upon objects which concern America.[1]

I have the honor to be with the most profound respect Sir, Your very humble & very obedient Servant   JAMES MILNE

Mr: Franklin à Passy

Addressed: A Monsieur / Monsieur Franklin / en son hotel / à Passy.

Notation: Milne Paris 19. May 1780.

To the Royal Academy of Brussels

Passy, printed by Benjamin Franklin; AL: Chicago Historical Society; AL (draft) and copy: Library of Congress

The Académie impériale et royale des Sciences et Belles-Lettres de Bruxelles did not, according to its own historians, produce a body of

---

spinning wool. He first addressed himself to Holker, who had him construct a carding machine and gave him an introduction to Necker. The French government, thinking his proposal to construct five different machines too expensive, turned him down, and Milne eventually established a cotton-spinning factory for François Perret. In late 1782 Milne and his brother John lured their father John Milne, Sr. (*c.* 1722–1804), the inventor, to leave Manchester and join them in France. There they remained, and in 1785 were installed by the government at the château de la Muette in Passy. Despite their successes and the significance of their role in the transfer of technology from England to France, the Milnes died in poverty. Charles Smith, "Episode in Cotton Trade History: Manchester Inventors in France," *Manchester Guardian*, Jan. 10, 1930, kindly communicated by Phyllis Giles through Prof. John Harris. See also Serge Chassagne, *Le Coton et ses Patrons: France, 1760–1840* (Paris, 1991), pp. 191–4.

1. The interview has left no trace. However, BF kept among his papers two engraved advertisements for machines invented and patented by John Milne, Sr. One was for dressing flour, the other for dressing oatmeal and barleymeal (APS). The former was patented in 1765: Bennet Woodcroft, comp., *Alphabetical Index of Patentees of Inventions* (reprint ed., London, 1969), p. 381.

No other letters from Milne have survived, but three lengthy memoirs by him, probably written in 1783, are among BF's papers at the Hist. Soc. of Pa. and will be discussed in future volumes. They detail his career in France, list his inventions, and ask for financial backing.

work of enduring value during its founding decade. It was formed in 1772 in an attempt to raise what had been a small literary society from a level of "frivolity." By incorporating the sciences, the academy hoped to become a serious institution.[2] One of its chief activities in its early years was to organize and judge intellectual contests, for which it devised questions and awarded medals.[3] At a meeting of October 13 and 14, 1779 (the report of which was not published until the following May), the society announced four questions for the upcoming year. The first three were literary and historical. The final one, in mathematics, was proposed "au lieu d'une question physique": given a certain geometric figure, how could one determine the greatest number of smaller figures that could be contained inside the first?[4] Franklin found the question so ridiculous, especially in light of its being advertised as having a practical value, that he penned this sarcastic response.

He was pleased enough with the essay to print it as one of the bagatelles, but uneasy enough at its "grossiereté" to explicitly request William Carmichael not to publish it in Spain.[5] In September, 1783, writing to Richard Price after the peace treaty had been signed, Franklin was reminded of the topic of "inflammable air" while describing the French balloon craze. He enclosed a copy of this bagatelle, calling it "a jocular Paper I wrote some Years since in ridicule of a Prize Question given out by a certain Academy on this side the Water." But, realizing that Price was a mathematician and might see merit where he had seen none, Franklin then suggested that his friend simply forward it to Priestley, "who is *apt* to give himself *Airs* (i.e. fix'd, deflogisticated, &c. &c.) and has a kind of Right to every thing his Friends *produce* upon that Subject."[6] If Franklin read the volume of the Academy's memoirs published that year (1783), he would have learned that the prize question was withdrawn because it had not been satisfactorily resolved.[7]

2. See *L'Académie royale de Belgique depuis sa fondation (1772–1922)* (Brussels, 1922), pp. 11–13. See also Richard E. Amacher, *Franklin's Wit & Folly: the Bagatelles* (New Brunswick, N.J., 1953), pp. 63–5.

3. *L'Académie royale de Belgique,* pp. 12, 15.

4. *Mémoires de L'Académie impériale et royale des Sciences et Belles-Lettres de Bruxelles,* III (1780), xliii–xlv. BF quotes from this question at the beginning of the bagatelle.

5. To Carmichael, Jan. 23, 1782, Smyth, *Letters,* VIII, 369.

6. To Price, Sept. 16, 1783, Library of Congress.

7. *Mémoires de L'Académie . . . ,* IV (1783), p. xxiv.

[after May 19, 1780]⁸

To the Royal Academy of * * * * *

G E N T L E M E N ,

I Have perused your late mathematical Prize Question, proposed in lieu of one in Natural Philosophy, for the ensuing year, viz. *"Une figure quelconque donnée, on demande d'y inscrire le plus grand nombre de fois possible une autre figure plus petite quelconque, qui est aussi donnée."* I was glad to find by these following Words, *"l'Académie a jugé que cette découverte, en étendant les bornes de nos connoissances, ne seroit pas sans UTILITÉ "*, that you esteem *Utility* an essential Point in your Enquiries, which has not always been the case with all Academies; and I conclude therefore that you have given this Question instead of a philosophical, or as the Learned express it, a physical one, because you could not at the time think of a physical one that promis'd greater *Utility.*

Permit me then humbly to propose one of that sort for your consideration, and through you, if you approve it, for the serious Enquiry of learned Physicians, Chemists, &c. of this enlightened Age.

It is universally well known, That in digesting our common Food, there is created or produced in the Bowels of human Créatures, a great Quantity of Wind.

That the permitting this Air to escape and mix with the Atmosphere, is usually offensive to the Company, from the fetid Smell that accompanies it.

That all well-bred People therefore, to avoid giving such Offence, forcibly restrain the Efforts of Nature to discharge that Wind.

That so retain'd contrary to Nature, it not only gives frequently great present Pain, but occasions future Diseases, such as habitual Cholics, Ruptures, Tympanies, &c. often destructive of the Constitution, & sometimes of Life itself.

---

8. The date on which volume III of the *Mémoires,* containing the satirized prize question, was announced for sale: Edouard Mailly, *Histoire de l'Académie impériale et royale des sciences et belles-lettres de Bruxelles* (Brussels, 1883), p. 267.

Were it not for the odiously offensive Smell accompanying such Escapes, polite People would probably be under no more Restraint in discharging such Wind in Company, than they are in spitting, or in blowing their Noses.

My Prize Question therefore should be, *To discover some Drug wholesome & not disagreable, to be mix'd with our common Food, or Sauces, that shall render the natural Discharges of Wind from our Bodies, not only inoffensive, but agreable as Perfumes.*

That this is not a chimerical Project, and altogether impossible, may appear from these Considerations. That we already have some Knowledge of Means capable of *Varying* that Smell. He that dines on stale Flesh, especially with much Addition of Onions, shall be able to afford a Stink that no Company can tolerate; while he that has lived for some Time on Vegetables only, shall have that Breath so pure as to be insensible to the most delicate Noses; and if he can manage so as to avoid the Report, he may any where give Vent to his Griefs, unnoticed. But as there are many to whom an entire Vegetable Diet would be inconvenient, and as a little Quick-Lime thrown into a Jakes will correct the amazing Quantity of fetid Air arising from the vast Mass of putrid Matter contain'd in such Places, and render it rather pleasing to the Smell, who knows but that a little Powder of Lime (or some other thing equivalent) taken in our Food, or perhaps a Glass of Limewater drank at Dinner, may have the same Effect on the Air produc'd in and issuing from our Bowels? This is worth the Experiment. Certain it is also that we have the Power of changing by slight Means the Smell of another Discharge, that of our Water. A few Stems of Asparagus eaten, shall give our Urine a disagreable Odour; and a Pill of Turpentine no bigger than a Pea, shall bestow on it the pleasing Smell of Violets. And why should it be thought more impossible in Nature, to find Means of making a Perfume of our *Wind* than of our *Water?*

For the Encouragement of this Enquiry, (from the immortal Honour to be reasonably expected by the Inventor) let it be considered of how small Importance to Mankind, or to how small a Part of Mankind have been useful those Discoveries in Science that have heretofore made Philosophers famous. Are there twenty Men in Europe at this Day, the happier, or even the easier, for any Knowledge they have pick'd out of Aristotle? What Comfort can the Vortices of Descartes give to a Man who has Whirl-winds in his Bowels! The Knowledge of Newton's mutual *Attraction* of the Particles of Matter, can it afford Ease to him who is rack'd by their mutual *Repulsion*, and the cruel Distensions it occasions? The Pleasure arising to a few Philosophers, from see-ing, a few Times in their Life, the Threads of Light untwisted, and separated by the Newtonian Prism into seven Colours, can it be compared with the Ease and Comfort every Man living might feel seven times a Day, by discharging freely the Wind from his Bowels? Especially if it be converted into a Perfume: For the Pleasures of one Sense being little inferior to those of an-other, instead of pleasing the *Sight* he might delight the *Smell* of those about him, & make Numbers happy, which to a benevo-lent Mind must afford infinite Satisfaction. The generous Soul, who now endeavours to find out whether the Friends he enter-tains like best Claret or Burgundy, Champagne or Madeira, would then enquire also whether they chose Musk or Lilly, Rose or Bergamot, and provide accordingly. And surely such a Lib-erty of *Ex-pressing* one's *Scent-iments*, and *pleasing one another*, is of infinitely more Importance to human Happiness than that Liberty of the *Press*, or *abusing one another*, which the English are so ready to fight & die for. ——In short, this Invention, if compleated, would be, as *Bacon* expresses it, *bringing Philosophy home to Mens Business and Bosoms.*[9] And I cannot but conclude, that in Comparison therewith, for *universal* and *continual UTIL-ITY*, the Science of the Philosophers abovementioned, even with the Addition, Gentlemen, of your *"Figure quelconque"* and the Figures inscrib'd in it, are, all together, scarcely worth a

F A R T-H I N G.

---

9. From the dedication to the 1625 edition of *Essayes:* Francis Bacon, *The Essayes or Counsels, Civill and Morall* (Michael Kiernan, ed., Oxford, 1985), p. 5.

To James Russell, Silvanus Grove and Osgood Hanbury

Copy: Library of Congress

Gentlemen   Passy May 20. 1780.

I have just received from his Excellency Thomas Sim Lee Governor of Maryland a Letter dated at *Annapolis in Council* the 4th. of January, requesting me to transmit to you the Copy of an Act (which I inclose accordingly) and to desire your immediate answer, whether you will transact the Business, sell out the Stock, & accept and pay the Bills drawn in pursuance of the Act?[1] If you aggree to execute this Trust, they direct that the stock be immediately sold, and that the Money be plac'd by you in the hands of Some Capital Banker in Amsterdam or Paris, Subject to your Drafts in Case Bills should be drawn on you. If you decline the service, you will see by the Act that I am impowered to take certain Steps,[2] which makes it necessary for me to know previously your determination. I therefore request to have it as soon as possible. With great Respect I have the honour to be. Gentlemen &c.

p.s. You will please to return me the Act if you do not under take to execute it.

Messrs. Russel, Grove and Hanbury Merchants, London.

From John Torris

ALS: American Philosophical Society

Honnd. Sir   Dunkerque the 20th. May 1780.

I have had the Honnor to write your Excellency on the 13th. Inst. relative to the Prise Flora Capt. Roodenberg, & on the Titles in your Hands which Prove that the Brig Friendship Capt.

1. Governor Lee's letter (xxxi, 336–8) enclosed an act of the Maryland Assembly for withdrawing bills of credit from circulation. He asked BF to inquire of Maryland's trustees in London (Russell, Grove, and Hanbury) if they would sell the state's stock in the Bank of England so it could honor its engagements.
2. *I.e.*, to choose a successor to the trustees. On April 19, above, JA had suggested Edmund Jenings.

Pretty John, & Schooner Peter Capt. Thos. Byrne, were maned by British Subjects, therefore were English Bottoms & subject to Condamnation favour of the Captor; & I hope your Excellency has allready drawn & forwarded these Condamnations.

I am advised that the Celebrated mr. Groult has sent to your Excellency his memorial Proving on authentic Testimonies & Authorities, that, the Cargoe of the Prise the Flora, Rooden-berg, was Legally acquiered by the unfortunate Black Prince.[3] I have a Copy of this memorial, & endeed, it Leaves me nothing to wish on the Legitimity of the Prise, & I am now convinced, that, all motives of Interest & Justice will prompt your Excellency to Pass forthwith Judgement of Condamnation on it. & as I find that, Mr. *De Maussallée mon avocat aux Conseils,* Can add but few arguments on the matter, & your Excellency wants none further, we might not Trouble him in the affair. However, He will Call to Take the Commands of your Excellency.—

Subjoined the Report on oath from Capt. Dowlin, which has been veriffied & attested by Two of his officers, which Prove the knowledge of the Parjured Capt. Roodenberg in the English Tongue, & the Fidelity of his first & Genuine Report In Berck,[4] which mention his Cargoe being for account & risk of the Merchants in Dublin it is Consigned to.—

If your Excellency desires an other declaration on these Subjects from Mr. Boulanger the English Brocker who Served in this report at Berck, I shall then requiere it, But I think your Excellency is now well Satisfied on the Head.

I am with greatest respect Honnd. Sir your Excellency's most obedient & most Humble servant   J. TORRIS

His Excellency Dor. Franklin Minister of the united States

Endorsed: May 20

Notation: Mr. Torris May 20. 1780—

3. Chantereyne sent the memorial with his letter of May 6, above.
4. Where Capt. Rodenberg made his deposition after reaching safety following the wreck of the *Black Prince:* Clark, *Ben Franklin's Privateers,* p. 130. Groult's memorial provides details.

From Jonathan Williams, Jr.

ALS: University of Pennsylvania Library; copy: Yale University Library

Dear & honoured Sir.   Nantes May 20 1780.

I have duely received your Favour of 10th Instant & have kept
it by me some time in hopes of being able to give some satisfactory answer to it, but I have not yet found any way of getting the
Goods out unless I were to buy a Ship and fit her for the Purpose,
this would undoubtedly be the most eligible Plan if Funds were
plenty, because the amount of the Freight will be more than half
as much as the Cost & outfit of a Ship, and in the one Case it is
all expence in the other the Ship remains worth her Cost; But in
the State of our Finances I do not suppose you would relish a
Plan which would require a great Disburse.

Mr de Montieu who has more Ships, and has let more to Government than any Man I know, was two days here in his Passage
from Brest to Paris, I spoke to him and he said he would immediately on his arrival confer with you and Mr de Chaumont on
the Subject; you may perhaps decide something together. I find
by my Letters from Brest that it will not do to send anything
thither, for what is there already cannot go out in the second Division, as there are more Stores to carry for Government than
there are Ships to take them: Mr Bersole has I suppose written
the same thing to M. de Chaumont.

If you think proper to execute that Part of Congress Order
which relates to Frigates a large Ship might be purchased & fitted according to the Direction of the Committee, they would
then have the materials they want & the Ship too; but in such a
Case I would reccommend not to arm her compleatly, for a 36
Gun Frigatte compleatly manned & armed has little or no room
for a Cargo, 10 Guns & about 40 Men would be enough for a
Transport Ship & the remainder of her Guns shott &c would be
a good part of Ballast which she must necessarily have & the
Room which would be necessary for 6 months Water & Provision for 200 men would remain for the Cargo, and a large Ship
so fitted to go under the Convoy of the Alliance would answer
all your Purposes. If this is thought an eligible Plan the Serapis
might be bought for the Purpose, or if you think that will not do
I can purchase a very fine Ship here & I could find americans

enough to man her. There happens to be a very fine Ship now on Sale, she has been launched but about two months and may be bought for less than she Cost, she is an excellent Frigate.—

Your Letter gives me, I imagine, full authority to act in this matter, and I would willingly save you all the Trouble I can, but I dare not take so much on myself without a provision of Funds, if you will therefore supply me with the Funds at the End of 4 & 6 months, I will give you no further Trouble in the Business and all shall be done with the utmost Expedition.

Mr. Ross is at L'orient. I could not therefore have a personal Consultation with him but I have written to him and offered to meet him half way on the Road for the Purpose:[5] When I hear from or see him, I will write the result of our Consultation.

I have not been able to have many Shoes made for such as are usualy made here are wretched indeed. I have therefore agreable to your Opinion prepared Leather of which I have a considerable Quantity ready to Ship; I have bought only sole Leather because I think our own upper Leather is much superior to what I can buy here.

I have Letters from Phila of the 16 April by a Brig arrived at L'orient. Mr Bache & all your Family were then well; the Last news they had then from Clinton was of the 18 March when he had done nothing, our army is 7000 Strong against him. Mr Gruel of this Place has failed for a considerable Sum.—[6] I am ever your dutifull & affectionate Kinsman   JONA WILLIAMS J

The Hon. Doctor Franklin

Notation: J Williams May 20. 80

5. A copy of JW's letter, dated May 14, is at the Yale University Library.

6. The previous November, Gruel had signed a *traite* to his creditors for almost one and a half million *l.t.:* L. Rouzeau, "Aperçus du role de Nantes dans la guerre d'indépendance d'Amérique (1775–1783)," *Annales de Bretagne,* LXXIV (1967), 273–4.

To Poellnitz
Copy: Library of Congress

Sir,   Passy, May 21. 1780.
I received the Letter you did me the honour of writing to me
the 13th. Inst. I think your determination is prudent, to wait for
a Peace, in order to make your Voyage to america. The Inconvenience of being taken by the Enemy, is too great to hazard with
your Lady and Family. Be pleased to make my Respects acceptable to her, and believe me to be, with great Regard, and best
Wishes for your Prosperity, Sir, Your m. o. & m. h. s.

Mr. Le Baron de Poellnitz près de la Porte D'albret, Maison de
l'architecte Bayle à Bordeaux.

From Achille-Guillaume Lebègue de Presle
ALS: American Philosophical Society

a chatillon sous Bagneux ce 21 mai 80
Je prie votre Excellence de recevoir mes remercimens du renvoy
que m'a fait mr Grand des Livres de Londres venus sous votre
nom;[7] et mes excuses d'avoir différé jusqu'a ce jour a m'acquitter de ce devoir. Le retard a ete causé par mon deplacement qui
m'a donné des occupations pressantes et des distractions de toute
espece.
Les soins de mon depart, au moment ou les livres m'ont ete
apportés, m'avoient fait oublier de vous envoyer par mr grand,
avec les deux livres qui vous etoient destinés, L'ouvrage du
Lord mahon dont je vous avois offert de vous procurer la lec-

7. This shipment had already been the object of two letters sent by
Lebègue to WTF. On April 30 he explained that Jean-Hyacinthe de Magellan,
in England, had entrusted a number of books destined for BF to someone who
had sent them to Ostend, addressed to the Doctor. (That person was Thomas
Digges; see his letter of March 17.) Since the parcel also contained books
meant for other people, Magellan, as soon as he became aware of the mixup, sent Lebègue the list of books and of people to whom they belonged. As
soon as WTF lets him know that the bundle has reached Ostend, Lebègue will
clear them through customs and proceed to the distribution himself (APS).
He wrote again on May 5 to announce that the books had arrived and he
needed a signed note from BF to take possession of them (APS).

ture.[8] Jai cru que le moyen le plus court pour vous faire parvenir ce dernier livre, etoit de le faire porter au bureau de mr Brillon, persuadé qu'il se feroit un plaisir de vous l'envoyer promptement. Ainsi Monsieur, vous devez avoir recu

1° un Exemplaire in 4° relié de votre dernier ouvrage;[9]

2° un Exemplaire in 8° destiné a feu mr Dubourg;[1]

3° un petit paquet que votre lettre m'a servi a retirer de la messagerie en y cherchant le balot de livres;

4° le livre du Lord Mahon que vous pouvez monsieur ne lire qu'a loisir, parceque je reste encore a la campagne 10 a 12 jours; et que la lecture de votre dernier ouvrage m'instruit plus utilement en differens genres.

Je ne manquerai pas a mon retour a Paris d'aller chez mr Grand le rembourser de la portion des frais dont mon paquet a augmenté votre envoi; ce que je lui ai demandé par un billet remis au porteur des livres et auquel il n'a pas repondu.

Jai recu la semaine derniere une lettre de mr Ingen-houzs qui m'envoye quelques notes pour l'Edition francoise de son ouvrage;[2] mais il ne me dit pas s'il reviendra passer quelques jours a Paris comme il l'esperoit en partant. L'impression de son ouvrage doit etre commencée, mais je n'ai point encore recu d'epreuve.

Jay lhonneur d'etre de votre Excellence le tres humble tres obeist serviteur   LEBEGUE DE PRESLE

Permettez moi je vous prie de presenter ici mes tres humbles civilités a Monsieur votre fils et de le remercier des peines qu'il a prises pour mon Paquet.

Notation: Le Begue de Presle Chatillon 21 may 1780.

8. Charles Stanhope became Lord Mahon upon the death of his brother Philip in 1763. He published in 1779 his *Principles of Electricity . . .* , probably the work alluded to here. A public trial of Franklin's and Stanhope's experiments in lightning-conductors is said to have taken place at the Pantheon under the superintendence of Edward Nairne, the electrician. *DNB.*

9. *Political, Miscellaneous, and Philosophical Pieces.* On May 15, BF inscribed a copy "To M. Le Ray de Chaumont le fils, from the Author": auction catalog of Nouveau Drouot, *Collection R.G.: lettres et manuscrits autographes, livres, portraits, mercredi 19 juin 1996,* p. 33.

1. Dubourg had died in December, 1779: XXXI, 237n, 242.

2. Ingenhousz's *Expériences sur les végétaux,* the French translation of his *Experiments upon Vegetables,* appeared in Paris in 1780. See XXXI, 122–3, 140n.

From Edme-Jacques Genet

ALS: American Philosophical Society

A Versailles ce 21. mai 1780

J'ai remis, Monsieur, à Mgr. le Cte. de Vergennes une traduction de la piece en langue angloise ci jointe.[3] Le ministre m'a ordonné de vous en envoyer une copie que je joins pareillement ici, avec quelques gazettes Américaines, en attendant les autres que je vous ferai passer Successivement. J'ai l'honneur d'etre avec un sincere attachement Monsieur Votre très humble et très obéissant Serviteur

GENET

Notation: M. Genet Versailles 21. may 1780.

From Arendt

AL: American Philosophical Society

Paris ce 22me May 1780.

Le Baron de Arendt présente Ses trés humbles rêspects et répète Ses adieux a Monsieur Le Docteur Francklin, il est trés mortifié d'être obligé de l'incommoder encore car il n'aime pas d'être a charge à quelqu'n, mais se trouvant dans la plus grande peine par le refus que M. Le Docteur lui fit hier,[4] il L'invite d'avoir la complaisance de dire seulement au Congres—que le Bon [Baron] lui a été recommandé par M. Le Comte de Vergennes sur les fortes instances que l'Envoyé Prussien a fait a ce dernier, et qu'il se justifieroit lui même chês le Congres sur sa trop longue absence par des lettres de M. Lee qu'il a entre ses mains— Le Bon. espère que M. le Docteur ne trouvera point sa demande indiscrette, par ce qu'elle est fondée dans la verite, et il se flatte qu'il lui fera avoir cette lettre au Congres par le même Exprès qui Lui a remis celle cy, pour quelle bonte il L'ui aura des trés grandes obligations.

Le Bon. èspere d'autant plus que M. Le Docteur lui accordera sa demande, comme il Lui avoit promis de le faire la semaine passée.

---

3. Probably the letter that JA sent to Genet on May 17 in order to refute an address made to the House of Commons on May 5 by Gen. Conway. Translated into French, this letter appeared on June 3 in the *Mercure de France: Adams Papers,* IX, 321–4.

4. Arendt must not have considered BF's safe conduct of May 18, above, an adequate recommendation.

Addressed: A Monsieur / Monsieur Francklin / Ministre Pleni-potentiaire / des Etats unis de L'amerique / près le Roi / Passy

Notation: Arendt le Baron de Paris 22 may 1780.

To Samuel Huntington

LS[5] and transcript: National Archives; copy: Library of Congress

Sir,   Passy May 22. 1780

The Baron d'Arendt, Colonel in the Armies of the United States, having express'd to me his Desire of returning to the Service in America, tho' not entirely cur'd of the Wound which occasioned his Voyage to Europe, I endeavour'd to dissuade him from the Undertaking. But he having procured a Letter to me from M. De Vergennes, of which I send your Excellency a Copy herewith,[6] I have been induced to advance him twenty five Louis, towards enabling him to proceed.— To justify his long Absence, he intends laying before Congress, some Letters from the honble Mr. Wm. Lee, which he thinks will be sufficient for that purpose.— With great Respect, I have the honour to be, Your Excellency's most obedt. & most humble Servant

B FRANKLIN

His Exy. Sl. Huntington Esq.

Notation: Letter from honble. B Franklin May 22. 1780— Read Decr. 4. Referred to the board of War[7]

From William Carmichael   Copy: Library of Congress

Dear Sir,   Aranjuez 22d. may 1780.

I have defered writing to you since my last of the 27th. Ultio.[8] in Hopes of profiting by the Ct. De Montmorin's Courier, but as

---

5. In WTF's hand.
6. Vergennes' letter of May 11, above.
7. *JCC*, XVIII, 1116.
8. April 22[–27], above.

it is not certain when one will be dispatched I venture to inform you by the ordinary post that Sir J.D. presented a memorial to the Ct. De FloridaBlanca, containing certain propositions tending to an Accomodation of the present differences between the Belligerent nations. On Application to the Ct. De Vergennes, you will undoubtedly be furnished with a Copy of his memorial and from the perusal of it will be able to judge whether it doth not merit the Derision with which it appears to have been received. The author is probably at Paris. I take the Liberty of advising you that M. Jay means to transmit Copies of it to Congress,[9] which perhaps you may think proper to do, as the Writer seems to found his hopes of Success on your interference and Wisdom I leave him with pleasure in your Hands.[1] Considering all things, the Operations for this Campaign have been pushed with much Vigor in this Country. I shall not mention American News because I am informed that you have received much later advices than have reached us. You will oblige me very much by permitting my friend and namesake to Copy a letter which you wrote to a Lady of the moulin Jolie,[2] several people of Distinction here are desirous of seing it and I own candidly that it will give me much pleasure to have this proof of your Confidence. M. Jay and family are at madrid and therefore I cannot present to you those compliments on their part, which I intreat you

9. Jay did send a lengthy letter, which included both a description of Sir John Dalrymple's visit and a copy of his memorial in which he proposed not only that BF help arrange a compromise peace with Britain, but also that the belligerents guararantee each other's colonial possessions: Wharton, *Diplomatic Correspondence*, III, 726–31. Dalrymple had given Chief Minister Floridablanca permission to transmit copies to BF as well as to the French government.

1. WTF made a notation in the margin, "Prive Corr." Probably written when he was preparing his edition of his grandfather's correspondence, he was marking the letter down through this point for possible inclusion. He did not publish this particular letter, however, but did include both BF's June 17 response (below) and Carmichael's copy of Dalrymple's memoir: *The Private Correspondence of Benjamin Franklin, LL.D., F.R.S. &c.* (3rd ed.; 2 vols., London, 1818), I, 61–3; II, 430–41.

2. "The Ephemera": XXVII, 430–5. Carmichael's friend and namesake was WTF.

to make to these for me who do me the Honor of remembring me.

I am with much respect, Your Excellency's most obliged & humble servant.   (signed) W. CARMICHAEL.

His Excellency B. Franklin Esqe.

From the Duchesse d'Enville

LS: American Philosophical Society

La Rocheguyon ce 22. mai 1780.

Le Séjour de M. votre petit fils à Genève, Monsieur, me fait espérer que les Citoyens de cette ville ont quelques droits à vos bontés; c'est dans cette Confiance que je vous les demande pour deux Jeunes gens que l'amour de la gloire et de la liberté font voler en Amérique: l'un se nomme Gallatin, il est âgé de 19. ans, fort instruit pour son âge, très sage jusques ici, et né avec des talens. Le second s'appelle Ser;[3] ils ont fait un mystère à leurs parens du projet qu'ils vouloient éxécuter, on ignore par conséquent le lieu où ils débarqueront; on suppose qu'ils vont à Philadelphie ou à l'armée Continentale; c'est un de mes amis qui m'instruit de tout ce détail en me priant de vous engager a les recommander; je partagerai sa reconnoissance et vous prie, Monsieur, de ne point douter des sentimens avec lesquels J'ai l'honneur dêtre Votre très humble et très obéissante servante

LAROCHEFOUCAULD D'ENVILLE

Addressed: A Monsieur / Monsieur franklin / A Pacy / près Paris.

---

3. Albert Gallatin and his Genevan friend Henri Serre had departed from Geneva in April without telling their families. By May 16 they were at Paimboeuf, and on July 14 they landed at Cape Ann (now Gloucester, Mass.): XXVI, 541n; Henry Adams, *The Life of Albert Gallatin* (Philadelphia, 1879), pp. 17–19, 23, 26. Gallatin's family made every effort to secure recommendations from prominent Americans for the young men. Adams, *Life,* pp. 22, 24. BF obliged the request within two days, responding to the present letter and writing to his son-in-law, May 24, below.

Notation: La Rochefoucauld d'enville la Rocheguyon le 22 may 1780

From Balthazar-Georges Sage

ALS: American Philosophical Society

Monsieur   Ce 22 mai [1780?]

J'ai appris par Mr. Leschevin que vous aviez eté voir à versailles Le Cabinet de Minéraux de Mr Son frere;[4] Les objets qu'il renferme sont tous beaux, bien choisis, le Catalogue en a été fait par Mr Delisle,[5] et je me suis chargé avec plaisir de le Completer de sorte que Les Morceaux qui n'y Sont point indiqués sont etiquetés par moi. Cette Collection fera partout une superbe base de Cabinet.

J'aurais eû Lhonneur d'aller vous Rendre mes devoirs si je n'etois pas aussi occupé.

Je suis avec Respect Monsieur Votre très humble et très obeissant serviteur   SAGE
                                    De lacademie a la monnoie

Mr francklin.

4. *Contrôleur de la Maison de la comtesse d'Artois,* in Versailles, he may have been the brother of the lady who invited BF, in December, 1778, to witness some experiments conducted by Sage: XXVIII, 239n. His *cabinet d'histoire naturelle* is mentioned in L.V. Thiéry, *Almanach du voyageur à Paris* (Paris, 1783), p. 127. The celebrated mineralogist Philippe-Xavier Leschevin de Précour (1771–1814) was his son. *Nouvelle Biographie.*

5. Jean-Baptiste de Romé de l'Isle (1736–1790) had published, in 1772, his *Essai de cristallographie.* . . . In it he argued that mineralogy should be considered a separate discipline rather than a branch of chemistry. A revised edition in 4 vols. entitled *Cristallographie* . . . appeared in 1783. See René Taton, ed., *Enseignement et diffusion des sciences en France au xviiie siècle* (Paris, 1964), pp. 370–1; Quérard, *France littéraire,* VIII, 135–7. L.V. Thiéry calls de l'Isle's cabinet of crystallography the most beautiful in France: *Le Voyageur à Paris* (Paris, 1790), p. 131

To John Diot and Co.

Copy: Library of Congress

Gentlemen, Passy, May 23. 1780.

I received the honour of yours (without date) but enclosing three Papers from the Admiralty, relating to a Prize called the Betsey.[6] As none of her Papers have been produced, and the only Person of her Crew that was brought in, was missing when he should have been examined, I find no Grounds to go upon in condemning her. This Vessel is the Third brought in, without papers or Persons to be examined, The Peter of London and the friendship being the other Two. I can condemn none under such Circumstances; and if this Practice is continued, I Shall suspect that they are neutral Vessels, and must with draw the Commission. If the Cargoes are perishable you can apply to the admiralty to Sell them, and to keep the money in their hands as a deposite for the Use of those who shall appear to be the Owners, after Proofs brought, either that the Prizes were English in which case they will be condemned, or that they were neutrals, in wich Case they must be restored with damages. I have the honour to be, Gentlemen, Your, &c.

Mesrs. John Diot and Co. Merchants at Morlaix.

To Ferdinand Grand

Copy:[7] American Philosophical Society

Sir Passy May 23d. 1780

Pay to W.T. Franklin ten Louis d'Ors he having advanced the Same by my order to Several American sailors to assist them in getting to LOrient Vizt.

6. The covering letter and the enclosures are missing. Diot & Co. had twice written BF in January about the *Betsey*, a prize made by the *Black Princess*, but her papers had been misdirected: XXXI, 378–9, 429–30, 465n; Clark, *Ben Franklin's Privateers*, pp. 107–8.

7. In the hand of Henry Grand.

Nous Benjamin Franklin,
Ecuyer, Miniſtre Plenipotentiaire des
Etats-Unis de l'Amerique, près Sa
Majeſté Très Chretienne,

PRIONS *tous ceux qui ſont à prier, de*
vouloir bien laiſſer ſeurement & librement paſ-
ſer Joseph Plummer, Charles Herbert
Benj. Carr & Benj. Taylor, Matelots
de la Frigate Alliance allant en la Virginie
ſans leur *donner ni permettre qu'il* leur *ſoit*
donné aucun empéchement, mais au contraire
de leur *accorder toutes ſortes d'aide et d'aſ-*
ſiſtance, comme nous ferions en pareil Cas,
pour tous ceux qui nous ſeroient recommandés.

EN FOI DE QUOI *nous* leur
avons délivré le préſent Paſſe-port, valable
pour un Mois *ſigné de notre main,*
contre-ſigné par l'un de nos Secretaires, & au
bas duquel eſt le Cachet de nos Armes.

DONNÉ *à Paſſy, en notre Hôtel, le*
23 May *mil ſept cent* quatrevingt

B Franklin

GRATIS.
Par Ordre de M. le Miniſtre Plenipotentiaire.

W. T. Franklin ſe.

7

Passport for Joseph Plummer, Charles Herbert,
Benjamin Carr, and Benjamin Taylor

To Bury [Benj] Taylor   48 *l.t.*
To Benj Carr.   48
To Ch. Herbert   48
To Joseph Plummer[8]   48
To James Tille   24
To Frank Foster[9]   24
    £240

Charge the Same to the publick Account of sir Your humble servt[1]   Sigd. B. FRANKLIN

To M. Grand Banker in Paris

Notations by William Temple Franklin: sign'd W.T. FRANKLIN / Copy of an Order on Mr. Grand.

8. The first four names on the list were members of Thomas White's crew on the *Alliance* who had come to France at BF's direction; see BF to White *et al.*, May 10. Charles Herbert recorded in his journal that on May 23, 1780, the sailors each received two guineas (48 *l.t.*) for travel to Lorient, their board was paid, and they received a pass: *A Relic of the Revolution . . .* (Boston, 1847), p. 242. BF's Cash Book reflects the payment of their "Acct at the Inn" (31.6 *l.t.*, "omitted" at its proper place but recorded on June 11), and the printed passport he issued them on May 23, valid for one month, is made out to "Joseph Plummer, Charles Herbert, Benj. Carr & Benj. Taylor, matelots de la Frige. l'Alliance allant à l'Orient." Ernest Merrill (Bronxville, N.Y. [1956]).

That document is the earliest known example of the second Passy passport variant. (See xxx, 181–2, for the first variant and a brief history of the forms.) The type is identical to the first Passy passport, but BF added a single rule border along the sides and across the top. Two other examples of this printing have come to light; their dates are Sept. 11 and Oct. 8, 1780. Randolph G. Adams reproduces the last example, classifying it as "Livingston 31b," in his article, "A Passy Passport," *The Journal of the Rutgers University Library*, v (1941–2), facing p. 8.

9. Promissory notes from both Tillee (or Tilee) and Foster are at the APS. See the Editorial Note on Promissory Notes, at the beginning of this volume, where Foster is listed as having received what may have been an additional sum on May 27. Only the present payment to him is listed in the Alphabetical List of Escaped Prisoners.

1. At some point, probably in 1780, BF printed a blank draft on Grand for money to assist the bearer, "lately from Prison in *England*," to return to America. A few of the blank forms survive; they are at the APS and at the Yale University Library.

From Samuel Cooper

ALS: American Philosophical Society

My dear Sir   Boston N.E. May 23'd. 1780.

I received some Months past your Letter from Passy dated
Octr. 27. 1779,[2] and lately a Copy of it by The Marquiss Fayette,
who arrived here in the Hermoine with M. Corny.[3] As the Arrival of the Marquiss diffused a general Joy, every Expression of
it was given here that Circumstances would allow, and particular Respects paid by the Government, as well as the People to this
prudent and gallant young Nobleman, who keeps the Cause of
America so warm at his Heart:[4] In these Respects Mr Corny
had his Share, as well as Captain La Touche Commander of the
Frigate.[5] The former, a Gentlemen of Letters and great Politeness, who acquired much Esteem in this Town in a little Time, is
gone on to Head Quarters, and from thence to Congress: the latter, who offer'd the Service of the Frigate he commanded to the
Government of this State, in the true Spirit of the Alliance, has
just returned from a short Cruize on our Coast, undertaken at
the Desire of the Council. He has visited Penobscot, taken a
near View of the Fort at Baggaduce, made two British Sloops of
War commanded by Mawett[6] who burnt Falmouth, retire up the
River, brought us an accurate Plan of the Fortress, and done
every Thing that Time and Circumstances would allow for our
Service. The Presence of this Frigate, under the Command of so
brave an Officer, and so warmly affected to the common Cause,

2. xxx, 597–9.

3. Dominique-Louis Ethis de Corny (xxiii, 332n), a *commissaire de guerre*,
was sent ahead with Lafayette to purchase provisions for Rochambeau's
army. Cooper arranged membership for him in the new American Academy
of Arts and Sciences (of which Cooper was vice president): Idzerda, *Lafayette
Papers*, iii, 20–4; Charles W. Akers, *The Divine Politician: Samuel Cooper and
the American Revolution in Boston* (Boston, 1982), p. 316.

4. Lafayette was greeted by fireworks, bonfires, banquets, and other fes-
tivities: Louis Gottschalk, *Lafayette and the Close of the American Revolution*
(Chicago, 1942), pp. 77.

5. Louis-René-Madeleine Le Vassor de La Touche-Tréville: xxvii, 78n.

6. Capt. Henry Mowat. For his destruction of Falmouth see John A.
Tilley, *The British Navy and the American Revolution* (Columbia, S.C., 1987),
pp. 59–60, and for his current command in Penobscot Bay, Gardner W. Allen,
A Naval History of the American Revolution (2 vols., Boston and New York,
1913), ii, 419, 438, 592. Castine is on the Bagaduce peninsula.

will be of great Advantage to the Trade of this State, and particularly to the Supply of this Town with Wood. Which has been at an exorbitant Price since the Enemy have taken Possession of Penobscot. Such Instances of Friendship and Aid make the most agreable Impressions on the Minds of the People here, and cultivate the Alliance; and I cannot but observe with Pleasure evident Marks of the growing Friendship between the two Nations.

It is impossible, my dear Sir, that I should ever loose the deep Respect and the Affection I have for you, *Dum Memor ipse mei, dum Spiritus hos regit artus.*[7] Your Friendship has united two Things in my Bosom that seldom Meet, Pride and Consolation; it has been the Honour and Balm of my Life. It has much affected me that the Turbulence and Uncertainty of the Times, together with the Weakness of my Nerves which has often unfitted me for Writing, should occasion to your View any Semblance of Neglect. I confess I have not written So often as my Heart dictated; but I have written repeatedly, particularly by the la sensible Capt. Chavagnes who carried my Grandson to France; but whither I gave the Letter to my Boy, to deliver with his own Hand, or to any one else who sailed from hence in that Ship, I do not now remember:[8] I wrote you largely by Mr. Austin, who carried my first Letter after the Convention of Saratoga,[9] and who left us again last Winter, of whose Arrival we have heard Nothing. I have been the more concerned at the Miscarriage of my Letters because they contained some Things relating to the Count d'Estaing, for whom I have the greatest Respect;[1] whose great Talents as a Commander, whose Intrepidity, Vigilance, Secrecy, Assiduity, quick Decision, Prudence, and unabated Affection to the common Cause, united with a surprizing Command of himself in delicate Circumstances and on the most trying Occasions, an Instance of which we had at Newport, I can never sufficiently commend. I thought it ought to be known at the Court of France in what high Estimation he was held here, but for whose un-

7. "As long as I have memory, as long as breath rules my body." Apuleius, *Florida*, XVI, 113–14.
8. In November, 1779, Cooper had sent letters of introduction for his grandson and for a Boston merchant: XXXI, 85–6, 92.
9. XXV, 103–11.
1. See XXVIII, 339–40.

common Prudence the Alliance might have received from the Indiscretion of some among us, an early Wound.

Mr. Bradford to whom I comit the Care of this Letter,[2] intended to have sailed directly to Holland, in his Way to France: but the Owners have altered the Destination of the Vessel first to Gottenberg— As another Vessel will soon sail for France or Holland, I hope to write more particularly by that. And am Sir, with every Sentiment of Esteem and Friendship Your obedient humble Servant   SAML: COOPER.

The Letters enclosed with this were sent me by Capt. la Touche, and M. de Corny to be committed to your Care.

Notation: Dr. Cooper May 23. 1780

From Dumas

ALS: American Philosophical Society; AL (draft): Algemeen Rijksarchief

Monsieur   La haie 23e. May 1780

Depuis ma derniere, j'ai écrit une Lettre très-soumise au Gd. Facteur où je lui demande pardon pour la 3e. ou 4e. fois. Il ne répond pas. Je ne puis donc rien faire de plus, jusqu'à-ce que vous me prescriviez quelque chose de plus, que d'avoir patience & d'attendre qu'il revienne. Je n'en serai pas moins prompt à lui rendre service si je puis, & s'il le veut. S'il arrivoit quelque grande nouvelle d'Amérique, je me recommande pour la savoir, s'il est possible, le premier, afin de pouvoir la lui annoncer. Cela pourroit devenir le véhicule du racommodement.

On me mande d'Amsterdam, qu'il y est entré un petit navire du Continent Américain, Cap. Moses Brown, consigné à Mr. Hodson, Maison qui ne passe pourtant pas pour être amie des Américains.[3] Mais cette phrase devroit-elle jamais sortir de ma bouche,

---

2. Probably Samuel Bradford (XXVIII, 278n), who had made a quick trip to Europe the preceding year: XXIX, 358.

3. Moses Brown (1742–1804) from Newburyport was presently commanding the brigantine *Mercury*, 10: Claghorn, *Naval Officers*, pp. 37–8; Mrs. E. Vale Smith, *History of Newburyport . . .* (Newburyport, 1854), 352–6. The firm may have been John Hodshon & Zoon: Butterfield, *John Adams Diary*, II, 444n.

après les cuisants chagrins qu'elle m'a causés? Le Cape. du navire n'avoit pas encore délivré ses Lettres.

Un Vaisseau parti de St. Eustache au commencement d'Avril, a apporté la nouvelle, qui y étoit parvenue de la part des Anglois-mêmes, de l'extrême embarras où ils se trouvent dans ces mers-là; leurs forces etant divisées, & une des divisions bloquée à Ste. Lucie.[4]

Mrs. Van De Perre & Meyners m'ont écrit fort poliment pour m'accuser la reception de votre Lettre, & de celle du Commodore Jones. Je leur avois joint une copie de la résolution du Congrès touchant le vaisseau portugais dont vous leur avez fait mention.[5]

La Requête d'Amsterdam a été retardée par l'opposition de deux ou trois fortes maisons, soufflées par certaines gens ici qui continuent de mettre des entraves à toutes ces bonnes choses. On m'assure néanmoins qu'elle sera présentée. C'est les mêmes gens qui ont fait nommer, pour aller négocier un Corps de Matelots au Danemark,[6] un homme élégant qui a voyagé en Italie, &c. & qui joue joliment dans des Proverbes & dans des Drames de Société. Si l'Etat accepte le 3e. Matelot de la Marine, notre Ami m'assure que cela seul donneroit le Corps de Matelots dont on a besoin; car la Hollande & la Frise seule emploient, dit-on 5000 vaisseaux au Commerce de la Baltique, de la France, de l'Espagne, du Portugal, & de la Méditerranée. Ainsi le Virtuose pourra revenir jouer ses drames en Hollande.

Je suis avec un très-grand respect Monsieur, Votre très-humble & très-obéissant serviteur   D

Nous ne doutons pas, notre ami & moi, qu'on ne cherche ici, dans le fonds, qu'à faire naître des prétextes pour ne point convoyer; à moins qu'on n'y soit forcé par les premieres dépêches qui arriveront de Russie.

---

4. The British Leeward Islands fleet was split into two squadrons in February, but was reunited in March: W.M. James, *The British Navy in Adversity: a Study of the War of American Independence* (London, New York, and Toronto, 1926), pp. 196–7.

5. Of April 23, above.

6. Attempts to procure sailors from Denmark proved futile. Amsterdam, Rotterdam, and other cities, as well as individuals, proposed various expedients to man the Dutch Navy: Fauchille, *Diplomatie française*, p. 500.

Je vous ai dit que la Requête a trouvé de l'opposition, & qu'on envoie un Damoiseau pour négocier des Matelots: voici un troisieme trait: c'est qu'on a mis en commission & envoyé au Texel une quantité trop grande de vaisseaux pour le peu de Matelots qu'on a; ainsi, aucun n'étant complet, on a un beau prétexte pour dire qu'on manque de matelots. C'est notre Ami qui m'a dit tout cela ce matin.

Passy à S.E. M. Franklin

Addressed: à Son Excellence / Monsieur B. Franklin, / Esqr. Min. Plenipe. / des Etats Unis &c. / Passy./.

Notation: Dumas la haie. May 23. 80

From Dumas

ALS: American Philosophical Society; AL (draft): Algemeen Rijksarchief

Monsieur   La Haie 23e. May[–June 13] 1780.

Je donnai ces jours passés une Lettre d'Introduction auprès de Votre Exc. à Mr. Corn. van Oudermeulen,[7] Directeur de la Compe. des Indes-or. [orientales] de la Chambre d'Amsterdam, qui se propose d'aller dans peu à Paris, exprès pour avoir quelques entretiens avec Vous, comme aussi avec Mr. 891,[8] sur des idées interessantes, dont j'ignore le sujet.— Il laissera, m'a-t-il dit, son secret cacheté entre les mains de Mrs. les Bourgue-maîtres d'Amsterdam, pour n'être ouvert & connu que lorsqu'il en sera temps.— C'est un homme connu pour avoir de grandes lumieres sur le Commerce en général, auteur d'un Livre estimé, imprimé depuis peu chez Rey à Amsterdam sous le titre de *Recherches sur le Commerce* in 8°. Il est ami de Mr. Temmink Bourguemaître regnant d'Amsterdam.[9] Il se plaint d'avoir des désagrémens de la part d'un puissant Parti ici, & d'être toujours

---

7. Cornelis van der Oudermeulen (1735–1794) was the author of *Recherches sur le Commerce ou Idées relatives aux intérets des différens peuples de l'Europe* (Amsterdam, 1778): *NNBW*, VI, 1085–6.

8. "Vergennes."

9. Egbert de Vrij Temminck (1700–1785): *NNBW*, V, 895–7.

en différend avec les Avocats de la Compe., qui ont une influence considérable dans toutes les affaires de cette Compe. Il y a déjà plusieurs semaines qu'il a intention de faire ce voyage: mais un entretien qu'il eut avec le 373. 657y. 610. 395,[1] où on lui déclaroit, que les soupçons que feroit naître contre lui un tel voyage pourroit lui faire perdre son Poste, l'a retenu. Depuis lors, le 30 lui ayant aussi fait un meilleur accueil, il avoit pensé que la prudence demandoit qu'il se conduisît avec ménagement, & qu'il convenoit d'attendre une occasion pour faire une telle démarche sans cette conséquence: or, dans la situation présente, où l'on n'ose plus ici montrer tant de partialité pour l'Angleterre, cette occasion lui paroît être venue.

Notre Ami, qui ignore d'ailleurs, ainsi que moi, quel est le secret que ce Monsieur veut vous confier, m'a confirmé ce que j'ai eu l'honneur de vous dire ci-dessus de sa capacité.

Je souhaite de tout mon coeur, que ce qu'il a à vous communiquer soit avantageux aux Etats-Unis. Vous en jugerez, Monsieur, quand il vous en aura fait la confidence.

Je suis avec un grand respect, Monsieur Votre très-humble & très-obéissant serviteur DUMAS

P.S. Cette Lettre étoit écrite, lorsque Mr. Oudermeulen m'a prié d'en suspendre l'envoi, jusqu'à-ce qu'il m'ait écrit d'Amsterdam où il retourne ce soir.

13e. Juin 1780

Après avoir différé pour plusieurs bonnes raisons jusqu'à présent d'exiger que je fisse partir cette Lettre, Mr. Oudermeulen m'a prié ce matin de vous la faire parvenir, & de vous prévenir en même temps, qu'avant de faire lui-même le voyage de Paris, il vous écrira d'Amsterdam une Lettre, où il vous fera je pense entrevoir ses idées & ses vues.

Je viens de recevoir l'honorée vôtre du 5e. Juin & les papiers qui y sont joints, dont je ferai [*torn:* usage?], quand l'occasion s'en offrira; En attendant réponse à ma derniere concernant l'affaire de Mrs. Van de Perre & Meyners Je vois un passage, Monsieur, dans votre Lettre, qui m'a vivement frappé: *before I*

---

1. "Grand pensionary of Holland," *i.e.*, van Bleiswijk. "Le 30" in the next sentence is "the stadholder."

leave Europe. Comment dois-je entendre cela? Je crains de l'interpréter.

Sir J. Y. a fait insérer dans la Gaz de la H— & d'Amst. ce qui suit.

Nous sommes autorisés *de source* d'assurer le public, que la Lettre, insérée dans la plupart des Gazettes de l'Europe, comme écrite par le Genl. Clinton, sous la date de Savannah le 30 Janv. *1780,* est une pure fiction, pour donner de fausses idées de la situation des affaires en Amérique; & que pareille Lettre n'est jamais sortie de la plume du Général Anglois, étant directement contraire au contenu de toutes celles qu'il a écrites.[2]

Passy à Son Exc. Mr. Franklin

Addressed: à Son Excellence / Monsieur B. Franklin, Esqr. / Min. Plenipe. des Etats-unis / &c. / à Passy./.

Notation: Dumas la haie May 23. 80

To Richard Bache   ALS: New-York Historical Society

Dear Son,   Passy, May 24. 1780

Messieurs Galatin & De Serres, two young Gentlemen of Geneva, of good Families and very good Characters, having an Inclination to see America; if they should arrive in your City, I recommend them to your Civilities, Counsel and Countenance. I am ever, Your affectionate Father   B FRANKLIN

Richard Bache Esqe

Addressed: To / Richard Bache Esqe / Postmaster General of the / United States / Philadelphia

---

2. The preceding two paragraphs, written on a separate sheet of paper, give Sir Joseph Yorke's denial of the authenticity of Clinton's supposed letter to Germain (discussed in our annotation of Samuel Wharton's letter of May 15). This denial was published in the June 13 issue of the *Gaz. de Leyde* (no. XLVII, supp.).

To [the Duc de la Rochefoucauld][3]

Reprinted from Henry Adams, *The Life of Albert Gallatin* (Philadelphia, 1879), p. 24.

Dear Sir, Passy, May 24, 1780.

I enclose the letter you desired for the two young gentlemen of Geneva. But their friends would do well to prevent the voyage.

With sincere and great esteem, I am, dear sir, you most obedient and most humble servant, B. FRANKLIN.

From Thomas Digges   ALS: Historical Society of Pennsylvania

Dr. Sir London 24 May 1780

I took the liberty, in a letter of the 9th. Inst. to solicit the favour of You to help me to a full length portrait of yourself.[4] It is to oblige a deserving and ingenious Engraver who means to employ his present time in producing a good print therefrom, & to take the plate with Him to a Country where his prospects for future happiness & success are greater than he can promise himself by staying here— He hopes too by Landing with him a good full length print of a person whom America looks up to as Her first Citizen, that it will pave his way to future employment & to a good settlement. We have several good bust & half-length likenesses of you in England but none at full length— What we want is one of these either setting or standing, with such ornaments and emblems to the portrait as You may chuse. The size of the Print is meant to be about two feet by 18 Inchs. more or less as the decorations may require. The nearer the drawing or picture is made to that size the better for my friend the artist. If you can possibly give up but a few hours to this my request, it would be a very grt obligation to me, besides the pleasure I shall

---

3. In answer to his mother's letter of May 22, above. The enclosure is BF's letter to RB, the preceding document.
4. Digges's letter was thrown overboard when the ship carrying it was captured: Digges to BF, June 10, below.

receive in holding forever in my possession the likeness of the man to whom my Country owes the first & most extensive obligations. If the favour could be done me, the drawing, painting, or Craons would find its way safely & expeditiously to me, if it could be forwarded from You to Monsieur Francois Bowens Negt. at Ostend. I shall forward to that gentn. on Saturday next a small deal box which contains a portrait of a Divine who is much respected by yourself & every person of his acquaintance, & what will make it more valuable to You, it is done by the fair hand of his amiable Daughter Miss Georgiana, in return for a present from You which I frequently hear commended and very much prizd.[5] I know of no private oppery [opportunity] to send it; I can get it safe to mr Bowens, & shall charge him not to forward it but by a very safe conveyance from Ostend.

We have been long impatiently waiting a line from You relative to the Captives in this quarter, as by what you last wrote Mr. H——n we had reason to expect another letter in a few days;[6] neither him nor Mr H——y can do any thing with a certain board until another letter is recd from You. In the meantime nothing is expected nor even is another cartel talkd of, but many of the prisoners have been lucky lately in getting themselves liberated. As Mr H——n wrote you the 12th Int., & my letter of the 9th also mentiond these circumstances we are in hopes another post or two will bring one of us a letter.

We are still without authentic news from America, but every day produces a new report about the Fate of Clinton; many people here are wicked enough to hope the present one (wch comes from France) to be true, & which says He has been repulsd at Ch. Town & flying towards Georgia.[7] A Ship is arrivd at Cork which saild from N York the 6th of April with the Reinforcement for Clinton 20 *transports with 3,000 men under convoy of the Rainbow only*—this ship left them on the 12th not far on their way, but steering South with a fair wind.

5. BF's present was the snuff box which is used as the frontispiece to volume XXXI; the portrait is the one promised by Georgiana Shipley in her May 26 letter, below.

6. BF's letter to Hodgson is that of April 11, above. H——y is Hartley.

7. This false report appeared in the May 24 issue of the *London Courant, and Westminster Chronicle.*

Our Wt Inda. fleet of near 250 sail is still detaind at Torbay for a fair wind. The N York will probably sail (50 or 60 ships) abot. the middle June. I hear of no troops or ships of considerable force going with them. Sr. C. Hardy is dead, & Adml Geary got the Channel fleet which we are told is to be 25 sail & to be ready in June. There are accots. to day from the west, that the Ardent man of war is retaken in the Bay Biscay by two fiftys— She appears to have been on a cruise by herself, & we rejoice exceedingly at getting our old Ship again.[8]

I formerly took the liberty to mention a Mr Burn of Lisbon to you & to ask yr. interest to him to procure a passport from Turin to Paris; I expect He is by this time in Paris & will probably make use of my Name (or an introductory Letter I had lodgd for Him at Paris) with you. He is a very deserving Young Man & in several instances been servicable to your Country, & I believe the only well wisher to its cause that can be found among the British factory at Lisbon. I am to beg your usual civility may be extended to Him, & you may safely trust any letters or parcells to him which you may have occasion to send hither. I am sir yr mo obligd & obt. Sert   W S. C

Addressed: Monsieur Monsieur B.F— / Passy

Endorsed: May 24. 80

Notation: May 24. 80

8. Francis Geary (*DNB*) sailed on June 8 with twenty-one ships of the line: W.M. James, *The British Navy in Adversity: a Study of the War of American Independence* (London, New York, and Toronto, 1926), pp. 243–4. Commodore Walsingham's West India convoy was finally able to sail from Torbay the same month, but the provisions convoy for New York did not depart until August: Elias and Finch, *Letters of Digges,* p. 164n; R. Arthur Bowler, *Logistics and the Failure of the British Army in America, 1775–1783* (Princeton, 1975), p. 135n. The *Ardent,* 64, was not recaptured by the British until 1782: James, *British Navy,* p. 344.

From John Kearsley Read[9] ALS: American Philosophical Society

My dear sir   Richmond, Virginia 25 May 80

I take the liberty to introduce to your particular regards, Mr. Joseph Mayo a gentleman of the first character & fortune in this country—[1] I have not a doubt but his Situation in France, will be extremely elegible when patronized by you,—& shall consider yr. favours to him as done to myself.—

I wrote you by the fair [Fier] Rodrigue, enclosing letters to my freind Jones,[2] since which I hear he is on the coast,— My Father[3] &c join in affection & believe me to be My dear Uncle yr. affec. Nephew   J.K. READ

Dr. Franklin

Addressed: His excellency Benjn. Franklin Esqr. / Paris— / Hond. by / Jos. Mayo Esqr.

To the Judges of the Admiralty of Cherbourg

LS:[4] New Jersey Historical Society; copies: Library of Congress, National Archives; Archives du Ministère des affaires étrangères; transcript: Library of Congress

Gentlemen,   Passy 26 May 1780[5]

I have received the *Procès Verbaux* and other Papers which you did me the Honour to send me, agreable to the 11th. Article

---

9. DF's nephew (X, 69n), who, as far as we know, had not written BF for almost four years. His latest extant letter is printed in XXII, 567–8.

1. A future member of WTF's circle of friends, he was in France by mid-September: Mayo to WTF, Sept. 18, 1780 (APS). Almost certainly he was the Joseph Mayo of Henrico County who died in 1785 while en route to Boston from Lisbon. His neighbors in Virginia were astonished by his will, which freed his 150–70 slaves: *Jefferson Papers,* VIII, 342–3.

2. In November John Paul Jones acknowledged receiving several letters from him. Read apparently asked him for a loan: Bradford, *Jones Papers,* reel 6, no. 1262.

3. John Read, Jr., seems to have maintained little contact with his brother-in-law BF; we have no record of any letters since 1766: XIII, 319–20.

4. In WTF's hand.

5. The copies and transcript bear the date May 16. Internal evidence does not conclusively establish which is the correct date. By mid-May BF proba-

of the Regulation of the 27th. Sep 1778. These Pieces relate to the taking of the Ship Flora, whereof was Captain Henry Roodenberg, bound from Rotterdam to Dublin, and arrived at Cherbourg in France, being taken the 7th Day of April 1780. by Capt. Dowlin, commander of the American Privateer the Black Prince.

It appears to me from the above mentioned Papers, that the said Ship Flora is not a good Prize, the same belonging to the Subjects of a Neutral Nation: But that the Cargo is really the Property of the Subjects of the King of England, tho' attempted to be masqu'd as neutral.

I do therefore request that after the Cargo Shall be landed, you would cause the said Ship Flora to be immediately restored to her Captain, and that you would oblige the Captors to pay him his full Freight according to his Bills of Lading, and also to make good all the Damages he may have sustained by Plunder or otherwise. And I farther request that as the Cargo is perishable you would cause it to be sold immediately, and retain the Produce deposited in your Hands, to the End that if any of the Freighters, being Subjects of their High Mightinesses the States General, will declare upon Oath that certain Parts of the said Cargo were bonâ fide shipp'd on their own Account and Risque, and not on the Account or Risque of any British or Irish Subject, the Value of such Parts may be restored: Or that if the Freighters or any of them should think fit to appeal from this Judgment to the Congress, the Produce so deposited may be desposed of according to their final Determination.

I have the honour to be, Gentlemen, Your most obedient and most humble Servant.   B FRANKLIN
Minister Plenipotentiary from the
United States of America
at the Court of France.

To Messrs. the Judges of the Admiralty at Cherbourg

---

bly had received the now missing documents from the Admiralty of Cherbourg: Torris to BF, May 13, above. BF enclosed the present letter with his of May 27 to Torris, below.

To ——— Milhas le jeune   Copy: Library of Congress

Sir,   Passy, May 26. 1780.

I received the Letter you did me the honour of writing to me relative to public Contract made in Charlestown, for 3050. Pounds Money of Carolina.[6] Those Contracts were as I suppose made by the Government of that particular State, with whose affairs I have no Concern, and know nothing of the Value of their Paper, nor what Provision they have made for redeeming it, nor where the Payment either of Interest or Principal is to be made. But I believe it is not in Europe, and that when such Paper is brought over hither, it is generally with an Intent to deceive, by the high nominal Value of what is in reality at present very low. I have the honour to be, Sir, &c. &c.

Mr. Milhas le Jeune à la Chapelle St. Jean, à Bordeaux.

To Vergennes

L:[7] Archives du Ministère des affaires étrangères; copy: Library of Congress

[on or before May 26, 1780][8]

Note for his Excellency Monsieur le Comte de Vergennes.

When the Alliance Frigate arrived in France, Mr. Franklin was desirous of employing her in annoying the English Trade, and obtaining Prisoners to Exchange for the Americans who had long languished in the Prisons of England.

A Cruise with a small Squadron, under Commodore Jones round the Coast of Britain being about that time intended, M. Franklin was requested by his Excellency the Minister of the Ma-

6. Milhas had asked on Feb. 19 when the interest on his contract would be paid: XXXI, 10–11.

7. In WTF's hand.

8. The date that it was given to Vergennes, according to a notation on a French translation of it; a second notation indicates a copy of it was sent to Sartine on May 31 (AAE). The Library of Congress letterbook copy, however, is dated May 16.

rine to join the Alliance to that Squadron.—[9] He chearfully complied with that Request, and in his Instructions to Capt. Jones, he encouraged him by the Hopes of his being useful to his Country in delivering so many poor Prisoners from their Captivity.

As the Squadron acted under American Commission and Colours and was commanded by an American Chief and was thence understood to be American, our Countrymen in the British Prisons rejoiced to hear of its Success, and that 500 English were made Prisoners in the Cruise, by an Exchange with whom they hoped soon to obtain their Liberty, and to return to their Families and Country.

The Alliance alone took Vessels containing near 200 of those English Prisoners. The Bonhomme Richard, which was mann'd chiefly by Americans took in the Serapis a great Part of the Remainder.

The Ambassador of France at the Hague, applied to Comme. Jones for those Prisoners, in order to execute a Cartel enter'd into with the Ambassador of England. Comme. Jones declined delivering them without Orders from Mr. Franklin. The Ambassador did Mr. F. the honour of writing to him on the Subject, acquainting him that Mr Jones had urged the Exchanging them for Americans, and promising to use his Endeavours for that Purpose.[1]

Mr Franklin thereupon immediately sent the Orders desired, expressing at the same time his Confidence in the Ambassador's Promise.[2]

The Prisoners were accordingly deliver'd; but they were actually exchang'd for French.[3]

His Excellency M. De Sartine afterwards acquainting Mr. Franklin, that he had not English Prisoners enough at L'Orient to fill an English Cartel then there,[4] Mr F. gave Orders that 48 he had in that Port should be deliver'd up for that Purposed 38 others at Brest to be employed in the same Manner.[5]

9. XXIX, 345–6, 382–3.
1. XXXI, 150–1; see also XXXI, 202–3.
2. XXXI, 203–4.
3. See XXXI, 120n, 240n.
4. XXXI, 477.
5. XXXI, 478–9. We have no record of the orders about the prisoners at Brest, however.

M. Franklin was afterwards informed by Mr de Chaumont, that Mr. De Sartine had assured him that other English Prisoners should be furnish'd to exchange for those so given up, in Holland and in France.

M. Franklin wrote accordingly to England,[6] and a Cartel Vessel was thereupon order'd from Plymouth to Morlaix with 100 Americans. As soon as M. F. was acquainted with this, he apply'd thro' M. De Chaumont to M. De Sartine for an equal Number of English who readily agreed to furnish them, and promised to send Orders immediately to march 100 from Saumur to Morlaix.

The Cartel arrived, landed the 100 Americans, but was sent back empty with only a Receipt from the Commissary of the Port, no English being arrived for the Exchange.

Mr. F. has since received Letters from England acquainting him that he is charged with Breach of Faith, and with deceiving the Board which had the Charge of managing the Exchange of Prisoners; and a Stop is put to that Exchange in Consequence.

The Poor American Prisoners there, many of whom have been confined two or three Years, and have bravely resisted all the Temptations, accompanied with Threats, and follow'd by ill Usage, to induce them to enter into the English Service, are now in Despair, seeing their Hopes of speedy Liberty ruined by this Failure.

His Excellency M. De Sartine has kindly and repeatedly promised by M. De Chaumont, to furnish the Number wanted, (about 400) for exchanging the said Americans.

But it is now said that the Kings Order is necessary to be first obtained.[7]

Mr. Franklin therefore earnestly requests his Excellency M. le Comte de Vergennes, to support the Proposition in Council, and thereby obtain Liberty for those unfortunate People.

Endorsed: M. de R[8] fin de May 1780. pour(?) traduire.

6. XXXI, 483–4. See also XXXI, 550–1.

7. A somewhat strained reading of Sartine's letter of April 24, in which he tried to warn that the matter had become moot because of British unwillingness to take French-made prisoners in lieu of American.

8. Rayneval; as far as we know, the foreign ministry did nothing beyond sending a translation of BF's memoir to Sartine, who let the matter drop.

From Peter Allaire

ALS: American Philosophical Society

Sir/   Paris 26 May 1780

I am very sensible of all your civilities. I shall take the first Oppertunity to return them. I beg you will Deliver the Bearer the Paper of Powders & Edens letters to Carlile.[9]

I am with Respect Your Excellencies Most Obied H Servt

P. ALLAIRE

His Excellencie Benj. Franklin Embassador from America

Addressed: His Excellencie / Benjn: Franklin / Embassadore / A Passy

Notation: Aller P. 26. May 1780.

From Dumas

ALS: National Archives; AL (draft): Algemeen Rijksarchief

Monsieur   La haie 26e. May 1780

Je vis hier Mr. Van de Perre. Il forme avec Mr. Meyners la plus forte maison de Commerce à Middelbourg en Zélande. Il m'a prié d'appuyer la réclame qu'il a faite du Vaisseau le Berkenbos sa propriété, destiné de Liverpool à Livourne, chargé de harengs & de plomb pour compte hollandois & Italien, pris par Mr. Jones & envoyé comme prise en Amérique, de l'appuyer, dis-je, tant auprès de vous qu'en Amérique. Mr. Van de Perre est de la famille la plus distinguée de Zélande, Directeur de la Compagnie des Indes-orientales, Neveu de Mr. Van Berkel Pensionaire d'Amsterdam, *de notre Ami.* Je crois n'avoir pas besoin de dire un mot de plus, pour vous faire juger, Monsieur, combien il importe que la plus prompte Justice soit faite à l'égard de ce Vaisseau. On lui a fait de fortes instances de la part des Anglois et leurs adhérens pour porter sa plainte à leurs H.P. directement, parce qu'on eût voulu faire de cette affaire quelque usage désavantageux à l'Amérique: mais il a mieux aimé avoir son recours à la justice du Congrès. Je crois, Monsieur, vous avoir déjà dit,

9. Which he had sent on Jan. 31. See XXXI, 428–9.

que je lui ai fourni la Résolution du Congrès touchant le Vaisseau Portugais, dont vous lui parliez dans votre Lettre.[1] Je suis mortifié que cela soit arrivé précisément à des gens alliés avec notre meilleur ami en ce pays. Ils demandent non seulement la restitution de tout, mais aussi des dommages & fraix, & entre autres de ceux que leur causent leurs Matelots, qu'on a ôtés du vaisseau, & placés sur l'*Alliance*.[2] Je suis toujours avec un très grand respect, Monsieur, Votre très-humble & très-obéissant serviteur   DUMAS

P.S. J'allois fermer ma Lettre, quand on m'a apporté celle dont Mr. Adams m'honore en date du 21 de ce mois en m'envoyant de votre part la Lettre attribuée au Genl. Clinton.[3] J'ai eu beaucoup de satisfaction de recevoir cette faveur de Mr. Adams; elle vient parfaitement à propos, pour me rassurer contre ce qu'on m'avoit rapporté il y a peu de jours, qu'on cherchoit à donner de mauvaises impressions contre moi à Mr. Adams.

Quant à la piece, je n'ose en faire usage: car je vois clairement que c'est une piece forgée, & que Clinton ne peut pas avoir écrit cela. Je la montrerai cependant au Gazetier de Leide,[4] qui en portera certainement le même jugement que moi. Mais je ne crois pas pouvoir en faire usage ni auprès de notre Ami, ni auprès du Gd. Facteur; ce que je regrette. Il paroît que la derniere Lettre très-soumise que j'ai écrite au dernier, l'a enfin touché; car il m'a fait dire par Son Secretaire aujourd'hui, qu'il l'avoit reçue, & qu'à Son retour d'Utrecht, pour où il part demain, il me fera dire d'aller chez lui. J'espere donc de le trouver appaisé, & que tout ceci, qui m'a presque fait mourir de chagrin, sera entierement

---

1. *I.e.*, in his letter to the Dutch firm of April 23, above, which Dumas had forwarded.

2. Dumas enclosed a French translation of extracts from a March 19 letter from Capt. Ary (or Arÿ) de Neef (or Neif) of the *Berkenbosch*. The captain described the Jan. 8 encounter with Jones's *Alliance*, which led to his ship being taken over by a prize crew and eventually captured by the British off Martinique. The National Archives holds a number of depositions (in Dutch, French, and English) on the incident: John P. Butler, comp., *Index, The Papers of the Continental Congress* (5 vols., Washington, 1978), I, 420. For Jones's account of the incident see XXXI, 389–90.

3. *Adams Papers*, IX, 330–1.

4. Jean Luzac.

fini: si seulement il n'insiste pas sur une rétractation en faveur de
... [5] car il m'est impossible de la donner: d'ailleurs ce Seroit
justifier le vol de la Lettre. S'il arrive quelque bonne nouvelle au-
thentique d'Amérique, faites-moi, la grace, Monsieur, de me la
faire parvenir d'abord, afin que je l'aie, s'il est possible, le premier, pour pouvoir l'apprendre au *gd. Facteur,* & à d'autres,
avant de la fournir aux Gazettiers.

Passy à S.E. Mr. Franklin

Addressed: à Son Excellence / Monsieur B. Franklin, Esqr. /
Ministre Plenipe. des Etats-unis / &c. / Passy./.

Notation: Mr. Dumas to Dr. Franklin

From Joachim Reallon   ALS: American Philosophical Society

Sir   St. Jean de luz 26 May 1780
   I hope your Exelency will Excuse me if I take the Leberty of
writting you this few Lines for to Lett you Know that I agreed
with Richard Graham & Compy.[6] to take the Commander of the
Sloop Canister from Dunfrise potomack river in virginia For a
Voyage to France, which I have had the misfortune to be taken
and Carried to England and from there Exchangéd, and as I
made an agrément with the Said graham & Compy that if in
Case that I Should be taken they were to pay me the sum of
twenty pound sterling, and as I am not acquainted with any Body
I hope your Exelency will Introduce me, How to have the Said
Sum of twenty pound therefore, I Sent you a Copy, of my agrement if you want the original I Shall Send you. Expecting from
you this favour with an answer. I am with respect Sir Your most
humble and obt. servant   JOACHIM REALLON

Copy of my agrement.

Sir   Dunfrise October 21. 1778.
Please to pay Joachim reallon twenty pound sterling on account
of Sir Your most Humble servant   RICHARD GRAHAM & COMPY

5. A reference to Georges Grand.
6. A Philadelphia merchant firm: *Jefferson Papers,* XI, 656–7.

To David francks Esqre. agent of British prisonners New York[7]

To the Honorable Dr. Frankling

Notation: Joachim Reallon. Dunfrise Oct. 21. 1778

From Georgiana Shipley

ALS: American Philosophical Society

My dear Doctor Franklin   Bolton Street May 26th 1780

I now send you the only return I can possibly make for your most valuable present, it is a drawing done by myself after a picture of Sir Joshua Reynolds's & as I have applyed myself entirely to painting in water-colors this last twelve-month I hope both you and your grand-son will be agreed as to the improvement I have made, otherwise I shall have spent much *time* & *labor* to little purpose.[8]

I have had the sincere pleasure of hearing, from several of our friends, repeated assurances of your good health & good looks these accounts make us happier than you can easily conceive, since every year rather encreases than lessens the love & admiration we feel for our much-valued friend. At times I continue to flatter myself that we shall meet again, yet I almost despair, when I reflect how many important changes must take place before that wish'd-for event.

I believe we shall set off for St Asaph the beginning of June, as my father is impatient to leave town, & we have no parliamentary business likely to detain him. It is now almost two years since I saw my brother, who lives entirely in Wales, I have also

7. David Franks: XXIII, 204n.

8. Reynolds, a close friend of the Shipley family who tutored Georgiana in art (XVIII, 200n), had painted a half-length portrait of Bishop Shipley in 1777. Georgiana entrusted her copy of it to Digges, who wrote BF on May 24 (above) that he would take care of forwarding it. The picture was lost in transit and became the subject of many anxious inquiries over the next seven months. It eventually arrived early in 1781; BF acknowledged its receipt in a letter, now fragmentary and without a date, written after Jan. 17, 1781 (Library of Congress). For the Reynolds portrait see Algernon Graves and William Vine Cronin, *A History of the Works of Sir Joshua Reynolds, P. R. A.* (4 vols., London, 1899–1901), III, 891.

a little nephew, whom I have never seen, so I have many inducements to make me think the journey agreable.[9]

Electricity is at present the fashionable *cure* for all complaints, it is certain that many people have received great benefit only from the electrical air, the shock & spark are seldom tryed, except in a few particular cases. Saturday we are to go to Mr Nairnes in order to see an electrical machine he has lately finished, & which is intended for the Empress of Russia.[1] Your friend Dr Priestley has been extremely ill with a bilious complaint, he is at present much better, yet looks far from well. He & Mr Bryant have had some literary desputes, which I fear have vexed him a good deal.[2]

In a large company the other day, a gentleman, who had lately traveled by Land from the East Indies, was mentioning the intense coldness of the nights during his passage over the desart. The extreme cold was confined to the desart & not perceivable on any other part of the Continent: none of the Company could assign a reason for this.

I returned you my thanks for the beloved picture by Mr Caslon,[3] but I can not conclude without repeating them, indeed I had no idea that a picture could make me so happy. It has however one *bad* effect, the temptation it gives me to take snuff, as an excuse for looking at it very very often.

Assure yourself of our constant good wishes, & believe me, as usual, Yours affecately & much obliged

GEORGIANA SHIPLEY

9. Her brother William Davies Shipley (1745–1826), dean of St. Asaph, married Penelope Yonge in 1777. Their eldest son was born in 1779: *DNB*.

1. Edward Nairne may have been developing the design which eventually became the "insulated medical electrical machine" for which he was granted a patent in 1782: W.D. Hackmann, *Electricity from Glass: the History of the Frictional Electrical Machine 1600–1850* (Alphen aan den Rijn, 1978), pp. 133–4.

2. In April, Jacob Bryant, the antiquary and author (*DNB*), had attacked Priestley in a 136-page treatise entitled *An Address to Dr. Priestly upon his Doctrine of Philosophical Necessity* (London, 1780). Priestley countered immediately with *A Letter to Jacob Bryant, Esq. in Defence of Philosophical Necessity* (London, 1780).

3. See XXXI, 444.

From John Torris   ALS: American Philosophical Society

Honnd. Sir   Dunkerque 26th. May 1780.

I have had the Honnor of writing your Excellency the 13th. &
20th. Insts., very satisfactory, I hope, relative to the Condamnation expected, for the Prises to the Poor Black Prince; The Brig
Friendship Capt. Pretty John, the Schooner Peter Capt. Thos.
Byrne, & the Dutch Brig the Aurora[4] Capt. Hy. Roodenberg
who had a Cargoe Clearly attested & proved to be the Property
of the Ennemy.

I have the Honnor to forwd. to your Excellency a Declaration
given upon oath Before a Nottary Publick, by Mr. Boulanger the
English Brocker in St. Vallery, who Interpretted the report of
Capt. Roodenberg.— But I hope this fresh Testimoney, can add
but Little to the Clear Persuasion your Excellency allready had,
on the Truth & fidelity of the Report in Berck, & on the Just &
undeniall Claim of the Captor on the Cargoe of the Aurora, of
which I beseech Your Excellency, to Hasten the Condamnation,
on account of the Immense decay of the merchandizes & the
Havey Charges the delay daily occasion.

I am advised from Morlaix that the Admiralty has sent to your
Excellency a Bill of Lading for the Cargoe of the Brig Friendship Capt Pretty John. I hope it will In fine determine your Excellency to grant an Immediate Condamnation thereof.—

I am in Hopes your Excellency will not requiece & wait for
such, to Condamn the Schooner Peter & her Cargoe, & that you
will be Satisfied for granting it, with the report Sent by the admiralty, with the Crew's signed Exchange or Parole Bill, & with
the Paragraph of the New Lloyd's List of the 21st. march advertising this Prise.—

My Correspondants writes me these Cargoes are daily Spoiling, & endeed, it occasions the Crew & the Concerns of the Poor
Black Prince an Immense Prejudice.—

I am with greatest respect Honnd. Sir your Excellency's Most
Humble & most obeidient Servant   J. TORRIS

His Excellency Dr. Franklin Minister for America—

4. *I.e.*, the *Flora*.

Endorsed: May 26.

Notation: Mr. Torris—May 26. 1780.

To John Torris

Copy: Library of Congress

Sir   Passy, May 27 –80
I received duly your Letters, of the 13th. 20th and 27. Instant.[5]
Inclosed I send the judgement upon the Ship flora and cargo.[6] As
to the other Vessels which have been brought in contrary to instructions without a Prisoner to be examined, or any Papers belonging to them, it is impossible that I can condemn them under
such Circumstances. There having been time sufficient to send
me up the Papers which are however not come, I begin to suspect that they are witheld merely because they would show that
the Vessels were Neutral. You mention as a Proof an Agreement
sent to me as sign'd by the Prisoners when discharg'd acknowledging themselves English &c. I received that Paper but I observed that the names were all sign'd in one hand Writing, which
is another suspicious Circumstance;[7] tho' otherwise it would not
have been sufficient Evidence. I have the honour to be sir, &c.

Mr. Torris Negt. a Dunkerque.

From Duvivier

ALS: American Philosophical Society

Monsieur   Paris ce 27 may 1780
Les Medailles que Vous m'avez demandées sont frappées; jat-
tends les noms des personnes que vous devez m'envoier pour les

5. All three of these are above, although the third has a date of May 26.
6. To the judges of the Admiralty of Cherbourg, May 26, above. On
May 28 BF also sent a copy of the judgment on the *Flora* to Vandenvyer frères
& Cie., a Paris banking firm (Lüthy, *Banque protestante,* II, 322) who presumably represented the vessel's Rotterdam owners. Library of Congress.
7. Apparently the masters of the *Peter* and *Friendship* filled in the names
of their crewmen: Clark, *Ben Franklin's Privateers,* p. 144.

faire graver comme nous en sommes convenus,[8] et je vous
prierois en meme temps en visitant ces memes papiers de prendre un parti sur les autres médailles a Graver. La belle saison
m'excite a vous faire cette demande.

Jai lhonneur d'estre tres respectueusement Monsieur, de
Votre Excellence Le tres humble et tres obeissant serviteur

B DuVivier

Addressed: a Son Excellence / Son Excellence Monsieur /
Franklin Ministre des Etats / unis d'amerique près le Roy / de
france / a Passy

Notation: Duvivier Paris 27 may 1780.

From Thomas Digges

ALS: Historical Society of Pennsylvania

Dr. Sir
London 29 May 1780

A friend of mine, Mr Renny of Phia, promising to put this
into the post Office at Ostend, I set down to mention what I omitted to do in my two last letters the 24 & 26th. inst,[9] which was
only to offer you from Mr Sam Hartley some more good Jama.

---

8. BF and Duvivier had evidently discussed using the die cast for Fleury's
medal to produce the two other Stony Point commemorative medals for
Wayne and Stewart (xxx, 416n). This would require reingraving only the
names and mottos. BF was concerned about the medals' expense and, as he
explained to Huntington in his letter of May 31 (below), he was in the process
of trying to locate a less costly engraver.

BF never answered the present letter. On June 18 Duvivier wrote again,
this time to WTF, asking whether BF had forgotten about Fleury's medal having been completed. Would WTF please write out the names to be engraved
on the next medals, once the letters were erased, and ask his grandfather
about the other medals that Congress had commissioned? On June 20, in response to a now-missing reply, he wrote again to WTF: he has only struck
medals in silver and bronze, not knowing that BF also needed one in gold.
(Fleury requested an extra medal in gold in a letter published above, at the
end of March.) He will strike a gold medal, erase the letters as requested, and
deliver the items "un de ces matins." APS. Duvivier exhibited Fleury's
medal in the Salon of 1781, where it was praised by a reviewer: Bachaumont,
Mémoires secrets, XIX, 323.

9. The latter of which is missing. "Renny" is John Rainey.

Rum (wch He has laying at Dunkirke) and of wch. you once before had a little. If any is wantd, we can with yr. assistance & direction contrive to get a small Cask from Dunkirque to Paris.

We are yet without any letters from you relative to the further proceedings in the Cartel matter, & we are anxious for such letter from you, as every thing for want of it is stopd at the office of sick & hurt.

I expect Mr. Wm. Burn of Lisbon, whom I formerly recommended to yr. attention & askd a passport for from Turin to Paris, is now at Paris, & will soon move this way on his way back to Lisbon. He will take particular care of any thing you may have to send to yr. friends here, & be assurd He merits your usual civility & attention.

We have no news yet from Clinton, but every body seems to give up his Expedition as a lost one & I beleive a great majority of this Country would be glad to hear a certainty of it.

I forwarded to Monr F Bowens a few days ago a small box containing a picture of Her Father from Miss Georgiana.[1] I hope it will reach you in safety. It will make me happy to have a request in my last for a *full length* Drawing of yourself complied with. My friend waits. I have only time to add that I am with the highest Esteem Dr. sir Yrs. &c &c   W.S.C

The Inclosd is a Letter sent to me by Dr. Logan from Liverpoole[2] from which port I expect he saild in a *direct* voyage to His home on Wedny last. I was pleasd to have it in my power to get him forwarded by so desirable a conveyance.

Addressed: Monsieur / Monsieur B. Franklyn / Passy

Endorsed: May 29. 80

1. Shipley. William Caslon had also promised his help in forwarding the picture; on June 20 he told WTF he had not heard from her (APS).
2. Missing.

437

From Dumas

ALS: American Philosophical Society; AL (draft):[3] Algemeen Rijksarchief

Monsieur,   Lahaie 29e. May 1780

Vendredi passé la Résolution passa aux Etats d'Hollande de prendre le troisieme matelot de tous les navires marchands qui voudront sortir des Ports de la province.[4] Je devois commencer par dire, que la requête des Marchands d'Amsterdam, dont j'ai eu l'honneur de vous parler dans plusieurs de mes dernieres, avoit été présentée le même jour.

Voici le commencement de la Lettre de Clinton insérée.[5] Je l'envoie aussi au Courier du Bas-rhin, & je la ferai passer aussi à Hambourg pour être mise en Allemand là. J'ai peut-être été trop severe en la jugeant Supposée par quelque bon fils de la liberté. Je croirois cependant qu'on l'a interpolée.

Il vient d'arriver une chose, qui m'inquiete beaucoup tant pour le crédit de 65.[6] que pour WYXCTPER 484.[7] Il a paru à 68 deux 114 DTBPPC au nom du 196. sur lui; & il n'est pas encore 78.[8] Je sais que Mr. De N—— a promis d'en 653 au moins 624. Si ce n'est MYDS.[9] Mais qui Sait combien d'autres suivront; & qui Sait où est WYXCPTER 484. J'attends que Mr. N—— me donne des nouvelles ultérieures de cela, & je vous informerai Monsieur de ce que j'en saurai.

---

3. Dated May 30.

4. The preceding Friday was May 26. The resolution included fishing boats and East Indiamen among the ships expected to furnish a third of their crews to the Dutch navy. La Vauguyon predicted that opposition to the measure would center in Zeeland, but that this province would not block the unanimous consent needed by the States General of the Netherlands: La Vauguyon to Vergennes, June 2 (AAE).

5. A French translation of the spurious letter appeared in installments in the May 30, June 2, and June 6 issues of the *Gaz. de Leyde* (nos. XLIII–XLV, sups.).

6. "America." BF wrote the decoded or deciphered words above their respective numbers or letters.

7. "Monsieur Laurens."

8. The words in code or cipher are, in order: "Amsterdam," "bills," "tirees," "Congress," and "arrived."

9. "De N——" stands for De Neufville. The encoded or enciphered words are "pay" (decoded by BF as "payer"), "one," and "both."

438

Je suis à la hâte avec un grand respect, Monsieur Votre très-humble & très obeissant serviteur   DUMAS

Passy à Son Exc. Mr. Franklin.

Addressed: His Excellency / B. Franklin M. Plenipy. / of the United States &c / Passy./.

Notation: Dumas la haie May 29. 80

From Landais   Two ALS:[1] American Philosophical Society

May it Please Your Excellency   [May 29, 1780]

I have been waiting ever Since I came to L'Orient for your order to me to Retake the Command of the frigate Alliance, thinking you would reflet how She was taken from me.

I Should look upon my Self culpable to remain a tame Spectator, while my athority on board her is usurped by another, Since I have been placed to that Command by a resolve of the Honble Congress.

It appears to me upon consideration, that nothing can authorise your Exy to this proceeding of displacing me; I am persuaded that even the Congress themselves would never pretend to exercise a power so arbitrary as to overthrow their officers without Tryal, were their reasons ever so well founded, much less upon a parcell of scandalous charges intended to Cover the Ignorance & misbehaviour of a man who would freely Sacrifice the reputation of the Officers & men of a whole fleet to Establish himself.

I consider it my duty to return to my Station on board her, I know of nothing that I have done that can justify your detaining me from this; I am responsible to them that intrusted the Ship to my Charge, to return her to them again.

If you have any express authority for depriving me of my

1. One of the ALS has the dateline "Lorient May 29 1780." It lacks the postscript, the enclosure, and BF's endorsement. Landais later said that he wrote a "duplicate" on May 30, the version printed here: Landais, *Memorial*, p. 97. The two versions differ in some details of punctuation, capitalization, and wording.

command I must Beg a copy of it & will pay due Obeidience to it, other ways I must consider my Self as Captain of the Ship & I beg that Dr Franklin will not encourage any Body to interfere with me in my duty, but give me all the assistance in his Power. It appears moreover that I am considered as the Captain of the Alliance by the Admiralty office of the united States, the letter of which I have the honour to inclose your Excellency a Copy.[2] I must beg a Speedy answer to this, & if your Exy is still determined to withhold me from my Station, you must be answerable for any disagreable Consequences that may take place, which I Should wish to avoid.

I am Your Excellency Most Obedient & most humble Servant
P: LANDAIS

P.S. I know that both Officers and men wish to have me return to my Command.[3]

His Exy Bn Franklin Minister Plenipotentiary of the united States of America

Addressed: To / His Excellency Dr. B. Franklin / Minister plenipo. to the United / States of America / Passy, / near Paris

Endorsed: Capt. Landais From L'Orient without Date. Suppos'd about the End of May 1780

---

2. Landais copied onto the verso an April 1 letter from John Brown, secretary of the American Board of Admiralty, which asked that the *Alliance* bring him two or three boxes or trunks to be delivered by Penet & Co. It was addressed to "Captain Peter Landais or the Commanding Officer of the Continental frigate *Alliance*." Landais enclosed another copy with his letter of June 14, below; it too is at the APS. A third copy (in Landais' hand) is at the National Archives.

3. Landais later claimed that he was led to write the present letter by the invitation of the officers and crew of the *Alliance* and that he had refused Port Commandant Thévenard's offer of the command of the *Serapis*, wishing to return to America for vindication: Landais, *Memorial*, pp. 96–7.

From Jean de Neufville & fils

ALS: American Philosophical Society

Honour'd Sir.   Amsterdam the 29th. May 1780.
    May it please your Excellency;
    That we lay before her, that by bills of Exchange drawn on
Henry Lawrence Esqr. as Commissioner of the United States, to
reside in Amsterdam, it appeard to us that it was expected in
America this Gentleman was to be here before this; butt neither
here nor at the Hague we could have the pleasure to learn anything about it. That in this Circumstance we have engaged directly to Accept some of them, if Mr. Laurence should not appear in a fourthnight; others we have purely engaged to wait the
time, as we do not know how farr those draufts may extend, and
whatever were our goodwill to assist the American it could very
shortly exceed our power to provide for the payment without
proper provisions were made. Those bills we find are drawn at
6 Month sight, and in the meantime we flatter ourselfs at least
that this matter must be settled, we therefor begg your Excellencys advice and assistance, to know at all events your Excellency
could or would procure us rimbursement, in case those bills
should not be rimbursed, and to which Amount, that we may
regulate ourselfs accordingly; This we hope may on new convince Your Excellency of the Zeal we bore and still bear to the
American Cause, which we are willing to defend and protect as
much as it lays in our power.
    Wishing that it may please Your Excellency again to honour
us with her Answer, We remain Constantly in particular with all
devoted Regard. Honourd Sir Your Excellencys most faithfull
and Most obedient humble Servants,

JOHN DE NEUFVILLE & SON

To Ferdinand Grand

ALS: Dibner Library of the History of Science and Technology, Smith-
sonian Institution

Sir,   Passy, May 30. 1780
    This is to request that you would cause to be paid in London
for me to Mr James Woodmason the Sum of Twenty Pounds

441

Eight Shillings and six pence Sterling, being for Paper of a particular kind which he has furnished by my Order and sent hither, for printing the Congress Promises.—⁴ I have the honour to be, Sir, Your most obedient & most humble Servant   B Franklin

P.S. Mr. Woodmason is a Stationer near the Exchange, London

To Mr Grand. Banker, at Paris.

Addressed: A Monsieur / Monsieur Grand / Banqr / Rue Montmartre

Notation: Dr. franklin / May 30th.

To Sartine   ls:⁵ Archives de la Marine; copy: Library of Congress

Sir   Passy May 30. 1780
    I am under the greatest Uneasiness to find, that great Part of the Cloathing sent to Brest to be shipt for America, was left behind, and that the Alliance alone has not sufficient Room, to receive it with the Arms and Gunpowder, which the King has been so good as to order for us, and which are all so much wanted in the American Armies. A Proposition has been made of asking to borrow the Ariel to assist in carrying these Things.⁶ It is said that a sufficient Number of Men and Officers can be furnished for her out of the Alliance. I am so unacquainted with Ship Business that I cannot judge of the fitness of that Vessel. But if your Excellency should approve of the Proposal, and be inclined to favour

4. For this paper, which BF had ordered in June, 1779, see xxx, 609–12. We cannot be certain when the shipment arrived at Passy; by July 25, BF learned that it was in Rouen (to Woodmason, July 25, Birmingham Assay Office, England). On May 31 Grand debited BF's account 507 *l.t.* 2 *s.* for payment to Woodmason: Account VI (xxiii, 21).
    5. In WTF's hand. A French translation is also at the Archives de la Marine.
    6. The *Ariel*, 26, was a captured British sloop of war placed under repair at Lorient after returning from the West Indies: Morison, *Jones*, pp. 301–2; Thévenard to Sartine, March 31, 1780, Archives de la Marine, B³DCLXXXII, 88–9. On May 26 Sartine indicated that Jones had requested the *Ariel* and that if no other vessel were available the king would order that the *Ariel* be given to him: Archives de la Marine, B⁴CLXXII, 178.

us with the Loan of that or any other Ship more convenient for the Purpose, it will be an essential Service to the United States, and for which they will be under great Obligation.

With the greatest Esteem I have the honour to be, Your Excellencys most obedient and most humble Servant B FRANKLIN

His Exy M. De Sartine./.

To John Torris

Copies: Library of Congress, National Archives, Archives du Ministère des affaires étrangères; transcript: National Archives

Sir,   Passy, May 30. 1780

In my last of the 27th. Instant, I omitted one thing, I had intended, viz, to desire you would give absolute orders to your Cruisers, not to bring in any more dutch Vessels, tho' charg'd with Enemy's goods, unless contraband. All the neutral states of Europe seem at present disposed to change what had before been deemed the law of Nations, to wit, that an Enemy's Property may be taken wherever found and to establish a Rule that free Ships Shall make free Goods. This rule is in itself so reasonable, and of a nature to be so beneficial to mankind that I cannot but wish it may become general. And I make no doubt but that the Congress will agree to it in as full an extent as france and spain.[7] In the mean time, and until I have received the Orders on the Subject, it is my Intention to condemn no more English Goods found in Dutch Vessels, unless contraband; of which I thought it right to give you this previous Notice; that you may avoid the Trouble and Expence likely to arise from such Captures and the Detention of them for a Decision, with great Regard, and best Wishes for the success of your Enterprizes, I have the honour to be, sir, &c.

M. Torris.

7. Congress did so in the autumn of 1780: *JCC*, XVIII, 864–7, 905–6, 1097–8.

From Benjamin Franklin Bache

ALS: American Philosophical Society

Mon cher grand Papa   Genève ce 30 may 1780.

Vous ne sauries croire combien m'a fait de plaisir vôtre lettre, parcequ'il y avoit longtemps que je n'avois de vos nouvelles, et j'etois tres en peine de vous, je vous ecrirai le plus exactement que je pourrai, j'ai été fort content d'apprendre qu'Adams avec son frere viendront peut être à Geneve, parceque cela m'entretiendra beaucoup mon anglois.[8] Les lettres de mon cher papa et de ma chere mama m'ont fait beaucoup de plaisir, parcequ'il y avoit longtemps que je n'avois reçû de leurs nouvelles; je leurs ecrirai à la premiere lettre que je vous ecrirai, ainsi qu'a mon cher frere, et je leurs envoyerai une piece de dessin; je languis bien d'avoir fini mes etudes pour aller les voir. J'aimerois beaucoup que vous et ma famille vinssiès faire un tour à Geneve; je desirerois aussi beaucoup que Cockran vint avec Adams en pension chez Mr Marignac; je m'y trouve très bien mon cher Grand papa je ferai tous mes efforts pour être plus diligent dans la suite; vous m'aves demandés les livres anglois que j'etudiois j'explique les petits livres anglois que vous m'aves donnés. Je m'aplique beaucoup à mon latin et à mes autres études, pour aller vite revoir ma patrie; mais je crois que je n'y irai pas de longtemps si je fais mes etudes je vous prie d'exhorter Cockran de venir en pension à genéve avec moi cela me ferait un grand plaisir.

Mon cher grand papa je suis avec un profond respect Votre tres humble et très obeissant petit fils   B Franklin B

Dites s'il vous plait à cockran que je lui ecrirai le mois prochain Mr et Me marignac vous presentent bien leurs respects.

Addressed: A Monsieur / Monsieur Franklin Ministre / plénipotentiaire des Provinces unies / de L'Amérique auprès de sa Majesté / très Chrétienne. Adressée à Monsieur / Grand Banquier ruë Montmartre / A Paris

---

8. John Quincy Adams, Charles Cochran, and BFB had all attended the Pension Le Coeur in Passy: xxv, 646; Taylor, *J.Q. Adams Diary*, I, 34n. Neither John Quincy Adams nor his brother Charles or Charles Cochran joined BFB in Geneva.

From Bondfield, Haywood & Co.[9]

Copy: Massachusetts Historical Society[1]

Sr.   Budeux 30 May 1780

Not doubting but we should find every encouragement that a mutual Intercourse of Commercial Connections could produce, we had formed our plans in consequence, when to our disappointment upon presenting our Entrys at the Custom House, we are refused to be admitted to load, but on the footing of Foreign nations unprotected by Special Treaties, and subject to heavy duties thereby, accruing to explain ourselves more amply, the following is our case: not being able to Insure our Vesels from France to the United States, we were obliged to turn our views into other Channels, and in consequence, freighting part of our Ships to the Contractors, bought Wine & Flour to Compleat our Cargoes for the French Islands, intending there to take on board the produce of the Islands to Philidelphia, and from thence with Tobacco for France our Vessels being ready, we sent our Broker to the Custom House to make the entry, and were told they could only be admitted upon paying the Alien Duties say 28 *l.t.* per Ton on wines &c. Taking only this case for a Bare, we humbly represent to your Excellence that unless some modification take place we must entirely relinquish all Commercial Connections we have only the opening to petition M. Necker for leave to load to the Frence Islands Provissions and Goods under the same restruction as is allowed to subjects of France, and without other incumbrances, without which we are unabled to pursue any trade with this Kingdom.

The treaty of Commerce Subsisting betwixt this Kingdom & the United States, has not been transmitted officially to the respective officers in this City;[2] they allow us to act by Curtosy we are wholly exposed to the Caprice of the officers in place, and the want of knowing the extent of our priviledges makes us depended to there pleasure, by which we must either submit to their

9. For Bondfield and William Haywood's firm see xxvi, 278n.

1. Where it is in the Adams family papers.

2. A year earlier, the American merchants at Nantes had to request a copy of the Treaty of Amity and Commerce from the American commissioners: xxviii, 357, 374, 406.

will or write up to Paris for explanations, thereby retarding our operations and subjecting us not only to heavy unnecessary Charges, but also to a laberinth of perplexities.

We take the Liberty to inclose to you a letter for M. Necker,[3] humbly praying he will be pleased to grant us leave to load on board our Ships provissions the produce of this Kingdom to the french Islands, on the footing the french Merchants are admitted, to dispose thereof as is accustomed, and load at the Islands the produce for Virginia. This is an operation every way National, and we flatter ourselves to be indulged by him with his aprobation in Course, permit us to sollicit the honor of your protection in our favor with the Ministry, from whom by your Interest we hope for Success. We have the Honor to be with due respect. Sir Your Very humble and Most Obedient Servts.

signd B. H. & Co

His Excell B Franklin Esq

From Thomas Digges

ALS: American Philosophical Society

Dr Sir   London May 30th. 1780

I am very sorry to be so frequently troublesome and repeatedly asking favours of You; But when I reflect on your readiness to do good, & that my present application is to help a deserving Man, I flatter myself I shall stand forgiven.

Dr. Upton Scott of Annapolis in Maryland is necessiated to seek His way back to His Country, Family & Home, by the same route (probably in the same ship) with our friend Mr. L——d in the next New York fleet. He is solicitous to me to aid Him in asking the favour of You (to whom He formerly had the honour

3. Which presumably BF sent on. With the present letter at the Mass. Hist. Soc., however, are copies of two related communications. One is a May 30 request from Bondfield, Haywood & Co. to Sartine for permission to send two vessels to the French West Indies under the American flag. The other is a June 10 letter from Sartine to *commissaire* Lemoyne (XXV, 321n) at Bordeaux ordering him to assure the company they could pursue their plan, as neutral ships would be treated like French on both their departure and arrival. A notation on the letter indicates the orders were being executed.

to be known)[4] to procure Him if possible some written Instrument, which may save His Baggage & Effects from seizure should the vessel on which He Embarks fall into the hands of an American Cruizer; in which case, tho the Doctor is a good friend to His Country, He may loose his Baggage, from the People who takes him not knowing any thing about Him or His worth.

Dr Scott is an old & respected Citizen of Annapolis, where He practisd Phisick with reputation for many years, and left that Country about four years ago with the approbation & good wishes of the Province, in order to look after a paternal inheritance in Ireland, from which Country He has lately returnd to seek a mode for getting home,[5] & which He thinks He can easiest accomplish by getting past the lines of New York. The fleet for that quarter will most likely sail in 3 weeks tho the Convoy is not yet nominated; and if such an instrument of writing as I now solicit can be got without any impropriety or inconvenience to You, I should esteem it a very great favour to have it forwarded by *the first post* to me. The letter may be directed to me in propria persona and inclosd in a cover to Messrs. Wm. Hodgson & Co. or Messrs. French & Hopson Brokers, wch last may be probably more safe than the former; tho I beleive He has never yet missd any of yrs.

I have the honor to be with very great Esteem Dr Sir Yr obligd & Obt Ser   TD

Addressed: Monsieur / Monsieur B: F——n / Passy

Endorsed: May 30. 80

Notation: T.D. London May 30. 1780.

4. Upton Scott (1722–1814) had been the personal physician to Gov. Horatio Sharpe: Elias and Finch, *Letters of Digges*, p. 215n. We have no record of his previous acquaintance with BF. L——d is Richard Bennett Lloyd, who was planning his own return to America: to BF, March 10, above.

5. Scott eventually did return safely. Although his reasons for going to Ireland were suspect, Maryland did not confiscate his property. In his later life he was plagued with gout, the beginnings of which at least one observer blamed on the claret he had consumed in Belfast: Walter B. Norris, *Annapolis: Its Colonial and Naval Story* (New York, 1925), pp. 242–3.

To Samuel Huntington

Two LS:[6] National Archives; ALS (draft): Library of Congress; copy: Library of Congress; transcript: National Archives

Sir,   Passy May 31. 1780.

I wrote to your Excellency the 4th. of March past, to go by this Ship, the Alliance, then expected to sail immediately. But the Men refusing to go 'till paid their Shares of Prize Money, and sundry Difficulties arising with regard to the Sale and Division, she has been detained thus long to my great Mortification, and I am yet uncertain when I shall be able to get her out. The Trouble & Vexation these Maritime Affairs give me is inconceivable. I have often express'd to Congress my Wish to be relieved from them,[7] and that some Person better acquainted with them, and better situated might be appointed to manage them. Much Money as well as Time would I am sure be saved by such an Appointment.

The Alliance is to cary some of the Canon long since order'd, and as much of the Powder Arms and Cloathing (furnish'd by Government here) as she, together with a Frigate, the Ariel, we have borrowed, can take: I hope they may between them take the whole, with what has been provided by Mr Ross.— This Gentleman has, by what I can learn, served the Congress well, in the Quality and Prices of the Goods he has purchased; I wish it had been in my Power to have discharged his Ballance here, for which he has importun'd me rather too much. We furnished him with about 20,000£ Sterling to discharge his first Accounts, which he was to replace as soon as he received Remittances from the Committee of Commerce: This has not been done, and he now demands another nearly equal Sum; urging as before that the Credit of the States as well as his own will be hurt by my Refusal.[8] Mr. Bingham, too, complains of me for refusing some of

6. The one from which we print is in WTF's hand. The other, in L'Air de Lamotte's hand, is marked "Duplicate."

7. See, for example, XXIX, 555–6 and XXX, 469, as well as his March 4 letter to Huntington, above.

8. In June, 1777, the American commissioners to France provided Ross 450,000 *l.t.* (approximately £20,000) to purchase supplies for Congress: *Deane Papers*, III, 30, 32. For BF's inability to pay the £18,000 still owed Ross see XXIX, 378n; XXX, 197–8.

his Drafts as very hurtful to his Credit, tho' he owns he had no Orders from Congress to authorise those Drafts.[9] I never undertook to provide for more than the Payment of the Interest Bills of the first Loan.[1] The Congress have drawn on me very considerably for other Purposes, which has sometimes greatly embarrass'd me, but I have duly accepted and found means to pay their Drafts: so that their Credit in Europe has been well supported: But if every Agent of Congress in different Parts of the World is permitted to run in Debt, and draw upon me at pleasure to support his Credit, under the Idea of its being necessary to do so for the Honour of Congress, the Difficulty upon me will be too great, and I may in fine be obliged to protest the Interest Bills. I therefore beg that a Stop may be put to such irregular Proceedings. Had the Loans proposed to be made in Europe, succeeded, these Practices might not have been so inconvenient: But the Number of Agents from separate States running all over Europe and asking to borrow Money, has given such an Idea of our Distress and Poverty as makes every Body afraid to trust us. I am much pleased to find that Congress has at length resolved to borrow of our own People, by making their future Bills bear Interest.[2] This Interest duly paid in hard Money to such as require hard Money, will fix the Value of the Principal; and even make the Payment of the Interest in hard Money, for the most Part unnecessary provided always that the Quantity of Principal be not excessive. A great Clamour has lately been made here by some Merchants, who say they have large Sums in their Hands of Paper Money in America, and that they are ruined by some Resolution of Congress which reduces its Value to one Part in Forty: As I have had no Letter explaining this Matter, I have only been able to say that it is probably misunderstood, and that I am confident the Congress have not done, nor will do any thing unjust towards Strangers who have given us Credit.[3]

I have indeed been almost ready to complain that I hear so lit-

9. XXXI, 557–8. See also XXIX, 29–30; XXX, 420–1, 462.

1. See XXIII, 471; XXV, 210n.

2. In a resolution of March 18, 1780: *JCC*, XVI, 262–7. Excerpts were published in the May 23–25 issue of the *London Evening Post*.

3. The complaints were all too justified; the same resolution effectively revalued "old" continental money at a fortieth of its face value: Ferguson, *Power of the Purse*, pp. 51–2.

tle and so seldom from Congress, or from the Committee of Correspondence: but I know the Difficulty of Communication, and the frequent Interruption it meets with in this Time of War. I have not yet received a Line this Year, and the Letters wrote by the Confederacy, as I suppose some must have been written by her, have not yet come to hand.

I mentioned in a former Letter[4] my having communicated to Mr Johnson of Nantes, the Order of Congress appointing him to examine the Accounts, and his Acceptance of the Appointment. Nothing however has yet been done in pursuance of it; For Mr Deane having wrote that he might be expected here by the Middle of March,[5] and as his Presence would be very useful in explaining the Mercantile Transactions, I have waited his Arrival to request Mr Johnson's coming to Paris, that his Detention here from his Affairs at Nantes, might be as short as possible. Mr Deane is not yet come; but as we have heard of the Arrival of the Fendant in Martinique, in which Ship he took his Passage, we imagine he may be here in some of the first Ships from that Island.

The Medal for M. Fleury is done and deliver'd to his Order, he being absent. I shall get the others prepared as soon as possible by the same Hand if I cannot find a cheaper equally good; which I am now enquiring after; 2000 Livres appearing to me a great Sum for the Work.[6]

With my last, I sent a Copy of my Memorial to the Court of Denmark. I have since received an Answer from the Minister of that Court for Foreign Affairs, a Copy of which I inclose. It referr'd me to the Danish Minister here, with whom I have had a Conference on the Subject.[7] He was full of Professions of the Good will of his Court to the United States, and would excuse

4. Above, March 4.
5. In his latest letter to BF, written on Dec. 24, 1779, Deane predicted he would embark for France on the *Fendant* in two or three weeks: XXXI, 272. He chose to wait for another ship, however.
6. BF was referring to the medals for Anthony Wayne and John Stewart. As he told Huntington on March 4, the cost was 1,000 *l.t.* per medal; the sum of 2,000 *l.t.* was paid, according to Account XXVII, on May 12. See also the annotation to Duvivier's letter of May 27, above.
7. BF's last to Huntington is above, March 4. The response from Denmark is Bernstorff's of March 8, and it referred BF to the baron von Blome.

the Delivery of our Prizes to the English, as done in Conformity to Treaties, which it was necessary to observe. He had not the Treaty to shew me, and I have not been able to find such a Treaty on Enquiry.[8] After my Memorial, our People left at Bergen were treated with the greatest Kindness by an Order from Court, their Expences, during the Winter that they had been detained there, all paid. Necessaries furnished to them for their Voyage to Dunkerque, and a Passage thither found for them, all at the Kings Expence. I have not dropt the Application for a Restitution, but shall continue to push it, not without some Hopes of Success. I wish however to receive Instructions relating to it; and I think a Letter from Congress to that Court might forward the Business; for I believe they are sensible they have done wrong, and are apprehensive of the Inconveniences that may follow. With this I send the Protests taken at Bergen against the Proceeding.

The Alliance in her last Cruise met with and sent to America a Dutch Ship, supposed to have on board an English Cargo.[9] The Owners have made Application to me. I have assured them that they might depend on the Justice of our Courts; and that if they could prove their Property there it would be restored. Mr Dumas has written to me about it.[1] I inclose his Letter and wish Dispatch may be given to the Business, as well to prevent the Inconveniences of a Misunderstanding with Holland as for the sake of Justice. A ship of that Nation has been brought in here by the Black Prince, having an English Cargo.[2] I consulted with Messrs. Adams and Dana, who informed me that it was an established Rule with us in such Cases to confiscate the Cargo, but to release the Ship paying her Freight &ca. This I have accordingly order'd in the Case of this Ship and hope it may be satisfactory. But it is a critical Time with respect to such Cases. For whatever may formerly have been the Law of Nations, all the Neutral Powers at the Instance of Russia, seem at present dis-

8. The Anglo-Danish treaty was 110 years old; on May 30 British Secretary of State Stormont proposed adding an explanatory article on shipping rights to it: Isabel de Madariaga, *Britain, Russia, and the Armed Neutrality of 1780: Sir James Harris's Mission to St. Petersburg during the American Revolution* (New Haven, 1962), p. 188.

9. The *Berkenbosch:* XXXI, 389–90.

1. Above, May 26.

2. The *Flora.*

posed to change it, and to inforce the Rule that *free Ships shall make free Goods,* except in the Case of Contraband. Denmark, Sweden and Holland have already acceded to the Proposition, and Portugal is expected to follow. France and Spain in the Ansrs. have also expressed their Approbation of it.[3] I have therefore instructed our Privateers to bring in no more neutral Ships, as such Prizes occasion much Litigation, and create ill Blood. The Alliance Capt. Landais took two Swedes in coming hither, who demand of us for Damages one upwards of 60,000 Livres, and the other near 500£ sterling;[4] and I cannot well see how the Demand is to be settled. In the News Papers that I send, the Congress will see authentic Pieces expressing the Sense of the European Powers, on the Subject of Neutral Navigation.[5] I hope to receive the Sense of Congress for my future Government, and for the Satisfaction of the Neutral Nations now entring into the Confederacy; which is consider'd here as a great Stroke against England. In Truth that Country seems to have no friends on this Side the Water: No other Nation wishes it Success in its present War, but rather desires to see it effectually humbled: No one, not even their old Friends the Dutch, will afford them any Assistance. Such is the mischeivous Effect of Pride, Insolence & Injustice, on the Affairs of Nations, as well as on those of private Persons! The English Party in Holland is daily diminishing, and the States are arming vigorously to maintain the Freedom of their Navigation. The Consequence may possibly be, a War with England; or a serious Disposition in that mad Nation to save what they can by a timely Peace.

Our Cartel for the Exchange of American Prisoners has been some time at a Stand. When our little Squadron brought near 500

3. None of these states had as yet signed a treaty with the empress; Denmark did so on July 9, Sweden on August 1, the Netherlands at the turn of the year, and Portugal in 1782: Madariaga, *Britain, Russia, and the Armed Neutrality,* pp. 188, 190, 289, 381. For the French and Spanish replies to her declaration see Sir Francis Piggott and G.W.T. Omond, eds., *Documentary History of the Armed Neutralities, 1780 and 1800* (London, 1919), pp. 206–8, 213–15.

4. Litigation over Landais' captures had by now been going on for more than a year: XXIX, 496–7.

5. Perhaps including Empress Catherine II's Declaration of Armed Neutrality, which was published, for example, in the April 7 issue of the *Ga𝑧. de Leyde* (no. XXVIII, sup.).

into Holland, England would not at first exchange Americans for them *there*, expecting to take them in their Passage to France: But at length an Agreement was made between the English and French Ambassadors, and I was persuaded to give them up, on a Promise of having an equal Number of English deliver'd to my Order at Morlaix. So those were exchanged for Frenchmen: But the English now refuse to take any English in Exchange for Americans that have not been taken by American Cruizers. They also refuse to send me any Americans in Exchange for their Prisoners released and sent home by the two Flags of Truce from Boston.⁶ Thus they give up all Pretentions to Equity and Honour, and govern themselves by Caprice, Passion, and transient Views of present Interest.

Be pleased to present my Duty to Congress, and believe me to be with great Respect, Your Excellency's, most obedient and most humble Servant.   B FRANKLIN

To his Excellency Samuel Huntington Esquire, President of Congress.

Notations in different hands: Letter May 31. 1780 from Doctr. Franklin. recd. Feb. 19. 1781 / orig read Sepr. 1 1780 Alliance not sailed pressed for Money by Mr. Ross—Affair with Denmark. A Dutch Vessel captured by the Alliance.

From Edme-Louis Daubenton

AL: American Philosophical Society

au jardin du Roy ce 31. may. [1780?]⁷
M. Daubenton le jeune a l'honneur de presenter son hommage à Monsieur franklin et de l'assurer de son respect en lui envoyant

6. The *Bob* and the *Polly:* XXXI, 418.
7. We originally assigned this note to 1773 and explained the address as being Le Roy's rather than BF's: XX, 219, 320n, 487n. Dr. Horst Dippel, however, has argued that "les nouveaux Cayers des oiseaux enluminés" were not an installment of "les planches enluminées" sent with Daubenton's note of July 20, 1773, but the color plates issued seven years later, and that this note of May 31 therefore belongs to 1780 or 1781: *Amerikastudien*, XXIII (1978), 347–8. We find his argument convincing, and are republishing the note in what we now believe is its earliest likely place.

les nouveaux Cayers des oiseaux enluminés qui lui manquent pour completer son exemplaire. Il aura grand soin de mettre a part ceux qui restent à faire et de les envoyer à Monsieur franklin.

Addressed: A Monsieur / Monsieur franklin / membre de plusieurs academies / pres de la muette / à Passy.

From Jean-Jacques de Lafreté

AL: American Philosophical Society

ce 31. mai 1780.
M. Lafreté a reçû a la Campagne le petit Billet de Monsieur franklin, sans quoi il auroit eu l'honneur de le remercier plustôt de la lettre de M. Robert Morris qu'il a la bonté de lui communiquer, et qu'il lui renvoye ci joint.[8]

Il a laissé a 15. lieües de Paris, Made. Lafreté, qui l'a chargé de la rappeller au souvenir de Monsieur francklin elle le prie de ne pas égarer une certaine lettre qu'elle lui a confié, et de la mettre dans sa poche la premiere fois qu'il viendra la voir à Surênes,[9] où elle viendra dans une 15ne. de Jours.

Mr. Lafreté présente ses Respectueux devoirs à monsieur francklin.

Notation: M. Lafreté 31. may 1780.

From the Officers of the *Alliance*

LS: University of Pennsylvania Library

Please your Excellency   L'Orient 31 May 1780
We had the honor of addressing your Excelly. the 12 of April, requesting that you would be so good as to take our case into consideration, that you would endeavour to have our wages and prize money faithfully paid us, and the Ship sent back to Amer-

8. Morris' March 31 letter (I), above.
9. Suresnes, near Passy; see XXVII, 52.

ica, where we all desire to be, and from which we have been so long absent.

Your Excellency has not yet answer'd us, or at least no answer from you has come to our hands, which makes us impatient to trouble you again in order to know if possible what we are to Expect. The Ship is now and has been for some months past in this place useless and expensive to the States, and by no means proffitable to us. While we Lament her loss to our country for so long a time, we cannot but feel for our own Scituation and that of the people, many of whom have families at home pining in misery & want. We know that much is due to us if what we have taken be justly accounted for by the concern'd in fitting out the expedition on which we were last year, and we make no doubt but that we shall find in your Excellency a firm intention to see us contented.

Captain Landais has inform'd us that your Excellency had sent a memorial to the Court of Denmark, requiering payment for those vessells which went into Bergen, and which that court deliver'd up to our Enemies. The answer to that memorial we are perfectly ignorant of, but yet we hope that you will be so good as to let us know the result as soon as possible, that we may satisfy the clamours of the people and know how to regulate our private affairs: the Ships were valuable, and there was a report that they were paid for.

It is with regrett that we find Captain Landais deprived of his command, under him we engaged on board the Alliance and with him we wish to return to America.[x] Notwithstanding the reports that have gone forth respecting the Battle with the Serapis, in which our shame is connected with our Captain's dishonor, we flatter ourselves that your Excellency entertains a higher opinion of our honor as officers and duty as men than to suppose that we would deliberately execute the orders of any man, when those orders tended to the distruction of our friends, when those orders contradicted the duties of humanity and the voice of reason founded on such duties.

Captain Landais gave particular orders about fighting, shewed the different Ships, which was the Bon homme Richard & which the Serapis, and we perfectly understood and executed his orders. If from the unhappy position of the two Ships, some

455

of our Shott passed into the Bon homme Richard, it was not his nor our fault, it was inevitable in that Case, and let the blame lie where it is due.

Your Excellency will we hope pardon this address, we speak feelingly because we think our characters injured, but we trust the time will come when the officers of the Alliance will be able to vindicate their honor and clear their reputation in the eyes of the world. We have the honor of being with the greatest respect Your Excellency's most obedient & most humble Servants

JAMES WARREN 1st. Lt. Marines
THOMAS ELWOOD 2d. Lt. Marines
ARTHUR ROBERTSON Midshipn.
CHIPN. BANGS Steward
ISAAC CARR Sail Maker
JAMES DEGGE 1st. Lieut.
JOHN BUCKLEY 2d Lieut.
JAMES LYND 3d Lieut.
JOHN LARCHAR JUNR: Mn.
BENJAMIN PIERCE Gunr.
JAMES BRAGG Carpent.
THOS. HINSDALE Mr. Mate
N BLODGET Purser
JOHN DARLING Boatswain

I sign to the foregoing all but respecting Captain Landais & fighting the Ships on the 23. Sep. 1779

A: WINDSHIP Surgeon quarter'd below.

I sign to all but what respects the fighting last cruise being absent JOHN SAWRIS Midshipn.

I sign to all but the clause marked x & to that also provided Capt. Jones does not go in the alliance   M PARKE Capt. Marines

His Exy. Dr. Franklin

Addressed: To / His Excellency Dr. B. Franklin / Minister plenipo. to the United States/ at / Passy/ near Paris

Endorsed: 24 / Officers of the Alliance May 31. 1780

From the Baron de Wulffen[1]   L: American Philosophical Society

Excellence   [before June 1, 1780][2]
   Jean Henry Baron de Wulffen, natif de Magdeburg, ci-devant
Lieutenant & Aide major au Regiment Infanterie de general
major de Rohrt au Service de S. M. Le Roi de Prusse, a présent
Capitaine de Dragons au Service des 13. provinces unies d'Amerique, fait prisonnier en octobre 1779, a Amboy province de Jersey, Echangé le 18: Avril, est arrivé d'Angleterre a Morlay, Sans
Souliers, Sans chemise, Seulement avec les habits d'un Simple
matelot; Actuellement a Paris, graces aux soins genereux du
Regiment de Normandie en garnison a Rennes, occupé a la
guerison de Ses blessures, demande le remboursement de Ses appointements & de Ses Rations non recus l'espace de 8: mois.

A Son Excellence Monsieur de Franklin Ministre plenipotentiaire des 13. provinces unies d'Amerique, auprès de Sa Majesté
très Chretienne.

Notation in Temple Franklin's hand: Baron de Wulffen

To Samuel Huntington

                LS[3] and transcript: National Archives; copy: Library of Congress

Sir,   Passy 1st. June 1780.
   Commodore Jones, who by his Bravery and Conduct has
done great Honour to the American Flag, desires to have that
also of presenting a Line to the Hands of your Excellency.[4] I
chearfully comply with his Request, in recommending him to
the Notice of Congress and to your Excellency's Protection, tho'

   1. Or Wolff, according to his sister, M.A. de Sonnemaens, who wrote BF
on March 15, above.
   2. The date on which BF sent Wulffen 192 *l.t.*, presumably in response to
the present letter. He wrote in his Cash Book: "To a poor Prussian Officer
Baron Wulffen wounded in our Service, and Sick, *8 Louis.*"
   3. In WTF's hand.
   4. See Jones's April 20 letter. Sartine also wrote Huntington on Jones's
behalf: Mrs. Reginald de Koven, *The Life and Letters of John Paul Jones*
(2 vols., New York, 1913), II, 79–80.

his Actions are a more effectual Recommendation, and render any from me unnecessary. It gives me however an Opportunity of showing my Readiness to do Justice to Merit, and of professing the Esteem & Respect with which I am, Your Excellency's most obedient & most humble Servant.   B FRANKLIN

His Exy S. Huntington Esq.

Notation: Letter from Doctr Franklin dated June 1st: 1780 read Feby. 19. 1781.[5] recommending *Commodore* Jones

To John Paul Jones

LS[6] and copy: National Archives; two copies: Library of Congress

Sir,   Passy, June 1. 1780
I have received a Letter from the Board of Admiralty, containing their Orders for the Return of the Alliance, a Copy of which is annex'd for your Government;[7] and I hereby direct that you carry the same into Execution with all possible Expedition.

With great Regard, I am, Sir, Your most obedient & most humble Sert.   B FRANKLIN

To the honble Commodore Jones Commander of the Alliance Frigate in the Service of the United States.

Notation: From his Excellency Dr. Franklin Passy June 1st. 1780— Enclosed an order from the Board of Admiralty—Philada. March 28th 1780

5. *JCC*, XIX, 174.
6. In WTF's hand.
7. The letter is that of March 28, above.

From Jean de Neufville & fils

ALS: American Philosophical Society

Most Honourable Sir!   Amsterdam the [1] June 1780[8]

We had the honour to write to Your Excellency by last maill,[9] acquainting her that we were willing to protect the American Creditt in accepting personally some bills drawn by order of Congress on Henry Lawrence Esqr. residing in Amsterdam; for whose arrivall we still wait. Our generall private connections with America are already so large that the assistance of money for those transactions cannot be expected from us, and your Excellency may be acquainted with some of them.

We doubt not butt on the bills that may be coming with Mr. Lawrance for a loan there might be methodes found for it if this should be the basis of those operations; How that may be, this is at least a circumstance as Criticall as unexpected, and your Excellency will judge with us that those bills for publicq use at all events must be honourd, if only we considere what influence of lost could attend them if they were protested, and the Consequence of further Publicq Credit.

To prevent all this, and to prevent all further inconvenience we have the honour to propose to your Excellency the following expedient.

We do not suppose the bills given out will exceed 2 or three hundred thousand Gilders, before they should hear in America of Mr. Lawrences arrivall here, and know there how matters were settled. Your Excellency may know more about it; butt be this as it will;

We offerr to Accept those bills which will offer, if your Excellency will give us leave to draw on her for what summs we may Accept & that she will accept our draufts for Acct. of Congress, and for those Drawn on Mr Laurens at 6 Month sight (and we have seen no others yett) we shall make our draufts on Yr. Excy. at 7 or 8 Month date with proper advice, if now she would approve of this our plan and give us Assurance that she will Ac-

8. It could hardly have been written any later, as BF answered it on June 6, below.
9. Above, May 29.

cept of those our bills directly after drawing we shall not lett any bills suffer butt continue to Accept them immediately. In this manner the whole matter is settled at once, and Your Excellency keeps up the Credit of Congress without advancing one farthing. Henry Laurens Esqr must arrive here within that time or his commission must be heard of, and there hath been Certainly measures provided for the payment of those bills butt we must fixe on some plan for the moment & we assure your Escellency we think this is absolutely the best.

We will not dwell on fixing beforehand any Comission for those operations, our principle for the American Cause makes us offer it without any view of intrest and even for nothing.

The sooner Your Excellency could find proper to honour us with an answer the better it would be; even by express as in this season of the Year every day there may apear new bills.

We have the honour to be with all devoted Regard Honour'd Sir. Your Excellencys most surely obedient & most humble Servants   JOHN DE NEUFVILLE & SON.

Notation: Neuville & fils. June 1780

From John Diot & Co.   ALS: American Philosophical Society

Honored Sir   Morlaix the 2d June 1780

We Receiv'd Your Excellency's honored Letter 23d. May in answer to the One we had the honnour to Write to you the 10th. Do.[1] but whereon we forgot to put the date.

We are Very Sorry to See what your Excellency is pleased to mention about the Prize Betzey, and are Surprised that the Papers relative to that Vessell have not been produced to you, as We have deliver'd 'em to the Admiralty office in Brest, which, Thro' mistake or Ignorance has forwarded the whole to the french Ministry and there was no other papers but a Customhouse Clearance wherein the Number and Sorts of goods that Composed her Cargoe was mentioned and her destination. If the admiralty had Committeed a blunt, We Shou'd think they

1. The firm's letter is missing; BF's is above.

Shou'd put things to Rights; If Your Excellency wou'd be pleased to inquiere after these papers, We don't doubt sir, but you'd find things as they ought to be.

We do not know what to Say in regard of the Two other prizes Peter and Friendship; The Want or loss of the Papers and Clearances of Said Vessells is undoubtedly owing to the hard weather they bore, and difficulty of Keeping So many prisonners in So Small a Craft; We fore See that Captn. Dowling's neglectfullness will prove hurtfull to his owners, unless your Excellency was pleased, after a Certain Time and no Claim enter'd, to Condemn them.

Rather than to See the goods damaged, We have petitioned the admiralty office to put them to Sale peremptorily, under Condition to deposite the proceeds.

Now We have the honnour to Acquaint Your Excellency with the Safe arrivall the day 'ere yesterday in this Road, of The Black Princess american privateer, Captn. Edward Macatter Commander, after a Very Warm Engagement with Three English privateers for 7 hours, Wherein the Princess desabled and dismasted One of her foes and by the bravery of her Crew and Swiftness of the Vessell got Clear of the Two others.[2]

She had all her Sails Tatter'd and Rigging Cut to pieces, but Luckily no body Killed nor Wounded, and She was forced to put in here to Repair.

She deliver'd us 6 hostages for five Ransoms amounting to £5505-.- St and took a brig Called The . . . . . ., loaded with Barley from   bound to   ; All the Crew had Left her at the first Gun that the Privateer fired at her, and there was no body left on board but the English Captain, who is Still aboard with the Prize master and three men of the Cutter.

Subjoin'd, Your Excellency has an abstract of her Journal, and a Declaration of Captn. Edward Macatter and his officers[3] Whereby, you'll See that against the use of all Nations against Humanity and all the Laws of People, the Three English Privateers Which the Princess did fight with, made use of Glass

2. The *Black Princess*'s opponents were H.M.S. *Racehorse* and the privateers *Unicorn* and *Alligator:* Clark, *Ben Franklin's Privateers*, p. 134.

3. Missing.

bottles which they Clapt into their guns, and We found it Sticking into the Mast Yards &ca.—and there was above a bushel taken up.

We thought 'twas our duty to Lay the Case before you, sir, to prevent the bad and dreadfull Consequences arising from So Illegal practices, and humanity Requieres that Your Excellency Shou'd Represent the matter to the English Ministry, For any man that is wounded So, is unrecoverable, which proved So, by a privateer out of DunKirk who had 33 people wounded and they all died— Besides Reprisalls might ensue, and We know Captn. Macatter and his people's Temper So well, that we are Sure that he wou'd Sink any English privateer that wou'd henceforth use So illegal a practice.

We think it fit to Observe to your Excellency, that american Privateers are not used in this part of France as they Shou'd. The commissary of the Marine here,[4] declared us yesterday that he gave orders to the Castle not to let the Princess go out untill further orders from The french Court, because the night of her departure from Cherbourg as She was under Sail, Fifteen french Sailors came in a Small boat and offer'd themSelves for the Time of the Cruize. Captn. Macatter who was in Sad want of hands took 'em on board, thinking no harm in doing So, but last night the Commissary Claimed them, and wee deliv'erd 'em up to day Except 3 that are on board of the prize that is not Come in as yet.

We Shou'd think the Commissary ought to be Satisfyed when Captn. Macatter Returned the people he Claimed and that is unproper for him or any person to stop the Cutter, when he got satisfaction.

We Jointly with Captn. Macatter beg your Excellency wou'd use her Interest at Court and Contrive means to have The Black Princess cleared that She might without loss of time Sett Sail in order to proceed into her Cruize against our Ennemies.

Waiting for the favour of your Excellency's answer, We have the honnour to be With due Respect Honored sir Your most obedient & most Humble Servants   JN. DIOT & CO

P.S. Since the above is Wrote, Three of the Eleven frenchmen Ran away, which inveterated the Commissary So much against

4. Boucault.

Captn. Macatter, that he positively threatened to order him to be Clapt in Gaol and used Very mean and ungentlemanlike Expressions, altho' Said Macatter, ignorant as he is of what gave lieu to all these disturbances, is Very innocent, as Your Excellency may Judge by an abstract of his declaration at the admiralty office, Signed by his Two first officers and by Four of the french Sailors, which are Owning that it was out of good and free will that they came on board the Princess and that Capn. Macatter did not know of Their being there.[5]

We can't conceive what Reason the Commissary may have to detain the Privateer any longer, it's Surely owing to his Spitefull and Rough ungentlemanlike Temper and Endeed, it's Shocking the way that americans are used by him.

We Earnestly beg Your Excellency will Speak to the Minister and applanish all difficultyes by Releasing the arrestment of the Privateer.[6]

To His Excellency Benj. Franklin Minister Plenipotentiary for the United States of North america, at the Court of France Passy

Endorsed: M. Diot June 2. 1780

Notation: Diot June 2d. 1780.—

From Dumas

ALS: American Philosophical Society; AL (draft): Algemeen Rijksarchief

Monsieur,   La Haie 2e Juin 1780

Mrs. J. De Neufville & fils ont promis d'accepter les deux Traites dont j'ai eu l'honneur de vous parler dans ma Lettre de mardi dernier, afin d'empêcher qu'elles ne soient protestées.[7] Le

5. This four-page extract is signed by *greffier* Rinquin of the Morlaix Admiralty. APS. See also Clark, *Ben Franklin's Privateers,* p. 135.

6. The firm wrote on June 5 to ask again for BF's intervention on Macatter's behalf, arguing that he might be able to capture part of Walsingham's convoy (for which see Digges to BF, March 3). It also asked BF to obtain French permission for recruiting Americans among the British prisoners at Dinan Prison. APS.

7. The preceding Tuesday was May 30, the date Dumas wrote on his own copy of the letter we publish under the 29th, above.

fils a été ici exprès, non seulement pour savoir si j'étois instruit de quelque chose concernant Mr. 484,[8] mais aussi pour voir avec moi ce qu'il y auroit à faire. Ce qui inquiete le plus ces Messieurs, c'est qu'ils ne savent pas la somme totale précise à quoi se montent les Traites que 196[9] peut avoir lâchées de cette maniere, & que nous ne savons aucune circonstance de cette émission: par conséquent il n'y a pas moyen de parler à personne; autrement nous aurions pu essayer de proposer à quelques personnes d'obliger en cette rencontre essentielle 196. Mais ne pouvant rien proposer qui ne soit vague obscur & incertain, personne n'y entreroit; & la proposition feroit plus de mal que de bien. Il faut espérer que M. 484 paroîtra incessamment sur l'horizon. Je ne m'étendrai pas davantage là-dessus, parce que ces Messieurs doivent vous avoir écrit de leur côté sur ce sujet.

L'affaire de la prise du Vaisseau hollandois le Berkenbos par Mr. Jones, devient de jour en jour plus facheuse. Mr. Van de Perre a été chez moi, avec une Lettre de son Capitaine, datée d'Antigoa, où il a été conduit, après avoir été pris par les Anglois. Il paroît par cette Lettre, que Mr. Jones a visité tous les papiers, & décacheté toutes les Lettres de cet homme, sans avoir rien pu trouver qui autorisât de simples soupçons. Sir J. Y.[1] & les Anglomanes rient de cette affaire, & en plaisantent: ce qui chagrine d'autant plus Mr. Van de Perre, qui est venu me faire ce récit, avec priere, Monsieur, de vous le faire parvenir.

Je suis avec tout le respectueux attachement qui vous est voué pour tout le reste de ma vie, Monsieur Votre très-humble & très obéissant serviteur   DUMAS

Mr. l'Ambr. n'est pas encore de retour d'Utrecht. Il va demain delà à Bruxelles, audevant de Made. la Duchesse,[2] & vraisemblablement il ne sera ici que mardi.

Voici la suite de la Lettre confidentielle. J'ai toujours de la peine à me persuader que Clinton ait pu écrire sur ce ton.

S'il arrive quelque bonne nouvelle de Charlestown, il est es-

8. "Laurens."
9. "Congress."
1. Sir Joseph Yorke.
2. The duc de La Vauguyon had married Antoinette-Rosalie de Pons, daughter of the vicomte de Pons, in 1766: *Dictionnaire de la noblesse*, XVI, 582

sentiel que je l'aie au plus vite, & que je puisse la faire valoir tant à Amsterdam, où j'irai exprès pour cela & en poste, qu'ici: comme aussi, si vous avez, Monsieur, des nouvelles de M. 484.

Passy à S.E. Mr. B.F—

Addressed: His Excellency / B. Franklin Esqr. Min. Plenipe. / of the united States &ce. / Passy./.

Notation: Mr Dumas la haie Juin 2. 1780

From Le Roy

ALS: American Philosophical Society

My Dear Doctor   Paris friday morning [June 2, 1780?][3]
    You would be very kind and very obliging if you were So good to give me a Copey of The French Translation of the Two letters of Genl Clinton &c taken upon The New York's pacquet boat Or if you cannot Spare it be So kind to lend it me to have it Copied out and you may be Sure I' will Send it you back faithfully. In doing my that favour you will oblige The Russian Ambassador Prince Bariatinskoy[4] for I must tell you it is for him That I beg of you that favour And I believe he writes this very day to his Court So that he is the more desirous to have it if it is possible quickly. If you can do me that pleasure you will oblige two persons very much and the Prince and I. Accept My Dear Doctor of my best compliments   LE ROY

P.S. Will you be So good my Dear friend to lett me know whether Captain Jones is gone a way or if he is Still in Paris.
    Give me leave to make my best compliments to M. Franklin your Grand-Son.

Addressed: a Monsieur / Monsieur Franklin / Ministre Plénipotentiaire / des Etats Unis en Son hôtel / à Passy

Notation: Le Roy

3. Our best guess, based on two clues from the letter. On June 2 Jones left Paris to return to Lorient. This is eighteen days after Wharton had sent from Lorient a copy of the spurious Clinton letter, long enough for BF to have had a French translation made.
    4. For whom see XXIV, 49n.

To Richard Bache

Dear Son   Passy, June 3. 1780.

I seldom hear from you or Sally, but I have lately had the satisfaction of hearing of you, that you and yours were all well the Begining of april last. I send you in a Parcel by this Opportunity some of the Correspondence betwen Ben and me. He was well a few weeks since, and very kindly notic'd where he is, by some respectable People. I continue, Thanks to God, well and hearty; and am ever, your affectionate father. My love to Will and the little ones.

M. Bache.

To Robert Morris

LS:[5] Mrs. Henry Sage, Albany, New York (1958); copy: Library of Congress

Dear Sir,   Passy June 3d 1780.

I received your kind Letter of March 31. acquainting me with your having engaged in M. De la Frétés Affairs on my Recommendation. I thank you very much; and beg you to be assured, that any Recommendation of yours will be regarded by me with the greatest Attention. The Letter you inclosed to M. Dumas is forwarded to him. We are impatient to hear from America, no Account of the Operations before Charlestown later than the 9th of March, having yet come to hand. Every thing here in Europe continues to wear a good Face. Russia, Sweden, Denmark and Holland are raising a strong Naval Force, to establish the free Navigation for Neutral Ships, and of all their Cargoes, tho' belonging to Enemies, except contraband; that is, military Stores. France and Spain have approved of it, and it is likely to become henceforth the Law of Nations, that *free Ships make free Goods*. England does not like this Confederacy. I wish they would extend it still farther, and ordain that unarm'd Trading Ships, as well as Fishermen and Farmers, should be respected, as working

5. In WTF's hand.

for the common Benefit of Mankind, and never be interrupted in their Operations even by national Enemies:[6] but let those only fight with one another whose Trade it is, and who are armed and paid for the Purpose.

With great and sincere Esteem, I am ever, Dear Sir, Your most obedient & most humble Servant.   B FRANKLIN

Robt. Morris Esq.

Endorsed: Passy 3d June 1780 Benjn Franklin Esqr.

From Sartine Copies: Library of Congress (two),[7] National Archives

A Versailles le 3. Juin 1780.

J'ai reçu, Monsieur, la Lettre que vous m'avez fait l'honneur de m'écrire le 30. du mois passé pour demander qu'il soit joint un Bâtiment du Roi à la fregate Americaine l'Alliance pour le transport des Armes, des Munitions de Guerre et des habillements destinés pour les Etats Unis. J'ai donné sur le champ des Ordres à l'Orient pour qu'il soit pourvu à cet Objet de la Maniere la plus convenable aux Intérêts du Congrès; et J'ai prescrit au Commandant et au Commissaire de ce port de procurer à M. Paul Jones toutes les facilités et tous les Secours qui pourront accélérer son Armement et Son Depart.[8] Ce Commodore ayant assuré que l'Alliance pourroit fournir un nombre suffisant d'offi-

6. BF repeated the list to Dumas on June 5 and in a letter of the following year: Smyth, *Writings*, VIII, 263. In a July 10, 1782, letter, probably to Benjamin Vaughan, he added "Artists & Mechanics . . . in open Towns": Public Record office; Bigelow, *Works*, XII, 56.

7. We print from the copy in BF's letterbook made by L'Air de Lamotte. The second one, prepared by Thomas Hutchins, is among Jones's papers. Copies of a June 4 forwarding letter from WTF to Jones (Bradford, *Jones Papers*, reel 5, no. 1099) are at the National Archives and the Library of Congress.

8. On June 12 Thévenard promised Sartine to accelerate repairs to the *Ariel*'s sails, there being no other ships at Lorient proper to carry supplies to America. He estimated that the sloop of war could carry 200 tons of cargo (of the 500 tons being assembled), sixteen cannon, and a crew of sixty: Archives de la Marine, B³DCLXXXII: 186-7. JW estimated that the *Ariel* could carry no more than 150 tons: JW to BF, June 23, below.

ciers et de Marins pour composer l'Equipage du Second Bâtiment; il y a lieu de croire qu'il sera incessamment en état de mettre à la voile.

J'ai l'honneur d'etre avec la plus parfaite consideration, Monsieur, Votre très humble et tres obeissant Serviteur

(signé) DE SARTINE

M. Franklin

From Clark & Cie.: Bills for Tableware

(I) and (II), printed forms with MS insertions, signed:
American Philosophical Society

This invoice and *lettre de voiture*, or consignment note, signal the first
significant purchase of tableware for an American foreign mission,
one perhaps connected with the upcoming celebration of the Fourth
of July. In previous years Franklin had rented tableware and other necessities,[9] but by 1780, possibly believing that the war was far from
over, he may well have decided that it would be cheaper to buy.

Ignoring the various French *faïences,* he chose an English product
quite recently launched on the continental market. Generally known
as creamware (in French, *faïence fine*), it had been perfected during the
1760's by Josiah Wedgwood;[1] one of its innovations was that it
replaced the traditional tin glaze by a transparent lead glaze. Once
he obtained Queen Charlotte's patronage, Wedgwood called it
Queen's Ware, and such was the appellation that Sally Bache used in
1773 when, writing from Philadelphia, she urged her father to send
some dishes over from England for the family's use.[2] She thought the
raised pattern, or "sprigs," was particularly elegant. We do not know
whether Franklin obliged, but this was a line of goods with which he
was certainly familiar.

Creamware eventually became so popular ("to be found in every
inn from Russia to Spain")[3] that it helped provoke the collapse of tra-

9. See xxx, 44.
1. As early as 1766, Wedgwood had made a medallion of BF in profile (XIII,
523n); he remained a lifelong friend and eventual partner in the fight for the
abolition of slavery.
2. XX, 453.
3. See Donald Towner, *Creamware* (London and Boston, 1978), p. 13.

Creamware Plate from Pont-aux-Choux

ditional earthenware-making techniques in England, France, and Holland.[4] Its advantages were a refreshing neoclassical simplicity after a surfeit of rococo, easier handling because of its lighter weight, and greater resistance to chipping; its drawback, in some people's eyes, was that it opened the way to industrialization.

Such characteristics were certain to please Franklin, but it seems surprising to see him "buy British" at the very time he was filled with a burning hatred against Britain. The clue to this paradox may have to do with industrial espionage. The French government, recognizing that France lagged behind England in technology, did its best to lure English workmen across the Channel, going as far as offering them a bribe to convert to Catholicism or a dowry to marry a French woman.[5]

Such was the case for the creamware factory that opened in 1775 in Montereau, a pottery center southeast of Paris, long known for the excellence of its clay.[6] A contract signed in 1774 specifies that the new company was financed by a 40,000 *l.t.* fund provided half by Holker *fils,* the son of Franklin's Rouen friend John Holker, and half by Antoine and Robert Garvey, two brothers, who were also established in Rouen. It was run by two *émigré* Englishmen, William Clark of Newcastle and George Shaw of Burslem, to whom the French government promised a ten-year annual subsidy of 1,200 *l.t.*[7] Their Parisian outlet was in the hands of M. Maisonneuve.[8] It was from his shop on the

4. The massive imports of Wedgwood had a "disastrous effect" on the French national art of painted *faïence:* Jeanne Giacomotti, *French Faience,* (George Savage, trans., New York, 1963), p. 236. See also pp. 5–7.

5. See John Harris, "Industrial Espionage in the Eighteenth Century," in John Harris, *Essays in Industry and Technology in the Eighteenth Century: England and France* (Hampshire, England, and Brookfield, Vermont, 1992), p. 168. His "British Entrepreneurial Attitudes to the Transfer of Technology in the Eighteenth Century" is to appear in the 1996 Proceedings of the Consortium on Revolutionary Europe Conference.

6. In a book entitled *L'Art de fabriquer la poterie façon anglaise* (Paris, 1807), the authors, M. O*** and M. Bouillon-Lagrange, repeatedly single out the greyish clay from Montereau as producing, given the right temperature, the whitest of dishes.

7. From information kindly provided by M. Jacques Bontillot, director of the Musée de la Faïence in Montereau. See also Jana Kybalová, *European Creamware* (Prague, 1989), p. 59. On Oct. 20, 1779, Holker *père* wrote his son, then French consul in the United States, about the death of an English workman employed by Clark and the problems caused by the death of Clark's own son, to be replaced by Clark's son-in-law, Jean Hall. Yale University Library.

8. See A. Lesur et Tardy, *Les Poteries et les faïences françaises* (2 vols., Paris, n.d.) II, 1198.

rue St. Jacques that Josiah Wedgwood's friend and partner, Thomas Bentley, traveling through France in the summer of 1776, purchased two small *compotiers* of Queen's Ware for 24 *sous*. Unimpressed with the quality of this French counterfeit, the Englishman noted in his journal that "The models and glaze in general are very indifferent and the workmanship bad. . . . This ware is manufactured at Montremi [*i.e.*, Montereau] sur la route d'Auxerre."[9]

I.

[June 3, 1780]
MANUFACTURE . . .[10] DE FAYANCE ANGLOISE, des Sieurs CLARK & Compagnie, établie à Montereau-faut-Yonne, en vertu d'Arrêt du Conseil du 15 Mars 1775, sous la dénomination de QUEENS WARE, ou Marchandises de la Reine.

Livré à *Monsiegneur francklin à Passy* par lesdits Sieurs CLARK & Compagnie, Entrepreneurs de lad. Manufacture, les Marchandises ci-après;

SAVOIR:

1. Grande Soupiere ronde avec le Plat à 7 l.t.		*7.*
2. Ditto moins Grande avec idem à 6 l.t.		*12.*
2. Terrines ovales avec idem à 24 l.t.		*48.*
12. douze. Assiettes dt.[dont] *2 douze. a Soupe à 6 l.t.*		*72.*
8. Plats ronds pr. Entremets à 18 s.		*7. 4.*
4. Ditto d'Entrée à 24 s.		*4. 16.*
2. Ditto à 36 s.		*3. 12.*
1. Ditto à 48 s.		*2. 8*
4. Plats ovales à 18 s.		*3. 12*

9. Thomas Bentley, *Journal of a Visit to Paris, 1776*, Peter France, ed., (Brighton, England, 1977), p. 71. From information kindly forwarded by Helen Anderson Sinclair Smith. In spite of Bentley's reassuring words, Wedgwood was worried enough to publish, in 1783, a twenty-four page pamphlet entitled *An Address to the Workmen in the Pottery, on the Subject of Entering into the Service of Foreign Manufactures* (Newcastle, Staffordshire), in which he warned Englishmen against the perils, physical and psychological, of emigration.

10. The word *Royale* was heavily crossed out here and in the following document from Montereau. Our best guess is that by 1780 the royal patent had lapsed.

4. *Ditto à 24 s.*	4. 16.
4. *Ditto à 36 s.*	7. 4.
2. *Ditto à 48 s.*	4. 16.
2. *Saucieres et Plateaux à 44 s.*	4. 8.
4. *Saladiers moyens à 30 s.*	6.
2. *Moutardiers et Cuillieres à 12 s.*	1. 4.
2. *huilliers à 4 l.t. 10 s.*	9.
2. *Beuriers a 50 s.*	5.
2. *Sucriers à desserts et Cuilliere à 3 l.t. 10 s. 7.*	7.
2. *Verriers à 12 s.* Verres à *5 l.t. 10 s.*	11.
1. *Ditto a 8 Idem a 4 l.t. 10 s.*	4. 10.
2. *Seaux à Bouteilles à 3 l.t. 10 s.*	7.
24. *Ditto à Verres à 20 s.*	24.
2. *Pots à L'Eau et Cuvettes à 3 l.t. 10 s.*	7.
1. *Grande Ecuelle et Plateau à 30 s.*	1. 10.
1. *Moyne.* [Moyenne] *Ditto et Idem à 25 s.*	1. 5.
1. *douze. Gobelets et Soucoupes à 5 s.*	5.
1. *douze. Tasses et Soucoupes à 5 l.t.*	5.
1. *Theyere à 36 s.*	1. 16.
1. *Pot à lait à 25 s.*	1. 5.
4. *Salières à 18 s.*	3. 12.
4. *Petites Bolles à 12 s.*	2. 8.
2. *Ditto à 24 s.*	2. 8.
1. *Ditto à 40 s.*	2.
1. *Ditto à 3 l.t.*	3.
2. *Sucriers à 15 s.*	1. 10.
4. *Compotiers à 15 s.*	3.
4. *Ditto à 20 s.*	4.
4. *Ditto à 24 s.*	4. 16.
4. *Plats quarré à 15 s.*	3.
4. *Ditto à 24 s.*	4. 16.
4. *Ditto à 30.*	6.
Pour La harrasse¹ Paille &a.	3.
	322. 16.
	10 7
	333. 3

1. Harasse, an openwork kind of crate to handle fragile ware.

A Montereau Le 3. Juin 1780./.

MACKINTOSH
Pour Messrs. Clark & Compie.

Notation: Pd by an Order on M. Grand.[2]

II.

MANUFACTURE... De TERRE-POTERIE, façon d'Angleterre, des Sieurs CLARK & Compagnie, établie à Montereau-faut-Yonne, en vertu d'Arrêt du Conseil du 15 Mars 1775,[3] sous la dénomination de QUEENS-WARE, ou Marchandises de la Reine.

Monsieur,   du *4 Juin 1780.*
   A la garde de Dieu & conduite de *Mrs les Entrepreneurs du Coche de Montereau* nous vous envoyons *une harasse* de notre Marchandise Terre-Poterie, façon d'Angleterre, numérotées & pezant comme en marge *trois cents cinquante Livres* poids de marc lesquelles vous étant rendues bien conditionées dans l'espace de *trois* jours, vous lui payerez sa voiture à raison de *Vingt Sols pr % pezant jusques a Paris* & rien autre chose, & dans

---

2. Grand's payment to Clark of 333 *l.t.* 3 *s.* is recorded on June 1 in Account VI (Thomas Barclay's Review of Franklin's Accounts, XXIII, 21) and Account XXVII. This would indicate that BF considered the set as a public purchase, in which case he would have left it behind for Jefferson's use. Less than three months after BF's departure, however, the new American minister to France was ordering a large quantity of table-china, hoping the pattern would match his own (*Jefferson Papers*, x, 436–7). Did Franklin, then, bring back the Montereau set to Philadelphia? In the course of the archaeological digging that preceded the erection of Franklin Court on Market Street, almost a quarter million shards were discovered, many of them fragments of cream-colored plates. But, as the Associate Curator of Independence National Park, Robert L. Giannini III, pointed out, BF's house was demolished as early as 1812 and the inhabitants of the row houses built on the spot used a vacant lot adjacent to it to discard their broken household goods all through the nineteenth century.

3. "Clark, Shaw et cie." had applied for this *arrêt de conseil* to expand their manufacture by importing two more English workmen and taking on apprentices. They also presented eight demands, including the exemption of Clark, Shaw, and all the English workers and their families, from the *droit d'aubaine* and from military service. The *arrêt* of March 15, 1775, granted everything they requested. Clark, Shaw & Co. to Trudaine de Montigny, Oct. 10, 1774, Archives nationales; communicated by Professor John Harris.

le cas de retard vous diminuerez le tiers de la voiture; & ce suivant l'avis de Vos très-humbles Serviteurs.

CRETTÉ[4]

pr Mrs Clarck et Compie. Entreprs.
de la Manufre. de terre facon
d'angleterre A Montereau
faut-yonne

[*In the margin*]: Numéros. Poids
50 *350*

A Monsieur, Monsieur *Maisonneuve au maga{z}in anglois rue St Jacques au Coin de Celle la Parcheminerie A Paris*
A *Monsieur Monsieur Le Docteur franckelin, agent de l'amerique A Passy*

Notation: voiture de montreau a paris de paris a pasy oficiés fort

Endorsed: Acct of Pottery 333 *l.t.:* 3.0

To Jean de Neufville & fils

LS:[5] National Archives; copy: Library of Congress

Gentlemen, Passy June 4th. 1780.

I received the Letter you did me the honour of writing to me on the 29th past, relating to certain Bills drawn on Mr Lawrens and requesting to know if I will engage to reimburse you, if you in his Absence, accept & pay them. As I have received no Orders nor any Advice relating to any such Bills, know not by whom they are drawn, whether for private or publick Account, or whether they are true or Counterfeit, what Quantity or Value there are of them, nor in short any one Circumstance relating to them, it would be inconsistent with common Prudence for me to enter into any such general Engagement. All I can say is that if they are really drawn by order of Congress, I make no doubt but

4. Louis-Auguste Cretté was the *receveur des droits de la rivière* in Montereau. Information sent by M. Bontillot.
5. In WTF's hand.

care will be taken to place Funds in time for the punctual Payment of them. I thank you in behalf of the Congress for the Readiness with which you kindly offer your Service in the Case, but I can say nothing farther at present to encourage your Paying such Bills.— I have the honour to be, with much Esteem Gentlemen, Your most obedient & most humble Servant,

B FRANKLIN

Mess. De Neufville & Son.

From Caffiéri[6]

ALS: American Philosophical Society

Monsieur   Paris ce 4 juin 1780

Je vien D'aprendre par les papiés Public que Le Congrés De Philadelphie en reconnoissance des services rendu par Le feu comte Pulawski Brigadier General, a résolu qu'un monument public Seroit élevé à La memoire de cet officier et que L'execution en Seroit Confiée a un artiste francois. D'apres cet article je prens La liberté de vous Ecrie pour vous priér de vouloire bien vous Resouvenire que vous avé eu la bonté de me promette de me charger de L'execution de touts Les Tombeaux que les Etats hunis americquen feuroit faire à l'avenire; Comme il a Du temps quil est question de ce Tombeaux peut-être que J'ay, quel que Concurrent, Sependant a merit Egale jose esperée avoire la preferanc, Pour obtenire Ce monument, j'ay en vous Monsieur une plaine Confience.

J'ay lhonneur D'etre avec respect Monsieur Votre Tres humble et tres obéïssant Serviteur   CAFFIERI

Notation: Caffieri. Paris 4 Jan 80.

6. The entry in the *DBF* on the famous sculptor notes that he avidly sought success and honors, importuned the Academy with his requests, and was never satisfied with what he was given. He did not obtain this particular commission (for which see *JCC*, xv, 1324, 1357); apparently neither did anyone else.

From Conrad-Alexandre Gérard[7]

ALS: American Philosophical Society

Monsieur   A Versailles le 4. Juin 1780.

Vous verrés par les lettres cijointes[8] qu'une boite de pelleteries arrivées ici par meprise, appartient à Mr. Keith, et les motifs qui m'engagent à vous prier de vouloir bien charger quelqu'un de disposer de ces effets. Je presume, Monsieur, que vous voudrés bien donner vos ordres à ce sujet, s'agissant de menager les interrets d'un de vos compatriotes.

J'ai l'honneur d'etre avec un respectueux attachement Monsieur Votre très humble et très obeissant serviteur   GERARD

M. le Dr. franklin

Notations in different hands:[9] M. Gerard concerning the Furs / Versaille 4 Juin 80

To Dumas

LS:[10] American Philosophical Society; copy: Library of Congress; transcript: National Archives

Dear Sir.   Passy June 5. 1780.

The Gentleman whose Name you wish'd to know in one of your late Letters,[1] is M. Westhuysen Echevin & Conseiller de la

---

7. As far as we know this is the last extant letter to BF from the former *premier commis* and minister to Congress. In ill health, he returned to his native Alsace in 1781 and died there nine years later: Meng, *Despatches of Gérard*, pp. 121–2.

8. Gérard must have sent a March 17 letter from Chaplain Robert Keith of the frigate *Confederacy* (on which Gérard had traveled from Philadelphia to Martinique), asking if Gérard had accidentally taken a box of furs belonging to him (APS). He also included his reply to Keith of June 4 (a copy of which is with the present letter). Gérard therein sent his apologies, explaining that the furs, by now virtually ruined, were discovered among the possessions of Pierre Penet, who had traveled with him from Martinique to Europe. He would, nonetheless, return the furs in case they still had some value.

9. The first of which is WTF's.

10. In WTF's hand.

1. On May 4.

Ville de Harlem. I shall probably [send an order?] to that Place for some of the Types, of which you have sent me the Prices, before I leave Europe. I think them very good and not dear.[2]

A Dutch Ship belonging to Mess. Little Dale & Co: of Rotterdam, being brought into France as having an English Cargo on board, I have followed your Opinion with regard to the Condemnation of the Cargo, which I think the more right, as the English have in the West Indies confiscated several of our Cargoes found in Dutch Ships.[3] But to shew Respect to the Declaration of the Empress of Russia, I have written to the Owners of our Privateers, a Letter of which I enclose a Copy, together with a Copy of the Judgement, for your Use if you hear of any Complaint.[4] I approve much of the Principles of the Confederacy of the Neutral Powers, and am not only for respecting the Ships as the House of a Friend, tho containing the Goods of an Enemy, but I even wish for the Sake of Humanity, that the Law of Nations may be farther improved, by determining that even in time of War, all those kinds of People who are employed in procuring Subsistance for the Species, or in exchanging the Necessaries or Conveniences of Life, which is for the common Benefit of Mankind; such as Husbandmen on their Lands, Fishermen in their Barques, and Traders in unarmed Vessels, shall be permitted to prosecute their several innocent and useful Employments without Interruption or Molestation, and nothing taken from them, even when wanted by an Enemy, but in paying a fair Price for the same.

I think you have done well to print the Letter of Clinton; for tho' I have myself had suspicions whether some Parts of it were really written by him, yet I have no doubt of the Facts stated, and think the Piece Valuable as giving a true account of the State of British and American Affairs in that Quarter. On the whole it has

2. We have found no evidence that BF ever placed an order with Enschedé and Sons.

3. The Dutch ship must be the *Flora*, as on June 6, below, Torris mentions "Little Dalle & Co." in conjunction with it. Dumas offered advice on May 4, above.

4. BF sent the judgment of the *Flora* to the Admiralty of Cherbourg on May 26. He sent cautionary letters to both Diot & Co. (May 23) and John Torris (May 27). All these are above.

the Appearance of a Letter written by a General who did not approve of the Expedition he was sent upon who had no Opinion of the Judgement of those who drew up his Instructions who had observed that preceding Commanders, Gage Burgoyne, Keppel, and the Howes had all been censur'd by the Ministers for having unsuccesfully attempted to execute injudicious Instructions with unequal Force; and he therefore wrote such a Letter not merely to give the Information contained in it but to be produced in his Vindication, when he might be recalled, and his want of Success charged upon him as a Crime, tho' in Truth owing to the folly of the Ministers who had order'd him on impracticable Projects and persisted in them notwithstanding his faithful Informations, without furnishing the necessary Number of Troops he had demanded.— In this View much of the Letter may be accounted for, without supposing it fictitious; and therefore if not genuine it is ingeniously written: But you will easily conceive that if the State of publick Facts it contains were known in America to be false, such a Publication there would have been absurd and of no possible Use to the Cause of the Country. I have wrote to Mr. Neufville concerning the Bills you mention.[5] I have no Orders or Advice about them, know nothing of them, and therefore cannot prudently meddle with them; especially as the Funds in my Power are not more than sufficient to answer the Congress Bills for Interest, and other inevitable Demands. He desired to know whether I would engage to reimburse him if he should accept and pay them; but as I know not the Amount of them I cannot enter into any such Engagement: For tho' if they are genuine Congress Bills, I am persuaded all possible Care will be taken by Congress to provide for their punctual Payment, yet there are so many accidents by which Remittances are delayed or intercepted in this Time of War, that I dare not hazard for these new Bills, the Possibility of being render'd unable to pay the others.

With great Esteem I am, Dear Sir your most obedt and humble Servt   B. FRANKLIN

p.s. I cannot prescribe as you desire anything relating to your affair with 62.[6] Your own Judgement ought to guide you. I shall be

5. On June 4, above; Dumas had mentioned the matter on May 29, above.
6. BF undoubtedly meant "64" for "Ambassador." "62" stands for "also."

careful to furnish you early with any good News we may receive. If the 732.[7] cannot be immediately made, it may with Prudence come on by Degrees./.

[*In the margin:*] (The Copy of the Judgement will be sent by next Post.)

M Dumas.

Endorsed: 175 Passy 5e. Juin 1780 Mr B Franklin

Notation: Benjamin Franklin

From Andrew and David Gallwey[8]

ALS: Historical Society of Pennsylvania

Nantes 5 June 1780.

The proofs we have of the writer of the annex'd letter & his companys good dispositions towards our american friends, the many attempts they have made to serve them, some of which have been attended with great success & a firm persuasion of their good wishes for that country to which they are so strongly attach'd that they have fix'd a resolution to retire thither with their familys & fortunes as the times permit, induce us to trouble your Excellency & to sollicit the grant of the favor they demand.[9]

7. "Reconcile."
8. Members of a Jacobite family from Cork that settled in Nantes. In 1732, merchant David Gallwey had formed an association with William Ellis: Meyer, *Armement nantais*, pp. 107, 112; Richard Hayes, *Biographical Dictionary of Irishmen in France* (Dublin, 1949), pp. 100–1. In 1789 another Gallwey, John, also an established merchant in Nantes, was recommended to Thomas Jefferson as a man of absolute trustworthiness and a friend to America: *Jefferson Papers*, XIV, 588–9.
9. The enclosure was an unsigned abstract of a letter written from Dublin on May 5: three vessels fitting out to carry salt, linens, and hardware to Virginia need passports. Would the Gallweys ask BF to provide passes for Christopher Sheridan, Richard Sheridan, and John Macabe, or if three letters are not possible, then only one for Christopher Sheridan? BF should be willing to grant this request, as the parties have already served his friends.

Mr. de Sartine & his predecessors in all the wars since the year 1730 granted us Passeports for these same friends by which means large importations of provisions for the navy have been made and considerable exportations of the produce of this kingdom to the great advantage of its trade.

Tho' we have not the honor of being known to your Excellency, we flatter on enquiry from the minister of the marine or the Director general you'll think we are not unworthy of your confidence.

Mr. Ross who is kind enough to present this to your Excellency, will give you any other information you may think proper to take on our account.

We have the honour to be with great respect Your Excellencys Most obedient & devoted Servs.

ANDW: & DD: GALLWEY

His Excellency Benj. Franklin Esqr.

Notation: Papers relative to the Passport given to Christ. Sheridan going from Ireland to settle in Ama[1]

From Jonathan Williams, Jr.

ALS: University of Pennsylvania Library; copy: Yale University Library

Dear & hond Sir.   Nantes June 5. 1780—

I wrote you the 20th of May to which I refer, as I have no answer I have not taken any decisive Step relative to a Ship to carry out the Goods. Mr Ross is since arrived here & I have consulted with him, I shew him the Letter I wrote you the 20 Inst & find

---

The answer should be sent under cover of John Brown. On May 22, the anonymous "firm" followed up its letter with a second, more urgent appeal, also addressed to the Gallweys: their "M. C" is determined to emigrate to Virginia before next September, and will swear an oath of allegiance on arrival. A copy of this letter (Hist. Soc. of Pa.) was forwarded to John Ross, who brought it to Paris and forwarded it to BF: Ross to WTF, June 16, APS.

1. BF issued a passport for Christopher Sheridan on June 25. Only a letterbook copy survives, and that has blanks left for the names of the ship and captain, the crew size, and tonnage. Library of Congress.

479

his Opinions and mine exactly agree. It is certain no man will freight at this Time without being paid a very high Price, & his Ship insured into the Bargain. Congress must therefore run all the risque and pay in Freight a large Sum of money, which Sum of money would go a great way towards purchasing & fitting a Ship & the risque would be no more. In the one case the freight paid is a dead Expence, in the other the Ship is always worth her Cost & the whole Freight is gained. The large Ship I mentioned to you in my last is yet unsold & may be bought if you can command Funds at 3, 6 & 9 months this vessell armed as I have already mentioned would answer our Purpose, or if you do not choose a new Ship I could buy 2 or 3 Smaller Ones which would be much cheaper but they would not answer the purposes of Congress when on the other side of the Water.—

Mr Ross has concluded to take a Trip to Paris to consult with you in Person on this Business and I shall do nothing 'till I hear the Result of your Conference.[2]

I am ever with the greatest Respect Yours most dutifully and affectionately   JONA WILLIAMS J

Notation: J Williams June 5. 1780

To Jean de Neufville & fils

LS:[3] National Archives; copies: Library of Congress, National Archives

Gentlemen,   Passy June 6. 1780.

Since writing to you by yesterdays Mail, I have received the honour of yours,[4] proposing to accept Bills drawn on M. Laurens, if I will authorise you so to do, and accept your Bills to

2. Ross left the following morning, and JW wrote to WTF on that day suggesting that he hand Ross the copy of JW's accounts, certified by BF, that WTF had agreed to have made. If WTF could not find a copyist, then he should ask BF's permission to send the original to Nantes and let JW have it copied there. APS. JW had first requested that WTF arrange for a copy (at JW's expense) on March 27, since he had sent his own to America with Lafayette. He had reminded WTF of that request on May 9: APS; Yale University Library.

3. In WTF's hand.

4. BF's letter is above, June 4; the firm's is printed under the date of June 1.

equal Amt. Having no Orders about those Bills, or even any Advice of such being drawn, and knowing that the English have plai'd many villainous Tricks with our Paper, I cannot think of giving Power to another, who may be less acquainted with our American Handwritings & Printings, to accept Bills which I have never seen, and therefore cannot judge whether they are counterfiet or genuine, and in this may make myself or the Congress accountable for unknown Sums. I believe no prudent Man would so expose himself or the Government of his Country. I thank you however for the Zeal and Readiness you show to support our Credit. When Mr Lawrens arrives, he will doubtless accept any good Drafts made upon him, and accept them as of the Date when they would have been presented if he had been at Amsterdam when they were received; because this is just; and I make no Doubt but they will be punctually paid. As to Loans in Holland, I believe the Congress have laid aside all Thoughts of them, having fallen upon means of borrowing at Home of their own People, by issuing Paper Money bearing Interest, which appears better and more advantageous to the Country than paying Interest abroad. You may see their Scheme, as resolved March 18. printed in the London Evening Post of May 25. And having come to this Resolution I fancy they cannot have drawn many Bills on Mr Lawrens.

With great Regard, I am, Gentlemen, Your most obedient & most humble Servant.   B FRANKLIN

Mess. J. Neufville et Fils—

From Antoine-Alexis Cadet de Vaux[5]

ALS: American Philosophical Society

Monsieur   Ce 6 Juin 1780
Monsieur le lieutenant Général de Police[6] fera Jeudi 8 du courant, à 11 h. précises l'Inauguration de l'Ecole de Boulan-

5. Cadet de Vaux's collaboration with BF and Parmentier in matters relating to bread and potatoes has been documented in XXVII, 520–21, 578; XXX, 310.
6. Jean-Charles-Pierre Lenoir.

gerie, Rue de la grande Truanderie. M. Parmentier et moi prononcerons un discours Sur les avantages de cet Etablissement. Il Serait flatteur pour nous et honorable pour la chose que vous veuilliés bien y assister; nous consacrerions dans les fastes de cette Ecole que Monsieur franklin en a honoré l'ouverture de Sa présence. J'ai flatté Monsieur Le Noir du plaisir de vous y rencontrer, au moins lui ai-je promi de faire tous mes efforts pour obtenir de vous cette faveur.[7]

Je Suis avec le plus profond respect, Monsieur, Votre très humble et très obeissant Serviteur

CADET
Censeur Royal R. St antoine

Notations: Cadet. 6 Juin 1780. / June 6 80

From Dumas

ALS: American Philosophical Society

Monsieur, La Haie 6e. Juin 1780

Rien de nouveau ici, Sinon que le Courier arrivé ici depuis peu de jours à l'Envoyé Russe, n'a rien apporté qu'une réponse générale de l'Impératrice aux Etats-Généraux sans entrer dans des détails,[8] sur lesquels l'Envoyé attend un autre Courier dans 8 ou dix jours. Je joins ici le reste de la Lettre de Clinton. Tout ce qui est dans ce feuillet, mérite votre attention, Monsieur, Si

7. We have found no evidence that BF attended the ceremony. The file on Parmentier at the Académie des sciences relates merely that a free baking school was opened on June 8 by Parmentier and Cadet. Another source reports that bakers from various provinces attended the courses given there twice a week to teach better ways of baking white bread for the Ecole militaire and brown for the jails (Hillairet, *Rues de Paris,* 1, 597). A lengthy account of the opening speeches was given in the *Jour. de Paris* for June 11, not surprisingly since Cadet was the *Journal's* founder.

8. To Dutch higher officials the Russian response was disquieting; instead of sending a draft treaty the empress indicated her desire that negotiations for an alliance of neutrals be held in St. Petersburg: Fauchille, *Diplomatie française,* pp. 502–3.

vous ne l'avez pas encore lu, particulierement l'article de Leide du 5e. Juin, qui remplit le bas de la 3e. & toute la page suivante.[9]

Je n'apprends rien encore du Voyageur[1] dont j'ai eu l'honneur de vous parler dans mes deux dernieres, ni n'ai des Lettres d'Amsterdam. La Cour n'est plus ici. Mr. l'Ambassadr. avec Made. l'Ambassadrice de F——ce doivent arriver incessamment. Tout semble endormi ici. Je suis avec un très-grand respect, Monsieur Votre très-humble & très-obéissant serviteur

DUMAS

Cette Lettre n'a pu partir Mardi: il n'etoit plus temps au Bureau.

Passy à S. E. Mr. B. Franklin

Addressed: à Son Excellence / Monsieur B. Franklin, Esqr. / Min. Plenipe. des Etats-unis / &c. &c. / Passy./.

Notation: Mr Dumas la Haie Juin. 6. 80

From Samuel Nuttle[2]   ALS: American Philosophical Society

Havre de Grace 6 June 1780 chez Mr. David Chauvel.
May it Please your Excellency

I take the Liberty of applying to your Excellency for that Protection, which every true American has always found in your Excellency; the last time I was at Paris & that I had the honour of being Presented to your Excellency, your Excellency was Pleased to promise it to me; it is with the Greatest Sorrow, that I see myself Confined in France at the Same time, that my Country & my Countrymen are Engaged in a most Glorious War; I should think myself very happy if I could Join them & Partake

9. Dumas is probably referring to an article about the violation of Dutch neutrality by three British colliers. It appeared on the third and fourth pages of the supplement to the June 6 issue of the *Gaz. de Leyde* (no. XLV).

1. Henry Laurens.

2. A former merchant ship captain who had carried across the Atlantic letters to and from BF: VII, 254; VIII, 231; XIV, 23–4. He had last written BF from the same address twenty months earlier: XXVII, 615–16. He sent the present letter under a covering letter to WTF (APS).

their Dangers; I quited my Country in her own Service, but had the misfortune of being Cast-away on the coast of Portugal. I have Since done my best to return, but as ill luck would have it, I was allways opposed, be it for want of means, or Speculations, which had no Success; detaind allways in hopes, I have passed 18 months in France, but seeing no Prospect of accomplishing my wishes I Accepet'd of a 1st. Leuitenants birth aboard the Josephine Privateer mounting 36 Guns; the Captn. thereof Mr. Favre, being a very experienced Commander, very well known & respected for his Courage & Science. I hoped to acquire under that brave man all nessasary qualifications, that might render me on my return more Servisable to my Country. We have been very unlucky in our last Cruise, allways chased by English men of war Superior to our force, we spent the best part of our time in avoiding them, & made but few prises; the Owners little satisfy'd dont chuse to rearme her 'till the begining of the Winter, when they promiss to continue me in the birth of 1st. Leiutt. being very well Satisfyed with my Conduct in the Several Engagements we were obliged to Sustain; they would gladly employ me as second Captn. but it lays out of their Power, as being Contrary to the ordinances of France to admit to that Post a Stranger who has not served the Campagnes necessary in the french Service, so that I am reduced to remain the whole Sumer without Employ & no hopes of preferment the next winter. I therefore apply to your Excellency for one in the Service of my Country or a dispensation from the Minister, that I may be admited as a Captn. in the french Merchand Service.

The Inclosed certificate which I take the Liberty to lay Before your Excellency will prove that I am Capable of fullfilling that place.[3]

I remain with the Greatest Respect Your Excellency's Most Obedt. Humble. Sert. SAMUEL NUTTLE

3. Capt. Jean-Louis Favre's enclosed statement (dated June 3) says that Nuttle has filled his post as first lieutenant with the utmost exactitude. Nuttle's thirteen or fourteen years' experience qualifies him for a captain's post, which he has demonstrated he could fill worthily. On July 31 Nuttle wrote WTF to renew his request. If BF is unsuccessful, he wishes to serve aboard the frigate *South Carolina*, presently at Amsterdam. Both of these documents are at the APS.

From John Torris   ALS: American Philosophical Society

Honnd. Sir   Dunkerque 6th. June 1780.

The Letter you did me the Honnour to write me the 27th. ulto. I have recd. a few days Past, & Inclosed the Judgment to give up the Ship aurora⁴ & to Condamn, under Some hard restrictions, the Cargoe.

I beg Leave to make a few observations to the Justice of your Excellency.

The acknowledgment that the Cargoe is really the Property of the Ennemy, altho' attempted to be masked as Neutral, does assert that, your Excellency is Justly convinced that Roodenberg, the master, is a Parjure, & doth allow us to Claim he shou'd be Punisht for Same, & not Treated so Partially as he is; otherwise, 'Twill encourrage the worst behaviour by him & others in future. I beg Leave to Submit this observation to your Excellency.

Altho' the Judgment seems severe on the Captors, & does expose them to the dishonnest dispositions of Some of the Freighters, they have such a respect for the determination of your Excellency, that an appeal to Congress is far from their mind; This Judgment requieres, however, a few explanations, & I Beseech your Excellency Will Let me know wether it is not understood that the Freight is to be Paid by the admiralty, out of the Produce of the Cargoe? This appears very Just; Because, the goods Condamned to the Captors, & those Claimed by neutral right owners, are to Pay it according to the Bills of Lading, & their Proportion of the expences? We Cannot apprehend that your Excellency wou'd requiere from the Captors so Considerable an advance as this Freight, when you deprive them of the Produce of the Cargoe for an unlimited Time.

I further observe to your Excellency, you did omit to fix the Customary space of Time for the Freighters to Lay in their Claims & for to appeal to the Congress. Also for the Captors to Claim from the admiralty the Produce of the Sale. I Beseech your Excellency will Limit the Same; Because, the Marchandize Belonging to the Ennemy, & those Claimed as the Property of

4. *I.e.*, the *Flora.*

Neutral Subjects, have Latly been asserted by acts & Declarations before Nottary Public at Rotterdam, which have been signiffied to Mr. De Chantereyne our Correspondant at Cherbourg; & I Send them to Mr. De Maussallé. The whole Cargoe is acknowledged by Messrs. Little Dalle & Co. & by Messrs. Herman & Vanyzendoorn, to be but shipt by them, & not their Property; except 31. Bales of Clover Seeds P.K. & X.M. shipt & Claimed by Mr. Peter De koker as his own Property.[5]

I have the Honnor to be with great Respect Honnd. Sir Your Excellency's most humble & most obedient servant   J. TORRIS

His Excellency Dr. Franklin minister at the Court of France

Endorsed: June 6

Notation: Mr. Torris. June 6. 1780

From Wulffen
LS: American Philosophical Society

Monsieur   Paris 6. Juin. 1780.

J'ai abandonné patrie, parents, Fortune, tout, pour voler, a l'exemple de tant de braves guerriers, en Amerique venger la liberté opprimée, & punir l'Orgueil Anglois. Couvert de Onze blessures, J'ai été pris, & n'ai eu rien de plus pressé, au Sortir des prisons, que de venir rendre compte a Votre Excellence, de ma triste Situation actuelle. Je brule d'un désir que Je Sens mieux que je ne puis exprimer d'aller verser le peu de Sang qui me reste pour l'honneur des 13: provinces unies, de la France, de toutes les puissances alliées, & pour tirer une vengeance personelle des traitements affreux que J'ai Souffert des Anglois, l'espace de Six mois que j'ai eté dans les cachots chargés de chaines. Manquant de tout pour le présent que puis-je, a qui m'adresser—Si ce n'est au Ministre de la nation pour la quelle J'ai combattu. Vous n'ignorez pas, Monsieur, les avances que m'a fait Mr. de Baÿer commandant du Regiment de Normandie.[6] Il faut que J'y Satisfasse.

5. Torris enclosed a two-page notarized statement of May 18–27, detailing the cargo of the *Flora*.

6. Antoine-François-Raymond de Boyer (1734–1805) at the time was only a lieutenant colonel, but probably he was the senior officer present when the regiment extended its help to Wulffen: *DBF; Etat militaire* for 1780, p. 157.

Privé de l'honneur de porter, faute de moyens, mon propre & véritable uniforme, J'en attends un autre de vous, Monsieur. J'espere que Votre Excellence après avoir ordonné au Banquier le remboursement de mes appointements de Capitaine non reçus l'espace de huit mois, voudra bien elle même taxer la Somme a la quelle peuvent monter mes rations journalieres que Je n'ai pu avoir, durant ma prison. Je crois avoir ce droit Sur la générosité & la justice de Votre Excellence. Je compte aussi, Monsieur, que je vous devrai de nouveaux & prompts ordres pour me rembarquer, & aller en Amerique montrer mes blessures encor ouvertes à tous mes Camarades. Ces braves officiers ne pourront qu'etre indignés en entendant, de ma bouche, le reçit de la barbarie des Anglois a mon égard, & tous unis ensemble nous vaincrons où nous mourrons.

Je Suis trés respectueusement Monsieur. De Votre Excellence Le trés humble & très obéissant Serviteur   BON. DE WULFFEN

To Landais

LS:[7] University of Pennsylvania Library; copies: Harvard University Library, Library of Congress, National Archives (two)

Sir,   Passy, June 7th. 1780.

I receiv'd yours of the 29th. past, and after the Manner in which you quitted the Ship, my clear and positive Refusal of replacing you contained in mine of March the 12th. and my furnishing you with a considerable Sum to enable you to go to America for a Trial, I am surpris'd to find you at L'Orient when I thought you had long since been on your Voyage, and to be told that "you had been waiting ever since your Arrival there for my Orders to retake the Command of the Alliance," when I had never before heard of your being there, or given you the least Expectation of the kind.— The whole Affair between us will be laid before our Superiors, who will judge justly of the Consis-

7. In L'Air de Lamotte's hand, except for the complimentary close, which is in BF's, and the address sheet, which is in WTF's. The copy at the Harvard University Library is certified by James Warren, Jr., and Fitch Pool to be a true copy. Their notation indicates that the letter was sent to Jones, who then sent it to Matthew Parke: Bradford, *Jones Papers*, reel 5, no. 1111, enclosure 1.

tency and Propriety of your Conduct and of mine. I wave therefore any farther Dispute with you. But I charge you not to meddle with the Command of the alliance or create any Disturbance on board her, as you will answer the contrary at your Peril. I am, sir, Your most obedient & most humble Servant   B FRANKLIN

Honble. Capt Landais, late Commader of Alliance, L'Orient.

Addressed: To, / The honble. Captain Landais / late Commander of Ship Alliance / now at L'Orient.

Notation by James Moylan: I presented this Letter—to Captain Landais on board the Alliance the 18th day of June 1780 and desir'd he wou'd give me a receipt for it, agreeable to the orders of the Honble. Doctor B. Franklin; the said Cap: Landais refused to receive it. saying it had been adress'd to the late commander of the Alliance.[8] This I do hereby attest & certify.

JAMES MOYLAN L'Orient 10th July 1780

To Officers of the *Alliance*

LS: National Archives;[9] copy: Library of Congress

Gentlemen   Passy, June 7. 1780.

I received your Letter dated the 12th. of April past, expressing that you were in necessitous Circumstances, and that you were allarmed at having received neither Wages nor Prize-Money when the Ship was so nearly prepared for Sea.

Having had nothing to do with the Prizes, and understanding that they could not soon be turn'd into Money, I had answer'd the purpose of your Letter in the best manner in my Power, by advancing twenty four thousand Livres, to supply the most urgent of your necessities, till the Prize-money could be

---

8. On June 18 James Degge gave Moylan a signed receipt (now at the University of Pa. Library) for BF's letter of this date to the officers of the *Alliance,* immediately below. At the same repository is an unsigned receipt for the present letter.

9. In L'Air de Lamotte's hand. BF made minor corrections to Lamotte's effort and signed it. It is marked "Copy."

obtained.[1] With regard to your Wages, I thought the Expectation of having them paid here was wrong. Nobody in Europe is impower'd to pay them. And I believe it is a Rule with all maritime States to pay their Ships only at home, by an Office where the Accounts are kept, and where only it can be known, what Agreements were made with the Officers and men, what advances they have received, and what their families or Attorneys may have receiv'd in their Absence.[2] I had many Letters and Informations from L'Orient acquainting me with the Discontent among the People of the Alliance at the Method proposed of Valuing the Prizes in order to their being paid for by the king, and that our Ship could not possibly be got out, unless that Method was chang'd and the Prizes fairly sold at Auction to the highest Bidder. I then apply'd to have the Change made, and it was readily agreed by Minister of the Marine, that they should be so sold: But to sell them suddenly, would again have been liable to Objection, and therefore time was given in the Advertisements that distant Purchasers of Ships might know of the Sale, and a greater Number of Bruyers give a Chance of a highter Price for your Benefit. Had the first Method been comply'd with, I am inclin'd to think, from his Majesty's known Generosity, a better Price would have been obtained (as similar Instances have proved) than is likely to be got by the Sale, and you would have had your Money sooner. I consented to Change to satisfy and if possible please you. The Delay was by no means agreable to me, as it occasioned a great Additional Expence, and I heartily wish'd the Ship in America.

I did, as you have heard, send a Memorial to the Court of Denmark, claiming a Restitution of the Prizes or of their Value. This Memorial was received long before they sailed from Berghen. They were neverthless allow'd to depart for England: and the only Answer I have had from that Court is, that the Restitution was made in pursuance of Treaties between the two Crowns. I am not satisfy'd with this Answer, but have laid the

1. To Jones, March 18, above.
2. The British Navy placed restrictions on paying its sailors, chiefly in order to prevent desertion: N.A.M. Rodger, *The Wooden World: an Anatomy of the Georgian Navy* (London, 1986), pp. 130–5.

whole Matter before Congress,[3] desiring their Instructions. You may be assured that not a Penny of the Value has been paid; and that if ever any thing is recover'd while I am concerned in the Business, Strict Justice shall be done you, which I have also no doubt will be done with Regard to the Serapis and Countess of Scarborough.

Having received several Letters from you formerly, complaining in Strong Terms of Capt. Landais' Conduct in the Government of the Ship, and his ill Treatment of all the Officers except the Purser;[4] and having received also from Captain Landais himself a Letter dated at L'Orient May 15. 1779. in which he says "you all join'd together against him even before he left Boston; that he was promised another Set, but being ready to sail; the Navy-board thought your Behaviour would be better when at Sea; on the contrary it grew worse and worse, and was come to that Pitch, that he was compell'd to acquaint me with it, that I might take a proper Method to remedy it; and if no other was to be found, he would rather chuse to leave the Command than continue with such Officers."[5] After all this, it is a little surprizing to me, that Capt. Landais, who came to Paris only to vindicate himself from some Charges against him, and there voluntarily as I thought, (and in pursuance of his former Resolution) relinquish'd the Ship, by desiring me repeatedly to give an Order for taking out of her the Things he had on board;[6] and who never once during all the Time he staid here, express'd the least Wish or gave the least Hint of a Desire to be continued in her, till he heard She was upon the Point of Sailing; and that now he should demand to be replac'd over you, and that you Should wish to be again under his Command; I know not how to account for this Change. But having agreed to what I imagin'd from the Letters on both sides would be agreable to both you and Capt.

3. In his letter of May 31 to Huntington, above.
4. These complaints began soon after the *Alliance*'s arrival in France: XXIX, 25–6. Landais blamed them on First Lt. Stephen Hills and Second Lt. Joseph Adams and said that once they had left the ship (XXIX, 645–6, 709), matters quieted: Landais, *Memorial*, p. 109.
5. XXIX, 497–8.
6. See, for example, XXXI, 380. On March 1, above, BF told Jones to deliver Landais his things.

Landais, and plac'd another Captain in the Ship, I cannot now comply with your Request. I have related exactly to Congress the Manner of his leaving the Ship and tho' I declin'd any Judgment of his Maneuvres in the fight, I have given it as my Opinion after examining the affair, that it was not at all likely, either that he should have given Orders to fire into the Bonhomme Richard, or that his Officers would have obey'd such orders if he had given them. Thus I have taken what Care I could of your Honour in that particular; you will therefore excuse me if I am a little concern'd for it in another. If it should come to be publikly known, that you had the strongest Aversion to Capt. Landais, who had used you basely, and that it is only since the last year's Cruize, and the Appointment of Commodore Jones to the Command, that you request to be again under your old Captain, I fear Suspicions and Reflexions may be thrown upon you by the World, as if this Change of Sentiment must have arisen from your Observation during that Cruize, that Capt. Jones lov'd close fighting, that Capt. Landais was skilful in keeping out of Harm's-way, and that therefore you thought yourselves safer with the Latter. For myself, I believe you to be brave Men, and Lovers of your Country and its glorious Cause; and I am persuaded you have only been ill advis'd, and misled by the artful and malicious Misrepresentations of some Persons I guess at. Take in good Part this friendly Counsel of an old Man, who is your friend. Go home peaceably with your Ship. Do your Duties faithfully and chearfully. Behave respectfully to your Commander, and I am persuaded he will do the same to you. Thus you will not only be happier in your Voyage, but recommend yourselves to the future favours of Congress, and to the Esteem of your Country. I have the honour to be Gentlemen Your most Obedient and most humble Servant.   B Franklin

To Lieutenant James Degge of The Ship Alliance, and other Officers of the said Ship, at L'Orient

Copy

Notation: Letter from Doctr Franklin to the Officers on board the Alliance June 7. 1780 No 1.

From the Officers of the *Alliance*

LS: University of Pennsylvania Library; copy: National Archives

Please your Excellency   LOrient June 7. 1780

We had the honor of addressing your Excellency the 31st. May, in which we gave some account of our present situation and Requested your Excellency to have us paid off and sent home with all the Expedition your Excellency could afford us.

We also made some mention of our Captain Landais, whose Loss we regreted, and under whose Command we wished to Return to America; as we did not then express our minds fully on that subject, We beg Leave to do it now by Representing to your Excellency that we have reason to think there never was a Ships Company of Officers and men more unanimous for a Captain, than the Alliance's in this Instance for Captain Landais; and since Congress has given him so good a right to Command us we hope your Excellency will condescend to Restore him to us— It was always our oppinions that he was a Capable & good Captain, his behaviour in the Engagement was such as certainly envinced it, The aspersions of his Enemies may have prevailed over your Excellency's Goodness, but your Excellency may believe us sincere when we assure you that we all fore & Aft wish to see him reinstated.

We would also beg Leave to represent to your Excellency that according to the Customs and Regulations of our Navy we hold ourselves bound to obey him and no other as Commander while our Engagement continues, unless he is removed by the forms prescribed in our Rules.

Your Excellency's Kind Indulgence in the few reasonable things we have presumed to ask, will Restore to us tranquility and induce us to return your Excellency our unfeigned thanks.

We are with the profoundest respect your Excellencys most obedient & most devoted humble Servants

James Degge	Thos Hinsdale
John Buckley	Isaac Carr
James Lynd	James Warren
John Larchar Junr.	Thos. Elwood
Benjamin Pierce	Arthur Robertson
James Bragg	Chipn. Bangs

JOHN DARLING   N BLODGET

Addressed: His Excellency Dr. Benja. Franklin / Minister plenipo to the United / States / at Passy / near Paris

Endorsed: Officers of the Alliance June 7. 80 L'Orient—

From John Torris

ALS: American Philosophical Society

Honnd Sir   Dunkerque 7th. June 1780.

I have Shown to Capt. Dowlin the Letter your Excellency did me the Honnor to write me concerning the Peter & Friendship, his Truely British Prises.[7] Your entertained suspicions grieved him to the Soul; He is no Pirate & wishes, for the amazing Suspicion, he never had a Commission from the Congress. Your Excellency is witness he made an honnorable use of it, therefore, he deserves Commandation, as well as his Consort the Intrepid Macatter, & not, indeed, such a Terrible reward! My sorrows & anxiety on the head are no Less than his own. He did Search Immediatly the few Papers he saved from Berck, & we Luckily, for his Vendication, found 2. Letters, a Bill of Lading, a Draught, & 2. accounts, fully Proving what The Friendship & her Cargo are. He deposited them at our admiralty with a full report, to be by them sent to your Excellency. The Circumstances therein mentd., will I hope, & at last, determine the Condamnation of the Peter & her Cargo; our admiralty says that the Councill at Paris wou'd requiere no other Proof in Such Particular Cases.[8] Your Excellency sees the reasons why the masters & mates of the Two Vessells Signed for them & their Crew, we hope 'Twill be Satisfactory. Capt. Thos. Byrne of the Peter had Capital motives to throw his Papers over Board with his Bags of Letters, before Striking.

Messrs. J. Diot & Co. have sent to your Excellency the Duplicates of the *Procès Verbeaux* relative to the Betsey, as early as

7. Above, May 27.
8. Torris enclosed a five-page inquest (dated June 6) of the Admiralty of Dunkirk concerning the *Black Prince* and her prizes *Peter* and *Friendship*.

the 10th. ulto., but I have not yet heard that the Condamnation was granted?

The Same Gentlemen have Sent your Excellency the short Journal of the New Black Princess. I hope your Excellency will do Justice to the Intrepidity of Capt. Macatter & his Brave Boys, who fought 9. hours 3. Guernsey Privateers of 18. guns 6. Pounders each, under Cap Lezard, in a Calm, haveing 6. Ransomers on Board, & they Cutted every one To Pieces.

Capt. Ryan has greatly distinguisht himself in the Fear nought, who is now here under repairs to Continue shortly his Cruise.[9]

I have sent to Morlaix the directions your Excellency addressed me the 30th. ulto. relative to Neutral Vessells.

I have the Honnour to be with greatest respect Honnd. Sir your Excellency's most obedient & most Humble Servant

J. TORRIS

His Excellency Dr. Franklin

Endorsed: June 7

Notation: Mr. Torris. June 7th. 1780

From Dumas   ALS: National Archives; copy: Algemeen Rijksarchief

Monsieur,   La Haie 8e. Juin 1780.

Mr. Van de Perre, Directr. de la Compe. des Indes or. pour la Zélande, & en société de Commerce avec Mr. Meyners, m'a parlé plusieurs fois de l'affaire du Vaisseau, tant chez moi que chez lui à l'Hôtel des Indes. Enfin sur le billet, dont ci-joint copie,[1] j'ai été lui protester que je ne pouvois rien de plus que ce

---

9. The *Fearnot*'s first cruise had begun with her departure from Dunkirk on March 24; it is described in Clark, *Ben Franklin's Privateers*, pp. 125–8. She did not sail again until about July 8: *ibid*, p. 157.

1. On June 7 van de Perre asked for Dumas' suggestions on how to proceed in the affair of the *Berkenbos* (*Berkenbosch*), "considérant que tout ce que je ferai pour la réclame sera pour indemniser autant que possible le Congrès, qui, en second lieu a son recours à leur Officier Paul Jones." A copy of this note, in Dumas' hand, is with the present letter at the National Archives and presumably is the "billet" in question.

que j'avois déjà écrit, n'ayant aucun pouvoir. Il m'a avoué alors, que le Billet étoit pour que je vous en fisse parvenir copie, Monsieur, avec la substance de la Lettre de son Patron de Navire, que j'avois déjà préparé;[2] ajoutant *confidemment,* que le Premier Noble de Zélande lui avoit conseillé de faire cette démarche auprès de vous par mon canal, pour éviter un éclat désagréable à la Rep. & aux Etats-Unis, s'il étoit obligé de faire réclamer le navire en Angleterre en s'adressant pour cet effet à L.H.P.; & que la Cour d'Angleterre, en ce cas, ne demanderoit pas mieux que de renvoyer les réclamants à ceux par qui la prise s'est faite. Il a tout lieu d'espérer, que sans cet éclat, qui gâteroit l'affaire, le vaisseau &c. sera relaché à Antigue sur la foi des papiers, qui sont en ordre & authentiques: en ce cas, il n'importunera pas les Etats-Unis pour la répétition des fraix; il se consolera généreusement de ce dommage. Mais si, contre son attente, le bâtiment n'étoit pas restitué à Antigue, il s'attendra à la Justice des Etats-Unis pour ravoir ce qui lui appartient.

Il me charge donc de demander à V. Exce., comment il doit se conduire? Doit-il s'adresser à Leurs H.P., & par-là à la Cour d'Angleterre? ou non? Quelle est l'alternative, Monsieur, que Vous lui conseillez, comme la meilleure, & pour les Etats-Unis, & pour lui?

Ayez la bonté, Monsieur, de ne parler d'aucune autre chose dans la réponse que vous me ferez là-dessus, afin que je puisse la produire au besoin à Mr. Van de Perre, à qui j'ai dû promettre d'envoyer copie de la dite réponse en Zélande dès que je l'aurai reçue.

Je suis avec un très-grand respect, Monsieur, De V. Exc. le très-humble & très-obéissant serviteur   DUMAS

Passy à Son Exce. M. Franklin

Notations in different hands: Mr. Dumas to B. F. and Mr. Van de Perre to Mr. Dumas June 7. 1780 / June 8. 80

2. See our annotation of Dumas to BF, May 26.

From Arthur Lee

ALS: Historical Society of Pennsylvania; AL (draft): National Archives

Sir,   L'Orient June 9th. 1780.
I have now waited here three months for the Alliance, & see
no probability of her sailing. The discontent of the Crew has in-
creasd to such a degree, as in my judgment to threaten the most
ruinous consequences, if their demands are not satisfyd.[3]
I feel it as a duty to the Public to give you this information; &
have the honor to be, with respect, Sir, Yr. most obedient humble servant   ARTHUR LEE

The Honble. Dr. Franklin. Minister plenipotentiary

Notation: June 9. 1780 A Lee to B Franklin had waited at L'orient
3 months for the sailing of the Alliance. Discontent of the Crew

From Jonathan Williams, Jr.: Two Letters

(I) ALS: University of Pennsylvania Library; copy: Yale University Library; (II) ALS: American Philosophical Society, copy: Yale University
Library

I.

Dear & hond Sir   Nantes June 9 1780
Inclosed is a Memorial from my Friends Messrs V & P French
& nephew of Bordeaux to the Director of the Finnances, relative to a Seizure of some Tobacco to their address in consequence of an erroneus Declaration, which is the sole Effect of
Ignorance of the real Quantity as you will see by the Memorial.

---

3. The crew's main demand was for Landais to resume command. On
June 12, in response to Landais's request for advice, Lee gave him his opinion that an officer entrusted with command of a ship was bound to keep,
guard, and defend that ship until he saw a congressional resolve giving command to another. Thus, Landais should keep command of the *Alliance* until
formally relieved: National Archives; Landais, *Memorial,* pp. 99–100.

I think there can be no doubt of Redress if the Fact is fairly known, and I therefore request you will kindly give the Memorial your Sanction and send it to Mr Necker.—[4]

It is a hardship on Trade in general to be obliged to make a Declaration of what the Person who declares cannot be certain, & yet be subject to Penalty, if it is not true; Ridiculous as this appears it is no less the Law, and the Custom House Officers never allow any Interpretation than what the Letter of the Law exactly conveys.—

I beg to repeat my Request to let the inclosed be sent to Mr Necker & am ever with the greatest Respect Dear & hond Sir Yours most dutifully & affectionately   JONA WILLIAMS J

The Honble Doctor Franklin.

Notation: Jona Williams June 9 80

II.

Dear & hond Sir   Nantes June 9. 1780.

Since my last by Mr Ross, Capt Jones has passed through this Place & I find by him that he has obtained the Frigate Ariel to carry out the arms at L'Orient and part of Mr Ross's Goods; although I understood that there would be as much as the Ariel would Carry, I have determined to send at least 2000 Suits of Cloathing in hopes to get them on board even if some of the arms should be left, for our army want Cloathing more than Guns. I have likewise determined to go myself to L'Orient & if possible to find a Ship there to join the Alliance & carry out the remainder of the Cloathing, in which Case I shall order those at Brest as well as the remainder here to be sent to L'Orient by Land with the utmost Expedition, but if I do not succeed immediately I will take a Trip to Paris to consult with you on some means of putting this matter into Execution for if our Cloathing does not get out this Summer our Troops must suffer much next Win-

4. They sent their memorial (missing) to JW on June 7; he acknowledged receipt on June 11, assuring them that he had forwarded it to BF (Yale University Library). BF in turn sent it to Necker on the 19th; see Necker's letter of June 26. The firm had been doing business with America since at least 1776: *Jefferson Papers,* I, 519.

ter.— The new Frigate I mentioned in my last is sold it is therefore too late to think of that Plan.— Vessells ready fitted should now be the Object in order to detain the Alliance as short a Time as possible, at all Events that Ship ought not to leave these Goods behind her.—

Please to drop me a Line directed to me at Mr Moylans L'Orient & let me know if you have concluded anything with Mr Ross.

Mr de Chaumont in his last Letter seems to think that he has not been readily enough supplied with Funds to answer my Bills on him. I supposed he would have received the Payments destined for this Object at the several Periods you mentioned to me, one is past & the second near at hand, which should make half the Sum required. I told him I would write to you on the Subject, tho' I do not in Fact know how the matter Stands. The Payments at the Periods fixed should answer the Purpose for I have always pushed my Bills at so long a Date as not to take anything in advance from those periods.—

It is reported here that lamotte Piquet is gone to Charlestown with his Divisions, if this is true & he arrives in Time Mr Clinton will have another baulk.—

I am with the greatest Respect Dear & hond Sir Yours most dutifully & Affectionately   JONA WILLIAMS J

I have been confined 8 Days with a wounded Leg which is the reason my Journey to L'Orient has been delayed.

Endorsed: M. de Chaumont's Complaint that Funds had not been furnished to pay his Acceptances—(not founded) as he had then near 100,000 livres in his Hands

Notation: Jona Williams June 9 1780

From Marie-Françoise Le Ray de Chaumont: Bill for a Horse and Carriage[5]

DS: American Philosophical Society

[June 10–October 2, 1780]

Monsieur franklin doit pour dépenses Ci a Pres

Savoir

Loyer d'une Voiture pendant trois mois à Compter du 10. juin der. [dernier] au 10. court. [courant][6] à 360. Chaque mois	1080
Nourriture d'un Cheval de Main pendant Le dit tems cest 92. jours à 32. sols	147. 4
ferrages du Cheval pour 3. mois	9.
brosses étrilles, Longes, graisse &a. le tout pour 3 mois à 5 *l.t.*	15.
	£1251. 4

Je reconnois avoir reçû de Monsieur le Docteur franklin La somme de douze cent cinquante une livre quatre sols pour le montant des depenses ci dessus faites pour son Compte à Passi ce. 2. Octobre 1780. Pour sol de tout conte pour ce qui conserne la depance de lecurie   LERAY DE CHAUMONT FILLE AINÉE

N.B. M franklin voudra bien indiquer depuis quel tems Le Cheval de main est au compte de Mr. Deane pour qua l'avenir La dépense qui le concerne [*soit*] retranchée des memoires de Mr. franklin

5. Although BF's accounts (in particular Account VI, XXIII, 21, and Account XXIII, XXIX, 3) record periodic payments for a carriage, coachmen, saddle horses, harnesses, and other accoutrements, this is the first bill we have found. The previous recorded payment to Mlle de Chaumont, made on Feb. 16, was for 1,871 *l.t.*: XXXI, 5. See also XXVIII, 4n, where we describe WTF's analysis of the financial advantage of buying a carriage, instead of continuing to rent.

6. The bill had been drawn up on Sept. 12. Mlle de Chaumont changed the date (just above her signature) to Oct. 2, the date on which the payment was recorded in Account VI.

From ——— Destouches[7]

ALS: University of Pennsylvania Library

Monseigneur,   Dunkerque ce 10e. juin 1780.

J'ai L'honneur d'informer vôtre Excellence, que jai fait porter ce jour a la poste aux Lettres La Grosse des Suplemens des procedure dinstruction des prises Le Pierre et L'amitié faites par le Capne. Patrice Dowlin Commandant Le Corsaire ameriquain Le Prince noir, Les quelles deux prises ont eté conduittes a morlaix.[8] Le Raport fait pardevant les officiers de cette amirauté, instruira vôtre Excellence des motifs de ces procedures. Je joins icy Les Certificats de cet Envoy, du directeur du Bureau de la de. Porte.

Je Suis avec un tres profond Respect, Monseigneur De Vôtre Excellence, Le tres humble et très obeïssant Serviteur.

DESTOUCHES Greffier En Chef

From Thomas Digges   ALS: Historical Society of Pennsylvania

Dr. Sir   Camberwell 10th June 1780

I find my letter to you of the 9th. ulo. was lost by the Packets being taken & the mails thrown overboard. Those of the 24th advising of the Bishops picture being sent you via ostend to the care of Mr Bowens, that of the 26 by Post inclosing the Gazette, & that of the 29th. offering you from Mr S—— H——tl—y any part of some Good Rum that he has lying at Dunkirque, I could not yet in course hear had got safe to yr. hands.[9] I should be glad of a line to the former direction (*W.S. Church*) when the picture gets in safety for the partys are anxious about it. I should also be very glad to know the fate of my application for *an other picture* which I have very much at heart.

7. The clerk of the Admiralty of Dunkirk, with whom BF had corresponded previously about prizes of the *Black Prince:* XXX, 513–14. This letter's dateline might also read "16."

8. On June 7, above, Torris told BF that the admiralty would forward documents about the *Peter* and *Friendship* (probably the package herein enclosed and now missing).

9. Digges' May 24 and 29 letters are above, but that of the 26th is missing.

I am much with Mr. H——s——n, & D H——,[1] & we have been many weeks in expectation of a line (as promisd in yr. last to Mr H——s——n) relative to the Cartel, about which no one step has been yet taken here owing to the Expectation by every post of getting an explanatory letter from you, & which is also wishd for by the Board who seem inclinable to let another Cargoe go.— There is not now above 260 in all.

Not a syllable lately from the Westward, & from the late very alarming tumults & insurrections in & abot. London, there is no more talk abot Clinton or America than if no such Country existed. The Bearer of this is a young man taken lately in a ship of Monsr Chamonts,[2] and I have sent by him 8 or 10 News papers, which, with his own accot of what He saw, will more fully explain than I can do in sheets of Paper the late disturbances, Riots, insurrections, & Conflagrations, which have happend.[3] I inclose you a news-paper plan of the ground wch abot. 100,000 People took on the 2d Int., from wch time until yesterday all Law, Police, or Government, seemd totally at a stand, & the whole City & suberbs were in the hands of a set of People revelling in distruction to private Property as well as the publick Goals, in riot, drunkenness & disorder. The *Bank of England* was in the most imminent danger; for had not some zealous patriot led the mob from the Flames of New-gate to Lord Mansfields house in Bloomsbury, in one hour the Bank might have been put in flames & the whole funds & Country set compleatly afloat. *All* the Civil as well as Mility. force (wch in all did not amot. to 5,000 men) were placed to protect the western parts of the Town, so that about 50 resolute fellows were left uninterruptedly to destroy new gate & many other Edifices. In one hour

1. Mr. Hodgson and David Hartley. BF's latest letter to William Hodgson was that of April 11, above.

2. The bearer was James Barnett, Jr., captain of a ship partly owned by Chaumont: XXVI, 415n, 677; XXVIII, 69–70, 322; XXIX, 328; Elias and Finch, *Letters of Digges*, p. 216.

3. The Gordon riots, the most violent mob episode in London during the eighteenth century: Christopher Hibbert, *King Mob: the Story of Lord George Gordon and the London Riots of 1780* (Cleveland and New York, 1958); Colin Haydon, *Anti-Catholicism in Eighteenth-Century England, c. 1714-80 . . .* (Manchester and New York, 1993), pp. 204–44.

& a half the Strongest prison in Europe was forcibly enterd &
the whole Edifice in flames—half that period would have done
for the Bank of England, & the danger it was then in & has been
since by the threats of the Mob, causd a considerable run thereon
Tuesday & *Wedy* last. The Riot seems now compleatly over. The
Bank is guarded very strong, but even till yesterday the Excha.
was more a Barrack for Troops of Horse & foot soldiery than
the walk of Merchants— Never was a City in such confusion—
It would be impossible to describe it to You without filling pages.
The privy Council on Wedy. issued a proclamation for Martial
Law, or rather to give power to the Soldiery to act as majestrates
& punish with immediate Death all disorderly Persons in consequence of which a great number have been killd & wounded—
This martial Law still subsists & in consequence of it neither
house of Parliamt can sit nor Courts of justice do Business—
The head quarter of justice *now* is at the Horse Guards, & the
Commander of the army is Lord Chief Justice— The cat is let
out of the bag, & if there is one sovereign in Europe more happy
than another at this present moment it is the Defender of the
Faith— now at the head of his *Respectable* military. By His man-
date aided by a party of horse as well as foot—Lord G Gordon[4]
was yesterday at 5 o Ck. taken up, underwent some artful Examn
at *the Horse Guards,* & was committed to the Tower in the night
for High Treason. How this may opperate the Lord knows, but
there seems a flame among the People even in distant parts of the
realm not to lett the matter rest quiet, & I should not be surprizd
to hear of 40,000 Protestants from the North rising to demand
His release. Your predictions have all come right about this
Country—surely there never was an instance of *Greatness* getting so rapiddly down to insignificance & contempt; but *the People,* even yet, do not seem to understand the cause of it all. This
is the Country, the mighty & all powerful people who were to
bring America to unconditional submission!!!— Adieu my

4. Lord George Gordon (1751–1793), the president of the Protestant Association, who at the head of 60,000 people had presented an anti-Catholic
petition to the House of Commons, precipitating the riots. At his trial the following year, however, he was found not guilty of treason: *DNB;* Namier and
Brooke, *House of Commons,* II, 513–15.

Good Sir, may Heaven favour all Your undertakings & turn the
hearts & Minds of Men to what is right & fit— Yrs mo truly

ALEXR BRETT

I forgot to mention to you that the Cartel wch was seizd at Bristol has been paid for to Mr Mitchell her owner[5] by the Admiralty
2918:8:8 after his dancing attendance 4 or 5 mos. However it is
an *ample* sum for the vessel & loss of time to the concernd.

I wrote you the 30th ulo. for a pass for Dr Upton Scotts Baggage in case of his being taken by an amn privateer on his way
to N York— He goes I believe in the same ship with Loyd— He
has been formerly known to you as a phisical man in Annapolis
has been some years from there after some property in Ireland
& is a good man respected by the Country & came away with
full approbation of the People. If it can be given please to inclose
it to me under cover to Messrs. W Hodgson & Co or Messrs.
French & Hopson.

Endorsed: June 10. 80

From Wulffen LS: American Philosophical Society

Monsieur   Paris 10: Juin 1780.

J'ai l'honneur de joindre ici 3. Lettres que je supplie Votre Excellence de vouloir bien faire passer en Amerique. Leur contenu
ne renferme autre chose que l'annonce de mon arrivée, & de
mon séjour en cette ville. Cÿ-inclus aussi les 3. Billets tous signés
en vous suppliant de vouloir bien me remettre le billet que le
Medecin-chirurgien de Mr. Le Bon. de Golz ministre prussien a
eu l'honneur de vous faire.

Souffrez, Monsieur, que je vous remercie très humblement
des 12. Louis;[6] Votre Excellence voudra bien me permettre de lui
en demander trente (30) autres pour la huitaine s'il est possible,
& d'en agir ainsi pour le reste de la somme qui m'est duë: n'ayant

5. Henry Mitchell was owner of the *Polly.*
6. Which Wulffen signed a promise to repay on June 8; see our editorial
note on promissory notes, above. The transaction was recorded as "12
Guineas more" (under the date of June 10) in BF's Cash Book.

pas le tems d'ecrire dans quelques unes de mes terres, Je ne saurois, sans cela, vivre, autrement qu'à l'aide d'autrui, sorte de vie qui n'entre pas dans mon Système.

Je vous Supplie, Monsieur, de vouloir bien m'honorer de vos ordres pour que Je puisse après la guerison de mes blessures me rembarquer, & aller en Amerique satisfaire les désirs de mon coeur, vanter votre administration en france, & Signer de mon Sang La reconnoissance, & le profond respect avec lequel je me ferai gloire de mourir Monsieur Votre très humble & très obéissant serviteur   BARON: JOHAN HENRICH DE: WULFFEN

Le Baron de Wulffen Capitaine & chef dun Corps de Cavalerie Legere au Service des 13. Etats Unies de L'amerique a l'hotel des Mousquetaires gris dans le fond de la deuxieme cour rue du Bacque fauxbourg St Germain.

To Wulffen   AL (draft): American Philosophical Society

Sir,   Passy, June 11. 1780

I shall take care to send your three Letters to America as you desire. I am sorry you are not satisfy'd with the 20 Guineas I have lent you but demand 30 more. I know nothing of what may be due to you, nor have I any Authority to pay it. I sent you Word with the last Money, that you were not to expect any more of me, and I now confirm it; there are too many exchang'd Prisoners continually applying to me for Relief, and I cannot advance to every one such Sums as in consideration of your Wounds I have advanc'd to you.— Nor can I advise you to return to America in the Condition you are in; for if you should be taken and put again in an English Prison, it may be fatal to you. Your Family, particularly your Sister Madame Sonnemaens would be happy to have you at home with them. I have the honour to be, Sir, Y. m. o. h. S.

M. le Baron de Wulffen, Hôtel des Musquetaires gris, dans le fond de la deuxieme Cour, Rue du Bacque faubourg St Germaine à Paris

From John Torris

ALS: American Philosophical Society

Honnd. Sir   Dunkerque 11th. June 1780.

My Correspondants at Morlaix & Capt. Macatter send me a Copy of their report & of the Letters they had the Honnor to write to your Excellency.[7] The Circumstances & great Losses attended with the abusive detaintion of the Black Princess, are a havey Strock on us, as they are not only missing the Best opportunities to make Prises & to destress the Ennemy, but the expences to maintain so many men are very great endeed; & Instead of Proffitting by the fitting of so Stout & good a Cutter, if she is not Instantly Let at Liberty to sail, we will be apt to loose.

I can answer to your Excellency for the Innocence of the good Natured & Brave Capt. Macatter in the affair, & also for the Truth of their report & of their representations.

It is not the first Complaint we have to make against the Commissary at Morlaix.[8] He is the Prime Cause of the Loss of the Poor Black Prince By disbanding all her Crew; He is really watchfull of all opportunity to mollest all americans & Specially the Captains & officers of our Privateers; He has the weakness to be affected with Jealousy for their Bravery & Success! He exceeds by far his orders & the dispositions of his *Superieurs*. I Beseech your Excellency will represent this Busey Commissary's Behavior to My Lord De Sartine, who's Intention, I am sure, is not to give a longer Chance to the Ennemy, by detaining so good a Privateer in Morlaix, & To the Immense Loss of all Concerns & Contrary to the Laws of Nations & to the Treaties Subsisting with America: Supose, nay, Capt. Macatter shou'd appear Blamable; But I do Insist his fault does proceed from Ignorance, & endeed, so good & so Brave a man as he Proves to be, deserves all Indulgences from his allies. His Ennemy wou'd show him generosity.

I Beseech your Excellency will Claim the departure of the Princess without any farther delay & we expect the Same from

7. The Admiralty extract described in Diot to BF, June 2, above, is filed with the present letter at the APS, so Torris may have enclosed both Diot's letter and the extract. Macatter's communication is missing.

8. Torris complained of Boucault on April 15, as Diot did on June 2, both above.

your Justice. I am with all respect Honnd. Sir your Excellency's
Most Humble & most obedient Servant   J. TORRIS

P.S. Your Excellency might easily obtain the asked for Prisonners
from my Lord De Sartine, If you wou'd apply, & you will add
to our gratitude.

His Excellency Dr. Franklin minister at the Court of France.

Endorsed: M. Torris June 11.

Notation: Mr. Torris June 11th. 1780

To John Paul Jones

LS:[9] National Archives; copy:[1] Library of Congress

Dear Sir,   Passy June 12. 1780.
     Saturday Morning last, I received a Letter Signed by about 115
of the Sailors of the *Alliance*,[2] declaring that they would not
raise the Anchor nor Depart from L'orient, till they had six
Months Wages paid them, and the utmost farthing of their Prize
money, including the Ships sent into Norway, and until *their legal Captain P. Landais* is restored to them; or to that Effect, for
I have not the Letter before me: this Mutiny has undoubtedly
been excited by that Captain, probably by making them believe
that satisfaction has been received for those Norway Prizes de-

9. In the hand of L'Air de Lamotte.
1. Also in Lamotte's hand. A lengthy extract is at the Harvard University
Library. Dated "Boston, 26th. Augt. 1780.," it is certified by James Warren,
Jr., and Fitch Pool as a true copy of one sent by Jones to Capt. Parke while
at Lorient. Warren was an officer of the *Alliance*, Pool (XXIX, 38) the captain's clerk. It is reproduced in Bradford, *Jones Papers*, reel 5, no. 1111, enclosure 4.
2. The crew's letter of June 1 is discussed in our annotation of the April
12 letter from the officers of the *Alliance;* BF is correct, below, about Landais'
interlineation. Landais' covering letter must be his of May 29, above. The
preceding Saturday was June 10.

liver'd up to the English, which God knows is not true; the Court of Denmark not having yet resolv'd to give us a Shilling on that Account. That he is concern'd in this Mutiny, he has been foolish enough to furnish us with Proofs, the Sailors Letter being not only enclos'd under a Cover directed to me in his hand Writing, but, he has also in the Same Writing interlin'd the Words, *their legal Captain P. Landais* which happen to contain his Signature. I went immediately to Versailles to demand the Assistance of Government, and on showing the Letter by which his Guilt plainly appear'd, an Order was immediately granted and sent away the same evening, for apprehending and imprisoning him, and Orders were promis'd to be given at the same time to the Commissary of the Port, to afford you all kind Assistance[3] to facilitate your Depart.[4] Mr. de Chaumont being with me, and assisting warmly in obtaining these Orders, we thought it best at the same time to give Directions, that those Sailors who have signed this Letter should not be favour'd with receiving any Part of the Money order'd to be advanc'd in part of what it is supposed the Serapis and Countess may be sold for, unless to such as express their Sorrow for having been so misled, and willingness to do their Duty; and that they may be known, their Letter was sent down to M. de Monplaisir;[5] but care should be taken, that it be return'd as it contains the Proofs abovementioned against Landais, who will probably be try'd for his Life, being consider'd by the Ministers as an Emigrant without the king's Permission and therefore still a frenchman, and when found in france still subject to its Laws.— When that Advance was ordered, it was Supposed the Vessels might have been got away without waiting for the sale, and that the People who had a Right to share them, receiving this in Part to relieve their present Necessities, might have appointed Some Agent to receive and remit the rest to them in America; but the Delays have been so great that the Time of Sale now approaches, and perhaps the Produce may be

3. In the copy, "all kind of Assistance".
4. On June 19 Port Commandant Thévenard and *Commissaire* Grandville were told officially that the King had ceded the *Ariel* to the United States for a campaign: Archives de la Marine, B²CDXIX: 9.
5. Montigny de Monplaisir appears to have been acting as Chaumont's representative in Lorient: Chaumont to BF, June 19, below.

known before you can be ready to depart with the Ariel, and, if ready Money is paid, the Division may be made at once. If any unforeseen Difficulties Should arise to prevent this, I see no other way but to Separate those who cannot trust to their Country to do them Justice, and put them on shore, and let them wait for their shares at their own Expence, for tis unreasonable to keep the Ship here at so monstrous an Expence to the Publick, for their private Advantage or Humours. As to Wages, I have no Authority or Means of paying Wages here; and I believe that all maritime states pay their ships at home; for it cannot be supposed that Pay-Offices are to be kept in every Part of the World to which ships may happen to go; besides It cannot be known here what their families or Attorneys have receiv'd for them.— I see you are likely to have a great deal of Trouble. It requires Prudence. I wish you well thro' it. You have shown your abilities in fighting. You have now an Opportunity of showing the other necessary Part in the Character of a great Chief, your Abilities in governing.— Adieu

Yours sincerely, B FRANKLIN

Honble. Commodore Jones Commander of the Alliance frigate at L'orient.

Notation: From his Excellency Dr. Franklin Passy June 12th 1780 No. 35.

From Alexander Gillon   LS: American Philosophical Society

Sir   L'Orient 12 June 1780

When I had the pleasure of seeing you last,[6] I acquainted your Excellency that there was strong hopes, that I should want Seamen & requested your Aid which you was pleased to promise me, observing that there was no men wanted for the immediate Service of the Continent, as the Alliance had more men than she wanted, I have now the direction of One Vessell for the Service

6. Probably the preceding September, before Gillon left for Germany and the Netherlands: XXXI, 183n.

of the State of South Carolina[7] and am about buying others, thus have come here to accept of the Services of such American Officers & Seamen as are under no Engagements to any, but as there appears difficulties that I wish to avoid, I have done but my Duty in Stateing Facts to His Excellency Monsr. De Sartine and as your Excellency was Nominated by the Rulers of America as their Representative here, I cannot do wrong in Troubling you with a Copy of said Letter,[8] & Stateing to you what is Necessary you should know, requesting in the Name of the State of South Carolina your support; the Seamen here, at Nantes, Morlaix, St. Malo, Havre de Grace & Dunkirk, that are disengaged & that are Americans I am about entering in to the Service of that State & have therefore as you see, wrote his Excellency requesting him to acquaint the proper Officers at the above different Ports of this my business, that they may not impede it, but furnish me with the proper Passports for such Americans as I have engaged in the State Service—

As I have Officially been applied to this day, by the Officers of the Continental Frigate of War the Alliance, I conceive it to be my Duty to acquaint your Excellency therewith & therefore inclose you my reply thereto,[9] that you may be aufait of all I do herein & to avoid misrepresentation, and that by your Superior Influence, you may direct the alarming consequence to be prevented that must follow, should any Arm'd force of this Country interfere in the regulations of the Navy of America, which Regulations have been established by our Rulers, thus no Officer can Err that abides by them & Acts conformable to the Laws of the Land—

Your Excellency well knows that I have ever avoided interfereing with the Officers & direction of any of the Continental

7. The frigate *South Carolina*, formerly *Indien*, which Gillon leased on May 30: XXXI, 184n.

8. A June 12 letter to Sartine in which Gillon has asked the support of the French *commissaire* at Lorient for his efforts to obtain crewmen from the *Alliance*. A copy of it at the APS bears BF's notation, "Commodore Gillon to M. de Sartine."

9. Also written on June 12, Gillon's letter (Landais, *Memorial*, pp. 99–100) expressed the opinion that Landais was "in honor and duty bound to directly take and keep command of the said Alliance." A copy is with BF's papers at the APS.

Ships in Europe, otherwise I should have avoided all that has now happned, as you know I was clear of opinion last year, that all Vessells that appeared to be Continental in this Harbour last June & July should have directly proceeded to the Relief of the Country whose Flagg they hoisted, excepting your Excellency or the Captains of such Ships had positive orders to send them on other Cruizes, and as a further proof, you know I at same time offerd to go with all the State Officers under my direction as Volenteers in that Fleet then fitting out here if going to America, This I say proves I did not seek to interfere with Continental Officers, but Sir, when ever I am Officially called on for my opinion, I should be wanting in my Duty, did I neglect giving it, I therefore gave it (as per inclosed Copy) as an Officer and as a Citisen of America, and so Clear am I in it, that I shall trouble the Honble. the Continental Congress with a relation of all I do in this & every of my business in Europe, & shall also request the Governor of the State under whose particular direction I am, to lay my Conduct in this Matter regularly before Congress, if I have erred in this opinion it can only proceed from being Ignorant of any Order Congress has sent to Capt. Landais, to deliver up the Alliance to you, to appoint another Captain, because as Capt. Landais has a possitive Order from Congress for the Command of the Alliance & that the Admiralty or Navy Board, still address Capt. Landais as Capt. of the Alliance,[1] he and every proper Officer in the Service must conceive it to be his Duty to take Care of his Ship, your Excellency may therefore I presume easily rectify this dispute by complying with what every officer has a right to demand before he obeys, that is, by your directing any person whom you Nominate to Superceed Capt Landais to produce your Order you gave to your Officer; to Capt. Landais, as also to the next Officer on board the Alliance, when ever your officer goes on board to take Command, and I moreover think, that Capt. Landais has a right to Demand from you a Copy of any Order that Congress has given you relative to him & the Alliance, & I also Conceive that if Capt. Landais should not be on board the Alliance, when your Officer goes on board to take Command, the first Lieut. of that Ship should also see that Order.— This Sir is Usual in all Services,

1. In the April 1 letter described in our annotation of Landais to BF, May 29.

else any man might go on board of any Ship & take Command
of her.

I hope your Excellency will do me the justice to believe that
all my Conduct herein proceeds from no other motive but a true
regard to the Country I ever will revere & from a Justice that is
due to every Officer in our Service, and because I am called on
Officially in this unhappy business; which I conceive is in your
power to redress in a few words, by furnishing Capt Landais
with a Copy of Congress's Order about him & the Alliance that
orders him out of the Ship, or else by letting him act conformable
to his Orders & to the Rules, our Rulers have prescribed—

This Sir may prevent very fatal Consequences, as I ever will
maintain the Doctrine that no foreign Power has a right to interfere (particularly by Force) with an American Naval regulation,
& that no Officer can be divested of his Command but by those
who gave it him & Even then by a regular Court Martial.

Another affair causes me now to interfere in a line of Command that I never wished to see canvass'd but at home, it is Sir
Abt. a number of American Officers & Seamen that are here disengaged, some of which are on board the Alliance which Ship
has her full Complement of Men & most of those Surplus men,
came out of a long confinement in England went on board of the
Alliance to keep themselves from Starving,[2] These very men are
now prevented from coming on Shore to Enter into Actual Service & to return home, and are threatned if they leave the Ship
to Enter with me, they will be carried on board by an Armed
Force of this Country, This being the Case it behoves me to support those men as Freemen, who knows no Compulsion, & thus
to prevent as much as in me lies this takeing place: I must therefore Crave your Excellency to join your Endeavours to procure
me Letters from Monsr. De Sartine to the proper Officers at the
different Sea Ports, to grant me passes for such men as I Ship that
are not Engaged & that are Americans, also that they will grant
me the Aid, Allies have a right to request—

Your Excellency will also observe it is my Duty to purchass
the Seraphis Prize Ship of War, if the Government does not

2. Arthur Lee later accused James Moylan, acting as Jones's agent, of attempting to starve the crew of the *Alliance:* Lee to James Warren, Oct. 30,
1780, Mass. Hist. Soc. *Collections,* LXXIII (1925), 143.

want her, and as I Know what Aid has been given to Ships of Warr of America I presume I am also intitled to it, and may with propriety request it, I am not in the least Alterd in my Zeal for to Serve the Country I revere, disapointment wets invention; the more difficulties the more Honnor, & tho I cannot exactly conceive from what Quarter, I've been so uniformly opposed since I have been in Europe, yet as I am now at Actual Service & am fitting out, I am Clear of Opinion any future opposition must proceed from a Superior Power & force, this I do not now presume will take place as the Matters are too farr gone to be stopt but by an opposition from Government & Ministers, Your Excellency will please to consider I address you Officially and do not mean to Offend, but to Act, Speak & write as every Freeman of America has a right to do; with every respect I have the Honor to be Your Excellency's Most obedient & most Humble Servant

A. GILLON
Commodore of the Navy
of the State of South Carolina

Your Excellencys reply per return of Post will oblige me under Cover to Messrs. Heretiers Foucaud Merchts. here.

His Excellency Benjamin Franklin Esqr.

Endorsed: Recd. Monday Morning near 10 oClock June 19.— / Commodore Gillon's Letters to B F. inclosing one to M. de Sartine another to Capt. Landais.

Notation: 12 June 1780

From John Rainey[3]

ALS: American Philosophical Society

Sir   Amsterdam June 12h: 1780.

I hope your Excely. will Excuse my taking the Liberty of troubling you with my Affairs, all the Excuse I can alledge is my Nessesity. In the Year 78, I remitted Dry Goods &c in Difft. Ves-

3. Claiming to be a relative of Deputy Quartermaster General John Mitchell, Rainey brought to Europe a letter of introduction from RB: XXXI, 46.

sels to America, to the Amot. of 4500£, Exclusive of Insurance all of which Arrd. Saife but abt £500, but at that time Sold Verey Low, as the money was in much better Credit at that time, and went After I had Ship't the whole Amot. to Virginia, I had wrote to the Merchts. I Ship't the Goods to, to put the money in the America funds, but found On my Arrival, there was but 5100 Dolls. put in, which was in March 78, wch. yr. Excely. will See in the Inclos'd Accot. of Certifs.,[4] and found the money was much Depreciated, so much so that the whole Amount of what I Ship't, If I had purchas'd Bills would not have brought me half my money. I had Nothing left to do but put the paper money in the funds as fast as I reced. it, and all I have for the Above Sum of 4500£ with Intrest upwd. of 2 Years and a half, is the 74900 Dolls. Certife. and 10,000 Dollars Certificates, wch. I had not reced. from a Gentn. in Virginia, taken out in Jany. 79, with the Intrest on the whole Since it was put in, when I left America I came in the Ship Luzann Capt. Thos. Bell,[5] and waited on your Excely. with a Letter of recomendn. from Mr. Beach which my relation Mr John Mitchell got for me & your Excell. gave me along with two Others a Pass. I went Over to London, my Views in going there was, I was Indebted to Some friends there abt 1500£ and it was the Opinion of many of my friends there that I could Sell money in the America funds better there than in France, or here, and I was of the Same Opinion, as I Judg'd the People there must be fully Convinc'd that America would maintain her Independance, but I found the People as much Deluded as ever, by the Ministry and their Creatures, and that there was no person would buy into our funds. The Paper money had got Such a Character, I was able to bring but a Trifle of money to Bear my Expences, and the greatest part of what I Owe in England, is owing to a Gentn. who is a real freind to America, and is in Distress for it at this time, and I have no Other way left to pay him but to Sell those Certificates, and I would not Offer to Ne-

4. Rainey enclosed a one-page list of his 56 certificates. They were dated between March 3, 1778, and Aug. 31, 1779. He noted that their interest had not been settled when he left Philadelphia and that he had ordered a Mr. Foster to receive the interest and deposit it in the loan office.

5. The *Chevalier de La Luzerne*, Thomas Bell commander, arrived in France before Jan. 25, 1780: XXXI, 501–2n.

gociate them here so I Acquainted your Excely. as it might be a Detriment to the Credit of the States, as I was Inform'd by Mr. Mitchell, Mr Lawrance was coming Over to this Country to Negotiate a Loan & Other matters here, this kept me so long in England expecting him Over, I beg your Excely. will advise me if it is proper to Offer them for Sale here in France or Spain. I forward a Letter by this Poast from Mr Diggs,[6] und. Cover to Monsr. Grand. I was detain'd a Considerable time at Margate & on the road and did not get here to last Saturday. I request your Excely. will not take it Amiss my troubling you in this Matter as I mention'd before nothing but the Nessesity I am in Could Justifie the freedom I have taken, I Supose your Excly. has hard that Lord G. Gordon went up to the Parlimt. House with 50000 Men with a Petition against the Popery Bill and that the [they] Burn'd a Roman Chapel & Destroy'd the Inside of Another, and a private Letter mentions that New Gate was all in flames and the Prisoners all Set at Liberty & Several Houses on fire, and Nothing but Anarchy & Confusion. There is a Vessel Arrd. from Boston left it the 4h. May, She brings nothing new. She had a Pacquet from the marquis le fyet,[7] which she threw Overbord, as She was Chas'd by a French Privateer, undr. English Colours, it is the Opinion of all the People I have Convers'd with in London If Charlestown can hold out and not be taken the English will Draw all there troops from the 13 united States, I Should be glad to Offer America my poor Services in any Manner I could be useful, at any risque, but your Excly. not having any knowledge of my Stediness in the Cause, I cannot Expect you will put any Confidence in me. Of Course I can only Offer up my prayer to the Almighty to Succor & help Ama. in the Day of Battle—

I am Yr. Excellys. Obedt. & Hum. Servant   JOHN RAINEY

His Exclly. Benjn. Franklin Esqr.

Notation: Rainey John. Amsterdam June 12. 1780.

6. Digges of May 29, above.
7. Details of Lafayette's arrival in Boston were carried in the June 13 issue of the *Gaz. de Leyde* (no. XLVII, sup.).

To John Jay

LS:[8] Columbia University Library; AL (draft): Library of Congress; two copies: Library of Congress

Dear Sir,   Passy, June 13. 1780.

It was a Mistake of a figure in my Letter that occasion'd you the Trouble of writing yours of the 28th. April. I find you charg'd only with 2564 Livres, 18.10 and not with 4564.18.10. *l.t.*[9] That Bill is paid, as also another drawn since for 3596. livres, 13. Sols. 0 dated March 20. In setting right these Money Matters, it is fit to mention a small Mistake that you have made; The Order of Congress required me to furnish you with 1000 Louis, or 24000 Livres. Your first Bill that came to my hands was for 4079 livres, which being paid and deducted left the sum of 19921. Livres, for which I lodg'd a Credit by means of M. Grand with M. d'Yranda, at your Disposal. But I have since paid the following Bills drawn on me by you, viz

One from Martinique Livres	3379. 8. 0.
One from Cadiz Mar. 3.—	2564.18.10.
One from Do. Mar 20.—	3596.13. 0.
Amounting to	9540.19.10.

Which Sum should also have been deducted from the 24000. *l.t.* but I lately understand from Mr. Grand that you had taken up the whole remaining 19921. Livres, by which means you are become indebted to me for those three Bills paid over and above the Order of Congress.[1] Let us excuse one another.

Yesterday, and not before, is come to hand your favours of April 14. with the Pacquets and Dispatches from Congress, &c. which you sent me by a french Gentleman to Nantes. Several of them appear to have been opened, the Paper round the Seals being smok'd and burnt as with the flame of a Candle us'd to soften the Wax; and the Impression defac'd.— The Curiosity of People in this Time of War is unbounded; some of them only want to see News, but others want to find (thro' interested Views)

---

8. In L'Air de Lamotte's hand. WTF inserted the complimentary close.

9. BF used a British pound sign before the number, which we have corrected to *l.t.*

1. For these bills see XXXI, 286–7, 409–10, and Jay's letters of March 3 and 20. For his subsequent explanation see Morris, *Jay: Revolutionary*, p. 793.

what Chance there is of a Speedy Peace. Mr Ross has undertaken to forward the Letters to England. I have not seen them; but he tells me they have all been opened. I am glad, however, to receive the Dispatches from Congress, as they communicate to me Mr. Adams's Instructions,[2] and other Particulars of which I have been long ignorant.——

I am at a Loss to conceive how it happened, that the Marquis d'Yranda, having receiv'd Orders from M. Grand to hold the Sum of 19921. Livres at your Disposition, by his Letter of the 22d. of february, should not acquaint you with so material a thing till the 14th. of April. I have desired Mr. Grand to give me Copies of his Letters, and I send them to you enclos'd. He had represented the Marquis to me, as a Man who had much Acquaintance, and Influence in that Court, and who might be useful to you on many Occasions; and he tells me that the Marquis both formerly and lately complains that you are shy and reserved towards him.

I am very sensible of the Weight of your Observation, "that a constant Interchange of Intelligence and Attentions between the public Servants at the different Courts are necessary to procure to their Constituents all the Advantages capable of being derived from their Appointment." I shall endeavour to perform my Part with you, as well to have the Pleasure of your Correspondence, as from a Sense of Duty: But my time is more taken up with Matters extraneous to the function of a Minister, than you can possibly imagine. I have written often to the Congress to establish Consuls in the Ports and ease me of what relates to maritime and mercantile Affairs; but no Notice has yet been taken of my Request. Bills of Exchange and other Money-Matters give me also a good deal of Trouble: And being kept in constant Expectation of a Secretary to be sent me, I have not furnish'd myself with the Help I Should otherwise have endeavoured to obtain. But I rub on, finding my Grandson daily more and more able to assist and ease me by supplying that Deficiency.

A Number of Bills of Exchange said to be drawn by Order of Congress on Mr. Lawrens, are arrived in holland. A merchant

2. JA's instructions (Butterfield, *John Adams Diary*, IV, 181–4) undoubtedly were enclosed with President of Congress Huntington's Oct. 16, 1779, letter, which BF received only on June 12: XXX, 542–4.

there³ has desired to know of me whether if he accepts them I will engage to reimburse him. I have no Orders or advice about them from Congress: do you know to what amount they have drawn? I doubt I cannot safely meddle with them.

In yours of April 27. you mention your Purpose of sending me some interesting Papers. They are not yet come to hand. Inclos'd I send you Copies of what has pass'd in writing, between the Danish Court and me.⁴ I have had also the Conference propos'd to me with the Minister of that Court here:⁵ He said much of the Good Will of his Court and Nation towards the United States, with assurances of a kind Reception in their Ports to our Ships, provided they would only use the Precaution of coming in under french Colours, in which Case, no Enquiry would be made or Demand to see their Papers. But he made no Proposition of Restitution, alledging that the giving up the Prizes to the English, was what they were obliged to by Treaties. I do not however find any such Treaty. I see they are embarrass'd and not well pleas'd with what they have done; but know not well how to rectify it. After my Memorial, our People at Berghen were treated handsomely, their Charges defray'd, and a Vessel provided to carry them to Dunkerque at the king's Expence. I shall continue to push them, but wish to know the Sentiments and receive the Orders of Congress.

Mrs: Jay does me much Honour in desiring to have one of the Prints that have been made here of her Countryman. I send what is said to be the best of 5 or 6 engraved by different hands, from different Paintings.—⁶ The Verses at the Bottom are truly ex-

3. Jean de Neufville.
4. Copies of BF's Dec. 22, 1779, memorial to Danish Foreign Minister von Bernstorff (XXXI, 261–5) and Bernstorff's reply of March 8, 1780, above, are among Jay's papers at Columbia University Library.
5. Graf von Creutz.
6. Juste Chevillet's engraving of the magnificent portrait by Joseph-Siffrède Duplessis that is the frontispiece to volume I of this edition. The Chevillet engraving is the frontispiece to the current volume. See our List of Illustrations, and Sellers, *Franklin in Portraiture*, pp. 133–5, 249.
The verse at the bottom, composed by the poet Feutry, reads "Honneur du nouveau monde et de l'humanité, / Ce Sage aimable et vrai les guide et les éclaire; / Comme un autre Mentor, il cache à l'oeil vulgaire, / Sous les traits d'un mortel, une divinité."
Feutry had sent BF the verse in April, 1777, for the St.-Aubin engraving

travagant. But you must know that the Desire of pleasing by a perpetual use of Compliments in this polite Nation, has so us'd up all the common Expressions of Approbation, that they are become flat and insipid, and to use them almost implies Censure. Hence Musick, that formerly might be sufficiently prais'd when it was call'd *bonne,* to go a little farther they call'd it *excellente,* then *Superbe, magnifique, exquise, celeste,* all which being in their turns worn out, there remains only *divine;* and when that is grown as insignificant as its Predecessors, I think they must return to common Speech, and Common Sense: As from vying with one another in fine and costly Paintings on their Coaches, Since I first knew the Country, not being able to go farther in that Way, they have return'd lately to plain Carriages, painted without Arms or figures, in one uniform Colour.—

The League of neutral Nations to protect their Commerce is now establish'd. Holland offended, by fresh Insults from England is arming Vigorously. That Nation has madly brought itself into the greatest Distress, and has not a friend in the World.

With great and sincere Esteem, I am Dear Sir, Your most obedient & most humble Servant.   B FRANKLIN

His Excellency John Jay Esqe. M. P.— &c.

Endorsed: Doctr Franklin 13 June 1780 Recd 27 June 1780

From Louis Filleul

L: American Philosophical Society

Mardy 13 apres midy [June 13, 1780][7]
M. filleul a l'honneur de vous faire part que Md filleul est heureusement acouchée d'un garçon. La mere et l'enfant se portent bien.

Addressed: A Monsieur / Monsieur franchlin / A Passy

(XXIII, 620). Although it was not used there, he included it in his collection entitled *Nouveaux opuscules* (Paris, 1779), under the title, "Pour le Portrait Du Docteur Benjamin Franklin." (p. 59).

7. The date puzzles us. Anne-Rosalie Filleul (XXIV, 571n; XXIX, xxxiii) is recorded as having given birth to a son, Louis-Auguste, on June 14, 1780, a Wednesday, at the château de la Muette: Félix Bouvier, "Une Concierge de Passy en l'An II," Société historique d'Auteuil et de Passy *Bulletin,* v (1905–6), 116. See also Lopez, *Mon Cher Papa,* pp. 227–9, 231.

From Joshua Johnson

ALS: American Philosophical Society

Sir   Nantes 13 June 1780

I have the honor to hand you inclosed four Letters that has this moment arrived by a Ship from New London & who departed 9 Ultimo.[8] I am with esteem Sir Your most Obed. Serv

JOSHUA JOHNSON

His Excellency. Benjn. Franklin Esqr.

Notation: Johnson Jonathan, Nantes 13. June 1780.

From John Paul Jones

ALS: American Philosophical Society; copy: National Archives

Sir   L'Orient June 13th 1780

On my arrival here I found that Captain Landais, encouraged as I believe by Mr. Lee & Mr. Gillan, had raised a party Spirit on board the Alliance:—[9] I have been however on board a considerable part of the time since my return and have always been well received and duely Obeyed.— As I found that my Commission and Authority had been called in question, I had a Copy of my Commission as well as your Orders Read on board yesterday for the satisfaction of every Person; and I soon afterwards discovered that Captain Landais had written the within Letter to Lieutenant Degge which he had read to the Crew,[1] and which I communicated last Night to the Commandant. This Day I came a shore in the forenoon to make some necessary Arrangements with the Commandant respecting the dispatch of the Ariel.— In my absence from the Alliance Captain Landais went on board

---

8. These must have been brought by the *Négresse;* see our annotation of Jonathan Trumbull's April 12 letter and that of Jonathan Williams, Sr., of April 25.

9. Lee wrote Jones on the 13th, taking Landais' side: Bradford, *Jones Papers,* reel 5, no. 1107; *Lee Family Papers,* reel 6, no. 683. Lee and Gillon each wrote Landais, supporting his position: Landais, *Memorial,* pp. 99–100.

1. In the enclosed letter, dated June 12, Landais told Degge to assure the officers of the *Alliance* he would resume command of the ship as soon as he heard from BF. Until then Degge should keep command: Bradford, *Jones Papers,* reel 5, no. 1105, enclosure.

declaring that he came to take Command of the Ship and was determined to Support himself by force against any person who would dispute his Authority. I thought it the most prudent method to make the within Written application to the Commandant of the Marine[2] who with the Commandant of the Road advises me to send an Account of the Matter to your Excellency by Express and to await your orders in consequence in concurrence with the orders of Government.

Several of the Brave officers who served with me in the Bon Homme Richard have already been treated with indignity on Board, and my First Lieutenant Mr. Dale this moment tells me that himself and some others have been turned a shore. Before I came a shore this forenoon, the Crew being assembled I demanded whither any one of them could say a word to my disadvantage. They answered they could not. There was then every appearance of general contentment and Subordination. I am certain that the people in general Love and would readily Obey me.[3]

The Armament of the Ariel is advancing very fast and I expect will be nearly compleated when the Express returns, as the Commandants both of the Marine and Road have assured me of their Utmost Assistance. I have reason to expect that the Clothing that can be embarked in the Ariel will arrive here in a very few Days as there was a Vessel engaged at Nantes for that pur-

2. Jones wrote Port Commandant Thévenard on the 13th to inform him of Landais' actions and to ask for his protection: Bradford, *Jones Papers*, reel 5, no. 1106.

3. As might be expected, Landais' account is quite different. When his barge arrived at 3:00 P.M. on the 13th the crew supposedly gave him "three huzzas." Landais summoned the officers of the *Alliance* to the captain's cabin where they said they had no objection to his resuming command and promised to obey cheerfully his orders. Landais then read his commission and his congressional appointment as captain to the crew, who gave him three more huzzas. He then put the former officers of the *Bonhomme Richard* ashore and informed the commandant of the port, the commandant of the harbor, and Jones that he had resumed his command: Landais, *Memorial*, pp. 100–1. The *Alliance*'s log reported (under June 12) that Landais had come aboard and taken command, he said by orders of Congress. His orders were read to the officers and crew and he ordered ashore all the former officers of the *Bonhomme Richard* and any other officer who would not acknowledge his authority: John S. Barnes, ed., *The Logs of the Serapis-Alliance-Ariel under the Command of John Paul Jones 1779–1780* (New York, 1911), pp. 89, 137–8.

pose. The Alliance will also be able to carry a considerable quantity of Clothing, besides the Articles that are already embarked on board that Ship; and upon the whole I expect the two Ships will be able to carry out the Articles that are most essentialy and immediately wanted. I wish to know whither you would chuse that I should leave out some part of the Musquets and take Clothing in their stead. It is the Opinion here that Musquets will be less wanted when we arrive in America than Clothing.

I send you inclosed the Letter from the Secretary of the Admiralty on which I understand Captain Landais founds his present pretentions to Command the Alliance.

My Conduct in this affair will I hope meet with your Excellencies Approbation. I have strictly followed the advice I have received from the two Commandants here. I have communicated to them the Verbal Orders you gave me at parting to ask their Assistance in Case it should be wanted; but they cannot, they say, act without Written Orders from you in concurrence with the Court.

I have the honor to be with great Esteem and Respect Your Excellencies Most Obliged and most humble Servant

JNO P JONES

His Excellency B. Franklin Esqr. &c. &c.

Endorsed: 35 / Capt. Jones Acct of the Proceedings of Capt Landais

Notation: L'Orient June 13. 80

From Arthur Lee

ALS: American Philosophical Society; AL (draft): National Archives

Sir/   L'Orient June 13th. 1780

The Passport you gave me[4] being expird & useless; I shall be obligd to you for sending me another.

4. Probably in February, when BF approved Lee's taking passage on the *Alliance.* BF at the time had expected the frigate to leave in a fortnight or three weeks. Lee suspected the delay was a plot: XXXI, 500–1; Lee to James Lovell, June 16, 1778 [*i.e.*, 1780] (National Archives).

JUNE 13, 1780

I have the honor to be with great respect, Sir, Yr. most obedt. Humble. Servt.   ARTHUR LEE

The Honble. Doctor Franklin

Addressed: The Honble / Doctor Franklin / Minister plenipotentiary / from the United States / at / Passi

Notation: A. Lee L'Orient June 13. 1780.

From Jonathan Nesbitt

ALS: American Philosophical Society

Sir/   L'Orient June 13th: 1780—

I shall leave it to others to inform you particularly of the disturbances on board the Alliance in Consequence of the late Machinations of Captain Landais & some others.— To the astonishment of almost every person here, he has this day assumed the Command of said Frigate, & as is said with a determined resolution to keep possession at all Events.— I think it my Duty as an American subject to give you my oppinion on this affair;— which is that Captain Landais has been instigated to take the present measure, by some designing person, (an Enemy to his Country) whose design it is to throw every thing into Confusion, and to prevent, if possible, the supplies now going out to America from getting there in due time.— If Captn: Landais had any pretentions to the Command of this Frigate, why did not he go on board on his first arrival here? But so far was he from having such an Idea, that he apply'd to Captain Thomas Bell of the Luzerne, *in Writing* for a Passage out to America on board his Ship.— Therefore his taking on himself the Command of the Alliance at this Critical Period, can be with no other design, (as I have already said,) than to create confusion & delay.— I must request your Excellencys Pardon for taking the Liberty to trouble you with my private Sentiments on this affair.— But I am considerably Interested in the termination thereof, being determined, (if Landais is continued in the Command of the Alliance) to send the Luzerne, wch: is under my care, immediately to Sea, not having any Confidence in such a Convoy.—[5]

5. Bell wrote Landais on June 26 to ask convoy protection from the *Alliance* (National Archives).

I have the honor to remain with Sentiments of great respect.— Sir Your most Obed. Servt   JONATH: NESBITT

Endorsed: 32/ M Nesbit Alliance

Notation: L'Orient. 13 June 80

From James Russell   ALS: American Philosophical Society

Sir   London 13 June 1780

Your favour 2oh Ulto: directed to Messr Hanbury Grove and Self came duely to hand. As Mr Hanbury is at Bath for his health, I wr'ote to him desireing to See him in Town to answer your letter,: he writes me the 10 Currt: acquainting me he is drinking the waters for his health, and Says he will certainly be in Town in a month or Sooner. When he comes you may depend on our answer. I am respectfully Sir Your oblidged hum Ser

JAMES RUSSELL

Addressed: Benjamin Franklin Esqr. / Passy / near / Paris / Via Ostend

Notation: Russel James 13 Juin 1780.

From Landais

Two LS:[6] American Philosophical Society; copy:[7] National Archives

Please your Excellency   L'Orient 14 June 1780

I wrote a Letter of the 29th. May & Duplicates and have received no answer. I beg'd your Excellency would inform me by what authority, I was kept from my Ship, I inclosed a Copy of a Letter from the Secretary of the Honble. Navy board, at

6. We print from the one that BF endorsed. The underlining in the second paragraph is his. The other LS, marked "Duplicate," has minor differences in capitalization, spelling, and punctuation.

7. In Landais' hand. At the Archives de la Marine (B⁴CLXXII: 219–23) is a French translation and a June 16 covering letter from Thévenard to Sartine.

Philadelphia the purport of which was, to take in a few goods for his use as the Ship was ordered home by Congress; My Officers & Crew inform me they have also wrote to your Excellency begging that their Lawfull Commander might be restored to them again— As they knew of no other Commander but me; they inform me that no answer has come to their hands—

I have Sir, *with the Advice of the Prinsiple americans,* and the desire of my officers & Crew, taken the Command yesterday as my right, and *am determined to keep her,* & Carry her to america *as required by Congress, in the Letter from the Secretary of the Honbl. Navy board that I inclosed to you,* I therefore beg you will have the Officers and Crew paid their prize Money and send me your Dispatches that I may fulfill the orders of Congress— On my going on board My Officers and men Received me very Cheerfully and acknowledged me to be their Lawfull Commander and no other till they see a Resolve of Congress For another Captain. I am ready to sail whenever you will be pleased to pay the people and send me your Dispatches—

I am with the greatest Respect your Excellencys most obedt and very humble Servant   P: LANDAIS

His Excellency Dr. B Franklin Minister plenipo to the United States at Passy Near Paris—

Addressed: His Excellency Dr. B. Franklin / Minister Plenipot: / To the united States / at Passy / near Paris / Chargé / recommandé

Endorsed:[8] 34 / Letter from Capt. Landais June 14 80 That he is advis'd by the principal Americans. Will keep the Vessel & follow the Orders of the Secretary of the Navy Board.

8. BF also made a notation on the enclosed copy of the April 1 letter from Secretary of the Board of Admiralty Brown, "Capt. Landais Suppos'd new Commission from the Secretary of the Navy board."

From Samuel Wharton

ALS and copy: American Philosophical Society

Dear Sir   L'Orient June 14 1780

I Am sorry to have Occasion to write you on the Subject of all the Letters, which are addressed to you by this Courier. Captain Jones, Messrs. Moylan and Nesbit will inform you of the particulars of the outrageous Behaviour of Captain Launday, and the (original) Officers, and Crew of the Alliance, in taking Possession of Her.[9] I will take the Liberty of giving my private Opinion of the Cause of this extraordinary Conduct. It is said by the partisans of Captain Launday, That you assumed a Power, not warranted by the Nature of your Ministerial Office in suspending Him and giving Captain Jones the Command, and therefore Captain Launday, as being accountable to the States for the Frigate was warranted in going on Board, and taking Charge of Her. I apprehend, Captain Launday is only made Use of, as an Engine, To create Confusion, and a Delay of the publick Stores, for the purpose of grounding a Complaint against You. It is difficult at present to collect such Facts, as would positively authorise me to say, That Mr. Lee is at the Bottom of this Affair, But from combining a Variety of strong Circumstances, I think, That When the Parties shall be properly examined on Oath by Congress, or the Admiralty Board, It will be found, He has employed every indirect Means in his power for that End.[1]

I have the Honor of being with the highest Respect, and Consideration Dear Sir your most affectionate humble Servant.

SAML. WHARTON

His Excellency Benjamin Franklin

(Private)

Endorsed: 31 / Mr Wharton Alliance

Notation: L'Orient June 14. 80

9. Jones and Nesbitt wrote on June 13, above.

1. Lee in turn said that no honest man could be safe among Wharton and his set: Lee to Lovell, June 16, 1778 [*i.e.*, 1780] (National Archives). Wharton elected not to return to America on the *Alliance;* for the passenger list see our annotation of BF to Jones, March 1.

From Jonathan Williams, Jr.

ALS: University of Pennsylvania Library; copy: Yale University Library

Dear & hond Sir   Nantes June 14. 1780.

I arrived here late last night and had only Time to see Capt Jones depart for Paris. He will inform you of the extraordinary Revolution which has happened on board of the Alliance, which from what I can learn is principaly owing to the pernicious Councils of a certain industrious Genius[2] near here who I believe would disturb the Tranquility of Heaven if he was admitted there.— One Good I hope however will result from this Evil for the Detention of the Alliance will give Time to procure Shipping to carry out the Cloathing under her Convoy, and now Capt Jones is at Paris I think he may be able to obtain from Government a Ship for that Purpose. I have yet had no Time to look round me but my next shall inform you what Ships there are here; the Serapis I find is to be sold the 22d Inst. I wish Government would buy her & let her carry out the Goods for us, their Assistance to us would then be compleat, otherwise it is not, for their Kindness in supplying us with the means to get Cloathing is lost if they do not also give us the means to get that Cloathing out.— I wait only to hear from you to give Orders for all to be brought hither. 2000 Suits are now on the Way.—

I hope the News we have here of the Capture of St Christopher, will turn out true, as it comes from Paris you will no doubt have heard it.—

I am with the greatest Respect Dear & hond Sir ever yours most dutifully & affectionately.   JONA WILLIAMS J

A Brig is just arrived from Phila, you have your Packets by the Post. Nothing decisive before Charlestown the 10 April.

Notation: J Williams June 14. 80

---

2. Arthur Lee. See also JW's letter of June 23.

526

From Jacques-Donatien LeRay de Chaumont

AL: American Philosophical Society

[before June 15, 1780][3]

M. de Chaumont à L'honneur de rèprèsenter à Messieurs les Ministres plènipotentiaires du Congrès que les Marchandises d'Europe seront à des Prix Excessifs en amerique pendant la Guerre, si on n'ouvre pas aux Nègociants un moyen d'aprovisionner L'amerique à meilleur Compte.

Fait

Une aune de Drap qui coute en Europe 20 *l.t.* revient en amerique à 80 *l.t.* a cause des frais d'assurance qui sont à 50. pr. % pour L'aller et 50 pr. % pour le retour.

Preuve

achat en Europe d'une aune de Drap	20 *l.t.*
Prime d'assurance pour L'aller à 50 pr. % Sur 40	
l.t. afin d'en recevoir 20 *l.t.* en cas de perte	20
Prime d'assurance pour le retour à 50 pr. %	
Sur 80 *l.t.* afin d'en recevoir 40 *l.t.* en cas	
de perte	40
Balance	80

20	L'aulne de Drap
20	de Prime d'assurance pour L'aller
40	Idem pour le retour
80.	

3. Certainly this document precedes Chaumont's confrontation with JA about the congressional devaluation of American currency to a fortieth of its face value: *Adams Papers*, IX, 431–3. Chaumont was a major holder of American currency and his financial affairs never fully recovered from the devaluation: Thomas J. Schaeper, *France and America in the Revolutionary Era: the Life of Jacques-Donatien Leray de Chaumont, 1725–1803* (Providence, R.I., and Oxford, Eng., 1995), pp. 295–302. While the "Ministres plènipotentiaires du Congrès" could be BF and JA, the reference is more likely to the American commissioners and we now believe this letter belongs to 1777 or 1778, like those printed in XXVIII, 316–20.

Il faut remarquer que je ne fais icy aucune mention des Bènéfices et comme il ne Sagit que de la valeur intrinsèque de L'aune de Drap chargée des frais indispensables.

Il doit s'en suivre que L'amerique devra à L'europe moitié plus que si cette premiere avait un èchange à offrir en Europe.

Cet Echange est tout trouvé. Les Promesses des Ministres plenipotentiaires portant interet, devraient ètre Echangès contre des Rècepissés du papier monnoye de L'amerique qu'on dèposerait au Congrès.

Cette opèration en rèduisant la Masse du Papier monnoye d'amerique rèduira celle des Taxes.

C'est à mon avis le meilleur employ que le Congrès puisse faire du Crèdit qu'on cherche en Europe: prendra qui voudra de ce papier-monnoye mais L'interet y amenera, parceque ceux qui n'en prendront pas ne pourront pas faire le commerce de L'amèrique en concurrence de ceux qui en prendront. La Nècessité servira à ètablir la confiance dans ce nouveau Papier, et une fois cette confiance ètablie par la nècessité, Le Congrès pourra Employer ce meme papier à tous ses Besoins.

Endorsed: Hint from Mr Chaumt

To Benjamin Vaughan
Copy: Library of Congress

Dear Sir   Passy, June 15. 1780.

I received duly the large Parcel of Letters and Papers you favoured me with by Mr. Austin, to which I shall when I can get a little time, answer particularly.[4] I received also a Box, containing 12 of the 4tos. and 4 of the 8vos. in boards, with the spanish Dictionary and Grammar,[5] and I think some Pamphlets. A bound 4to. is also come to hand, I know not whether from you or some other friend, but suppose it from you. I have given most of these away to friends here who have presented me with their Works; and I wish to have another Dozen half 8vos. and half

4. See Vaughan's letter of April 23.
5. BF's accounts record a purchase of a Spanish dictionary and grammar during the previous months: XXXI, 5.

4tos.—and to know what Number was printed, and whether they are likely to sell, for I should be sorry that M. Johnson were a Loser.[6]

I can now only answer yours of the 2d. Instant relating to Ld. Tankerville's Affair, which you represent as pressing.[7] If his past Conduct has been as you intimate, it will undoubtedly have weight on Occasion. I know nothing of the Existence of the Law you mention. The Congress make no Laws, and each State gouverns its particular Affairs by its own internal Laws which rarely come to my hands here. I think an Attorney or Attorneys Should be appointed, to sollicit if necessary, and transact the Business. A Memorial to the Congress would be improper; it must be (if such a thing is found necessary) to the Government of Virginia. I have not time just now to look for the Papers you formerly sent me relating to this Business; but I will peruse them, and If then any thing occurs to me worth while, I will mention it to you. Remember me affectionately to your father and the good family to Drs. P and P. and present my Respects to L.S[8] if you think they may be acceptable. I just now hear, that the Mob have burnt several Houses of the Ministers. If they went no farther, I should be less concern'd at their Extravagancies; as such a Taste of fire may make those Gentlemen sensible of the Wanton malice with which they have encouraged the Burning of Poor People's Houses in America!— Mr. S. Wharton, lately here gave me for

6. Vaughan's edition of BF's writings had been published by Joseph Johnson the preceding December. It was available in quarto and octavo volumes: XXXI, 211.

7. Vaughan's letter of the 2nd is missing. The case may have involved the estate of Charles Bennett, third earl of Tankerville. He inherited in 1755 extensive holdings in Virginia from his mother's first cousin John Colvill, although they were severely encumbered with debt. Tankerville himself died in 1767, apparently leaving most or all of his Colvill inheritance to his younger son Henry Bennett: W. W. Abbot, Dorothy Twohig, *et al.*, eds., *The Papers of George Washington: Confederation Series* (4 vols. to date, Charlottesville and London, 1992–), I, 66n. Washington, who had been an executor of the will of John Colvill's brother Thomas, declined a 1783 request from Charles Bennett, fourth earl of Tankerville, to take a further part in the matter: *ibid*, 65, 66n. We find no evidence in BF's papers that he played any role either.

8. Drs. Priestley and Price and Lord Shelburne.

you a Copy of one of my Letters to him, which he says he show'd to some of the Ministry as soon as he receiv'd it, But they were incapable of being the better for any Warning. I send it you inclos'd and am ever my dear friend. Yours most affectionately.

Mr: Benja. Vaughan.

From Dumas

ALS: American Philosophical Society; copy: Algemeen Rijksarchief

Monsieur,   Lahaie 15e. Juin 1780.

En vous confirmant mes précédentes, & notamment celles qui concernent Mrs. *Van de Perre & Meyners & Mr. Van Oudermeulen.* J'aurai l'honneur de répondre à l'honorée votre du 5e. Le Mr. que vous me nommez, m'est connu de réputation pour un fort galant homme; & je sais qu'il fait des affaires avec Mr. 165.[9] Quant à ce qu'il vous a dit, je suis persuadé présentement qu'il ne peut l'avoir dit que dans de bonnes intentions, quoiqu'il n'en ait parlé que fort inexactement, pour l'avoir ouï sans doute de quelqu'un qui lui-même étoit peu instruit. Quoiqu'il en soit, laissons meurir la chose même entre les mains de *notre ami* seul. Il m'avertira quand il sera temps d'y penser & d'agir.

J'attends le Jugement que vous me promettez par premiere Poste touchant le Vaisseau Flora. En attendant soyez sûr, Monsieur, que je ferai divers bons usages de votre Lettre aux Armateurs de nos Corsaires. J'ai dessein d'abord d'en faire parvenir une Copie à Mr. le G—— F——. Le 2d. Pense. d'Amst., à qui je viens d'en parler, l'approuve; mais j'attends *notre Ami,* qui n'arrivera ici que Lundi, pour savoir *S'*il l'approuve aussi; après quoi je n'hésiterai pas.

J'ai lu avec beaucoup de Satisfaction vos réflexions sur la Lettre du Gl. Clinton. Mr. Adams m'a fait l'honneur de m'écrire sur le même sujet.[1] Je ferai usage de cela aussi, discretement, dans les gazettes, d'autant mieux, qu'on a mis dans la Gazette de La Haie,

---

9. Chaumont, although the code number for him actually was 166 (165 was "Charlestown"). Westhuysen probably saw him when he visited BF at the Hôtel de Valentinois: BF to Dumas, April 23 and June 5, above.

1. *Adams Papers,* IX, 330–1.

par autorité, & *de source*, que c'est une fiction. On m'a assuré que c'est le Juif *Pinto*, l'Ame damnée de S. J. Y. qui travaille à cette gazette-là.[2]

En remettant la 732[3] à mon propre jugement, comme vous faites, Monsieur, vous me faites redoubler de sévérité contre moi-même: & si l'on n'exige rien de trop humiliant, je Sacrifierai au bien du service Américain autant de mon amour propre qu'il sera possible.

Je crois inutile, Monsieur, de vous parler de ce qui se passe à Londres, de Gordon à la tête d'une Pétition de 150,000 souscrivans, de l'émeute de 50,000 de la populace, du pillage de 2 chapelles & de plusieurs hôtels de Seigrs. Catholiques, de Newgate réduit en cendres, de nombre de Catholiques qui arrivent de Londres à Ostende chercher un asyle, &c. Les gazettes & notamment celle de Leide de demain 16e. No. 48 qu'il faut avoir vous diront tout cela.[4] J'ajouterai que je suis informé de bonne part, que bien des gens en ce pays en sont consternés, & que notamment S. J. Y. fait du très-mauvais sang. Il doit avoir reçu 2 ou 3 Exprès de suite.

Je suis avec un très-grand respect, Monsieur Votre très-humble & très-obéissant serviteur   DUMAS

S. E. Monsr. B. Franklin

Addressed: à Son Excellence / Monsieur B. Franklin / Min. Plenipe. des Etats-unis / &c. / Passy./.

Notation: Mr Dumas la Haie Juin. 15. 80.

From James Moylan   ALS: American Philosophical Society

Honord Sir   L'Orient 15th. June 1780

Yesterday evening I received intelligence from Lieutenant Dale[5] that a certain number of Midshipmen & Sailors belonging

2. As a British publicist, Isaac Pinto was an ally of Sir Joseph Yorke; see XXII, 410n.
3. "Reconcile," *i.e.*, "reconciliation."
4. A discussion of the Gordon riots did appear in the supplement to issue XLVIII (June 16, 1780) of the *Gaz. de Leyde.*
5. The former first lieutenant of the *Bonhomme Richard* (XXX, 454, 631)

to the *United States Service* and under the immediate command of Cap: J. p. Jones, had engaged with Commodore Gillon of So. Carolina and that he had sent the said Midshipmen & Sailors to some town in Holland, by Land.— Cap: Jones having left written directions with me, (copy of wch. you will find herewith) to prevent such desertion, caused me to apply to the Commandant of this port for his consent to have them made prisoners, wch. he immediately granted and by the lawfull means always used on such occasions in this Country, I had them arrested at Hennebon, about six miles from hence, last night and they were this morning lodged in the prison of this port at about the hour of four.— Commodore Gillon represented to the Commandant & Commissary[6] that my proceedings were illegal & totally unjustifiable and claimed these prisoners under the articles of agreement they had enter'd into with him.— On compairing the same with those they had formed prior a long time thereto with Captain Jones, we found that the said Commodore Gillon had absolutely engaged twelve men, (whose names and quality's you will find inclosed) under the discription I had the honor of giving you at the other side, and five others who had been releived by my house with money at the request of Doctor Bancroft for your acct. and who had been daily fed on board the Frigate Alliance since their releasement from the English prisons. The rest, (for you'll please to observe there had been Twenty two men taken at Hennebon,) we cou'd not produce proper papers to justify Cap: Jones's right to, but wch. Mr. Mease tell's me is unfortunately owing to Captain Jones's absence, in whose possession they are, and for the confinement of those last, Commodore Gillon threatens me with the vengeance of this Country, the rigours of the American Law and one of his Officers avows he will make use of personal resentment. You will likewise please to observe, that on a mutual investigation of this affair in presence of the Commandant & Commissary of this port, they advised us to enlarge such of those men from Confinement, as, in behalf of Cap: Jones I cou'd not produce any written engagements for, wch., with the concurrence of Lieutenant Dale I agreed to with a promise from the Commandant & Commissary of not furnishing them any pass-

6. Thévenard and Grandville.

port untill your & the Ministers decision on the matter shou'd be known.

Under this last class, comes those five men we (Gourlade & Moylan) had advanced money to on your account and the remaining five are those, whose engagements with Cap: Jones we are not acquainted with from the reasons already assign'd.

This, Sir, is a faithfull representation of the transaction; the Commandant, Commissary & Commodore Gillon write to Monsieur De Sartine by this post respecting it,— I doubt not he will communicate such intelligence as he receives from them on the subject, to you by wch. means you will be furnish'd with the necessary information to draw a conclusion and give your directions, wch. I pray may be don with as much dispatch as your convenience will admit of and that the necessity of the case requires.

It is a lamentable consideration to me, that while I think I am thus faithfully obeying my directions & thereby preventing much real injury to America, I shou'd be exposed, not only to Lawfull authority, but to personal resentment and danger. The former I shall ever most cheerfully submit to, & I have too high an opinion of America, (the Country of my adoption since my first knowledge & sight of it) to fear its judgmt. of my conduct on this or any other occasion, and your protection Sir, as it's Minister, I only request, while you think I am worthy of it.— I must now beg leave to remark, that if some effectual measures are not immediately fallen on to prevent it, the number of American seamen now in this place will soon be so much diminish'd as to prevent the vessels intended for the transportation of the supply's of cloathing &c. for the use of the united States of America geting out there in proper season.—

I have the honor to be Hond Sir Your most obt hl svt

JAMES MOYLAN

The Honble. B. Franklin Esqr. Minister Plenipotentiary from the United Sates of America &c. &c.

Endorsed: 37 / Mr Moylan's Letter relating to Comme Gillon's debauching the Sailors

Notation: 15 June 80

From Jean de Neufville & fils

ALS and AL: National Archives

Amsterdam the 15 June 1780

Honourd and Dear Sir! May it please your Excellency,

That in Consequence of our former information, we have accepted all those bills which hath appeared to us drawn on the Honourable Henry Laurens in Amsterdam, untill the receipt of those letters she hath favour us with dated 4th and 6th instant, which came to hand by last Mail, we inclose the list of our Accept.[7]

How willing we might be again to go further, the reasons of Common prudence Suggested by your Excellency made us Stop at once, that however we may not have, anything left to reproach our Selfs, we have the honour to inclose to your Excy. one of our accepted bill, which we discounted on the purpose, we have confronted them with Several hundreds, but find no Countrefeiting therein. We have all morall assurances besides that Such bills have been distribued by Congress, and had the Cap: who was Charged with the last dispatches from the Marquis de la Fayette, not distroyed his papers we Should have already gott Some our Selfs.

We will in the meantime desire all those who might present to us Such bills again, to wait Some days, that we may Receive your Excys. answer.

May it then please your Excellency again to Consider what ought to be and can be done, and what may be the Consequence of those bills being protested as they will be Directly by want of acceptance, and in Case M. Laurens might not arrive, as a Sea passage is Exposed to infinite dangers, the Credit of Congress, we are Sorry So [to] Say it, hath before already Sufferd to much in Holland, and the first bills from America being protested there, Should ruin it Entirely and hurt the Credit of all her bills in Europe.

7. Among BF's papers at the APS is an undated document, "List of the Bills of Exchange drawn by F. Hopkinson at 6 Months Sight, on the Honourable Henry Laurens Esqr. Commissioner for the united States of North America, in Amsterdam. Accepted by absence of the Honourable Henry Laurens Esqr. the First June by John De Neufville & Son fr. Bank Money." It lists twelve bills (for a total of $9,344) and notes that they were countersigned by Thomas Smith, commissioner of the continental loan office in Pennsylvania.

We beg your Excellency to return us the inclosed bill[8] and to favour us again with her orders, assured of our Sentiments for the Common wealth of America and that in particular Honnourd and Dear Sir We have the honour to be with due respect Your Excellencys most Devoted And most obedient Humble Servants.   JOHN DE NEUFVILLE & SON

To his Excy. B Franklin Min Plenipot. of the United States of North America at the Court of France

Copy

From John Rainey   ALS: American Philosophical Society

Sir   Amsterdam June 15th. 1780
I had the Honour to write your Excly. the 12th. Inst, but by Mistake did not mention to whose care to Direct to, If your Excely. is so good as to favr. me with an Ansr. please to Direct to the Care of Messrs. John de Nefville & Son— Since Writing my Last there is no Mail Arrived from England, which Alarms people here, as the Wind has been fair this 3 days, There is Some letters comes by fishing Boats, wh. says the Guards has fired on the People, & many kil'd,— it is thought affairs is in great Confusion in London, there is a Ship Arrived from St. Eustatia left it the 26th. Aprl. it is reported She brings Account of the French, and English, Fleets, having another Battle, and that the English was Defeated,[9] I have not yet been able to find out any person has a Letter,—
I am with respect Your Excelys. Most Obedt. Servt.
                    JOHN RAINEY

His Excly. Benjn. Franklin Esqr

8. Probably the bill of exchange for 824 guilders filed with the AL at the National Archives. It had been signed over to them by Elkanah Watson, Jr.
9. Guichen and Rodney's battle off Martinique on April 17, the first of several inconclusive engagements between the two admirals: *Gaz. de Leyde*, no. XLVIII (June 16, 1780); W.M. James, *The British Navy in Adversity: a Study of the War of American Independence* (London, New York, and Toronto, 1926), pp. 198–204.

JUNE 15, 1780

Addressed: To / His Excely. Benjn: Franklin Esqr. / at Passey near / Paris

Notation: Rainey John, Amsterdam June 15. 1780.

From Cornelis Van der Oudermeulen

ALS: Library of Congress

Monsieur.   Amsterdam le 15 Juin 1780.

J'ai l'honneur de remettre cijoint a votre Excellence un Memoire contenant mes Idées pour établir le Commerce entre Votre Etat et les Européens du continent.[1]

Dèsque j'ai cru le tems favorable pour les mettre en execution, j'ai pensé de faire le Voÿage pour vous les communiquer, ainsi qu à Monseigneur Le Comte de Vergennes, mais depuis aiant réflechi qu'il convenait d'agir avec toute la prudence, j'ai preferé de Vous faire parvenir au préalable la presente, afin de ne rien hazarder que lorsque je Saurai que mes idées meritent quelque attention. Si donc Monsieur, Vous les goutés je viendrai desque j'aurai recu Votre reponce, (où le plutôt que mes petites affaires le permetteront) pour m'abboucher avec Vous, & consulter sur cette affaire Votre Excellence et les Personnes qu'Elle jugera convenables.

En attendant Votre Excellence observera la distinction que Je fais de Compagnie previligiée et particuliere, elle Se trouve analogue aux objets que j'ai en vue. Ces Idées demandent des explications plus detaillées, & c'est dans le tems que je m'en occuperai tres Volontiers. Je previens cependant Votre Excellence que je ne desire pas d'avoir part dans les Administrations publique, qui pourront en resulter.— Au reste il est certain que le bon succes

1. The enclosed two-page memoir proposed establishing one or several privileged commercial companies in America and one or several private companies in Europe. These would open a trade between selected European ports (such as Amsterdam, Bruges, Dunkirk, or Hamburg) and America via St. Eustatius, St. Croix, and St. Thomas. The memoir has numerous contemporary underlinings and bracketings, perhaps made to assist BF in preparing his response of June 22, below.

536

de ces sortes d'Entreprises, dependent principalement et en grande partie de la maniere qu'on les établit dans leur principe.

Je prie instamment Votre Excellence de secretter mon nom, ainsi que je le fais à Msgr. Le Cte de Vergennes, et de me faire parvenir la reponce par une voÿe soure, car une fois nos liaisons connu, votre correspondance avec moÿ sera bien observée.

Jai lhonneur d'être avec toute la Consideration possible, Monsieur De Votre Excellence Le tres humble & tres obeissant Serviteur   Cs. Van der Oudermeulen

p.s. Jai encore en vue que si une fois le commerce pouvoit setablir Sur le pied que je propose, & S'animer par les profits, qu'alors on pourra après quelques Expeditions trouver facilement les moÿens de fournir des Especes par anticipation, ainsi vous sentez Monsieur que mes idées ne Sont pas bornés.

To Landais

Copies:[2] Library of Congress, Harvard University Library, National Archives (two)

Sir,   Versailles, June 16. 1780.

I am much surprised to learn that you have contrary to the express Orders contain'd in mine of the 7th. Instant taken upon your self the Command of the frigate. I do hereby repeat those Orders, and charge you to quit the ship immediately.[3] I am, Sir, your &c.

Captain Landais.

2. The copy at the Library of Congress is in L'Air de Lamotte's hand. The one at the Harvard University Library is attested by James Warren, Jr., and Fitch Pool to be a true copy. One of the copies at the National Archives is in Landais' hand.

3. Landais received this letter a week later; on the same day he moved the *Alliance* to an anchorage off the Ile de Groix to prevent Jones's regaining control of the ship: Landais, *Memorial*, pp. 102–3.

To the Officers and Seamen of the *Alliance*

Copies:[4] Library of Congress, Harvard University Library, National Archives (two)

Gentlemen,   Versailles, June 16. 1780.

Having judg'd fit for the Service of the United States, to appoint Comme. Jones to the Command of the Alliance in her present intended voyage to America, I hereby direct you to obey him as your Captain, till farther Orders shall be given by the honourable Congress. I am, Gentlemen, Your friend and humble servant.   B.F.

Minister Plenipotentiary from the U.S. &c.

To the Officers and Seamen of the Alliance frigate.

To Sonnemaens

Copy: Library of Congress

Madam,   Passy, June 16. 1780.

I received duly the Letter you did me the honour of writing to me the 15th. of March past, inquiring after your Brother Jean Henry Baron de Wolff, aid de Camp. of General Washington. I was not able at that time to give you any Information concerning him, but purposed writing to America to obtain it for you. He was taken Prisoner by the English in America, very barbarously treated, and sent to England, where he was exchanged. He is now strongly bent to return to America. As he is almost a Cripple, having received eleven Wounds, four with a Bayonet after he had surrendred, which Wounds are not yet all healed, I have advised him to return to his family and repose himself. But he will not take my Counsel. Perhaps you may have more Weight with him. A Letter from you under Cover to me will reach him here, if it comes within a fortnight from this Date.[5] I have the honour to be. Madam, your &c.

Madame M. A. de Sonnemaens née Baronesse de Wolff a Venlo.

4. Like the immediately preceding letter, the copy at the Harvard University Library is attested by Warren and Pool. One of the copies at the National Archives is attested by Matthew Parke, another of the *Alliance*'s officers.

5. BF wrote to Wulffen on June 11, above. The lady received this letter on June 28 and promptly followed BF's suggestion. On July 1, together with her

From Landais

LS: American Philosophical Society, University of Pennsylvania Library; copy:[6] National Archives

Please your Excellency   L'Orient 16 June 1780

My last to you was of the 14 Instant in which I informed your Excellency that I had retaken the Command of the Ship Alliance, which I left in the charge of my Lieutenant.[7]

There are on board this Ship sixty seven cases containing small arms and two hundred & sixteen barrells of powder,[8] which are claim'd by Mr. Thavenard Commr. of the Port of L'Orient. I know not on whose account, to whom they belong, or by whose order they are placed here. There are also on board some Cannon in the same predicament, except that they have not been claim'd. If it is by your order you will please to Acquaint me with it, and let me know what I am to do with them.

I have repeatedly desired your Excellency to have my people paid their prize money, but I have never had the honor of receiving an answer; I shall only add now, that I am sure it would be for the Interest of the United States that no more time be lost by that delay.

As I have only shewn your Excellency my commission, I have now the honor of inclosing you a copy of it, with documents sufficient to convince your Excellency that I have the sole right of commanding the Frigate Alliance,[9] and if your Excellency has

---

husband Col. Sonnemaens, she wrote in Dutch to her brother, urging him to come to Venlo and convalesce with his family (APS). The same day, the Colonel informed BF that they had invited Wulffen to recuperate in their home and begged for BF's protection of their relative (APS).

6. In Landais' hand.

7. James Degge.

8. Far less than the *Alliance* could have carried. In August, 1780, BF announced that the smaller *Ariel* would carry to America roughly twice that quantity of arms and powder: Lopez, *Lafayette*, p. 197.

9. Among BF's papers are two copies of a March 1, 1777, American commission Deane provided Landais as commander of the armed cargo ship *Heureux*, which was taking supplies to the United States (APS and University of Pa. Library; there is also a copy at the National Archives). With the copy at the University of Pa. Library (and the one at the National Archives) are copies of a May 9, 1778, resolution continuing Landais as a captain in the American Navy (*JCC*, XI, 484–5) and a June 19, 1778, resolution appointing him captain of the *Alliance* (*ibid.*, p. 625).

any orders or dispatches for America for me, I am ready to receive them, if circumstances permitt me to wait for them. It will be necessary for me to receive permissions from your Excellency for those Gentlemen you think proper to give a passage in this Ship. I write your Excellency by duplicate and desire to be answer'd so, that I may be sure to receive your Letters. I have the honor to be with due respect Your Excellencys most humble Servant.   P: LANDAIS

his Exy. Dr. Franklin

Addressed: His Excellency B Franklin Esqr. / Minister plenipotentiary to the / United States / Passy / near Paris

Notation: P. Landais L'Orient 16. June 80

From Jacques-Donatien LeRay de Chaumont

AL: American Philosophical Society

[after June 16, 1780][1]

M de Chaumont a L'honneur de prevenir M. franklin que C'est aujourdhuy Le Courier de Bretagne[2] et que S'il veut que L'alliance reste a L'orient Comme Cela est Bien Necessaire il est interessant qu'il envoye Ses ordres aujourdhuy au Capitaine.

Notation: Chaumont

To William Carmichael

Copy: Library of Congress

Dear Sir,   Passy, June 17. 1780.

Your favour of the 22 past came duly to Hand. Sir J.D.[3] has been here some time, but I hear nothing of his political Opera-

1. On the assumption this note postdates BF's unsuccessful attempt of June 16 to force Landais to leave the *Alliance.* BF does not seem to have issued further orders to the naval captain to remain in Lorient; Landais moved the *Alliance* from there on the 23rd.

2. Postal couriers left for Lorient on Monday, Wednesday, and Saturday: *Almanach Royal* for 1780, p. 616. June 16 fell on a Friday in 1780.

3. John Dalrymple. Carmichael answered BF on Aug. 12 that the supposed finds were a hoax (Library of Congress).

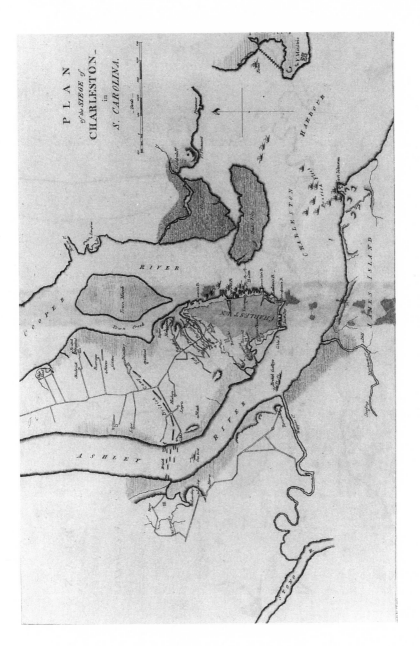

Plan of the Siege of Charleston

tions. The Learned talk of the Discovery he has made in the Escurial Library, of 40 Epistles of Brutus, a missing Part of Tacitus and a Piece of Seneca, that have never yet been printed which excite much Curiosity. He has not been with me and I am told by one of his friends that tho' he wished to see me, he did not think it prudent. So I suppose I shall have no Communication with him; for I shall not seek it. As Count de Vergennes has mentioned nothing to me of any memorial from him I suppose he has not presented it, perhaps discouraged by the Reception it met with in Spain. So I wish, for Curiosity's Sake, you would send me a Copy of it. The Marquis De La Fayette arrived safely at Boston the 28th. of April. And it is said gave expectation there of the coming of a Squadron & Troops— The Vessel that brings this,[4] left new-London the second of May; her Capt. reports that the siege of Charlestown was raised, The troops, attack'd in their retreat, & Clinton killed; but this want Confirmation. London has been in the utmost Confusion for 7 or 8. Days the Begining of this Month. A Mob of fanaticks join'd by a mob of Rouges have burnt and destroy'd property to the amount it is said of a Million Sterling. Chappels of foreign ambassadors, Houses of members of Parliament that had promoted the act for favouring Catholics; & the Houses of many private Persons of that Religion pillaged and consumed, or pulled down to the Number of 50. Among the rest, Lord's Mansfield's is burnt with all this furniture Pictures, Books and papers, Thus he who approved the Burning American Houses, has had fire brought home to him. Had the mob burnt none other, we might have more easely excused them. He himself was horribly scar'd, and Govr. Hutchinson it is said died outright of the Freight.[5] The mob tired with roaming(?) and rioting seven Days and Nights were at length suppressed and Quiet restored on the 9th. in the Evening. Next Day Lord George Gordon was committed to the Tower.

Your Namesake[6] will send you Copies of what passed between M. Lee & M. Grand. What relates to the Difference between Sir Geo. & M. Dumas I may tell you some time or other.

4. Probably the *Négresse*.

5. Hutchinson died of a stroke on June 3, the second day of the rioting: Bernard Bailyn, *The Ordeal of Thomas Hutchinson* (Cambridge, Mass., 1974), p. 373.

6. WTF. No letters between the two prior to 1781 are extant, however.

It is not very important to you to know at present and is improper to write. M. Lee has been long at L'Orient waiting for a Passage on board the Alliance. I have yesterday received Several Letters acquainting me with a Mutiny on board that Ship, which he is supposed to have instigated. I have obtained and sent down Orders to apprehend and imprison some of the Chiefs, which I hope will produce Quiet. That restless Genius, wherever he is, must either find or make a Quarrel.—

I received the Act you mention from the State of Maryland, with a Letter from the Governor[7] desiring me to forward a Copy of it to the Trustees in London, and to learn from them whether they would execute it, by selling the Stock and paying the Bills to be drawn on them. I have accordingly sent the act—, and written to them, requesting an answer, but have yet received none. It is only in Case of their Refusal to act that I am impowered to name one of the Several Persons mentioned; and I apprehend that if they refuse, it will be on this Principle that they were appointed and intrusted by an act of the old Government; that the News is not yet acknowledged in England sufficiently to authorise the Operation it requires; and that if by the fortune or War the old should be restored, they may be subject to a suit for Breach of Trust in complying with the Directions of a Law not made by due authority &c. I also think that if they refuse, my Nomination of another will also be deemed insufficient by the Bank, which never pays Money it has been intrusted with but to the Order of the Persons who actually deposited it, and who in this Case were the Trustees. I remember that having when in London about thirty Thousand Pounds in my Hands belonging to the assembly of Pensylvania,[8] which I was ordered to deposite in the Bank, Subject to their Drafts, the Bank refused to receive it on such Condition, acquainting me that they never took in Money for Account of Persons residing in other Countries, never but for Account of Persons residing at the Time in London, on whose Drafts, only it was to be repaid so that I was obliged to deposite the Money as in my own Name; and the assembly to draw upon me. This I imagine that if the Trustees

7. XXXI, 336–8.
8. He had such a sum in 1760: IX, 28n, 241–2.

refuse the Act will prove abortive: for it is does not seem likely that the Bank, even if it would formerly have paid Respect to an Act of Assembly, will in this Case take upon itself to acknowledge the authority of the new State, before it is acknowledged by Government and pay to a Person of my Nomination Monies deposited with them by Messrs. Hanbury &c. But if it shall prove that I am mistaken, I will then as you decline the Service, take your Advice in the nomination of another.

Inclosed I send you the little piece you desire.[9] To understand it rightly you should be acquainted with some few Circumstances. The Person to whom it was addressed is Mde. Brillon a Lady of most respectable Character and pleasing Conversation. Mistress of an amiable family in this Neighbourhood, with which I spend an Evening twice in every Week. She has among other Elegant accomplishments that of an Excellent Musician, and with her Daughters who sing prettily, and some friends who play, She kindly entertains me and my Grandson with little Concerts, a Dish of Tea and a Game of Chess. I call this my Opera; for I rarely go to the Opera at Paris. The *Moulin Joly* is a little Island in the Seine about 2 Leagues from hence, Part of the Country Seat of another friend, where we visit every Summer and spend a Day in the pleasing Society of the ingenious learned and very polite Persons who inhabit it. At the Time when the Letter was written, all conversations at Paris were filled with Disputes about the Musick of Gluck and Picciny, a German and an Italian Musician, who divided the Town into Violent Parties.— A friend of the Lady having obtained a Copy of it under a promise not to give another, did not observe that Promise so that many have been taken, and it is become as publick as such a thing can well be that is not printed. But I could not dream of its being heard of at madrid. The Thought was partly taken from a Little Piece of some unknown Writer which I met with 50 years since in a newspaper, and which the sight of the Ephemera brought to my Recollection. ADieu my Dear friend, and believe me ever, Yours most affectionately   (signed) B. FRANKLIN

M. Carmichael.

9. On May 22 Carmichael had requested a copy of the "Ephemera."

To Gourlade & Moylan

Copy: Library of Congress

Gentlemen   Passy, June 17. 1780.

I am much obliged by your favour of the 13th. Instant. I am persuaded that your Conjecture of the Adviser and Promoter of the Mutiny, is well founded.[1] Measures are taken that I hope may be successful in suppressing it. With great Esteem, I have the honour to be. Gentlemen Your &c.

Mrs. Gourlade and Moylan.

To John Paul Jones

ALS: National Archives; two copies:[2] Library of Congress

Sir,   Passy, June 17. 1780

Having been informed by several Gentlemen of & from L'Orient, that it is there generally understood the Mutiny on board your Ship has been advised or promoted by the honourable Arthur Lee Esqe, whom I had ordered you to receive as a Passenger; I hereby withdraw that Order, so far as to leave the Execution of it to your Discretion; that if from the Circumstances which have come to your Knowledge, it should appear to you, that the Peace and good Government of the Ship during the Voyage may be indangered by his Presence, you may decline taking that Gentleman; which I apprehend need not obstruct his Return to America, as there are several Ships going under your Convoy, and no doubt many of their Passengers may be prevail'd with to change Places. But if you judge these Suspicions groundless, you will comply with the Order aforesaid. I have the honour to be, Sir, Your most obedient & most humble Servant

B FRANKLIN

Honble. Commodore Jones

1. We have not located the firm's letter, but they must have blamed Arthur Lee. He had been a critic of Gourlade for years: xxv, 84n.

2. One is in L'Air de Lamotte's hand; the other was made at Lorient in August, 1780, and certified by Thomas Hutchins.

Addressed: A Monsieur / Monsieur le Commodore / Jones. / chez M. Gourlade / Ngt. / à L'Orient

Notation: From his Excellency Dr. Franklin Passy, June 17th 1780 Informed by several Gentlem from L'orient that the mutiny had been advised or promotd by the Honble A: Lee &c.

To Jonathan Nesbitt

Copy: Library of Congress

Sir   Passy, June 17. 1780
I thank you for the information contained in your favour of the 13th. Instant. Orders are gone down from the Government to secure Capt. Landais, and assist Capt. Jones in recovering the Command of his Ship.[3] I am sensible the Officers and Men must have been misled most probably by the Person you suspect, as much as by Capt Landais, and I doubt not their returning to their Duty; and that your Ship will have the Benefit of being under the Care and Convoy of that brave Commander. With great Regard I have the honour to be Sir, &c.

Mr. Jonathan Nesbit.

To Samuel Wharton

Copy: Library of Congress

Dear Sir,   Passy, June 17. 1780.
You oblig'd me very much in sending me Clinton's Letters.[4] I sent Copies to England and Holland, where it has been printed. Some have doubted its being genuine: My Answer, is, that whether written by him or not, it contains in my Opinion a True State of American and British Affairs in that Quarter. The Protestant Mob in London, beginning soberly the 2d. Instant with the attendance on a Petion to Parliament on a refusal to take it into

3. On June 20 Port Commandant Thévenard issued orders to have arrested any officer or seaman of the *Alliance* whom Jones designated: Charles H. Lincoln, ed., *A Calendar of John Paul Jones Manuscripts in the Library of Congress* (Washington, D.C., 1903), p. 154.
4. On May 15, above.

immediate Consideration, proceded to Violence, treated ill several Members, burnt several Ambassadors Chapels and being on the seven following Days join'd by all the *disorderly* Rogues of the two Cities pillag'd and destroy'd the Houses of Catholics and favourers of Catholiks to the number of near fifty; among them Lord Mansfield's House with all his furniture, Pictures, Books, Papers, &c, and himself almost frighten'd out of his Wits. If they had done no other Mischief, I would have more easily excused them, as he has been an eminent Promoter of the American War, and it is not amiss that those who have approved the Burning our poor Peoples Houses and Towns should taste a little of the Effects of fire themselves. But they turn'd all the thieves and Robbers out of Newgate to the Number of three hundred and instead of replacing them with an equal number of other Plunderers of the Publick, which they might easily have found among the Members of Parliament, they burnt the Building. It is said they also attempted to plunder the Bank. The Troops fired on them, and kill'd 33.— They were not finally suppress'd till the 9th. at Night; and then chiefly by the City associated Troops. Lord George Gordon is committed to the Tower. Damage done is computed at a Million Sterg. I thank you for yours of the 14th. I have Letters signed by the very officers who now join Capt. Landais, complaining of his Conduct to them in the strongest Terms; and the like from him against them, declaring that he would quit the Ship rather than serve with such a Set.[5] When he came up to Paris, which was only to explain his Conduct, he had no Desire, at least he express'd none to me of returning to the Ship, but on the Contrary worry'd me for an Order to have his things out of her which I declin'd because I would not do an act that should look like punishing him before he was tryed by a Court Martial, that could be only had in America.[6] The separating him and his Officers one would think should be a pleasure to him as well as to them, especially when it appeared his own Act. His Attempt therefore to resume the Command af-

5. For the past animosity between Landais and his officers see XXIX, 25–6, 236–7, 494–5, 497–8, 645–6; for their change of attitude see above, May 31 and June 7.

6. On March 12, above, BF *did* authorize Landais to take his things from the *Alliance.*

ter another was appointed, & when he had received a considerable Sum, advanced to assist him in taking Passage on another Ship, in order to obtain a Trial, and this by exciting a Mutiny just when the Alliance was on the Point of Sailing, is not only unjustifiable but criminal. I have no doubt but your suspicion of his Adviser is well founded. That Genius must either find or make a Quarrel wherever he is. The only excuse for him that his Conduct will admit of, is his being at times out of his senses. This I always allow, and am persuaded that if some of the many Enemies he provokes do not kill him sooner, he will die in a Madhouse.—[7] As to Capt. Landais, I have no other Powers relating to the Alliance, than what are imply'd in my Ministerial office. He was instructed strictly by the Admiralty in America to obey my Orders.[8] He disobey'd them. It is not necessary to discuss those Matters here. We are accountable at home. I am heartily sorry that you have been so long detaind.

I have done every thing in my Power to prevent it. You can have no Conception of the Vexation these Maritime affairs occasion me. It is hard that I who give others no Trouble with my Quarrels, should be plagu'd with all the Perversities of those who think fit to wrangle with one another— I wish you a good Voyage at last, and that I could mend your Company. A Dieu I am ever. Yours affectionately.　　　　　　　　　　　　　　BF.

M. Wharton.

To Jonathan Williams, Jr.

ALS (draft): American Philosophical Society; copy: Library of Congress

Dear Jonathan,　　　　　　　　　　　Passy, June 17. 1780.

I received yours of the 9th. We have applied for another Frigate besides the Ariel, but it cannot be had. My Instructions now are, after talking with Mr. Ross; Get on board the two Frigates all you can of your Clothing, which is to be prefer'd to Mr Ross's Cloth; then estimate the Bulk of what Remains, with

7. BF had long questioned Lee's sanity: XXV, 472n; XXVI, 223.
8. See XXVII, 651–2; XXVIII, 255–6.

that Cloth, and other things belonging to the Publick; and if nearly sufficient to load another Vessel, and you can find one so ready that she may be fitted in time to go with the Frigates, you are to agree for her upon Freight, & ship the whole.

I do not understand M. de Chaumont's Complaint, Funds as I am inform'd being lodg'd with his Banker to pay the Bills as they become due. Indeed I never understood why they were drawn on him at all. They might as well, for what I can see, have been drawn directly upon me.— Try if you can beat this Business into my head. I am ever Your affectionate Uncle   BF

Notation by Franklin: BF. to J. Williams June 17. 1780 M. Chaumont's Complaint not understood; nor why the Bills were drawn on him. Funds were provided.

From the Duc de la Vauguyon   Copy: Library of Congress

La haye 17 Juin 1780.

Permettéz, Monsieur, que j'aye l'honneur de vous adresser Mr. Dumont[9] qui vous remettra ma Lettre, et que je vous prie d'accueillir favorablement. Monsieur, le Comte de Vergennes pourra vous donner sur lui des Eclaircissements plus étendus, et je me refere aux Notions qu'il voudra bien vous communiquer. Je saisis avec Empressement cette occasion de vous renouveller l'assurance des Sentiments de la consideration la plus distingue avec laquelle J'ai l'honneur d'être, Monsieur, votre tres humble et tres obeissant Serviteur   signé LE DUC DE LA VAUGUYON

M. Franklin.

9. An alias being used by an Englishman who recently had come to La Vauguyon's residence in The Hague with a plan to arm an uprising in Cornwall. He had called himself Montagu Fox and claimed that during the Gordon Riots he had stolen documents from Lord Sandwich, been arrested, and escaped from the Tower. La Vauguyon provided him a passport to go to Paris. In reality, "Montagu Fox" was a British agent. For a detailed account of his career see Richard B. Morris, *The Peacemakers: the Great Powers and American Independence* (New York, Evanston, and London, 1965), 112–31.

From Sartine

a Versailles le 17. Juin 1780.

Le Lieutenant General de l'Amirauté de Vannes et de l'Orient m'informe, Monsieur, que vous lui avez écrit pour demander que le Vaisseau le Serapis soit vendu pardevant les Juges de cette Jurisdiction.[1] Vous vous rappellerez certainement que dans le Principe, J'avois proposé de faire estimer le Bâtiment dont il s'âgit, et d'en faire remettre la valeur pour être repartie aux Etats-Majors et Equipages qui ont été employés sous les Ordres de M. Jones.[2] Ce Commodore ayant présumé depuis que la Serapis ne seroit porté à Sa Juste Valeur qu'autant qu'il seroit vendu par adjudication, J'ai ordonné dès le 22. Avril dernier au Commissaire en Chef de l'Orient, d'Annoncer cette vente par des Affiches. Comme il paroit que d'après ce que vous a mandé M Jones, vous preferez de faire faire la vente par l'Amirauté, je vous prie de me marquer si je puis revoquer les Ordres qui ont été donnés. Je vous observe cependant que la forme que j'avois proposée n'étoit nullement dispendieuse, mais qu'il n'en sera pas de même, Si vous jugez que la vente du Vaisseau dont il s'agit, doive être faite par l'Amirauté.

J'ai l'honneur d'être avec la plus parfaite consideration, Monsieur, Votre très humble et tres obeissant Serviteur./.

(signé) DE SARTINE.

M. Franklin.

1. Above, May 18.
2. Jones was concerned with distributing money from the sale among them as soon as possible; he even had BF deliver to Sartine a May 27 memorandum urging him to make an immediate bid for the *Serapis* (and possibly the *Countess of Scarborough*) or to advance money to the *Alliance*'s crew: Bradford, *Jones Papers*, reel 5, nos. 1063, 1077, 1090, 1093, 1095.

From Vergennes

L (draft):[3] Archives du Ministère des affaires étrangères; copy: Library of Congress

a Versailles le 17. Juin 1780

J'ai l'honneur de vous envoyer, M. copie au 10. Juin d'une lettre de M. de Sartine, ainsi que de celle qui a été addressée à ce Ministre par m. l'ambassadeur de Hollande.[4] Vous y verrez que le Corsaire le Prince noir a enlevé un navire Hollandois appellé la flora: je ne doute pas, M, que vous ne condamniez ainsi que nous le procédé de ce Corsaire, et que vous ne lui ordonniez la restitution immédiate de Sa prise avec dommages et intérets. Cet acte de justice de votre part me Semble d'autant plus nécessaire, qu'il Sera une conséquence des justes menagements que nous avons pour les puissances neutres, ainsi que des principes qui font l'objet de leur association; D'ailleurs il est de la Sagesse du Congrès de menager toutes les nations, et d'eviter avec le plus grand Soin tout Sujet de discution, et toute démarche qui pourroit exciter leur mécontentement. L'evenement qui fait l'objet de cette lettre est dans ce cas, et je Suis persuade, m., que vous Sentirez comme moi, M, que vous ne Sauriez trop vous empresser de prévenir les plaintes auxquels il ne manqueroit pas de donner lieu si vous en laissiez l'auteur impuni.

M. franklin.

3. In the hand of Gérard de Rayneval. The copy contains a complimentary close, but the other differences are minor.

4. La Vauguyon's May 22 letter to Sartine complained that the *Black Prince* had not only failed to respect the flag of the *Flora* (even though her papers were in order), but had forcibly removed most of her crew. If such proceedings were tolerated, French privateers would begin flying the American flag. He asked the return of the crew, release of the ship, and indemnification of the captain. Sartine in his covering letter agreed with him and asked Vergennes to arrange the matter with BF. Copies of both are included with the copy at the Library of Congress.

John Paul Jones: Memorandum on Landais

AD: Library of Congress

Versailles June 17th. 1780.

When the Treaty of Alliance with France arrived in America Congress feeling the most lively Sentiments of Gratitude towards France, thought how they might manifest the Satisfaction of the Continent by some public Act. The finest Frigate in the Service was on the stocks ready to be Launched and it was Resolved to call her the Alliance. M. Landais a french subject who had then arrived in America from France as Master of a Merchant Ship Laden with public Stores had reported that he had been Captain in the Royal Navy of France, had Commanded a Ship of the Line been a Chief Officer of the Port of Brest and was of such worth and estimation for his great abilities that he could have any honors or advancement in his own Country that he pleased to accept:[5] But that his desire to Serve America had induced him to leave his own Country and even to Refuse the Cross of St. Louis that he might be at Liberty to abjure the Religion of his Forefathers, which he did accordingly.— Congress believing M. Landais to be a Man in heigh esteem at the Court of Versailles and thinking with reason that it would give pleasure to his Majesty to find that one of his worthy Subjects had been treated with distinction in America, appointed him Captain of the Alliance. Now considering his late Conduct it would be rendering a very acceptable service to Congress if the Kings Ministers would please to transmit to the President, their Opinion of Captn. Landais both before he went to America, and since in Europe while under the Command of Commodore Jones: For it is necessary for Congress to know whether the account he gave of himself in America was true.

Memorandum

Notation: No. 35 Memo. regarding Capt. Landais 17 June 1780[6]

5. Landais' services in the French Navy had been varied but considerably more modest than his claims: Six, *Dictionnaire biographique*, II, 51; Charles O. Paullin, "Admiral Pierre Landais," *Catholic Historical Review* XVII (1931–2), 296–8; Jean-Etienne Martin-Allanic, *Bougainville navigateur et les découvertes de son temps* (2 vols., Paris, 1964), I, 498, 502, 615, 619–20, 629–30.

6. See BF's list of papers relating to the *Alliance* [before June 26], where this is number 35.

To Vergennes

LS:[7] Archives du Ministère des affaires étrangères; copy: Library of Congress

Sir,   Passy, June 18. 1780.

I received the Letter your Excellency did me the honour of writing to me the 17th. of this Month, together with the Letters inclosed of M. De Sartine and of the Ambassador of Holland, concerning the Ship Flora, which had been brought into Cherbourg by the Black Prince Privateer: Your Excellency will see by the inclosed Papers, that I had already given Orders for the Release of the Vessel, with Payment of Damages, before M. the Ambassador's Complaint was made.[8] And by my Letters to the Owners,[9] may be seen what my Sentiments are with Regard to the Principle about to be established by the Neutral Powers. This single Cargo I nevertheless condemn'd to the Use of the Captors, excepting what should be reclaimed on Oath by the Subjects of Holland. My Reasons for doing so were,

1. Because the Law has been settled in America, that Enemies Property found in neutral Ships, might be taken out of the same paying the Freight that would have been due if the Ships had compleated their Voyages, together with all Costs & Damages.[1] Of this there has been already several Instances; and Foreign Owners have been so well satisfy'd with the handsome Treatment their Ships met with when carried into our Ports on such Occasions, that I never heard of any Complaint.

2. Because the English have always condemn'd and confiscated American Property found in Dutch Ships, of which there have been, as I am informed, many Instances in America; and neither the Dutch Captains nor Owners, have ever complained of this as a Violation of the Flag of their Nation, nor claimed its

7. In WTF's hand. A French translation is at the AAE and a fragment from BF's draft is at the Harvard University Library.

8. BF enclosed copies of his letter of May 26 to the Admiralty judges at Cherbourg and of May 30 to Torris, both above; docketing on the copies at the AAE indicate they were enclosed with the present letter.

9. Meaning Torris, the owner of the *Black Prince.*

1. The principle that British goods aboard any vessel were liable to capture was established by Congress prior to the Declaration of Independence: *JCC,* IV, 343; V, 453.

Right of Protecting our Goods in their Ships, but have deliver'd them up to the English on receiving their Freight.

3. Because a Treaty has been long since offer'd to Holland, in Behalf of the United States, in which there was an Article, that free Ships should make free Goods;[2] but no Notice has been taken of that Offer: And it was understood, that 'till such a Treaty was enter'd into, the old Law of Nations took Place, by which the Property of an Enemy was deem'd good Prize wherever found. And this Vessel, charged with English Property, being brought in; on the Captain's Voluntary Declaration that it was such, before the Intention of the Neutral Powers to change that Law could be known, it was thought that the Captors Right to the Cargo, could not be fairly refused.

I hope these Reasons, and the Orders I had given, will be satisfactory to his Exy the Ambassador of their High Mightinesses, whom I highly esteem & Respect. I am perfectly convinc'd of the Wisdom of your Excellency's Reflections on the Subject; and you will always find me pursuing a Conduct conformable to those just Sentiments.

With Regard to the Observation of M. De Sartine on the "Inconvenience resulting from American Privateers, fitted out as the Black Prince is, by Frenchmen, and yet not subject to the same Forms and Laws, with your Privateers"; I beg leave to observe, that by the Express Words of the Commission, granted to them, they are directed to submit the Prizes they shall carry into any Port in the Dominions of a Foreign State to the Judgment of the Admiralty Courts established in such Ports or States, and according to the Usage there in force.[3] Several of our first Prizes brought into France, were, if I mistake not, so judged; and it was not upon any Request of mine, that such Causes were afterwards referr'd to me, nor am I desirous of continuing to exercise that Jurisdiction.— If therefore the Judgment I have given in the Case of the Flora, is not approved, and the Council of Prizes will take the Trouble of re-examining and trying that Cause and

2. In Article XVIII of Lee and Neufville's draft treaty of amity and commerce of Sept. 4, 1778: Wharton, *Diplomatic Correspondence*, II, 796.

3. See the initial commission of the *Black Prince*, which is reproduced opposite p. 52 of Clark, *Ben Franklin's Privateers;* see also XXVIII, 632.

those of all other Prizes to be brought in hereafter by American Cruisers, it will be very agreable to me; and from the very Terms abovementioned of the Commission I think it will also be agreable to the Congress. Nor do I desire to encourage the fitting out of Privateers in France by the King's Subjects, with American Commissions. I have had many Applications of the kind, which I have refused, advising the Owners to apply for the Commissions of his Majesty. The Case of the Black Prince was particular. She had been an old Smugler on the Coasts of England and Ireland; was taken as such, and carried into Dublin; where her Crew found Means to break Prison, cut their Vessel out of the Harbour, and escaped with her to Dunkerque. It was represented to me, that the People being all English and Irish, were afraid to continue their smugling Business, lest if they should be again taken, they might be punished as British Subjects for their Crime at Dublin: and that they were willing to go a Privateering against the English, but speaking no other Language, they imagined they might if taken, better pass as Americans if they had an American Commission, than as Frenchmen if under a French Commission.[4] On these Grounds I was applied to for a Commission, which I granted,[5] believing that such a swift Vessel, with a Crew that knew so well all Parts of the Enemy's Coasts, might greatly molest their Coasting Trade: Her first Successes occasioned adding the Black Princess, by the same Owners; and between them they have taken and sent in, or ransom'd or destroyed, an amazing number of Vessels, I think near eighty.—[6] But I shall continue to refuse granting any more Commissions, except to American Vessels and if, under the Circumstances above represented, it is thought nevertheless inconvenient that the Commissions of the Black Prince and Princess should continue, I will immediately recal them.[7]

4. XXX, 203–4, 215, 368–9.

5. XXX, 536.

6. During the five cruises of the *Black Prince*, one of the *Black Princess*, and two joint cruises the privateers had made 61 captures: Clark, *Ben Franklin's Privateers*, pp. 89, 111, 153, 177.

7. As Clark points out there is less to this offer than first appears: the *Black Prince* had been wrecked, and BF avoids any mention of the *Fearnot: ibid.*, p. 142.

With the greatest Respect, I am Sir, Your Excellency's most
obedient and most humble Servant   B FRANKLIN

His Exy: the Ct. De Vergennes.

Notation: M. de R.

To John Fothergill

Reprinted from William Temple Franklin, ed., *Private Correspondence of
Benjamin Franklin* (2 vols., London, 1817), I, 64–5.

Passy, June 19, 1780.

My dear old friend, Dr. Fothergill, may assure Lady H. of my
respects, and of any service in my power to render her, or her
affairs in America. I believe matters in Georgia cannot much
longer continue in their present situation, but will return to that
state in which they were when her property, and that of our common friend G. W. received the protection she acknowledges.[8]

I rejoiced most sincerely to hear of your recovery from the
dangerous illness by which I lost my very valuable friend P.
Collinson. As I am sometimes apprehensive of the same disorder, I wish to know the means that were used and succeeded in
your case; and shall be exceedingly obliged to you for communicating them when you can do it conveniently.[9]

Be pleased to remember me respectfully to your good sister,
and to our worthy friend David Barclay, who I make no doubt

8. The letter from Fothergill that prompted BF's reply is missing. "Lady
H.," Selina Shirley, Countess of Huntington (1707–1791), was contributing
to an orphanage established in Georgia by George Whitefield and had
asked Fothergill how it was doing: Betsy C. Corner and Christopher Booth,
eds., *Chain of Friendship: Selected Letters of Dr. John Fothergill of London,
1735–1780* (Cambridge, Mass., 1971), p. 500n; Lewis, *Walpole Correspondence*, XLVIII, 2, 450–1.

9. Collinson had died in 1768 of strangury: XV, 257; Norman G. Brett-
James, *The Life of Peter Collinson, F.R.S., F.S.A.* ([London, 1926]), p. 38.
Fothergill's Oct. 25, 1780, reply to the present letter describes in some detail
his urinary tract disorder and the remedies he employed to alleviate it: Corner and Booth, *Chain of Friendship*, p. 497.

laments with you and me, that the true pains we took together to prevent all this horrible mischief proved ineffectual.[1]

I am ever, Your's most affectionately,   B. FRANKLIN.

To William Hodgson   Incomplete copy: Library of Congress

Dear Sir,   June 19. 1780.
I received your several favours of March 28. and may 12. I thank you for the Justice you did me at the sick and hurt Office, in the assurances you gave that it was not my Intention to deceive, nor my fault that an equal Number of Prisoners did not return with the Cartel. On my consenting to give up the 500 Prisoners we carried into Holland, I had the Promise of an equal Number of English to be given me, to exchange for americans. You will see by the enclos'd from Mr. de Sartine[2] what account is given of the Disappointment in that Instance at Morlaix but since your information that the Board would not receive English Prisoners captur'd by the french in lieu of those captured by Americans, tho' they had in Holland received English. . . .[3] English Prisoners be if possible reserved from all exchanges, and not delivered up till after the Conclusion of a Peace. I send you enclos'd a Copy of the Paroles that have been given by near 500 English NOT ONE of whom has had the Virtue to comply with his Solemn Engagement. What is become of your National Honour?— I send you also an Account of the brave Conyngham's Treatment when a Prisoner, written by Himself.[4] Also An Account of the Treatment of a poor harmless Quaker in Pensilva-

1. Fothergill's sister was probably Ann, who managed his household when BF knew them in London: x, 170. David Barclay had collaborated with Fothergill on the abortive peace negotiations of 1774–75: XXI, 361–8, 541–3, 551–64, 583–8.
2. Presumably Sartine's letter of April 24, above.
3. Half a page of the letterbook has been torn out at this point.
4. Immediately following the present letter in BF's letterbook is a lengthy extract of Conyngham to BF of Dec. 1, 1779. See XXXI, 182n, where we describe BF's emendations to that letter.

nia by your Troops, which I lately received from his father.[5] A Book is preparing in America containing a great Number of Authenticated Accounts of such Barbarities among which is the Covering with Pease Straw 15 american soldiers wounded and disabled in a fight near a Barn in New Jersey, and setting fire to the straw, whereby they were burnt to death. Engravings are intended to be made of each Transaction, proper to be printed in the Book.[6] You may judge what Impression this is likely to make in the Minds of Children, and what Effect it may have on Posterity, with regard to any future Union or even Good Will between the two Nations if the printing it is not prevented—

I am much surpriz'd at the Conduct of the Person you mention,[7] and his Letter in the Morning Post. Be pleased to present my affectionate Respects to the Club, and believe me ever, with sincere Esteem Dear Sir, &c.—

Mr. Hodgson.

5. Following the passage cited above is this "Extract of a Letter from Philadelphia":

"My sixth Son Anthony, settled about 12. miles on t' other Side Schuylkil, fell into the Enemies hands, who after they had plundered his house, of his (& my sent there for safety) even to the little bed in a Sucking Childs Cradle, met with most Cruel Treatment; Cut and mangled when he was thrown from his horse, and while he was on the ground, utterly disabled from rising by wounds in 29 places, stabb'd thro' both his Cheeks, a slitt down his nose, and cross his upper lip, several fingers cut off and his hands disabld by his wounds, in short was cruelly mangled, and this by a Noble Lord and Peer of G.B. who at last bid the others, cut the damn'd Rebel in two, and come away, which they attempted to do, as they passed their horses over his Body; through all this, by the mercy of God he yet lives, to help his family, contrary to all our Expectations, Judge what Shocking News this was to his poor Mother and family in our desolate Retreat."

6. See XXIX, 590–3, especially item 17.

7. David Williams.

To Sartine

LS:[8] Archives de la Marine; incomplete copy:[9] Library of Congress

Monsieur   a Passi ce 19 Juin 1780

J'ay receu La lettre que Vostre Excellence m'a fait L'honneur de m'ecrire Le 17 de ce mois, Sur unne lettre qu'elle a Reçue du Lieutenant general de L'amirauté de Vannes et de L'orient, qui L'informe que J'ay ecrit au dit Lieutenant general pour que le Vaisseau le Serapis Soit vendu par devant Les Juges de Cette amirauté. J'ay L'honneur, Monsieur, de vous observer a ce Sujet, que les Capteurs americains etant tenus d'obtenir mon Consentement Sur la validité des prises qu'ils peuvent faire, J'escris alors aux officiers des amirautés ou Sont Conduittes ces prises, Lorsqu'elles me paraissent faittes Sur L'ennemy de L'amerique, qu'ils peuvent en faire la vente, *Lorsqu'ils en Seront Requis;* Ce qui ne me parait pas, Monsieur, autoriser Les officiers de L'amirauté de vannes a Pretendre que la vente du Serapis Soit faitte devant eux, des que vostre Excellence a Jugée plus Expédiant d'en ordonner La vente par devant Les officiers de la Marine du Port de L'orient, et Je la Suplie de Prescrire aux officiers de L'amirauté tout Ce que Bon luy Semblera a ce Sujet.

Je Suis avec un tres Respectueux attachement Monsieur vostre tres humble et très Obeissant Serviteur   B FRANKLIN

M. de Sartine

Notation: Le meme jour il a eté ecrit a Mrs. Thevenard et de la Grandville.[1] Rep. le 23 Juil.

---

8. In Chaumont's hand.

9. Through the word "obtenir"; the remainder is missing.

1. Apparently a reference to Sartine's June 19 orders to Thévenard and Grandville at Lorient ceding the *Ariel* to the United States for a campaign.

From Benjamin Franklin Bache[2]

ALS and copy: American Philosophical Society

Mon cher grand papa   Genève ce 19 juin 1780

J'avois promis de vous envoyer dans ma première lettre une pièce de dessin, mais ce sera pour une autre fois, m'empressant de vous écrire aujourdui pour vous apprendre que j'ai remporté le prix pour avoir mieux traduit un morceau de latin en françois que les autres écoliers; ce prix se donne publiquement dans léglise cathédrale et par le premier magistrat. Mr De Marignac, à qui cela a fait un grand plaisir, vous prie d'agréer ses felicitations, et son respect; Je sens trop, mon cher grand papa, toutes les obligations, que je vous ai, pour ne pas faire tous mes efforts pour vous contenter; Jéspére que vous vous portès bien, ma santé est très bonne, grace à dieu. J'aimerois beaucoup que mon frère vint à Genève, de même que les fils de monsieur Adams; outre le plaisir, que j'aurais, à faire mes etudes avec eux nous pourrions souvent parler en anglois; je languis beaucoup de les voir; J'écrirai au premier jour à mon papa et à ma mama; faites mes compliments, s'il vous plait, à mon cousin et à cockran.

Jai l'honneur d'être avec un profond respect Mon cher bon papa, Vôtre tres humble, et obeissant, petit fils,

B. Franklin B.

Comme c'est l'ordinaire de donner un gouté, je vous prie dites moi le plus vite que vous pourrés ou plutôt priés cockran de m'écrire, si vous voulès que j'en donne un.

Madame cramer, qui a toujours beaucoup de bontès pour moi, a reçu la lettre que vous lui avès envoyée et vous repondra ces jours ci, elle vous assure bien de ses respects.

---

2. The sophisticated and highly grammatical style of this letter is certainly not BFB's own. See Marignac to BF, under the same date, below, for more details about the *goûter*.

From Jacques-Donatien Le Ray de Chaumont

ALS: American Philosophical Society

Monsieur,   Passi ce 19 Juin 1780

J'ay L'honneur de Remettre a vostre Excellence unne Lettre en datte du 14 de ce mois de M de Montplaisir[3] un des Correspondants a L'orient que J'ay Chargé de La Suitte de L'Expedition de L'Escadre Qui etoit Sous les ordres du Commodore paul Jones, vous verrez dans La Susditte Lettre Ce que vous avez deja pu apprendre par ailleurs, que Mr. lée qui a été un de vos Confreres Lors de L'alliance de L'amerique avec la france, encourage publiquement par Son approbation la Conduite très Reprehensible des Equipages de la fregatte L'alliance. Il n'a fallu qu'un fou Comme Lord gordon en angleterre, pour y exciter la plus honteuse de touttes les Seditions, et L'exemple encouragé de L'equipage de L'alliance par un homme du Caractere de M. Lée est Capable de faire unne tres grande impression dans un port du Roy. Vous Seriez au desespoir, Monsieur le Docteur, qu'un peu de Negligence a arrester La Cause du Soulevement de L'Equipage de L'alliance occasionat des Punitions Rigoureuses Contre Cet Equipage tandis qu'ils paraissent se Laisser aller aux suggestions de vostre ancien Confrere et Du Soit disant Commodore Guillon au Cordon Rouge.[4] Permettez moy de vous proposer de Communiquer a M. le Comte de vergennes La Susditte Lettre de M. de Montplaisir qui est un Negotiant Sage et Moderé et incapable de faire un faux Rapport. Peutestre Ce Ministre Jugera t'il apropos de proposer a Ces Messieurs de S'eloigner du port de L'orient du moins tant que L'alliance y Sera dans la Radde.

Je Suis avec Respect Monsieur vostre tres humble et tres obeissant serv   LERAY DE CHAUMONT

M franklin

Notation: Le Ray de Chaumont 19. June 80.

3. Montigny de Monplaisir's letter describes how Landais gained control of the *Alliance* and notes that Lee and Gillon had strongly approved his conduct. University of Pa. Library.

4. A reference to the ribbon Gillon wore across his chest (which provoked Jones's sarcasm, too): John Trumbull to Jonathan Trumbull, Oct. 11, 1781, Mass. Hist. Soc. *Collections*, 7th series, III (1902), 286; Bradford, *Jones Papers*, reel 5, no. 1124.

From Marignac   ALS and copy: American Philosophical Society

[*c.* June 19, 1780][5]

Franklin demande à son bon grand Papa la permission de donner un gouter à ses amis à l'occasion de son prix, en lui disant que c'est l'usage, Il est très vrai que les Genevois le font, Mais les étrangers n'y sont pas absolument tenus, quoique la plus grande partie le fasse, Je ne crois pas qu'on voye avec peine qu'il n'en donne point; ce sera donc uniquement un plaisir & une marque de Contentement, que son grand Papa lui donnera, en sacrifiant à cela près de quatre Louis:

Oserois-je ajouter ici mes félicitations, l'assurance de mon contentement & du profond respect avec lequel j'ai l'honneur d'être Monsieur Vôtre très Humble & très obeissant Serviteur

G L De Marignac

Je recevrai avec reconnoissance & intérêt les jeunes gens, que Monsieur Franklin semble me promettre.[6]

From John Torris   ALS: American Philosophical Society

Honnd. Sir   Dunkerque 19th. June 1780.

I have the Honnor to forwd. your Excellency the Declaration made by Capt. Thos. Byrne, Late of the Schooner Peter, Before Notary Public in London the 16th. Inst., that, the said Schooner Peter, was Taken as a Prize on the 26th. Febry., by the Black Prince Privateer, Capt. Dowlin, Between the Landsend & Ushant.[7] I am happy this Free declaration is Conform in every point, to the report made by the Prise Master & the People who Brought

5. Dated on the basis of BFB's letter of this day, above. The two letters are written on the same sheet of paper.

6. Apart from BFB, four young Americans were eventually enrolled at the College of Geneva: Samuel Cooper Johonnot, Robert Montgomery, who came to the school in the summer of 1781, and the two sons of Robert Morris, Robert, Jr., and Thomas, who arrived in June, 1783. For their vicissitudes see Claude-Anne Lopez, "A Story of Grandfathers, Fathers, and Sons," *Yale University Library Gazette*, LIII (1978–79), 177–95.

7. Capt. Byrne's declaration of June 16 was attested by Joseph Cotissos, notary public. It notes that the schooner *Peter* was carrying a cargo of staves and flour from London to Madeira when she was captured. APS.

her Into Morlaix, & To the Dito of Late By Capt. Dowlin & his Officers.— I am also Happy that Messrs. Chs. & Edwd. Hague[8] my Correspondants in London, had Interest enough to Procure the Same, & therewith Justiffy, we did not deserve the Suspicions which your Excellency has been pleased to entertain on this Prise not being really English.

I hope your Excellency will have no further reasons to refuse the Immediate Condamnation thereof, the Same I expect you have allready done, for the Friendship Capt. Pretty John's.

I have not yet heard on the release of the Poor Princess & of her Brave People!

I am with all respect Honnd. Sir your Excellency's most obedient & most hble Servant   J. TORRIS

His Excellency Dor. Franklin.

Endorsed: M Torris June 9. 1780

Notation: Mr. Torris. June 9. 1780

From Jonathan Williams, Jr.

ALS: University of Pennsylvania Library

Dear & honoured Sir.   L'Orient 19 June 1780.

This will be presented to you by Doctor John Foulke & Mr Fox who are warmly reccommended to me from Philadelphia. I beg leave to introduce them to you & shall be particularly obliged by your Civilities to them.

I am with the greatest Respect Dear & honoured Sir Your dutifull & affectionate Kinsman   JONA WILLIAMS J

The Honable Doctor Franklin

Addressed: A monsieur / Monsieur Franklin / Ministre plenipotentiaire / des Etats unis de l'amerique / Septentrionale en son Hotel / A Passy prés Paris.

Notation: Jona Williams 19 June 1780

8. Merchants of Mark Lane, London: *Kent's Directory for the Year 1779*, p. 77.

From the Marquise de Lafayette[9]

ALS: American Philosophical Society

ce 20 Juin 1780

On m'a dit, monsieur, qu'on avoit eu des nouvelles de Charlestown. Elles m'interessent trop vivement, pour que je n'aye pas quelques droits, a vous demander ce que vous pourriés, et ce que vous voudries bien m'en dire; et Si ce qu'on debitoit, il y a quelques jours de La deroute des anglois, et de la mort du Gal. [General] Clinton se confirme. Ce ne peut être, monsieur, qu'a titre de bonne americaine, et de femme de celui qui recoit des americains, et de vous en particulier, des marques de bonté, si precieuses pour nous, que j'ose vous importuner de toutes ces questions. Pardonnes Les moy je vous en Supplie, rendés justice a La Sincerité de mes sentimens et receves en lhommage.

Jai lhonneur detre, monsieur, votre tres humble et très obeissante servante NOAILLES DE LA FAYETTE

Notation: Me. De Lafayette 20. Juin 1780.

From Joseph Gardoqui & fils

ALS: American Philosophical Society

Sir Bilbao the 21st. June 1780.

The safe arrivall in our River after a passage of 34 days from Sallem in New England of the ship the Generall Pickering Capt Jonathan Haraden,[1] gives us by the desire of the Master an opportunity of Troubling your good self with the present lines, & will serve to Informe you that he haveing either misslaid, or the Board of warr not haveing delivered him a letter for us with a very large order to ship on his Vessell many Articles presisly

---

9. Whose anxiousness for news may indicate she had not yet received the letters her husband wrote the first week of May, telling her of his safe arrival in Boston: Idzerda, *Lafayette Papers*, III, 8–10.

1. Haraden (1744–1803) was from Gloucester, Mass. During the war he captured sixty British ships: Claghorn, *Naval Officers*, p. 138.

wantted for that Continent as we are for the want of the letter & order deprived of the pleasure of serving that Honourable Corporation finds that he will have a good deal of room to spare on Board his ship; therefore rather than to take any goods on freight on any privatte Account, he has requested us to make you an offer of what room there may be left on his ship after he receives the Articles that Can be purchased with the value of the cargoe of Sucars that he has delivered us.

The Ship is upwards of 200 Tons Burden, New, Sailes Imconparably well, armed with 16 guns 6 pounders & Two nine pounders, & will be manned before he departs with between 50 a 60 good hands; Therefore should you think proper to proffitt of this opportunity you may be assured that what ever orders you shoud be pleased to honour us with for the purpose, will be attended to, with the utmost punctuality & Care.

We sinerely offer you the Tenders of our abillitys in this place, & remmain with the highest respectt Sir your mt obligd obt hble Serts,   JOSEPH GARDOQUI & SONS

We Trouble you with an Account of the Engagment sustained by Capt Haraden against a Lugger of Triple his force. a Governo[2]

His Exelency Benjamin Franklin Esqre.

Addressed: His Excellency / Benjamin Franklin Esqr. / Minister Plenipottenciary / from the United States of / America &a In / Paris

Notation: Gardoqui Joseph & Sons Bilbao 21. June 1780.

---

2. An Italian phrase, meaning "for guidance." Haraden's engagement was against the *Achilles*, carrying 43 cannon; he succeeded in retaking his prize, the *Golden Eagle*, from her: John A. McManemin, *Captains of the State Navies during the Revolutionary War* (Ho-Ho-Kus, N.J., 1984), p. 130.

From John Paul Jones

LS:[3] American Philosophical Society; AL (draft): National Archives[4]

Sir.   L'Orient June 21st. 1780

I was detained at Versailles forty hours from the time of my arrival, and was then informed by M de Genet that an express had been sent from Court with the necessary orders to the Kings Officers at L'Orient respecting Captain Landais and the Alliance. I found myself here early yesterday morning fifty four hours after leaving Versailles. The Alliance had the Evening and Night before been warped and towed from the Road of L'Orient to Port Louis and no Express from Court had arrived here, M. de Thevenard the Commandant however made every necessary preparation to stop the Alliance as appears by the inclosed document on the Subject.[5] He had even sent his orders in the Evening before I was aware to fire on the Alliance and sink her to the bottom if they attempted to approach and pass the barrier that had been made across the Entrance of the Port. Had I even remained Silent an hour longer the dreadful work would have been done.— Your Humanity will I know Justify the part I acted in preventing a scene that would have rendered me miserable for the rest of my life.— The Alliance has this Morning been warped and towed through the Rocks and is now at Anchor without between Port Louis & Groa.[6] In this situation I at Noon sent out Lieutenant Dale with a letter to Captain Landais

3. Two minor spelling mistakes have been corrected from the draft. The postscript is in Jones's hand.

4. A French translation is at the Archives de la Marine. Jones sent this letter to Edme-Jacques Genet, the foreign ministry's chief of interpreters, for forwarding (see Bradford, *Jones Papers*, reel 5, no. 1117), and Genet had the letter translated: BF to Jones, July 5 (Library of Congress).

5. Jones enclosed a two-page document in French dated June 20 (University of Pa. Library) listing the ships and shore batteries ready to oppose by force the departure of the *Alliance*. This document also discusses the French decision (made at Jones's request) to refrain from using force until the arrival of the King's orders: Bradford, *Jones Papers*, reel 5, no. 1116, enclosure.

6. Landais' account of the crisis does not attempt to explain the French naval officials' change of heart: Landais, *Memorial*, pp. 102–3.

whereof the within is a Copy.—[7] When Lieutenant Dale returns I will render you an Account of the event.—

Yesterday Morning the within letter was brought me from Mr. Lee, tho' I had never even hinted that his Opinion or advice would be acceptable.[8] He has however pulled off the Masque, and I am Convinced is not a little disapointed that his Operations have not produced Blood-shed between the subjects of France and America, Poor Man.

Yesterday every thing that Perswasion or threatning could effect was attempted. I sent on board the inclosed letter to Captain Parke of the Marines[9] with copies of yours of the 16th. to Captain Landais and to the Officers and People of the Alliance and an Extract of *the agreeable part* of your letter to me of the 12th. respecting money matters & ca. and I added a Postscript desiring an answer or a personal interview, and assuring them that they would on returning to their duty be done strict Justice with respect to their Interest in a few days, and all my influence should be exerted to obtain their excuse for the past.— The letter was delivered but I have as yet received no answer.— M de Thevenard on his part sent the deputy of M: Sweighauser on board with your letters *under his own cover* to Captain Landais and to the Officers and Men of the Alliance. The one was delivered to Captain Landais the 'other to the Lieutenant Degge.— M De Thevenard also sent on board an Officer with the Kings order to arrest Captain Landais who refused to surrender himself.— Mr Lee and his party pretend to Justify their measures because they say you did not put Captain Landais under Arrest,— according to them you Cannot displace him however great in Crimes! If this Government does not interfere to crush that despicable party, France and America have got much to fear from it. I verily believe them to be *English* at the bottom of their

7. In this communication, dated June 21, Jones asked Landais to deliver the former crewmen of the *Bonhomme Richard* and Jones's personal effects: Bradford, *Jones Papers*, reel 5, no. 1114.

8. In a June 13 letter to Jones, Lee defended Landais' right to command the *Alliance: ibid.*, no. 1107.

9. Jones advised Parke, "Open your eyes.": *ibid.*, no. 1111. A copy of that letter is filed with the present one at the APS. Landais placed Parke under arrest on the evening of the 21st: Landais, *Memorial*, p. 103.

hearts.— I am ever with the highest Esteem and most profound respect. Dear sir, Your affectionate and most humble Servt.

JNO P JONES

N.B. Mr. Dale has this moment brought me the within impertinent Note from Capt. Landais.[1] I understand that the Alliance is to remain under Groa till the Prize Money is Paid.

Notation: J.P. Jones L'Orient June 21. 1780

From Jonathan Williams, Jr.

ALS: University of Pennsylvania Library; copy: Yale University Library

Dear & hond Sir.   A L'Orient le 21 Juin 1780

I have not written you since the 14 Instant because everything has been here in such a State of Confusion and Suspence and I chose to say nothing 'till I could say something decisively.[2] I must now inform you that there is no prospect of Capt Jones's

1. An undated response to Jones's letter of June 21, now with BF's papers at the University of Pa. Library. In it Landais questions Jones's right to command the *Ariel*. It bears WTF's notation, "Impertinent Note of Capt. Landais's to Commodore Jones."

2. Tempers were flaring in Lorient. On June 18, JW ran into Thomas Lee, the young nephew of Arthur Lee (XXVII, 294n; XXXI, 500–1), and evidently "Publickly insulted" him. The next morning Lee sent two seconds to challenge JW to a duel. E. Brush and Joseph Brown, Jr., presented Lee's complaint; JW refused to apologize and, to the acute alarm of the seconds, he accepted the challenge "with the Greatest Pleasure." Lee, who was then summoned, offered JW his choice of pistols. When asked as to the place, JW answered "*here*"; as to the distance, JW suggested the nearer the better, as Lee was to have the first shot. The rivals faced one another at a distance of four yards. At JW's insistence the seconds reluctantly stepped aside, whereupon "Mr Williams with a surprising fortitude receiv'd the fire from Mr Lee, which fortunately miss'd him." JW offered Lee a second shot, which he emphatically refused. JW then announced that he would not reciprocate the fire, and "discharg'd his pistole out of the Window." The matter was now considered "honourably Settled," JW having exhibited "amazing Intrepidity & firmness," and Lee, for his part, displaying "Every appearance of true Bravery." Testimony of E. Brush and Joseph Brown, Jr., June 20, 1780, Yale University Library. Brown and Brush were in Lorient awaiting passage to America on the *Alliance:* BF to Jones, March 1, above.

regaining the Alliance, she is under Groix and nothing but fair Combat and Superiour Force can alter the Government of her. For the Detail of this Affair I refer you to other Letters which you will receive no doubt by this Post.

The 2000 Suits of Cloaths are arrived & I have 2000 more on the Way, besides which all that remained at Brest M. de Chaumont has ordered hither, thus we shall have more than the ariel can carry and I have no other Ship except a small Brig of Mr Moylans nor do I see a prospect of getting one unless Government should grant us one. I hope you will approve the Steps I have taken and favour me with your answer.—

You will hear from Nantes that News is come there of the Marquis de la Fayettes safe arrival in Boston.

I am ever with the greatest Respect Dear & hond Sir Your most dutifull & Affectionate Kinsman   JONA WILLIAMS J

Addressed: A Monsieur / Monsieur Franklin / Ministre Plenipotentiaire / des Etas Unis en son Hotel / a Passy prés Paris

Notation: Jona Williams 21 June 80

To Dumas: Two Letters

(I) and (II) copies: Library of Congress, National Archives[3]

I.

Dear sir   Passy, June 22. 1780.

I received duly yours of May 23. June 2, 6. 8. and 15.— Inclosed you have a Letter for the Gentleman you recommended to me.[4] He seems to be a man of Abilities.

---

3. An LS of (I) in WTF's hand was offered for sale in 1976 by The Rendells (Newton, Mass.); the verso of the letter is reproduced in their sales catalogue no. CXVIII (August, 1976), p. 19. An LS of (II), with the date of June 28, 1780, is listed in the C.F. Libbie & Co. (Boston) sales catalogue, Dec. 18–19, 1907, p. 62; the catalogue prints the first sentence and a half of it.

4. To Van der Oudermeulen of this date, below; see Dumas to BF of May 23–June 13 for his recommendation and for the inquiry answered in BF's next paragraph. Dumas' June 2 letter mentions Neufville's bills, while that of the 15th inquires about the judgment of the *Flora*. BF's second letter to Dumas of the present date, immediately below, was written in response to Dumas' of June 8.

568

The Words *before I leave Europe*, had no Relation to any Particular immediate Intention, but to the General one I flatter myself with, of being able to return and spend there the Small Remains of Life that are left me.

I have written distinctly to Messrs. de Neufville concerning those Bills. I hear that 484⁵ was at New Bern the 12th. of April, and soon to sail from thence or from Virginia for france. Probably he might not sail in some Weeks after, as Vessels are often longer in fitting out than was expected.— If it is the fier Rodrigue a 50 gun Ship, that he comes in, I have just heard that She would not sail till the Middle of may.

Herewith you have the Judgment relating to the flora, which I thought had been sent before.

The Mischiefs done by the Mob in London are astonishing! They were, I hear within an Ace of destroying the Bank with all the Books relating to the funds, which would have created infinite confusion. I am grieved at the Loss of Charlestown.⁶ Let us hope soon to hear better News from the Operations of the french and Spanish forces gone to America.

With great Esteem, I am ever Dear Sir, Your &c.

M. Dumas

II.

Dear Sir   Passy, June 22. 1780.

As the English do not allow that we can make legal Prizes, they certainly cannot detain the Dutch Ship the Berkenboos, on Pretence that it was become american Property before they took it, for the rest there is no doubt but the Congress will do what shall appear to be just, on a Proper Representation of facts laid before them, which the Owners should appoint some Person in America to do. Those Gentlemen may depend on my rendering them every service in my Power. I am &.

Mr. Dumas.

5. Henry Laurens; see our annotation of Webster's May 2 and Dumas' June 2 letters.

6. The news of Clinton's May 12 capture of the city had recently been published in the London papers (*e.g.*, the *London Courant, and Westminster Chronicle* of June 16).

To Joshua Johnson

Sir   Passy, June 22. 1780.

I duly received the Honour of your Letter acquainting me with your Acceptance of the Trust you were appointed to by Congress, and your Readiness to enter upon the Execution of it.[7] I have delayed hitherto requesting your coming to Paris for that Purpose, because Mr. Deane, who had the Chief Management of all the Mercantile affairs, and whose Presence as well as Papers might be necessary to explain those transactions, has been long daily expected here, having written to me in December last from Virginia, that he was there in his Way to france, was to sail in the fendant, a French Man of war for Martinique, and thence take a passage hither.[8] We have heard some time of the arrival of the Fendant at that Island, but I hear nothing of Mr. Deane. When I reflect on my time of Life I grow more impatient to have those Accounts settled: If therefore M. Deane Should not arrive in the Course of a Month, I must then desire you would come up, bring with you if you can, a good Clerk that is an Accountant, to copy &c. and let us do the Business together as well as we can.

On the Receipt of the Act of assembly from Maryland relating to their money in England, I wrote to the Commissioners there, sent them the Original Act after taking a Copy, and desired their immediate Answer whether they would execute the Trust, as something was required of me to be done in case of their Refusal.[9] I have but just learnt by a Letter from Mr. Russel, that mine got to hand. He wrote me of the 13th. Instant, that Mr. Hanbury being at bath for his Health, he had written to him desiring to see him in town to answer my Letter; that the Answer dated the 10th Current, was, he should certainly be in town in a Month or sooner; and Mr. Russell adds, when he comes you may depend on our Answer.

I have the honour to be, Sir.

Mr. Johnson.

7. Johnson had agreed to audit the accounts of BF and his former fellow commissioners: XXXI, 564–5.

8. XXXI, 272.

9. To James Russell, Silvanus Grove, and Osgood Hanbury, May 20, above.

To Jean de Neufville & fils

LS:[1] National Archives; copy: Library of Congress

Gentlemen,   Passy June 22. 1780.

I received duly your respected Letter of the 15th. current, inclosing one of the Bills drawn on Mr. Lawrens, which I return herewith. I am satisfy'd that the same is a genuine Bill, and that it will be accepted by Mr Lawrens, when he arrives, as of the Date when it would have been presented if he had been at Amsterdam: But I have no Advice or Orders relating to those Bills; and as that Gentleman may be daily expected, I think it not proper for me to meddle with them at present; nor indeed does it seem necessary, since they may without Prejudice to the Holders remain noted, according to what I am told is the Custom of Merchants, 'till the Expiration of the Term, and if Mr Lawrens should not in that Time appear, I might pay them if I should have Funds in my Hands; if not they may then be protested and sent back. Inclosed I send to your Care a Letter for Mr Lawrens which I have just received from Philadelphia: It came from thence with others dated the 5th. of May, when it must have been supposed there that he was on his Passage.

With great Regard, I have the Honour to be, Gentlemen, Your most obedient & most humble Servant.   B FRANKLIN

Messrs: J. De Neufville & Sons.

To John Rainey

Copy: Library of Congress

Sir   Passy, June 22. 1780

I wrote to you in Answer to yours of the 12th. as Mercht: in Amsterdam, not knowing how to direct to you more particularly. Since that Letter we have received news from America which may be agreable to you. It is that the Congress, to prevent any loss to those who have lent them money, arising from the subsequent Depreciation of the Paper, have made a Resolution to re-

---

1. In WTF's hand.

pay the same according to its full value in the time of lending.[2] This fixes your Property and secures you from the Loss you might otherwise have apprehended, on which I congratulate you; and am, Sir &c.

Mr. John Rainey.

To Van der Oudermeulen Two copies:[3] Library of Congress

Sir, Passy. 22. June. 1780

I received the Letter you did me the Honour of writing to me, the 15th. Inst. containing the Sketch of a Plan for commerce with America by establishing there and in Europe Companies with Privileges for that Purpose, upon which you desire my Sentiments.

I cannot from so small a Sketch understand fully the Extent of your Plan: But I will mention what occurs to me in Perusing it.— There is no doubt but that Merchants in Europe may if they think fit, form themselves into Companies for carrying on the Commerce of America, with such Privileges as they can obtain from their Sovereigns; but the general Principle in America being for a free Trade with all the World, and to leave every one of their Merchants at Liberty to prosecute it as he may judge most for his Advantage, I do not think such Companies can be established *there* with any exclusive Rights or Privileges. And this open commerce being free to all Nations, and more profitable to Europe than to America, which can very well subsist and flourish without a Commerce with Europe; a Commerce that chiefly imports Superfluities & Luxuries; it concerns those Nations principally to protect that Commerce, in which Protection there is no doubt but France will bear her Part; but that she should take the whole upon her, is too much to be ask'd or expected by America. We have besides a common Opinion, that Business is

2. This resolution was passed on April 18: *JCC*, XVI, 374–5. Congress had already begun corrupting the integrity of loan office certificates, however, by using them as currency: Ferguson, *Power of the Purse*, pp. 53–5.
3. The one from which we print is in WTF's hand; the other is in L'Air de Lamotte's.

best manag'd and to most Advantage by those who are immediately interested in the Profits of it; and that Trading Companies are generally more profitable to the Servants of the Company than to the proprietors of the Stock, or to the Publick.

I have the honour to be, Sir, Your most obedient & most humble Sert   signed. B. FRANKLIN

M. Van der Oudermeulen

Copy.

Notation in Franklin's hand: Papers & Letters Relating to a Company propos'd to be formed in Europe for the American Trade

From John Adams

LS:[4] Archives du Ministère des affaires étrangères; AL (draft): Massachusetts Historical Society; copies: American Philosophical Society, National Archives; transcript: National Archives

Sir   Paris June 23d. [*i.e.*, 22][5] 1780
I have this Day the honour of a Letter from his Excellency the Comte De Vergennes, on the subject of the Resolutions of Congress of the Eighteenth of March, concerning the Paper-Bills; in which his Excellency informs me that the Chevalier De La Luzerne has Orders to make the strongest Representations upon the Subject.[6]

I am not certain whether his Excellency means that such Or-

4. In the hand of Francis Dana.

5. On the National Archives copy Dana added a note that the letter was actually written and sent on the 22nd, but misdated the 23rd.

6. *Adams Papers*, IX, 453–9; for background see *ibid.*, 427–33, 449–50. JA's dispute with Vergennes over the effects of Congress' 40:1 devaluation of American currency (on March 18, 1780) upon French creditors helped lead to his becoming virtually persona non grata with the French court. JA's role in the controversy has been subject to different interpretations. Charles Francis Adams, ed., *The Works of John Adams* ... (10 vols., Boston, 1856), I, 314–16, for example, portrays him as an innocent victim of circumstances, while James H. Hutson, *John Adams and the Diplomacy of the American Revolution* (Lexington, Kentucky, 1980), pp. 61–4, argues that he was imprudent and hence largely responsible for his own troubles.

ders were sent so long ago, as to have reached the hand of the
Minister at Congress, or whether they have been lately expe-
dited;[7] if the latter I submit it to your Excellency, whether it
wou'd not be expedient to request that those Orders may be
stopped until proper Representations can be made at Court;[8] to
the end that if it can be made to appear, as I firmly believe it may,
that those Orders were given upon Misinformation, they may be
revoked, otherwise sent on.

Your Excellency will excuse this because it appears to me a
matter of very great Importance. The Affair of our Paper is
sufficiently dangerous and critical and if a Representation from
his Majesty shou'd be made, Advantage will not fail to be taken
of it, by the Tories, and by interested and disappointed Specula-
tors who may spread an Alarm among many uninformed People
so as to Endanger the public Peace— I have the honour to be
with much Respect Your Excellency's most obedient and most
humble Servant   JOHN ADAMS

His Excellency Dr. Franklin

From Dumas   ALS: American Philosophical Society

Monsieur   Lahaie 22e. Juin 1780.
Quelle funeste nouvelle nous venons de recevoir. Charlestown pris; & toute la Garnison (6000 h.) prisonniere.[9] Cette derniere circonstance est pire que la perte de la Ville. Il auroit mieux

7. Vergennes wrote La Luzerne on June 3, instructing him to lobby Con-
gress for an exemption for Frenchmen from the currency devaluation: *Adams
Papers*, IX, 458–9n; Hutson, *John Adams*, p. 60.
8. JA is implying either that he wants BF to make these representations or
that he will need more time to prepare them himself. BF assumed the latter:
BF to Vergennes, June 24. That assumption was wrong, as JA on June 22 wrote
Vergennes a lengthy memorandum on the subject: *Adams Papers*, IX, 460–70.
Hutson, *John Adams*, pp. 64–5, accuses JA of deliberately misleading BF (a
case which would be stronger if the present letter actually had been written
on June 23, as Hutson assumes). JA apparently did send BF a copy of his memorandum with his June 29 letter, below.
9. The news of which appeared in the next day's issue (no. L) of the *Gaz.
de Leyde*.

valu abandonner celle-ci; & avec les 6000 h. empêcher l'ennemi de pénétrer dans le pays qu'on auroit par-là sauvé & conservé: au lieu que le voilà exposé aux courses de l'ennemi; & les Etats Unis privés de la quote part que cette riche Province fournissoit à la Caisse commune. Mais à quoi servent d'inutiles regrets? Si ce n'est à augmenter la douleur de ce fatal évenement, qui consterne tous nos amis ici, nuit au crédit de l'Amérique, & releve celui de l'ennemi. J'en suis malade, & ne trouve de soulagement qu'à mêler ma douleur avec la vôtre. Je me persuade néanmoins, que ce coup ne sauroit changer la destinée de l'Amérique, & que finalement l'ennemi restera la dupe de l'histoire. Le gd. F——r, qui s'est adouci à mon égard, & que j'ai déjà visité 2 ou 3 fois, est aussi de ce sentiment.

Pour faire voir que ce coup n'abat point les Américains, ni leur serviteur ici, J'ai porté aujourd'hui copie de votre Lettre aux Armateurs, & de celle à l'Amirauté de Cherbourg au G—— P——[1] avec cette courte Lettre.

"M. Les 2 pieces ci-jointes m'ont été envoyées de Passy, pour en faire l'usage que je croirai convenable ou nécessaire. Je les crois dans le cas de devoir être communiquées à V. E., & de ne pouvoir que Lui être agréables, puisqu'elles interessent les sujets de cette République. Je suis avec un profond respect, &c."— (Le tout sous un couvert cacheté que j'ai laissé à son Domestique.) Le gd. F——r & *notre Ami* approuvent cette démarche. Notre ami est fort affecté du malheur de Charlestown. Je l'ai rassuré tant que j'ai pu sur les suites. Je ne saurois me rendre raison de cette catastrophe, qu'en supposant qu'il y a eu de la trahison.

J'attends de votre réponse, Monsieur, quelque beaume pour la plaie qui saignera jusque-là. Je suis, dans le malheur comme dans le bonheur, Monsieur, avec le plus respectueux attachement Votre très humble & très obéissant serviteur   DUMAS

Passy à Son Exc. M. Franklin

Notation: Dumas la haie Juin 22. 80.

Addressed: A Son Excellence / Monsieur B. Franklin, Esqr. / Min. Plenipe. des Etats-unis / &c. / *Passy./* .

1. Dumas must have sent Grand Pensionary van Bleiswijk the enclosures to BF's letter of June 5, above.

From Vandenyver frères & Cie.

ALS: American Philosophical Society

Monsieur   Paris ce 22 Juin 1780

Nous avons recu la Lettre que vous nous avés fait Lhonneur de nous ecrire le 28 may der [dernier] avec La Copie du Jugement pour le Navire La flore et Son chargement, nous avions esperès quil auroit eté plus favorable aux proprietaires du dernier, mais nous L'avons envoyés Sur le champ a Cherbourg pour le faire mettre a execution et ce n'est quen datte du 17 de ce mois quon nous mande que le Navire est dechargé et en etat de repartir pour la hollande mais quil est retenu par le défaut de Ses passeports et autres papiers de bord qui nont pas eté renvoÿés a L Amirauté du dit Lieu.

Nous Supplions Votre Excellence d avoir la bonté de faire tenir les dits passeports Connoissemens et autres papiers par premier Courier a Lamirauté de Cherbourg pour que le Navire puisse mettre a la voille et Se Soustraire aux dangers dont ce port paroit etre menacé.

Nous Sommes avec le plus profond Respect Monsieur Vos tres humbles & tres Obeissants Serviteurs

VANDENYVER FRERES & COMP

a Monsieur franklin a Passy

Notations in different hands: Vandeniver freres, Paris 22. Juin 1780. / Ansd[2]

From Vergennes

Copy: Library of Congress

Versailles le 22. Juin 1780.

M. Dumont, Monsieur, qui vous est annoncé par M. Le Duc de la Vauguyon[3] desire que je me joigne à cet Ambassadeur pour vous engager à l'entendre. Je defère Volontiers à sa Sollicitation et je profite avec plaisir de cette Occasion pour vous renouveller

---

2. We have not located the response.
3. Above, June 17.

les Sentiments distingués avec lesquels J'ai l'honneur d'être. Monsieur, votre tres humble et très obeissant Serviteur.

(signé) De Vergennes

M. Franklin.

Invitation to the Fête Apollonienne[4]

D: American Philosophical Society

[before June 23, 1780]

Fête
Apolloniene à St. Cloud
le 27. juin 1780

On partira à 7. heures du matin en Batelets. Musique Militaire Sur l'Eau à midi, assemblée académique jusqu'à une heure et demie. Il y sera fait lecture de divers morceaux d'Eloquence et de Poësie. Il y aura exposition de differens ouvrages de Peinture, de Sculpture, d'Architecture et de Gravure. A deux heures Le Banquet, Ensuite Concert et Divertissement champêtre.

Les Billets d'entrée ne pourront servir que pour les Personnes dont ils porteront les noms, et qui seront inscrites Sur le Régistre du Comité établi pour veiller au bon ordre de la fête.

Les Billets des Dames leur seront remis chés elles par un des membres du Comité.

Il ne sera donné des Billets qu'à ceux qui seront sur la Liste des personnes invitées à la fête, et on n'en délivera aucun aprés le 23. Juin./.

4. The Société apollonienne, presided over by Court de Gébelin, was created in 1780. A kind of free university, it was called the Musée de Paris as of 1781 and lasted until 1785. See Pierre Chevallier, *Histoire de la franc-maçonnerie française: la Maçonnerie: école de l'égalité (1725–1799)* (Paris, 1974), p. 286.

To Arthur Lee

Sir,   Passy, 23 June 1780.

I received the Letters you did me the honour of writing to me, the 23th.[5] Inst: informing me of the Passport I had before given you being expired and desiring another. Inclosed I have the Honour of sending it to you.[6]

With great Respect, I am sir, your most obedient and most humble Servant   BF.

Honble. A. Lee Esq.

From John Paul Jones

LS:[7] American Philosophical Society; AL (draft): National Archives; copy:[8] United States Naval Academy Museum

Honored and Dear sir   L'orient June 23d. 1780

I by the last post gave you an account of the events here respecting Captain Landais and the Alliance, and inclosed all the necessary papers to explain circumstances.—[9] Yesterday the Serapis was publicly sold for I think 240,000 livres.—[1] Mr. Wil-

---

5. Actually the 13th, above.

6. We have not located the passport. The present letter was, as far as we know, the last communication between BF and Lee until 1786. Lee's return voyage to the United States aboard the *Alliance* was far from comfortable, according to an Oct. 30, 1780, letter he wrote James Warren: Mass. Hist. Soc. *Collections*, LXXIII (1925), 142–4.

7. The final sentence of the postscript is in Jones's hand and does not appear in the AL (draft) or the copy.

8. Made at Lorient in August, 1780, and attested a true copy by Thomas Hutchins.

9. Jones to BF, June 21, above.

1. Although the French government did purchase the *Serapis* for 240,000 *l.t.*, she did not serve thereafter with the French Navy. Instead, a former captain in the East India Company named Roch received the king's permission on Sept. 8 to arm her for privateering in the Indian Ocean. After being doubled in copper, she sailed from France on Feb. 21, 1781, and was destroyed on July 31 in an accident near Ste. Marie Island, off Madagascar: Archives de la Marine, B¹XCIII: 33, 48; B²CDXIX: 7, 9, 12; B³DCLXXXIV: 207–8; B³DCCV: 29.

liams and myself have been looking after a ship on freight to transport from France the remainder of the 5 a 600 Tons of public stores that are now so much wanted in America.— No Merchant Vessel however can be found here for the purpose. There will remain 400 Tons after the Ariel is filled up; for the estimation that M. De Chaumont has made is short more than half the quantity of the reality.

I know his self Sufficiency[2] would laugh at this, were I alone in thus widely differing from him, but when he knows that my Calculation does not exceed that of the Commandant and Commissary here he ought to have modesty enough to confess that he is unacquainted with Marine affairs. The Serapis will be Masted and fitted for sea in a very short time, as soon perhaps as the whole cloathing &c can be collected here.— Mr Williams assures me that no suitable Ship can be had on freight even at Nantes nor any where else in the Kingdom to his knowledge.— If the Government would condescend to lend the Serapis, that Ship armed in Flute,[3] would with the Ariel armed for War, Just answer the purpose, and there would be no Room in either ship left vacant— The Serapis might carry her lower Battery in the hould & might sail with 150 Men, the two ships might sail in Company and would be a good protection for the Stores, against any of the Enemies Cruising Ships.— The Serapis might be full armed and manned for War immediately on her Arrival in America, and might with the Ariel and some other Continental Frigates be sent without loss of time directly from America on some of the services, that are hinted at in the Project that I had the honor to present to Government,[4] This last Idea you know agrees with your Opinion on the services proposed in my Project; I therefore hope you will support it with your Credit, and I am convinced that if adopted it will be Productive of very good Consequences.

As to manning the Serapis and Ariel, I believe firmly that little or no difficulty will be found in effecting it, 300 Men will be

2. Chaumont.

3. With part of her gun battery removed to make room for cargo.

4. Jones had submitted to the French government plans for amphibious operations with a squadron incorporating some French Navy frigates: Bradford, *Jones Papers*, reel 5, no. 1087; Morison, *Jones*, p. 290.

sufficient for both Ships. There are an Hundred Officers and Seamen now here on shore, and on board the Alliance that belonged to the Bon Homme Richard, besides from 50 a 80 of the Volunteer Soldiers, who are still waiting here at their own expence, in hopes of serving again under my Command, and from the hourly applications that are made to me here, if I had authority, I could soon compleat the remainder.

I am with real Affection & Profound respect, Your Excellencys Most Obliged and Most Humble Servant   JNO P JONES

M De Thevenard has this day sent a new requisition to Captain Landais for the Seamen &ca on board the Alliance, who served with me in the Bon Homme Richard. I have recd. yours of the 17th.— Money would make the people of the Alliance do anything.

His Excellency. Benja Franklin Esqr. & &

Notation: J.P. Jones L'Orient June 23. 1780

From Sartine

Copy: Library of Congress

A Versailles le 23. Juin 1780.
J'ai reçu, Monsieur, la Lettre que vous m'avez fait l'honneur de m'écrire le 19. de ce mois.

J'ai fait prevenir les officiers de l'Amirauté de Vannes que la Vente du Vau. Le Serapis se feroit à L'Orient par le Commissaire des Ports et arcenaux de la Marine en ce Port. Vous serez tres incessamment informé du Prix auquel ce Bâtiment aura été porté et l'adjudication n'aura occasionné aucun frais.

J'ai l'honneur d'être avec une parfaite Consideration Monsieur, Votre tres humble et très obeissant Serviteur./.

M. Franklin.

From Jonathan Williams, Jr. ALS: American Philosophical Society

Dear & hond Sir.   L'Orient June 23. 1780
I have received your Favour of the 17 Inst and should be happy immediately to execute your Orders, but the Frigate Al-

liance has not only fled and deprived us of her Assistance but the Bonhomme Richards men are in her & are loaded with Irons because they want to join their old Commander. Thus does this Fool & madman sacrifice the dearest Interests of our Country, by following the pernicious Councils of your late Colleague. It is in my Opinion beyond a Doubt that Landais Brain (if it ever was right) is turned, and AL moves the distracted machine taking Care however to keep the Springs out of Sight.—

I do not find the possibility of freighting merchant Ships. I have consulted M. de Thevenar the Commandant of this Port, and I have the pleasure to find his Opinion & mine agree; The Bulk of the Stores is not less than 500 Tons and I think rather more; the Ariel when she is armed *en guerre* cannot carry more than 150 Tons of these Goods, from 3 to 400 Tons will then remain. There are here belonging to the King the following Ships which have no actual mission. The Serapis (bought for the King yesterday at 240,000 *l.t.*) The Terpsicore a fine Frigate acknowledged to be the best Sailor in the Marine, rather old but now fitting and may be soon compleat.[5] La Chimere a good Frigate but will require too long an outfitt— Either of the two first of these Ships may be ready to go with the Ariel and if armed as a Transport will at Once carry out the whole of the Stores to our suffering Country— Please to look at the Letter I wrote you from Nantes just before my Departure reccommending the new Frigate there and the manner of arming her,[6] that plan may be executed either with the Serapis or the Terpsicore and it is approved by the Commandant here as well as by Capt Jones. It will cost little more than to freight, even if you could freight, & the Ship so much gained; if then you would buy either of these Ships of a private Person why not of the King? and if you could get money of Government to pay for them, or pay for the Freight if you could hire why can't Government give a Ship at once or let one? Where lies the difference? To enforce this reasoning we may surely return to our old argument "their Kindness in assisting us with the means to procure Cloathing is lost if we can't get that Cloathing out."

5. The *Terpsichore*, 30, was built in 1763: Dull, *French Navy*, p. 356. John Paul Jones had sought to obtain her: Morison, *Jones*, pp. 306–7.
6. JW must mean his of May 20, written several weeks before he left for Lorient. The "new Frigate" had been sold; see JW's letter of June 9.

I would set off to see you if it was not for the Situation of Mrs Williams. You know she has already made one miscarriage and she is now three months gone with very alarming appearances of a second misfortune.—⁷

I am ever with the greatest Esteem & Respect Your dutifull & affectionate Kinsman JONA WILLIAMS J

As to the propriety of drawing on Mr de Chaumont rather than you I never understood more of it than his Directions to have it so, and as you refered me to him for Orders I supposed you understood each other, the Reason he gave me was that your political capacity was incompatible with these commercial Transactions.— JW

Endorsed: M. de Chaumont's Reason given to Mr Williams for drawing on him.— Mr W. suppos'd I had agreed to it.—

Notation: Jona Williams June 20 1780

From Gérard de Rayneval
Copy: Library of Congress

A Versailles le 14. Juin [*i.e.*, June 24]⁸ 1780.
M. Le Cte. de Vergennes a remis avant hier, Monsieur, une Lettre pour vous à M. Dumont qui desireroit fort de vous entretenir; S. Éce. vous seroit infiniment obligé si vous vouliez bien lui dire si le dt. Dumont vous a éffectivement vû, et lui confier les Ouvertures qu'il peut vous avoir faites. Mon Exprès a ordre d'attendre votre Reponse.

J'ai l'honneur d'etre avec un parfait attachement, Monsieur, Votre très humble et tres obeissant serviteur.

(signé) GERARD DE RAYNEVAL.

M Franklin.

7. Mariamne delivered a healthy girl, Christine, on Dec. 29: I, lviii; JW to BF, Dec. 30, 1780, University of Pa. Library.
8. Probably mistranscribed by L'Air de Lamotte. Vergennes introduced "Dumont" on the 22nd, above, and BF replied to the present letter on the 24th, immediately below.

To Gérard de Rayneval

ALS: Archives du Ministère des affaires étrangères

Sir   June 24. 1780

The Person who calls himself Dumont was with me yesterday Evening, bringing Notes to me from M. de Vergennes & M le Duc de Vauguyon.[9] He said his Business was to solicit a Supply of 4000. Stand of Arms to be landed in the West of England, for the Use of the Petitioners who were become sensible that Petitioning signified nothing, and that without using Force it was impossible to prevent the total Loss of Liberty and the Establishment of arbitrary Government in England; that the Appearance of 4000 Men in Arms, would be sufficient to draw together a great Body from different Parts, the whole Nation being dissatisfied with the present Government; that even the Army was disaffected, & the Navy so much so, that Admiral Geary had been ordered to put to Sea with the Fleet, to prevent a Revolt which was apprehended among the Seamen.[1] I mention'd the Difficulty of Landing such a Quantity of Arms in England, without being observed, & Troops sent to seize them, or to defeat the People that should undertake to use them, before they could be disciplin'd; and that it was not probable such an Aid could be obtained, without its being well known whose Hands the Arms were to be put into, what Persons of weight were likely to be concern'd, and other Circumstances that might satisfy there was a Chance of Success. He said all relating to the Reception & Use of the Arms was already arranged; and Persons of Note concern'd in the Affair, would discover themselves as soon as they could be assur'd of obtaining the Supply: but otherwise it was dangerous & could not be expected. He desired me to forward & favour the Business if my Opinion should be asked; but made no particular Offers or *Ouvertures* to me. I do not know him. He ask'd my Opinion of the Design. I told him I could form none, without knowing more Particulars of it than he had communicated, and also the Persons who were to conduct it. He said he

9. Above, June 22 and 17, respectively.
1. Geary's fleet actually spent most of June at sea looking for the French and Spanish fleets: G.R. Barnes and J.H. Owen, eds., *The Private Papers of John, Earl of Sandwich* . . . (4 vols., London, 1932–38), III, 275–6.

was to see M. de Vergennes, & that he would call again upon me after that Interview.[2] If he communicates any thing farther worth Notice, I shall immediately acquaint Mr de Vergennes with it, to whom be pleased to present my sincere Respects. I have the honour to be, with perfect Esteem, Sir, Your most obedient & most humble Servant   B FRANKLIN

M. de Raynevall

To Gourlade & Moylan   Copy: Library of Congress

Gentlemen,   Passy, June 24. 1780.

I received your favour, acquainting me with a Desertion from the Alliance and your having stopt the People.[3] Your Letter is not before me, having put it with other Papers into the Hands of Messrs. Adams and Dana, and requested their Advice, they being, much better acquainted with maritime Law than myself. I cannot therefore answer it fully till next Post. This is just to acquaint you, that I approve of your discharging such as had enter'd into no Engagement, tho' they had received Relief in their Necessities. The Prisoners who came exchanged from England, are freemen and may engage with who they please: but if they are immediately wanted to help out with the Stores to be sent to Congress in the Alliance and Ariel, Commodore Gillon surely will forbear enticing them from that Service.[4]

By the enclosed Note which came in yours, it Should Seem that Provisions for the Alliance have been Stopt,[5] and that the Signature J.P. Jones is a Mistake for P. Landais. If the Stoppage has not been a measure of Government I could wish it taken off as Landais will otherwise obtain them from Mr. Schweighauser's

2. Vergennes also wanted more proof. The British double agent soon returned to the Netherlands, and for the next year kept producing fictitious or misleading information: Richard B. Morris, *The Peacemakers: the Great Powers and American Independence* (New York, Evanston, and London, 1965), pp. 116–27.

3. Moylan to BF, June 15, above.

4. Gillon attempted to recruit from the *Alliance* for his new frigate: Gillon to BF, June 12, above.

5. The note is missing. Moylan told the purser of the *Alliance* that he would

Agent by Virtue of a former Order to Schweighauser from the Navy board and that will bring an Expence upon me.[6] Besides it will seem hard that the Poor People exchanged Prisoners and other honest men on board, should be famish'd for the folly of that Gentleman.

I have the honour to be Gentlemen &c.

Messrs. Gourlade and Moylan.

To Landais

Copies: Library of Congress, National Archives

Sir   Passy, June 24. 1780

You have written several Letters peremptorily demanding of me the Prize Money which you say is due to the People of the alliance[7] and in yours of the 16th. which I have received thro' the Hands of Mr. Schewighauser, you speak of time lost by the Delay of that Payment to the Prejudice of the Interest of the United States. Your two first Prizes were Swedish Ships, the Owners of one of them demands 500£ Sterling, and those of the other upwards of 60,000 Livres, damages on account of illegal Capture.[8] Another if I remember right was a Brigantine from Ireland under Protection of the king's Passport, which I apprehend is already or will be adjuged no good Prize and Perhaps Damages will also be demanded.[9] The three Prizes sent into Norway have been delivered up to the English by the Danish Government, and not a farthing received on their Account, or even promised.[1] I do

---

continue to supply the ship as before, but the purser accused him of not doing so: Moylan to Nathan Blodget, June 17, and Blodget to Moylan, June 18 (APS); see also our annotation of Gillon's letter cited above.

6. We have not located the Eastern Navy Board's orders to Schweighauser, but its orders to Landais recognized the authority of the local commercial agent: XXVIII, 255. The agent in Lorient was Schweighauser's representative, Puchelberg, who did supply the *Alliance:* Puchelberg & Cie. to BF, July 10, 1780 (APS).

7. Above, June 14 and 16.

8. The *Victoria* and *Anna Louisa:* XXVIII, 563, 632; XXIX, 18; XXX, 224–5, 295n, 353–4, 506; XXXI, 362–3.

9. The *Three Friends,* which appears in vol. 30.

1. The *Union, Betsy,* and *Charming Polly:* XXX, 336, 591–3.

not recollect any others but the Serapis and the Countess of Scarborough which you know were not sold when you wrote your last Letter, and therefore none of the Produce of Such Sale could be in my Hands, or in the Hands of any body; nor do I intend ever to meddle with the Receipt or Payment of any such Money. But your Letters tho' directed to me are written to be read in America where the facts not being known, it may seem from those Letters that I had Money in my hands which I unjustly detained.— As to the prejudicial Delay of the sailing of the Alliance, it has been owing to the mutinous Declarations of the People, which you have promoted, (as appears by your having interlined one of their Papers with your own Hand and Signature)[2] that they would not weigh an Anchor &c. till they were paid, the utermost farthing of their Prize Money &c and the Sale not being till the 22d. of this Month, such Payment was as before impossible.

The other Particulars in your Letter I Shall answer by next post, and I am, Sir, &c.

Capt Landais

To Jean-Daniel Schweighauser   Copy: Library of Congress

Sir   Passy, June 24. 1780.

I last Night received your respected Letter of the 20th. Instant; inclosing one from Capt. Landais to which the Within is an Answer sent open for your Perusal.[3] I should make no Objection to your Supplying the Alliance with such Provisions as might be necessary for the present Subsistance of the People that are on board her, many of whom are exchanged Prisoners, honest and good Men who ought not to suffer famine for the folly of that Gentleman: But the king having given Orders for paying all

2. As he had; see our annotation of BF to Jones, June 12. BF's recognition that Landais' letters were intended to be made public may also have some merit; Landais published his June 14 and 16 letters in his *Memorial*, pp. 102–3.

3. The preceding document. None of Schweighauser's letters to BF over the previous twelve months are extant; the latest surviving one is published in XXIX, 632–3.

the necessary Charges of that Ship during her present Rélache at L'Orient, I do not see why the Application has been made to you, unless the Provisions furnished ever since her Arrival there have been lately Stopt, which I have not heard; because this is unnecessarily bringing a present Expence upon me, which I am ill provided to bear, besides commencing a new Account of Disbursements in another House, that will rather tend to confuse the affair, and answer no good Purpose, I Shall therefore write by this Post to L'Orient, requesting that if the Provisions have been stopt on Acct. of Capt. Landais Misconduct, they may nevertheless be continued, for the sake of the Poor People.[4]

With regard to the Goods in the Arsenal[5] it has long been my desire that they Should be Shipt to America. If it was not before ordered, I now request you would take the first good Opportunity of doing it. The old Iron I must leave to your Judgment, and as you think it better to dispose of it, the Charge of transporting it being more than it is worth, I desire you will sell it as well as you can.

Your other Letters I will fully answer in a few Days. I have constantly paid your Drafts; and have the honour to be, Sir.

M. Schweighauser.

To Vergennes

ls:[6] Archives du Ministère des affaires étrangères; copy: Library of Congress

Sir,   Passy June 24. 1780

In consequence of the enclosed Letter which I have received from M. Adams,[7] I beg leave to request of your Excellency, that the Orders therein mentioned if not already sent, may be delayed, 'till he has prepared the Representations he proposes to

4. To Gourlade & Moylan of this date, above.
5. Schweighauser had taken over jw's arms manufactory: xxvii, 463; xxviii, 414.
6. In wtf's hand.
7. Above, under the date of June 22. The recipient's copy of that letter is now at the AAE.

lay before you on that Subject, by which it will appear that those Orders have been obtained by Misinformation.

With great and sincere Respect, I am, Your Excellency's most obedt & most humble Servant   B FRANKLIN

His Exy. M. le Comte De Vergennes

Notation: rep. le 30 Juin

From ———— de Illens   Copy:[8] American Philosophical Society

Monsieur!   Marseille 24. juin 1780

Un de mes Vaisseaux nomé le Diligent comandé par Capne. GrosJean, aborda heureusement à Charlestown en 1778 avec une Cargaison considérâble, & quoiqu'il fut d'une Portée assez forte, il ne pût point raporter avec luy les fonds de la Cargaison. En conséquence, mon Cape. GrosJean laissa au Trésor du Congrès environ 40 mille Pounds de Caroline, pour laquelle Some on luy délivra un contract, Soit une Déclaration des Trésoriers ou Comissaires du Trésor, Només Wilhelm ParcKer;[9] & John Alx Croll No. 411. Sous la date du 27e. Janvier 1779, dont on m'a transmis Copie, l'original restant en mains de Mr Plombard,[1] Consul de france au dit Charlestown, porte 7% d'intéret annuel.

Je désirerois Monsieur de retirer ces fonds. Si la chose n'est pas trop onéreuse, à défaut j'attendrai le retour de la Paix avec patience—

Mais je suis, come d'autres Négoicians, qui ont des fonds en main du Congrès, fort allarmé Sur le sort de ma Créance. Les papiers publics, nous parlent tous d'une réduction que le Congrès vient de faire à 2 ½% de Sa Valeur du Papier monoye. Je pense que l'on n'aura pas Sacrifié les Créances de la Nation, j'ose vous prier, Monsieur, de daigner me donner quelqu'éclaircissement

8. Made by Illens and enclosed in his follow-up letter of July 28. APS.

9. In 1778–79 the commissioners of the continental loan office in South Carolina were William Gibbes, William Parker, and Edward Blake: *JCC*, XI, 497; XV, 1123. We do not recognize the following name.

1. J. Plombard, appointed consul at Charleston by French Minister Gérard in October, 1778: David R. Chesnutt *et al.*, eds., *The Papers of Henry Laurens* (14 vols. to date, Columbia, S.C., 1968–), XIII, 6n.

Sur le Sort, que doit attendre le Comerce françois, de tous Ses fonds deposés au Trésor.

Copie

Notations: De Illenen Marselle 4. Juin 1780. / 24 Juin

From Jean de Neufville & fils

ALS:[2] American Philosophical Society

Honourd Exy   [after] June [24?] 1780.[3]

We have gott the honour to trouble your Excellency with the explication of Sevall. bills drawn on the Honourable Henry Laurens Esqr. Comissioner fr. the United States of North America residing in Amsterdam, we have since ask'd a fourthnight that we expected an Answer[4] butt an English house having presented a bill the 24th. send word today that she would have it protested, we have return'd(?) the bill copy'd with . . .

. . . certify by this present that the . . . above is a Copy was . . .

This . . . which influences it may . . . Excellency to Accept of . . . again to prevent those . . . and if we had gott some . . . Excellency about . . . then that by . . . your Excy should . . . on all such bills as . . . this we fell upon as the only . . . of a publicq protest however . . . that your Excellency will . . . some [?] that we may delay . . . as long as possible in hopes that Hy Laurens[?] may arrive Soon, Resolved that before this bill which only bears fr. five hundred fifty Gild. should be protested we will Accept of it;

How farr our Caracter answers fr. the benefitt of the American Cause from principle, we have shown sufficiently to your Excellency and the whole world, we will continue in the same manner of thinking where there may be an occasion to show it; our private conections in America already are something large. We

2. A large tear running diagonally across the page has destroyed several words on many of the lines. We have reconstructed as much as we can and indicate with ellipses the missing portions.

3. Dated on the basis of their reference to a bill of the 24th.

4. Probably a reference to their letter of June 15, above.

have in three days gott Lately three Vessells with Tabac from one house in Alexandria butt we should be . . . of the two Republicqs that . . . to render every good office to the . . . Any notion of we . . . all Regard. . . . Excellency's most . . . faithfull humble Sts

JOHN DE NEUFVILLE & SON

To Thomas Digges   Copy: Library of Congress

Dear Sir   Passy, June 25. [1780]

I received yours[5] inclosing a very obliging Letter from Mr. President Banks. The Congress cannot be said to have ordered the Instructions I gave, tho' they would no doubt have done it, if such a Thing had been mentioned to them. It is therefore not proper to use any farther Endeavours to procure a Medal for them. I do not indeed perceive that one is intended for me as you imagined, and tho' it would certainly give me Pleasure if voluntarily order'd I would not have it obtain by Sollicitation.

I thank Mr. Hartley much for his kind offer of more Jamaica Rum.[6] But as I have Still a great deal left of what he was before so obliging as to send me, a fresh Quantity is unnecessary. I wish you would hint to me how I could make him some acceptable Return.

The Portrait you mention is not yet come to hand nor have I heard anything of it. I am anxious to see it, having no hopes of living to see again the much lov'd and respected Original.[7]

I have at the request of friends sat so much and so often to painters and Statuaries, that I am perfectly sick of it. I know of nothing so tedious as sitting Hours in one fix'd Posture. I would nevertheless do it once more to oblige you if it was necessary, but there are already so many good Likenesses of the face, that if the best of them is copied it will probably be better than a new

5. Of April 6, above.

6. For which see Digges's letters of May 29 and June 10. The merchant Gamba, who knew Samuel Hartley, had sent BF rum from an unnamed friend (XXVI, 324n), probably Hartley.

7. A portrait of Bishop Jonathan Shipley: Digges to BF, May 24, May 29, and June 10.

one, and the Body is only that of a lusty man which need not be drawn from the Life: any Artist can add such a Body to the face. Or it many be taken from Chamberlain's Print.[8] I hope therefore you will excuse me. The face Miss Georgiana has, is thought here to be the most perfect.[9] Ornaments and Emblems are best left to the fancy of the Painter.

As the Board after receiving the 500 English Prisoners we carry'd into Holland, in Exchange for frenchmen, refus'd to take other frenchmen (which the Government here had promised me) in Exchange for Americans, I gave over all Thoughts or Expectations of continuing the Cartel. I have however wrote to Mr. Hodgson about it by the Opportunity.[1] We are much obliged to that good Man for the Pains he has taken in that affair. Finding that the Prisoners are like to be longer detained. I desire they may be paid from me the little comfort I can afford them of Six pence per week each. I will answer your Drafts for the Sums necessary.

I received Mr. Hartley's excellent Letters printed and manuscript, which I have sent to America,[2] where he will ever be revered for his incessant Endeavours to procure Peace, which endeavours however, I imagine he will find, from the late success of the King's Troops at Charlestown less attended to than they have been, and that desirable Event more remote than expected.

I send you herewith the Passport for Mr. Scot. I have, you see, great faith in your Recommendation.

With great Regard and Esteem, I am Dear Sir Your most obedt. humble Servant.   FRANCIS LYN.

Mr. Digges.

8. A mezzotint of a portrait by Mason Chamberlain: x, frontispiece and xv.

9. A miniature of the Duplessis portrait of him: I, frontispiece and xix; XXIX, 635n; XXXI, xxix, 444n.

1. Above, June 19.

2. BF is probably referring to David Hartley's *Two Letters to the Committee of the County of York* (London, 1780): XXXI, 469n.

To John Jay

LS:³ Columbia University Library; two copies: Library of Congress

Sir   Passy, June 25. 1780.

Mr. Ross having been employed by the Committee of Commerce to purchase Goods for the Use of the Army, has advanced and engaged his Credit for near 20,000£ Sterling more than he has been supply'd with by that Committee; several ships they had sent with Tobacco for that Purpose having been taken, and what arriv'd having been previously mortgag'd to the farmers General so that they could not be applied to his Use. He is much distressed by this Disappointment. I would help him if it were in my Power, but the funds I have, are not more than sufficient to pay the Congress Bills for Interest. He has requested me to recommend him to your Excellency, which I do most heartily, that if you should be enabled by any Loan or Subsidy put into your hands, to extricate him, you would do it; as he has been a faithful Servant of the Publick, and I am persuaded the Congress would approve of any Assistance you may afford him. His Accounts have been examined here by Skilful and impartial Persons, and found perfectly just and regular.— I have the Honour to be, with great Esteem and Respect, Your Excellency's most obedient and most humble Servant   B Franklin

His Excellency. J. Jay Esqe. &c.

Endorsed: Dr Franklin 25 June 1780 Recd 8 July 1780

From Dumas

ALS: American Philosophical Society

Monsieur   La haie 25 Juin 1780

Je fais de mon mieux pour pallier & exténuer ici le mal de Charlestown; & j'y reussis passablement. Si je pouvois produire un mot de votre part sous les yeux de *notre ami* là-dessus, ce ne seroit pas mal. Il craint que cela n'ébranle la constance du Congrès: & je m'évertue à le rassurer là-dessus. Je fus avant hier matin chez le Prince de Galitzin Envoyé plénipe. de Russie, qui

3. In L'Air de Lamotte's hand.

me connoît depuis longtemps. Je lui donnai copie de votre Lettre aux Armateurs, & le morceau de la vôtre à moi, où vous me dites, que pour montrer votre respect à S. M. l'Imperatrice de Russie vous ne condamneriez plus la propriété angloise trouvée dans des bâtimens neutres.[4] Il a reçu ces pieces avec plaisir, & fait entendre qu'il en fera part à sa Cour.

Je tiens de *notre ami,* qu'on a voulu brûler l'Escadre *Russe* dans le Port où elle est;[5] le feu étoit déjà dans un des vaisseaux. Heureusement on l'a éteint, avant qu'il soit parvenu aux poudres pour le faire sauter au milieu des autres. On a tout de suite dépêché un Exprès à l'Impératrice pour lui faire part de cette tentative dont tout le monde soupçonne des gens que je n'ai pas besoin de vous nommer. Ceci est sûr; car c'est le Resident de la Rep. à Petersbourg, Mr. Swart qui l'écrit à L.h.P.

Je crois avoir oublié, Monsieur, de vous marquer, à la priere de Mr. D'Oudermeulen, qu'il vous a écrit le 15 de ce mois une Lettre[6] sous couvert de Mr. Jean Teissier[7] Marchd. d'Amst., qui l'a adressée à un Négociant ou Banquier de Paris, & qu'on s'attend à une réponse par mon canal. Je suis avec un très-grand respect, Monsieur Votre très-humble & très obéissant serviteur

DUMAS

Passy à S.E. M. Franklin

Addressed: His Excellency / B. Franklin, Esqr. M. Plenipe. / of the United States, &c. / Passy./.

Notation: Dumas la haie June 25. 80

4. BF to Dumas, June 5, with its enclosures, above. Russian envoy Golitsyn, a fellow scientist, had written BF soon after the latter's arrival in France: XXIII, 248–52.

5. The Russian fleet, 15 ships of the line strong, sailed from its base at Kronstadt, near St. Petersburg, on June 19: *Courier de l'Europe,* VIII (1780), 49, issue of July 25.

6. Above.

7. Possibly the international moneylender Jean Texier, for whom see Pieter J. Van Winter, *American Finance and Dutch Investment 1780–1805 . . .* (trans. by James C. Riley, 2 vols., New York, 1977), I, 381n.

From Montbarey

Copy: Library of Congress

A Versailles Le 25. Juin 1780.

Vous savés, Monsieur, que j'ai donné des Ordres le 1er. avril dernier pour qu'il fût delivré au Capitaine Paul Jones, des Magazins de l'Artillerie du Port Louis, pour être embarqués sur la Fregate l'Alliance en Armement à l'Orient; 15. mille Fusils de Soldat et cent Milliers de Poudre;[8] il a été deja remis 67. Caisses de fusils et 20. Milliers de Poudre. Mais une Contestation s'étant élevée pour le Commandement de cette Fregate entre les Srs. Paul Jones et Landais, celui ci s'en étant même mis en possession en vertu du Pouvoir qu'il dit en avoir du Congrès et l'ordre que j'avois addressé pour faire remettre les dits Effets, portant que la Delivrance en seroit faite au premier, nominativement, le Directeur de l'Artillerie a cru devoir faire suspendre la delivrance du Surplus, jusqu'a ce qu'il fût informé au quel de ces Capitaines il auroit à la faire. Je vous prie donc, de vouloir bien, aussitôt la Reception de ma Lettre de me faire connoitre celui des deux qui doit commander cette Fregate, afin que j'autorise ce Directeur à lui faire remettre ce qui reste à livrer suivant la Reconnoissance qu'il en prendroit.

J'ai l'honneur d'etre avec un parfait attachement, Monsieur, Votre tres humble et tres obeissant Serviteur.

LE PCE. DE MONTBAREY

M. Franklin

From James Moylan

ALS: American Philosophical Society

Honor'd Sir   L'Orient 25th. June 1780

In consequence of the Note that you forwarded me with two Letters, one adress'd to the Honble. Cap: Landais late Commander of the Ship Alliance, and the other, to Lieutent. James Degge and the other Officers of the said Ship[9] I gave immediate advice of their reception and that I was ready to deliver them

---

8. BF informed Jones about the arms and gunpowder on April 1, above.

9. The letters that BF forwarded to Moylan are above, June 7, although we have not found a covering letter to him.

agreeable to my instructions. No other notice being paid to this advice, than a messuage from Captain Landais desiring I shou'd go on board the Alliance, (wch. for a few days before he had possess'd himself of the command) there to deliver them. I thought proper at that period to reject the proposal, from a suspition of his intention of injuring my freedom. But concluding, the contents of those letters to be of interesting import to the United States of America and that they had remain'd in my possession three days, further unsaught for; I resolved with the advice of some friends to go on board the ship Alliance and there deliver them according to your orders. On the 18th. of this month I went on board her for this purpose, accompany'd by Mr. Jonathan Williams and there acquainted Cap: Landais with the object of my Bussiness and that on his signing the receipt wch. I presented him agreeable to it's copy here inclosed, I wou'd deliver him the letter. The receipt he read more than once and consented to sign it; but when he had begun his signature, as you will see, he abruptly turn'd round & told me he wou'd not receive the Letter, because it was adress'd to the *Late* Commander of the Alliance. This he said on returning me the proposed receipt and his letter remains in my possession untill further orders from you regarding it.[1] Lieutenant James Degge recd. the one adress'd to him for wch. you will find the receipt inclosed.—[2] It wou'd be tedious to mention the threat's used by Captain Landais on this occasion both to Mr. Williams & myself. I will therefore only add, that he will authenticate the relation I now give you of this affaire, and that my time (wch. has been very disagreeably employ'd since then,) did not admit my giving you sooner advice thereof wch. I pray your excuse for.

I have the honor to be respectfully Hond. Sir Your most obt & most humble St   JAMES MOYLAN

1. Landais' account of the meeting claims that it was Moylan and JW who were inflexible: Landais, *Memorial*, p. 102. With BF's papers at the APS is a letter dated June 17 from Moylan to Nathan Blodget, purser of the *Alliance*, expressing a desire to deliver the two letters with which BF had entrusted him. Blodget replied the following day that as Moylan had refused a receipt from Landais for the letter, he knew of no method for delivering it that would be satisfactory to Moylan. APS.
2. For the receipt see our annotation of BF's letter to Landais.

The Honorable B. Franklin Esqr. American Ambassador &c. &c.

Notation: James Moylan L'Orient June 25. 1780

From Sartine: Two Letters

(I) Copies: American Philosophical Society,[3] Library of Congress, Archives Nationales; press copy: Library of Congress; (II) copy: Archives Nationales

I.

à Versailles le 25. Juin 1780.

J'ai eu l'honneur, Monsieur, de vous marquer par ma Dépêche du 26. May 1779, que Je chargeois les Administrateurs de la Guadeloupe, de regler, d'après les Connoissances qu'ils pourroient se procurer sur les Lieux, L'indemnité que le Roy vouloit bien accorder aux Armateurs du Brigantin Corsaire le Fair Pley, coulé bas aux Attérages de cette Colonie.[4] Sur le Compte que j'ai rendu a Sa Majesté des éclaircissement qui me sont parvenus à ce Sujet, elle a ordonné qu'il seroit payé aux Propriétaires du Corsaire, Quinze mille Livres, Argent de France, qu'ils pourront toucher à Paris, chèz le Tresorier de mon Departement. Ce traitement vous paroitra d'autant plus favorable que le Brigantin n'a péri que par la Faute du Sr. Giddins qui le Commandoit.

J'ai l'honneur d'être avec la plus parfaite Consideration, Mons., Votre tres humble et tres Obeissant Serviteur

(signé) DE SARTINE.

Copie d'une Lettre de Son Excellence Mr. De Sartine à Mr. Franklin.— Colonies.

Notation: Monsr: De Sartine's Letter to Dr: Franklin June 25th. 1780.

---

3. In L'Air de Lamotte's hand.
4. Sartine's letter is printed in XXIX, 546. For the *Fair Play* incident see also XXVIII, 350; XXIX, 393–4, 480–1, 486–8, 560, 664–5; XXX, 544–5, 550.

II.

A Versailles le 25. Juin 1780.

J'ai reçû, Monsieur, avec la lettre que vous m'avez fait l'honneur de m'ecrire le 19. de ce mois, celle des Srs. Bondfield, flaipoood et Compagnie, Négociants Américains, établis à Bordeaux, qui demandent la permission d'expédier, sous pavillon Américain, pour les isles françoises, deux Bâtimens destinés à y prendre des retours pour l'Amérique septentrionale.[5] Ces Négocians m'en avoient déja adressé une semblable, sans signature, que j'ai renvoïée à M. le Moyne, Commissaire général Ordonnateur à Bordeaux, en lui écrivant la lettre dont je joins ici copie. Cet Ordonnateur me marque qu'il en fait part aux deux Negocians Américains. Je suis tres aise d'avoir prevenû vos desirs.

J'ai l'honneur d'etre avec la plus parfaite considération M; votre très humble et très obeissant serviteur

A M. franklin

From Wulffen

ALS: American Philosophical Society

Monseigneur [*c.* June 25, 1780][6]

Bien vivement penétré Des Soins, que Votre exellence, a pris La peine de Se Donner a mon occasion; je Serois bien enchanté que vous Daignassiéz reçevoir L'etendue de ma vive reconnoissance, qui egaleroit Les biens faits Signalés, que j'ai eprouvés de votre Bonté et qui ne Sortira jamais de ma mémoire.

L'objet qui m'intéresse, est le Certificat que vous à remis L'embassadeur Du roy de Prusse, qui m'est indispensable, pour parvenir en hollande.[7]

Je Suplie Votre Exellence de Vouloir Bien me le délivrer n'ayant D'autre Empressement à mon arrivée que De vous le

---

5. Bondfield was a partner of William Haywood; see our annotation of their May 30 letter to BF for the one to Sartine that BF had enclosed.

6. Based on Wulffen's impending departure from Paris. He changed his mind and finally went to visit his sister, M.A. de Sonnemaens. He must have left Paris around June 25 as he was in Brussels by June 29 and with her in Venlo by July 7: Dumas to BF, July 4 (APS); Wulffen to BF, July 7 (APS).

7. Presumably the certificate he requested on June 10, above.

faire repasser De Suite. Je me plais à vous renouveller ma recconnoissance, et L'etendue Du plus profond respect. J'ai L'honneur D'etre avec La Plus parfaite Soummission De Votre Exellence Le plus humble & Le plus obeissant Serviteur Monseigneur
BARON JOHAN HENRICH DE WÜLFFEN
Captain de cavallerie aux services Le unis lâ d'amerique[8]

A Son Excellence Monseigneur De Franklin ministre Plenipotentiaire Des Etats unis D'amerique

A Son Exellence

Queries for John Adams[9]

D: Massachusetts Historical Society,[1] National Archives; drafts: Library
of Congress, American Philosophical Society

[before June 26, 1780][2]
M. Adams, after having perused the inclosed Papers,[3] is desired
to give his Opinion on the following Questions.

8. This is the only time in corresponding with BF that he signed his last
name with an umlaut. His claim to the rank of captain is spurious; see our
annotation of his sister's March 15 letter.
9. These queries may have been posed during a conversation among BF,
JA, and Dana: *Adams Papers,* IX, 475n. The document as sent to JA was preceded by two drafts that are still extant. Both are in the hand of Edward Bancroft, who may well have been present at the discussion. What appears to be
the first of these drafts (Library of Congress) bears the heading "Questions
put Mr. Adams, on the part of Dr. F." and contains some interlineations and
changes in wording made by Bancroft. What would seem to be the second
draft (APS) incorporates the changes Bancroft made on his first one and contains additional modifications in phrasing in BF's hand. The numbering of the
three paragraphs and the heading "M. Adams, after having . . . " are part of
this second draft. It bears a notation in BF's hand, "38./Queries.—to Mr
Adams." The D at the Mass. Hist. Soc. follows the format and wording of the
APS draft, and the one at the National Archives follows the version at the Library of Congress.
1. In L'Air de Lamotte's hand.
2. The date of JA's response, below.
3. From JA's response we know that BF enclosed a bundle of thirty-seven
papers; a list of them is given immediately below. The present document is
number 38, "Queries on the whole."

1st. Whether Captain Landais, accused as he is, of Capital Crimes, by his Senior and late Commanding Officer, after having apparently[4] relinquished the Command of the Alliance frigate, by with drawing his Effects from the same, after having asked and received money by Order[5] of the Minister Plenipotentiary, in order to transport himself to America, and take his Trial there, upon the said Accusation,[6] and after having for that Purpose, *in writing*, requested a passage to be procur'd for him,[7] was intituled, *at his pleasure*, to retake the Command of the Alliance, (contrary to the positive order of the Minister Plenipotentiary, whose orders the said Landais was by the Navy Board instructed to obey), and to dispossess his successor, the oldest naval Officer of the United States, in Europe, who had commanded the said frigate near eight months,[8] and brought her to the Port where she now is?

2dly. Whether the Conduct of Captain Landais, at L'Orient in exciting the Officers and Seamen of the Alliance, to deny the Authority of Captain Jones under whose Command they had voluntarily come, and remained there, and encouraging the said Seamen to make unlawful Demands on the Minister Plenipotentiary for the United States, and to enter into a mutinous Combination, not to put to Sea with the Alliance until the said Demands should be complied with, thereby retarding the Departure of the said frigate and of the Public Stores, on board, be not highly Culpable?

3dly. Whether after Captain Landais's late Conduct and the manner in which he has retaken the Command of the frigate Alliance, it be consistent with good order, Prudence, and the Public Service, to permit him to retain the Direction of her, and of

4. Preceding word interlined by BF.
5. Preceding two words interlined by BF.
6. In Bancroft's first draft the paragraph continues, "and after having applied for a passage in the Private ship Luzerne was intituled, at his pleasure, to retake the Command of the said Frigate contra to the express orders of the Minister Plenip whose orders he had been instructed to obey & to dispossess . . ."
7. Preceding five words interlined by BF.
8. The preceding three words substitute for Bancroft's "during two voyages after Captain Landais's departure".

the Public Stores intended to be sent with her, accused as he is of Capital Crimes by his late Commodore, and for which if he arive in America, he must of Course be tried?[9]

Endorsed: from Dr Franklin. June 1780.

In Franklin's hand: Queries

Franklin's List of Papers relating to the *Alliance*

AD: University of Pennsylvania Library

[before June 26, 1780][1]

List of Papers.

N° 1. Letter from the Navy Board. Dec. 21. 1778. mentioning the Orders to Capt. Landais to obey the Orders of Mr Franklin

2. Second Letter from the Officers of the Alliance complaining of Capt. Landais Feb. 2. 1779. Note, Another in stronger Terms was receiv'd & sent to America.

3. Another from Ditto complaining of Short Allowance March 3. 1779

4 Letter from Capt. Landais complaining of his Officers. May 15. 79

5 Answer, on that Subject

6. Marquis de la Fayette & Col. Gimot, on the same, speaking of the Animosities as dangerous

---

9. Bancroft had drafted the paragraph as, "Whether after Captain Landais has by such Conduct Obtained Possession of the Alliance Frigate, it be consistent with Prudence, good order & the public Service, to permit him to retain the Command of her, and of the Public Stores intended to be sent with her, accused as he moreover is of Capital Crimes by his late Commodore, & for which if he arrive in America, he must in Course be tried."

1. On June 26, below, JA acknowledged receipt of the thirty-seven items (and the queries based on them, the immediately preceding document) which are enumerated here. Among BF's other papers at the University of Pa. Library is a two-page list in L'Air de Lamotte's hand of letters written to Landais, to Gillon, and to the officers of the *Alliance*, the latest of which are dated June 16. One of the letters, BF to Gillon, May 28, 1779, is no longer extant. The list is partly in French, partly in English.

7. Orders to Capt. Landais to join Capt. Jones, and put himself and Ship under his Command April 28. 1779

8 Letter from Capt. Landais, he complies with the Orders, May 12. 79

9 Farther Orders to Capt. Landais July 28. 1779—

10 Letters between Capt Jones & Capt Landais at Sea. Refusal [*to*] obey Orders.

11 Lieut Col. Wuybert's Certificate of such Refusal & other Misbehavior

12 Capt Ricot, of the Vengeance; his Certificate of Ditto.

13 Officers of the Vengeance their Certificate of Ditto.

14 Mr. Mease's Certificate of ditto

15 Charges against Capt. Landais from Commodore Jones, attested by Officers

16 M. de Sartine's Letter desiring an Enquiry into Landais' Conduct

17 Letter to Capt. Landais, calling him to Paris.

18 Letter to Navy Board relating to the Enquiry.

19 Letters to Capt. Landais, answering about his Things left on board the Alliance. Feb. 12, & March 1, 1779.

20 Letter from Capt. Landais, demanding to be replac'd in the Alliance March 11. 1780

21 Answer to Ditto. March 12. refusing

22 Letter from Capt. Landais at L'Orient

23 —from Officers of the Alliance April 12, 1780

24 —from Do. May 31.

25 —from Do. June 7.

26 Mutinous Paper sign'd by 115 of the Sailors of the Alliance interlin'd & sent to BF. by Capt Landais

27 Letter to Capt. Landais, June 7.

28 Letter to the Officers June 7.

29. Orders to Capt. Landais & the Officers, sent by Advice of the Minister of the Marine.

30 Letter from Capt. Landais with a Copy of his Commission. June 16. 1780

31 —from Mr. Wharton ⎫
32 —from Mr Nesbit ⎬ relating to the Proceedings
33. —from Mr Moylan ⎭ on board the Alliance

34 —from Capt. Landais June 14. that he is advis'd by the

principal Americans, will keep the Vessel and follow the Orders of the Secretary of the Navy Board

35 Capt. Jones's Acct of the Proceedings of Capt Landais

36 Letter from Commodore Gillon, enclosing Copy of one to M. de Sartine & one to Capt. Landais

37 Mr Moylan's Letter relating to Sailors entic'd from the Service of the States by Comme. Gillon.

38 Queries on the whole.

List of Papers relating to the Alliance Frigate

To Montbarey
Copy: Library of Congress

Passy, June 26. 1780. 7. a Clock.

I have just received the Letter your Excellency did me the Honour of writing to me yesterday concerning the fusils and Powder the Delivery of which had been ordered into the Hands of Commodore Paul Jones, then Commander of the alliance frigate. As he is at Present deprived of that Command, and these Stores are exceedingly necessary to be sent as soon as possible to America. I am obliged to request your Excellency to order as much of the Remander as can be taken in by that Ship to be delivered on board her to the Commanding Officer for the Time being, to whom I shall give Orders to receive and take Charge of the same. I am, with greatest Respect, Your Excellency's most obedient and most h. S.

Prince de Montbarey.

To John Torris
Copy: Library of Congress

Sir
Passy, June 26. 1780.

Herewith you have the Judgments on the Prizes the Peter and the Friendship: as to the Betsey, taken in December last, I do not find that Proofs have yet been sent me of her being English Property: and whatever good Opinion I may have of the Uprightness of your Captains, it is not regular that I Should condemn without Proofs. The Instructions require not only the Papers, but one Prisoner at least for examination to be brought in with each Prize.[2] This has been in several Instances neglected. Pray give strict Orders to your Captains to be more observant.

I gave a Copy of my Judgment on the Flora to the Attorney for the Owners.[3] Perhaps they too may have some Objections, or desire some Explanations, and it would be most convenient for me to consider the whole together. I have not yet heard from them, but probably I may soon; when you shall have my Answer:

When a Commission was ask'd for the Princess, I was told that Cruizing together, there would be more convenience to stow and bring in Prisoners;[4] but the contrary has happen'd fewer being brought in than before. The Prisoners to exchange for Americans are all the Advantage I have for my Trouble in reading and examining the Admiralty Papers, and for the vast Expence of Postage those Pacquets of Papers, and the Correspondence relating to the Captures, occasion me. Not one American Prisoner has ever been return'd me from England in consequence of the Paroles given by the English Prisoners discharged at Sea. So that if that Practice is continued, I must decline farther Concern in the affair and withdraw the Commissions. The Instructions ought to be observed in that Instance, as well as those above mentioned.

I congratule you on the success of the Fearnought Capt. Ryan; and have the honour to be Sir.

M Torris

2. According to the fourth article of the April 10, 1776, congressional instructions to privateers: Sir Francis Piggott and G.W.T. Omond, eds., *Documentary History of the Armed Neutralities 1780 and 1800* (London, 1919), p. 97.

3. BF may be referring to Vandenyver frères & Cie., the owners' French representatives, to whom he wrote on May 28, above.

4. Coffyn had said this: XXX, 273–4.

From John Adams

LS:[5] American Philosophical Society; AL (draft) and copy: Massachusetts Historical Society

Sir   Paris June 26. 1780

I have read over all the Papers in the Bundle left with me, numbered to thirty seven. I have also read the three Queries stated to me.[6]

These Queries I apprehend can legally be answered only by Congress or a Court Martial: and therefore it would be improper in me to give any answer to them, because the Papers will appear before Congress or a Court Martial, who can judge of them better than I. They will also hear Captain Landais which I cannot do. My Opinion therefore would have no Weight either before the one or the other Tribunal—or supposing it to be admitted to be read and to have any Weight it ought not to be given, because I cannot be legally either a Witness or a Judge.

I cannot however think that the Instructions of the Navy Board to Captain Landais to obey the Orders of the Minister Plenipotentiary, contain Authority to remove him, without his Consent, from the Command of a Ship committed to him by Congress, because the Navy Board themselves had not as I apprehend such Authority.

Since those Instructions were given, as I was informed at Boston, Congress have given to the Navy Board Power, upon any Misbehaviour of an Officer, to suspend him, stating to Congress at the same Time a regular Charge against him—[7] But I do not find among these Papers such Authority given to any Body in Europe, nor do I find that any regular Charge against Captain Landais has been stated to Congress.

5. In the hand of JA's private secretary John Thaxter, Jr., except for the dateline, name of addressee and complimentary close, which are in JA's. The differences between the recipient's copy and the draft are discussed in *Adams Papers,* IX, 477n.

6. The queries for JA and a list of the thirty-seven papers are printed under the date of [before June 26].

7. A congressional committee appointed to prepare a plan for regulating the affairs of the American Navy unsuccessfully proposed that such powers be given to a superintendant of the Admiralty: Smith, *Letters,* XIII, 599–600. For the powers actually given to the newly-established Board of Admiralty see *JCC,* XV, 1217–18.

There has seldom if ever been in France a sufficient Number of Officers at a time to constitute a Court Martial, and our Code of Admiralty Laws is so inadequate to the Government of Frigates for any Length of Time in Europe, that it is presumed Congress in future will either omit to put Frigates under any direction in Europe, or make some Additions to the Laws of the Admiralty adapted to such Cases—for there is an End of all Order, Discipline and Decency, when disputes arise and there is no Tribunal to decide them, and when Crimes are committed or alledged, and there is no Authority to try or to punish them.

I have not observed among these Papers any clear Evidence of Captain Landais Consent to leave the Command of the Ship and therefore upon the whole, rather than bring the present disputes about the Alliance to any critical and dangerous decision here, where the Law is so much at a loose and there can be no legal Tribunal to decide, I should think your Excellency would be most likely to be justified in pursuing the mildest measures, by transmitting all the Papers and Evidence to Congress or the Navy Board for a Trial by a Court Martial and ordering the commanding Officer of the Alliance with the Stores and Convoy as soon as possible to America.

I give this Opinion to your Excellency, to make what use of it you think proper.

I have the Honour to be, with great Respect, sir your most obedient and humble Servant   JOHN ADAMS.

His Excellency Benjamin Franklin Esqr, Minister Plenipotentiary

Notations in different hands: June 26. 1780. / Answer to the Queries. / recd 11½ A.M. June 26. / John Adams

From Jacques Necker

Copy: Library of Congress

Paris Le 26. Juin 1780.

J'ai reçu, Monsieur, avec la Lettre que vous m'avez fait l'honneur de m'écrire le 19. de ce mois les deux memoires qui y étoient joints. L'un concerne M.M. Bondfield Haywood et Compe. qui demandent la Permission d'envoyer aux Isles Françoises deux

de leurs Navires sous Pavillon Americain.[8] Ces Négociants
m'avoient déja présenté cette Demande, Je leur ai marqué le 12.
de ce mois qu'il falloit un Passeport dans cette Circonstance et
qu'ils devroient pour l'obtenir s'addresser à M. De Sartines. Le
second mémoire est relatif à M.M. P. French et neveu de Bordeaux: ces Négociants se plaignent d'une saisie de 9. Boucauts
de Tabac manquant à la Cargaison portée par les connoissements
du Navire la Pedggy; ils m'avoient également fait passer leurs
Représentations.[9] J'ai chargé les Fermiers Gx. [Généraux] de me
rendre Compte de l'affaire, J'attends leur reponce pour donner
une Décision et je ne manquerai pas de vous en faire part.

J'ai l'honneur d'etre avec un sincere attachement, Monsieur,
votre très humble et très obeissant Serviteur   (signé) NECKER

M. Franklin.

From Benjamin Vaughan[1]   ALS: American Philosophical Society

My dearest sir,   London, June 26, 1780.
Dr. Priestley & Lord Shelburne have parted, as far as I can
understand, amicably.[2] The truth is, the two characters were
such as did not understand the one the other: The one did not
comprehend enough the nature & merit of a speculative scholar,
nor the other the situation and difficulties of a political actor. I

8. For this memoir see our annotation of Bondfield, Haywood, & Co. to
BF, May 30; BF's covering letter to Necker is missing.

9. See JW to BF, June 9. The *Peggy* had brought the tobacco from North
Carolina: *Adams Papers*, VI, 108–9. When JW visited Passy in July, he learned
that Necker had written to Bordeaux and assumed that the affair had been settled to the firm's satisfaction: JW to V. & P. French & Nephew, July 22, 1780
(Yale University Library).

1. Probably in answer to BF's letter of June 15, above.

2. For the background of Priestley's departure from his post as Lord Shel-
burne's secretary see XXXI, 123, 454–5, 456–7. Priestley had written to
Vaughan in March that he thought he could do would please
Shelburne: Robert E. Schofield, ed., *A Scientific Autobiography of Joseph
Priestley (1733–1804)* (Cambridge, Mass., and London, 1966), p. 181. See
also John T. Rutt, *Life and Correspondence of Joseph Priestley* . . . (2 vols.,
London, 1831–32), I, 206–7; Edward George Petty, Lord Fitzmaurice, *Life
of William Earl of Shelburne* . . . (2 vols., 2nd edition, London, 1912), II,
333–4.

labored, as *you* did, to prevent it; but œconomy was a farther motive (as appears to me) for separation. Dr. Priestley means to reside at Birmingham, near his brother in law; and a subscription is putting about to enable him to pursue his experiments at pleasure, which with the £150 a year he receives from Lord Shelburne upon *parting*, will probably set him at ease. Ld: Shelburne to some has put it upon the footing of the Dr's health; but Dr. Priestley says that Ld. Shelburne finding no farther use in him, had wished to see him settled otherwise, & talked of providing for him in Ireland, but that he chose to live in England and therefore claimed his £150 per annum: Had he lived 10 years with him, it would have been £250 per an. There have been no angry words; and the whole has passed through Dr. Price, to whom the circumstance was broken *after* the challenge from Fullarton & the night *before* meeting him, for reasons it should seem relative to the new situation accidents might produce.— Dr. Priestley has voided a number of gall-stones. He is weakened for the present, and has certainly suffered somewhat in constitution; but may yet live to do us all good.

I have nothing farther to add, but a common wonder with you at the new blunders of government through our late tumult; which certainly owes all its mischief to the stupidity & insensibility of government before its breaking out, & to their timidity & folly afterwards. All is now quiet, and perhaps the country may in consequence in some little degree think of arming. Many words[3] associated for the time, and some lastingly.

In some expectation of hearing from you about Lord Tankerville, I am my dearest sir, yours in every degree whatever and as ever.   B VAUGHAN.

From Samuel Wharton *et al.*   ALS:[4] National Archives

Sir   L'Orient 26 June 1780
We understand some Persons in the Town have written to the Ministers of France, That the Americans, who are here aproved

3. Possibly "wards."
4. In Wharton's hand. The letter is filed with a collection of documents used at the court martial of Landais upon his return to the United States.

Captain Landais' Conduct in Possessing Himself of the Frigate Alliance, which you had committed to the Charge of the Honorable Commodore Jones. For the sake of Truth, and undeceiving those,—Whom such Misrepresentations may have deceived,— We think it necessary to explain ourselves explicitly on this Subject. We have deeply lamented, Sir, the Behaviour of Captain Landais and his Advisers in agitating so unseasonable a Dispute, opposing your Orders, and ruining the Measures Your Excellency had adopted for the Supply of our Army with Cloaths &c and the Convoy of the American Vessels (laden with Merchandize, wherein our Friends and ourselves are interested to the Amount of near two Millions of Livres) Which We have detained here at a very heavy Expence in full Dependance on it. The Discretion and unexampled Bravery of Commodore Jones yielded us a reasonable and pleasurable Confidence, That our Vessels would arrive in Safety.— But now We feel, We assure you Sir, The utmost Doubt, and anxiety for the Preservation and arrival of the Publick Stores and our property.

We have the Honor of being Sir, your Excellency's most obedient and most humble Servant

SAML. WHARTON
JONA WILLIAMS J
THO. BELL
MATTHEW MEASE
THO. HUTCHINS
JAMES MOYLAN./.
JONATN: NESBITT
J. GRUBB

His Excellency Benjamin Franklin Esqr.

Notation: Letter from Saml Wharton &c to Doctr Franklin June 26: 1780 No 5

To Richard Bache

LS:[5] Mrs. Richard R. Wood, Wawa, Pennsylvania (1957)

Dear son,   Passy, June 27. 1780.

I have just received yours of may 2. with the Newspapers which you sent by M. Mease. He sent them up from the L'Orient, not coming to Paris himself. I have desired that you might send me the German Newspapers, but I suppose the Letters did not get to hand.[6] Pray take them in, and send them by Duplicates. They will much oblige some of my friends among the foreign ministers— I wish also to have some Graffs of the Newtown-Pippin when it is Seasonable to cut them.[7] They may be sent in a Tin Case solder'd up tight. When I was last in Philadelphia, Mr. Miller printed a little Book, containing a Number of Phrases of the Delaware Indian Language: I want a Copy of that.[8] Send

---

5. In L'Air de Lamotte's hand.

6. BF's request for German newspapers is missing. On Oct. 30 (APS) RB wrote that he was sending the "Dutch papers" printed by Styner and Cist, former apprentices to Mr. [John Henry] Miller (for whom see below). This would have been the *Philadelphisches Staatsregister,* which Melchior Steiner and Carl Cist founded in July, 1779; it lasted probably until early 1781, when their firm was dissolved. BF may have been thinking of two other German-language newspapers, however, which formerly existed in Philadelphia but were defunct by the time he wrote the present letter. They were Heinrich Miller's *Wöchentliche Philadelphische Staatsbote,* which suspended publication in May, 1779, and the *Pennsylvanische Staats-Courier,* a continuation of Christopher Saur's *Die Germantowner Zeitung* (with which BF would have been acquainted), which ceased to operate in 1778: Clarence S. Brigham, *History and Bibliography of American Newspapers, 1690-1820* (2 vols., Worcester, Mass., 1947), II, 945, 952, 962.

7. During BF's years as colonial agent in London he often asked for Newton pippin apples or grafts from the trees for planting; DF and his friends frequently obliged his requests. See, for example, VII, 369; IX, 25, 27; XII, 302–3; XIII, 525.

8. John Henry Miller, one of BF's journeymen who later became an important German printer in Philadelphia: IV, 260n; VIII, 99n; Isaiah Thomas, *The History of Printing in America* . . . (2nd ed.; 2 vols., Albany, 1874), I, 253–5. Miller printed *Essay of a Delaware-Indian and English Spelling-Book, for the Use of the Schools of the Christian Indians on Muskingum River* (Philadelphia, 1776), written by the Moravian Brethren missionary David Zeisberger (*DAB*). RB sent BF the work on Jan. 16, 1781: Musée de Bléran-court.

one by two or three different Ships, that I may be more sure of receiving them.

You have never given me a particular account of the State in which you found my Papers that were entrusted to the Care of M. Galloway. There were among them 8. Volumes of manuscript Collections concerning Agriculture, manufactures, Commerce, &c which I much valu'd. They cost me 60£ Sterling. There were also all the Books of my Letters containing my publick and private Correspondence during my Residence in England. I wish to know whether these are left or taken away.—[9] I shall Show every Civility in my Power to the Persons you recommend, particularly Messrs. Fox and Foulk. If the Regimt. of deux Ponts, or its Col. & Lieut. Colonel should come into your Parts, I recommend earnestly those two Gentlemen to your best Services. They are sons of a Lady my very dear Friend, Madame la Comtesse de Forbach, Dowager of the late Prince de deux ponts, whose Nephew I formerly recommended to you. I have wrote all about Ben in my Letter to Sally.[1] We continue well, & I am ever Your affectionate father   B FRANKLIN

M. Bache

Addressed: To / Richard Bache Esqr / Postmaster General of the / United States of Ama / at Philadela. / [*In Franklin's hand:*] Private

Notation: B.F. to RB. June, 1780

To Sarah Bache   LS:[2] Mrs. Martin M. Kendig, Chicago, Illinois (1955)

Dear Sally   Passy, June 27.[–August 12] 1780.
I received your pleasing Letters of Nov. 14.[3] Mr. aston whom you recommended to me has been here, and I treated him with

9. RB's report of the state of BF's papers had been very general, but alarming: XXVII, 89, 90, 605. We cannot identify the manuscript collections, but BF continued to inquire about them (BF to RB, Sept. 13, 1781, APS).
1. Of the same date, immediately below.
2. In L'Air de Lamotte's hand.
3. See XXXI, 95–6.

the Civilities you desired.[4] I was glad to hear that William, Betsy & Louis, tho' the two latter are yet Strangers to me, were all well & lively. Will was always lively. Tell me what Improvement he makes in his Learning. He ought to read and begin to write by this time. I hope to have a Letter from him soon. Ben writes to me often. He is very glorious at present, having obtained the Prize of his School for a best Translation from the Latin into French; which was presented to him in the Cathedral Church by the first Magistrate of the City. I send you his Letter and his Master's containing the News of this Important Event.[5] He gives a Treat on the Occasion to the rest of the Scholars for which I shall pay with much Pleasure. If this gets Safe to your hand, you will receive with it a little Portrait of him, sent me by a Lady that is his friend. I inclose one of her Letters.[6] I received the Newspapers you were so kind as to send me by M. Gerard, but you may imagine they were very old before I got them. Lately I have got some fresher with yours of may 2. giving me the good Tidings of your Child's being safely thro' the Small Pox. M. Mease himself by whom you sent that Letter is not yet come to Paris. Messrs. Foulk and Fox are just arrived, & will do Temple & me the favour to take a family Dinner with us. Letters by them from a number of my old Friends, occasion me much Pleasure in renewing the remembrance of them. I continue in health, but have too much to do.— The Congress have kept me in constant Expectation of being assisted by a Secretary; but he has not yet appeared, and Temple and I are absolute Drudges. I am ever My dear Child, Your affectionate Father   B FRANKLIN

Temple present his Duty.

[*in Franklin's hand:*] Augt. 12. All continue well— BF.

Mrs. S. Bache.

Addressed: Mrs. S. Bache / Philadelphia

4. George Ashton of Philadelphia: XXXI, 95–6.

5. See BFB's letter of June 19 and schoolmaster Marignac's of *c.* June 19, both above.

6. The enclosure is missing, but almost certainly the lady was Mme Agathe Arthaud, who had taken the young Benny under her wing: XXX, 587.

To John Paul Jones

LS:[7] National Archives; copy: Library of Congress

Dear Sir,   Passy June 27. 1780. 6 oclock PM.

I have this Minute received yours of the 23d. The Letter you mention having sent me by the last Post, inclosing the necessary Papers to explain Circumstances, is not come to Hand; so that I am much in the dark about your present Situation. I only learn by other means, that the Alliance is gone out of the Port, and that you are not likely to recover & have relinquished the Command of her. So that Affair is over. And the Business is now to get the Goods out as well as we can. I am perfectly bewilder'd with the different Schemes that have been proposed to me for this purpose by Mr Williams, Mr Ross, yourself and M De Chaumont. Mr Williams was for purchasing Ships; I told him I had not the Money, but he still urges it. You and Mr Ross proposed borrowing the Ariel. I joined in the Application for that Ship. We obtained her. She was to carry all that the Alliance could not take. Now you find her Insufficient.[8] An additional Ship has already been asked and could not be obtained. I think therefore it will be best that you take as much into the Ariel as you can, and depart with it. For the rest I must apply to the Government to contrive some means of transporting it, in their own Ships. This is my present Opinion. And when I have once got rid of this Business no Consideration shall tempt me to meddle again with such Matters, as I never understand them.

With great Esteem, I have the honour to be Sir, Your most obedient & most humble Servant   B Franklin

Honble. Come. Jones.

Addressed: A Monsieur / Monsieur le Commodore Jones / chez M. Moyland, Negt / à L'Orient

---

7. In WTF's hand. BF added "6 oclock PM" to the dateline and "as I never understand them" to the final sentence before the complimentary close.

8. Jones inserted a marker above this word and commented in the margin: "The Ariel when Armed *en Flute* as I proposed would have carried all the Cloathing that the Alliance could not take. But I never thought her Sufficient to carry 600 Tons of Goods!"

Notation: From his Excellency Dr. Franklin Passy, June 27th. 1780

To Landais   Two copies:[9] National Archives

Sir,   [June 27, 1780]
   You are hereby directed to receive on board the said Frigate as many Cases of Fusils and as much of the Gun powder, ready to be delivered to you by Order of his Excellency the Prince de Montbarey, Minister of War, as you can conveniently Stow, giving a Receipt for the same; and the same, together with the Powder, Arms and Cannon, already Ship'd, to transport to Philadelphia; and deliver the whole to the Board of Admiralty there for the Use of the Congress for doing which this Order Shall be your Warrant.[1]
   Given at Passy this 27th Day of June 1780.
                                        (signed) B. FRANKLIN
                                        Minister P. &c. &c.

To the Commanding Officer for the time being of the Frigate alliance belonging to the United States of North America.

Notation in Franklin's hand: Copy of the Orders sent to Capt. Landais

   9. We print from the one in L'Air de Lamotte's hand. The other contains a postscript: "The Cases of Fusils and Gun Powder are in the Kings Arsenal at Port Louis."
   1. These orders were moot: the *Alliance* had already left Lorient for an anchorage off the Ile de Groix. She delivered in Boston only the 67 cases of arms and 216 barrels of powder already on board: Lopez, *Lafayette*, p. 196.

To Sartine[2]

Copy:[3] American Philosophical Society; press copy and incomplete copy:[4] Library of Congress

Sir,   Passy June 27. 1780.

I am very thankful to his Majesty in Behalf of the suffering Owners of the Brigantine Fair play: for his Goodness in ordering to be paid them Fifteen Thousand Livres out of your Treasury. But as that sum is conceived by your Excellency to be a favourable Allowance, in consideration that the Misfortune happen'd by the Fault of Capt Giddins, and the Owners apprehed there was no fault on his Part, (being so informed by Depositions upon Oath) and none was mentioned or supposed in the Governor of Guadloupe's first letter to your Excellency on the Subject, I fear they will think the Sum very small as an Indemnification for the Loss of their Vessel, valued at 26,666⅔ Spanish mill'd Dollars or 6,000£ Sterling.[5] I therefore request your Excellency would be pleased to examine with some attention the said Depositions and the Valuation (of which I enclose the Duplicates) and if on the whole you should judge the matter improper to be offer'd at present for his Majesty's Reconsideration, you would at least favour me with the Informations that have been sent to your Excellency from Guadaloupe of the blamable Conduct of the Captain: as by communicating those Informations to the Owners, I may more easily satisfy them of the Favourableness of the Sum his Majesty has been pleased to grant them.

2. In answer to Sartine's first letter of June 25, above.

3. In the hand of Gurdon Saltonstall Mumford, the sixteen-year-old nephew of Silas Deane who arrived in Paris in mid-August, 1780, and worked as BF's secretary for more than a year. He will be more fully identified in vol. 33. BF marked this "Copy."

4. Both are in L'Air de Lamotte's hand, the former having been taken from an "original" copy written by Lamotte and bearing his descriptive notation (in French). The latter is from the legation letterbook, and the page on which it was continued is missing. All three versions of this letter are virtually identical, and the language is sufficiently awkward in places that we wonder whether it was written by someone other than BF, or was translated from a French draft.

5. At the current exchange rate of 23.5 *l.t.* per pound sterling, 15,000 *l.t.* was worth about £640.

Your Excellency will perceive by their Letter, which I send herewith, that they desire Mr: Jonathan Williams of Nantes might receive for them the Sum that should be granted.[6] I am therefore farther to request that your Excellency would be pleas'd to give Order to your Treasurer, to accept and pay his Drafts for the said fifteen thousand Livres.

I am with great Respect, Sir, Your most Obedt & most humble Servt: (signed) B FRANKLIN.

M. de Sartine.

Copy

Notation: Copy of Dr: Franklins Lett: to Monsr: De Sartine June 27th. 1780

To Jonathan Williams, Jr.

Copy: Library of Congress

Dear Jonan.   Passy, June 27. 1780.

To get rid of all farther Projects and Propositions which I never understand relating to the Shipping of the Goods, I entrusted you with that Business and impower'd you to freight a Ship or Ships. But I have not succeded, for in yours of the 23d. you send me new Schemes. No other Man of War to go under the Command of Comme. Jones can at Present be obtained. Assist him in getting out with the Ariel after that you and Mr. De Chaumont may unite in finding some means of sending the rest of the Goods. You and he can agree and assist each other; but there never can be any Union of Counsels or Endeavours between the Commodore and him.— I was told that if we would obtain the Ariel, she would do our Business. I join'd in the Application and we obtained her. Now she is too Little and another is wanted. I will absolutely have nothing to do with any new Squadron Project. I have been too long in hot Water plagu'd almost to Death with the Passions, fegaries and ill humours and Madnesses of other People. I must have a little Repose. This to yourself and believe me ever. Your affectionate Uncle

6. XXIX, 486–8.

P.S. If the Alliance is not totally gone, you have inclos'd an Order which I promised the Prince de Montbarey[7] to send down for her Reception of more arms &c. tho' I fear She will be carry'd into England, either by her Crew or by an Enemy.

Mr. Williams

From Genet

ALS: American Philosophical Society

Monsieur   a Versailles ce 27. juin 1780

Par le désir du Commodore Paul Jones j'ai fait traduire et remis à Mgr. de Sartines toutes les pieces contenues dans le paquet ci joint que j'ai l'honeur de vous addresser.[8]

J'ai l'honeur d'etre avec respect Monsieur Votre très humble et très obéissant serviteur   GENET

Notation: Genet, Versailles 27. Juin. 1780.

From Joseph Myrick[9]

LS:[1] American Philosophical Society

Excellent Sr,   St Maloes June, 27th. 1780

I having Recd. Commission as Capt. to Cruize against the English in the Cutter called the American Union Mounting 4 Carriage and ten Swivel Guns, most of the Crew and myself be-

7. On the previous day, above. The order to Landais is that of June 27, also above.

8. Genet's bureau of interpreters served not only the foreign ministry, but also the navy, army, and finance ministries: *Almanach de Versailles* for 1780, p. 244. Jones wrote him on June 21 asking him to forward documents after showing them to the French government, but not specifying what they were: Bradford, *Jones Papers*, reel 5, no. 1117.

9. Myrick was from Nantucket. He was captured and confined to Mill Prison in September, 1780, but a year later was released to serve in the British Navy: Claghorn, *Naval Officers*, p. 217.

1. The letter, and probably the signature, are in the hand of Timothy Kelly, the former clerk of the *Black Prince*, who was now a member of the crew of the *American Union:* Kelly to BF, July 4, 1780 (APS).

ing formerly on board of the Black Prince Privateer under the Command of Capt Marchant and Capt Dowlin, their Commission Signed by yr Excellency our Prize Money we have given Power to Mr. Poreau & Compy. of Dunkerque² to Receive the same when paid by Mr Torris, our Commission is French, but as all of us are American Subjects Claims yr. Excelency's protection in the following Case we left Dunkerque May 30th, on our Cruize, which we Continued in the Channell when on the 26th Inst. at 3 in the Morning was Chased by two English Frigates and one Cutter who Continued the Chase for 8 hours untill we got Safe into this port. This day has Recd. Orders from the Commissary of this port that our privateer is Stopped in this harbour by Order of Mr. Sartine— Claims as Americans Yr. Excellencys timely Assistance to twenty four of us here detained, yr. Excellency's Commands we are Ready to obey, Remains with Respects to yr Nephew and the Rest of American Gentlemen

 Yrs   JOSEPH MYRICK

Addressed: His Excellency Benjamin / Franklin, Minister for the / United States of North America / at Passy near Paris

Notation: James Myrick June 27. 1780

From Arendt   ALS: American Philosophical Society

Monsieur, L'orient (au Cheval blanc) ce 28me Juin, 1780.

Son Exçellençe n'attribuera pas a une indiscretion que je La supplie de me faire avoir une passage au Bord de La fregatte L'alliance. Il m'a été impossible d'en trouver par tout ou je me suis présenté, par ce que tous les vaissaux etoint remplis de monde, et comme mon voÿage est trés préssante et asses interressante pour Votre patrie et qu'il a encore asses de place sur L'alliance et que j'offre de paÿer la passage et la nourriture, j'êspere que Son Exçellençe eù egard a tout cela ne me refusera point ma demande et m'enverra la permission avec le premier Courier qui retour-

2. Apparently BF had recommended Marchant to the Dunkirk firm of Poreau, Mackenzie & Cie.: XXVIII, 591.

nera.³ J'ai l'honneur d'etre avec beaucoup de respect Monsieur de Votre Exçellence Le trés humble et très obeissant serviteur

BARON DE ARENDT.
Colonel americain

Notation: Baron de Arendt. L'Orient 21 Juin 1780—

From Montbarey
Copy: Library of Congress

A Versailles Le 28. Juin 1780.
Je vous donne avis, Monsieur, qu'en consequence de la Lettre que vous m'avéz fait l'honneur de m'écrire le 25. de ce Mois, J'ai mandé à M. de Malherbe Directeur de l'Artillerie, que le Commodore Paul Jones n'ayant plus le Commandement de la Frégate l'Alliance, c'étoit au Commandant actuel de ce Batiment que devoient être remis les 15,000 fusils et les 100. Milliers de Poudre que M. Minard De Saleux⁴ avoit eu Ordre au Commandant actuel de fournir une Réconnoissance des d. [dits] Effets, sur la remise qui lui en sera faite.

J'ai l'honneur d'être très parfaitement, Monsieur, votre très humble et tres obeissant Serviteur

(signé) LE PCE. DE MONTBAREY.

M. Franklin.

From Puchelberg & Cie.
LS: American Philosophical Society

My Lord,   L'Orient 28h. June 1780
We beg leave to inform your Excellency, that we are authorised by the officers and Crew, of the American fregatte the Alliance, by way of procuration to be their lawfull Atorneys and

---

3. After returning to the United States Arendt did not go back to military life. Instead, he sought reimbursement for past services and pursued his interest in fostering trade between Prussia and the U.S.: Smith, *Letters,* XVI, 529n; *JCC,* XIX, 29–30.

4. A subordinate of the military governor of Lorient and Port Louis: *Etat militaire* for 1780, p. 47.

agents, to Receive all the money that may be found due to them by way of prizes, made by the said fregatte alone or in company with other vessels.

We are desired to acquaint Your Excellency of this, and to ask of your Excellency the money that is due to them of the prizes Brigs Fortune & May flower, that were sold about last September,[5] their part of the prize Ship Serapis, lately sold and whether the Countess of Scarborough, that was into Dunkirk is sold, also if the prizes sent into Bergen are paid for, that they may Receive their proportion of those.

We beg Your Excellency's Information and assistance in behalf of this ship and Remain with the greatest Respect My Lord Your Excellencys Most obedient humble Servants

PUCHELBERG & CIE.

Notation: Puchelberg L'Orient 2. June 1780.

From John Adams

LS:[6] American Philosophical Society; copy: Massachusetts Historical Society

Sir   Paris June 29th. 1780

I have the honor to inclose a Copy of the letter of the Comte De Vergennes, to me, of the 21st. of this Month, and a Copy of my Answer to his Excellency of the 22d.[7]

This Correspondence is upon a subject, that has lain much out of the way of my particular pursuits, and therefore I may be inaccurate in some things, but in the principles I am well persuaded I am right— I hope that things are explained so as to be intelligible, and that there is nothing inconsistant with that decency, which ought in such a Case to be observed.

5. The two prizes had been sent into Lorient and sold in October: xxx, 306, 308, 360–1.

6. In Dana's hand except for the postscript, which is in JA's.

7. The APS holds a copy of Vergennes to JA, June 21 (*Adams Papers*, IX, 453–9) and a signed copy of JA's lengthy June 22 memorandum to Vergennes (*ibid.*, 460–70). Copies of those letters provided by the French foreign ministry (for which see our annotation of Vergennes to BF, June 30) are also at the APS.

If your Excellency thinks me materially wrong in any Thing, I shou'd be much obliged to you to point it out to me, for I am open to Conviction.

This Affair in America is a very tender and dangerous business, and requires all the Address, as well as Firmness of Congress to extricate the Country out of the Embarrassments arising from it: And there is no possible System, I believe, that cou'd give universal Satisfaction to all, but this appears to me, to promise to give more general satisfaction than any other that I have ever heard suggested. I have the honor to be with much Respect Your Excellency's most obedient and most humble Servant

JOHN ADAMS

I have added Copies of the whole Correspondence.

His Excellency Dr. Franklin

From Thomas Digges   ALS: Historical Society of Pennsylvania

Dr. Sir   London 29. June 1780

Since my letter of the 8th Int. by Mr Barnet, I have wrote you the 10th. & 23d. Instants;[8] and hearing that my Lisbon friend Mr. B,[9] whom I took the liberty to introduce to You, is about this period to Leave Paris, I am in some hopes of getting by him a line from you, which may answer three or four requests I have made in late letters: I mean in respect to Dr. Upton Scotts Pass *for His Baggage* in case He is taken by an Amn. Privateer on the voyage to N York He meaning to push out in the next fleet to that place in order to get to Annapolis, which pass I took the liberty to apply to you for by Post the 30th of last month;— For a Spectacle glass that would sute your sight in order to oblige a Genn. who means to present you with a pair made of Cherokee Cristal; To know what I am to expect relative to a request for a full length drawing or picture of Your self which is wanted for the purpose of getting a good print; and also to know what hopes of release remain to our captive Brethren &ca.

8. Only the letter of the 10th, above, is extant.
9. Presumably William Burne, whom Digges introduced on March 15, above.

I advanced Mr Jas Barnet £12:12:0 on a bill He gave me on Monsr. Rey De Chamont, & I find from my friend Mr Bowins at Ostend He made further use of my introduction and took up a few guineas more of Mr B on a similar bill. I should be obligd to you to give Mr. Barnet a hint to have these two Bills taken care of, for I am not in circumstances to bear well the protest of them. I am led to give this hint to Him from having lately experiencd inconveniences of protests on four bills, amotg [amounting] to upwds. of 60£, given me by americans in a similar situation to Barnet, on people in Nantes & Bilboa; as well as one lately given me by an acquantance of Barnets who drew for 10 Guineas on his unkle in Scotland, & who declard He would pay the bill of no *Reebel*.

Nothing of any consequence has come to my knowlege from the west since my last, save an accot. from the West Indies of a second Brush between the French & English fleet, in which the English Ships sufferd most tho they remaind *as is the boast here* Masters of the Sea. A Packet from St Kitts the 25th. May, brings accots, which from the collecting the whole, stands pretty nearly thus. On the 13th of May Rodney descried the French fleet to windward of Him & not far distant, when Martinique bore W by No. 12 Leagues; The french apparantly meaning to ply to windward & to get into Martinique. After much manœuvring the Van of the English fleet (*six* Ships the best sailers from being copperd) got up with & attackd the Rear of Monsr. Guichens Squadron. The other part of Rodneys fleet being rather distant on accot of light winds could not get up, till the English Ships were pretty roughly handled, particularly the Conqueror the Cornwall & another, who were mauld considerably, tho not so disabled as to be obligd to quit the Seas;— On the getting up of the other ships of Rodneys fleet, *it is said* the French retreated back to Guadeloupe leaving Rodney, as they express it in the City, Lord Paramount of the Seas. The accots go to no further particulars than that the English lost in the engagement 220 Men *killd*.[1] Every person but the immediate dependants & runners of

1. Guichen returned to Martinique on May 22, a week after the Battle of St. Lucia Channel, described above. In this action and another on May 19 Rodney's squadron suffered a total of 68 killed: W.M. James, *The British Navy in Adversity: a Study of the War of American Independence* (London, New York, and Toronto, 1926), pp. 209–13.

ministry look upon the accots. as a very bad one, and one strong suspicion of it is, that the Government give the public no Gazette accots of the action altho the packet brought dispatches. The Gents at Loyds look a little black upon it, & visibly seem to fear for the Islands as well as the Ships on their way out. This news, as well as the present situation of things in consequence of the late curious Insurrection, would have thrown a deadly damp upon the spirits of the whole Country, had it not been for the oppertune arrival of what they call *good news* from South Carolina. It is impossible for me to describe to you how much the minds of the people are elated at it, & how universal the opinion now is, That america must in consequence be subdued; That the whole southern Colonies must fall; That is a certain fact that of No Carolina have submitted; That the Congress are routed by an Insurrection at Phila; The french Minister obligd to fly &ca. &ca &ca— These reports, all aided by the assertions of Ministry, and even hinted by them in the House of Commons as *Facts*, have had an effect on the minds of the people which you may better guess at from knowing their folly, than I can describe. They have Servd to raise the Stocks above three pr Ct. and to bring over a number of people, who thought rationally before, to an opinion, that the game is totally up with America, That *Rebellion* there has got its death blow, & that one years vigorous war more will assuredly bring that Country to the unconditional submission to this. You cannot think sir, how generally this opinion possess's even the better & more thinking sort of people as well as the Houses of Parliament. In the Debates on Hartleys last motion for terms to be offerd Ama. the ministry were more impudent than ever;[2] & did in very plain terms persuade the House, that all which I have before stated abot. the distressd situation of America were facts.— Genl. Conway (whom I do not mean to mention as a virtuous or good Character) did as much declare that the last farthing of this Country ought to be tryd against Ama. & that if ten would not

2. Hartley's bill to invest the crown with power to make peace with America was debated in the House of Commons on June 27 before being defeated 93 to 28: J. Almon, ed., *The Parliamentary Register* ... (17 vols., London, 1775–80), XVII, 751–3.

do send 20,000 Men more to reduce it rather than offer Independence *now*.[3]

You may depend upon it (and I wish to impress it upon Your mind) that every remaining exertion in the power of this Country will be sent forth against America— Fleets & armys will be sent to ruin if they cannot subdue it, provided fleets & armys can be got; and they will effect in great measure the ruin of other places in america, provided france & Spain do not act more vigorously at Sea, and go to *work* instead of making a Parade. I fear much from the discontents in america with regard to non assistance of Ships from their allies. Five ships of the Line cruising on the Coasts south of Phia. in the months of March, April, or May, would have effectually securd Chas Town & capturd a British army— The very same mischiefs will happen in No Caroa. & Virga if those Coasts are not guarded & protected this summer. *One* Engs. Line of Battleship (wch has been for months lying up at Hallifax) and six or eight of the size of 44 Gs [guns] & frigates, have been *all* the Force of England in Ama since the month of Feby.[4] & with this trifling naval guard, they are conducting small armys to Quebec, Hallifax, & other parts of the Coast. Adml. Graves with 8 of the line may be expected to arrive at N York about this period, & his intention is to watch the movements of Tierneys Squadron.[5] Our Idea here is that when walsinghams fleet of six Ships gets to the Wt Indies the Engs. will be superior to the french by 3 Ships.[6]

You, who have often laughd at the follys of this Country would wonder now at the infatuation that seemingly possess's

3. Although generally an opponent of the American war, Col. Henry Conway considered himself "no enemy to Government": Namier and Brooke, *House of Commons*, II, 246.

4. As of July 1, H.M.S. *Portland*, 50, was stationed in Canadian waters and the *Robust*, 74, *Europe*, 64, *Raisonable*, 64, and *Renown*, 50, in American waters: Dull, *French Navy*, pp. 365–6.

5. Graves reached Sandy Hook with his six ships of the line on July 13, three days after Ternay reached Newport with his seven: John A. Tilley, *The British Navy and the American Revolution* (Columbia, S.C., 1987), p. 193.

6. Walsingham rendezvoused with Rodney on July 12 before proceeding to Jamaica. A week earlier, however, Guichen and an accompanying Spanish squadron had sailed for St. Domingue, effectively ending the year's campaigning in the West Indies: James, *British Navy in Adversity*, pp. 217–18.

every one— The Exultation abot. Chas Town & the supposd excellent state of their affairs in america surpasses all belief, in short they are as much upon Hobby[7] as ever they were since I had any knowlege of them. If one may judge rightly from the actual state of things against this Country as well in america & the West Indies as in Europe in general, one would be apt to think, that before many weeks are elapsd they would be flung from this hobby & be as much in the dumps as Englishmen are used to be on the receiving bad news. I wish you every blessing & am with the most sincere regard Sir Yr very ob Sert

P.S. A frd. is to put this in the Post office at Amm. [Amsterdam]

Notations: June 29. 1780. / June 29. 80

To Cabanis

Reprinted from John Bigelow, *The Life of Benjamin Franklin, Written by Himself* (5th ed.; 3 vols., Philadelphia, 1905), II, 496b–496c

Dear Sir,   [June 30, 1780]
Daily expectation of having a printed copy of the enclosed paper[8] to send you (which I did not receive till last night) has made me too long omit answering your kind letter of the 10th of last month. I imagine you may collect from it all that is necessary to be known in order to erect properly a conductor for securing a house from lightning. A private dwelling will not require such complex and costly machinery as the lofty Tower of Strasburg. A simple rod of iron of half an inch in diameter, tapering to a point, and extending nine feet above the highest part of the building, and descending into the earth till four or five feet below the surface, will be sufficient. We often talk of you at Auteuil, where everybody loves you. I now and then offend our good lady who cannot long retain her displeasure, but, sitting in state on her sopha, extends graciously her long, handsome arm, and says, "la; baisez ma main: je vous pardonne," with all the

7. *I.e.*, a subject or plan unduly occupying one's attention.
8. BF and Le Roy's report on the protection of the cathedral of Strasbourg, May 12, above.

dignity of a sultaness. She is as busy as ever, endeavoring to make every creature about her happy, from the Abbe's[9] down thro' all ranks of the family to the birds and Poupou.[1] I long for your return, being with great and sincere esteem, Yours most affectionately,   B FRANKLIN.

Present my respects to your father and my thanks for getting so valuable a son. My grandson joins his compliments.

To M. Cabanis fils dated Passy, June 30, 1780.

From Gérard de Rayneval   AL: American Philosophical Society

à vles. [Versailles] le 30 Juin 1780
Monsieur franklin trouvera ci-joint la lettre originale de M. adams;[2] M. de Rayneval le prie de vouloir bien la luy renvoyer, aussitôt qu'il en aura fait tirer copie.[3]

Notation: De Raynval, Versailles le 10. Juin 1780.

From Vergennes

LS: National Archives; draft:[4] Archives du Ministère des affaires étrangères; copies:[5] American Philosophical Society, Library of Congress, Massachusetts Historical Society; transcript: National Archives

A Versailles le 30. Juin 1780.
Je n'ai reçu qu'hier, Monsieur, la lettre que vous m'avez fait l'honneur de m'écrire le 24. de ce mois.

9. André Morellet and Martin Lefebvre de La Roche.
1. Possibly "Pompon," Mme Helvétius' dog. She had a great fondness for all sorts of animals: Lopez, *Mon Cher Papa*, p. 248.
2. Presumably the recipient's copy, now at the AAE, of JA's June 22 memorandum to Vergennes, for which see JA to BF, June 29.
3. Among BF's papers at the APS is an undated letter from Rayneval to Chaumont, asking him to press for the return of the Adams correspondence.
4. In the hand of Gérard de Rayneval.
5. The one at the APS is in L'Air de Lamotte's hand, the one at the Mass. Hist. Soc. in James Lovell's.

Vous demandez, en conséquence de l'invitation que vous en a faite M. Adams, que les ordres donnés à M. le Chev. de La Luzerne relativement à la resolution du Congrès du 18. mars dernier soient revoqués ou au moins suspendus, parceque ce Plénipotentiaire est en état de prouver que ces ordres ne sont fondés que sur de faux raports.

M. Adams m'avoit adressé dés le 22. une très longue discution sur la matière dont il s'agit; mais elle ne renferme que des raisonnements abstraits, des hypotéses et des calculs qui n'ont que des bazes idéales ou, tout au moins, étrangères aux sujets du Roi, enfin des principes qui ne sont rien moins qu'analogues à l'Alliance qui subsiste entre sa Majesté et les Etats-unis.

Vous pouvez juger par là, Monsieur, que les prétendües preuves annoncées par M. Adams n'étoient point de nature à nous faire changer de sentiment, ni, par conséquent, à opérer la revocation ou la suspension des ordres donnés à M. le Chev. de La Luzerne.

Le Roi est si persuadé, Monsieur, que votre opinion personnelle sur les effets de la resolution du Congrès, pour ce qui concerne les étrangers et surtout les françois, différe de celle de M. Adams,[6] qu'il n'apréhende pas de vous mettre dans l'embarras en vous requerant d'apuier auprès du Congrès les réprésentations que son Ministre a été chargé de faire à ce Senat; et pour que vous puissiez le Faire avec une entière connoissance de cause, Sa Majesté m'a ordonné de vous envoyer copie de ma lettre à M. Adams, des Observations de ce Plenipotentiaire et de La réponse que je viens de lui faire.[7] Le Roi s'attend que vous mettrez le tout sous les yeux du Congrès, et Sa Majesté se flatte que ce Sénat imbu d'autres principes que ceux que M. Adams a

6. BF might be expected to take a more conciliatory line because of his less confrontational attitude toward diplomacy. The differences between BF and JA's negotiating styles are discussed in Gerald Stourzh, *Benjamin Franklin and American Foreign Policy* (2nd ed., Chicago, 1969), pp. 154–64, and Jonathan R. Dull, *Franklin the Diplomat: the French Mission* (Philadelphia, 1982) (APS *Transactions*, LXXII, part 1), pp. 68–9.

7. BF's papers at the APS contain one or more copies with French notations of the following documents, all of which are printed in *Adams Papers*, IX: JA to Vergennes, June 16, 20, and 22 (two letters); Vergennes to JA, June 21 and 30.

développés, convaincra Sa Majesté qu'il juge les françois dignes de quelqu'attention de sa part, et qu'il sait aprécier les marques d'intérêt que Sa Majesté ne cesse de donner aux Etats-unis.

Au surplus, Monsieur, le Roi n'indique pas au Congrès les moïens qui pourroient être emploiés pour indemniser les françois porteurs de papier monnoye; Sa Majesté s'en raporte entièrement à cet égard à l'équité comme à la sagesse de cette Assemblée.

J'ai l'honneur d'être très parfaitement, Monsieur, votre très humble et très obéissant serviteur   De Vergennes

M. franklin

M. Franklin

Notations: Letter from Ct. de Vergennes to Doct. Franklin June 30. 1780—with 5 Numbers from 1 to 5 inclusive / Origal Letter from Count Vergennes to Dr Franklin.

From Bethia Alexander   ALS: American Philosophical Society

ce mardy matin [*c.* June, 1780]
Une Dame, qui j'aime assez quoique je la connois peu, vient de m'ecrire, mon cher Docteur, pour me demander une grace qui malheureusement depende de vous. Je dis malheureusement car je vous connois tant d'occupation que je n'ai entrepris de vous ecrire qu'a regret—voici L'affaire—Madm: la Comtesse Dillon[8] a plusieurs de ses amis, et je crois même son Mari sur L'escadre de Monsieur de Terney qu'on croit etre destiné pour L'ame-

---

8. Born Thérèse-Lucy de Rothe (1751–1782), Countess Dillon was lady-in-waiting to Marie-Antoinette. Her daughter, Henriette-Lucy (1770–1853) became the famous marquise de la Tour du Pin, author of the *Journal d'une femme de cinquante ans,* the liveliest memoir on French emigration: *DBF,* xi, 355; Bodinier, *Dictionnaire,* p. 142. On Sept. 25, the Countess thanked BF for all his trouble and asked him to forward another letter (APS). She sent him two more notes, both undated, both asking him to forward letters to America (APS). One of them was meant for a relative of the Dillons, either Dominique Sheldon or François de Sheldon de Bickford. Both men appear in Bodinier, *Dictionnaire.*

rique,[9] elle voudrois pouvoir leurs donner de tems en tems de ses nouvelles mais elle ne sait pas comment s'y prendre, c'est sur cela qu'elle demande votre avis et votre aide— Voyez, mon cher Docteur, si vous voulez entreprendre de lui faire part des occasions qui se trouverons pour ce pays Lâ, et de dire au Soin de qui elle doit adresser ses lettres.— Mon: le Comte Dillon s'est si bien battu contre nous autres pauvres Anglois, que sa femme merite a ce qu'il me semble, cette petite service de votre part—si vous etes du même avis faites le moi savoir par une petite ligne—et dites moi en même tems si j'ai encore quelque place dans votre Coeur,? ou si les quatres Grands lieus qu'il y a entre vous et moi m'en ont tout a fait chassée? Rappellez moi au Souvenir de Madame Helvetius, et ses amis— Adieu mon cher Docteur que vous m'aimez toujours ou que vous ne m'aimez plus je serois pour la vie Votre affectionnée   BETHIA ALEXANDER

Addressed: A Monsieur / Monsieur Franklin—Passy / Pres / Paris

9. Ternay's squadron sailed on May 2 (hence our dating of the present document) but the Countess' husband, Arthur Dillon (1750–1794), was not a part of it, being in the West Indies at the time. He fought in Grenada, St. Lucia, Savannah, and Tobago, was made governor of Tobago in 1786, and represented Martinique at the *Etats généraux*. Falsely accused of instigating a royalist conspiracy, he was guillotined in 1794. *DBF;* Bodinier, *Dictionnaire.*

Index

Semicolons separate subentries; colons separate divisions within subentries. A volume and page reference in parentheses following a main entry refers to an individual's first identification in this edition.

Bentham, Jeremy: identified, 236n; sends book, 236; letter from, 236
Bentham, Samuel (Jeremy's brother), 236n
Bentinck, William Henry Cavendish, 3rd Duke of Portland, 302n
Bentley, Thomas, 83, 470
Berck (Normandy): *Black Prince* aground near, 241, 259–60, 307, 402n
Berckel, Engelbert-François van, Pensionary of Amsterdam ("notre ami") (xxiv, 430n): and Dumas, 20–1, 95, 166, 173, 191–2, 226, 246–7, 263–4, 303, 351, 351–2, 395, 417–18, 419, 430, 530, 575, 592–3: Bleiswijk, 21, 303, 575: Hartsinck, 351; provides news, 20–1; van de Perre is nephew of, 221n, 429; political activities of, 303; predicts general peace, 351; is dismayed by news of Charleston, 575, 592
Bergen: *Alliance*'s prizes at, 10, 21–2n, 37–8, 75–6, 130, 223, 363–4, 450–1, 455, 489–90, 506–7, 517, 585, 619; American merchant ship arrives at, flying French colors, 239, 242; American prize crews repatriated from, 239, 241–2, 363–4, 413n, 451
Berkenbosch (brigantine), 221, 271–2, 294–5, 296, 298, 352–3, 417, 419, 429–30, 451, 464, 569
Berkenhout, Dr. John, 191
Bernstorff, Count Andreas Peter von (Danish foreign minister): discusses use of Danish ports by American ships, 75–6; tries to excuse Danish return of Bergen prizes, 75–6, 450–1; does not favor American independence, 76n; letter from, 75–6
Bersolle, Emmanuel-Yves (Brest merchant, xxvi, 319n), 162n, 202–3, 269, 403
Besongne, Jacques-Jean (printer, bookseller): identified, 77n; seeks advice on ties with booksellers in America, 77; letter from, 77
Bessière, ———, 387n
Betsey (prize), 196, 412, 460, 493–4, 602
Betsy (prize), 585n
Bibles: BF ordered to supply, 174n
Bibliographie encyclopédique (Pougens), 275–6, 362
Bibliothèque royale, 275
Bieuville (Beauville, Beuville), ———: salary of, for working in foundry, 5
Bilbao, Spain, 563
Billion des Gayeres, ———: Mme Brillon seeks recommendation for, 78–9; recommended to R. Morris, 79

Bills of exchange: for supplies, 4; W. Finnie writes concerning, 44; Cossoul writes concerning, 45; BF accepts, 54n, 91, 235n; Digges asks about, 66, 125–6; J.F. Frin remits to Grand, 77–8; BF asks for, obtains guarantee of, 91–2; Wulffen presents to Neufville & fils, Congress honors, 111n; E. Bird sends to J. Nesbitt, 235; forwarded by *Diana*, 235; J. Nesbitt sends to BF, 235; of Wilcocks, 325; RB sends, care of Meyer, 337n; give him trouble, complains BF, 516; on Congress, BF to pay, 592. *See also* Laurens, Henry
Bingham, William (former American agent at Martinique, xxii, 443n), 112–13, 137, 223, 448–9
Bion, ———: seeks news of son, the *Chasseur*, 49
Bion, Wilfrane(?), 49
Blackit, Peter: claims is held in prison unjustly, 181–2; letter from, 181–2
Black Prince (privateer): Torris principal owner of, 196n, 552n; prizes of, 196–7, 210, 212, 259, 359, 385–6, 401–2, 412, 424–5, 434, 451, 461, 485–6, 493, 500, 550, 552–4, 561–2, 576, 602–3; crew, cruises of, 210–11; shipwrecked, 241, 307, 402n, 505, 554n; journal of, 306, 307n; commission of, 553–4; former crew members of, serve on *American Union*, 616–7; mentioned, 51n
Black Princess (privateer): Collins to sail on, 179–80; at Roscoff, 181; Blackit serves on, 181; Torris principal owner of, 196n; prizes of, 196–7, 212, 412, 460–1, 493 &c, 554, 602; cruises of, 210, 461–2, 494; crew of, 257, 462–3, 505–6; name transferred to new ship, 257n, 260; at Morlaix, 461–2, 505–6, 562; commission of, 554, 603
Blake, Edward (S.C. loan office commissioner), 588n
Bland, Theodorick, Jr. (Va. delegate to Congress), 122
Bleiswijk, Pieter van (Grand Pensionary of Holland): and Berckel, 21, 303, 575: Dumas, 93–4, 227, 240, 575: Oudermeulen, 419: La Vauguyon, 575
Blodget, Nathan (purser of *Alliance*, xxix, 31): and Landais, 96, 490; requests wages, prize money, reappointment of Landais, 243–4, 454–6, 488–91, 492–3; and Moylan, 584–5n, 595n; letters from, *inter alia*, 243–4, 454–6, 492–3; letter to, *inter alia*, 488–91

Cuming (Cumming), James (*continued*)
asks for *Serapis*, 199–200; letter from, *inter alia*, 199–200
Currency, American: Congress devalues, liv–lv, lvii, 71, 339, 449, 481, 527n, 571–2, 573–4, 587–8, 588–9, 619–20, 626–7; depreciation of, liv–lv, 53, 112n, 160, 170–1, 338–39, 513–14, 571–2; paper money in S.C., 426; Chaumont's memoir on, 527–8. *See also* Exchange rates
Customs regulations, French, 497
Cutting, Nathaniel: asks for *Serapis*, 199–200; letter from, *inter alia*, 199–200

Dale, Richard (former first lt. of *Bonhomme Richard*), 520, 531–2, 565–7
Dalibard, Thomas (botanist), 389
Dalling, John (gov. of Jamaica), 25, 126
Dalrymple, Sir John, 290–1, 409, 540–1
Dalton, Tristram (Newburyport shipowner, xxix, 486n), 596, 614–15
Daly, James: requests wages, prize money, reappointment of Landais, 243–4, 488–91; letter from, *inter alia*, 243–4; letter to, *inter alia*, 488–91
Dana, Francis (xxii, 8n), 114, 186, 451, 573n, 584
Daphne (schooner), 358–9
D'Argentré (merchantman), 44n
Darling, John: requests wages, prize money, reappointment of Landais, 243–4, 454–6, 488–91, 492–3; letters from, *inter alia*, 243–4, 454–6, 492–3; letter to, *inter alia*, 488–91
Dartmouth, Eng.: ship to, captured, 197, 386; privateer from, 361n
Daubenton, Edme-Louis: sends color plates for *Histoire naturelle des oiseaux*, 453–4; letter from, 453–4
Davesne, ———, 146
David, ———, l'aîné (Morlaix merchant): seeks consulship, 47
De Amicitia (Cicero), 263n
Deane, Silas (former commissioner, xxii, 183n): accounts of, with F. Grand, 4; returns to France, 41, 450, 570; and Finlay, 64n: auditing of commissioners' accounts, 99, 450, 570: Arthur Lee, 133–4n: saddle horse, 499: Landais, 539n; R. Morris praises character of, 193–4; investigation into finances of, 194n; recommends commission seekers, 225; recalled by Congress (1777), 225n; Mumford the nephew of, 614n

Deane (frigate, U.S.N.), 162n
De Berdt, Dennys, 133n
Degge, Lt. James: requests wages, prize money, reappointment of Landais, 243–4, 454–6, 488–91, 492–3; Moylan delivers letters to, 488n, 566, 594–5; should see BF's orders, says Gillon, 510; appointed temporary commander of *Alliance*, 519, 539; letters from, *inter alia*, 243–4, 454–6, 492–3; letter to, *inter alia*, 488–91
Dei Conduttori per preservare gli edifiʒi da' fulmini (Toaldo), 374n
De la Félicité publique (Chastellux), 135n
Delaware Indians, 609
Delisle. *See* Romé de l'Isle
Delleville, Philippe de (lieutenant general of Bayeux admiralty): writes concerning American prisoners escaped from Portsmouth, 233; BF acknowledges hospitality of, to escaped American prisoners, promises to reimburse, 255; letter from, 233; letter to, 255
Deneker Riedy & Comp. (Nantes merchant firm), 228
Denies, Phillips, 181–2
Denmark: BF corresponds with government of, 10, 38, 75–6, 130, 223, 363–4, 450–1, 455, 489–90, 506–7; returns prizes from Jones's cruise, 10, 21–2n, 37–8, 75–6, 130, 223, 363–4, 450–1, 455, 489–90, 506–7, 517, 585, 619; and League of Armed Neutrality, 21n, 452n, 466; permits American ships under false flags to enter ports, 76n, 239; repatriates American prize crews, 239, 241–2, 363–4, 413n, 451; treaty between Britain and, 279n, 451; Dutch may seek sailors from, 417
Depotien Duboishalbrand, ———, chevalier: wishes to exchange Pa. dollars, 44
Désaleux, ——— Minard, 203n
Descartes, René, 400
Descriptions des arts et métiers (Académie royale des sciences), 117n, 300n
Desgrange, ———: seeks commission, 147
Deshaises, ———, abbé, 275
Deshayes, ——— (*commissaire des classes* at Cherbourg), 257
Destouches, ——— (clerk of Dunkirk admiralty): sends prize documents, 500; letter from, 500
Deux-Ponts, Christian, comte de (duchesse de Deux-Ponts' son), 101–2, 137, 229, 610
Deux-Ponts, Guillaume, comte de (duchesse de Deux-Ponts' son), 101–2, 137, 229, 610

Durey de Meinières, Jean-Baptiste-François, 297n, 298

Durey de Meinières, Octavie Guichard: identified, 297n; BF plans to call on, with Mme Helvétius, lix, 297–8; encourages BF's visit, 298; letter to, 297–8

Du Rouzeau, Thomas, abbé (secretary of Neuf Soeurs): invites BF, WTF to Neuf Soeurs induction feast for Jones, 330–1; invites BF to Neuf Soeurs meetings, 331n; letter from, 330–1

Duties, French: prevent Bondfield, Haywood & Co. from trading with West Indies, 445–6. *See also* Farmers General

Duvivier, Pierre-Simon-Benjamin (engraver): identified, 273n; engraves medals, 39n, 201, 273, 349, 435–6; letters from, 273, 435–6; letter to, 349

Dwyer, Thomas: seeks prize money, wages, 137–9; letter from, *inter alia*, 137–9

Eastern Navy Board: sends *Alliance* to Europe, 104n; BF informs about Landais inquiry, 104–7; sends orders to Schweighauser, Landais, 585; letter to, 104–7

East Indies: ship from Lorient believed bound for, 71

Eckhardt, Anton Georg: identified, 247n; answers BF's letter, 247; and brother have perfected manufactory, 248–9; encloses memoirs, 249; letter from, 247–9

Eckhardt, Francis Frederick (inventor, Anton Georg's brother), 248–9

Ecole de boulangerie: Cadet de Vaux announces inauguration of, 481–2; teaches methods of breadmaking for jails, Ecole militaire, 482n

Ecole royale militaire, 101n, 482n

Economy: and industry, extolled as republican virtues, 282n

Eden, William, 429

Edinburgh, University of, 114n

Education: BF recommends Geneva for, 115; at Cheam School, 206; for women, at Mrs. Wilkes's school, 209: at French convent, 267n; of young Americans in Europe, 314–15

Edward IV, King of England, 275

Electricity: Rittenhouse observes, 326; C. Millon comments on, 370–1; electrical air as fashionable cure, 433. *See also* Franklin, Benjamin, science; Lightning rods

Elizabeth (wife of King Edward IV), 275

Ellis, William, 478n

Ellwell, Elias: BF aids, 7

Elwood, Thomas: and other *Alliance* officers request wages, prize money, reappointment of Landais, 243–4, 454–6, 488–91, 492–3; letters from, *inter alia*, 243–4, 454–6, 492–3; letter to, *inter alia*, 488–91

Emigrants, would-be: collectively described, 14–17; BF asked to help, discourages, 74n, 421; Digges recommends, 261

Emigration: constitution of Pa. will encourage, says BF, 134

Encylopédie (Diderot), 300n

England: invasion of, advocated, 33n. *See also* Great Britain

Englehard, ——— (surgeon): wishes to emigrate, 15

Ennius (poet), 263n

Enschedé, Johannes, 128, 174, 227, 303

Enschedé & Sons (Dutch firm), lviiin, 476n

Enville, Marie-Louise-Nicole-Elisabeth de La Rochefoucauld, duchesse d' (La Rochefoucauld's mother, xxiii, 213–14): requests recommendation for Gallatin and Serre, 410, 421; letter from, 410–11

Ephemera, The (BF), lix, 409, 543

Eskimos, 280

Espréménil, Jean-Jacques du Val d' (Leyrit's nephew), 324

Essai de bien public . . . (Collignon), 32

Essai de cristallographie . . . (Romé de l'Isle), 411n

Essai sur les principes de la greffe (Cabanis), 365n

Essayes or Counsels, Civill and Morall, The (Bacon), 400

Essay of a Delaware-Indian and English Spelling-Book . . . (Zeisberger), 609–10

Essay on Public Happiness, An (Chastellux), 135, 136

Estaing, Charles-Henri, comte d' (French admiral, xxiii, 67n): fails to recapture Savannah, lix; captures ship, 27n; rumored to receive command of ships escorting Rochambeau, 73; fêted at Bordeaux, 88; and auxiliary officers in French navy, 88n; accepts dinner invitation, 98; wounded at Savannah, 98n, 230n; S. Cooper praises, 415–16; mentioned, 45–6, 179; letter from, 98

Eudel, A. M. (*contracteur général des fermes*): asks BF to locate Tardiveau, forward letters, 48

Europe, H.M.S. (ship of the line), 623n

Evans, Lewis (cartographer), 332

Evans, Sarah, 46

Eveillé (French ship of the line), 229

Franklin, Benjamin (*continued*)
cates, 449, 477; directs Bancroft to assist former prisoners, 532; may withdraw privateering commissions, 554, 603; refuses American commissions to French privateers, 554; involvement with commercial affairs incompatible with BF's ministerial duties, claims Chaumont, 582
—music: sends song to Hopkinson, 119
—portraits: Chevillet engraving, xxix, 517; frontispiece to *Œuvres de M. Franklin*, 160; images of, as "changeable as the moon," 160; S. Jay requests print of, 316–17, 517; portrait of, by Duplessis, 350; Fournier le jeune requests, receives permission for portrait of, 349–50, 362–3; Digges requests portrait of, for English engraver, 421–2, 437, 503, 590, 620; miniature of, on snuffbox, 422, 433, 591; BF is tired of sitting for, 590; print to be made from Chamberlain's portrait, 591
—printer: considers, purchases type, xxix, lviii, 128, 173, 227, 297, 300, 303, 309–10, 328–9, 350, 363, 476; foundry of, lviii, 174n; prints new variant of Passy passport, xxx, lviii, 413n: promissory notes, 6: bagatelles, 217n: blank form for prisoners' receipts, 413n; sends type to Watson, 69, 304n; orders paper for promissory notes, 441–2
—science: corresponds with Ingenhousz on electricity, lightning rods, conductivity of metals, lvii, 341–6, 346–9; on lightning rods for Strasbourg Cathedral, lviii, 373–6, 624; recommends Bartram's seed nursery, 55; requests seeds for Malesherbes, 55; describes Rochon's micrometer, 120; praises Ingenhousz's discovery of photosynthesis, 120; Eckhardt sends description of rolling parallel rule to, 247n; corresponds with Eckhardt, 247–9; writes "An Attempt to explain the Effects of Lightning on the Vane of the Steeple of a Church in Cremona . . . " 348n; attends pump demonstration, 370; trial of experiments of, in lightning-conductors, 406n; visits Leschevin's mineral collection, 411; invited to inauguration of Ecole de boulangerie, 481–2; describes requirements for lightning rod on private dwelling, 624
—social activities: and WTF, invited by Sarsfield, lix, 231: invited by Deux-Ponts, 151–2: dine with Fox, Foulke, 611; during Jones's visit to Paris, lix, 312–13n; with Mme Brillon, lix, 79,

369–70, 543: Mme Helvétius, lix, 297–8, 624–5: Malesherbes, 54, 265; entertains fellow Americans, 50n; comte de La Luzerne calls on, 54; plays chess, 54, 543; reports on public diversions at Paris, 55–6; d'Estaing dines with, 98; enjoys company of JA's sons, Johonnot at dinner, 117; invited by Holkers to visit Rouen, 143: to dinner at Girardot de Marigny's, 312–13: by Caffiéri to view statue in his Louvre studio, 340–1; rarely attends opera, 543
—views and opinions: praises French cordiality, good will, lv, lix, 41, 117–18, 185, 224, 285: good laws, just dealings of U.S., 298–9; on freedom of trade in wartime, lx, 466–7, 476: the advantages of great states at war, 55–6: aging, 116: European, American hospitality, 118: Associated Counties Movement, 122–3: Britain, British, 123, 452–3, 469, 476–7, 481, 546, 556, 591: Spain's delay in joining alliance, 185: portraits as presents, 350: Gordon riots, 529, 541, 545–6, 569: European commerce in America, 572–3: the profit motive, 572–3; hopes for a good peace soon, 54; describes France as martial country, 57; expects to see U.S. flourish after war ends, 57; says Pa. constitution will draw many to emigrate, 134; does not believe "free ships, free goods" applies in *Berkenbosch, Flora* cases, 296, 552–3; applauds "free ships, free goods," 443, 452, 466–7, 476, 552–3; believes war far from over, 468: *Alliance* officers good men, but misled, 491; can form no opinion of Fox's plan to land arms in England, 583; says JA, Dana better versed than is he in maritime law, 584; takes less confrontational attitude toward diplomacy than JA, 626n
—writings: "To the Royal Academy of Brussels," lviii–lix, 396–400; "The Ephemera," lix, 409, 543; use of outlining, 36–7n; *Œuvres de M. Franklin*, 160n; "The Whistle," 217n; German translations of, 301; *Political, Miscellaneous, and Philosophical Pieces*, 301, 406, 528–9; *Exper. and Obser.*, 301n
Franklin, Deborah, 161
Franklin, William Temple: invitations to, lix, 151–2, 231; wig for, 3; accounts of, 5–6; and Brown, 9n: Digges, 25, 249: Richard Neave, 59: H. Grand, 99: Carmichael, 178, 188, 289–90, 409, 541: JW, 222, 480n: Jones, 265, 467n: Ross 284n, 286n, 480n: Pougens, 362n: Caslon, 437n; letters, documents, in hand of,

Hutton, James (*continued*)
tine, 281; requests new passport, 281–2; letter from, 280–2
Hyland, Benjamin: signs promissory note, 7

Illens, ——— de (Marseilles merchant): ship owned by, arrives in Charleston, 588; wishes information on money deposited in America, 588–9; letter from, 588–9
Independence Day: BF's 1779 party for, 116n; 1780 celebration of, 468
Independent Ledger (Boston paper), 117n
India: French loss of, 323. *See also* Pondicherry
Indians, American. *See* Delaware Indians; Iroquois
Indications des ouvrages . . . relatifs à la saisie des bâtiments neutres (Groult), 359n
Indien. See South Carolina
Indigo: cloth offered in exchange for, 31
Ingenhousz, Jan (physician, XIV, 4n): discusses electricity, lightning rods, conductivity of metals, lvii, 341–6; BF thinks worthy of membership in APS, 116; writes on photosynthesis, 116, 120; invents "new" electrical machine, 342n; visits Paris, 342n; and Le Roy, 344; introduces Walckiers de St. Amand, 345–6; sends notes for *Expériences sur les végétaux* to Lebègue, 406; letter from, 341–6
Ingraham, Duncan, Jr., 9n
Inoculation: Bond defends, 116
Inquiry into the Original State and Formation of the Earth, An (Whitehurst), 379
Insects, 314
Insurance: importance of, in commercial contracts, 161; cost of, cited by Chaumont, 527
Intelligence reports: collectively described, 70–3, 229–30n
Introduction to the Principles of Morals and Legislation, An (Bentham), 236n
Invalides, Eglise royale des, 340
Invincible, H.M.S. (ship of the line), 250
Ireland: plan to menace, 8; political unrest in, 27, 40, 292, 319; revolt of, advocated, 33n; captain from, seeks aid, 42–3; Landais captures ship going to, 50n; BF expects to obtain complete liberty, 122; *Bonhomme Richard* squadron takes prizes off, 266, 368; U. Scott's inheritance in, 447, 503. *See also* Dublin
Irish: confined in Dinan Prison, willing to serve America, 391
Irish Seminary (Paris), 50

Iron: price of, at Philadelphia, 339; BF authorizes Schweighauser to sell, 587
Iroquois: attack N.Y., Penn. frontiers, 284
Irwin, Matthew, 44
Izard, Ralph, 9n, 22, 46, 187, 288n

Jackson, John (lawyer), 25
Jackson, John (pilot), 94n, 173, 240
Jamaica: fears for safety of, 26; British convoy to, 463n. *See also* Port Royal
James (merchant ship), 23–4, 103n
Jameson, ———, 22n
James's Island (S.C.), 318
Janot. *See* Volange, M.-Fr. Rochet
Janssoone (?), ———, 373n
Jarvis, Jno.: requests wages, prize money, reappointment of Landais, 243–4, 488–91; letter from, *inter alia*, 243–4; letter to, *inter alia*, 488–91
Jason (French ship of the line), 73n
Jason, H.M.S. (20-gun warship), 234n
Jay, Sir James, 133
Jay, John: accounts with BF, 28, 37, 184, 223–4, 253–4, 315, 321–2, 515–16; at Cadiz, 28n, 37, 222; and Yranda, 37, 317, 515–16: Littlepage, 52n, 53: A. Lee, 252, 254: Nesbitt, 390; Spanish court receives unofficially, 92; praises Gérard, 108n; in Madrid, 178n, 409; BF hopes for financial assistance from, 185: discusses means of communicating with, 186–7: hopes will visit Paris, 187; Yranda complains of, 186; and BF have no secrets, says BF, 187; outlines precautions for sending mail, 252–4; forwards letters, papers, 288–9; health, 290; sends greetings, 290; informed about Dalrymple proposals, 290n, 409; praises French court, people, 316; greetings to, 318; Congress draws bills on, 390; asked to assist Ross, 592; letters from, 28–9, 252–4, 315–17, 321–2; letters to, 222–5, 515–18, 592
Jay, Sarah Van Brugh Livingston (xxx, 555n): at Cadiz, Madrid, 28n, 178n; greetings to, from, 225, 290; health, 290, 316; requests print of BF, xxix, 316–17, 517; mentioned, 254n
Jebb, Dr. John, 380–1
Jefferson, Thomas, 75n, 175n, 472n, 478n
Jenings, Edmund (XXI, 216n; XXIII, 320n), 270
Jennings, Theobald: BF, Delleville correspond about, 233, 255; escapes from Forton Prison, asks for help, 234–5; letter from, *inter alia*, 234–5

Parker, William (S.C. loan office commissioner), 588

Parliament, British: North's majority in, 26; public will prefer representatives of Associated Counties Movement over, believes BF, 123; triennial, proposed, 218; petitions presented to, 218–19; efforts to shorten duration of, 302n; and power to legislate for Ireland, 319n; during Gordon riots, 502; contains "Plunderers of Publick," says BF, 546; and American war, 622. *See also* Commons, British House of

Parliament, Irish, 27

Parmentier, Antoine-Augustin: collaborates with BF and Cadet de Vaux, 481n; and Cadet de Vaux open Ecole de boulangerie, 482

Paroles. *See* Prisoners, American

Passports: BF drafts, xxx, liv; printing history of, lviii, 413n; for Carpenter, 23, 103: Burne, 109–10, 126–7, 423, 437: Gridley, 167: J. Cazneau, 220: Andrews and Shaw, 232: Hutton, 280–2: type, 294n, 304n: Bergen sailors, 413n: Scott, 446–7, 503, 591, 620: Sheridans and Macabe, 478–9: J. Rainey, 513: Lee, 521, 578: sailors recruited by Gillon, 532–3: *Flora*, 576; use of, advocated, 33n; Allaire requests, is denied, 387; French, wished by Gillon for sailors, 509, 511: for *Three Friends*, 585: for Bondfield, Haywood & Co., 606

Passy: plan to bring hostages to, 8; Péchigny boarding school at, 46, 117, 150n; Le Roy hopes to settle in, 50; d'Estaing's country house in, 98n; Jones arrives in, 265n; Adams, Cochran, BFB attend Pension Le Coeur in, 444n

Patriote (brig), 256

Paulus, Father ———: wishes to emigrate, 14

Paulze, Jacques (farmer general, xxiii, 130n): and JW, 69, 158, 158, 162: duties on JW's uniforms, 183–4, 190, 222: Prost de Royer, 275

Péchigny, ——— Devillier, 46, 117

Péchigny, ——— Devillier, Mme, 46, 117

Peggy (brig), 606

Peirce, Jeremiah: signs promissory note, 7

Pembroke Prison, Wales, 179

Penelope. *See* Bob

Penet, d'Acosta frères & Cie., 256, 440n

Penet, Pierre, 256, 475n

Penn, Richard, 310n

Pennsylvania: issues loan office certificates, 63; disputes over constitution of, subside, 134;

party politics in, 283n; Indian attacks on frontiers of, 284; Test Act in, 317

Pennsylvania Assembly, 195n, 283n, 313n, 317n, 542

Pennsylvania Gazette, 154n

Pennsylvania Hospital, 283n

Pennsylvania Packet (newspaper), 119n, 389

Pennsylvanische Staats-Courier, 609n

Penobscot Bay, 73, 308n, 340, 414

Penthièvre, Louis-Jean-Marie de Bourbon, duc de (admiral of France, xxx, 534n), 196–7, 385

Percy, Hugh, 383n

Perret, François, 396n

Peter (prize), 197, 212, 307, 386, 402, 412, 434, 435n, 461, 493, 500, 561–2, 602

Peters, Richard (secretary of continental board of war, xxiii, 274n): recounts financial difficulties, 169–71, 322; BF recommends Angély to, 225; recommends Foulke, 322n; letters from, 169–71, 322–3; letter to, 225

Peters, Sarah Robinson (Richard's wife), 322

Peters, William (Richard's father), 169–70, 322

Petit Châtelet (Paris prison): R. Haines held at, 46

Petit Cousin (transport), 360n

Petry, ——— (Jean-Baptiste's brother), 330n

Petry, Jean-Baptiste, 329–30

Pets: of Mme Helvétius, 625

Pettice, Capt. ———, 262

Philadelphia: BF prefers as destination for *Alliance*, 130, 613: wishes to send military supplies to, 197–8; Board of Admiralty wishes *Alliance* sent to, 163, 458, 523–4; property in, suffers from depreciation, 170; bountiful harvest at, 198; Beaulieu on parole at, 335n; people, authorities of, are reportedly optimistic about Charleston, 390; price of wood in, 390; severe winter in, 390; plan to load tobacco in, 445; brig from, arrives at Nantes, 526; ill treatment of Quaker in, by British, 556–7; German language newspapers in, 609n; rumor of insurrection in, 622

Philadelphisches Staatsregister, 609n

Philip (prize), 197, 212, 307

Photosynthesis: Ingenhousz discovers, 116, 120

Piccinni (Piccini), Niccolò (composer), 55, 543

Pierce, Benjamin: requests wages, prize money, reappointment of Landais, 243–4, 454–6, 488–91, 492–3; as intermediary for *Alliance* crewmen, 245n; letters from, inter alia, 243–4, 454–6, 492–3; letter to, inter alia, 488–91

Pierce, Dr. John Harvey: wishes to emigrate, 261

Stevens, Capt. John, 234

Stevenson, Margaret, 205, 208

Stewart, Maj. John, 436n, 450n

Stocks: British, rise in price, 622

Stono Ferry, S.C., 318–19

Stores, naval: Mitchell to carry, 23; Dutch convoy for, 163n

Stormont, David Murray, Viscount, 46

Strange, Robert (engraver, xxiii, 226n), 208

Strasbourg Cathedral: engraving of, discussed, xxix; BF, Le Roy's report on lightning rods for, lviii, 373–6, 624

Stuart, John, third Earl of Bute, 383n

Stürler vom Altenberg, Johann Friedrich, 165n

Sugar: price of, at Philadelphia, 339; delivered to Gardoqui & fils, 564

Sullivan, Gen. John, 284n

Sullivan's Island (S.C.), 339

Supplies, military: from France, requested by Congress, lv–lvi, lx, 3, 18n, 41, 185; Lafayette solicits, obtains for U.S., 9n, 17–18, 41, 185; carried by *Chasseur*, 49: *Marc Antoine*, 51: *Heureux*, 539n; Rochambeau can bring to America, 74n; P. Richard sends to U.S., 112n; BF petitions French government on behalf of Md. for, 143n: said to oversee shipment of hemostatic powder to U.S., 154: does not know how to send from Lorient to America, 364; Louis XVI asked for warship to carry, 197–8; American need for, 288, 316, 364, 442; Arendt to deliver to Va. for W. Lee, 392n; can be carried by frigate, 403; JW recommends purchasing ship to carry, 403–4, 497–8; *Ariel* to carry, 442, 448, 467, 520–1, 539n, 579–80, 584, 612; Jones wishes *Serapis* to carry, 579–80; J. Ross to purchase, 592. See also *Alliance*

Surveillante (French frigate), 40n

Sussex, Eng.: projected attack on, 8

Swallow (brigantine), 103n

Swallow (packet), 138

Swart, Johan Isaac de (Dutch minister in St. Petersburg): identified, 94n; sends Russian news, 94, 393–4, 593

Sweden: and League of Armed Neutrality, 21n, 452n, 466; 1772 coup d'état in, 165n; protests Landais captures, 452, 585

Symmachus, Quintus Aurelius, 341

Symmer, Robert, 348

Syng, Philip, Jr. (silversmith, i, 209–10n), 116

Tableware: BF purchases, xxx, 468–73

Tacitus, 541

Talamuth, ——— (lawyer): seeks publication of memoir, 33

Tankerville. *See* Bennett, Charles

Tanner, Benjamin, xxx

Tardiveau, Barthélemi, 48

Taxes: imposed by Va. to halt currency depreciation, 53; American, Webster recommends to replace loans, 338n

Taylor, Benjamin, 413

Taylor, John, 27

Tea: price of, at Philadelphia, 339; BF drinks with Mme Brillon, 543

Technology: transfer of, from England to France, 395–6n: to U.S., 396

Teissier. *See* Texier

Temminck, Egbert de Vrij, 418

Temple, John (x, 389–90n), 191, 220, 252

Ternay, Charles-Louis d'Arsac, chevalier de, 72–3n, 102, 157, 229–30n, 269n, 623, 627–8

Terpsichore (French frigate), 581

Terry, Nath., 91–2

Test Act (Pa.), 317

Texel, Netherlands: British prisoners exchanged for French at, 20, 39, 237, 305, 378, 427, 453, 556, 591; warships at, may lack sailors, 418

Texier, Jean de (financier), 593n

Textiles: firms producing, create consortium for commerce with America, 31; sought for Mass., 31; offered for America, 31–2. *See also* Cloth

Thayer, George (exchanged prisoner), 138n

Théâtre Italien, 55n

Théâtres des boulevards, 55–6n

Theobald, James, 208

Thévenard, Antoine-Jean-Marie (commandant at Lorient, xxx, 87n): and sale of *Serapis*, 299n, 558: Landais, *Alliance*, 440n, 519–21, 523n, 539, 545n, 565–6, 580: *Ariel*, 467n, 507n, 520, 558n, 579: dispute between Moylan, Gillon about *Alliance* sailors, 532–3

Three Friends (prize), 29, 585n

Thuillières, Jean-François de, 230

Tickell, Mary, 205n

Tillee (Tille, Tilee), James, 6, 413

Timber. *See* Naval stores

Toaldo, Giuseppe, abbé, 374

Tobacco: cloth offered in exchange for, 31; Mason enters trade in, at Nantes, 62n; sent from Va. to Europe, 239, 590; Bondfield, Haywood & Co. want to bring from Philadelphia, 445; seized by farmers general, 496–7, 592, 606; sent by committee of commerce to pay for supplies, 592; from N.C., brought by *Peggy*, 606n